MAGILL'S
SURVEY
OF
AMERICAN
LITERATURE

MAGILL'S SURVEY OF AMERICAN LITERATURE

Volume 2

Crane–Harte

Edited by

FRANK N. MAGILL

Marshall Cavendish Corporation
New York • London • Toronto • Sydney • Singapore

Published By
Marshall Cavendish Corporation
2415 Jerusalem Avenue
P.O. Box 587
North Bellmore, New York 11710
United States of America

∞ The paper used in these volumes conforms to the American National Standard for Permanence of Paper for Printed Library Materials, Z39.48-1984.

Library of Congress Cataloging-in-Publication Data
Magill's survey of American literature. Edited by Frank N. Magill.
    p. cm.
  Includes bibliographical references and index.
    1. American literature—Dictionaries. 2. American literature—Bio-bibliography. 3. Authors, American—Biography—Dictionaries. I. Magill, Frank Northen, 1907.
PS21.M34 1991
810.9′0003—dc20
ISBN 1-85435-437-X (set)   91-28113
ISBN 1-85435-439-6 (volume 2)   CIP

PRINTED IN THE UNITED STATES OF AMERICA

CONTENTS

HART CRANE

Born: Garretsville, Ohio
July 21, 1899
Died: Caribbean Sea
April 27, 1932

Principal Literary Achievement

A consummate lyric poet, Crane was also one of the few of his time who wrote against modernist despair, sharing Walt Whitman's invincible hope for the American people's future.

Biography

Harold Hart Crane was born in Garretsville, Ohio, on July 21, 1899, the son of Clarence and Grace Hart Crane. He was an only child, stuck between incompatible parents who each demanded his allegiance. His father, a successful businessman who founded what became a prosperous candy company, wanted his son to follow in his footsteps. His mother, who resented her husband's absences and abuse, pressed the boy to develop in a more artistic direction.

When he was nine, the family recriminations exploded so fiercely that his mother had a nervous breakdown and entered a sanatorium, while the boy was sent to live with his grandmother in Cleveland. Eventually the whole family relocated to Cleveland where Crane went to East High School. He was an introverted adolescent, occupying his free time taking long walks alone or in voracious reading. His high school years were punctuated by a trip to visit his grandmother's plantation on the Isle of Pines, Cuba. Although the trip was ruined by marital discord, it introduced Crane to the tropical regions to which he would return and which he would picture so magically in his last poems.

In November, 1916, Clarence Crane moved out and his wife filed for divorce. The marriage was over. The young Crane, who had been viewing the Greenwich Village arts explosion from a distance and had already had his first poem published in one of its small magazines, *Bruno's Weekly*, a few months previously, quit high school and set off for New York City. Over the next few years he was to get to know many literary figures, such as Allen Tate and Waldo Frank; although he was to achieve a measure of success and even become associate editor of another small magazine, *The Pagan*, he never seemed able to commit himself to poetry or to one place.

Certainly, it was no easy task to be a poet in the United States in the 1920's. Many

writers settled in Europe, where literary pursuits were more respected; in France and Italy, particularly, one could live more cheaply than in the United States. Crane chose to stay largely in his own country, restlessly moving back and forth from the Midwest to the East Coast and from job to job. He was handicapped by his lack of education but found work in advertising, as a salesman for his father, and as a traveling secretary for a stockbroker. He was further handicapped by an ever-growing alcoholism and the type of homosexuality that led to a fascination with sailors and a constant involvement in barroom brawls.

Throughout these years, he kept publishing and polishing his verse, often, when unemployed, staying with friends and receiving financial aid from his father. In 1925, he obtained a degree of recognition when a wealthy arts patron gave him money to continue work on his book-length poem *The Bridge* (1930). His first book of poems, *White Buildings*, was published in 1926. As was the case for all of his work, reviews of the book were mixed. Most reviewers recognized and applauded the unmatched lyrical intensity, but there were also many complaints over obscurity and density. Meanwhile he was plowing ahead on the larger canvas of *The Bridge*, which was to occupy him for seven years and would range over America's geography and history. Working sporadically, he, too was ranging; in the years between 1925 to 1930 (the year this second book was published), he moved from New York to Cuba, then to New Jersey, California, Majorca, and Paris.

With the publication of *The Bridge*, again to mixed reviews, Crane received a Guggenheim Fellowship to work on a project in Mexico. In Mexico, he stayed at an artists' colony and had as fellow members such luminaries as the American novelist Katherine Anne Porter and the Mexican muralist David Siqueiros, who did a portrait of Crane. In the spring of 1932, Crane decided to sail back to the United States on the S.S. *Orizaba* to help settle his father's estate. Depressed and drinking heavily on the voyage, on April 27, near noon, Crane committed suicide by jumping overboard.

Analysis

If his late poems, brilliant but few in number, are set aside, Hart Crane's poetry can be divided into two phases. The first is that of apprenticeship, when he was composing the poems to go into the volume *White Buildings*. "Apprenticeship" should not be taken in this case to denote any immaturity or lack of mastery, but rather that in the individual short lyrics of this book he developed a language and outlook and worked with a variety of poetic forms that in his second period he would weld into one vast multifaceted commentary on the United States in his long poem *The Bridge*.

In his first phase, he tried many forms: epithalamions, elegies, and love cycles, as well as many types of versification, such as free verse, quatrains, and heroic couplets. He could work within highly constricted metrical structures naturally, never showing off this aspect of his poetry, never using this formal mastery for attention-getting effects. The most outstanding of his technical skills was his command of rhythm. Paralleling the content of his poems, which generally would describe a persona moving from a flaccid, uninspired, ordinary moment to one of heaven-sent revelation and uplift, the rhythmic movement would begin sluggishly, bogged down with caesuras (pauses in the middle of lines) and multiple uses of parataxis (clauses arranged with no apparent subordination), but the pace would gradually increase, building to an impassioned forward flow at the close.

What many readers experienced as the difficulty of entering a Crane poem is not only attributable, however, to the purposely stumbling meter at the beginning, but also to both the poem's language and manner of linking concepts. Crane had a voracious love of words from all levels of discourse, and he mixed into his poems such things as racy slang, scientific terms, everyday speech, and advertising slogans. Such combinations were common in the poetry of the day, but Crane's approach was unusual. Where poets such as T. S. Eliot and Ezra Pound juxtaposed high and low vocabulary to make a comment on modern vulgarity, Crane was trying to create a fused compound, almost a new tongue, where many lexical fields would blend together for a unified effect. His usage here paralleled his belief that the United States was, or rather would be, great because of its ability to meld together all the world's races.

What caused even greater difficulties for readers was his presentation of a startling, allusive sequence of concepts. Many serious readers could not follow the leaps of this argument and imagined that his writing was the product of some sort of poetic frenzy. In actuality, his texts exhibited incredibly compressed and subtle trains of thought that recall the lightning-like logical discussions appearing in poems of John Donne and other seventeenth century British metaphysical poets, whom Crane much admired.

To illustrate the uncomprehending reception accorded his works, one could consider the response of Harriet Monroe, editor of *Poetry*, one of the most prestigious magazines of the period, who chided him about a submission: "Your poem reeks with brains. . . . [T]he beauty which it seems entitled to is tortured and lost." She consented to publish the poem only with Crane's explanation appended. In his clarification, Crane outlined his doctrine of the "logic of metaphor." He argued that "emotional dynamics are not to be confused with any absolute order of rationalized definitions." He went on to ask: "Isn't there a terminology something like shorthand as compared to usual description . . . which the artist ought to be right in trusting as a reasonable connective agent toward fresh concepts, more inclusive evaluations?" That is, in order to depict accurately the flickering play of emotions as they intersect with intellection and the objects of feelings, what is needed is a style of writing that moves associatively and quickly inside language.

As mentioned, the theme of these shorter poems is transcendence. More specifically, and in keeping with his youth, the poems centered on such adolescent themes as appreciation of other writers or artists from whom the poet had learned, in pieces such as "Chaplinesque" (1921) and "At Melville's Tomb" (1926), or of longing for experience, in such poems as "Repose of Rivers" (1926). The writer may (for example, in "Chaplinesque") begin by meditating disconsolately on the nature of life but then see suddenly how great art finds and gives importance to the small victories that are still possible.

In his monumental *The Bridge*, Crane again must work his way from despair to hope, but in this work his melancholy turns on the sorry state of the crass, materialistic United States—a country which the writer eventually sees revealed, in an apotheosis, as the center of light and democracy that it could be, symbolized in the image of a bridge. His final poems, darker and yet still as lyrically intense—poems such as "The Broken Tower" (1932)—portray a bid for elevation that fails as the poet's own force seems insufficient for renewing vision.

AT MELVILLE'S TOMB

First published: 1926
Type of work: Poem

The poet visualizes nineteenth century American novelist Herman Melville sadly meditating on the destructive force of the ocean but then rising toward acceptance.

"At Melville's Tomb" is the poem that caused *Poetry* editor Harriet Monroe such trouble in interpretation and called forth Crane's famous reply in which he expounded his theory of composition. The sixteen-line poem pays homage to the nineteenth century American novelist, Herman Melville. In the manner of many poems by young writers addressing their forebears, it manages both to praise the older writer and to suggest that he shares the younger writer's outlook. Crane pictures Melville as meditating on one of Crane's own favored themes, the dual nature of the sea, beginning the lyric with the imaginative depiction of the novelist watching breakers roll onto a beach. Certainly Melville, a sailor, wrote knowingly about the sea, but his major novel, *Moby-Dick* (1851), to which Crane alludes, is little concerned with this topic and centers on fraternal and hierarchical relations in a small community of men on a whaling ship.

As Crane depicts the ocean that Melville is observing, it is a place both of death and of eventual resurrection as men overcome their fears and create a faith in something higher. Water has traditionally been viewed as connected to rebirth in baptism and other rituals. As Melville looks into the surf, he sees "the dice of drowned men's bones" and thinks of the wrecks and lost lives in the depths. His thought rises up, though, to a vision of men at sea finding a spiritual solace in the sky as "silent answers crept across the stars."

The poem is written in four-line stanzas in iambic pentameter. The strict meter and stanzaic form play against an irregular rhyme scheme that is used to reinforce the argument. The only heroic couplet (consecutive rhyming lines), for example, occurs in the climactic lines at the end of the third stanza where Melville finds metaphysical rest.

The terrific condensation of image and argument make the poem difficult to read easily, and, it should be noted, this difficulty starts with the title. "At Melville's Tomb" suggests that the piece to be presented will describe the poet pondering the novelist's tombstone. Yet from the first line, setting the poem on a deserted beach, it becomes evident that the "tomb" denoted by the title is not one in which Melville is buried, but the place where many of his characters, such as the crew of the *Pequod* in *Moby-Dick*, are buried—that is, the bottom of the sea. This redirection of the reader from an individual grave to a more universal resting place can be seen as symbolizing the way an artist redirects a reader's gaze from his or her own personal problems to the universality of the human condition.

FOR THE MARRIAGE OF FAUSTUS AND HELEN

First published: 1926
Type of work: Poem

Crane presents mythic characters from the Trojan War as embodiments of human energies that can still be unearthed in humankind's midst by the poet-seer.

It would be appropriate to begin the analysis of "For the Marriage of Faustus and Helen" with its title. The reader will search in vain for any mention of a marriage or of Faustus in the three-part piece; however, a study of the title leads directly into an understanding of Crane's ideas about historical correspondence. He wrote that in this poem he was trying to find "a contemporary approximation to an ancient human culture." In the case of Helen, considered the most beautiful woman in the classical world, Crane sought to reconstruct in "modern terms . . . the basic emotional attitude toward beauty that the Greeks had." Thus, in the poem's first part, the narrator sees Helen in modern garb stuck in rush-hour traffic.

This attitude toward the past offers a strong rebuff to the outlook of Crane's pessimistic contemporaries. An example of this more prevalent, darker attitude is to be found in Ezra Pound's *Cantos* (1917-1970). In this work, the poet, disavowing the present, imaginatively envisions previous times in history, in Renaissance Italy or feudal China, for example, when a man could combine writing verse with living a socially and politically active life. Crane refuses to follow Pound in entering the past as a refuge, but insists that every possibility for heroic life that could be found in other periods is still to be found.

As if to prove this assertion, his poem finds modern equivalents for specific events in the life of the mythological Helen of Troy, mentioned in the poem's title. In the original myth, Helen had been kidnapped from her Greek husband, Menelaus, by Paris, son of the king of Troy, which precipitated a war between the two countries. In the first section of Crane's poem, the narrator locates the modern Helen in a street-car: "some evening," he muses, "I might find your eyes across an aisle." In the next part, he finds the contemporary version of the revels at Menelaus' court in a hot jazz club. Then, in the last part, he depicts a modern version of the Trojan War in the bombings and dogfights of World War I.

Even after all of this, however, the reference in the title to Helen marrying Faustus remains to be explained. The poem's epigraph is from an Elizabethan playwright, which suggests that the story Crane is recalling is not the Homeric epic, but this tale as it is refracted through Christopher Marlowe, who wrote *Doctor Faustus* (c. 1588). If Helen is the ideal of beauty, Faustus, in this play, is the ideal of learning and scholarship, who, though he has to sell his soul to the devil to obtain his desires, is able to call up Helen of Troy from hell to be his paramour. In Crane's poem, Faustus is never clearly identified, or even mentioned, but it is implied that he is represented by the narrator, who has drawn Helen out of the hell of a modern traffic jam. The narrator's ability to recognize the woman who embodies beauty and offer her "one inconspicuous, glowing orb of praise" indicates that he, a poet, is the modern equivalent of Doctor Faustus, who should be rewarded with the highest prize, her hand, and that the world owes him gratitude for his ability to perceive something valuable — her beauty — that is unrecognized.

In its view of the poet's function, then, this piece can be seen as an extension of themes in Crane's earlier Melville poem. There the writer wrested meaning from drowned men's bones, here from a tarnished modern world where "The mind has shown itself at times too much the baked and labeled dough," too willing to accept pat answers rather than seeking truth for itself. Crane's use of words from different levels of language parallels his work on myths. The poet shows both that a woman as beautiful as Helen is in our midst and that modern American English, even the vulgarized words of advertising copy, if properly combined with other words, can yield delightful harmonies.

VOYAGES

First published: 1926
Type of work: Poem

In a dual movement, the poet describes his deep, conflicting feelings toward a friend and the sea.

The six-part poem "Voyages" holds the last place, a position considered most important by Crane, in his first volume, *White Buildings*. In many of his shorter lyrics and in sections of *The Bridge*, the central figure is scarcely individuated, a near anonymous observer who undergoes a visionary experience rooted in the coming to a deeper appreciation of language and the human lot but not involving any biographical self exposure. In "Voyages," however, Crane strikes a more intimate note, dealing with the pain of parting and being apart from someone loved.

Given the scandal that would have accompanied a writer's admission of homosexuality in this period, Crane's reticence about given intimate details of his life in his works and his indirection in speaking about the objects of his affection are understandable. In this piece, two stylistic traits compound the difficulty of comprehending, while adding to the originality of the description of, his relation to his friend on which the poem is centered.

It is expected that a poem of friendship will be addressed to the friend, but Crane adds to such addresses numerous apostrophes. The literary use of apostrophe occurs when a poet speaks to an inanimate object as if it were a human interlocutor. Thus Crane writes, "O rivers mingling toward the sky// . . . let thy waves rear/ More savage than the death of kings." The reader may notice in this passage the ascription of a personal pronoun, "thy," to the water. The poet also grants the rivers a human will, indicating that he believes they can alter the height of their waves to answer his entreaties. By this apostrophizing practice, the love for his friend and his feeling for the sea are mingled in a complex web.

Not only are the sea and other bodies of water put into a human dialogue, but water is humanized with anthropomorphic descriptions as well. Crane depicts the Caribbean by saying, "Mark how her turning shoulders wind the hours." The "shoulders" are the waves that move in predictable tides.

It is in the many passages of description in the poem that the second stylistic feature mentioned occurs (a feature that is even more prominent in *The Bridge*). This involves the presenting of a number of adjectival clauses, ambiguous in reference, before the noun they modify in such a way that until that noun appears it is difficult to identify the description's object. The first stanza of the second section, for example, speaks of "this great wink of eternity" and "her undinal vast belly" before identifying that it is the ocean that these clauses are describing.

One effect of this usage is that, combined with the apostrophes and anthropomorphic references, the water and the poet's missing friend are easily confused, which suggests there is some equivalence between the two. Crane is not arguing that the sea is actually partially human, but rather the profound point that a man's feelings toward nature and his fellows may hold similar depths of emotion.

It has already been suggested that Crane's poems characteristically move from a feeling of disconnectedness and melancholy to a realization of underlying integration. In this piece, by adopting almost a pantheistic position—that is, the belief that the world as a whole has a single soul and so is necessarily one—Crane seems to be prejudging his case. If the world is united in substance with the human, then it is easy to find resemblances between the two. The poet is not writing a philosophical argument, and it is not necessary for him to prove anything, but it might seem that the reason for his stress on this unifying underpinning is so that he can shift attention to another disturbing disharmony, not between man and nature but within each. In plumbing his feelings, he finds that he has a love/hate relationship with both his friend and the ocean. His friend, after all, has left him; the sea, after all, is what separates him from this friend, who is pictured watching the receding waters on a ship.

The very first section of the poem presents this duality. The narrator is observing children playing and feels it necessary to warn them that the "bottom of the sea is cruel." This simple contrast between two features of the sea is expanded through the rest of the poem. Crane, for example, explores how the ocean is more than a place for children to swim; it is freighted with a symbolic and linguistic history that has played a part in the narrator's own life and friendships. The movement of the poem is through a continual deepening of material. The narrator's social and psychic connections to water are uncovered until the ending note, which affirms poetry as the one vehicle that can convey such a complex emotional and intellectual intertwining.

THE BRIDGE

First published: 1930
Type of work: Long poem

The poet finds that the United States, if it will be nourished on its own myth and history, can overcome its contemporary doldrums.

The book-length poem *The Bridge* far surpasses in scope anything else Crane attempted. In "For the Marriage of Faustus and Helen," he had indicated how the energies of ancient mythic symbols still exist all around modern man. In this larger work, he attempts to explain how primary American myths are embedded in current consciousness and, further, how these myths are basically emancipatory, pointing the United States to a future of ethnic harmony and a valuing of artistic achievement.

One thing that spurred Crane to the creation of this work was his reading of T. S. Eliot's *The Waste Land* (1922). In looking at the work, he was both awed by Eliot's technical mastery and irritated by his hopelessness. Eliot, too, drew on mythology to create his work, turning to agrarian cultures for his theme. In those cultures, there was often a myth of a king or hero who died in the autumn, but who was reborn in spring with the new crops. Eliot, as his title suggests, stopped the unfolding of this story halfway, depicting modern society as one that had lost all of its legitimate authorities and was stuck in a winter without hope of resurrection.

A look at the manner in which Crane treated the story of Rip Van Winkle in the second part of his poem will indicate his contrasted approach. The folktale is presented in a way that is both wittily irreverent and personal. It is not called up in a portentous meditation but by recalling how it first was learned by the author in a primary school lesson, where the pupil "walked with Pizarro in a copybook." The story is interpreted positively, as charting the capacities of the human mind. Rip Van Winkle woke up in a confused state in which events that for him occurred yesterday had actually taken place twenty years ago. Crane presents his mature narrator effortlessly, vividly recalling his school days, and so indexes Van Winkle's juxtaposition of time periods to the human ability to recapture the past. This point validates, in turn, the broader project of the poem, which argues for the centrality of memory. If, the poem argues, the United States' historical and mythic apprehension were fully utilized, the nation would be regenerated.

It should not be thought that Crane's fervent optimism meant that he underestimated the problems of America. Two of its major defects, as he diagnosed them, propelled his work. The country had lost touch with its past, he says, and this is shown in a number of ways. For one, the omnipresent clamor of advertising and other distractions, as described in the opening of "The River" section, tricks the people into a pointless immersion in contemporary ephemera. A related point is that the lack of historical circumspection has undercut an appreciation of who really built the country. "The River" section casts light on the lives of transient workers, roustabouts, and ne'er-do-wells who, then and now, worked the farms and factories. He speaks of "hobo-trekkers that forever search/ An empire wilderness of freight and rails" as the true fathers of the country. This group has come to know the physical terrain of the nation in a way the comfortable never could by their daily harsh contact with it.

A second fault that Crane spies is the United States' mistreatment and ignorance of the American Indian. This represents another loss of the country's own past, for, in conceiving of America, Crane is thinking not primarily of the history of the United States since the thirteen colonies, but of the history of the geographical land mass. His sensitivity in examining the symbolic, personal, and interpersonal connotations of the Caribbean Sea in "Voyages" had prepared him for the similar examination he carries out in this work of his own country's topography. In studying this terrain, he repeatedly finds evidence of a layer of history and myth left by the Indians. The section "The Dance" focuses on Indian ceremonials and beliefs, which he reveals need to be acknowledged and integrated into his country's awareness.

With themes as powerful as these handled with such boldness and lyricism, it is not surprising (or pretentious on Crane's part) that he was to compare his poem to the Roman epic poem by Vergil, *The Aeneid* (first century B.C.). In the most elementary of ways, *The Bridge* is not an epic, since it lacks both a straightforward narrative and an epic hero, but it does employ a number of epic devices and is guided by an epic theme.

A standard epic poem begins with an invocation of the muse, the goddess of poetry who the writer hopes will inspire him on his high venture. Crane, believing in no gods, calls on the image of the Brooklyn Bridge, which he could see close at hand from his window during some of the time he was writing this work. He calls to it, "Unto us lowliest sometime sweep, descend." The Brooklyn Bridge is one of the most beautiful bridges in the world and so reveals to the poet that America can on rare occasions use its mechanical, pragmatic genius for the construction of lovely objects.

A second important device Crane re-employs is the epic guide. In *La Divina Commedia* (c. 1320; *The Divine Comedy*), for example, the poet narrator is led through hell by the ghost of his predecessor, Vergil. In the "Cape Hatteras" section of Crane's poem, the shade of Walt Whitman, nineteenth century American poet, appears. Whitman also had seen his country on the rack, since he served as a male nurse in the Civil War, and yet had felt the country's promise as Crane does. The poet of *The Bridge* feels his vigor renewed by contact with this earlier giant.

Finally, epic poems are often concerned with the founding of cultures or countries. *The Aeneid* concludes with the founding of Rome, John Milton's *Paradise Lost* (1667) with the origins of the Christian world in the Garden of Eden. *The Bridge* sets out to refound America by pondering its origins. The first section of the poem, "Ave Maria," concerns Columbus' discovery of America for the Europeans. The next section, "Powhatan's Daughter," however, undercuts the finality of Columbus' discovery both by discussing the Indians, who came to the land long before Columbus, and by noting that it was anonymous workers and farmers, not great men, who did most of the work of discovery. The following sections develop the narrator's own sense of the past and explore how the past is sedimented in every landscape. In "Quaker Hill," for example, Crane's visit to the New Avalon Hotel, a building that had once been a Quaker meeting house, leads to reflections on the political and spiritual changes one area of New England has undergone in its history. The last section, "Atlantis," returns to the Brooklyn Bridge, playing off the multiple associations of its architecture to dream of what happiness the future will hold if only the nation can follow the lead of its poets in grasping hold of its own myth and life history.

Summary

It is easy to imagine that writing for Crane was strenuous, even painful, for what he demanded of his verse was both lyrical intensity and intellectual density. At the core of his thought was a depiction of transcendence, a bursting of the bonds of received perception that led to a fuller recognition of how the past and myth were entwined with the present moment. He argued that his country, addled in the 1920's by materialism, could be regenerated by an increase in self-knowledge that could be gained by listening to its poets.

Bibliography

Bennett, Maria F. *Unfractioned Idiom: Hart Crane and Modernism.* New York: Peter Lang, 1987.

Berthoff, Warner. *Hart Crane: A Reintroduction.* Minneapolis: University of Minnesota Press, 1989.

Brunner, Edward. *Splendid Failure: Hart Crane and the Making of "The Bridge."* Urbana: University of Illinois Press, 1985.

Clark, David R., ed. *Critical Essays on Hart Crane.* Boston: G. K. Hall, 1982.

Combs, Robert. *Vision of the Voyage: Hart Crane and the Psychology of Romanticism.* Memphis, Tenn.: Memphis State University Press, 1966.

Giles, Paul. *Hart Crane: The Contexts of "The Bridge."* London: Cambridge University Press, 1986.

Lewis, R. W. B. *The Poetry of Hart Crane: A Critical Introduction.* Princeton, N. J.: Princeton University Press, 1967.

Schwartz, Joseph. *Hart Crane: A Reference Guide.* Boston: G. K. Hall, 1983.

Schwartz, Joseph, and Robert C. Schweik. *Hart Crane: A Descriptive Bibliography.* Pittsburgh: University of Pittsburgh Press, 1972.

Unterecker, John. *Voyager: A Life of Hart Crane.* New York: Farrar, Straus & Giroux, 1969.

James Feast

STEPHEN CRANE

Born: Newark, New Jersey
November 1, 1871
Died: Badenweiler, Germany
June 5, 1900

Principal Literary Achievement
Despite his short life and small output, Stephen Crane was a major American fiction writer, crucial in the development of modern psychological realism.

Biography

Stephen Crane was born November 1, 1871, in Newark, New Jersey, the fourteenth and last child of the Reverend Jonathan Townley Crane and Mary Helen Peck Crane. Dr. Crane was an eminent Methodist ecclesiastic, one consequence of which was that the family moved frequently: in 1874, 1876, and finally, in 1878, to Port Jervis, New York, a town which would figure in Stephen Crane's late fiction as Whilomville (*Whilomville Stories*, 1900). Dr. Crane died suddenly in 1880. Stephen Crane's universal skepticism has, as one plausible source, rebellion against his religious upbringing. His rootlessness and death-haunted fiction may have been influenced by the crucial events of his early childhood. On the positive side, Crane grew up exposed to good books; though few specific details of his reading are known, clearly he absorbed enough to give him the literary background he needed, despite a weak formal education.

In 1883, Crane's mother took him to Asbury Park, a resort town established by the Methodists on the beaches of southern New Jersey. Here among her co-religionists, Mrs. Crane re-established her family as best she could. Asbury Park had a sinful side, however—prostitution, liquor, and gambling were all present—and Crane, by now an adolescent, was pulled in two directions. Presumably he remained innocent of "bad women" (he was rarely able to portray women convincingly in his fiction). Primarily an observer, he nevertheless ran with a fast, sporting crowd; he developed a passion for baseball and took up smoking.

His mother, having lost control of her young rebel, attempted the traditional solution: She sent him away to school. He went first to Pennington Seminary, of which his father had been principal before the Civil War, then, in early 1888, to the Hudson River Institute in Claverack, New York. This military school was weak academically, but it gave Crane some background (and presumably, from the Civil War

veterans on the staff, provided him with some anecdotes) which would prove useful when he came to write *The Red Badge of Courage: An Episode of the American Civil War* (1895). In September, 1890, he entered Lafayette College as an engineering student; he failed and entered Syracuse University in January, 1891. He played catcher and shortstop on the varsity baseball team; his first published story appeared in *The University Herald*, and he probably began drafting *Maggie: A Girl of the Streets* (privately printed, 1893; published, 1896). That summer he reported Asbury Park news for his brother Townley, who owned a news agency, and for the *New York Tribune.* He met Hamlin Garland, a writer well known for his realistic stories of midwestern farm life. In the fall he did not return to Syracuse; his formal education was over.

Instead, he moved to New York to seek his fortune; more specifically, he moved to his brother Edmund's house in Lake View, New Jersey, close enough for forays— job-hunting, adventuring, observing urban life—into the city.

During this period, as throughout his adult life, he was destitute much of the time; his frequent malnourishment probably contributed to his early death. With the death of his mother on December 7, 1891, he was more than ever on his own. He tried salaried journalism (much of his life's work would consist of features, notably war correspondence, for newspapers) but, in early 1892, lost a briefly held job with the *New York Herald.* Straight reporting bored him, and he did not get along well with reporters. Whatever his intentions at the time, he was above all serving a literary apprenticeship. His explorations of the Bowery, the most notorious New York slum of the time, gave him the material for *Maggie: A Girl of the Streets,* and in 1893 he began *The Red Badge of Courage.* He had *Maggie: A Girl of the Streets* privately printed because no one—given its prostitute heroine, its (rather mild) profanity, and its lurid scenes of slum life—was bold enough to publish it. Few read it, but one who did, and greatly admired it, was William Dean Howells, foremost American novelist and champion of realism of his day. Crane thus gained a crucial friend and ally.

Crane continued to write: the poems that would go into *The Black Riders and Other Lines* (1895), and *George's Mother* (1896), another novella of slum life. Excerpts from *The Red Badge of Courage* published in 1894 by the Bacheller Syndicate gained for him some notoriety; during the next year, the syndicate sent him west as a correspondent, providing him with background for some of his finest stories. In October, 1895, *The Red Badge of Courage* was published; by December, Crane was an international literary celebrity. Unfortunately, from this point on, his life went steadily downhill.

He became the subject of envious, malicious gossip, especially as a result of his defense—against the corrupt New York police—of Dora Clark, who may or may not have been a prostitute. He fled this uncomfortable atmosphere in November, 1896, for Jacksonville, Florida, to report on the Cuban insurrection; there he met the madam of a brothel, Cora Taylor, with whom (though she was married to a husband who would not divorce her) he was to live as husband and wife. In January, 1897, he was shipwrecked from the steamer *Commodore* off the Florida coast, an experience which led him to write his masterful short story "The Open Boat" (1897), collected in *The Open Boat and Other Tales of Adventure* (1898).

In 1897 he moved to England with Cora, traveled to Greece to report the Turkish war, then, in 1898, returned to the United States to volunteer for service in the Spanish-American War; he was turned down, probably because of a diagnosis of pulmonary tuberculosis, but went anyway as a correspondent. He thrust himself into danger at every opportunity, perhaps even seeking his own death. From Havana, in 1899, he returned to England, where he lived in Brede Place, an ancient manor house that Cora had found; he wrote frantically in a losing effort to generate income that would keep up with Cora's extravagance. At Christmas he suffered a massive tubercular hemorrhage; that spring, Cora took him to Badenweiler, Germany, where he died at the age of twenty-eight on June 5, 1900.

Analysis

Stephen Crane might best be regarded as an inexplicable literary phenomenon: a brief, bright comet, brilliantly distinct from every other writer of his time. Such an approach, however—metaphorically throwing up one's hands and standing back in wonder—is not very satisfying to literary critics, who have expended vast amounts of energy attempting to fit him into various pigeonholes. Thus the student of Crane will soon wander into a bewildering maze of theory: The author is referred to as naturalist, realist, impressionist, and ironist. It may be useful to discuss these concepts, then, before examining Crane's principal theme and the lasting value of his fiction.

Literary naturalism was imported to America from Europe, mainly by way of the French novelist Émile Zola, and found its chief American expression, around the beginning of the twentieth century, in the novels of Theodore Dreiser and Frank Norris. It is a literary method based on the idea that the physical world is all that exists; it denies the supernatural. The novelist's approach is that of the scientist: to examine phenomena, rigorously and objectively, with a view to proving a thesis about the human condition. Typically, this thesis is that people are indistinguishable from animals—that their lives are strictly governed by heredity and environment, making them essentially victims of biological and social forces which they are helpless to oppose. Probably the most readable works of American naturalism are Norris' *McTeague* (1899) and Dreiser's *Sister Carrie* (1900). The fiction of Stephen Crane has some naturalistic elements, in that it is skeptical, probably agnostic, and generally pessimistic. Yet even in *Maggie*, the work to which the term most readily applies, it is not clear that the characters are purely victims of their environment. At key turning points they are offered opportunities to act kindly—to change the course of Maggie's life—but fail to take them. Nor is the deep moral outrage which pervades the story typically naturalistic. Crane knows what good is and takes his stand for it, even if the realist in him sees that, in the Bowery, the good generally fails.

Realism in its most basic form refers simply to getting things right—careful observation and rendering of detail. For example, the realist Mark Twain felt that a famous American romantic novelist, James Fenimore Cooper, had made egregious errors of detail that robbed his work of conviction. In this sense Crane is certainly a realist; he was an expert reporter, and the details of his work ring true. Much of his writing, though by no means all, centers on probable and everyday occurrences. In this aspect he stands firmly in the camp of such leading realists as Hamlin Garland and William Dean Howells. He was more concerned than either of those writers, however—and herein lies a clue to his greater significance for most modern readers—with inner reality: not merely with what happened, but with how it felt and why it mattered. Thus, his realism is more subjective. He describes Civil War battles not as they might appear to a disembodied observer floating above them, but as they looked and sounded to a terrified soldier in the middle of them. His method is in turn affected. In *The Red Badge of Courage*, in particular, the narrative is far more disconnected and the imagery more dreamlike than in the social realism of Garland and Howells. It is these qualities which have caused some critics to refer to Crane as an impressionist. Impressionism, an extremely vague term as applied to literature, suggests an attempt to render the subjective aspects of a scene as opposed to the verifiable events—what could be filmed by a documentary filmmaker, for example—that make it up.

The greatest fiction writers are able to view events from multiple perspectives, a quality readily apparent in Crane's best work: He is at once the frightened correspondent in "The Open Boat," concerned only with survival from moment to moment, and the survivor observing the foibles, pretensions, and ultimate helplessness of man; he is both the runaway soldier wallowing in self-justification and the dispassionate witness. It is out of this multiplicity of vision that Crane's pervasive irony arises. It is not to be confused with a simple irony of tone, a kind of sarcasm whose purpose is to proclaim the author's distance from and superiority to the people and events he is describing. Instead, it expresses a complex, deeply imagined and unsentimental vision. If humans need their illusions to survive in an indifferent universe, in a state of war with one another and with the natural world, let them have them; nevertheless, let them back off from time to time and see those illusions for what they are. It is only in such moments of clarification that human beings, understanding their true place in the scheme of things, come together as brothers.

In Stephen Crane's universe, everyone is indeed at war: The statement is a critical commonplace and is self-evident to any reader once alerted to it. Usually ("The Open Boat" is a notable exception) the enemy is human and the cause of the conflict is human blindness—failure of observation and imagination, leading to an inability to see others as sentient beings capable of suffering. It is difficult to shoot down one's brother, face to face, but in *The Red Badge of Courage* the Confederate soldiers are cogs in a war machine that has been aimed at another war machine. To the Swede, in "The Blue Hotel" (1899), the other characters are murderers out of pulp adventure fiction. Rarely do Crane's characters connect in any significant way; all too often they lash out blindly to save whatever is precious to them, whether self-image, social status, or life itself. Crane's vision, then, is essentially tragic. His stories do not necessarily make comforting reading. Yet they are above all passionately honest, revealing an integrity found only in the finest fiction. They have much to say to a world which remains at war.

MAGGIE: A GIRL OF THE STREETS

First published: 1896 (privately printed, 1893)
Type of work: Novella

Cast out by her family and abandoned by her lover, a young girl comes to a sad end.

Maggie: A Girl of the Streets presents more difficulties to modern readers than other major work by Crane. The heavy dialect and outmoded slang can be distracting, but a more central problem lies in the characterization, or lack of it, of the protagonist. The harrowing pictures of life in a New York slum, however, still ring true.

The fundamental law of life in the Bowery is revealed in the opening scene—and depicted as absolute throughout the story. Maggie's brother Jimmie Johnson appears as a small boy fighting a group of boys from Devil's Row "for the honor of Rum Alley." As he is about to be overwhelmed, an older boy, Pete, happens along and pitches in on his side. With the enemy routed, Jimmie goes home to a family also at war; here the mother is victorious, the father driven out to drown his sorrows in a neighboring saloon. So it goes throughout: The powerful prey on the powerless and are preyed upon themselves in turn. Power may stem from physical prowess, from socioeconomic position, or from sexual desirability. Whatever its source, however, power is universally exploited for pleasure or vindication. Because the characters lack any vestige of self-knowledge or empathy, inevitably their behavior is revealed as at best futile, at worst destructive. Jimmie fights for the "honor" of Rum Alley, but Rum Alley has no honor. Maggie's mother ultimately banishes her in the name of conventional respectability, but she herself is a ranting and raving alcoholic. The streets and tenements that make up the urban jungle are strewn with victims. Maggie, from the first scene in which she appears, is only one of many.

Maggie: A Girl of the Streets consists of nineteen brief sections; in the first four, Maggie and Jimmie are children. In these sections, Crane is highly successful in evoking the milieu. It is in the fifth—with Maggie grown and engaged in near-slave labor as a seamstress—that he begins to run into trouble. She has become "a most rare and wonderful production of a tenement district, a pretty girl." As additional characterization, Crane reveals that "when a child, playing and fighting with gamins in the street, dirt disgusted her." That statement essentially marks the limit of his conception of Maggie. For the story to rise above pathos, its heroine would have to reveal some divine spark, or, in practical terms, considerable spunk in her attempts to make a new life for herself. The potential for triumph or tragedy is present in the situation; unfortunately, however, the protagonist, in her timid passivity, remains nothing more than a victim of circumstances.

Her good looks and vulnerability make her a natural target for Pete, Jimmie's rescuer in the opening scene, who has become a bartender and a swaggering man about town. He begins squiring her about—more because she is a decorative prop to his ego than out of any real feeling—and Maggie, naturally enough, falls in love with him. Thus, ominously, the power is all on Pete's side. Interspersed with scenes of the courtship are scenes with Jimmie, now a truck driver and minor league swaggerer himself, and Maggie's mother, widowed but unchanged in her alcoholic, sanctimonious violence. At the end of section 9, the midpoint of the story, the mother throws Maggie out. With nowhere to go except with Pete, Maggie now (it is indicated discreetly) loses her virginity—she is "ruined." The sexual double standard comes into darkly ironic focus: Jimmie, who has been "ruining" girls for years, proclaims that "Maggie's gone teh d' devil." The mother responds with a curse biblical in intensity, but with imagery straight from the Bowery: "May she eat nothin' but stones and deh dirt in deh street. May she sleep in deh gutter an' never see deh sun shine again."

After a dramatic scene in a saloon, in which a fight between Jimmie and Pete over Maggie's honor escalates into a riot, the beginning of the end for Maggie comes quickly. By now, with no one else to turn to, her "air of spaniel-like dependence had been magnified and showed its direct effect in the peculiar off-handedness and ease of Pete's ways toward her." In a dance hall they meet Nell, "a woman of brilliance and audacity" whom Pete had known previously, and whom he wants more than she wants him. As a result of this shift in the balance of power, Maggie is very soon abandoned. Her mother refuses to take her back in, effectively condemning her to a life of prostitution.

To this point Crane's techniques have been realistic. Now, in section 17, Maggie's remaining life is foreshortened into a few pages, as she is shown first well dressed in a brilliantly lit theater district, then walking down darker, grimier streets, being rejected finally by boys and drunks, coming at last to the river, into which she will deliver up her life. How much time has passed cannot be determined exactly, but it is presumably several years. The power of this section depends on the extent to which the reader has come to identify with Maggie in the earlier, more fully developed ones; many will find it more puzzling than anything else.

After a scene depicting the downfall of Pete, *Maggie: A Girl of the Streets* ends with the announcement to her family of her death. In the last line of the story, her mother, utterly unconscious of what she has done to her daughter in her vindictive failure of love, screams "Oh, yes, I'll fergive her! I'll fergive her!" It is one of the most harrowingly ironic endings in all fiction and anticipates the greatness of the work to come.

THE RED BADGE OF COURAGE

First published: 1895
Type of work: Novel

In the course of a series of Civil War skirmishes, a young Union soldier is initiated into manhood.

The Red Badge of Courage is as hard to classify as is Crane's work in general. It is a war story in the sense that the major external action consists of clashes between opposing armies, but certainly it is unconventional in what it omits. No geographical place names are given, except for a single casual mention of the Rappahannock River, so that the action—all the more surreal for this reason—cannot be located on a map. Similarly, no dates are given; it is impossible to tell what strategic significance, if any, the series of inconclusive actions might have had. In fiction that is intended to justify one side in a war, much is generally made of the justice of the cause; moreover, the soldiers on "our side" are portrayed as brave and noble, the enemy as evil. In *The Red Badge of Courage*, on the other hand, the cause is never described, and, though the enemy remains mostly faceless, it becomes clear at last that the only difference between Union and Confederate soldiers is the color of their uniforms. The novel is distinctly modern in this sense, much in the spirit of the fiction engendered by the Vietnam War. In its vivid depiction of the futile suffering brought about by war, it is an antiwar novel.

It is also, and perhaps primarily, a coming-of-age story. According to traditional readings, Henry Fleming, the young protagonist, moves in a series of stages from boyhood, marked by his cowardly flight from his first battle, to manhood, marked by his leading a charge and capturing a Rebel flag. In the fiction of Stephen Crane, however, as ironic a writer as ever lived, nothing is ever quite that simple. The question of just what it is that Henry Fleming learns (and in turn, just what it is that war teaches any of those condemned to fight in it) remains open, to be answered by each reader by closely following the details of the story.

The Red Badge of Courage moves back and forth between traditional realism, partly from Henry's point of view and partly from Crane's ironical one, and the surreal, disjointed imagery of nightmare. Thus, in the opening paragraph, from the camp of Henry's untested regiment one can see "the red, eyelike gleam of hostile campfires set in the low brows of distant hills"—a picture of a war monster. Next the story turns to a matter-of-fact description of camp life, including small domestic arrangements, quarrels, and the inevitable buzz of rumor. By these varied techniques, Crane accurately expresses the flavor of Henry's existence—mostly ordinary, a life dominated by trivial events and emotions, but always haunted by the specter of the fearful unknown.

At length the regiment begins its march to action; before any fighting actually occurs, Henry begins to feel his helplessness to alter the onrushing course of events. His regiment "inclosed him. And there were iron laws of tradition and law on four sides. He was in a moving box." It is this kind of statement which has caused some critics to describe *The Red Badge of Courage* as naturalistic and Henry as simply a victim of historical forces. Yet it is important to remember that these are Henry's perceptions, not Crane's, and that Henry is often self-deluded. A moment later, he reflects that he "had not enlisted of his free will," when in fact he had. He made that choice and, like the characters in "The Blue Hotel," will have others to make as well.

His first crisis occurs when his regiment has to withstand an infantry charge. At first he "suddenly lost concern for himself, and. . . . He became not a man but a member. . . . He felt the subtle battle brotherhood more potent even than the cause for which they were fighting." This is reminiscent of the brotherhood in "The Open Boat," but it is ironically undercut by its arising from war (Henry's state is described as "battle sleep") and by its being so very short-lived. Soon, when a few men run, Henry runs too.

He runs blindly, without conscious volition, and his adventures while away from his regiment, chapters 6 through 12 of the twenty-four in the book, make up the dramatic heart of the novel. He pictures himself initially as being pursued by dragons and shells with "rows of cruel teeth that grinned at him." Soon, as he calms down, he begins to justify himself: Since his regiment was about to be swallowed, running was an intelligent act. Yet when he overhears some officers saying that the regiment held, he feels more than ever isolated: He grows angry at his comrades for standing firm and actually thinks of them as his enemy.

Throughout the novel, in typical adolescent fashion, Henry undergoes wild mood swings that color the ways he sees the external world. Distanced for a time from the fighting, he enters a forest and comes to "a place where the high, arching boughs made a chapel. . . . There was a religious half light." Then, in a type of violent juxtaposition that Crane uses frequently, he sees that he is "being looked at by a dead man," a decaying corpse Crane describes in graphic detail. Henry disintegrates: "His mind flew in all directions," matching the chaos of the day's events. It is when he comes to a road filled with wounded men that he most acutely feels his shame, hence the need for a wound of his own, a "red badge of courage." He falls in with a "tattered man" who befriends him and with a "spectral soldier," a dying man he recognizes with horror as Jim Conklin, formerly known as the "tall soldier" of his own company. Henry and the tattered man accompany Jim on his death walk as he searches, seemingly, for the right place to die. At his death occurs the most famous and controversial image of the novel: "The red sun was pasted in the sky like a wafer." One prominent critic has interpreted this sun to be a metaphor for a communion wafer, and an elaborately worked-out system of religious references as giving the book its underlying structure; others, probably with better reason, discount the religious element and see the source of the image as the red seals that were commonly pasted on envelopes.

Henry, in his shame, now abandons the badly wounded tattered man. As he frantically questions a soldier in a routed mass of Union infantry, the man hits him on the head with his rifle, thus bestowing on him a profoundly ironic red badge. As the day ends he staggers on into the dark, only to be rescued by a mysterious "cheery man" whose face he never sees. This cheery man, with almost magical prowess and rare good will, restores him to his regiment.

It is typical for heroes of epic myth to make a trip to the underworld, a trip which explores their own deepest fears and from which they are reborn to a higher self. Henry has now completed such a journey; when he wakes the next morning, "it seemed to him that he had been asleep for a thousand years, and he felt sure that he opened his eyes upon an unexpected world." The difficulty with this sort of mythic reading, however, is that in many ways Henry seems unchanged and continues to behave badly. Wilson, a comrade formerly known as the "loud soldier," has been genuinely humbled; there have been models of brotherhood in the tattered man and the cheery soldier, and of heroism in the dignity of Jim Conklin's death. Yet Henry never tells the truth about his wound, and he is not above wanting to humiliate Wilson for having revealed his fears. At the end, he is tormented not by having abandoned the tattered man but by his fears of being found out. It is as though whatever meaning the mythic story might have had for Crane was overwhelmed by his clear-eyed realism.

Henry does become heroic, or at least stalwartly successful, in conventional military terms, and he turns at the end to "images of tranquil skies, fresh meadows, cool brooks—an existence of soft and eternal peace." On the face of it, there is a happy ending. Henry has basked euphorically in nature before, however, only to be brought up short by a rotting corpse. The war is by no means over; there is little peace to be had, and there is no convincing evidence that Henry will experience unbroken inner peace. So the meaning of the ending remains decidedly ambiguous. Exactly what lessons has Henry Fleming learned—that appearance matters more than reality, or that peace of mind is best attained by internalizing the values of society? If so, *The Red Badge of Courage* is a darker book than has generally been recognized.

THE OPEN BOAT

First published: 1897
Type of work: Short story

Four men shipwrecked in a ten-foot dinghy struggle to survive.

"The Open Boat" is considered by some critics to be Stephen Crane's masterpiece. Summarizing the rudimentary plot—the struggle of four shipwrecked men to survive in a rough sea in a ten-foot dinghy—suggests little of the story's abiding interest. At its center lies not the question of who will survive, ultimately revealed as a matter of chance anyway, but rather the progressively revealed nature of human life and the place of humanity in the universe. The theme is not presented as an abstract philosophical statement; it emerges, rather, from a brilliantly compelling rendition of life in an open boat, vividly portrayed and psychologically exact.

The events immediately preceding those of "The Open Boat" are recounted in "Stephen Crane's Own Story," published January 7, 1897—five days after the *Commodore* sank—in the *New York Press*. The short story can be appreciated without reading the journalistic narrative, though knowing the context is useful as background. It is instructive, nevertheless, to compare the openings. "Stephen Crane's Own Story" begins, after the dateline, "It was the afternoon of New Year's. The Commodore lay at her dock in Jacksonville"—functional journalistic prose, whose sole purpose is the objective presentation of facts. The opening of "The Open Boat," on the other hand—"None of them knew the color of the sky"—is one of the most famous sentences in modern literature. Arrestingly, with the utmost concision, it reveals the essentials of life in a ten-foot dinghy: One's world is reduced, one's attention is focused solely on survival from moment to moment. What the men know about, in frighteningly intimate detail, is the waves that threaten to swamp the boat.

The four men in the dinghy are the captain of the *Commodore*; the oiler, who worked in the engine room; the ship's cook; and the correspondent, Stephen Crane himself. They have come together by accident, strangers whose names—except for the oiler's, given incidentally in dialogue—are not even mentioned. This deliberate omission comes to suggest, by the end, that the men are Everyman, that everyone, in a symbolic separated sense, lives in an open boat without knowing it. They are separated from the sea by "six inches of gunwale." The correspondent rows and wonders "why he was there"—in that boat, in that particular place and time—but the wonderment is also about his life and about human life in general. Many of the details in the story have a similar double significance, coming as they do from two different angles: The correspondent is sitting in the boat six inches from the waves, and is at the same time reflecting on the events afterward as he writes the story.

The surface structure of "The Open Boat" is that of the journey itself; an almost random movement as the boat, sometimes controlled by the struggling oarsmen, sometimes by wind and waves, works its way up and down the Florida coast. Land and safety are within sight but are unattainable because of the pounding surf. A more significant movement lies in the rapidly altering perspectives of the men as they experience hope and fear, confidence and despair, anger, puzzlement, and love for one another in the brotherhood of the boat—a lifetime's range of emotions. Ultimately, however, the controlling factor is irony: In the contract between what humanity is and what it thinks it is, layer after comforting layer of illusion is stripped away.

The source of the ironic revelations that, by the end, make the men think "that they could then be interpreters" is a radically altered perspective. From the open boat, everything looks different. A seagull, ordinarily harmless and indeed afraid of people, tries to land on the captain's head; if he tries to shoo it away he might swamp the dinghy. The men see people on the shore but cannot make their need understood; the people on the beach, the purported lords of the earth, are not merely ineffectual but ludicrous.

Night falls and the correspondent, the only man awake in the boat, learns something about real power from a shark: "It cut the water like a gigantic and keen projectile." In the end, as the boat founders in the surf, it is the oiler, the strongest swimmer of the four, who drowns. Human strength and resourcefulness are no match for the power of a universe which has revealed itself to the correspondent as "flatly indifferent."

Yet the philosophy that emerges from "The Open Boat" is not unmitigatedly dark. For all the hardship, fear, and disillusionment, the correspondent recognizes "even at the time" that his boat ride is "the best experience of his life." The wellspring of this paradox is love, "the subtle brotherhood of men." Brotherhood is no hedge against mortality, but it does make life in the open boat, life without illusions, worth living. "The Open Boat" is a timeless and moving tale of struggle, not merely for physical survival, but also for understanding and acceptance of man's fate.

THE BLUE HOTEL

First published: 1898
Type of work: Short story

A quarrel over a card game in a storm-bound Nebraska hotel leads to tragedy.

In "The Blue Hotel," a group of strangers comes together in a small isolated hotel, a refuge from the storm outside. Isolating characters in this way is a common plot device in both mainstream and mystery fiction—and Crane's story is a suspense thriller, whatever its larger meanings. People in such a situation, unconstrained by the laws and traditions of a larger society, become a society in themselves; under the additional pressure imposed by unfamiliar and unpredictable events, they reveal their truest and deepest values. In this story, as in "The Open Boat," the implications are universal.

"The Palace Hotel at Fort Romper was painted a light blue . . . screaming and howling in a way that made the dazzling winter landscape of Nebraska seem only a gray swampish hush." What is the significance—beyond the spelled-out realistic one that it makes the hotel visible to travelers—of the unusual color? Bright primary colors, as in *The Red Badge of Courage* and "The Bride Comes to Yellow Sky," appealed to Crane. Here the color occurs again later, when the characters go outside to fight: "The covered land was blue with the sheen of an unearthly satin." The suggestion is fundamental to an understanding of the story: The blue hotel is no refuge from the storm, because the characters carry the storm—uncontrolled violence and hatred—within them.

The three guests who come to the hotel owned by Pat Scully, and run by him with the help of his son Johnnie, are "a tall bronzed cowboy," "a silent little man from the East," and a "shaky and quick-eyed Swede"—characters from widely spaced places who, as in "The Open Boat," are never given names. That the hotel is anything but a safe harbor, a place of peace and love, is revealed at once; the small room "seemed to be merely a proper temple for an enormous stove, which, in the center, was humming with godlike violence." Johnnie Scully is playing cards and quarreling with an old farmer. Pat Scully loudly "destroys the game of cards," sending his son up with the baggage. The guests then hear his "officious clamor at his daughters."

The potential for violence, then, is already present. It is the Swede, who sits silently "making furtive elements of each man in the room," who provides the catalyst. The others play cards and again quarrel; the Swede, who is badly frightened by his own preconceptions of the wild West, at length speculates—to everyone's astonishment—that "there have been a good many men killed in this room." No one is able to reassure him, and at length, in his growing hysteria, he bursts out with "I suppose I am going to be killed before I can leave this house!" In his literal insanity—he has fabricated a world which connects with reality hardly at all—he carries within him the seeds of his own death.

Scully finally does manage to placate him, whereupon he turns into an arrogant bully. He views all human relationships in terms of power; interpreting Scully's overtures as signs of weakness, he concludes that the power is on his side now, and, as everyone does in *Maggie: A Girl of the Streets*, he abuses it. He joins the card game, accuses Johnnie of cheating, and the two go out into the storm to fight. The scene that follows is full of animal images: Scully turns on the Swede "panther-fashion"; the combatants watch each other "in a calm that had the elements of leonine cruelty in it"; they collide "like bullocks." Meanwhile, the cowboy, whose animal nature has surfaced as well, urges Johnnie, "Kill him."

The Swede wins, however, and walks into town, goes into a bar, and arrogantly attempts to browbeat a group of men into drinking with him. In a brief melee, and more or less in self-defense, one of them, a quiet, respectable gambler, stabs him: "[A] human body, this citadel of virtue, wisdom, power, was pierced as easily as if it had been a melon." The dead Swede lies with his eye on a sign on the cash register: "This registers the amount of your purchase." By his failures of "virtue, wisdom, power," he has bought his death.

If the story ended here, as it logically might, it would be naturalistic, portraying humans revealed as animals, helpless in the grip of their bestial emotions. Crane added a kind of coda, however, a scene later between the cowboy and the Easterner. The Easterner reveals that Johnnie really was cheating at cards; he himself was too cowardly to reveal what he knew and forestall the fight, while Scully permitted it and the cowboy fueled it with his rage. All of them, in a sense, collaborated in the murder; all could have made different choices which would have prevented it. Naturalism, with the characters in the grip of forces too great for them to oppose, cannot rise above pathos; "The Blue Hotel," on the other hand, is tragic. The characters have a chance to live up to their highest human potential. Because they fail, a man needlessly dies.

THE BRIDE COMES TO YELLOW SKY

First published: 1898
Type of work: Short story

A showdown in a Western town concludes with a comic twist.

"The Bride Comes to Yellow Sky," half the length of "The Blue Hotel" and "The Open Boat," lacks the narrative density and philosophical depth of either. Instead it debunks some pervasive myths of the American West, with wonderfully comic effect. In the generally grim catalogue of Crane's work, this story offers a refreshing change of pace.

In the most primitive kind of Western story, the characters lack identifiable human characteristics. They are robotlike, standing for largely meaningless abstractions of good or evil; everything leads up to, and the interest of the story lies in, the climactic showdown. Marshal Jack Potter of Yellow Sky, Texas, on the other hand, is all too human. As he rides home on the train from San Antonio, his new bride beside him, he is thinking not of confrontations with badmen, but, anxiously and distractedly, of what the town will think of him in his new married state. This is a rite of passage in more than the ordinary sense. It marks Jack's transition from Old West lawman, the stereotypical hero of the American frontier, to solid married citizen of the New West, the self-conscious hero of domestic comedy. To mark the occasion, he has left his gun at home.

Meanwhile, back in Yellow Sky, the Old West seems alive and well in the person of Scratchy Wilson. In a scene out of any number of dime Westerns (the kind of story that fatally terrified the Swede in "The Blue Hotel"), a young man appears at the door of a saloon and announces that Scratchy is drunk and on the rampage. Nobody is tempted to become a dead hero; doors and windows are bolted and barred, and everyone awaits the return of the marshal, whose job is to fight Scratchy. It seems that he has fought him before (a detail which, to the experienced reader of Westerns, might seem odd—in the classic showdown, someone invariably dies).

In the next section, Scratchy himself appears, a badman with some details comically askew: His flannel shirt is "made principally by some Jewish women on the East Side of New York. . . . And his boots had red tops with gilded imprints, of the kind beloved in winter by little sledding boys on the hillsides of New England." On the streets of the deserted village there is no one to fight. He chases a dog to and fro with bullets, nails a scrap of paper to the saloon door as a target—and misses it by half an inch.

As Jack Potter and his new bride walk "sheepishly and with speed" toward his house, then, everything is set for the climax. Scratchy points his revolver at the unarmed marshal and sets out to play with him like a cat with a mouse; the only possible outcomes, seemingly, are tragedy or implausible heroism. Scratchy is enraged to discover that the marshal has no gun—what fun is that?

When he asks why, Jack replies that it is because he is married. The stunned Scratchy is "like a creature allowed a glimpse of another world"—as indeed he has been—and it is a new world with no place for him in it. In the showdown between old and new, Scratchy is armed with his six-guns, Jack with his wife. Jack wins hands down: Scratchy turns and walks away, leaving "funnel-shaped tracks in the heavy sand." Time and the prairie wind will soon efface them, and the Old West will be no more.

Summary

Stephen Crane is a crucial transitional figure in American literature. The psychological depths of Henry James, the master realist of Crane's lifetime, went virtually unrecognized at the time; the dominant figure was William Dean Howells, most of whose genteel social realism is unread today except by scholars. It was Crane who made the great leap inward—who, in *The Red Badge of Courage*, exhumed buried feelings to which the public responded with a shock of recognition. Such a response to a work so radically new is almost unheard of in the history of literature. For an instantaneous success to continue to speak to later generations is rarer still. Crane's fiercely unconventional honesty, above all, makes of his small body of fiction a treasure.

Bibliography

Beer, Thomas. *Stephen Crane: A Study in American Letters.* New York: Alfred A. Knopf, 1923.

Berryman, John. *Stephen Crane.* New York: Sloane, 1950.

Cady, Edwin. *Stephen Crane.* New York: Twayne, 1962.

Holton, Milne. *Cylinder of Vision: The Fiction and Journalistic Writing of Stephen Crane.* Baton Rouge: Louisiana State University Press, 1972.

LaFrance, Marston. *A Reading of Stephen Crane.* Oxford, England: Clarendon Press, 1971.

Nagel, James. *Stephen Crane and Literary Impressionism.* University Park: Pennsylvania State University Press, 1980.

Soloman, Eric. *Stephen Crane: From Parody to Realism.* Cambridge, Mass.: Harvard University Press, 1966.

Stallman, R. W. *Stephen Crane: A Biography.* New York: George Braziller, 1968.

Wolford, Chester. *Stephen Crane: A Study of the Short Fiction.* Boston: Twayne, 1989.

Edwin Moses

ROBERT CREELEY

Born: Arlington, Massachusetts
May 21, 1926

Principal Literary Achievement
Working in the modernist mode of Ezra Pound and William Carlos Williams, Robert Creeley's exceptional sensitivity to language and rhythm have made him one of America's leading poets.

Biography
Robert White Creeley was born in Arlington, Massachusetts, on May 21, 1926, two weeks before the birth of Allen Ginsberg in Newark, New Jersey. His parents were both from families that had been living in New England for generations, and his sister Helen was four years old when Oscar Slate Creeley, a physician married for the third time, and Genevieve Jules Creeley had their second child. When Dr. Creeley took his two-year-old son for a drive in an open car, a piece of coal shattered the windshield and a shard of glass cut Robert's eye, leading to a series of infections which culminated in the removal of the eye when the young boy was five—one year after his father's death. His mother moved to West Acton and became a public health nurse when Dr. Creeley died, and for the remainder of his childhood, Robert was reared in the care of aunts, grandmothers, and a maid named Theresa.

In 1940, Creeley entered Holderness School, a small boarding school in Plymouth, New Hampshire, where he published articles and stories in the *Dial*, the school literary magazine, which he edited in his senior year. Upon graduation in 1943, he entered Harvard University. After two years, Creeley joined the American Field Service and drove an ambulance in Burma and India; he then returned to Harvard for a second try. In 1946, he helped to edit the Harvard *Wake*'s special E. E. Cummings issue and published his first poem, "Return," there. During this year, his schoolmates at Harvard included the poets Robert Bly, Frank O'Hara, Kenneth Koch, and John Ashbery. Creeley had just married Ann McKinnon, however, and one semester short of his degree in 1947, he left school and moved to a chicken farm in New Hampshire. His son David was born in October, 1948. His wife's trust fund provided a meager subsistence, and he raised pigeons and chickens for additional income. His first public reading took place in 1950 on Cid Corman's radio program "This Is Poetry," and Creeley began to gather manuscripts from contemporary writers for an alternative magazine to be called *Lititz Review* (for Lititz, Pennsylvania,

the home of his coeditor Jacob Leed). Corman told Creeley about Charles Olson, the poet who was about to publish his ground-breaking "Projective Verse" essay. Creeley and Olson began a mammoth correspondence in which they both worked out the fundamental strictures of their poetic philosophies, and although the material for the magazine was not used immediately, Creeley placed some of it in *Origin I* and *Origin II* in 1951, including the first poems of Olson's *Maximum* sequence.

Creeley and his family (now three children) lived in France from 1951 to 1952, and then on the island of Mallorca from 1952 to 1955. His first book of poems, *Le Fou*, was published in 1952, and in 1953 he started the Divers Press, publishing his second book of poems, *The Kind of Act Of*, and publishing his first book of short fiction, *The Gold Diggers*, in 1954. In December of 1953, Olson, now the rector of Black Mountain College in North Carolina, asked Creeley to edit the *Black Mountain Review*; Creeley's first issue of the influential magazine appeared in March just before he arrived to teach at the college. He returned to Mallorca to try to repair his marriage, but came to North Carolina to teach and edit the review in 1955 after his divorce. That same year, his volume of poems *All That Is Lovely in Men* was published by Jonathan Williams. Creeley resigned from Black Mountain College in 1956, traveling to San Francisco, where he met Allen Ginsberg, Jack Kerouac, Gary Snyder, and other members of the San Francisco renaissance. Later in the year, he moved to Albuquerque, New Mexico, to teach in an academy for boys and was presented with a B.A. by Olson from Black Mountain.

He met and married Bobbie Louise Hoeck in 1957, began an M.A. at the University of New Mexico, and became the father of a daughter, Sarah, in November. Continuing his studies, he presented for his M.A. thesis a collection of poems and was granted the degree in 1960. He won the Levinson Prize from *Poetry* magazine for a group of ten poems and was included in Donald Allen's landmark anthology *The New American Poetry, 1945-1960* (1960). He remained at the University of New Mexico through 1962 as a visiting lecturer, and in 1962 his first book of poems to gain national attention, *For Love: Poems 1950-1960*, was published. In 1962-1963, he lectured at the University of British Columbia, then returned to New Mexico, remaining there from 1963 to 1966. In 1963, after completing the spring semester, he contributed to the Vancouver Poetry Festival, which brought together Olson, Robert Duncan, Ginsberg, Denise Levertov, and others Creeley had met while he edited the *Black Mountain Review*. Late in 1963, his novel *The Island* was published, and in 1964, he received a Guggenheim Fellowship. His friend Olson had begun to teach at the State University of New York at Buffalo, and Creeley participated in the Buffalo Arts Festival in 1965. In the following year, he accepted a position as a visiting professor at Buffalo, and in 1967 he was appointed professor of English there, a position he held until 1978.

Scribners published his second major collection of poems, *Words*, in 1967, and in 1968, Creeley returned to the University of New Mexico as a visiting professor for one year. Scribners published his next collection, *Pieces*, in 1969; a book of early and uncollected poems, *The Charm*, was issued by the Four Seasons Foundation in that year. Creeley also recorded two readings of his work. He spent the 1970-1971 academic year as a visiting professor at San Francisco State College and took part in poetry festivals in Texas and Belgium. In an attempt to conclude a peripatetic existence that had gone on for more than two decades, Creeley established a permanent residence in Buffalo in 1973 and began to take a very active interest in the cultural affairs of the city, working against the prevailing academic disinclination to bring literature to a wider segment of the population.

Continuing to travel extensively, Creeley took part in a poetry festival in Toronto in 1975 and spent the spring of 1976 reading his work in Fiji, New Zealand, Australia, the Philippines, Malaysia, Japan, and Korea, sponsored by the United States Information Agency (USIA). Scribners published a volume of his *Selected Poems* in 1976; *Mabel: A Story and Other Prose* was published by Marion Boyars in London, an indication of his growing international reputation. At the end of the year, he was divorced from his second wife, and in 1977, he married Penelope Highton. In 1979, Creeley began to publish poetry with the innovative, pioneering New Directions Press, founded and run by James Laughlin. Their association began with *Later* (1979), a volume that marked a ripening, more reflective turn in Creeley's style. Creeley returned to the University of New Mexico as a visiting professor in 1979, 1980, and 1981. In 1980, Black Sparrow Press published the first two volumes of his historic correspondence with Olson, an exchange of letters that was both a record of a special friendship and an epistolary analysis of postmodern poetry and poetics.

Creeley's son William Gabriel was born in 1981, the same year Creeley received the Shelley Memorial Award from the Poetry Society of America, a further indication of how much his work had become a part of the main current of American poetry, and in 1982, he augmented his position as a major figure in American literature with the publication of *The Collected Poems of Robert Creeley, 1945-1975*, a book that Creeley regarded as a coherent expression of his work which had "a sense of increment, of accumulation . . . that is very dear to me." New Directions followed this volume with Creeley's work over the past four years in *Mirrors* (1983), and in December of that year his daughter Hannah Highton was born. Creeley spent the winter of 1983-1984 in Berlin on a Berlin Artists Program Grant, then served on the National Endowment for the Arts (NEA) Literature Fellowship Panel in 1984. In that year, he turned again toward his New England origins by establishing a residence in Waldoboro, Maine, behind his sister Helen's house. In 1986 his third collection from New Directions, *Memory Gardens*, was published, a book which offered many reflections about members of his immediate family. The seventh and eighth volumes of Creeley's correspondence with Olson were published in 1987, and two years later, the University of California Press issued *The Collected Essays of Robert Creeley*, a companion volume to the *Collected Poems* and a book which, in gathering most of Creeley's theoretical, critical, autobiographical, and occasional prose into one collection, provided further evidence of the weight and influence of his thinking about literature. In 1990, New Directions published *Windows*, Creeley's eleventh book of poetry. Creeley continued to teach at the State University of New

York, holding the Samuel P. Capen Professorship of Poetry and Humanities, and he was honored by his community with the title New York State Poet for 1989-1991.

Analysis

Among the poets who took it as an obligation to explain the poetics of the evolving modernist continuation of the tradition in American literature which began with Walt Whitman and was developed by Ezra Pound and William Carlos Williams, Robert Creeley may be the most lucidly articulate as well as the most challengingly imaginative. With his friend and poetic brother Charles Olson, whose own theoretical suggestions (especially his "Projective Verse" essay of 1950) led to what Gilbert Sorrentino called "an encouragement for all young writers who felt themselves to be disenfranchised," Creeley accepted the task of demonstrating that his differences from the established strictures of the New Critics (such as John Crowe Ransome and Cleanth Brooks) were not failures of form but a different approach to the entire question of what form might be. In his essays and interviews, Creeley responded to the need for "the dignity of their own statement" felt by writers who shared his concerns, and although he rarely used his own poetry as an example of his theories in argument, preferring to cite the work of many colleagues he admires, his poems may be most clearly understood in the context of his own observations about the nature of writing.

Creeley's work has adhered to Olson's comment that "form is never more than an extension of content," a direct refutation of the idea common to academic criticism in the first half of the twentieth century that a poem should be a container of a specific design into which the poet arranged his words and images. Creeley has stressed the idea that, as Olson put it, "there's an appropriate way of saying something inherent in the thing to be said." That is, each specific occasion from which a poem emerges requires the suitable form and language of its particulars. Creeley claimed to feel "a rhythmic periodicity in the weight and duration of words to occur in the first few words, or first line, or lines, of what I am writing." Therefore, the crucial choice in the poem's opening established a measure—a much wider and subtler determinant than meter—to which the poet was compelled to respond as the poem continued. Put in another way, Creeley drew a parallel between a farmer plowing a field and a poet composing a poem. The first line, or furrow, determines direction; the second line solidifies it. Creeley saw the literal root of the word "verse" as a furrow, or a turning, just as the line turned in accordance with the requirements of emphasis, stress, breath units, and other elements inherent in the language as it was employed. While it is clear from Creeley's work that he is very much aware of the entire history of poetry in the English language (and that he regards it as "rather regrettable and a little dumb not to make use of the full context of what's been done"), he is also interested in the "possibilities of coherence . . . other than what was previously the case." Or, as he explains in his essay expressing his basic credo, "I'm *given* to write poems," he believes that it requires all of his intelligence to "follow the possibilities that the poem 'under hand' as Olson would say, is declaring."

Another crucial component of Creeley's poetic style is his use, in the spirit of Williams' arch claim that his poetic language came from "the mouths of Polish mothers," of the colloquial, with which he feels "very at home." Following the pioneering example of Williams' work, Creeley attempts to engage language at a level he regards as both familiar and active, so that the poem is an "intensely *emotional* perception," no matter how evident the poet's intelligence and education may be. This insistence on emotion recalls Whitman's dictum, "Who touches this book touches a man," and is a part of Creeley's determination to resist the academic theorists who emphasized an ironic distance that was part of a habit of diction that excluded many modes of speech as inappropriate for poetry. The use of a "commonly situated vernacular," however, does not mean that Creeley has neglected craft in the shaping of the language into a poem. One of the most distinctive aspects of his style is his precise arrangement of words so that a minimum of material is concentrated to produce an often complex series of meanings; a compact, even sparse poem—unadorned with rhetorical touches that mainly call attention to themselves—that answers Pound's insistence on condensation and compression. Because Creeley's poetry has removed some of the accumulated verbiage of previous conceptions of the "poetic," it has been mistakenly described as "thin," whereas it is more accurately lean or trim, with implication replacing unnecessary explanation. As Creeley points out, it is not that Williams restricted himself to a colloquial language which never utilizes words that are less frequently spoken. "What is common is the *mode* of address," Creeley observes, while the "sense of source in common speech" leads to an authenticity that supports Creeley's ideas that "the local is universal" and that language is the most basic instrument in permitting a poem to "exist through itself," as Olson insists.

While Creeley's poetics have remained relatively consistent during the course of their development, the poems he has written over four decades have continued to evolve in terms of their perception of his personal experiences. His first significant book, *For Love: Poems 1950-1960*, contains lyrics, many patterned after classical antecedents, which concentrate on the nature of love, but on a "strained, difficult love relationship" (as John Wilson remarks) in which Creeley, contrary to more recent social developments, attests a kind of primitive maleness endemic in American life. The erotic conditions which drew the poems, often in pain, from the poet's life are captured in language that seethes with erotic intensity while maintaining a decorum that elevates the work beyond mere confession. The poems are rife with wit, directed at the poet himself as frequently as at the world, but beyond the dark comedy of a man who called an earlier collection a "snarling garland," there is a gentleness, a poignancy that is very affecting. Poems such as "Ballad of the Despairing Husband" or "The Ball Game" use a comic mood to keep chaos at bay, while "I Know A Man" is "the poem of the decade . . . on a world gone out of control," according to Robert Hass, but beyond these, poems such as "The Name" (addressed to his daughters) or the extraordinary "The Rain" have a depth of feeling produced by words absolutely appropriate for the occasion.

Creeley's next collection, *Words*, moved further from the demands of formal concerns, employing a method Creeley called "scribbling" or "writing for the immediacy of the pleasure." Some of the most severe critical reactions Creeley suffered were directed at poems such as "A Piece," which reads in its entirety:

> One and
> one, two,
> three.

Creeley's concern here was to focus on the process of his thinking and to use both the rhythms of jazz and the techniques of a painter such as Jackson Pollock, whose paintings reflect the artist's actual placement of paint (words) on the canvas (the page) independent of specific representation. In addition to the poems which emphasize the singular effect of each word, there are longer, more intricate arrangements which move beyond the play of individual units of meaning to the human dimension.

Pieces moves even further in the direction of abstraction, but from the position that the poet is interested in establishing a harmony with the natural world. The structural openness that is declared in this collection and which marks Creeley's writing for the next ten years (through the collection *Hello: A Journal, February 29-May 3, 1976*, published in 1978) tends to break the "boundaries of individual poems" (as John Wilson observes) so as to emulate what Louis Zukovsky called "continuing song." Creeley, in quoting Robert Lowell, mentions that he moved back to a "more deliberate organization" at the point where he sensed he was at the "edges of incoherence." In *Pieces* and in other poetry written during the 1970's, Creeley depended on the pacing and rhythms to provide scraps of information; at times, a kind of minimalist reduction became so pervasive that Creeley was, as Louis Martz put it, "at the taut edge of poetic existence." The poems that appear in his next significant collection, *Later*, do not contradict Creeley's original intentions but give him a wider field for operation. The poetry of the first part of the 1970's utilized a method Creeley called "a continuity rather than a series of single instances," while *Later* and then *Mirrors* move again toward the strengths of the single poem, although always in the context of the other poems surrounding it. The major change in *Later* is a turn toward the reflective, as Creeley's characteristic expression of immediate thought and feeling in a very specific present is tempered by the reflection of a man who can see his own life as history combining occasion into pattern.

Creeley remarked that he felt *Later* was "a really solid book," and he stopped writing for nearly two years after its publication to take a "breathing space." Realizing in 1981 that he still had "a lot that I wanted to get out," he wrote the poems that were published in *Mirrors* in 1983. In this book, the poetry has a reflective range that does not lessen the impact of Creeley's "luminous austerity" but merges or mingles it with a new feeling of quiet acceptance. There is a troubled awareness of fatigue, failure, and aging in the poems, but the frustration and confusion expressed in "Age," in which the poet says

> He thinks he'll hate it
> and when he does die
> at last, he supposed
> he still won't know it,

is balanced, even countered, with the sentiments in "Oh Love": "Oh love/ like nothing else on earth!"

The strain of philosophical consideration, often presented with Creeley's dry humor, continues in *Memory Gardens*. The book has four sections, the first two containing many terse statements such as "I'll Win," in which the poet reviews his strategy of "being gone/ when they come" and summarizes its effect by saying mordantly, "Being dead, then/ I'll have won completely." These "cryptic epigrams" (as Dudley Fitts called Creeley's earliest poems) alternate with poems specifically written for various friends and several translations/adaptations (or as Creeley puts it, "free play on sounds and occasionally understood words") of poems by Richard Anders, whom he met in Berlin. The third section is Creeley's most comprehensive examination of his family background to this point in his life. This group includes meditations about his early life and poems about his parents such as the deeply affecting "The Doctor," in which images, like fragments of memory, recall the father he hardly knew. The poem closes with the poet's memory still charged with desire to uncover more information. After the psychic exhilaration and strain of the mental excursion into the realm of his past, Creeley again shifts to a more contemplative mood in section 4, in which a philosophic calendar with a poem for each month matches the spirit of the season to a specific kind of insight. This twelve-part sequence, with some variants on poets such as Thomas Wyatt and Ralph Waldo Emerson, leads toward Creeley's next book, *Windows* (1990), which is a display of virtuosity offering many of the most successful examples of Creeley's voice from previous collections in fresh and vital new poems. There is a lyric intensity in "Broad Bay," structural compactness in "Trec," explications of language in "Sight," considerations of relationships in "You," terse and penetrating philosophical discourse in "Age," more cryptic epigrams in "Improvisations," linguistic density in "Here," and the familiar sense of the poet working toward versions of his life as occasions of place. This collection suggests that Creeley's future work will maintain the vigor and clarity of what Charles Molesworth calls "the hard-won specificity of his voice, its timbre, its tremors" which is "like nothing else on earth."

THE RAIN

First published: 1962
Type of work: Poem

The poet, in a contemplative mood at night while listening to rain falling, wishes his love were content in his company.

Among his lyrics which use an image from the natural world as an occasion for an emotional revelation, "The Rain" is one of Creeley's most poignant and successful efforts. It opens with the direct, lean language that is Creeley's special signature:

> All night the sound had
> come back again,
> and again falls
> this quiet, persistent rain.

It then proceeds to a psychological correlative, where the poet asks "What am I to myself" and considers whether "hardness" is permanent, whether he is to "be locked in this/ final uneasiness" that even "rain falling" cannot alleviate. Then the poem moves beyond observation (of the self in the context of the phenomena of nature) to a fervent declaration of necessity:

> Love, if you love me,
> lie next to me.
> Be for me, like rain,
> the getting out
>
> of the tiredness, the fatuousness, the semi-
> lust of intentional indifference.

The plague of human frailty, which he condemns in three multisyllabic constructions that stand in stark contrast to the poem's other diction, is a part of the common affliction that dismembers relationships. As a remedy, Creeley then instructs his "love" to "Be wet/ with a decent happiness." The joining of rain, its properties of liquidity and fluidity, with a desirable human attribute unifies everything, and the mixture of the modestly hopeful and the idealistic in the last line perfectly captures the reserved or cautious optimism that is one of Creeley's most appealing features.

I KEEP TO MYSELF SUCH MEASURES . . .

First published: 1967
Type of work: Poem

Concerned about the nebulous nature of language, the poet seeks tangible coordinates with which to measure his perceptions.

The nature of language and its relationship to the physical world and the individual self ("speech is a mouth," Creeley exclaims with audacity in "The Language") is the subject of the poem "I Keep To Myself Such Measures . . ." The title, which is completed in the second line by the very personal ". . . as I care for," is an expression of the poet's interest in dimensions both in his art and in his daily life. The completing line of the first stanza, "daily the rocks/ accumulate position," uses a concrete object to stand for the accretion of experience, but then, in a dramatic reversal, Creeley qualifies the particularity of the rocks by observing, "There is nothing/ but what thinking makes/ it less tangible," expressing one of this most basic principles: the concern that language is nebulous and that the thought it renders can never be precise or final. Nevertheless, a position is established through the direction ordered by experience, even though that position is never so solid that it cannot be shaken. The consequence of Creeley's perception that "thinking makes/ it less tangible." compromises sanity itself, leading to uncertainty as a principle of existence:

> The mind
> fast as it goes, loses
>
> pace, puts in place of it
> like rocks simple markers,
> for a way only to
> hopefully come back to
>
> where it cannot.

The "simple markers" to which Creeley refers are the mental coordinates that prove unsatisfactory as permanent guidelines because of the motion—external and internal— that is the source of change in every form of life. The realization that the mind "cannot" come back to a previous position is the burden and fascination of the entire process of perception. Creeley's attempts to deal with this transitory universe are the focus of his measuring; his creation of the measures in his poems is a figure for a method of seeing that requires a measuring of everything in the personal realm. The "rocks" or "simple markers" cause him to say "My mind sinks" because measure is both a restriction and a point of reference, but because there is no alternative (if the mind is to be maintained at all as a functioning entity), Creeley concludes that "I hold in both hands such weight/ it is my only description." The word "such" retains the ambiguity of the shifting process of measuring, but the tangibility of "both hands" reinforces the importance of the process itself, for the man and the poet.

THERESA'S FRIENDS

First published: 1979
Type of work: Poem

The poet's recollections of his youth are informed by the Boston Irish cultural community that is his heritage.

Robert Creeley was reared by several women after his father died, including his mother, his grandmother, and a slightly retarded woman named Theresa whom his father had brought home to work as a maid. Creeley came to think of her as an "emotional ally" who was not as severe as his family and who needed his friendship in her alien condition. Among the poems Creeley wrote about his family, "Theresa's Friends" is a reminiscence that excludes some of the complex emotional intensity that sometimes almost overwhelms the poet so that here he can enjoy his reflections without feeling forced to wring nuance from every particle of memory.

"From the outset," he recalls, he was "charmed/ by the soft, quick speech" of Theresa's friends. Typically, it is their use of language that captivates him, the "endlessly present talking" that gave him his first sense of being Irish, which included the cultural mix of "the lore, the magic/ the violence, the comfortable/ or uncomfortable drunkenness." Each of these features is a source of recollective pleasure, not an element to be worried over, and as the poem narrows in focus, an ironmonger is depicted patiently telling the young man "sad, emotional stories/ with the quiet air of an elder." This is a feature of the oral tradition that informs Creeley's work as a poet of sound and speech, and the relaxed, conversational pace of the poem—more like a narrative than most of Creeley's works—sets the structure for a concluding insight that is especially dramatic because of its sudden increase in emotional pitch.

After the gradual preparation he has received from Theresa's friends concerning his cultural heritage, Creeley's mother tells him "at last when I was twenty-one" that "indeed the name *Creeley* was Irish," including him officially in the community of tale and mood toward which he has been drawn. The information comes with the effect of revelation, certifying all that Creeley had instinctively sensed about his origins, his destiny, and his gifts. In an unusually traditional concluding stanza, Creeley raises the level of language to inform and convince the reader/listener fully of the depth of his feeling:

> and the heavens opened, birds sang,
> and the trees and the ladies spoke
> with wondrous voices. The power of the glory
> of poetry—was at last mine.

THE EDGE

First published: 1983
Type of work: Poem

Uncertainty about everything plagues the poet, who continues to explore the world in language that is itself tentative and uncertain.

The insistent inspection and dissection of linguistic possibility for which Creeley is known reaches a kind of peak in "The Edge." The very short, elliptic word-unit common to Creeley's style throughout his writing life is fused into compact three-line stanzas, which are linked by a continuing focus on edges or boundaries in thought and action, poetry and life. Each stanza has a tentative hold, and then a release into the next one; a hesitancy that occurs after almost every unit of meaning. Creeley suggests that the poem itself is unclear in its way or course, "this long way comes with no purpose," just as the life it expresses seems unsure of its direction as the poet continues seeking, experimenting, testing, trying, and measuring language and form. Uncertainty does not preclude action, however; the poem's tentativeness is not an indication of paralysis but of an effort to discover a true course after many missteps. The poem itself expresses the poet's desire to construct or discover meaning through the repetition of small actions:

> I take the world and lose it,
> miss it, misplace it,
> put it back or try to, can't
>
> find it, fool it, even feel it.

There is no end to this, and the poem does not have an ending, only another thrust further into being, as the poet proclaims "This must be the edge/ of being before the thought of it/ blurs it. . . ." As Charles Molesworth aptly observes, poems such as this one are "a dramatization of the limits of Creeley's existential, improvisatory stance," statements where language and thought shift perception even as it occurs.

PLAGUE

First published: 1990
Type of work: Poem

The poet sees the isolation of patients at a leper hospital as a symbol of human loneliness and reaches for the consolation of human decency to avoid despair.

Although doubt and uncertainty are the climate of much of Creeley's poetry, there is a hard-won hope based on the trials of experience that resists despair or cynicism. In "Plague," a poem written in terse two-line units which are like semi-discrete couplets that lean into each other, the world is described in those times when it has become "a pestilence/ a sullen, inexplicable contagion" for the poet. Creeley reaches back toward the medical imagery of his father's life to form a figure for mental disorder, a figure which conveys the feeling of "a painful rush inward, isolate—" akin to a time in his own childhood when he saw "lonely lepers" he knew to be social pariahs "just down the street,/ back of shades drawn, closed doors." The closeness of the afflicted, the people damned by disease, reminds Creeley of how near to disaster all people are. In times of mental pressure or pain, the poet realizes, anyone may be similarly ravaged, forced to submit to a kind of universal aloneness in which the individual is transformed into an alien "them." "No one talked to them, no one/ held them anymore," he laments soberly. For a poet who is a master of the considered relationship, this complete absence of even the possibility of love is chilling to contemplate, but, as in an earlier poem in which Creeley called on the rain to inspire "decent happiness," here he reaffirms the reaching, sympathizing impulse in the human spirit in a symbolic evocation of "the faint sun":

> again, we look for the faint sun,
> as they are still there, we hope,
> and we are coming.

A poem such as "Plague" shows how the pared-down, lean lines and the open interconnected images produce "movingly rich emotional testaments" that are impressive explorations of language and self-consciousness—the kind of poetry that Creeley has made his own.

Summary

In one of the best reviews of Creeley's work, the poet and critic Robert Haas has said that Creeley's way "has been to take the ordinary, threadbare phrases and sentences by which we locate ourselves and to put them under the immense pressure of the rhythms of poetry and to make out of that what dance or music there can be." In a threefold pattern, Creeley uses the postmodern reliance on process (language in action) to reduce the chaos of abstraction, applies the analytic power of the mind to draw specific shape out of the promise of the process, and then applies the core instincts of the human heart striving for love to prevent the analytic reductions of the demands of form from turning all to abstraction again. Often difficult and even irritating, Creeley's poetry at its finest is, as many commentators have pointed out, unlike anything else in the language or literature of the twentieth century.

Bibliography

Allen, Donald, ed. *Contexts of Poetry: Interviews with Robert Creeley, 1961-1971.* Bolinas, Calif.: Four Seasons, 1973.

Edelberg, Cynthia. *Robert Creeley's Poetry: A Critical Introduction.* Albuquerque: University of New Mexico Press, 1978.

Ford, Arthur. *Robert Creeley.* Boston: G. K. Hall, 1978.

Fox, Willard. *Robert Creeley, Edward Dorn, and Robert Duncan: A Reference Guide.* Boston: G. K. Hall, 1989.

Terrell, Carroll, ed. *Robert Creeley: The Poet's Workshop.* Orono, Maine: National Poetry Foundation, 1984.

Wilson, John, ed. *Robert Creeley's Life and Work: A Sense of Increment.* Ann Arbor: University of Michigan Press, 1987.

Leon Lewis

E. E. CUMMINGS

Born: Cambridge, Massachusetts
October 14, 1894
Died: North Conway, New Hampshire
September 3, 1962

Principal Literary Achievement
Though he is recognized as a writer whose poetic experiments added significantly to the development of modern literature, E. E. Cummings also contributed to the development of other forms of literature, including autobiography.

Biography
The first of two children born to Edward Cummings and Rebecca Haswell Clarke, E. E. Cummings was reared in a curious milieu for a rebel poet. He virtually grew up in Harvard Yard and was surrounded by the most traditional aspects of Cambridge culture. His father, an instructor in sociology who later became a Unitarian churchman, instructed his son to pass the plate during certain church services. One of the few deviations from this elite, exclusive upbringing was E. E. Cummings' time in public high school, the result of one of his father's democratic ideas.

In 1911, Cummings entered Harvard University, living at home during the first three years of his university education. He wrote for the *Harvard Monthly*, publishing his first poems in that journal in 1912. He was graduated from Harvard magna cum laude in 1915, and he delivered the commencement address, entitled "The New Art." During his undergraduate years at Harvard, Cummings demonstrated a revolutionary and rebellious attitude toward traditional, conventional art and literature, an attitude that would be characteristic of Cummings throughout his life.

After receiving his M.A. from Harvard in 1916, Cummings moved to New York City and spent three months in an office job. The following year he sailed for France as a volunteer in the Norton Harjes Ambulance Corps of the American Red Cross. His four-month imprisonment by French authorities on suspicion of disloyalty provided the basis for his first autobiography, *The Enormous Room*, published in 1922. Released from prison on New Year's Day, 1918, Cummings returned to New York City, where he lived in Greenwich Village.

In 1920, Cummings made his first major appearance in *The Dial*, a literary magazine that was a vehicle for most of the leading artists of the time. From 1921 to 1923, he made his first trip to Paris, where he met many of the leading avant-garde

figures who found Paris to be a lively and stimulating place for art and artists. Cummings lived in Paris intermittently throughout the 1920's and made numerous trips abroad throughout his life. When he returned to the United States in 1923, Cummings took up permanent residence in New York City, spending the summers at Joy Farm, his family's summer home, in Silver Lake, New Hampshire. His return to New York coincided with the publication of the first of twelve volumes of poetry, *Tulips and Chimneys* (1923), all of which revealed Cummings' effort to experiment with language, structure, and ideas.

Cummings was married three times: first to Elaine Orr in 1924, then to Anne Barton in 1927, and finally to Marion Morehouse in 1932. While he was dealing with these personal changes in his life, he wrote prolifically: nearly eight hundred poems, plays, ballets, fairy tales, and autobiographies. He also produced a number of drawings and watercolors, having his first major showing of paintings at the Painters and Sculptors Gallery, New York City, in 1931. Other shows were held at the American British Art Center and the Rochester Memorial Art Gallery.

During his life, E. E. Cummings was recognized for both the quantity and quality of his work. He was awarded two Guggenheim Fellowships, the first in 1933—the year his book *Eimi*, based on a trip to Russia, was published—and the second in 1951. He was also awarded a fellowship of the American Academy of Poets in 1950 and a National Book Awards special citation in 1955. In 1957, Cummings received the Bollingen Prize in Poetry as well as the Boston Arts Festival Award.

Despite this public recognition of his work and despite his position as the Charles Eliot Norton Professor at Harvard during 1952-1953, Cummings was a private person. Toward the end of his life he made few public appearances except for a series of lectures at Harvard and readings of his poetry to mostly undergraduate audiences. He became partly crippled by arthritis and wore a brace that forced him to conduct these readings while sitting in a straight-backed kitchen chair. He would read for a half hour, rest, then return to finish the program, charming audiences with his poetry and personality. E. E. Cummings died in 1962, having worked to the last day of his life.

Analysis

Because of his idiosyncratic punctuation and typography, E. E. Cummings is often labeled an experimentalist, and indeed his art is innovative and revolutionary. One of the most curious aspects of Cummings' work, however, is that it combines experimentation with tradition, a point Gertrude Stein noted in her book, *The Autobiography of Alice B. Toklas* (1933):

> Gertrude Stein who had been much impressed by The Enormous Room said that Cummings did not copy, he was the natural heir of the New England tradition with its aridity and its sterility, but also with its individuality.

In all of his works—prose, poetry, drama, and autobiography—Cummings celebrated this quality of individuality, seeing it as the legacy of his New England upbringing and also as the outstanding characteristic of modernism. For Cummings, individuality was both a theme and a technique. Thematically, it was a faith in a world in which the independent, alive, living individual struggled against the cerebral, joyless nonindividual. Cummings celebrated the existence of the individual and satirized the boring, mechanistic lives of nonindividuals. Technically, individuality was at the core of Cummings' experiments with word coinings, free verse, innovations with typography and punctuation, and other strategies that make Cummings' literature, especially his poetry, look and sound different from almost any other artist's work, especially those who preceded him. Thematically and technically, then, Cummings was committed to individuality, a dedication he made clear during one of his six "nonlectures" at Harvard: "Let us pray always for individuals; never for worlds."

The individuals for whom Cummings prays and about whom he writes inhabit a particular kind of universe. It is, first of all, a place that is natural, not created by human beings, and it is a place in which nature is process, not product. To understand this place and the people within it requires intuition and imagination, not mere intellectualizing. Thus Cummings is constantly criticizing those who believe they can rely only upon reason, while he praises those who try to understand with their hearts and their emotions.

Cummings' true individuals are lovers, artists, clowns, circus people, or adolescents—those who, in his view, challenge both society and labels. They are connected by their freedom—their vital need to be independent—and they typically demonstrate that independence by challenging those who embody convention, tradition, and mechanization. Politicians, soldiers, bureaucrats, and "Cambridge ladies" are targets of their assault, for all those individuals not only represent categories themselves, but they also attempt to label, and thus limit, the freedom of others.

In his poetry, Cummings uses several strategies to explore his ideas about individuality. He coins words so that nouns are made of verbs, creating a sense of nonstop motion and forcing the reader to become actively involved in the poem. He also distorts the syntax of sentences so that it is impossible to read his works in a traditional way of identifying subject-verb-object. Still another strategy is visual—setting up the poem on a page so that it looks different from the traditional, linear lyric, thus compelling the reader to move back and forth within the poem, making meaning out of the motion of reading as well as out of the words being read. Taken together, these strategies emphasize process: the process of being alive—a hallmark of a true individual—and the process of reading.

His other literary forms demonstrate this same celebratory stance. In his autobiographies—*The Enormous Room* and *Eimi*—Cummings honors the individuals who transcend the boundaries of society. Whether they are the prisoners in the French Army camp or citizens in Russia, individuals who listen to and learn from their hearts and who are independent and self-reliant are the objects of Cummings' praise. In his plays and ballets and other works, the same kind of people are honored, and, by contrast, their opposites are parodied and satirized.

THE ENORMOUS ROOM

First published: 1922
Type of work: Autobiography

A self-portrait in which Cummings describes his captivity in a French prison during World War I.

The Enormous Room is E. E. Cummings' autobiographical narrative of the time he spent in La Ferté Mace, a French concentration camp a hundred miles west of Paris. Cummings and a friend, both members of an American ambulance corps in France during World War I, were erroneously suspected of treasonable correspondence and were imprisoned from August, 1917, until January, 1918. In this book, Cummings describes the prisoners with whom he shared his captivity, the captors who subjected their victims to enormous cruelty, and the filthy surroundings of the prison camp. Written in the form of a pilgrimage and modeled after John Bunyan's *Pilgrim's Progress* (1678), Cummings' narrative also shows the influence of early American black autobiographies. Like Christian in *Pilgrim's Progress* and the slaves who wrote their own stories, the narrator in Cummings' self-portrait faces an arduous journey to freedom, a voyage not unlike the ones described in many early black autobiographies also modeled on Bunyan's classic. In Cummings' voyage, the autobiographer emphasizes and celebrates his belief in individuality, especially as it is seen in the characters of the prisoners, including the gypsy dubbed Wanderer, the childish giant named Jean le Nègre, and the clownish captive called Surplice.

In *The Enormous Room*, the reader follows the enslaved Cummings along three legs of his journey: first, the period before La Ferté Mace; then, the period beginning with the second day in the enormous room; and finally, the departure from the French prison. During the first part of the autobiographical journey, Cummings appears as a rebellious American soldier parodying the rhetoric of wartime communication in his description of dissension within the ranks:

> To borrow a characteristic-cadence from Our Great President: the lively satisfaction which we might be suspected of having derived from the accomplishment of a task so important in the saving of civilization from the clutches of Prussian tyrany [sic] was in some degree inhibited, unhappily, by a complete absence of cordial relations between the man whom fate had placed over us and ourselves. Or, to use the vulgar American idiom, B. and I and Mr. A. didn't get on well.

Rebellious and independent, the young Cummings quickly learns the price of asserting these two qualities: He is imprisoned and joins a multitude of other captives who try desperately, and usually successfully, to retain their individuality despite their captors' efforts to rob them of this quality.

Enclosed in the space he calls "the Enormous Room," Cummings is entrapped in an oblong room 80 feet by 40 feet. This room in La Ferté Mace both restricts and unites an international menagerie of humanity (Dutch, Belgian, Spanish, Turkish, Arabian, Polish, Russian, Swedish, German, French, and English), including the American animal, E. E. Cummings. Among the most memorable of these fellow prisoners is Surplice—the court jester of the enormous room, the fool, the scapegoat, the eternal victim—who occupies an important spot in both the prison and the world, as Cummings notes: "After all, men in La Misère as well as anywhere also rightly demand a certain amount of amusement; amusement is, indeed, peculiarly essential to suffering; in proportion as we are able to be amused we are able to suffer." Cummings' description of this classic notion of scapegoating is especially poignant because he is describing himself as well as his readers: "I, Surplice," says Cummings, "am a very necessary creature after all."

Another memorable prisoner with whom Cummings shares his space is Zulu, thus called, says Cummings, partly because he looks like something Cummings had never seen, partly because the sounds of the two syllables appeared to relate to his personality, and partly because Zulu seemed to like the name. Cummings is particularly attracted to this prisoner because Zulu embodies the qualities that Cummings cherishes: individuality, vitality, emotion, and timelessness. Zulu is "A Verb; an IS," according to Cummings, meaning that he is an example of life and action—as a verb represents action—not a victim of passivity, the quality Cummings associates with nouns.

His insights into scapegoating and verbs are two of the many lessons Cummings learns during his captivity; they are lessons that contribute to the changes that occur within him and that result in his being a different person when he leaves La Ferté Mace. Having entered the prison as a youthful soldier who flippantly used language to parody wartime rhetoric and officials, he leaves the prison as a more thoughtful individual, one who sees the power of language to celebrate the wonders of life and individuality. As he prepares to leave the prison, he writes a poem, not only the first stanza of a ballad, as he had done in the beginning of his journey, when he had hoped that the next day he would write the second, the day after, the third, and the next day, the refrain—never having done any of it.

On the boat to America, Cummings is surrounded by strangers, and when he arrives in New York he is struck by the image of anonymous Americans, hurrying about in a frenzy of activity. He sees New York differently from the time he left it because he himself is different. This final scene in *The Enormous Room*, a picture of separateness yet potential connectedness, reflects the basic lesson that Cummings learned from his education in prison: He can neither completely nor permanently unite himself with others. He can, however, celebrate his individuality, his sense of self, and his gratitude for being alive and able to use language to describe his journey into and out of La Ferté Mace and the trips that lie ahead of him.

One of the strengths of *The Enormous Room* is that it explores several important issues, including war, society, and language. In the tradition of war novels, it protests the war, but it is more of a parody than a protest, since Cummings uses humor to present his view of people. Thus one has the *plantons*, the cruel jailers, whom

Cummings depicts with a mixture of mockery and sympathy, and the prisoners, whom Cummings describes with humor and joy as they find ways to remain individuals despite the efforts of their captors to dehumanize their innocent victims. *The Enormous Room* is a book about society insofar as it protests society's tendencies toward dehumanization, non-reflection, mechanization, and over-intellectualizing. Amid his descriptions of prisoners and jailers, Cummings inserts his protestations about education, government, and religion, suggesting that these institutions rob people of their individuality.

The Enormous Room is also about language, the vehicle that Cummings manipulates for two reasons: to show the dangers of empty rhetoric and to help readers see the world in a new way. Like other artists during and after World War I, including Ernest Hemingway, who objected to the lofty words that frequently concealed reality, Cummings protests the politicians' words that, in his view, were largely responsible for the "Great War." Cummings uses language as art—art that is intended to help people see in a new way. Thus he describes the prisoners, whom he calls Delectable Mountains, in poetic terms that force the reader to see these characters as beautiful individuals, not as dirty criminals.

Finally, *The Enormous Room* is about E. E. Cummings, the prisoner who begins his captivity as a young Harvard graduate and who grows through the process so that he is able to transcend his Cambridge roots and connect with prisoners whose lack of education and sophistication taught him who he was and wanted to be. At the conclusion of the book, when Cummings returns to New York, he is a different person, one who has recaptured the joy of childhood and the importance of being an individual who celebrates humanity, life, and love.

IN JUST-

First published: 1920
Type of work: Poem

A lyric about the time that immediately follows winter.

One of Cummings' most famous poems, "in Just-" reveals the poet's typically experimental approach, avoiding all punctuation to emphasize the nonstop vitality of a season he describes as "mud-/ luscious" and "puddle-wonderful." A goat-footed balloonman whistles; children play hopscotch, jump-rope, and marbles; and the world celebrates the season that can only be described as "Just-spring."

The poem is divided into five sections, with a format that matches the sense of dance and music that are described in the lyric. Contrasts are important—the slow tune of "Just-/ spring" and "mud-/ luscious" is juxtaposed with the speed of "and eddieandbill come/ running from marbles and/ piracies and it's/ spring." The poem, like the season, is a mixture of contrasts, from old balloonman to young children, from the slow, quiet time of growth to the rapid, explosive moments of ecstasy.

Taken together, these contrasts describe a season which has no word in the English language except for Cummings' coined phrase: "Just-spring."

ALL IN GREEN WENT MY LOVE RIDING

First published: 1923
Type of work: Poem

A poem that re-creates the myth of Diana slaying Actaeon.

"All in green went my love riding" is an example of Cummings' use of an ancient myth to communicate his message to a modern audience. The poem is about courtly love, and it alludes to the Roman and Greek myth in which Diana or Artemis, goddess and protectress of wildlife, is challenged by the hunter Actaeon. The goddess changes Actaeon into a stag, whereupon Actaeon's own hounds attack and kill him. Cummings retells this story, using fourteen stanzas, each of which paints a graphic picture that chronicles a part of this chase.

The poem is replete with colors: the green garb of a lover, the golden color of the horse, the silver dawn, the redness of the roebuck, the whiteness of water. It is equally specific in other details, such as numbers: there are four hounds and four deer. These and other details paint a picture that combines beauty with terror; the beauty of the place and the lover are enveloped in the ominous atmosphere of death.

Told from the view of Diana or Artemis, this poem describes the chase, beginning with Actaeon's departure and concluding with his death and Diana's swoon. Though the poem ends with these images, it is not a lyric about finality or mortality. On the contrary, it is about vitality and life, for the lovers are united in their ecstasy, just as the poem is united by its repetition (with the variation in the final line) of the first and last two stanzas. Thus the color green, the color of life, connects the lovers, who themselves are joined in the cycle of life and death.

THE CAMBRIDGE LADIES WHO LIVE IN FURNISHED SOULS

First published: 1923
Type of work: Poem

A poem that satirizes people whom Cummings viewed as aristocratic snobs.

A sonnet, "the Cambridge ladies who live in furnished souls" attacks a broad group of people who, Cummings believed, populated Cambridge, Massachusetts, and many other locales. These faculty wives, church women, and literary society ladies are described in careful detail, beginning with the first line, in which they are seen in terms of the stuffy Victorian rooms in which many of them resided. They have "comfortable minds," suggesting their lack of individuality and originality, and daughters who are like themselves: "unscented shapeless spirited."

These Cambridge ladies believe in Christ and the American poet Henry Wadsworth Longfellow, "both dead." They themselves are also dead, unaware that, above their stuffy rooms and beyond their stuffy lives, the "moon rattles like a fragment of angry candy." Isolated in their artificial world, they engage in meaningless banter, oblivious of the wonders of the natural world within and around them.

I SING OF OLAF GLAD AND BIG

First published: 1931
Type of work: Poem

The poem sings the praises of Olaf, a conscientious objector.

The opening line of "i sing of Olaf glad and big" announces the poet's intention: to sing, to celebrate, the greatness of an individual who bravely defies convention and who heroically dies because of his act of rebellion. Olaf's "warmest heart recoiled at war," so he became a conscientious objector, subjecting himself to cruel harassment at the hands of a "trig westpointer"—a graduate of the United States Military Academy at West Point. Like the Delectable Mountains in *The Enormous Room*, Olaf stands his ground and announces to his tormentor that he will not kiss the flag that he represents.

Described as "a conscientious object-or," Olaf becomes an "object" to the officers who treat him as cruelly as the *plantons* treated the prisoners in La Ferté Mace. Olaf continues in his opposition to war, however, and is thrown into prison for his defiant stance. His tragic, heroic death causes the poet to sing his praises and to question conventional notions of courage: "unless statistics lie he was/ more brave than me: more blond than you."

ANYONE LIVED IN A PRETTY HOW TOWN

First published: 1940
Type of work: Poem

A poetic portrait of a town in which humanizing and dehumanizing forces coexist.

"Anyone lived in a pretty how town" is a poem in which Cummings' wordplay is especially effective. The poem contrasts "anyone" and "noone" with "someones and everyones," the first pair being the hero and heroine who love each other, the second pair being the anonymous mass of nonbeings who live lives of quiet desperation, as another New Englander, Henry David Thoreau, once lamented. Eventually "anyone" and "noone" die, but their lives have been meaningful and enriching; the rest of the townspeople—the "someones and everyones"—continue to live, though their existences, like those of the Cambridge ladies, are characterized not by life but by living death.

In the first stanza, Cummings reveals a number of technical innovations. In addition to his inventive use of the pronoun "anyone," he plays with the phrase "a pretty how town," suggesting that the saying—"how pretty a town"—conceals something not so pretty after all. The second line is a syntactical jolt: "(with up so floating many bells down)." It is followed by a line in which four words, without punctuation, imply the tolling of those bells to signify the passing of time: "spring summer autumn winter." The final line of this first stanza returns to the first line and "anyone," who "sang his didn't he danced his did."

Unaware of and unconcerned about the "someones and everyones" who "cared for anyone not at all," the hero of the poem falls in love with "noone," whose celebration of life rivals that of her lover. As they live life and the rest of the town lives death, the cycle of nature continues. Bells continue to toll, children continue to be born, and the townspeople continue to say, not their prayers, but their "nevers." While these nonbeings "slept their dream," the lovers "anyone" and "noone" lived their dream, ultimately dying and being buried side by side, just as they had lived their full, vital lives. After their deaths, the "pretty how town" continued exactly as it always had, with "Women and men (both dong and ding)" pursuing their meaningless lives; they "reaped their sowing and went their came/ sun moon stars rain." Though dead, "anyone and noone" are alive because at least they once were alive; by contrast, "someones and everyones," though still breathing, are merely existing, surviving the seasonal change. Clones of one another, they are untouched by the individuality and vitality of their neighbors who loved and died singing their "didn'ts" and dancing their "dids."

PITY THIS BUSY MONSTER,MANUNKIND

First published: 1944
Type of work: Poem

The natural world is preferable to the restless, unsatisfying human world of "progress."

"Pity this busy monster,manunkind" is a poem that emphasizes Cummings' belief in nature and his opposition to those things—science, technology, and intellectual arrogance—that he believed attack the purity of nature. In the opening lines, Cummings makes it clear that man is un-kind—as opposed to being "mankind"—when he or she engages in "progress." In this case, "Progress is a comfortable disease," one which uses electrons and lenses to "deify one razorblade/ into a mountainrange;lenses extend/ unwish through curving wherewhen till unwish/ returns on its unself." For Cummings, progress contrasts with nature, as he suggests when he writes, "A world of made/ is not a world of born."

The speaker in this poem, as revealed in the last line, represents progress but suggests the promise of nature; "We doctors," he or she says, "know a hopeless case." Hopelessness is the human-made cycle of progress, scientific progress. There is a way out, however, as the speaker points out in the concluding lines of the poem: "listen:there's a hell/ of a good universe next door;let's go." Unlike this universe, composed of negative Cummings-created words such as "unwish" and "unself," the next-door universe consists of wishes and selves—that is, real emotions and real individuals. Those realities, for Cummings, are the true realities.

Summary

E. E. Cummings' works are testimonies to the self and the natural world which nurtures that self. They speak of the need to experience the world, not control it; they remind their readers of the importance of the present moment. They celebrate the individual over society, the self over selves. They honor emotion over intellect, feeling over thought. In Cummings' works, one hears a voice that speaks clearly and loudly to the modern world, a voice that both warns and celebrates. That combination of sounds is, in itself, one of Cummings' most significant contributions.

Bibliography

Baum, S. V., ed. *Cummings and the Critics.* East Lansing: Michigan State University Press, 1962.

Dumas, Elizabeth. *E. E. Cummings: A Remembrance of Miracles.* New York: Harper & Row, 1974.

Friedman, Norman, ed. *E. E. Cummings: A Collection of Critical Essays.* Englewood Cliffs, N.J.: Prentice-Hall, 1972.

Lane, Gary. *I Am: A Study of E. E. Cummings' Poems.* Lawrence: University Press of Kansas, 1976.

Norman, Charles. *E. E. Cummings: The Magic Maker.* Boston: Little, Brown, 1972.

Marjorie Smelstor

SAMUEL R. DELANY

Born: New York, New York
April 1, 1942

Principal Literary Achievement
One of the earliest and most influential black authors of science fiction, Delany has expanded the limits of the genre by blending it with stories drawn from myths and with modern interpretations of philosophical thought.

Biography
Samuel Ray Delany, Jr., was born into an upper-middle-class family in the Harlem district of New York City on April 1, 1942. His father had come to New York from North Carolina and, in the period before Delany's birth, had established a successful career as a funeral director. Delany's mother, the former Margaret Carey Boyd, was a library clerk with a long-standing interest in literature. In the late 1920's, she had been a friend of several authors in the literary movement kown as the Harlem Renaissance.

The prosperity of Delany's family allowed the young Samuel to attend a number of prestigious schools. Having been graduated from the private Dalton School, Delany enrolled at the Bronx High School of Science. There, a reading disorder which had troubled Delany throughout his early schooling was diagnosed as dyslexia. Despite his handicap, Delany was already making progress toward a literary career. While he was still in his early teens, he wrote several novels (none of them published) and served as coeditor of the *Dynamo*, his high school's literary review. Delany's early work won for him several local awards, and he was encouraged to continue with his literary pursuits.

On August 24, 1961, Delany married his former coeditor on the *Dynamo*, Marilyn Hacker. During that same year, he began taking courses at the City College of New York and became poetry editor of the college's literary journal, the *Promethean*. Marilyn, meanwhile, left school and began work as a science fiction editor for Ace Books. Because of Marilyn's encouragement and his own conviction that he could write more interesting science fiction than that being published at the time, Delany completed his first successful science fiction novel, *The Jewels of Aptor* (1962), when he was only nineteen. *The Jewels of Aptor*, like each of Delany's first eight novels, was published by Ace Books. At first, the novel appeared only in a heavily edited version, bound into the same volume as fellow science fiction author

James White's *Second Ending*. A revised edition of *The Jewels of Aptor* was issued by Ace in 1968, and the full text of the novel finally appeared in an edition published by Gregg Press in 1976.

Delany dropped out of college in 1963 and embarked upon an intense period of writing. While supporting himself as a musician, Delany published *Captives of the Flame* (1963), *The Towers of Toron* (1964), *City of a Thousand Suns* (1965), and *The Ballad of Beta-2* (1965). In each of those novels, he united the traditional narrative of the quest with a detailed account of imaginary civilizations. That same combination was to appear in much of his later fiction.

In 1965, Delany left the country to begin a quest of his own. On an extended journey throughout Europe and Asia Minor, he completed *The Einstein Intersection* (1967), publishing it upon his return to the United States. He then resumed work as a musician in New York City and continued to write novels and short stories. In 1966, with the publication of *Babel-17*, Delany reached a turning point in his career. *Babel-17* received a Nebula Award from the Science Fiction Writers of America and was the author's first novel to be read widely by the general public. Delany won a second Nebula Award for *The Einstein Intersection*; he would receive the award again for a short story, "Aye, and Gomorrah . . . " (1967), and a novella, "Time Considered as a Helix of Semiprecious Stones" (1969).

For a brief period during the late 1960's, Delany lived in San Francisco. Upon returning to New York City, he completed *Nova* (1968), a novel which proved to be another breakthrough for Delany. *Nova* was the author's first work to be published by a press other than Ace Books (it was issued by Doubleday) and his first novel to be printed in a hardbound edition.

In the early 1970's, Delany began experimenting with new media and avant-garde literary forms. He wrote, directed, and edited two short films, *Tiresias* (1970) and *The Orchid* (1971), developed plots for the comic-book series *Wonder Woman* (1972), and edited four volumes of *Quark* (1970-1971), a quarterly anthology devoted to experimental techniques of writing and analyzing science fiction. His coeditor of *Quark* was once again his wife, Marilyn Hacker. By this time, Marilyn had become an award-winning poet in her own right. She and Delany would continue to collaborate on various projects until their divorce in 1980.

Delany also began work on his most ambitious project to date, a long and difficult novel that was to be known as *Dhalgren* (1975). When *Dhalgren* was finally published, it met with a mixed reaction. The novel sold exceedingly well—more than half a million copies were eventually printed—but critical reviews were largely negative. Many critics were puzzled by the ambiguity of the novel's plot (its central character is an amnesiac whose uncertainty about his own past clouds the narrative at many points) and by Delany's radical departure from the accepted conventions of science fiction. Rather than taking place in an imaginary future locale, for example, *Dhalgren* is set in a strangely distorted version of the 1970's. The setting proves to be an extended metaphor for modern life, with many of the problems of contemporary society taken to their logical—or perhaps illogical—conclusions.

While *Dhalgren* was still in press, Delany completed another novel, *The Tides of Lust* (1973). This work represented another radical departure from Delany's earlier fiction. *The Tides of Lust* includes explicitly pornographic passages, a factor that seemed to alienate many readers. The book quickly went out of print. Nevertheless, Delany returned to the theme of sexuality in his next major novel, *Triton* (1976), which depicts a utopian society in which all restrictions on personal and sexual relationships have been removed.

In 1975, Delany was named Butler Professor of English at the State University of New York at Buffalo. While at Buffalo, Delany began devoting more of his energies to literary criticism and analysis than to fiction. He became a senior fellow at the University of Wisconsin, Milwaukee's, center for Twentieth Century Studies in 1977 and at Cornell University's Society for the Humanities in 1987. A few more novels were published by Delany during this period, including *Distant Stars* (1981) and the comic-book novel *Empire: A Visual Novel* (1978). Nevertheless, Delany's most important work throughout the 1970's and 1980's remained in the field of literary criticism. After writing two volumes that he called "notes on the language of science fiction," *The Jewel-Hinged Jaw* (1977) and *Starboard Wine* (1982), Delany served in 1988 as professor of comparative literature at the University of Massachusetts at Amherst.

Analysis

It is not surprising that so much of Delany's work in the late 1970's and the 1980's was in the field of literary criticism; even his early fiction reveals an extensive knowledge of literary theory and of mainstream literary traditions. For example, in *The Jewels of Aptor*, the quest for telepathic jewels places Geo, the hero of the novel, in the same tradition as numerous other protagonists of epic quests, including Gilgamesh, Jason, and Percival. Delany even makes an explicit association between Geo and Jason, the leader of the Argonauts, by adopting the name "Argo" for one of the central deities in the novel.

In traditional epics, heroes of quests begin their journeys because of a desire to seek adventure or a wish to recover some physical object. Delany's characters, however, are motivated more by a desire to seek knowledge than by any hope of material gain. Thus Rydra Wong, the heroine of *Babel-17*, begins her voyage hoping to obtain the information that she needs to decipher a strange alien dialect. Joneny, the protagonist of *The Ballad of Beta-2*, sets out to learn about the Star Folk. In traditional quest stories, physical journeys usually serve as a metaphor for the protagonist's inner journeys of self-discovery. Delany, aware of this tradition, has merely exposed the metaphor, making knowledge both the symbolic and the actual goal of the quest.

Delany's familiarity with modern philosophy and with anthropology has had a major impact upon his novels. The goddess Argo in *The Jewels of Aptor* was inspired by Delany's reading of *The White Goddess* (1947), an examination of religion and folklore by the poet and novelist Robert Graves. *The White Goddess* dealt extensively with the origins and influence of the pre-Greek goddess Cybele. Graves's exploration of Cybele's connection with the earth and fertility may be seen in Geo, *The Jewels of Aptor*'s protagonist, whose name is derived from the Greek word for "earth." Moreover, in such novels as *Triton* and *Tales of Nevèrÿon* (1979), Delany used the techniques of modern anthropology to analyze the fictional societies which he himself had created.

BABEL-17

First published: 1966
Type of work: Novel

An intergalactic poet attempts to foil saboteurs by breaking their code and learning their language.

Babel-17, Delany's first novel to receive a Nebula Award, was also the first to address issues found in many of his later works. Part novel and part philosophical inquiry, *Babel-17* explores the degree to which language shapes the perception of reality. Babel-17, the artificial language from which the novel receives its name, is described by Delany as lacking both first- and second-person pronouns. As a result, Delany suggests, speakers of this language would not have any ability to be "self-critical"—to separate reality from what the language has "programmed" them to see as reality. On the other hand, Babel-17's analytical superiority over other languages is said to ensure that its speakers develop technical mastery over most situations.

One of the questions raised by the novel, therefore, is how much one's language dictates the way in which one perceives the world. In Babel-17, the word for a member of the Alliance would mean something roughly translatable as "one-who-has-invaded"; this, Delany suggests, causes those who think in the Babel-17 language instinctively to view the Alliance as a hostile force that must be destroyed. As one reads the novel, one wonders how much one's own linguistic structures—including, for example, such expressions as "upper class," "Far East," and "New World"—not only reflect, but also actually determine, a system of values.

With a poet as its protagonist, *Babel-17* is also a work that explores the nature and power of literature. In the poetry of Rydra Wong, the novel's main character—as well as in the quotations taken from the poetry of Marilyn Hacker, Delany's wife, which serve as epigraphs for major sections of the novel—one finds poetry continually represented as an effective medium of communication. Rydra Wong's success throughout the galaxy is proof that words can unite individuals regardless of their backgrounds, cultures, or even the planets on which they live.

On yet another level, *Babel-17* functions as a sociological novel, exploring the ways in which people wrongly assume that social conventions reflect a universal law. In the intricately detailed world that Delany has created, many contemporary customs are presented in an exaggerated fashion so that the reader might view them from a new perspective. For example, a reader may be repulsed initially by the novel's description of "cosmetisurgery," a procedure by which lights, flowers, and mechanical devices are implanted into one's body as a decoration. Yet, in the characters' discussions of this practice, it quickly becomes apparent that surgical alteration of the body for purposes of beauty or hygiene has parallels to the familiar customs of circumcision, ear-piercing, and creating tattoos. In a similar way, the discomfort that some of the novel's characters experience when encountering a "triple" (a form of marriage among three people) is intended to reflect the discomfort of Delany's readers' own society when dealing with those whose sexual lives deviate from accepted norms.

THE EINSTEIN INTERSECTION

First published: 1967
Type of work: Novel

In the distant future, a musician attempts to defeat a mysterious figure who is murdering those who are "different."

The Einstein Intersection expands upon the theme of cultural diversity Delany had first explored in *Babel-17*. The alien race inhabiting the earth thirty thousand years in the future attempts to develop its "humanity" by imitating the traditions of the extinct human race. In the end, one of the lessons that the aliens learn is that they must accept their own unique natures and develop traditions more appropriate to themselves. Furthermore, frequent mutations cause differences to emerge among the aliens. The protagonist of the novel is one of those "different" beings—as is, ironically, the figure who has been destroying the mutants. Thus, failure to accept one's own fundamental difference from others leads, in the novel, to hostility and ultimately to violence.

The narrator of the story, Lobey, is a musician. In the course of the novel, he sets out to regain his lost love, Friza, who is later taken from him again. Delany calls Lobey's opponent in the novel "Kid Death." All these elements have been inspired by the Greek legend of Orpheus, Eurydice, and Hades (the god of death in Greek mythology), but the myth of Orpheus is only one of the mythic allusions central to *The Einstein Intersection*. Like many of Delaney's novels, the general structure of *The Einstein Intersection* is that of the quest. (Indeed, tying the plot of the story to his own artistic quest, Delany includes among the chapter epigraphs a number of passages taken from the journals that he kept during his travels throughout the Mediterranean in 1965.) Moreover, the novel's frequent reference to mutations, both among the aliens themselves and in nature, was influenced by Ovid's *Metamorphoses* (first century B.C.), a Roman epic in which the transformations of mythical characters was a unifying theme. The *Metamorphoses*, too, had retold the legend of Orpheus.

The Einstein Intersection explores those myths in much the same way that *Babel-17* had explored language. The novel treats mythology as a phenomenon capable of determining the way in which reality is perceived. By the end of the novel, Lobey must free himself from the mythic patterns that he has inherited. He must permit his own "different" nature to emerge. This, Delany suggests, will prove to be the redemption of Lobey himself and of his entire culture.

TRITON

First published: 1976
Type of work: Novel

In a future utopia, a judgmental young man struggles to find his place in society.

The role that language played in *Babel-17* and that mythic patterns played in *The Einstein Intersection* is assigned to traditional sexual identities in *Triton*. In this novel, Delany explores the way in which one's relationships, especially those dictated by the norms of society, determine one's self-image. *Triton* depicts a sexual utopia existing in the year A.D. 2112, a society in which all forms of personal relationships are permitted. Without any restrictions placed upon them, the inhabitants of this society are free to invent or develop whatever social and sexual identities they choose. Sex-change operations are common, as are "refixations," procedures through which a person's sexual orientation may be altered. The reader expects, at first, that this degree of personal freedom will be liberating, and it is liberating for most of the characters in *Triton*. For Bron, however, the novel's central character, the unlimited choices available in his society create only a profound sense of discontent.

Bron is Delany's first antihero. Self-centered, intolerant, and opinionated, he makes an unusual protagonist; Delany wants his reader not to identify with Bron. Like Kid Death in *The Einstein Intersection*, Bron cannot endure what is different, even in himself. While Kid Death's hostility was directed outward, Bron's intolerance has its greatest effects upon himself, providing the source of his unhappiness and alienation. Despite Bron's best efforts (including, in the end, a sex-change operation and refixation), he is never able to overcome his limitations, and the novel ends with Bron still unhappy and disillusioned.

Triton thus contains Delany's most complete commentary on the social effects of intolerance. Bron goes to extreme lengths to force himself and others into the sexual roles that he regards as right; however, Delany suggests that these sexual labels (and, by implication, any sorts of labels) can never bring one closer to understanding oneself or the identities of others.

Summary

Delany's central characters are usually individuals whose quest for knowledge leads them to a greater self-discovery. Frequently, this insight involves a realization that the very means that one uses to achieve understanding (for example, language and folklore) may actually be limiting in terms of what one is able to understand.

On the level of sociology, Delany's novels display a compassionate understanding for individuals who deviate from the norm. By presenting worlds that are exaggerations or distortions of the world known to Delany and his readers, he illustrates how illusory or arbitrary most societal norms really are and suggests that, if seen from a slightly altered perspective, each individual is "different" in some way.

Bibliography

Barbour, Douglas. "Cultural Invention and Metaphor in the Novels of Samuel R. Delany." *Foundation* 7/8 (March, 1975): 105-121.

_____. *Worlds Out of Words: The SF Novels of Samuel R. Delany*. Frome, Somerset, England: Bran's Head Books, 1979.

Govan, S. Y. "The Insistent Presence of Black Folk in the Novels of Samuel R. Delany." *Black American Literature Forum* 18 (Summer, 1984): 43-48.

McEvoy, Seth. *Samuel R. Delany*. New York: Frederick Ungar, 1983.

Nilon, Charles. "The Science Fiction of Samuel R. Delany and the Limits of Technology." *Black American Literature Forum* 18 (Summer, 1984): 69-74.

Peplov, Michael W., and Robert S. Bravard. *Samuel R. Delany: A Primary and Secondary Bibliography*. Boston: G. K. Hall, 1980.

Slusser, George Edgar. *The Delany Intersection*. San Bernardino, Calif.: Borgo Press, 1977.

Weedman, Jane B. *Reader's Guide to Samuel R. Delany*. West Linn, Oreg.: Starmont, 1979.

Jeffrey L. Buller

DON DeLILLO

Born: New York, New York
November 15, 1936

Principal Literary Achievement

DeLillo's novels, with their surrealistic and paranoid elements, zany characters, and comic set pieces, are an important contribution to post-World War II American fiction.

Biography

Don DeLillo was born in New York City on November 15, 1936. He was reared as a Catholic and grew up in Pennsylvania and New York City's South Bronx. He lived for a while in Greece, which became the setting for *The Names* (1982). He was granted a Guggenheim Fellowship, and in 1984 he received the award in literature from the American Academy and Institute of Arts and Letters. In 1986, he was honored with the American Book Award for *White Noise* (1985).

Among DeLillo's major works are the novels *Americana* (1971), *End Zone* (1972), *Great Jones Street* (1973), *Ratner's Star* (1976), *Players* (1977), *Running Dog* (1978), *The Names* (1982), *White Noise* (1985), and *Libra* (1989). His books were always favorably reviewed but did not gain a major breakthrough until *White Noise*, which caught many readers' attention with its depiction of a dangerous chemical leak. When DeLillo published *Libra*, a fictionalized version of President John F. Kennedy's assassination, he became firmly established in the canon of contemporary writers who are both successful in the marketplace and critically blessed by their appearance on college reading lists. Besides his novels, he has published short stories, as well as the plays *The Engineer of Moonlight* (1979) and *The Day Room* (1986). Under the pseudonym of Cleo Birdwell, he also collaborated on the novel entitled *Amazons* (1980). His rise to critical prominence in the 1980's was capped in 1990 by "Fiction of Don DeLillo," a special issue of *South Atlantic Quarterly* devoted to DeLillo's work.

DeLillo has never exploited his creative success by appearing on talk shows, and he has never been especially forthcoming about his private life. He has responded openly to interviews, however, thereby yielding a sense of how he feels about his work. In a 1979 interview, he explained his reticence by referring to his "silence, exile, cunning, and so on." He admits in the same interview that *Americana* is the novel that draws most deeply on his own life: "I was hurling things at the page. At

the time I lived in a small apartment with no stove and the refrigerator in the bathroom and I though first novels written under these circumstances ought to be novels in which great chunks of experience are hurled at the page. So that's what I did." As his career has progressed, DeLillo has learned to process his experience in the crucible of his imagination. The end result is the vision of America revealed in *Libra*.

Analysis

DeLillo's first novel is entitled *Americana*, and the title would serve well for his whole body of fiction. *Americana* is an account of a generally aimless trip around much of the country—New York City, Maine, the Midwest, and Texas—and its first-person narrator, David Bell, calls it a "mysterious and sacramental journey." The novel has two features that have distinguished all of DeLillo's work; a true gift for language and a talent for creating zany characters. These blessings have enabled DeLillo to evoke American life effectively without having to worry much about plot. It is no wonder that he came to write a novel based on John F. Kennedy's assassination: The characters in the story are often as dispossessed, as alienated, and as paranoid as the people he had been making up in his fiction, and they dwell in an America as surreal as his fictional universe.

His materials include rock music, football, mathematical logic, an "airborne toxic event," and scenarios of nuclear devastation. In treating such topics, implied criticism of the irrationality of much of American life is inevitable, but DeLillo's treatment of his characters is generally even-tempered rather than corrosive. He has even said of the unappealing Pammy and Lyle in *Players* that "I can't talk about them as people I love or hate. They're people I recognize."

One aspect of DeLillo's ongoing praise of folly is his extraordinary comic sense. The originality of his conceptions stands out immediately, but most of the discussions of this work try to keep this a secret. Examples include a man in *White Noise* who wants to hire a prostitute on whom to perform the Heimlich maneuver, a woman in *Ratner's Star* who is described as having no lap, and Esther and Vera Chalk, the two sisters in *End Zone* who host picnics with "meatless and breadless organic sandwiches." The novels are peopled through and through with these likeable oddities; *Ratner's Star* in particular is a virtual megalopolis of such types, many of whom seemed to have walked straight out of the pages of the third book of Jonathan Swift's satirical *Gulliver's Travels* (1726).

Of all of America's manic preoccupations during the 1960's, none was more intense or better publicized than rock and roll music and drugs. These two subjects are often intimately identified in the popular imagination, and they become the twin plot strands of *Great Jones Street*. This novel's rock and roll hero, Bucky Wunderlick, sings tunes of America's heartland such as "VC Sweetheart," "Cold War Lover," "Protestant Work Ethic Blues," and his signature song, "Pee-Pee-Maw-Maw." Bucky suddenly abandons his rock group in Houston, however, and goes into hiding in a "small crooked room, cold as a penny," on Great Jones Street in New York City. He is soon entangled in a bewildering plot to retrieve a package of a new, untried dope, and he is forced into illicit commerce with such figures as Epiphany Powell (a black female bodyguard), Azarian (a band member), and Bucky's manager, Globki. Prominent in the swirling plot is Opel Hampton, educated—at least for a year—at Missouri State Women's College in Delaware, Texas. The plot of *Great Jones Street* is trivial and the characters are comic strip jokes, but the language is always strong, and the hallucinatory world of rock music and psychedelic obsessions is turned into an effective piece of Americana. Bucky Wunderlick will appear again in various incarnations as the man who goes to earth to hide out from the madness of life, a favorite DeLillo character.

Great Jones Street, then, is a minor novel but is typical DeLillo work in several ways. It was followed by *Ratner's Star*, and along with *Americana* and *End Zone*, these early novels were mostly genial in mood. They featured protagonists who were vulnerable, human, and sympathetic. The next two novels, *Players* and *Running Dog*, introduced a cynical tone.

Players is a letdown after the long, boisterous *Ratner's Star*. Its two "players"— Lyle and Pammy, husband and wife—are, respectively, a Wall Street broker and a writer for the Grief Management Council. Their life together disintegrates when a terrorist murders a broker on the floor of the stock exchange and when, soon after that, Pammy learns of Lyle's affair with an office secretary. Pammy flees from their marital nightmare by accompanying two homosexual friends to Maine, but one of these men commits suicide, and Pammy is left to face chaos again. Meanwhile, Lyle meets (through his mistress) the members of the terrorist cell and gets involved as a double agent working for the FBI.

The theme of betrayal and intrigue introduced in *Great Jones Street* and developed in *Players* becomes more intense in *Running Dog*, which offers DeLillo's most elaborate plot to that point. The likeable looneys of the early novels are here replaced by pornography merchants, mobsters, and hired killers. The aging smut peddler Lightborne seeks "the century's ultimate piece of decadence," an amateur film supposedly depicting the last days in Adolf Hitler's bunker. Other characters include the CIA-trained Glen Selvy, a regular customer of Lightborne's who buys not for himself but for Senator Lloyd Percival. The sordid cast includes a mysterious figure known as Lomax, to whom Selvy sells information about Percival, who is investigating an intelligence unit called PAC/ORD. This group has a secret arm—Radial Matrix—that has prospered in its cover as a straight business firm under its chief, Earl Mudger, who is Lomax's boss.

Selvy acquires two female consorts, first Moll Robbins, a journalist from the magazine "Running Dog," and later Nadine Rademacher, a Texas girl who has been scraping through life in a Times Square sleaze joint telling dirty stories while almost nude. Selvy has to flee New York with Nadine when Mudger suspects him of dealing independently for the film and sends two Asian hit men to kill him.

His life in danger amid shadowy plots and subplots, Selvy does what DeLillo characters always do—he heads for cover where he can hold off the outside world. For Selvy, this hideout is The Mines, a bleak piece of Texas where the CIA trains its agents in violence. He faces his pursuers with only a bolo knife; when he is killed, his head is packed in a bag for delivery for Mudger.

The whole story ends rather flatly for all its main characters when Lightborne eventually gets the film and shows it to a Texas pornography king named Odell Armbrister, only to discover it is but a dull parade of women and children in innocuous pursuits, enlivened only by Hitler prancing around in the role of Charlie Chaplin playing Hitler. As the screening ends, a hoodlum named Augie the Mouse shows up and claims the film for Mudger.

Running Dog is significant for its preview of *Libra*; DeLillo has a sure feel for the riffraff that populate the darker corners of American life, and he sniffs out their ties to the powerful and respectable. The paranoia of his characters is mitigated by the fact that someone is after them and sinister forces are indeed at work to disrupt their lives. A century ago Bucky Wunderlick and Glen Selvy would have sought the anonymity available in the frontier, but in the 1970's they have to hunker down in uncongenial refuges in the outlands of Texas and New York City and wait out their tormentors. Pammy hopes for emotional relief in rural Maine, but she finds only more pain in the company of the two homosexual men who are wounded in their own way.

These early novels develop several distinct character types. There are the entertaining eccentrics, often oddly named, such as Epiphany Powell, the Chalk sisters, and the astonishing cast in *Ratner's Star*. They sometimes bear scars of psychic struggle, but they are more often comic constructions with no human interest. Then there are the central figures who retreat from defeat and humiliation, waiting for the end with a resignation born of their grim vision of the madness and meaninglessness of the world. In the more sour novels there are the pornography dealers, the hit men, and other vicious examples of human slag. The bleakness of DeLillo's universe derives more from metaphysical sources than political ones. That is, his anatomies of America and Americana expose the seven deadly sins as endemic throughout the body politic but their etiology traces to human nature rather than to political figures such as Lyndon Johnson or Richard Nixon.

The language in DeLillo's work always appeals strongly, and it is the product of much conscious attention. He explains his concern with language in an interview with Tom LeClair:

> What writing means to me is trying to make interesting, clear, beautiful language. Working at sentences and rhythms is probably the most satisfying thing I do as a writer. I think after a while a writer can begin to know himself through his language. He sees someone or something reflected back at him from these constructions.

DeLillo believes that the power of fiction goes deep enough that, over time, a writer might be able to "shape himself as a human being" through the language he uses, to "remake himself."

END ZONE

First published: 1972
Type of work: Novel

A young man copes with football and fears of nuclear war.

Gary Harkness is a talented young halfback with a troubled mind and soul, and Logos College in West Texas is a last chance for him. Gary's troubles begin with his father's saying about life: "Suck in that gut and go harder." His father had played football at Michigan State, and his life creed is an amalgam of clichés from Teddy Roosevelt as adapted by Knute Rockne: "(1) A team sport. (2) The need to sacrifice. (3) Preparation for the future. (4) Microcosm of life." This parody of the work ethic and the American Dream sticks in Gary's throat, making him a constant disappointment to his pharmaceutical salesman father.

His father, who had spent most of his time on the bench, makes a real football player out of Gary, who becomes all-state and receives twenty-eight scholarship offers. He goes first to Syracuse University, where he meets a girl who is hiding from the world and goes to ground with her—fortified by two boxes of Oreos and an economics text full of "incoherent doctrines." At Penn State the next fall, Gary succumbs to angst and retreats, this time to an Adirondack winter at home. Gary's next sojourn is at Miami, where all goes well until he becomes obsessed with the horrifying accounts of nuclear war that he finds in a textbook. Depression sends him home again, waiting out the year before moving on to Michigan State as an "aging recruit." When he and two other players hit an Indiana safety man so hard that he dies the next day, Gary gives up once more and stays in his room for seven weeks shuffling a deck of cards.

So Logos College is Gary's final chance. At Logos he finds himself playing for Coach Emmett Creed, who says of football, "It's only a game, but it's the only game." Gary's teammates are a colorful lot, notably Taft Robinson and Anatole Bloomberg. Taft is a transfer student from Columbia University, the first black student at Logos. He is brilliant in the classroom as well as on the football field, but he eventually gives up on football. Taft reads books about the Holocaust and ponders his claim that Rembrandt van Rijn and Johann Sebastian Bach had Masai blood in their veins. Taft is another DeLillo loner in retreat from the madness of the world.

Taft's roommate is Anatole Bloomberg, left tackle on offense. Anatole is also "a voluntary exile of the philosophic type." Anatole is overweight and suffers from enuresis. He is a Northerner who is, he says, "unjewing" himself in West Texas:

You go to a place where there aren't any Jews. After that your revise your way of speaking. You take out the urbanisms. The question marks. All that folk wisdom. The melodies in your speech. The inverted sentences. You use a completely different set of

words and phrases. Then you transform your mind into a ruthless instrument. You
teach yourself to reject certain categories of thought.

By these means he will relieve his "enormous nagging historical guilt."

Gary spends most of his time away from the football field with either Myna Corbett, a classmate in Mexican geography, or Major Staley, a Reserve Officers' Training Corps professor. Myna claims that she keeps her weight at 165 pounds to free herself from "the responsibility of being beautiful." Her Texas boots are studded with blue stars, and her mind is stuffed with the fantastic plots of science fiction novels. She is especially fond of the trilogy written by Tudev Nemkhu, a Mongolian with an epic imagination. Gary and Myna spend time on picnics with Esther and Vera, the Chalk sisters, who specialize in breadless and meatless sandwiches.

Whereas Gary's closest friends all seem burdened by some great spiritual wound, Major Staley is brisk and competent. Gary finds in Major Staley an agreeable accomplice for conjuring up awful visions of a nuclear future. Major Staley is not a war-hungry monster who wants to annihilate the Russians or anyone else. He cannot get the subject off his mind because he believes that "[s]omebody has to get it before the public regardless of language. It has to be aired in public debate, clinically, the whole thing, no punches pulled, no matter how terrible the subject is and regardless of language. It has to be discussed."

A second instructor to whom Gary is close is Alan Zapalac, who teaches exobiology. Zapalac voices the paranoia that many of DeLillo's characters feel: "I'm afraid of the United States of America. Take the Pentagon. If anybody kills us on a grand scale, it'll be the Pentagon. On a small scale, watch out for your local police."

With friends such as Taft, Anatole, and Myna, and professors of woe such as Major Staley and Zapalac, Gary's alienation gets worse and worse. At story's end he is confined to the college infirmary, being fed through plastic tubes.

End Zone is structured as a triptych, with the big football game between Logos and West Centrex Biotechnical Institute as its centerpiece. DeLillo's account of the game is a marvelous set piece. The ambience of college sports is evoked vividly. The dialogue rings true, and the game is convincing and entertaining—a narrative by someone who knows what happens in football. *End Zone* is, then, a sports story that gratifies with its knowledgeable game talk, an evocation of the terrible shadow of nuclear war as it was felt in the 1960's, and a picture of several unusual but ingratiating young people whose fates the reader cares about as they cope with an insane universe.

RATNER'S STAR

First published: 1976
Type of work: Novel

A boy genius tries to decode a mysterious signal from outer space.

Ratner's Star is a fantastic narrative in two parts built around an enticing plot idea. In part 1, "Adventures: Field Experiment Number One," Billy Twillig is summoned to a Connecticut think tank, the School of Mathematics of the Center for the Refinement of Ideational Structures. Billy is a boy genius, a fourteen-year-old winner of the first Nobel Prize in Mathematics who has done brilliant work with the "zorg," "a kind of number" but a "useless" one. The center occupies a huge cycloid—architecturally imaginative but impossible to visualize. Billy is summoned to the center to decode a mysterious radio signal that scientists believe is coming from a planet orbiting Ratner's star. The signal is fourteen pulses, gap, twenty-eight pulses, gap, fifty-seven pulses.

The signal has already been pondered at length by many of the great gurus of mathematics. The great mathematician Endor, for example, spent weeks on the pattern but ended up by going to live in a hole in the ground—a typical DeLillo loser who literally goes to earth. When Billy finds him in his burrow, Endor is subsisting on plants and worms. The other scholars who study the strange pulses are given some of the looniest of all DeLillo's loony characterizations: Peregrine Fitzroy-Tapps is one of the more amusing examples, hailing as he does from Crutchly-on-Podge, pronounced Croaking-on-Pidgett, a hamlet near Muttons Cobb, spelled Maternity St. Colbert. Another absurd pedant is Gerald Pence, a student of myths who dresses in "old khaki shorts, bark sandals, and a string headband ornamented with eucalyptus nuts." Pence blathers on about the occult in a rambling lecture that features a white-haired aborigine hidden beneath a white canvas on a miniature flatcar. The mystery beneath the canvas is not disclosed even when the canvas-shrouded creature moans and whirls, finally turning inside out before subsiding into a quiet heap.

Other incredibly named characters include a famous obstetrician, Hoy Hing Toy, who once delivered a baby and ate the placenta in "five huge gulps." Elux Truxl identifies his name as a mere "nom de nom," "the sound identity I have assigned to my nom." Elux is a con man from Honduras who heads a cartel that wants to control the "money curve" of the world. His Sancho Panza is Grbk, a very short person, "mal y bizarro," who is obsessed with exposing his nipples. Grbk is "a tragic person, very sadiensis." None of DeLillo's oddities, however, suffers a deformity more original, a physical deficiency more demanding of radical prosthesis, than does the young woman named Thorkild, a specialist in "decollation control." Billy chances upon her in her bath one day, but she will not allow him to view her naked because she has no lap.

Ratner's Star soon reduces to a parade of such original non-characters. Orang Mohole, a star of "alternate physics" who has twice won the Cheops Feeley Medal, glazes his audience's eyes with talk of the "value-dark dimension" and the "mohole totality." Orang conceives of the universe as a "stellated twilligon" and predicts its "eventual collapse in a sort of n-bottomed hole or terminal mohole." His feeding habits feature regular trips to a vomitorium. He takes Billy to a party where the atmosphere is enlivened by unusual fragrances from aerosol cans, such as "heaped garments" and "nude female body (moist)—sense of urgency arises." The Cheops

Feeley whom the medal honors suffers an uncommon spiritual malady; Cheops is, he says, a lapsed gypsy.

Making his way through this incredible throng, Billy gets to see the wizened Shazar Lazarus Ratner during a torchlight ceremony underneath the cycloid. Ratner lives on only thanks to the silicone injections he gets from his physician, a Dr. Bonwit, who keeps a yacht named the *Transurethral Prostatectomy.*

When he is not marveling at the doings of his co-workers, Billy is figuring out that the pulses derive from a "positional notation system based on the number sixty" and that they represent the number 52,137. His triumph is flat, however, because Billy is soon told by the chief mathematician, Dr. Softly, that work on Ratner's star is no longer needed and that he is to work on "a logistic cosmic language based on mathematical principles." Part 1 ends with the announcement of this assignment.

Part 2 is entitled "Reflections. Logicon Project Minus-One." DeLillo has explained that the two parts—"Adventures" and "Reflections"—refer to Lewis Carroll's *Alice's Adventures in Wonderland* (1865) and *Through the Looking-Glass* (1871). The parallels are structural, however, not thematic. DeLillo's lengthy commentary on *Ratner's Star* identifies numerous structural contrasts between parts 1 and 2 and notes that Pythagoras is the "guiding spirit" behind the work.

Billy learns in part 2 that "in the untold past on this planet a group of humans transmitted a radio message into space." This knowledge clears up the puzzle of the pulses: They came from Earth millions of years ago. Billy then deduces that the sixty-base notation suggests that 52,137 is a number of seconds and that the pulse sequence—fourteen, twenty-eight, fifty-seven—refers to twenty-eight minutes and fifty-seven seconds after two o'clock in the afternoon on the unspecified day. At the same time, Billy notices that the clock on the wall gives exactly that time; as the significance of the time sinks in, he hears a radio announcement of an unpredicted eclipse of the sun that is about to occur. Billy and Dr. Softly realize that the end is imminent, and both depart for Endor's hole, two more DeLillo characters digging in to wait for the end.

WHITE NOISE

First published: 1985
Type of work: Novel

A history professor copes with a deadly chemical spill and his wife's fear of death.

White Noise probably succeeded mostly for its dramatization of a topical issue: the danger to the environment—and to humankind—represented by the many substances continually issuing from chemistry laboratories. While death from chemical poisoning is a major theme of the novel, however, it is only subsidiary to the grim awareness of inevitable death and annihilation that seizes everyone's consciousness in this novel. White noise fills up all frequencies, creating a steady hiss. In DeLillo's imagination it becomes a sobering metaphor for that low, monotonous, but steady small whisper of human mortality constantly filling up the otherwise unused frequencies of an individual's mental processes.

White Noise has all the best features of a DeLillo novel: crazy characters presented with wit and imagination, language that carries its conceptions gracefully, several wonderfully conceived set pieces, and a major character who at the end braces himself against the world's madness. It also has the failure of plot that is not unexpected in a DeLillo novel.

White Noise is divided into three parts. Part 1, "Waves and Radiation," develops the comic characterizations and dwells on the ubiquitous noises that make up the background to everyday life; the "dull and unlocatable roar" of the supermarket, the "great echoing din" of the hardware store, and, most disturbing of all, a seven-hour spell of loud crying that inexplicably overtakes the protagonist's young son. Jack Gladney, the first-person narrator, chairs the department of Hitler studies at College-on-the-Hill. Jack suffers much unease over his inability either to read German or to speak it, a scholarly failure that leads to a comic interlude when Jack hosts a conference on Hitler studies but hides from all the German participants. His welcoming speech includes all the words he can find that are the same in both German and English, and it features many allusions to Hitler's dog, Wolf, whose name is the same in both languages.

Jack's two closest colleagues are Howard Dunlop, a self-taught meteorologist, and Murray Jay Siskind, a researcher in popular culture. Howard's correspondence school degree in meteorology authorizes him to teach that subject "in buildings with a legal occupancy of less than one hundred." Even this eccentricity traces to a preoccupation with death, since Howard came to the subject when he found in patterns of weather data a structure that helped him cope with the trauma of his mother's death. Murray Jay Siskind's comic obsessions—reading the advertisements in *Ufologist Today* and performing the Heimlich maneuver on a prostitute, for example—are rooted in his overwhelming loneliness. He seeks to present a "vulnerability that women will find attractive" but manages only a "half sneaky look, sheepish and wheedling." These three wounded academics are complemented by a friend of Jack's son, the teenaged Orest Mercator. Orest's desperation appears in his obsession with spending sixty-seven days in a cage of poisonous snakes.

Part 2 is "The Airborne Toxic Event," a sterile euphemism for the cloud of Nyodene derivative that drives everyone from the college town of Blacksmith for nine days. DeLillo invests the event with an appropriate menace and paranoia, and Jack Gladney's exposure to the toxic gas fills the back of his mind with a white noise exactly like the hum of nuclear warfare that settles into Gary Harkness' consciousness in *End Zone*. The deadly cloud forces everyone to face up to their thoughts of death, and it leads to the terrible human problem that Jack has to fight in the last section of the book.

Part 3, "Dylarama," reveals that Jack's wife, Babette, is overwhelmed by her fear of death. Jack learns of Babette's terror when he finds out that she is furtively taking an experimental drug, Dylar, that is supposed to neutralize the area of the brain in which fear of death arises. To pay for the Dylar, Babette sleeps with the distributor.

Jack's discovery of Babette's plight coincides with his realization that, given his medical history, he is doomed by his exposure to Nyodene. Suffering himself, he confronts Babette and persuades her to tell him her own nightmares about death and to tell of her sexual betrayal. They can only comfort each other.

At this point, the plot of *White Noise* disintegrates in a bizarre, surreal denouement prompted by a lecture on death that Murray gives to Jack. In Murray's interpretation of human nature, everyone must repress the fear of death to survive. Those who cope best are the killers, as opposed to the "diers." The killers feed on the lives of the diers and gain strength from "a fund, a pool, a reservoir of potential violence in the male psyche."

Swayed by Murray's vision of the weak and the strong, Jack distinguishes himself from those DeLillo protagonists who seek cover under stress. Jack takes a pistol left him by his father-in-law, steals his neighbor's car, and shows up at the hotel room of Willie Mink, the man who has sold Babette the Dylar and cuckolded Jack. The shootout that ensues is absurd: Jack shoots Mink twice, but Mink gets the gun and shoots Jack in the wrist. Jack drives them both to the emergency room and then returns his neighbor's blood-stained car, giving up on his destiny as a killer. The novel ends as it must, with no resolution to the constant haunting awareness of the death that everyone faces.

Much of *White Noise* is rendered poetically through DeLillo's careful attention to language. The comic creations, both funny and poignant, are among his best; the set pieces on the crying child, the Hitler conference, and the toxic event are excellent. The good people deserve the reader's concern, and the bad person, Willie Mink, is straight from DeLillo's special gallery of unsavory human predators. Most significant, perhaps, is the sense of the menacing white noise that lingers on in the reader's consciousness.

Summary

   Many of the interests of the first eight novels culminate in *Libra*, DeLillo's 1989 fictionalized version of the assassination of John F. Kennedy. Lee Harvey Oswald's paranoid careening into American history suits DeLillo's creative concerns quite neatly, and by making him the center of *Libra* (Oswald's astrological sign), DeLillo has a ready-made plot into which he can fit the kinds of characters he seems to understand intuitively. Jack Ruby and David Ferrie, for example, would seem right at home in any DeLillo novel. *Libra* lacks only the bright comic characterizations to make it completely representative of DeLillo's sensibility, but the likes of Myna Corbett and Orest Mercator would be out of place in the gray universe of Lee Harvey Oswald, Jack Ruby, and CIA operatives. Nobody else has re-created that universe quite so convincingly as Don DeLillo.

Bibliography

Bryant, Paula. "Discussing the Untellable: Don DeLillo's *The Names.*" *Critique* 29 (Fall, 1987): 16-29.

_____. "Don DeLillo: An Annotated Biographical and Critical Secondary Bibliography, 1977-1986." *Bulletin of Bibliography* 45 (September, 1988): 208-212.

Bryson, Norman. "City of Dis: The Fiction of Don DeLillo." *Granta* 2 (1980): 145-157.

DeLillo, Don. Interview by Tom LeClair. In *Anything Can Happen: Interviews with Contemporary American Novelists.* Edited by Tom LeClair and Larry McCaffery. Urbana: University of Illinois Press, 1983.

Johnson, Stuart. "Extraphilosophical Instigations in Don DeLillo's *Running Dog.*" *Contemporary Literature* 26, No. 1 (1985): 74-90.

Johnston, John. "Generic Discontinuities in the Novels of Don DeLillo." *Critique* 30 (Summer, 1989): 261-275.

LeClair, Tom. *In the Loop: Don DeLillo and the Systems Novel.* Urbana: University of Illinois Press, 1987.

Morris, Matthew J. "Murdering Words: Language in Action in Don DeLillo's *The Names.*" *Contemporary Literature* 30 (Spring, 1989): 113-127.

South Atlantic Quarterly 89 (Spring, 1990). Special DeLillo issue.

Frank Day

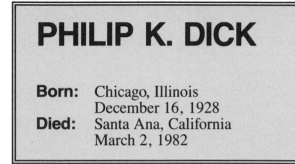

PHILIP K. DICK

Born: Chicago, Illinois
December 16, 1928
Died: Santa Ana, California
March 2, 1982

Principal Literary Achievement
Widely recognized as one of the leading science-fiction writers of his time, Dick contributed to the growing recognition of science fiction outside the boundaries of fandom.

Biography

Philip Kindred Dick was born in Chicago, Illinois, on December 16, 1928, the son of Edgar and Dorothy Kindred Dick. He and his fraternal twin sister Jane were six weeks premature; Jane, the smaller and more frail of the two, died on January 26, 1929. When Dick was still a small boy, his mother told him about his sister's death. As a surviving twin, he felt a mixture of guilt and anger; in later years, he sometimes attributed Jane's death to his mother's negligence, probably unfairly so.

Some months after Jane's death, the Dick family moved to California, where Edgar took a job in the United States Department of Agriculture's San Francisco office. In 1933, however, when Edgar was transferred to Reno, Nevada, Dorothy refused to go. A strongly independent woman (she was a feminist and a pacifist at a time when those convictions placed her in a distinct minority), she chose to remain in Berkeley with Philip. A custody battle ensued, as a result of which, in 1935, Dorothy and Philip moved to Washington, D.C., where she wrote pamphlets on child care for the Federal Children's Bureau. In 1938 they returned to Berkeley, where Philip attended high school and, very briefly, the University of California. Except for a period of a few weeks in 1972 spent in Vancouver, British Columbia, Canada, he lived in California for the rest of his life.

In Dick's own account, he began his career as a writer at the age of twelve. That was when he learned to type—a skill at which he had to become extremely proficient in order to keep up with the pell-mell flow of his imagination. It was at age twelve that he discovered his first science-fiction magazine, inaugurating a lifelong attachment. By that time, too, he suffered from a variety of phobias and other emotional problems, connected, in part at least, to childhood traumas. As an adult, he seemed to move from one emotional crisis to another—he was married five times,

486

attempted suicide several times, and experienced several breakdowns—but through it all he remained an immensely productive writer.

Anthony Boucher (the pen name of William Anthony Parker White), critic and writer of mysteries and science fiction and cofounding editor (1949) of *The Magazine of Fantasy and Science Fiction*, played an important role in the development of Dick's career. Though unimpressed by Dick's attempts at mainstream fiction, Boucher saw great promise in the young writer's more speculative fiction and encouraged him to develop his talent in that direction. In October, 1951, Boucher accepted Dick's story "Roog" for *The Magazine of Fantasy and Science Fiction*; it was Dick's first sale. In 1952, Dick sold four more stories. Soon, he had established himself as one of the most prolific writers in the genre; in 1953 and 1954 he sold more than fifty stories.

In the early 1950's there were many outlets for science-fiction short stories, as new magazines were appearing in abundance. By the mid-1950's, however, the boom was over; only a few magazines in the science-fiction field survived. At this time, Dick began to shift primarily to writing novels, though he continued to produce stories throughout his career; commercial considerations aside, the novel form offered much greater scope. *Solar Lottery*, Dick's first science-fiction novel, was published in 1955. By the end of the decade, he had published five more. (During the 1950's, Dick also completed a dozen mainstream novels, but publishers were not interested in his mainstream work. One of these novels, *Confessions of a Crap Artist*, written in 1959, was published in 1975, and several of the others were published posthumously.)

Dick continued to write at a feverish pace through the 1960's. His novel *The Man in the High Castle*, published in 1962, received the Hugo Award, science fiction's most prestigious accolade. In the next two years, 1963 and 1964, he wrote eleven novels, all of them readable, several outstanding. He was acknowledged as one of the leading figures in science fiction. Most of these books, however, earned only small advances and minimal royalties. Dick's sustained productivity came at a high cost. By the early 1960's he had become a heavy user of amphetamines and a whole pharmacopoeia of medications; his dependence on amphetamines increased as the decade passed. While Dick also experimented occasionally with other drugs, he was never the LSD-inspired writer of legend; later, he described the destructive impact of drugs on many of his friends—and on his own life.

By the end of the 1960's, Dick was in poor health both physically and mentally, and his output of fiction decreased considerably. In February and March, 1974, he had a series of mystical experiences that preoccupied him for the remainder of his life. He devoted some two million words to a running commentary which he called "An Exegesis," a philosophical/autobiographical journal in which he reflected on his life and works, on problems such as the nature of good and evil, and particularly on his firsthand encounter with the divine (which, according to his mood, he was inclined to interpret in various, often contradictory, ways, sometimes debunking it altogether). He also published several novels influenced by the experiences of 1974, including *Valis* (1981), *The Divine Invasion* (1981), and the posthumous *Radio Free Albemuth* (1985).

Only in his last years did Dick begin to enjoy financial security. (An impulsively generous man, he gave without ostentation to charitable organizations and to individuals in need.) Foreign rights—his books were particularly popular in France, Great Britain, and Japan—and reprints brought significant income, as did the film *Blade Runner* (1982), an adaptation of his novel *Do Androids Dream of Electric Sheep?* (1968). The film also attracted new readers to his work, but Dick did not live to see its premiere; he died in Santa Ana, California, on March 2, 1982, after a series of strokes.

Analysis

In his essay "How to Build a Universe That Doesn't Fall Apart Two Days Later" (written in 1978 but not published until 1985, as an introduction to the story collection *I Hope I Shall Arrive Soon*), Philip K. Dick outlined the principal themes of his fiction:

> The two basic topics which fascinate me are "What is reality?" and "What constitutes the authentic human being?" Over the twenty-seven years in which I have published novels and stories I have investigated these two interrelated topics over and over again.

Philosophers, it is sometimes said, are people who sit around asking "Is this table real?" The point of the caricature is to suggest that philosophy is too esoteric, divorced from the problems of everyday life. After all, except for the mentally ill, everyone knows what reality is, so why ask?

Dick was a writer of fiction, however, not a philosopher, and his concern with the nature of reality was anything but abstract. His stories and novels explore collisions between multiple realities—an experience familiar to anyone who watches the television news, where advertisements for cars and computers are bracketed by scenes of emaciated famine victims in Ethiopia and clips from the latest victory of the Los Angeles Lakers. Dick was particularly interested in the interplay between subjective and objective reality. As he noted in a letter written in 1970,

> I have been very much influenced by the thinking of the European existential psychologists, who posit this: for each person there are two worlds, the *idios kosmos*, which is a *unique* private world, and the *koinos kosmos*, which literally means *shared* world (just as *idios* means private).

To function as an "authentic human being," one must have these two worlds in balance. When the shared vision of the *koinos kosmos* ruthlessly dominates the private vision of the *idios kosmos*, the result is loss of identity, mindless conformity— a fear that was particularly strong when Dick began publishing in the 1950's, the decade that produced Sloan Wilson's novel *The Man in the Gray Flannel Suit* (1955) and Vance Packard's early study of the coercive power of advertising, *The Hidden*

Persuaders (1957). On the other hand, when one's private vision is not tempered by a "strong empathetic rapport with other people" (a fundamental value in Dick's worldview) and by an awareness of a reality that is greater than any individual, the result is delusion, even madness, destructive to oneself and often to others as well.

Science fiction allowed Dick to explore themes of multiple realities and cognitive dissonance more freely and thoroughly than he could in mainstream fiction. Many of his novels feature situations in which one character invades and distorts the perceptions of others, altering the way in which they experience reality. In *Eye in the Sky* (1957), for example, the premise is an accident at a particle accelerator. While the victims of the accident—a very diverse lot—lie unconscious, their inner worlds merge in some unexplained fashion; in this dreamlike state, the whole group experiences the world as it is seen by each of the group's members, one by one. Dick uses a similar plot device to good effect in *Ubik* (1969) and *A Maze of Death* (1970), and especially powerfully in *The Three Stigmata of Palmer Eldritch* (1964). Such science-fictional scenarios reflect real-life circumstances; one way to describe the Nazi era is to say that a single man, Adolf Hitler, with the complicity of many others, was able to impose his insane *idios kosmos* on an entire nation.

It would be very misleading, though, to suggest that Dick wrote stories and novels merely to explore certain recurring themes (no matter how important those themes might be). As a writer he was a consummate showman: funny, wildly inventive, with a sheer exuberance that could not be accommodated within the conventions of mainstream fiction. Even his best books are marked by inconsistencies, implausibilities, and stylistic rough edges aplenty. Yet these flaws go hand in hand with the qualities that make even his weakest books worth reading: the mind-twisting plots, the heady mixture of incongruous elements.

A typical Dick novel contains enough story ideas for four or five ordinary books. *Clans of the Alphane Moon* (1964), for example, takes its title from the inmates of a mental hospital on a distant moon, out of contact with Earth for twenty-five years as a result of a galactic war between humans and aliens. Left on their own, the inmates have divided into groups according to type of illness, the paranoids living in a state of constant suspicion, the depressives barely able to function, and so on; for their mutual benefit, the various groups maintain an uneasy coalition, threatened when a delegation from Earth arrives with plans to reinstitutionalize them. At the same time, the novel is about marital discord and reconciliation; Dick's depiction of the conflict between protagonist Chuck Rittersdorf and his brilliant wife, Mary, rings painfully true, with enough blackly comic exaggeration to make it funny. The novel also has a political angle (the war against the aliens has not ended the Cold War, and Chuck's job is to program simulacra—that is, humanoid robots—which are used to infiltrate Communist territories, where they will disseminate pro-American propaganda), and, like many of Dick's works, it contains an oblique self-portrait of the author. Stir in characters such as the telepathic Ganymedean slime mold Lord Running Clam (one of Dick's finest creations) and the themes discussed above, and the result is a uniquely Dickian concoction—imaginable only in science fiction.

Indeed, Dick employed the full panoply of the genre's props: aliens and androids, telepathy and precognition, parallel time tracks—his novel *Now Wait for Last Year* (1966) makes dazzling use of the latter—and all the rest. Yet along with these staples of science fiction, many of his books feature sharply rendered settings drawn from contemporary life, sometimes given a little twist to fit a futuristic scenario. *Time Out of Joint* (1959) depicts late-1950's suburbia; *Dr. Bloodmoney: Or, How We Got Along After the Bomb* (1956) is set in San Francisco and laid-back Marin County; *A Scanner Darkly* (1977) evokes the drug culture of the 1960's; *Radio Free Albemuth* (1985) ranges from Berkeley in the 1950's to Southern California in the 1970's.

Wherever they are set, most of Dick's novels are grounded in the clutter and trivia, the mundane cares and joys, of everyday life. Most of his protagonists, too, are ordinary people, such as repairman Jack Bohlen of *Martian Time-Slip* (1964). Dick had a hard time ending his books—he could not settle the metaphysical questions that fueled them—and so, typically, he concluded not with a cosmic resolution but with a modest affirmation of simple human virtues. The last lines of *Martian Time-Slip* are representative:

In the darkness of the Martian night her husband and father-in-law searched for Erna Steiner; their light flashed here and there, and their voices could be heard, business-like and competent and patient.

SOLAR LOTTERY

First published: 1955
Type of work: Novel

In the corrupt, feudalistic world of the twenty-third century, a troubled idealist refuses to conform.

Solar Lottery, Dick's first published science-fiction novel, was his best-selling book prior to *Do Androids Dream of Electric Sheep?* That fact says much about the audience for science fiction, for of all Dick's novels *Solar Lottery* most resembles the stereotypical and ephemeral products of the genre. Even in this early work, however, some of Dick's recurring preoccupations and distinctive gifts are apparent.

Most of Dick's novels are set in the near future (indeed, in certain instances, Dick's future has already become the reader's past). *Solar Lottery*, in contrast, takes place in the distant future, in the year 2203. In many science-fiction stories (especially those written in the period from the 1930's through the 1950's), the futuristic setting is never coherently or convincingly established. Rather than undertaking the difficult task of imagining a future society, the writer relies on the power of suggestion (simply to say "2203" is to conjure vague but exciting images), supplemented by a bit of technological extrapolation. Such is the case in *Solar Lottery*.

The world of 2203 is one in which space travel has long been a reality, yet in other respects humanity seems to have regressed. This future society is feudalistic. Skilled individuals must swear fealty to corporations or powerful figures. Loyalty is the highest virtue—but in practice, "loyalty" means blind obedience. Common people (unclassified, or "unks") are given a largely illusory measure of hope by an elaborate mechanism known as the Quiz; at the random twitch of a bottle, the single most powerful figure in the society, the Quizmaster himself, may be deposed, to be replaced by someone utterly obscure.

In this scenario one can detect familiar themes and issues of the 1950's, combined by Dick in a strange and whimsical amalgam: the growing influence of corporations in American life and the stultifying conformity they encouraged; the loyalty hearings conducted by Senator Joseph McCarthy; the appeal of television quiz shows, which were wildly popular at the time Dick was writing *Solar Lottery*; even the role of John von Neumann and Oskar Morgenstern's game theory in America's postwar nuclear strategy (the novel includes a mini-dissertation on game theory). Restless and dissatisfied in this static and unjust society, protagonist Ted Bentley ultimately rejects the system's overemphasis on loyalty and its complacent materialism. His inarticulate idealism is paralleled in a subplot involving the Prestonites, a sect inspired by the writing of maverick astronomer and linguist John Preston to search for a tenth planet in the solar system.

Solar Lottery concludes with a recorded message from the long-dead Preston, extolling "the highest goal of man—the need to grow and advance . . . to find new things . . . to expand." This platitudinous conclusion, unthinkable in Dick's later novels, actually has little connection with the conflicts that animate *Solar Lottery*— in particular the tension between Bentley and deposed Quizmaster Reese Varrick, the prototype for such ambivalently portrayed larger-than-life figures as Gino Molinari in *Now Wait for Last Year*, Glen Runciter in *Ubik*, and the Glimmung in *Galactic Pot Healer* (1969).

THE MAN IN THE HIGH CASTLE

First published: 1962
Type of work: Novel

In the alternate world imagined in his novel, Germany and Japan were victorious in World War II.

The Man in the High Castle belongs to the subgenre of science fiction known as alternate history. Most science-fiction novels postulate future developments (ranging from intergalactic travel to all manner of bionic devices) which have brought about a world much different from the reader's own. In contrast, alternate-history novels look into the past, imagining how subsequent history might have developed if the outcome of some key events or series of events had been different. Ward Moore's novel *Bring the Jubilee* (1953), for example, is based on the premise that the South won the Civil War. Kingsley Amis' *The Alteration* (1976) imagines a Europe in which the Reformation never took place. On a larger scale, Orson Scott Card in *Seventh Son* (1987) and its sequels has created an alternate history of American in the nineteenth century.

The Man in the High Castle imagines a world in which Germany and Japan, rather than the United States and the Soviet Union, are the two superpowers. In Dick's alternate history, President Franklin Delano Roosevelt was assassinated during his first term; the lack of his strong leadership was one factor that contributed to the Allies' defeat. The war ended in 1947; the action of the novel takes place fifteen years later, in 1962 (the year in which *The Man in the High Castle* was published).

The setting is a conquered America, divided into several distinct zones. The Pacific States constitute one such zone, under the relatively benign administration of the Japanese. The Rocky Mountain States form a buffer of sorts, controlled neither by the Japanese nor by the Germans but lacking any real power. From the Rockies to the Atlantic are the United States, under brutal German control.

There are several intersecting plot lines in *The Man in the High Castle*; in no other novel does Dick develop such a variety of characters so fully. Moreover, he shifts point of view rapidly from character to character, allowing the reader to view the world of the novel from many different perspectives; even deeply flawed characters are presented with a measure of sympathy. Robert Childan owns a shop in San Francisco, specializing in Americana (the Japanese are passionate collectors). He is an obsequious racist, a classic "little man," full of envy and bitterness. Juliana Frink is a judo instructor in Colorado; her estranged husband, Frank, makes jewelry in San Francisco and hopes to keep his Jewishness a secret. Rudolf Wegener is a captain in the German navy who is morally opposed to his Nazi superiors; he comes to San Francisco under a false identity to meet with a Japanese official, Nobusuke Tagomi, and warn him of a secret German plan to stage a border incident in America that will serve as a pretext for an all-out nuclear attack on Japan. Indeed, all of these characters are forced in some way to confront the horrors of Nazism. In the world of the novel, that includes not only the Holocaust but also a genocidal "experiment" in Africa that has resulted in the virtual depopulation of the continent. Yet *The Man in the High Castle* is not primarily concerned with the peculiar nature of the Nazi phenomenon. Rather, Nazism functions in the novel as an especially potent embodiment of primal evil.

Countless science-fiction novels depict an archetypal conflict between the forces of good and evil. Dick's treatment of this theme, however, is highly distinctive. Here, as Mr. Tagomi perceives in a moment of insight, evil is not simply a concept: "There is evil! It's actual like cement." Yet this palpable evil, Mr. Tagomi realizes, is not confined to the Nazis and their ilk: "It's an ingredient in us. In the world. Poured over us, filtering into our bodies, minds, hearts, into the pavement itself."

Such a recognition can be shattering; in a scene that is repeated with variations in many of Dick's novels, Mr. Tagomi finds that for a short time, reality itself appears to be dissolving before his eyes. What saves him from moral paralysis is a counter-recognition or intuition that, however muddled human attempts to do good and fight evil may be, they are in harmony with the order of things that underlies the world of appearances.

That such an order, though imperfectly perceived, really exists—that it is not merely a product of wishful thinking—is suggested in the novel in two ways. First, there is the role in the narrative of the *I Ching*, the ancient Chinese book of divination. To use this oracle, one tosses coins or yarrow stalks and then consults the text according to the patterns in which they fall. In the course of the novel, several of the characters repeatedly have recourse to the *I Ching*. The fact that its guidance generally proves to be reliable suggests metaphorically that beneath the seeming chaos of human experience there lies a meaningful order. At the same time, the fact that the oracle is frequently enigmatic, requiring considerable interpretation and never easily verifiable, suggests that human access to this immutable order will remain incomplete, always subject to distortion.

Second, there is the intriguing novel-within-a-novel, Hawthorne Abendsen's *The Grasshopper Lies Heavy*, which is read or alluded to by many of the characters in *The Man in the High Castle* and from which several passages are quoted. Abendsen's novel, banned in German-controlled territories (where it nevertheless enjoys clandestine circulation) and very popular in the Pacific States, describes an alternate history in which Germany and Japan were defeated in World War II. The world of Abendsen's novel, while it closely resembles the real world outside the frame of *The Man in the High Castle*, is not identical to it; for example, Rexford Tugwell, not Franklin Roosevelt, is President of the United States during the war. (In Abendsen's version, Roosevelt is president through 1940 and is thus able to prepare the country for war.)

The climax of *The Man in the High Castle* occurs when Juliana Frink, having killed a Nazi assassin who was on his way to kill Abendsen, seeks the novelist out in his home in Cheyenne, Wyoming. Abendsen, who is rumored to be entrenched in a fortress (the "High Castle" of the title), is in fact living with his family in an ordinary stucco house on a residential street. There, with Abendsen looking on, Juliana consults the *I Ching* about *The Grasshopper Lies Heavy*. (She has guessed, correctly, that the novelist himself used the *I Ching* when writing his book.) The oracle's verdict is at once clear and mysterious: the hexagram for Inner Truth. Abendsen's book is true.

Much of the fascination of alternate-history novels derives from the fact that, like allegories, they have two levels of meaning. On one level there is the imagined world of the story. At the same time, the reader is implicitly led to compare this fictional world with the actual historical world. In *The Man in the High Castle*, however, there is an added level of complexity, for in Dick's novel the characters themselves (some of them, at least) become aware of an alternate reality beneath or parallel to the surface reality of their world. This link between the situation of the characters and the situation of the reader is one of the features that makes *The Man in the High Castle* not only an exceptional example of the alternate-history novel but also one of the enduring classics of science fiction.

DO ANDROIDS DREAM OF ELECTRIC SHEEP?

First published: 1968
Type of work: Novel

Androids of the latest model are harder than ever to distinguish from the humans whom they are so cunningly designed to mime, but they still have one telltale flaw.

Thanks to the film *Blade Runner*, *Do Androids Dream of Electric Sheep?* is Dick's best-known novel. (A tie-in edition was issued in paperback under the title of the film, with Dick's original title given in small print.) That is ironic, since, as is often the case, the screenwriters omitted significant elements of the novel, changed others, and added material of their own.

Do Androids Dream of Electric Sheep? is a post-nuclear holocaust novel. This subgenre is one of the most crowded in science fiction, including masterpieces such as *A Canticle for Leibowitz* (1959), by William M. Miller, Jr., as well as countless forgotten books. Writers from outside science fiction have often contributed to this subgenre too; one notable example is Russell Hoban's *Riddley Walker* (1982).

Dick's novel, written in the mid-1960's and published in 1968, is set in 1992. World War Terminus and the resultant fallout have rendered much of Earth uninhabitable and much of the population sterile. Many of the survivors have emigrated to the barren landscape of Mars. Others, despite the hazards (there is a whole class of people damaged by radiation, known as "specials" or, more popularly, "chickenheads"), have chosen to remain on Earth.

This scenario is familiar enough, but Dick's way of developing it is characteristically fresh. Post-nuclear holocaust tales tend to veer toward cynicism or sentimentalism; *Do Androids Dream of Electric Sheep?* avoids both of these extremes. In the world Dick imagines, animals of all kinds have a special value. Some species are extinct, while others are greatly diminished. To own an animal is a mark of status; it is also to enjoy a living link with the pre-holocaust world. There is a marvelous humor in this—animals are graded in the manner of collectible coins or stamps, with regular catalogs issued, and neighbors keep close track of one another's acquisitions—mixed with deep poignancy. For those who cannot afford a real animal, there are substitutes, such as the electric sheep owned by protagonist Rick Deckard.

Deckard is a bounty hunter. His quarry are rogue androids (called "replicants" in *Blade Runner*), so sophisticated in design that they are almost impossible to distinguish from genuine humans. Almost, but not quite—for androids lack one vital human quality: the ability to empathize, to put oneself in another's place. Here, as in many of his novels, Dick uses the device of the android (the simulacrum) to raise disturbing questions about our identity as human beings. Such questions are high-lighted by Deckard's attraction to the beautiful android Rachel Rosen and by the kindness and wisdom of the hapless chickenhead John Isidore.

The theme of empathy is developed in an important strand of the novel entirely omitted from the film. Like many members of their society, Deckard and Isidore participate in a quasi-religious movement known as Mercerism. Gripping the handles of a "Mercer box," the communicant experiences "fusion" with the thousands of others who are performing the rite at that moment; together they all experience identification with the archetypal figure of Wilbur Mercer, a white-haired old man ascending a steep hill, tormented by rock-throwing antagonists yet pressing on. To be fair to the filmmakers, it should be noted that perhaps they omitted this strand of the novel because Dick's development of it is self-contradictory. Late in the novel, the androids expose Mercer as a fake. After this startling reversal, Dick pulls a counter-reversal; yes, Mercer is a fake, but somehow, and in a more important sense, he is also real. Here the conflict between Dick's persistent skepticism and his equally strong yearning to believe is revealed in its naked form.

Summary

Ezra Pound suggested that artists are "the antennae of the race." The novels of Philip K. Dick would seem to bear out that judgment. As technological developments increasingly blur the distinction between the human and the artificial, the real event and the simulated happening, the prescience of Dick's vision becomes increasingly clear.

No one book of Dick's stands out as a near-flawless expression of that vision. Taken together, though, his ten or twelve best books constitute a powerfully achieved and unmistakably individual body of work. Metaphysical probing, deliberately overloaded plots, quirky humor, a fascination with the "junk" of popular culture as well as with esoteric lore are a few of the salient features of the unique cosmos of Philip K. Dick.

Bibliography

Apel, D. Scott, ed. *Philip K. Dick: The Dream Connection*. San Diego: Permanent Press, 1987.

Gillespie, Bruce, ed. *Philip K. Dick: Electric Shepherd*. Melbourne, Australia: Nors-trilia Press, 1975.

Lem, StanisŁaw. *Microworlds: Writings on Science Fiction and Fantasy*. San Diego: Harcourt Brace Jovanovich, 1984.

Levack, Daniel J. H. *PKD: A Philip K. Dick Bibliography*. San Francisco: Underwood/Miller, 1981.

Mackey, Douglas A. *Philip K. Dick*. Boston: Twayne, 1988.

Olander, Joseph, and Martin Harry Greenberg, eds. *Philip K. Dick*. New York: Tap-linger, 1983.

Sutin, Lawrence. *Divine Invasion: A Life of Philip K. Dick*. New York: Harmony Books, 1987.

Warrick, Patricia. *Mind in Motion: The Fiction of Philip K. Dick*. Carbondale, Southern Illinois University Press, 1987.

Williams, Paul. *Only Apparently Real: The World of Philip K. Dick*. New York: Arbor House, 1986.

John Wilson

JAMES DICKEY

Born: Atlanta, Georgia
February 2, 1923

Principal Literary Achievement
One of the best of the post-World War II American poets, Dickey is also the author of the best-selling novel *Deliverance*.

Biography

James Lafayette Dickey was born on February 2, 1923, in Atlanta, Georgia, son of Eugene Dickey, an Atlanta lawyer, and Maibelle Swift Dickey. The Dickeys' first-born son, Eugene, died four years before James was born. Eugene's death from spinal meningitis at the age of six is the subject of Dickey's poem "The String," in which the poet's guilt feelings appear in the refrain "Dead before I was born."

The young Dickey was an excellent athlete who played football at North Fulton High School, from which he was graduated in 1942. He then enrolled at Clemson Agricultural College in South Carolina, where he played football before quitting school after one semester to join the Army Air Force. Dickey spent four years, 1942-1946, in military service, flying about a hundred missions for the 418th Night Fighters in the South Pacific. The poem "The Firebombing" and many of the other poems in *Helmets* (1964) and *Buckdancer's Choice* (1965) raise questions prompted by his participation as a pilot in the devastation of Japanese cities. Dickey has remarked that he first began reading poetry while in the Air Force. He frequented the library stacks, he says, while waiting for the librarian he was dating to finish work.

In 1946, his military service completed, Dickey transferred from Clemson to Vanderbilt University. He also gave up football for track and set the Tennessee state record for the 120-yard high hurdles. Dickey enrolled at Vanderbilt in the wake of three significant literary movements at that university: the fugitive period of the 1920's, the agrarianism of the 1930's, and the blossoming of the New Criticism in the 1940's. Although he has sympathized with the Vanderbilt writers in their skepticism about industrialization, he has kept literary movements at arm's length throughout his career and is not identified with any school.

Dickey married Maxine Syerson in 1948, and they had two sons: Christopher Swift, born in 1951, and Kevin Webster, in 1958. Maxine died in 1976, and later that year Dickey married Deborah Dodson. Their daughter, Bronwen, was born in 1981. Dickey received his A.B. degree from Vanderbilt in 1949, and the next year

was awarded an M.A. after writing a thesis on Herman Melville's poems. He was able to complete the fall semester as an instructor at the Rice Institute in Houston, Texas, before being called back into the Air Force to serve in the Korean War. Following his discharge from military service in 1952, Dickey returned to Rice for two more years and began writing poetry. A *Sewanee Review* fellowship in 1954 helped him support his family for a year in Europe, after which he returned in 1955 to teach at the University of Florida. His academic career proved a disappointment when he found himself loaded down with composition classes, and the final blow came when his reading of "The Father's Body" to a Gainesville audience led to demands for an apology. Rather than apologize, Dickey resigned from the university.

Dickey continued to write—and publish—poetry, but he did it while living in New York City, where he took a job writing advertising copy for the McCann-Erickson agency. In 1958, still with McCann-Erickson, Dickey returned to Atlanta; he soon switched to Liller Neal, a smaller firm, and then to Burke Dowling Adams, where he was creative director and vice-president.

His poetry accumulated during these years, and he published two collections, *Into the Stone and Other Poems* (1960) and *Drowning with Others* (1962). The Union League Civic and Arts Foundation Prize (1958), the Vachel Lindsay Prize, and the Longview Foundation Award (both in 1959) were followed in 1961 by a Guggenheim Fellowship. Dickey at this time left the advertising world to become a full-time poet and took his family to Italy, where he traveled and wrote for a year before taking up poet-in-residence appointments at Reed College (1963-1964) and San Fernando Valley State College (1964-1965).

Dickey's reputation as one of the nation's ranking poets was solidified by the publication of *Helmets* and *Buckdancer's Choice. Buckdancer's Choice* won the National Book Award for poetry, the Melville Cane Award from the Poetry Society of America, and the National Institute of Arts and Letters Award. With these honors in 1966 came a brief stint as poet-in-residence at the University of Wisconsin, Madison, and an appointment as consultant in poetry for the Library of Congress (1966-1968). In 1969, Dickey became Carolina Professor of English and writer-in-residence at the University of South Carolina in Columbia, where he has remained ever since.

Although he continued to publish poetry in the 1970's and 1980's, some of which was well received, it was the early work in *Helmets* and *Buckdancer's Choice* that critics valued most highly. His first novel, *Deliverance* (1970), was both a popular and a critical success, and it was made into a successful film starring Jon Voight and Burt Reynolds, with Dickey himself writing the script and playing the sheriff. His second novel, *Alnilam* (1987), on which he worked for more than a decade, was not so well received.

Besides his fiction and his poetry, Dickey has written some notable criticism, especially in *Babel to Byzantium: Poets and Poetry Now* (1968). An outspoken critic, he has given poor grades to such major figures as Robert Frost and William Carlos Williams and judged Allen Ginsberg an absolute failure. Among the poets he prizes are Theodore Roethke, Rainer Maria Rilke, and D. H. Lawrence.

In 1974, Dickey published *Jericho: The South Beheld*, a sumptuous coffee-table volume in which Dickey's prose poems were accompanied by illustrations by Herbert Shuptrine. It was a commercial success, but it seemed to his critics to be a diversion from a serious literary career. The children's book *Tucky the Hunter* (1978) and another volume of poems, *The Strength of Fields* (1979), rounded out another decade of diverse and generally well-received accomplishment. The 1980's were most conspicuously marked by the second novel, *Alnilam*, and *Puella* (1982), a collection of poems about a young girl's maturing.

Analysis

Dickey's essay "The Enemy from Eden" is a meditation on the metaphysics of snake hunting with a blowgun. The blowgun-wielding hunter — "the One," as Dickey identifies him—fashions his weapon from a length of aluminum pipe and arms it with sharpened lengths of coat-hanger wire guided by improvised vanes of typing paper scraps. With this weapon the snake hunter seeks his foe, alert not to walk "right into the fangs, the jungle hypodermic." When the "Universal Evil," the "Enemy from Eden," succumbs to the coat-hanger needle in the brain, his skin will become "something to have a drink with, at all times of day and night." After the kill, "For some reason, the One is well, full of himself and out of himself."

This brief essay contains much essential Dickey; he is an avid deer and snake hunter. Striding into the natural world, armed with the minimum of hand-fashioned weapons, and doing battle with the allegorical monster is an irresistible theme. It conjures up the Red Cross Knight in the Den of Error and Ahab pursuing the great white whale. It also relates directly to Dickey's concern in both his fiction and his poetry for the magic and mystery of nature and the dangers and satisfactions available to the man who will face up to the challenges.

The major Dickey themes are all exemplified in *Poems 1957-1967* (1967), a compilation from *Into the Stone*, *Drowning with Others*, *Helmets*, *Buckdancer's Choice*, and *Falling* (not previously published in book form). Several of the poems treat the death of Dickey's brother, Eugene, and the poet's ensuing guilt. Dickey's mother suffered from angina, and he became convinced that she would not have put herself through the exertion of bearing him if Eugene had not died. This view of his conception and birth troubled Dickey. "The Underground Stream" voices the poet's frequently stated urge to merge his identity with natural elements—in this instance, with the underground stream he perceives as he lives on the edge of a flowing well—and is infused with the poet's memory of his "one true brother,/ the tall cadaver, who/ Either grew or did not grow." Another early poem, "The String," recalls the story of his brother's having performed string tricks, "Incredible feats of construction," as "he lay/ In his death-bed singing with fever." The direct personal feeling of "The String" is strengthened by the elegiac refrain "Dead before I was born."

The same sense of the dead brother's haunting presence emerges in "Armor" and "In the Tree House at Night." The fantasy about armor conjures up a brother "whose features I knew/ By the feel of their strength on my face/ And whose limbs by the shining of mine." In the poem's moving resolution, the brother is armored in gold and the poet has

> let the still sun
> Down into the stare of the eyepiece
> And raised its bird's beak to confront
> What man is within to live with me
> When I begin living forever.

In the tree-house poem, it is the "dead brother's huge, freckled hand" that steadies the nails in the tree-house ladder; and it is his spirit that draws the speaker into the tree house at night, where he enjoys a mystical experience: "My green, graceful bones fill the air/ With sleeping birds. Alone, alone/ And with them I move gently./ I move at the heart of the world."

Of the numerous recollections of war in *Poems 1957-1967*, "The Performance" is perhaps the most stunning. It is one of the most powerful elegies to have been inspired by World War II. "The Performance" honors Donald Armstrong, master of the "back somersault, the kip-up," as the poet imagines the downed flier's execution. Doomed to dig his own grave before the enemy's "two-handed sword" falls on his neck, Armstrong does all his "lean tricks. . . . As the sun poured up from the sea/ And the headsman broke down/ In a blaze of tears," but at the end Armstrong "knelt down in himself/ Beside his hacked, glittering grave, having done/ All things in this life that he could."

"Awaiting the Swimmer" is one of Dickey's love poems. The speaker of the poem stands by a river, holding a white towel and waiting for a woman to reach him on the bank. He wraps her in the towel and leads her to the house, where he is overcome with feeling: "What can I perform, to come near her?/ How hope to bear up, when she gives me/ The fear-killing moves of her body?" Three other early love poems— "On the Hill Below the Lighthouse," "Near Darien," and "Into the Stone"—develop similar statements of awe at the power of love and sexual feeling. In each poem, the natural setting is important, with moonlight bathing the lovers in all three poems as the speaker works out his feelings in figures of light and shade, stone and water.

The early love poems contrast with some later ones in different moods, such as "Adultery," with its "Gigantic forepleasure," "wrist watch by the bed," and "grim techniques." This poem ends in a recital of illicit lovers' banalities and the speaker's lighthearted summing up: "We have done it again we are/ Still living. Sit up and smile,/ God bless you. Guilt is magical." In "Cherrylog Road," the speaker waits in a junked Pierce-Arrow for the archetypal farmer's daughter, here named Doris Holbrook. In the still heat of the junkyard, the hulks "smothered in kudzu," the young speaker and his consort "clung, glued together,/ With the hooks of the seat springs/ Working through to catch us red-handed." The wild ride over, they leave "by separate doors," and the speaker roars off on his motorcycle, "Wringing the handlebar for speed,/ Wild to be wreckage forever." Many of Dickey's best poems express a natural relationship between the world of man, as personified in the speaker, and the larger world of leaf and stone. These poems often evoke a natural creation trembling with transcendent spirit.

THE OWL KING

First published: 1962
Type of work: Poem

A father calls to his blind son, lost in the woods but bonded by natural sympathies to the owl king.

The eight-page poem "The Owl King" is arranged in three parts. Part 1, "The Call," is the father's hopeful search for his blind son. This one-page section is characteristic of much of Dickey's poetry in several ways. It is written in eight-line stanzas, for example, with the first line recurring at the end as a refrain in italics. Many of Dickey's poems, especially the earlier ones, are told in stanzas of five to eight lines, and the refrain is fairly commonly used (examples include "Dover: Believing in Kings," "The String," and "On the Hill Below the Lighthouse"). The stanzas are linked by enjambment, although this poem has rather less of that device than usual in Dickey. The unrhymed lines are mostly of eight syllables, with Dickey's typically heavy anapestic stress heard everywhere. The metrical pattern found most frequently in a Dickey line is an iamb followed by two anapests, and "The Call" offers perfect examples, as in "It whispers like straw in my ear,/ And shakes like a stone under water./ My bones stand on tiptoe inside it./ Which part of the sound did I utter?" The alliteration in these lines is not unexpected in a Dickey poem, and the word "stone" is perhaps the commonest word in Dickey's vocabulary.

The father's call is answered by the owl king's song, and the second part of the poem, two pages, is the owl's story; it is told in one long stanza. The owl king's vision allows him to see "dark burn/ Greater than sunlight or moonlight,/ For it burn[s] from deep within [him]." He hears, then sees, the blind boy with "His blue eyes shining like mine." They are immediately companionable, so that the father's call becomes a "perfect, irrelevant music," and they sit each night on the owl's oak bough. The blind boy achieves something of the owl's vision, with the boy's eyes "inch by inch going forward/ Through stone dark, burning and picking/ The creatures out one by one."

In the five-page third part, "The Blind Child's Story," the boy describes, in short lines, his journey into the forest and the relationship he achieves with the owl. Perched on the oak bough, the boy "learn[s] from the master of sight/ What to do when the sun is dead,/ How to make the great darkness work/ As it wants of itself to work." The owl weeps when the boy takes him in his arms in the glow of a heavenly light. The boy then walks through "the soul of the wood," for he can now "see as the owl king sees." The hints of religious allegory grow thicker at the end as the boy concludes, "Father, I touch/ Your face. I have not seen/ My own, but it is yours./ I come, I advance,/ I believe everything, I am here."

THE SHEEP CHILD

First published: 1967
Type of work: Poem

The myth of the sheep child—half human, half sheep—inspires a lyric celebration of the will to life embodied in sexual desire.

"The Sheep Child" is in two parts. In the first section, the poet revives the old legends of anomalous deformed births resulting from humans copulating with animals. Among these is the much-whispered-about story of the "woolly baby/ pickled in alcohol" somewhere in an obscure corner of an unnamed museum in Atlanta. Even though "The boys have taken/ Their own true wives in the city" and the sheep are now safe in the pasture, the story persists in· the "terrible dust of museums." Thus the poet imagines the sheep child saying, with his eyes, the story of his begetting, birth, and death. The sheep child's narrative, printed in italics, is a beautiful lyric of desire.

Speaking from his "father's house," the sheep child recounts his sheep mother's interlude in the west pasture, "where she stood like moonlight/ Listening for foxes." It was then that "something like love/ From another world . . . seized her/ From behind," and she responded to "that great need." From this event ensued the sheep child:

> I woke, dying,
>
> In the summer sun of the hillside, with my eyes
> Far more than human. I saw for a blazing moment
> The great grassy world from both sides,
> Man and beast in the round of their need,
> And the hill wind stirred in my wool,
> My hoof and my hand clasped each other,
> I ate my one meal
> Of milk, and died
> Staring.

From his birth in the pasture, the sheep child goes directly to his incarceration in the museum and his "closet of glass." He becomes a reminder of the taboo surrounding unnatural sex, driving the farm boys "like wolves from the hound bitch and calf/ And from the chaste ewe in the wind." The force celebrated in this poem is a terrible one and must be regulated. So, says the sheep child, "Dreaming of me,/ They groan they wait they suffer/ Themselves, they marry, they raise their kind."

DELIVERANCE

First published: 1970
Type of work: Novel

Four city dwellers take a canoe trip that leads to violence and death.

Deliverance, Dickey's first novel, was a successful adventure story that was made into a popular film starring Burt Reynolds and Jon Voight. Dickey turned his interest in hunting and the outdoors into a suspenseful narrative that pits the four main characters not only against a wild river in north Georgia but also against several of the savage mountain men who prowl the wilderness along the river banks.

The novel's two epigraphs are much to the point of the events that follow. The first, from the modern French writer Georges Bataille, translates as "there exists at the base of human life a principle of insufficiency." The second is from the Old Testament prophet Obadiah: "The pride of thine heart hath deceived thee,/ thou that dwellest in the clefts of the rock,/ whose habitation is high; that saith in his heart,/ Who shall bring me down to the ground?"

Bataille's observation explains well the urge that sends these comfortable professional men from Atlanta off on an arduous challenge to their bodies and their spirits. The ringleader is Lewis Medlock, a devotee of outdoor sports who must always be matching himself against some grueling physical challenge and who proposes the trip to the others. The narrator is Ed Gentry, an advertising agency executive, who begins the trip as more or less Lewis' second in command. Lewis and Ed are accompanied by Drew Ballinger, a sales manager for a soft drink distributor, and Bobby Trippe, a mutual funds salesman.

The trip these four men take down the treacherous Cahulawassee River has the features of an archetypal journey fraught with hazards of nature and human evil, and it is a modern masterpiece of this genre. The novel also inverts the genre, however, in the sense that these men do not have to make such a perilous journey. Their adventure is a bogus one, conceived as a deliverance from the ennui of modern city life and infused with the spirit of Lewis Medlock, who must always test himself. Ironically, the four men drive away from home in modern automobiles and then set themselves the task of getting home the hardest way possible. When it is all over, the decent Drew Ballinger is dead, and his body is submerged under tons of water. Bobby Trippe, the least equipped of the four for the strains of the mythical outdoors, has been sodomized and permanently embittered. Lewis Medlock has failed when confronted with the tense existential drama for which he has prepared himself through such a long novitiate. And Ed Gentry, the narrator, the skeptic, the apprentice to the guru Lewis, has taken on Lewis' responsibilities and accomplished his initiation triumphantly. Yet the question remains: From what has Ed been delivered?

Deliverance is tightly plotted and structured in three main sections of roughly equal length. A brief "Before" section introduces the characters and sets up the journey. The first day is narrated in "September 14th," and it takes the men by car to the little village of Oree, where they begin their journey to the camp where they will tent the first night. "September 15th" begins mildly, but soon reaches a narrative peak in a confrontation on shore with two backwoods yahoos who torment the travelers and rape Bobby before Lewis kills one with an arrow from his bow. The surviving backwoodsman escapes, and the four continue their trip in a grim frame of mind after burying the dead man. Their trip takes them through bad rapids; at this juncture, Drew falls over as if shot and upsets the lead canoe in which he is riding with Ed. Lewis mangles his leg badly while getting ashore, and leadership devolves upon Ed. Convinced that the surviving mountaineer is following them for an ambush, Ed scales a high cliff, climbs a tree, and waits for their tormentor as the second day ends. "September 16th" finds Ed in the tree waiting for their pursuer, who indeed dutifully appears to accept from Ed the arrow that kills him. The dead man's body is consigned to the waiting river, and the three survivors continue on to the town of Aintry after burying Drew's body and agreeing on a story of his accidental death. This classic plot pattern is completed by an "After" section in which their rickety story is questioned briefly but soon becomes part of the river's annals as the whole area is flooded, ensuring the eternal concealment of the three bodies.

Wherein does the deliverance lie in this story of violence and death? For the unfortunate Drew and Bobby, there were no consolations, only oblivion and humiliation. For Lewis there is deliverance from the compulsions that drove him to rigorous physical disciplines. As Ed observes of Lewis at the last, "He can die now; he knows that dying is better than immortality."

Ed has been delivered from a great hope, the aspiration to compensate for the insufficiency of life by heroic accomplishment. After Drew's death, when Lewis and Ed realize the predicament in which they are caught, Lewis observes that "here we are, at the heart of the Lewis Medlock country"; Ed exults in the challenge he faces in Lewis' role: "My heart expanded with joy at the thought of where I was and what I was doing."

Ed's exaltation on the river has been partly prepared by a sequence in the opening exposition. In the flurry of preparations for their trip, Ed's male attention is caught by the gaze of a model at his agency, a girl with a "gold-glowing mote" in her eye; she represents for Ed the call to overcome the insufficiency of civilized man's quotidian rounds. The promise of the "gold-glowing mote" is fulfilled in the joy Ed experiences on the river bank, a genuine deliverance from civilization's restraints. The culminating deliverance will come only later, in the journey's aftermath, when passions are stilled and peace is regnant. Then Ed reports that "the gold-halved eye had lost its fascination. Its place was in the night river, in the land of impossibility." Ed sees her now and again around the studio: "She is a pleasant part of the world, but minor. She is imaginary."

This, then, is the deliverance: the humiliation foreseen in Obadiah that beats out of recalcitrant, Faustian man the urge to surmount the sense that life is not enough.

Deliverance is thus a moral tale of the superiority of resignation, of the virtues of cultivating one's garden. At the conclusion, Ed Gentry sits with his wife, Martha, in marital companionability: "In summer we sit by a lake where we have an A-frame cottage—it is not Lake Cahula, it is over on the other side of the lake—and look out over the water, maybe drinking a beer in the evening." It is a life of muted pleasures, true, but it is a true deliverance from the exhausting pursuit of the promise in the "gold-glowing mote."

ALNILAM

First published: 1987
Type of work: Novel

A blind man struggles to discover how his son died when his plane crashed at a North Carolina training base during World War II.

Alnilam is completely different from *Deliverance*. Whereas *Deliverance* unfolds swiftly around a tightly structured plot, *Alnilam*—much longer at 682 pages— rambles along, often faltering under the burden of its sometimes awkward split point of view. The main character, Frank Cahill, is an amusement park owner in Atlanta who learns that his son Joel has died in a mysterious training plane crash at the North Carolina Air Corps base where he is stationed during World War II. Joel's body cannot be found, and Cahill, recently victimized by blindness brought on by diabetes, travels by bus to the training base with his German shepherd seeing-eye dog, Zack. He hopes to learn exactly what happened to Joel.

Cahill is received well by the camp authorities, and he meets Joel's officers and friends. He trudges over the site of the fatal accident. He even sleeps with one of the local girls well known to the airmen. He never discovers, however, exactly how Joel died. What he does discover is that Joel was the moving spirit of a mysterious cult named for the star Alnilam deep in Orion, the hunter constellation. Their goal is a transcendence of the earthly and physical through the experience of flight, an experience that to them becomes virtually mystical.

Many pages of *Alnilam* are printed in double columns. A column on the left in bold-face print renders the thoughts and sensations of the blind Cahill groping around the base in both literal and figurative darkness. A column on the right in normal print maintains the usual flow of omniscient third-person narration. The device sometimes intrudes on the reader's willing suspension of disbelief. When the double-column arrangement goes on for several pages, should the reader go all the way with the left column and then backtrack to the right column or try to keep up with both at once? At times, the tonal differences do not seem pronounced enough to warrant the extra effort of following two points of view.

Dickey has always been courageous about taking chances, however, and even if the split narration is not always successful, he does succeed in giving a moving impression of the blind Cahill's quest. Some of the scenes are memorable. The training plane fight, for example, is a gripping re-creation of a blind man's sensations at the controls of a PT-17 aircraft; and Cahill's night bundled up with the girl very effectively captures a different kind of experience.

Cahill's ordeal takes place in the dead of winter, and the cold contributes to the tactile imagery so necessary in recounting a blind person's movements around unfamiliar terrain. Cahill's adjustment to the sterile landscape of the base; his closeness to Zack, his dog (in whose fur he frequently fumbles for reassurance), and the slow revelation of what his son had been up to—all help give the story sufficient life for the reader often to forget the narrative contrivance.

Summary

The importance of the outdoors runs all through Dickey's work; the need for physical communion with the substantial world outside the all-consuming ego appears everywhere. *Deliverance*'s Ed Gentry scaling a two-hundred-foot cliff, embracing the solid earth of north Georgia, is emblematic of this longing for merging in Dickey's sensibility. With this spiritual yearning goes an acceptance of the violence that is built into nature and is a given of existence that is better acknowledged than shied away from. Dickey's criticism reveals a man of considerable breadth of learning, although his work is never literary and allusive in diction and symbol.

Bibliography

Calhoun, Richard J., ed. *James Dickey: The Expansive Imagination*. Deland, Fla.: Everett/Edwards, 1973.

Calhoun, Richard J., and Robert W. Hill. *James Dickey*. Boston: Twayne, 1983.

Heyen, William. "A Conversation with James Dickey." *Southern Review* 9 (1973): 135-156.

Kirschten, Robert. *James Dickey and the Gentle Ecstasy of Earth*. Baton Rouge: Louisiana State University Press, 1988.

Lieberman, Laurence. *The Achievement of James Dickey: A Comprehensive Selection of His Poems With a Critical Introduction*. Glenview, Ill.: Scott, Foresman, 1968.

Markos, Donald W. "Art and Immediacy: James Dickey's *Deliverance*." *Southern Review* n.s. 7 (July, 1971): 947-953.

Mills, Ralph J., Jr. "The Poetry of James Dickey." *Triquarterly* 11 (Winter, 1968): 231-242.

Frank Day

EMILY DICKINSON

Born: Amherst, Massachusetts
December 10, 1830
Died: Amherst, Massachusetts
May 15, 1886

Principal Literary Achievement

Dickinson's poems, in marked contrast to the sentimental, domestic style of her time, offer original ways of seeing the everyday through verse formulations that are distinctive, lyrical, and timeless.

Biography

Emily Elizabeth Dickinson was born in Amherst, Massachusetts, on December 10, 1830, elder daughter of lawyer Edward Dickinson and Emily Norcross Dickinson. Dickinson was the second of three children, a year younger than her brother, William, and three years older than her sister, Lavinia. She was born in a large house built by her grandfather, Samuel Fowler Dickinson; except for absences of about a year for her schooling and seven months in Boston, she lived in it all of her life and died there at precisely 6:00 P.M. on May 15, 1886.

It is paradoxical that a woman who led such a circumscribed and apparently uneventful life managed to acquire the rich perceptions that enabled her to write 1,775 poems unlike any others in the English language. Every one is recognizably her own, and many are masterpieces. The circumstances of her life, therefore, hold a special fascination for readers of her verse.

Dickinson's sharp perceptions and brilliant inner life arise primarily from her background. Her paternal grandfather, whom she never knew, remained an unseen presence in her family. A Trinitarian deacon educated at Dartmouth College, he became moderately prosperous through his legal practice, investments, and a number of appointive and elective government positions; he was also a visionary. His religious zeal led him to use his entire fortune to found two Trinitarian educational institutions: Amherst Academy (1814) and Amherst College (1821). It was he who built "the homestead" in 1813, the great brick house that defined the daily life of his poet-granddaughter. Having spent thousands of dollars in the cause of education, he had become insolvent by early 1833. On May 22, 1833, he was even forced to sell the homestead. He moved to Cincinnati, Ohio, where he did church-related work, then Hudson, Ohio, where he died of pneumonia on April 22, 1838.

His son Edward, the poet's father, succeeded where the elder Dickinson had failed. Edward continued in his father's position as trustee of the Amherst institutions. By the end of his term in 1873, Amherst College had assets of more than a million dollars. By March, 1855, he had repurchased the house his father had built and lost. Educated at Yale University, he managed to combine religious zeal with practical business ability. His daughter would remember his long absences—as representative to the Massachusetts state legislature, as chief financial officer of Amherst College, as land speculator with holdings in northern New England—but she clearly loved him in a way she never did her mother.

Edward was an undemonstrative man; he had struggled through Yale University with only the barest financial support of a father who ironically had directed all of his resources to the support of Amherst College. The elder Dickinson believed, in characteristic Puritan spirit, that he owed the most support to the greatest number, even though this meant stinting a member of his own family. Edward was, consequently, a man who had needed to stifle external emotions so many times that he had trouble expressing them at all. Many of the courtship letters he wrote to Emily Norcross Dickinson (the poet's mother) survive, but even during the emotionally charged period before marriage Dickinson found it possible to describe, entirely impersonally, what he considered the characteristics of an ideal wife. Edward also had found it disconcerting that he had to sacrifice an independent career, in effect, to redeem his father's good name. Despite his withdrawn nature and his long absences from home, he remained a primary figure in his daughter's life and poetry.

Dickinson did not have the same close relationship with her mother. Emily Norcross was not intellectual by nature—she barely understood much of her daughter's poetry—and was at least as undemonstrative as Edward. Many stories about the strange relationship of withdrawn mother and poet-daughter are embellishments of the apparently cruel comments the younger Emily made in letters; others follow from stories told by the relatively small number of persons admitted to the Dickinson circle. Most likely, the antagonism between mother and daughter arose from their different temperaments: the mother lonely and non-literary, the daughter keenly intellectual and entrusted by her father with many of the household responsibilities which properly should have been her mother's. Still, it would be wrong to assume that Dickinson's relations with her mother were filled with petty arguments. After her father's sudden death in 1874, during his first term in the Massachusetts House of Representatives, Dickinson and her mother grew closer. She nursed her mother faithfully, from 1875 to 1882, through the paralysis which ultimately took her life.

Dickinson's early relations with her only brother were competitive. In many ways they were alike; both were intellectual and ambitious. Though Dickinson's education was excellent for a woman of the mid-eighteenth century—coeducational training at Amherst Academy, from 1840 to 1845, and slightly more than a year at Mount Holyoke Female Seminary, in 1847 and 1848—it is likely that she envied her brother's ability to circulate in the larger world. They were always friendly rivals.

Dickinson's sister had a personality much like that of her mother, though there is no indication of antagonism between Emily and Lavinia. Indeed, were it not for her sister's efforts after Dickinson's death it is likely that a first collection of her poems would never have appeared. With Thomas Wentworth Higginson and Mabel Loomis Todd, she sorted out the nearly eighteen hundred poems, some of which were written on billheads, envelopes, and odd scraps of paper. They deciphered Dickinson's cramped handwriting and "corrected" and standardized her punctuation. Variations of this first edition, which first appeared in 1890, four years after the poet's death from kidney disease, remained substantially the only printed texts of Dickinson's verse until Thomas H. Johnson numbered and restored their original readings in his 1955 major edition. Dickinson had only eleven poems published during her lifetime.

The poet's surviving family members share some of the responsibility for creating the image of "the white nun of Amherst." This epithet refers to her habit of dressing exclusively in white after 1861. That she did this out of despair from some impossible love, either for young Ben Newton (her father's law clerk) or for Charles Wadsworth, a married Philadelphia minister with a family, is unlikely. It is possible, as has been suggested, that Wadsworth's acceptance of a pastorate in San Francisco was an attempt to avoid temptation, but contemporary critics generally argue against the image of a Dickinson desolate because of a lost love. Johnson assigns most of Dickinson's bridal poems to the 1860's, based on this unhappy romance, but one can easily question the Johnson chronology. If correct, it would mean that Dickinson composed two-thirds of her entire output of verse in eight years and an astonishing number (681) in the years from 1862 to 1864.

Dickinson family members recalled, destroyed, and sometimes severely edited much of the poet's personal correspondence. "The belle" or "queen recluse" personas they created by default were infinitely preferable at the close of the nineteenth century to the rebellious, unconventional, but thwarted genius that she actually was. Dickinson had close relationships with several men her own age, particularly with Samuel Bowles, editor of the Springfield, Massachusetts, *Daily Republican*. Newton, a clerk in her father's law office, was a friendly critic of her verse; however, it is difficult, and mostly unnecessary, to speculate about whether these were romantic attachments. Contrary to the widely accepted myth, Dickinson's literary friendships actually broadened during the last ten years of her life. Higginson reintroduced her to a girlhood acquaintance, Helen Hunt Jackson, an acclaimed writer and crusader for the rights of American Indians (Jackson's novel *Ramona* [1884] is her most familiar work to contemporary readers).

Another area of Dickinson's life obscured in the nineteenth and early twentieth century accounts is the poet's views on religion, and this directly affects the interpretation of many of her poems. Dickinson was reared in the conservative Trinitarian tradition of Jonathan Edwards. This places her background against that of the liberal Unitarians, whose most famous minister was, at the time, Ralph Waldo Emerson. Dickinson remained, however, the only member of her family never to undergo a conversion experience. This was something of a disgrace given the heady zeal of

Amherst, but Dickinson never compromised, though it meant being anathematized while in attendance at Mount Holyoke.

Some of her poems suggest science and empiricism as alternatives to unexamined belief; many others portray the particulars of church services against the need for reason. It is an indication of their tolerance that Dickinson's family never pressed her in these matters. Indeed, Dickinson's father provided his daughter with the kind of training which encouraged such inquiry. She was well read, particularly in the physical sciences, and she had ready access to her father's and the Amherst College libraries. The men of the family had read many of the same works as Dickinson, but these had merely strengthened their religious convictions. Dickinson always maintained her belief in a supreme deity, but she doubted that human institutions provided a necessary link.

Except for the vision problem which plagued her periodically as early as 1862, Dickinson's life was free of any medical incident until the uremic poisoning which ultimately took her life, swiftly and without pain, on May 15, 1886. Dickinson sought treatment for her severely blurred vision in Boston in 1864. Her stay there of seven months was the only period, aside from her year at Mount Holyoke, that she remained away from home, and her letters emphasize her desire to return home. The vision problem seems to have abated of its own accord in Dickinson's later years, though it appears in her handwriting throughout the 1860's.

The Dickinson that remains once one disregards myth and apocrypha is an immensely gifted woman born a century and a quarter too soon. Rebellious in matters of family and religion, she nevertheless remained dutiful to those who needed her. Far from being an active feminist (for this was nearly impossible during the Civil War period in conservative Amherst), she accepted the enclosed life of a well-born but unmarried New England woman. Had she lived more extensively in the larger world, her verse would probably not have resembled the legacy she left.

Analysis

Critics of Dickinson's verse generally note that the poems incorporate one or more of the following themes: death, love, religion, nature, and eternity. This observation, of itself, does not take into account the amazing thematic combinations she managed or the extraordinary variety of poetic voices she employed. These range from the almost embarrassing cuteness of poems such as 61 ("Papa above!") or 288 ("I'm Nobody! Who are you?") to the skepticism of 338 ("I know that He exists.") and the passion, with intended or accidental double meaning, of 249 ("Wild Nights—Wild Nights!"). Some of her poems are high serious meditations, such as 258 ("There's a certain Slant of light"); others amount to waspish commentary, such as 401 ("What Soft—Cherubic Creatures—"). That she could see herself as a nobody, a seething volcano, a mouse, or a loaded gun all within the compass of several hundred poems is an indication of the variety of unconventional metaphor she used.

Even more astonishing is the fact that her style undergoes no linear development. Many of the early poems are as excellent as the later ones; bathetic and coy elements also appear throughout the collection. Absence of end-line punctuation creates en-jambments that run for full stanzas, while dashes often create a hiatus at mid-line or end. Early critics ascribed these eccentricities to Dickinson's inability or unwilling-ness to punctuate (a characteristic her correspondence shares). Others see Dickin-son's unconventional style as a flaunting of convention, particularly since most nine-teenth century verse written by women was conservative in both form and theme. Still others, noting the lyric configuration of the dashes, compare her poems to the lyric measures of nursery rhymes or to the hymnal melodies then sung in Trinitarian churches. These interpretations do not necessarily exclude one another. What is im-portant is that the irregular rhythms these dashes create almost always improve the poetry.

Dickinson neither titled nor dated her poems, and this is one problem that John-son faced when preparing the 1955 major edition. The result is that he assigned the poems numbers, arranging them in what appeared a likely chronological order. Sometimes he arrived at relatively secure dating, as when a poem appears in dated letters, on dated billheads, or on postmarked envelopes. Unfortunately, this pre-cludes neither prior nor subsequent composition. Furthermore, because the poems show no radical shifts in style, the task of firm dating remains even more daunting.

A related curiosity of Dickinson's poems is their nearly complete exclusion of reference to external specifics. Number 61 ("Papa above!") might appear to imply her father's death, yet the Johnson chronology posits 1859 as its year of composi-tion. Since Dickinson's father died in 1874, accepting the Johnson dating means having to limit application of the first line to the poet's divine father alone. The poem becomes merely a coy parody of The Lord's Prayer rather than a simultaneous hope that the poet's own father might remember his little mouse.

The complete run of Dickinson's poems is so marked by genius that one tends to forget the occasional lapses of obviously unsuccessful works. These seem to occur most often when she reaches beyond the microcosm of her immediate world. A good example of this is poem 196 ("We don't cry—Tim and I,"). Dickinson here attempts to parallel the pathetic condition of the poet's persona and that of Tiny Tim, the patient crippled child of Charles Dickens' *A Christmas Carol* (1843). Un-fortunately, the effect is so cloying and sentimental that the poem descends to the bathetic, almost becoming parody. Similarly, poem 127 ("'Houses'—so the wise Men tell me—"), though it begins with a biblical simplicity akin to that of William Blake's child songs, strains to such an extent to evoke sympathy that the verse be-comes flaccid. What began as the Lord's promise of a mansion for His children quickly descends to sentimentality for its own sake: "Mansions cannot let the tears in,/ Mansions must exclude the storm!"

The mid-nineteenth century figures of Dickens' Tiny Tim and Little Nell thus continue to afflict Dickinson's verse at irregular intervals. In all fairness, so much maudlin sentiment pervaded the popular poetry of the time that it is a wonder Dick-inson's style remained as distinct and uniformly superior as it did. Her poetry is generally on its weakest ground when her dry wit or high serious reflection aims merely to imitate popular trends of the day.

Amherst, in Dickinson's time, was an enlightened, relatively well-educated community, surrounded even in the nineteenth century by institutions of learning, many of them associated in one way or another with the Trinitarian or Unitarian churches. From Dickinson's perspective, however, its people were all too comfortable in religious outlooks she rejected. Infant death was an even more common fact of life in the nineteenth than in the twentieth century. Regular influenza epidemics claimed the lives of adults as well as children every winter. Tuberculosis, then called consumption, claimed still more, and all those deaths appeared listed on the front page of the Springfield *Daily Republican*, the newspaper Dickinson read every day. The room in which Dickinson wrote overlooked the Protestant cemetery. At one period, the funerals of Amherst friends and acquaintances became so common that Dickinson felt she had to move her writing desk to the center of the room to spare herself. In short, Dickinson and her contemporaries lived with death in a way most present-day Americans can hardly comprehend.

Added to this is the fact that Dickinson steadfastly resisted the doctrine of "election," the view that some were marked from birth for salvation while others were damned. Proof of such justification lay in what Trinitarians called a "conversion experience." This generally took the form of some personal religious insight experienced at a critical stage in life. Dickinson's grandfather, father, and brother had all undergone such an experience during or just after their college years. Even at Mount Holyoke, however, Dickinson was among "the unredeemed." She was one of only three students so categorized. To be included among "the saved" she needed only to profess some religious experience, yet she refused to make this claim merely for social acceptance. By her late teenage years she had abandoned church attendance; for a New England woman reared in the tradition of nineteenth century Trinitarianism, this was anathema. It is little wonder, then, that particulars of the Congregationalist funeral service appear as they do in poem 280 ("I felt a Funeral, in my Brain"). Their droning monotony first causes the narrator's mind to go numb. Feet scrape the wooden floors of the frame church until the narrator feels "That Sense was breaking through—." The coffin seems to "creak across my Soul," and she is "Wrecked, solitary." Finally, "a Plank in Reason, broke," and the narrator "Finished knowing—then—."

Literally, the poet describes her own death, a familiar starting point for many of her poems. The particulars of the service are equally familiar, but her alterations are striking and reflect her nonconformist views. To the congregation, she is "wrecked" and "solitary." Reason breaks, and sense breaks through. She plunges downward into nothingness and finishes knowing because at death she has certainty. There is no mention here of heaven or hell. The "World" she hits "at every plunge" is that of her inner self.

Dickinson here reverses the "plank of faith" metaphor familiar to most New England Protestants in the nineteenth century. This plank, firmly grounded on either side, bridges an abyss. One negotiates it while holding firmly to the Bible. Look to either side and one must surely plunge into the depths. Dickinson's family, as most others of their station, owned William Holmes and John W. Barber's *Religious Allegories* (1848), which presents the metaphor accompanied by a woodcut showing one of the faithful attempting to cross the gap. Dickinson's plank is Reason, not Faith, however, and Reason does not break, it breaks through. To contemporary readers such nonconformity may not seem particularly striking, but one must imagine the effect it had on Dickinson's family and church-going acquaintances. This poem, them, synthesizes the death and religion one finds so often separately treated in Dickinson's verse; more important, it gives some impression of the extent to which the poet felt obliged to argue her convictions. She did not take her theological position merely for the sensation it no doubt created, and her religious views were certainly more heterodox than many critics indicate.

Contemporary critics who analyze Dickinson's work must storm the verbal fortress of commentary written by her family and friends who, with all good intentions of making Dickinson the stereotype of a nineteenth century spinster who happened to write poetry, came close to neutralizing the double meanings of many of her best poems. Higginson, whose advice she regularly sought on literary matters, is particularly blameworthy in this regard. During her lifetime, he repeatedly urged her not to publish, largely on the practical grounds that her verse was unsalable, though wider circulation of her poems would undoubtedly have brought her into correspondence with important writers of the day. One could also argue that this might have changed her style, made her less violently expressive, or rendered a life in Amherst impossible, but these are moot arguments.

Even after her death, Higginson was intent on perpetuating the Dickinson image he had helped to create. Typical is his famous disclaimer inevitably attached to commentaries on poem 249 ("Wild Nights—Wild Nights!"). The poem turns on the image of a storm; lovers in the safe harbor of their love can cast away both compass and chart and row in the Eden of their love. Higginson's scruples concerned the erotic implication of the poem's final lines: "Might I but moor—Tonight—/ In Thee!" Higginson feared to publish the poem "lest the malignant read into it more than that virgin recluse ever dreamed of putting there." One wonders, however, whether Higginson even noticed the much more perverse implications of a stormy Eden whose fallen lovers dispose of the compass and chart which would have kept them on the prescribed course—presumably, apart. Though one could argue that the erotic image of the moored lovers was unintended, it is much more difficult to reject the lovers' obvious abandonment of their set course. The reckless emotion of their love justifies the erotic implication of the final lines.

Comparable eroticism, in this case consummation of love, appears in poem 190 ("He was weak, and I was strong—then—"). Here the lovers alternate in conditions of strength and weakness. When the narrator becomes weak, her lover leads her "Home." The night is quiet, the lover says nothing. When "Day knocked" they had to part, neither the stronger: "He strove—and I strove—too—/ We didn't do it—tho'!" This final line refers to the lovers' refusal to part, but it also can imply their decision not to abandon the traditional rules of courtship. This naughtiness is an important element of Dickinson's verse. To deny it merely to create the image of a sainted recluse plays false with the facts and cripples the impact of her poetry.

Men much more than women were important to Dickinson the poet. She relied upon the literary judgments of Newton, a clerk in her father's office, and editors and Higginson, and she appears never to have questioned their separately expressed views that she should not attempt to circulate her poems more widely. They, no doubt as much as she, were affected by the stereotypes of domestic verse, the only kind considered suitable for a nineteenth century woman to publish. If one examines the poems Dickinson did place during her lifetime, it becomes obvious that they suit requirements of prevailing taste; were they the sole criterion by which to judge her as poet, she would have been considerably less important than contemporary critics agree she is. Of the 1,775 poems in Johnson's edition, only eleven appeared in Dickinson's lifetime, and six of those eleven were printed in the Springfield *Daily Republican*. Those six are poem 3 ("Sic transit gloria mundi," which appeared bearing a title "A Valentine"), poem 35 ("Nobody knows this little Rose"), and more substantive verse such as poem 214 ("I taste a liquor never brewed—," which was given the title "The May-Wine"), poem 216 ("Safe in their Alabaster Chambers—," called "The Sleeping"), poem 228 ("Blazing in Gold and quenching in Purple," entitled "Sunset"), and poem 986 ("A narrow Fellow in the Grass," which appeared as "The Snake").

This small list allows one to see how editors consistently attempted to render Dickinson's verse immediately intelligible, both by means of clarifying titles and standardizing punctuation. Though one could consider none of these poems inferior, they nevertheless fit within the parameters of what passed as "women's verse" in a way other of her works did not. It is easy to see how they are consonant with works published by Dickinson's female contemporaries: Charlotte Brontë's *Jane Eyre* (1847), Harriet Beecher Stowe's *Uncle Tom's Cabin* (1852), Elizabeth Barrett Browning's *Aurora Leigh* (1857), and George Eliot's *Middlemarch* (1872). By the time Eliot had published *Middlemarch*, Dickinson had written but not published—and had little hope of publishing—more than twelve hundred poems.

POEM 160 (JUST LOST, WHEN I WAS SAVED!)

First published: 1891 (as "Called Back")
Type of Work: Poem

One of Dickinson's anticipatory views of eternity.

Dickinson wrote this poem between 1860 and 1862, if one accepts the Johnson chronology. Her sister included it among the small selection of poems published after the poet's death. It appears that the title "Called Back" was appended based on a note the poet had written to her cousins on the day before her death. Perhaps she was inspired by the sudden conviction she was recovering that affects many terminally ill people, or (equally likely) she did not want her cousins to worry. In any event, she wrote, "Little cousins,—Called Back. Emily."

Dickinson's poems often focus on a proleptic view of the death experience; that is, they anticipate death yet present a living narrator to interpret the nearly experienced event. Not surprisingly, they are usually devoid of any overt Christian imagery; yet, there does appear, in this instance, the image of the "Reporter" who has stood before the apocalyptic "Seal." The narrator's wish to remain next time, to see "the things . . . / By Ear unheard,/ Unscrutinized by Eye—" corresponds to Saint Paul's words in 1 Corinthians 2.9. The speaker, however, is far more like Samuel Taylor Coleridge's Ancient Mariner or Herman Melville's Ishmael, the narrator of *Moby-Dick* (1851). All three have looked upon death and lived.

It is impossible not to sense the enlightened, humanistic tone of the poem's first two lines: "Just lost, when I was saved!/ Just felt the world go by!" The third line, which repeats the initial word of the first two and adds "girt," implies that meeting "Eternity" is akin to a struggle or a hero's encounter with an opponent. Eternity is predatory, and the paratactic arrangement of lines 1-3 emphasizes its insistent claim on the speaker. Even so, the "breath" of line 4 allows her to overcome its influence and to "feel," so that she can "tell" what she has seen. Poetry, whose words one feels as much as hears, thus provides the strength for the poet to return. The desire to be a "pale Reporter"—that is, to be a poet interpreting universal experience in an insightful way—is too great for her to succumb to death, at least this time. Nevertheless, Hercules' cry of "*Plus ultra*" ("still further"), shouted when he had erected Gibraltar and Ceuta at the edge of the world, has meaning for the poet, too. She desires to take language further than it has ever been, even though she faces the likelihood of destruction, or a poem without transcendent meaning. The death and rebirth which the poem describe thus resemble a fixed part of a mythic hero's experience, even as they correspond to the humanist insight of a poet who has gone beyond merely dabbling in verse and become a true poet.

POEM 187 (HOW MANY TIMES THESE LOW FEET STAGGERED—)

First published: 1890 (as "Requiescat"; also called "Troubled About Many
                    Things")
Type of work: Poem

Utilizes the burdened, domestic tone characteristic of many Dickinson poems which have domestic settings.

Though this poem was written during the same period as poem 160, the appearance of the housewife figure in poem 187 required an altogether more plodding, heavy tone. Dickinson achieves this through alternating dactyls and trochees. The woman's "—low feet staggered" so many times that "Only the soldered mouth can tell—." Sealed coffin and mute corpse challenge anyone who desires to understand the hardship under which she labored to "Try" to "stir the awful rivet" and "lift the hasps of steel!" The corpse's forehead is "cool" because in death it is free of labor. Dickinson repeatedly shifts the housewife's burden to the reader through the imperatives "Try" (used twice) and "Lift." Ironically, the domestic burden of the housewife's duties becomes the weight of the coffin and the dead weight of handling the corpse itself: "the listless hair" and the "adamantine fingers," stiffened in death. Their steel-like unyieldingness can no longer wear a tin thimble.

Predatory flies, a death and disease symbol which regularly appear in Dickinson's poems, batter and speckle the woman's once-clean chamber window. Both they and the sun are "Brave"; both sun and ceiling cobweb are "Fearless." Even so, despite this oppressive imagery, the housewife has finally become "Indolent," lain in a field of daisies. The poem thus resolves itself in a single line through the double implication of "indolent": lazy, but also free from suffering. There is no contradiction at all in the two views of death Dickinson takes in her poetry. Seen from the aspect of the poet or of a woman whom household burdens do not confine death becomes an awe-filled adventure contemplated with heroic anticipation. The moment the perspective becomes that of a housewife or a woman bound by domestic duties, death becomes a blessed release from labor.

POEM 214 (I TASTE A LIQUOR NEVER BREWED—)

First published: 1861 (as "The May-Wine")
Type of work: Poem

This poem describes the intoxicating feeling that poetry causes.

For the ancient Greeks, Dionysus, the god of the wine grape, was also the deity associated with dramatic poetry. Writing verse, and reading it, removed one from ordinary sense experience; Dickinson, though never invoking the god's name, makes all she can of the association between intoxication and ecstasy in poem 214. The rhythm of a reel (a whirling dance) supports this imagery. Significantly, this poem privileges the reading of verse to the writing of it. The speaker "tastes" the never-brewed liquor, which is held in pearl tankards, the mother-of-pearl covered verse anthologies of Dickinson's time. The "Frankfurt Berries," the hops used to produce fine beer, could never yield as rich a brew as can the well-distilled language of great poetry.

Those who consume the insubstantial metaphors of verse become drunk, debauched on air and dew; they reel through summers that never end from inns under eternally blue skies. The speaker is unrepentant for her drunkenness. She will stop consuming verse only when the "Landlords" of nature turn "the drunken Bee" from gathering pollen from flowers or when butterflies no longer gather their "drams"—in other words, when nature no longer furnishes precedents for the speaker's own behavior. When she dies, the seraphim, highest order among the angels, will toss their haloes, their "snowy Hats" in greeting, the saints come to their windows to see her, the "little Tippler" from the world of man—as well as from the wine-grape district of Spain, which she calls "Manzanilla."

This poem furnishes a good example of how early editors often diminished the strength of Dickinson's verse through alterations they believed would make the poetry more consonant with prevailing taste. After Dickinson's death, Higginson and Mabel Loomis Todd changed the last lines from "To see the little Tippler/ From Manzanilla come!" to "To see the little Tippler/ Leaning against the sun." Their change rendered even more vapid the innocuous 1861 alteration made by the Springfield *Daily Republican*: "Come staggering toward the sun."

POEM 216 (SAFE IN THEIR ALABASTER CHAMBERS—)

First published: 1862 (as "The Sleeping")
Type of work: Poem

A poem, written in several versions, that describes the justified dead awaiting resurrection.

Dickinson wrote several versions of this poem, sending them quite literally across the backyard hedge for the opinion of her sister-in-law. Unable to make a final decision, she sent two versions to Higginson, who printed the completely different final stanza of the second version together with the two stanzas of the first version, thereby creating a single poem one-third longer than Dickinson had intended.

There are curious implications in this poem that critics often overlook. Read straightforwardly, it states that the meek sleep safely in their satin-raftered, stone-roofed graves and confidently await their resurrection to ratify the salvation they already know is theirs. Breezes laugh in the castle above them; bees buzz "in a stolid Ear," and birds sing ignorantly in cadence. The poem concludes with a lament on the wisdom lost with the dead. In the second stanza of the 1861 version, the ages wheel by, crowns drop, and doges (Italian dukes) lose their power silently.

The cynical implication of the 1859 version's second stanza is that the breeze laughs at them as they wait, the bee gossips about them in the unyielding ear of creation, and the birds sing their meaningless songs in rhythm even as no resurrection occurs. In the 1861 version, years pass through the firmament, crowns drop, and power passes; it all happens silently, but the justified merely wait, safe in the comfort of their ignorance.

POEM 258 (THERE'S A CERTAIN SLANT OF LIGHT)

First published: 1890
Type of work: Poem

Compares afternoon winter light with the despair one encounters in a search for transcendent meaning.

This poem begins by noting the oppressive sound of church bells heard in the bleak atmosphere of a winter afternoon. They give "Heavenly Hurt," though they leave no external scar. Within six lines, Dickinson synthesizes a description of depression in terms of three senses: hearing, sight, and feeling.

This depression is, however, more than ordinary sadness. It comes from heaven, and it bears the biblical "Seal Despair." It hurts the entire landscape, its nonhuman as well as its human constituents, which listens, holds its breath for some revelation, yet perceives only the look of death. Significantly, the poet nowhere implies that no meaning exists; indeed, in other poems she is certain that a divine being exists and that there is a plan. Even so, the implications of what she writes are almost as devastating, for the apocalyptic seal of revelation holds fast, yielding no enlightenment to those below but the weak afternoon sun of a New England winter.

Read straightforwardly, the only means to combat this despair is, logically, faith, but in Dickinson's landscape one senses only its external sign: the weighty tunes of a cathedral carillon. The "internal difference," the scars of discouragement and despair, remain within all, though visible to none.

POEM 303 (THE SOUL SELECTS HER OWN SOCIETY—)

First published: 1890 (as "Exclusion")
Type of work: Poem

The poem explicitly notes that individuals choose the particulars of their own environment but also implies renunciation of traditional beliefs.

Critics note that poem 303 was written in 1862, the year Dickinson made her decision to withdraw from the larger world. The poem, read in this simple way, simply states the need to live by one's own choice. This reading, perfectly acceptable in itself, overlooks several important phrases which have larger implications.

The first of these curious choices of language is "divine Majority," in line 3. "The Soul" of line 1, not merely "a soul" or a person, shuts her door not only to people at large but also to the majority, even those who bear the stamp of divine sanction. Read this way, the poem also indicates the poet's decision not to join the society of the Elect, this even though "an emperor be kneeling" on her doormat. The conduit of grace, an analogy favored in the sermons of Jonathan Edwards, becomes "the Valves" of the soul's discrimination. Though she remains "unmoved," the soul is neither nihilistic nor solipsistic. Even as the capitalized letter implies zero, the soul chooses "One," then becomes deaf to all entreaties "Like Stone." To insist that this necessarily indicates preference for a Unitarian rather than a Trinitarian view carries the interpretation to a theological level which the poem's language will not sustain. Nevertheless, selectivity in all matters, including religion, is something the poet clearly favors.

On a complementary level, one notices the carefully crafted description of the woman not at home to any callers, except one or at most a few. Read this way, which merely supplements the other possible alternatives, the poem states the preference to live in a way unlike that of most nineteenth century women, spurning the conventions of social obligation and what society expects, even though an emperor might attempt to persuade her to join the larger group.

POEM 328 (A BIRD CAME DOWN THE WALK—)

First published: 1891
Type of work: Poem

Describes unexpected cruelty, distrust, ingratitude, and fear all within an apparently placid, idyllic setting.

This is the finest example of Dickinson's nature verse, for it perfectly juxtaposes elements of superficial gentility against the inner barbarity that characterizes the workings of the world. The narrator chances to see a bird walking along a pathway, but just as the scene appears perfect, the bird seizes upon a worm, bites it in two, and devours it. The bird drinks some dew on nearby grass (note the alternate for a drinking "glass"), then graciously steps aside, right to a wall, to allow a beetle to pass. The bird, like one fearful of being caught in an unacceptable action, glances around quickly with darting eyes.

"Cautious" describes both the demeanor of the bird and that of the observing narrator. Both feel threatened, the bird of the possible consequences of its savagery, the narrator because she is next on the bird's path. She "offered him a Crumb," not because she admires the bird, but out of fear and expediency. The bird, sensing that it has escaped any potentially harmful consequences for what it has done, struts a bit as "he unrolled his feathers" and "rowed him softer home—." Ironically, its walk is too casual, softer than oars dividing a seamless ocean or butterflies leaping into noon's banks, all without a splash. Behind its soft, charming, and genteel façade, nature is menacing, and its hypocritical attempts to conceal its barbarism make it more frightening.

POEM 465 (I HEARD A FLY BUZZ— WHEN I DIED—)

First published: 1896
Type of work: Poem

The most famous of the Dickinson poems that look ahead to death, set at the instant that lies between life and death.

This poem relies upon the poetic devices known technically as synesthesia (use of one sense to describe the workings of another) and paronomasia (wordplay). The predatory fly, functioning as in poem 187, waits to claim a corpse. The room is still, but this stillness resembles the interval between the heavings of a storm. Eyes had cried all they could; the patient, who is speaking, is beyond willing life, though she has willed her "Keepsakes." The language is both theological and legal: "when the King/ Be witnessed—/ in the Room—."

Then, hesitantly but unmistakably, the fly interposes itself between the dying speaker and the light. Its buzz is "Blue—uncertain stumbling." The windows fail, and the speaker cannot "see to see—." Characteristically, there is no enlightenment at the moment of death, merely a failing of the human objects designed to admit light. Thus, human sight does not allow human understanding. Dickinson once wrote to Higginson, using her distinctive capitalizations, that, "The Ear is the last Face We hear after we see." Clearly, she identifies the "eye" with the "I." The King is present to witness the death, but it remains a legal transaction. Neither He nor the speaker have the will to alter things, beyond ensuring that the material objects willed fall to the wills of their new owners.

POEM 640 (I CANNOT LIVE WITH YOU—)

First published: 1890
Type of work: Poem

The most famous of the love poems, often misread to argue for the poet's love relationship with Charles Wadsworth.

This poem's coherence results from the opposition of tensions which arise from Dickinson's dual understanding of life. To live with the beloved is impossible, for "it would be life." Life is, on the other hand, something eternal, the key to which resides with the church sexton, who keeps the key to the Lord's tabernacle. The cups of human life, however, hold no sacramental wine; the housewife discards them when they break or crack and replaces them with newer ware.

The speaker cannot die with the beloved, for the gaze of "the Other" intrudes; it can neither be shut out nor down. This apparent rival that spies on any possible pact is the metaphysical divine other that has first rights in matters of death as well as life. Similarly, it is impossible for the speaker to "stand by/ And see you—freeze"; the single death of the beloved denies death to the devoted speaker.

Even a joint resurrection of the lovers is impossible; this would anger Jesus and obscure the face of the redeemer. To this dual understanding of life the poet thus adds the stages of the Christian experience: life, death, judgment, and resurrection. When the beloved looked upon the "homesick Eye," grace would "Glow plain," but it would be "foreign" to him who sought a higher grace. Furthermore, "They'd judge Us," saying that he sought to serve heaven even though she could not.

The speaker could then no longer have her eyes on paradise; both would suffer damnation, but she would fall the lower and they would still remain apart. The effect would be the same even if the beloved were forgiven. The only alternative, "Despair," becomes their connection; their only conversation is their joint prayer, which allows them to link the immanent and the transcendent.

POEM 712 (BECAUSE I COULD NOT STOP FOR DEATH)

First published: 1890
Type of work: Poem

In the most famous of her eternity poems, Dickinson personifies death as a gentleman caller.

Death appears personified in this poem as a courtly beau who gently insists that the speaker put aside both "labor" and "leisure." He arrives in his carriage, having stopped for her because she could not have stopped for him, and he even submits to a chaperone, "Immortality," for the length of their outing together.

This death holds no terrors. Their drive is slow, and they pass the familiar sights of the town: fields of grain which gaze at them, the local school and its playground. Even so, the speaker realizes that this is no ordinary outing with an ordinary gentleman caller when they pass the setting sun, "Or rather—He passed Us—." She realizes that it has grown cold, that she wears only a gossamer gown and a tulle lace cap.

Death takes the speaker to her new home, "A Swelling of the Ground," whose roof is "scarcely visible." Though centuries have passed since the event, the entire episode, including the speaker's awareness of her death, seems less than a day in length. The poem fuses elements of the secular seduction motif, with elements of the medieval bride-of-Christ tradition, arguable through inclusion of details such as the tippet of a nun's habit.

POEM 754 (MY LIFE HAD STOOD— A LOADED GUN—)

First published: 1929
Type of work: Poem

The most famous of the paradox poems, dealing with the Christian and secular understandings of life and death.

This poem is written as a riddle that challenges the reader to identify the speaker. On the literal level the speaker is a gun, loaded to do its owner's bidding. Its "smile" is like a Vesuvian eruption, laying low its master's enemies. None survive "On whom I lay a Yellow Eye—/ Or an emphatic Thumb—." Though the master must live longer than the gun, the gun may also live longer than its master.

Critics have given this poem every variety of interpretation, almost none of them totally satisfactory. Most common (and least satisfying) is the argument that the poet is herself the loaded gun, waiting to be called by her master, the Lord, ready to fight her Lord's battles, willing to make His enemies hers. Yet how can one reconcile this with the possibility of the gun's outliving her master except by admitting the possibility of a mortal deity? Though Dickinson doubts and even despairs in some of her poems concerning matters of election and redemption, she never denies that a deity exists. In fact, poem 338 explicitly records her certainty that there is a divine presence. Similarly, it does no good to see this poem merely as an emblem of the poet's personal, creative, or sexual frustration, as some critics have done.

Were one to have asked residents of Dickinson's Amherst the solution to the final riddle stanza, however, it is likely that they would have answered that the master was Christ and the gun was death. Christ has authority over life and death as Son of the Father; even so, Christ died before death disappeared from the world of the living, and in this sense death outlived Him.

Another interpretation embraces a more classical alternative. Myth traditionally pictures deities dealing out death with weapons: Zeus uses thunderbolts, Apollo and Artemis bows and arrows, Wotan a spear fashioned from the great ash tree which underpins creation. Seen in this way, death is both master and means. It uses whatever tool stands at the ready and creates opponents even as it destroys creation. The single consolation to universal creation, which will one day encounter death, is that neither death nor the tools it uses have eternal life.

POEM 986 (A NARROW FELLOW IN THE GRASS)

First published: 1866 (as "The Snake")
Type of work: Poem

Presents the archetypal snake in the grass as a symbol of cunning.

One of the best-known Dickinson nature poems, poem 986 is more remarkable for its execution and technique than its content. The narrator unexpectedly encounters a snake in tall marsh grass. Far from tempting the narrator, as the serpent tempted Eve, it induces fear, panting, and a sudden chill. The first eleven lines describe the snake in a personified, almost amiable way. He sometimes "rides" through the grass, parting it like a comb does hair. Yet, when plain sight threatens to betray its exact location, the grass "closes at your feet/ And opens further on—."

The narrator of this poem is male, perhaps because boys rather than girls would be more likely to walk through marshes; however, the narrator's sex also underscores the phallic implications of this symbol. If one prefers to see this sexual imagery, it is possible to cite the sexual association of such words and phrases as "Whip lash," "tighter breathing," and "Zero at the Bone." In any event, reading the poem as a commentary on human cunning is entirely consistent with any further level of meaning. The narrator feels cordial toward "Several of Nature's People" but has only fear for the snake. In this, as in many Dickinson's poems, one must beware of mixing biographical folklore with the poem and forcing the reading offered by structuralist critics that the poem is Dickinson's confession of sexual fear.

Reading the poem's first line aloud causes the tongue to flicker, like that of a snake; sibilants abound in increasing number as the lines describe the snake's approach. These elements are certainly intentional. Poem 1670 ("In Winter in my Room") presents a similar encounter, though with a worm-turned-snake. Relating the events as a dream sequence, this narrator flees whole towns from the creature before she dares set the experience down.

POEM 1624 (APPARENTLY WITH NO SURPRISE)

First published: 1890
Type of work: Poem

Nature is presented as the victim of the elements and an approving God.

The situation described in this short poem is simple. Frost "beheads" a "happy Flower" even as it plays back and forth in a breeze. The flower is not surprised that it has died in this way, even if the frost's power was "accidental." The wordplay on axe, beheading, and accidental is clear. What is a surprise is that the real assassin is "blonde." It is clearly the sun, which withheld its warmth and allowed the frost to do its dirty job. The sun "proceeds unmoved," the oxymoron emphasizing that the sun simply observes the workings of nature from its high vantage point. It metes out a day, and God, higher still, approves it all as director of the conspiracy.

Summary

One can fully appreciate Emily Dickinson's originality only by placing her verse against that of her poet contemporaries. She is certainly more mystical—and is a better poet—than Ralph Waldo Emerson or Henry David Thoreau. Her poetic works have greater substance than those of Edgar Allan Poe. She writes poems far richer in content than the school poets: James Russell Lowell, John Greenleaf Whittier, and Henry Wadsworth Longfellow. The only American poet of her century with whom she is comparable is Walt Whitman.

In the nineteenth century, women generally wrote only domestic verse—material suitable for ladies' magazines—or wrote under male pseudonyms. Higginson's advice that Dickinson avoid publication makes most modern readers of Dickinson angry, as do the alterations made by Dickinson's early editors. One can be grateful that Dickinson's creative energy remained undiminished.

Bibliography

Anderson, Charles R. *Emily Dickinson's Poetry: Stairway of Surprise.* New York: Holt, Rinehart and Winston, 1960.

Benes, Peter. *The Masks of Orthodoxy.* Amherst: University of Massachusetts Press, 1977.

Bianchi, Martha Dickinson. *The Life and Letters of Emily Dickinson.* Boston: Houghton Mifflin, 1924.

Bloom, Harold, ed. *Emily Dickinson.* New York: Chelsea House, 1985.

Johnson, Thomas H. *Emily Dickinson: An Interpretive Biography.* Cambridge, Mass.: Harvard University Press, 1955.

Knapp, Bettina L. *Emily Dickinson.* New York: Continuum, 1986.

McNeill, Helen. *Emily Dickinson.* New York: Virago/Pantheon, 1986.

Miller, Cristanne. *Emily Dickinson: A Poet's Grammar.* Cambridge, Mass.: Harvard University Press, 1987.

Sewall, Richard B. *The Life of Emily Dickinson.* 2 vols. New York: Farrar, Straus & Giroux, 1974.

Wolff, Cynthia Griffin. *Emily Dickinson.* New York: Alfred A. Knopf, 1986.

Robert J. Forman

Principal Literary Achievement

Both as essayist and novelist, Didion has used a reporter's lean, precise prose to dramatize the decline in such traditional American values as self-reliance and respect for others.

Biography

Compensating for her own physical frailty and persistent childhood fears, Joan Didion has long identified with the resilience of her great-great-great-grandmother who, in 1846, left the Donner wagon train and followed a northern pass through the Sierras just before a Nevada blizzard isolated the main party and drove them eventually to cannibalism. That frontier example sustained her as her father, Frank Didion, an Army Air Corps officer, moved the family from base to base. She and her brother entertained themselves by watching films, and her mother advised her to keep busy by writing stories. Her sense of insecurity diminished only after their return to Sacramento, where the family land went back five generations. What remained, however, was her sense of the theatrical. Stories of her pioneer ancestors always included near disasters, life on the edge. Her early fears, therefore, of rattlesnakes, collapsing bridges, and atomic bombs were only partly based in reality. The other source was an imagination stirred to excitement but not wholly believing in actual tragedy.

During her senior year at Berkeley, in 1956, she won first prize in *Vogue*'s nonfiction contest, along with an apprenticeship that eight years later had turned into an associate feature editorship. In New York she never refused an offer to a party, though she usually remained a silent observer. Meanwhile, in 1963, she had published a first novel, *Run River*, an excessively melodramatic tale of a Sacramento valley dynasty overburdened with murder, suicide and near-incest. More successful was her marriage in 1964 to John Gregory Dunne, a writer for *Time*, who was as talkative as she was reticent. They moved from New York to California and, in 1966, after a miscarriage, adopted a baby girl whom they named Quintana Roo (after a place in the Yucatán).

Although dismayed by escalating violence on the West Coast and desirous of making her separate peace, she forced herself to examine her times and, in 1968, pub-

lished her essays on civil disorder in northern California as *Slouching Towards Bethlehem*. The effort cost her a serious breakdown. Although her second novel, *Play It As It Lays* (1970), was a best-seller, critics who admired its cinematic style overlooked her compassion for Maria, the distraught narrator, and her admiration for the young mother's perseverance.

During a visit to Colombia in 1973, she contracted nearly fatal paratyphoid fever, but that experience helped her write her third novel, *A Book of Common Prayer* (1977), which contrasts the irresponsible "flash politics" of South American men with two North American "marginal women" whose spirit maintains the core of civilization. The same image of submerged life-giving women provided the counterforce, in her 1979 collection of essays, *The White Album*, to the Charles Manson cult murders and the assassination of Bobby Kennedy. Consequently, that book is more balanced than *Slouching Towards Bethlehem*. It also gave her the courage, despite her health problems (her weight has rarely exceeded 100 pounds, and in the seventies she was virtually blind for six weeks from multiple sclerosis, later in remission), to travel to war-torn El Salvador in 1982. The result was *Salvador* (1983), a penetrating essay on the mindless terror, left and right, in that country's ongoing revolution and the naïveté of American foreign policy. Without any solutions to offer to a difficult dilemma, Didion had to be satisfied with providing an honest record of the facts, the lies, the contradictions. History, she implied, is simply remembered events. Whether or not it contains heroic deeds, simply remembering accurately is heroism enough—especially for Americans, who, she claims, too often consider themselves exempt from history.

In 1984, her novel *Democracy* further indicted an American government which, while supposedly relying on an informed public, withheld from them vital secrets about connections between corporate business and coercive foreign policy. Her extended essay *Miami* (1987) similarly goes beyond the status of Cubans in Florida to Washington's hidden agenda toward Fidel Castro's regime. Didion possesses an intense curiosity about how things work: from irrigation systems to new freeways, from organized government to personal behavior. She is even more interested in how she might gain some degree of control over her body, her pain, her life. Dunne and Didion wrote a number of screenplays together during the 1970's, because the pay freed them later to write their novels, but they resented letting a director make decisions of pace and texture which should be a writer's choice. For her own publications, Didion is an exacting taskmaster, requiring sometimes several years of revisions before her compressed short novels are released.

It was Didion's curiosity which, in the eighth grade, led her, note pad in hand, to walk calmly into the Pacific: It was a life wish, not a death wish. A wave slammed her back on shore. Some of that continuing openness keeps her young in her outlook. For all of her affection for northern California, it is also a symbol of a home from which it is safe to depart because it will always be there on her return. She and Dunne, in the mid-1980's, divided their time between Los Angeles and New York City; in 1988, they moved to New York.

Analysis

That Joan Didion's perspective on life is that of the witness who is both part of and apart from what she so critically observes can be substantiated easily from her essays and fiction. She is a loner, resistant to identification with any movement or label. She is a moralist who, however, does not offer herself as a model for others, in either thought or behavior. Yet even in the absence of high expectations for either herself or society, she does make great demands on both. While acknowledging the extent of natural disasters in ordinary lives, she requires a willed effort to probe constantly for whatever degree of self-control and self-affirmation is possible. This is what "living on the Edge" means to her, and therefore to her characters: the edge as impending cliff or as opening frontier.

In her earliest works, the two Californias represented these alternatives: the life-style of the north's work ethic; the death-style of Hollywood's illusory glamor. That contrast between the American Dream of opportunity responsibly accepted and the American Nightmare of destructive greed was already clear in the essays collected in *Slouching Towards Bethlehem*. It was reinforced with the further essays in *The White Album* (1979), as the drug culture came to dominate much of urban California, and in her novel, *Play It As It Lays*. By implication, the social dilemmas of the West Coast symbolized a growing national crisis as well.

As Didion fought to overcome her shyness, she also risked short visits beyond the continental United States—limiting herself always, however, to warm places: South and Central America and Hawaii. Her reportage has always been incisive and therefore useful as a portrait not only of political temperaments in tropical places, but also of the peculiarities of the United States' foreign policy. Too often, American alliances have been made with anti-Communistic regimes which have hardly been democratic alternatives. Such is the inference one draws from her novel *A Book of Common Prayer* and her nonfiction works *Salvador* and *Miami* (1987). Yet Didion does not pretend to be a social or political expert with an agenda of her own. She proceeds only from a carefully controlled mixture of detachment and compassionate interest in the possibilities of humane control of events. Her principal complaint is that American naïveté and arrogance have conditioned people to think that they are immune from reality and the forces of history.

The harshness of so much of reality, particularly for women such as those who are narrators or central characters in Didion's novels, might suggest a natural affinity between Didion and feminism; however, she astonished the more radical members of her sex by her critical comments in her 1972 essay "The Women's Movement" (reprinted in *The White Album*). There she asserted that women unaware of the Marxist roots of American feminism misunderstood how "networking" was being manipulated so that mass identity was substituted for the ideal of individual self-hood. Feminists in turn argued that Didion was one of them, so often did she picture women as helpless victims. Yet Didion has never blamed her personal problems on a patriarchal society, as some feminists have done. Furthermore, although it is true that her characters Maria, Charlotte, Grace, and Inez are considered marginal at best by the male characters in the books in which they appear, it is not their whims and weaknesses that Didion memorializes, but their courage and persistence despite their seeming powerlessness. Such women find centers in themselves in the midst of crises and are not interested in controlling anyone else. Only Marin in *A Book of Common Prayer*, perhaps, is an exception, and she is the young revolutionary, the terrorist without a grasp of reality or a genuine cause.

Joan Didion is prompted to write not from ideology but from curiosity. She writes not to persuade, not to incite to action, not to promote any movement; she writes, she has said, to find out what she is thinking. In part, this reliance on herself as her own most accessible reader originated in the insignificance still attributed to women writers at the middle of the twentieth century. Consequently, she was free to write for herself, and to find forms appropriate to her own perception of character and circumstance. Early in life she studied the techniques used by Ernest Hemingway to avoid abstraction and to particularize events. Her editor-in-chief at *Vogue* reinforced this hard focus, requiring exact language. Her essay "On Keeping a Notebook" (first published in *Holiday* and reprinted in *Slouching Towards Bethlehem*) explains that the accuracy of a factual record has never been quite as important to her as ambience, the associations resurgent in her mind as she rediscovers what otherwise passing moments have meant to her. Details are important most of all as clues to insights.

Her novels have particularly acknowledged the limitations of her narrators, the tenuousness of their hold on others' reality, and the often-interrupted continuity of their lives. Nevertheless, it is just such limited but sensitive narrators whom she respects and even admires. Although her novels are compact, they convey an intensity often lacking in the longer, plot-heavy novels of her contemporaries. The inner lives of her female characters are troubled, sometimes by their very "innocence." The greater menace, however, in Joan Didion's eyes, lies in the complacent, self-congratulatory, technology-oriented outer worlds in which moral ambiguities go largely unrecognized. She prefers outsiders, the *de fuera*, who—like herself—struggle to survive society's losses of memory and of meaning.

SLOUCHING TOWARDS BETHLEHEM

First published: 1968
Type of work: Essays

The anarchy of the 1960's in the United States must be recognized and confronted, although perhaps it cannot be fully survived.

Joan Didion rejected, but found that she could not ignore, the negative aspects of the drug culture associated with the anti-Establishment movements that grew out of the Beat Generation. Because it was threatening California's frontier traditions of responsible self-reliance, she decided to put aside her preference for privacy and describe the disorder. She discovered that in many ways the so-called counterculture mirrored the shallowness of the Establishment against which it purported to take its stand. The dropouts shared the same self-centeredness, indifference, and casual relationships that marked large corporations. For the greed that brought a "rush" or "high" to wealthy materialists, they simply substituted hallucinogenic drugs.

Many of Didion's articles from this period (including those on the hippies of the Haight-Ashbury district in San Francisco) first appeared in *The Saturday Evening Post*. She believed she was describing the nature of love and death in a "golden land," as revealed in sensational murder cases, or the limited realities of such film icons as John Wayne, splinter groups of Communists, drug addicts, such quiet peacemakers as singer Joan Baez and her disciples in Carmel Valley, or the Diggers, who tried to feed society's dropouts. Her descriptions are so accurate in their particulars that they seem impersonal; her anxiety over the slow erosion of solid citizenship can only be inferred from behind a mask of gentle representation. She had so successfully learned to distance herself through concreteness and compression—practiced by imitating Hemingway and that earlier journalist, Katherine Anne Porter—that individually the first essays hardly seem to warrant the warning implicit in her choosing William Butler Yeats's foreboding poem "The Second Coming" as an epigraph to her book. Yet they are crucial to her indictment of a decaying society.

The later sections subtitled "Personals" and "Seven Places of the Mind" proceed with equally quiet portraits, which tend to provide the positive values that she is remembering and, through memory, defending. "On Keeping a Notebook," for example, makes clear her invisible but close involvement in all that she describes—indeed, how each fragment is more essentially a clue to her feelings about herself than about the person or circumstance being reported. "On Self Respect" speaks of having the same courage to admit one's mistakes as one's disciplined ancestors had. "Notes from a Native Daughter" explains what it was about California in her childhood that brought her back to it from New York (whose own portrait is provided in "Goodbye to All That"). The code of conduct, an ethic of conscience, which she associates with her California is rendered somewhat abstractly in the essay "On Morality"; but its basis in family closeness is explicitly dramatized in "On Going Home." Without such positive affirmations, Didion's critique of her contemporaries' negative outlook would have made her seem supercilious: a mere rebel against rebels without a cause.

The two aspects of American culture—the destructively artificial and the compassionately profound—are brought together in "Letter from Paradise, 21° 19′ N., 157° 52′ W," a study of Hawaii. That island can be a state of mind, a place for tourists to enjoy their fantasies of all that glitters; or, as it was for Didion, visiting the sunken *Arizona* with all of its memorialized dead still submerged, a place of profound meditation on infamous betrayals and the death of innocence.

Her brief vignettes of racism and monopoly finance eventually became absorbed as background for her 1984 novel, *Democracy*. In the meantime, however, there were the increasing body counts from the Vietnam War, assassinations of political and spiritual leaders, and love communes turned into violent cults that so nauseated Didion that the apparent breakdown of the United States caused her own temporary breakdown. Recovering from that, her appeals in the essays in *The White Album* became more vehement, involving a broader spectrum of sources, high and low, of the nation's decadence, and finding stalwart figures of the true opposition no less difficult to identify. Aside from this escalation of insistence, as the will to recovery became more urgent, Didion's vision and manner of address remained as she had established them in *Slouching Towards Bethlehem*.

PLAY IT AS IT LAYS

First published: 1970
Type of work: Novel

Maria is more authentic and more substantial than Hollywood people, including her director husband and her "best friend," can ever realize.

The eighty-three brief scenes in this short novel at first appear to symbolize protagonist Maria Wyeth's anxious sense of being a displaced, discontinuous person; however, their interrupted continuity also comes to represent the failure of the film industry to comprehend her complexity and her needs. Maria's husband Carter never gets beyond his first image of her as an East Coast model; it is this superficial self that he prefers in the films which he makes of her. He is equally narrow in his attitude toward their daughter Kate, born defective. Carter has her institutionalized and attempts to prevent Maria from visiting her.

The fact that Maria's own mother died horribly, alone on the desert and attacked by coyotes, has reinforced Maria's maternal feelings. She identifies with her rejected child; both are marginal, considered outside the in group of the "beautiful people." Starved for simple assurances that she is really alive and lovable, Maria has an affair with scriptwriter Les Goodwin. When she becomes pregnant, Carter declares that she must either abort the fetus or never again see Kate. The fact that Les is already married drastically limits Maria's options. Forced to choose between her two children, both wholly helpless, Maria agrees to the abortion; as a result of her guilt, however, she suffers recurring nightmares, including children being led to extermination gas chambers.

Helene, who has always played the part of her closest friend, can provide neither understanding nor consolation. Instead she offers a partnership in a sado-masochistic *ménage à trois* with her producer husband BZ. Eventually, however, even BZ realizes the emptiness of his life-style and invites Maria to join him in a final overdose of drugs. She resists, still loyal instinctively to finding a purpose for herself and for Kate through a relationship whose pathetic aspects are offset by the desperation of her love, an obsessive need to be needed.

Didion takes enormous risks of misguiding the reader with several techniques that she chooses. She allows Carter and Helene to pass judgment on Maria before turning the novel over exclusively to her key character. Then Maria's experience is narrated largely in a nonrational, often disconnected, seeming disorder. Yet the author's faith lies with the reader's ability to contrast the strong feelings of attachment and resilience in Maria, despite all of her hardships, with the overripe and rotten opportunists for whom the American Dream (and its counterpart, the Western Dream) has reduced an imaginative vision to an imaginary delusion. Carter and Helene are captives, BZ is a victim, of the void concealed behind the spectacular pageantry of motion pictures. *Play It As It Lays* ("take it as it comes") enacts much of the wisdom inherited by Didion from old California's high regard for commitment and courage.

Hollywood comes to stand for negative aspects in American society at large as it becomes less and less productive in a postindustrial age and more and more directed toward services and entertainment designed to fill increasing leisure hours with stimulation. Didion sees in a self-satisfied First World nation such dangerous attributes as impermanence of human relationships and spiritual values; she sees either a lack of comprehension of, or an indifference to, the consequences of irresponsible behavior. It is a society out of control. Maria thinks that she is a born loser, but it is the culture around her, not Maria herself, which is mindless and insensitive. The distinctions between her immediate world and her inner self are so subtle that, despite a National Book Award nomination, many critics complained about the novel's nihilistic theme. Even though Didion and Dunne themselves wrote the screenplay for this novel, in 1972, the film could not convey all the necessary nuances. Nevertheless, *Play It As It Lays* records the struggle of one woman for meaning in a society which, far from commending her, can only hold her in contempt for not adapting to its capricious ways.

A BOOK OF COMMON PRAYER

First published: 1977
Type of work: Novel

Biochemist Grace Strasser-Mendana recovers an interest in intimate human affairs through symbolic sisterhood with fellow expatriate and agonizing mother Charlotte Douglas.

Concerned that readers had difficulty perceiving the admirable qualities of Maria in *Play It As It Lays*, Didion in *A Book of Common Prayer* has Charlotte Douglas, Maria's equivalent, observed and analyzed by an older, scientifically trained American woman. Grace Strasser-Mendana, early orphaned in the United States, is the widow of a Latin American president, probably killed by his brother in a struggle for power. What principally keeps Grace overseas in fictional Boca Grande is her desire to be close to her son Gerardo, though he too is toying with political violence. At first she is merely distracted by the antics of Charlotte Douglas, a newcomer, until she perceives parallels between their lives and values as "outsiders" in a world trained for irresponsibility—and therefore for destruction.

Charlotte, having been reared in an overprotected, middle-class environment, cannot cope with either Warren Bogart, her first husband who tries to compensate for his inadequacies through physical abuse of others; or with Leonard Douglas, her current husband, who pretends to be a liberal lawyer but is covertly a gunrunner. She turns all of her frustrated affection on her daughter Marin, who, however, has become a mindless radical revolutionary involved in the bombing of buildings. Charlotte believes that Marin may surface in Boca Grande simply because, for her as mother, it represents the cervix of the world. Part of the way southward, Charlotte brings with her a premature newborn who dies of complications. Douglas, its father, who cannot accept imperfection, wanted to let it die in a clinic. Charlotte, in contrast, writes on her visa application "Occupation: mother."

Gradually Grace comes to understand Charlotte's innocence and good will, to empathize with this woman in shock, and to recover her own capacity for the compassion that helps define human purpose. The two women become, in effect, a substitute family. When the brothers-in-law of Grace engage once again in coup and countercoup, and refugees flee, Charlotte remains behind to tend the sick and wounded; she is slain. Dying, she cries out not for herself but for Marin. Grace is also dying, of cancer, yet is the only person other than Charlotte devoted to life. Therefore, as principal narrator of *A Book of Common Prayer*, she memorializes this other woman who, though considered comic by society, struggled so heroically to rise above circumstances. It is Charlotte's resilience, not her victimization, which Grace is celebrating.

Didion, a lapsed Episcopalian, still retains respect for rituals from her childhood, and she considers this novel the equivalent of Grace's prayer for/to the essential goodness in Charlotte. If Boca Grande symbolizes the danger of failing to come to terms with history (that is, the consequences of human actions) and therefore of being doomed to repeat its mistakes, the novel's reliance on psalms and litanies implies a divinely orchestrated design to life, epitomized by the connection between Grace and Charlotte. The novel also functions as Grace's prayer of thanksgiving for Charlotte's inadvertent restoration of Grace to a faith in mankind, in spite of all its errors and horrors. That appeal to something eternal is paralleled by the time structure in this novel. The chronicle of events is only rarely linear. Instead, distant past, present, and near future tend to be looped together. At first this seeming disorder of cause and effect as well as of chronology conveys both the instability of Latin politics and the disconnectedness between Charlotte and reality. Eventually, however, what is conveyed is a kind of continuous present, with history the sum of all coexistent times. The loops become a sequence of knots, implying an eternal realization of what temporarily seems confused. The technique is moralist Didion's way of warning Americans that no one is immune from human events, from effects that he or she partially has caused.

DEMOCRACY

First published: 1984
Type of work: Novel

Democracy, which can hardly exist without a well-informed citizenry, has to take its primary example from open communication within the family.

While *Democracy* was still a work in progress, Didion referred to it as "Angel Visits," a Victorian term meaning brief encounters. Closely attached to her own ancestry and her immediate family, she might have been expected to offer the Christian family of Hawaii as a shining example for others; instead, the opposite is true. Paul Christian, the father, represents the overbearing baronial class that ruled Hawaii's agribusinesses. Worse, he has the same imperious relationship with his own wife and daughters. Although he is free to wander across the world, the other Christians are expected to remain in place, anticipating his unregulated return.

Paul's California wife, Carol, who expected a fuller life and greater stability through marriage, never is allowed any degree of self-worth. Finally, after second daughter Janet's wedding, Carol disappears on a cruise, never to return. Janet's husband, Dick Ziegler, invests the modest fortune which he made in Hong Kong housing in Oahu's windward real estate. Janet, however, conspires with her uncle, Dwight Christian, to circumvent Dick's plans; she is shot to death, along with business intermediary Omura, by her father late in 1975.

By that time her sister Inez, the novel's central character, is forty years old, apparently well-married, but still exceedingly unhappy because unfulfilled. Her husband, Harry Victor, has a political career that seems endlessly rising. From a liberal lawyer once assigned to the Justice Department, in 1969 he rose to appointive senator, replacing an incumbent who had died. In 1972, however, he failed to be elected to the same office. His dream of a possible presidency wavers. The greater loss, though, is to his sense of self. Making politics his career has required that Victor adopt so many positions on issues dear to lobbyists or constituents that his true identity is shredded. Inez, already suffering from the same self-alienation, tells a reporter that loss of memory is the price of public life. Her twin children are also adrift: Adlai, whose attitudes towards Vietnam ebb and flow, and Jessie, a drug addict out of touch with reality.

Consequently, Inez turns on occasion to Jack Lovett. Although he is a free-lance covert agent, dealing with war and multinational businesses, and is no more readily available than members of her own family, romantically she assumes that this mysterious figure has a secret self that he knows and nurtures. When Jack rescues Jessie from Saigon just before it falls, Inez offers him her gratitude and love.

In her own way, Inez is as much a defective narrator as Charlotte in *A Book of Common Prayer*. Both, at best, can supply certain necessary facts but never an understanding of their implications. In *Democracy*, Didion offers herself as the sensitive equivalent of Grace Strasser-Mendana. The character "Joan Didion" knew Inez briefly when they both worked at *Vogue*. Later in California, she read of the double slaying of Janet and Omura, and as acquaintance and as professional reporter, she came when summoned by Inez, who needed someone with whom to communicate her pain and confusion. Eventually Inez and Jack flee to Malaysia, where he suddenly dies of a stroke. The only identity left Inez is that of displaced person, and she decides to work with the Kuala Lumpur refugee camp. Didion, like Grace in the previous novel, recognizes that she is not the perfect witness to Inez' life. The novel's scenes are even more disjointed than those in *Play It As It Lays*. Though Didion withholds judgment of Inez, by implication she has indicted American politics, especially as the secret deals with the military-industrial establishment can involve in war whole populations ignorant of its true causes and aims. The amorality of those in power may be hidden temporarily, but finally such indifference to others not only destroys the nation's integrity, but also defeats the mercenaries themselves.

Summary

What sustains Didion in her writing is her faith in the possibility of a better life than what people allow one another to live. That faith rises from her experience of history. All persons, of whatever gender, suffer from natural limitations, reinforced by their own refusals to admit to those imperfections. Didion's exceptions are those women able to maintain their integrity, moral courage, and a vision of a more mutually considerate society, under the most trying circumstances. Their resilience, rather than their unremitting agony, is only gradually perceived because it is only slowly earned, with much difficulty.

Bibliography

Davidson, Sara. "A Visit with Joan Didion." *The New York Times Book Review*, April 3, 1971, p. 1.

Friedman, Ellen G., ed. *Joan Didion: Essays and Conversations*. Princeton, N.J.: Ontario Review Press, 1984.

Garis, Leslie. "Didion and Dunne: The Rewards of a Literary Marriage." *The New York Times Magazine*, June 22, 1979, sec. III, p. 8.

Henderson, Katherine Usher. *Joan Didion*. New York: Frederick Ungar, 1981.

Kakutani, Michiko. "Joan Didion: Staking Out California." *The New York Times Magazine*, June 10, 1979, sec. VI, p. 34.

Kuehl, Linda. "Joan Didion." In *Writers at Work*. 5th series, edited by George Plimpton. New York: Viking Press, 1981.

Winchell, Mark Royden. *Joan Didion*. Boston: Twayne, 1980.

Leonard Casper

ANNIE DILLARD

Born: Pittsburgh, Pennsylvania
April 30, 1945

Principal Literary Achievement

Annie Dillard, a twentieth century Transcendentalist, explores the place of humankind in the natural world.

Biography

Annie Dillard, born Meta Ann Doak to Frank and Pam (Lambert) Doak on April 30, 1945, in Pittsburgh, Pennsylvania, grew up as a member of the comfortable upper class. At the private schools that she attended, she was rebellious and dissatisfied. She was a bright, precocious young woman who felt that she did not fit in with her surroundings; she was frequently in trouble at school—she went joy riding and was suspended once for smoking. She wanted to escape the life that her family, school, and class seemed to believe was her destiny: marriage and the Junior League.

After she was graduated from high school, Dillard entered Hollins College, where she was inducted into Phi Beta Kappa and received her B.A. in English in 1967 and an M.A. in English in 1968. In 1965, when she was a sophomore at Hollins, she married her creative writing professor, R. H. W. Dillard, a poet and novelist. When she finished her graduate degree, Dillard began painting, concentrating on developing a talent she believed that God had given her. At this time she also began reading voraciously: natural history, literature and criticism, classics, and poetry. She also began keeping track of her reading and experiences in extensive journals, a practice she continues to follow. In 1971, after a serious case of pneumonia, Dillard turned her energies to exploring the natural world outside. Her experiences inspired and informed her first book of prose, *Pilgrim at Tinker Creek*, which was published in 1974, the same year as her first book, *Tickets for a Prayer Wheel*, her only book of poetry. Both books deal with finding meaning in a universe that, on the surface at least, appears meaningless and devoid of God.

After the publication of *Pilgrim at Tinker Creek*, Dillard became a contributing editor for *Harper's Magazine* and traveled to the Galápagos Islands. The resulting essay, "Innocence in the Galápagos," received the New York Presswomen's Award for Excellence in 1975. Dillard's fame brought problems for a woman who valued her privacy; she was besieged by offers of public appearances, readings, and film scripts. Her popularity troubled her, since she felt that it took her away from her

writing. Dillard, a writer who values her privacy and guards her energies, left Virginia in 1975 to take a position as a scholar-in-residence at Western Washington State University in Bellingham, Washington. In that same year she was divorced.

During the following years, Dillard contributed columns to *Living Wilderness,* the journal of the Wilderness Society, and began work on *Holy the Firm,* which was published in 1977. In 1976, while teaching at Western Washington State University, Dillard met anthropology professor Gary Clevidence, who taught at Fairhaven College. They moved to Middletown, Connecticut, where Dillard began teaching as a distinguished visiting professor at Wesleyan University in 1979. Dillard and Clevidence were married in 1980, and their daughter, Cody Rose, was born in 1984. They separated in 1987 and were later divorced. In 1988, Dillard was married to writer Robert D. Richardson, Jr., whom she met after writing to him a fan letter about his book *Henry David Thoreau: A Life of the Mind* (1986). She continues to teach as an adjunct professor at Wesleyan University and spends summers in South Wellfleet on Cape Cod.

Although reviewers and critics persist in describing Dillard's books as collections of essays, she insists that *Teaching a Stone to Talk: Expeditions and Encounters* (1982) is the only volume that truly fits that description. In addition, Dillard has published *Encounters with Chinese Writers* (1984), an account of her 1982 trip to China as a member of the United States cultural delegation; *Living by Fiction* (1978), a book about modern writers; *An American Childhood* (1987), and *The Writing Life* (1989). She also edited *Best American Essays, 1988.*

Dillard is a member of the usage panel of the *American Heritage Dictionary* and has been a jury member for the Bollingen Prize, the nonfiction Pulitzer Prize, and the PEN/Martha Albrand Award. Besides being awarded the Pulitzer Prize for *Pilgrim at Tinker Creek,* Dillard has been named a New York Public Library Literary Lion and has received the Washington State Governor's Award for Literature (1978), the Appalachian Gold Medallion from the University of Charleston (1989), and Boston's St. Botolph's Club Foundation Award (1989). *An American Childhood* was nominated for the 1987 National Book Critics' Circle Award.

Analysis

Annie Dillard is much more than the voice of her most popular book, *Pilgrim at Tinker Creek.* In fact, those readers and critics who view her as an untutored Appalachian local who both rhapsodizes about and is horrified by the natural world of rural Virginia misjudge their subject. That Dillard can make her readers share in such small and private activities as seeking out praying mantis egg cases or sitting quietly trying not to scare a muskrat attests both her powers of observation and her skill at descriptive narration. All of Dillard's writing displays this almost photographic evocation of place, a skill that has prompted critics to label her a naturalist. Dillard does not agree; for her, the natural world provides the only avenue by which to contemplate the ultimate, the absolute, the divine. Nature provides metaphors that describe human agonies and activities; nature, for Dillard, is the only place where she can catch glimpses of an otherwise silent and invisible God.

Surprisingly, to some people, Annie Dillard does not think of herself as an environmentalist nor as a champion of wilderness preservation; rather, she sees herself as someone for whom the world is her greatest subject because it allows her to consider those questions she sees as being most vital. Since she believes that it is a writer's goal to bring enlightenment, give clarification, search out answers, and provide inspiration, her writing probes the nature of being and the meaning of meaning. She looks to nature, to the concrete world, for examples of courage and inspiration, and sometimes her search is a painful one, for wherever she turns she confronts the hard realities of living in an eat-or-be-eaten world, a place where things are born only to die and where destruction seems to be waiting around the next corner. The mystery that infuses the natural world does not provide Dillard with easy answers to a question such as "Why am I here?" In *Pilgrim at Tinker Creek*, for example, she looks at the prolific activity of the insect world and comes away frightened by the ravenous and destructive appetites that even seem to compel females laying eggs to devour their offspring. What should be one of the most powerful images of hope— birth and the perpetuation of life—becomes an image of destruction. The explanation that she offers suggests that what Dillard hopes for is not affirmation through explicit religious salvation but acceptance of the great dance of birth, death, and renewal that surrounds and includes every living being on earth. From that acknowledgment comes tranquility, for Dillard can see herself as a part of, rather than apart from, the teeming activity that surrounds her at Tinker Creek.

The search for the answers, the quest to bring meaning to day-to-day events underpins all that Dillard writes. In *Holy the Firm* she again looks at pain, suffering, death, and chaos. She wants to find a reason for human suffering, and again her answer is to affirm that there does, indeed, exist a tie between living beings and God, but a tie that is not always immediately obvious in the daily round of accident, pain, and irrationality. In both *Pilgrim at Tinker Creek* and *Holy the Firm*, Dillard perhaps raises more questions than she answers, or at least so it seems to those critics who want her to tie up all the loose ends. Loose ends are precisely what Dillard is interested in, however, and the world as she sees it offers even the most practiced observer more loose ends than easy answers.

In *Teaching a Stone to Talk*, although Dillard ranges further afield than her immediate "backyard" and presents essays not only about the goings-on near Tinker Creek but also about the creatures of the Galápagos Islands and the Arctic Circle, her intention remains the same: witnessing nature. For Dillard, this witnessing is a religious act; in everything she sees and experiences, she seeks answers to primal questions. In this sense, one could say that Dillard's work reveals the nature of the writer intensely, yet she insists that she never writes about herself, that she works painstakingly to keep her personality out of what she has to show her readers.

Dillard brings her precision and sense of detail to *An American Childhood*, a book that deals with her growing up in Pittsburgh. In her earlier work, the person of Dillard remained behind the scenes; the reader saw what she saw, heard what she heard, and reacted. The personality of the narrator was somehow distanced, muted. Although Dillard insists that she is not revealed in *An American Childhood*, this book provides a much more intimate view of Annie Dillard than do any of her previous volumes. Most important, it lets readers gain insight into the careful observer and deep thinker that is the "voice" of all that Dillard writes. One important side of her personality that surfaces in *An American Childhood* is something that was also apparent in her earlier work: a voracious intellectual curiosity. Concrete knowledge serves as her catalyst, allowing her to spring from mere facts to a consideration of their metaphysical implications. In *Holy the Firm*, for example, when she describes a plane accident in which a young girl was horribly disfigured, the girl's burns become the vehicle by which Dillard can explore the meaning of pain and, by extension, the nature of a divinity that would allow such horrors to occur.

In *The Writing Life* (1989), Dillard examines the profession of writing: how one writes, what it means to write, why one writes. With her usual intimacy—but lack of concrete personal details—she discusses the solitary struggle that writing is. As in all of her earlier work, Dillard is concerned with knowing, meaning, and interconnectedness. For her, the world is both the palette and the canvas: She draws her materials from her surroundings and she colors her surroundings with the philosophical considerations that are her preoccupation. Like Henry David Thoreau, whose heir the late Edward Abbey said that she was, Annie Dillard travels far and rarely leaves home. Her universe starts in her study or at her back door and extends from there to the farthest corner of the universe and beyond.

PILGRIM AT TINKER CREEK

First published: 1974
Type of work: Nonfiction

The beauties and horrors of the natural world give the careful observer access to the divine.

In *Pilgrim at Tinker Creek*, Annie Dillard touches on all the important themes that will continue to inform everything she writes. At first glance, this book might appear to be a collection of occasional essays that track the changing seasons through one calendar year; in fact, that is how some critics have viewed this work—as essays on the perplexities of nature. While the book does take up this theme over and over again, it is not for the simple pleasure of holding up a quirk of nature for its cheap thrill value. Dillard carefully built this volume after months of painstaking observation of and research about both metaphysics and the natural world. The rhythms of the book are tightly controlled and depend on recurrent images and themes that surface over and over, allowing Dillard to focus on the key issues at the heart of the narrator's personal journey. As much as anything, this book is about seeing and about gaining the ability to see within oneself, into the surrounding world, and beyond to the divinity that informs the world.

The book opens with a startling image of violence, creation, and death with the bloody paw prints left on the narrator by her returning tomcat. The world she sees as she looks out from her cabin beside Tinker Creek in Virginia is one in which little seems to make sense. Wherever Dillard turns she sees the raw, brutal power of nature to reproduce itself, and she finds the sheer exuberance of the natural world startling, overwhelming, and stupefying. She cannot look at an insect laying its eggs, for example, without being reminded of all the instances in the insect kingdom where the mother devours its mate, its eggs, or its young—or is food for them in return for giving them life. What is the point, Dillard asks, in bothering to replicate oneself if one only serves as grist for the mill, food for the soon-to-be-born? In *Pilgrim at Tinker Creek*, Dillard questions the god that would set such a horror show in motion, and she wonders how one can go on in the fact of such depressing statistics: No matter what, everyone must die.

Yet Dillard wants to find an answer that will allow her to celebrate rather than be repulsed by what she sees, and, rather than being only a collection of essays about her observations of the natural world, *Pilgrim at Tinker Creek* traces Dillard's abundance and vitality. By looking carefully at the world around her confined neighborhood of Tinker Creek, Dillard discovers a pattern and gains some conviction that there is something more going on than a mad dance of death. She learns to look beyond the particular individual, past the moment, to a larger picture, and while some readers will find her answers depressing, others will see that she has achieved an acceptance of what she sees around her. Unlike many others, who look on the violence of nature and see no possibility for a divine plan, Dillard comes to believe that the endless cycle—birth, death, and transformation into atoms of other beings—is in itself a way of gaining transcendence over death and achieving immortality.

Certain central natural images, such as her cat's bloody paw prints, surface again and again after Dillard has once told their story. She stands transfixed beside the creek, at first seeing the water and a frog that seems to collapse as she looks on; then her eyes shift focus and she sees the giant waterbug that has just finished draining the captured frog. This picture of the malign side of nature hovering immediately below an apparently tranquil and innocent surface is one to which she will refer time and time again. Dillard sees the death's head behind the living form many times; she confronts nature's seeming blind preference for the species over the individual. She sees things up close and notices the ragged wings, the frayed leaves, the living things being ground to dust. A more timid person would have given up and perhaps turned suicidal. Dillard, however, continued to look for answers, realizing that there is more to nature than the surface turmoil and violence.

In one chapter, Dillard recounts the story of a young woman who was born without sight. When surgery allows the woman to see for the first time as a young adult, she at first cannot see anything, then sees but does not comprehend, then sees in distorted fashion because she has yet to gain the experience by which to interpret what her eyes show her. The young woman's image of the tree with the lights shining through it is one to which Annie Dillard returns many times in *Pilgrim at Tinker Creek*, and it becomes her metaphor for what she seeks in her journey through the natural world. She is looking for the divine power behind the everyday; its discovery is something that she comes to realize happens infrequently at best, but it does happen. When Dillard least expects it, the force behind the universe shines out and nearly blinds her.

In a sense, Dillard had to suffer though the deep, pessimistic despair she describes in many chapters of *Pilgrim at Tinker Creek* in order to emerge with the understanding she attains in the book's final chapter, "The Waters of Separation." Like many mystics before her, Dillard had to despair of ever finding God before she could apprehend the presence of the divine. By showing her readers the power, might, and violence of the world of Tinker Creek, she takes them along with her on her quest to make sense of a seemingly senseless world. She gains freedom or salvation by recognizing that she is a part of the great dance of birth and death that she has so carefully recorded.

HOLY THE FIRM

First published: 1977
Type of work: Nonfiction

Pain is a necessary part of living and does not deny the existence of a divinity.

In *Holy the Firm*, Annie Dillard explores the metaphysical and religious concerns that inform her first two books, *Tickets for a Prayer Wheel* and *Pilgrim at Tinker Creek*. In this book, Dillard looks more closely at the problem of pain: How can one reconcile the existence of pain, suffering, and death with a belief in a benevolent God? Set near Puget Sound, where Dillard lived at the time, the book is short, spanning only three days. In the first of its three sections, "Newborn and Salted," Dillard describes a moth being attracted to the flame of a candle and burned to death. The moth's death is an image to which she often returns in her discussion of the nature of the divinity. The second section, "God's Tooth," is concerned with Julie Norwich, a seven-year-old child who, with her father, survives the crash of his small plane. Unlike her father, however, the child is horribly burned, and her face is completely destroyed. When Dillard asks if God was responsible for this tragedy, she concludes that God cannot be present in a world where an innocent child is mutilated for no reason. "Holy the Firm," the book's third and final section, attempts to find a place for a merciful God in a violent world. The solution that Dillard achieves is that God owes humankind no explanations. Since God created humans and not vice versa, God is not required to answer to them.

Dillard also concludes that the control that people cherish so dearly is only an illusion, that humans are only passengers on earth, along for the ride rather than behind the steering wheel, and on a journey whose destination they cannot know.

For Dillard, accepting or affirming that God is the foundation for all things allows her to believe again in the unity of all things, even when some things—such as the disfigured child—seem unjust. Acceptance of the ineffable nature of God enables Dillard to reaffirm her desire to proclaim the mysteries of the universe through her art and her life, thereby reaffirming the essentially divine nature of creation.

Many people see *Holy the Firm* as a powerful visionary statement, a testament to the triumph of faith in a seemingly irrational universe. Dillard does not find the role of prophet a comfortable one and denies that her intention was anything other than to describe her personal visionary experience. As in *Pilgrim at Tinker Creek* and *Teaching a Stone to Talk*, Dillard struggles to work through her dark night of the soul, her bleakest despair. Like other mystics, she must find a way to come to terms with those things that challenge her belief in a divine purpose for the world. In *Holy the Firm*, Dillard reaches an understanding of God's relationship to or place in her world and the natural world that she observes around her. She seems able to resolve the contradictions by something that esoteric Christianity calls "Holy the Firm," a universal substance that keeps the human world in touch with God—a god who remains present but invisible and unknowable. This is enough to allow Dillard to believe that God exists and for her to worship him.

TEACHING A STONE TO TALK

First published: 1982
Type of work: Essays

By observing nature, both close to home and in remote places, one can discover the presence of the divine.

Teaching a Stone to Talk: Expeditions and Encounters resembles both *Pilgrim at Tinker Creek* and *Holy the Firm* in that Dillard is still seeking answers to what she considers to be key questions: What is the universe about? What is the god like who created such a place as this? How is it possible to make sense of a universe that contains so much destructive energy and violence? In this book she again hunts for the silent god who created the natural world that Dillard often finds disturbingly violent and indifferent. This time, rather than center her investigations around one locale, as she did in *Pilgrim at Tinker Creek*, she ranges far afield. Dillard is adamant that her other books are not, as some critics and reviewers have asserted, collections of essays; as far as she is concerned, only *Teaching a Stone to Talk* fits that description.

A trip to the Galápagos Islands provides her with the opportunity to examine evolutionary theory in her essay "Life on the Rocks: The Galápagos." In "The Deer of Providencia," she describes a small deer caught and suffering in a hunter's snare, unable to do anything but injure itself more severely as it struggles. "Total Eclipse" recounts her experiences in Yakima, Washington, during a total eclipse of the sun, when she felt overwhelmed by the power of nature as the moon's shadow slammed across the earth. She shared the primal fear that the sun's light would be extinguished forever. "Living Like Weasels" discusses the fierce competitive energy of these hunters, and Dillard wonders if, freed from the constraints of society, she could fight as viciously for her survival as they do every day.

As in *Pilgrim at Tinker Creek*, Dillard uses the things that surround her as starting points in her search for meaning in a violent, indifferent universe. Unlike in the earlier book, however, she occasionally interacts with other people. Here she tries to fit in, to feel comfortable in a world that seems to threaten from all sides and at all times. Sometimes the world looks like home, while at others it appears completely unfamiliar and aloof. In one of her essays, "An Expedition to the Pole," she interweaves a description of the Catholic church that she attends (after having given up her family's Presbyterianism when a teenager), an account of the ill-fated Franklin expedition to find the Northwest Passage, and her own trip to the Arctic Circle. In all three instances she finds herself in alien territory, yet at the essay's conclusion she joins in the song, frantically: What choice does she have but to become a part of the only congregation, the community of humankind?

Although Dillard says that *Teaching a Stone to Talk* is a true book of essays rather than a tightly knit series of pieces, the pieces in this book wrestle with what for Dillard are central issues. The title essay, "Teaching a Stone to Talk," clearly makes this point: In it she recounts the story of a man who kept a stone and each day tried to get it to utter a word. Absurd as this sounds at first, it is precisely what Dillard tries to do in almost everything she writes: get an answer back from the universe. She listens and listens to nature, hoping to hear the voice of the creator; sometimes, as in "An Expedition to the Pole," "Lenses," "A Field of Silence," and "Life on the Rocks: The Galápagos." she seems to detect a faint whisper in response to her questions, "Are You out there?"

AN AMERICAN CHILDHOOD

First published: 1987
Type of work: Nonfiction

Childhood experiences shape and prepare a person to be and to see as an adult.

In *An American Childhood*, Dillard starts with herself and her experiences growing up in Pittsburgh in order to examine the nature of American life. She claims that the book is not an autobiography, but is rather a capturing of what it means for a child to come of age in the United States. Dillard seems to be uncomfortable with revealing information about herself; despite the fact that *An American Childhood* is intensely autobiographical, she denies that that was its purpose. Nevertheless, it is her account of her inward intellectual journey: the book recounts incidents in her life through her mid-teenage years, when she says that the consciousness that directs her perceptions of the world as an adult was formed. She believes that it is as a child that one is truly alive, can feel most deeply, and is affected most strongly by experiences.

Perhaps Dillard feels compelled to attempt to escape the merely personal because she intends, as she says, to make a commentary on the universal nature of her experiences. Perhaps she also so strongly asserts the separation between her personal life and the life that she presents in her book because she is a genuinely private person. It is rare that Dillard gives interviews, does readings or lectures, or provides information about herself. She repeatedly insists that the personality of the writer is not what is important; rather, it is the ideas an individual conveys about the meaning of life, nature, and meaning that count and are what both readers and writers should pursue. She does not like the limelight, because it takes away from the time she needs to read, reflect, and write. *An American Childhood*, then, offers readers a rare glimpse of the private side of Annie Dillard.

Her intention was to use herself as an example so that she could examine the way in which a child comes to consciousness—that is, arrives at the perceptions and attitudes that will guide her as an adult. She is by no means the first writer—American or otherwise—to attempt such an undertaking: Marcel Proust's *À la recherche du temps perdu* (1913-1927); *Remembrance of Things Past*, (1922-1931); James Joyce's *A Portrait of the Artist as a Young Man* (1916), or William Wordsworth's *The Prelude: Or The Growth of a Poet's Mind* (1850) are three examples of this mode. *An American Childhood* is particularly reminiscent of Wordsworth's famous spiritual epic. Like Wordsworth, who is regarded as one of the most important poets of nature, Dillard provides her readers with accounts of those childhood events that caused her to have such a passionate regard for and interest in the natural world. Also like Wordsworth is Dillard's intense focus on the spiritual, mystical, and violent aspects of the natural world and her need to fit herself, and, by extension, all of life into a meaningful pattern that makes sense of the seemingly senseless aspects of the natural realm.

Like Wordsworth, Dillard was a youthful rebel, always out of place in her upper class environment. In *An American Childhood*, she explores the values that she could not adopt, the goals that she did not share, and the manners that she would not practice in order to examine the alternatives she ultimately chose.

Wordsworth was a child who needed solace; nature in all of its terrible majesty gave him the comfort that he could not find in other people. Dillard, too, needed an escape from her fears; for her, knowledge—in particular knowledge about the natural world—gave her the power to triumph over her fears.

An American Childhood also provides readers with glimpses of Dillard's family that tell more about Dillard than about her parents and siblings. It is not so important that these events be true as it is that she thinks that her interpretations of them are accurate. We see a loving family that does not quite know what to do with a daughter who rejects their Presbyterian religion, who craves and seeks out solitude, who is wild and unruly at school. The reader sees the psychic place in which Annie

Dillard grew up, and that view, no matter what she herself says to the contrary, offers readers a closer look at the person than did her earlier works. Even so, the book still maintains distance between the reader and the person of Annie Dillard.

Summary

Annie Dillard stalks the infinite by tracking the finite in the world of nature. A mystic who looks for a divine force behind the natural world, she is a deeply spiritual person who sometimes can only console her readers with the assurance that they are all participants in the great dance of the universe. That contradictions exist, that danger, terror, and destruction are part and parcel of the world she observes are all facts of life. Her interests revolve almost exclusively around making sense of the events that she observes in the natural world in order to gain entrée to the world of the divine. Dillard's prose is powerful, evocative and lyrical, and the subjects she examines are of universal interest.

Bibliography

Bischoff, Joan. "Fellow Rebels: Annie Dillard and Maxine Hong Kingston." *English Journal* 78 (December, 1989): 62-67.

Beuchner, Frederick. "Island Journal." *The New York Times Book Review*, September 25, 1977, pp. 12, 40.

Dillard, Annie. "PW Interviews Annie D." Interview by Katharine Weber. *Publishers Weekly* 236 (September 1, 1989): 67-68.

Ward, Patricia. "Annie Dillard's Way of Seeing." *Christianity Today* 22 (May 5, 1978): 30-31.

Wymard, Eleanor B. "A New Existential Voice: For Annie Dillard the World is an Epiphany." *Commonweal* 102 (October 24, 1975): 495-496.

Melissa E. Barth

E. L. DOCTOROW

Born: New York, New York
January 6, 1931

Principal Literary Achievement
Doctorow is one of the most important novelists of his generation, an award-winning innovator in the realm of historical and political fiction.

Biography
Born in the Bronx in 1931, Edgar Lawrence Doctorow has returned again and again to urban themes, to the life of New York City at the beginning of the twentieth century and in the 1920's and 1930's when he was growing up. Greatly influenced by the radical politics of the Depression and by the work of John Dos Passos, Doctorow has chosen to write an updated version of proletarian fiction, reflecting his concern with the domination of the means of production by government and industry; Doctorow sides with the masses—the immigrants, the minorities, and all the downtrodden, underdog characters who populate his novels. Unlike the proletarian fiction of the 1930's, however, Doctorow's work is rarely sentimental; rather, it is distinguished by an elegance and irony that perhaps in part is attributable to his formal education and to his early conventional and middle-class pursuit of a career. Writing a generation after the Palmer raids that rounded up and imprisoned radicals in the 1920's and the great industrial strikes of the Depression, he has had the opportunity and the incentive to meditate on both the persecution of American radicals and the failure of the left to mount a credible alternative to the capitalistic power structure.

Doctorow was graduated from Kenyon College with a major in philosophy. Known for its prestigious literary review and the presence of important writers such as the poet John Crowe Ransom, Kenyon provided Doctorow with examples of literary careers he could emulate, for he was educated in a college generation that had exposure to writers who were for the first time being placed in significant numbers in faculty positions. Writers continued to be critics of society while being employed by one of its influential institutions. This dual and ambiguous role has had an impact on the marginalized consciousness of writers such as Doctorow who earn a living from the society they criticize; writers in this context are both inside and outside the system and are subject to the social and antisocial attitudes, the bifurcated points of view of the rich and the poor, that mark so much of Doctorow's fiction.

After serving in the Army, Doctorow worked for publishers in New York City, editing the work of important writers, such as Norman Mailer, who came out of World War II with their hostility toward the status quo intact. Mailer, Doctorow has observed, was part of a wartime generation that believed that a writer had to fight for and win a reputation in a society inimical to writers. Doctorow, on the other hand, has eschewed Mailers' military metaphors and his sense of embattlement for a vision of the writer as ironic commentator—an elusive fictional narrator who is implicated in and yet aloof from the action he describes.

Doctorow's cool stance may also reflect his philosophical training. In his novels, he tries to infuse serious ideas into popular genres such as the Western in *Welcome to Hard Times* (1960), and science fiction, in *Big as Life* (1966). Identifying with the disadvantaged and with the dissenters, he has fashioned fiction with a leftist orientation, and on occasion he has joined his voice to public protests against government censorship and other forms of tyranny. With residences in New York City and New Rochelle, New York, he has divided his time between the city and the suburbs; he has taught at Sarah Lawrence College and New York University.

Ragtime (1975), a popular and critical success, catapulted Doctorow into prominence as one of the finest and most exciting novelists of his generation. With *Welcome to Hard Times* and *The Book of Daniel* (1971), he had already established a solid reputation, but the rave reviews of *Ragtime* and the subsequent film adaptation of the novel secured his place in contemporary culture. *World's Fair* (1985) won the American Book Award in 1986, and *Billy Bathgate* (1989)—nearly as successful as *Ragtime*—shows that Doctorow continues to explore the astute blending of fact and fiction and of history and literature that has distinguished his most important novels.

Analysis

E. L. Doctorow is a political novelist concerned with those stories, myths, public figures, and literary and historical forms that have shaped public consciousness. Even when his subject is not overtly political—as in his first novel, *Welcome to Hard Times*—he chooses the genre of the Western to comment upon the American sense of crime and justice. Knowing that the Western has often been the vehicle for the celebration of American individualism and morality, Doctorow purposely writes a fablelike novel in which he questions the American faith in fairness and democracy. At the same time, he writes from within the genre by maintaining the customary strong opposition between good and evil, between the bad guys and the good guys, and a simple but compelling plot line.

The struggle in *Welcome to Hard Times* is between the Man from Bodie, who in a fit of rage destroys a town in a single day, and Blue, the tragic old man who almost singlehandedly tries to rebuild it. The plot and characters echo classic Western films such as *High Noon* (1952), with their solitary heroes who oppose villains tyrannizing a community. Doctorow's vision, however, is much bleaker than the traditional Western and cannot be encompassed by the usual shoot-out or confrontation between the sheriff and the outlaw. In fact, Doctorow's novel implies, the West was chaotic and demonic, and order was not usually restored in the fashion of a Hollywood motion picture. The reality of American history has been much grimmer than its literature or its popular entertainment has acknowledged. Indeed, Doctorow's fiction shows again and again a United States whose myths do not square with its history.

It is a paradoxical aspect of Doctorow's success that his parodies of popular genres are themselves usually best-sellers. Perhaps the reason for this is that alongside his ironic use of popular genres is a deep affection for the literary forms he burlesques. The title of his first novel, for example, is a kind of genial invitation to have some fun with the pieties and cliches of the western. Doctorow is deadly serious about the "hard times" and grave flaws in American culture, but he usually finds a way to present his criticism in a comic vein.

There is not much humor, however, in *The Book of Daniel*—a major political novel about the Cold War period of the 1950's. Centering on a couple bearing a striking resemblance to the historical Ethel and Julius Rosenberg, who were executed for espionage in 1954 (they were accused of stealing the "secret" of the atomic bomb for the Soviet Union), Doctorow has one of their children, Daniel, narrate the novel and investigate what happened to his parents while trying to come to terms with his own sense of 1960's radicalism. Concerned less with whether the couple are actually guilty of spying, Doctorow has Daniel search for his own identity by tracking down and interviewing those closest to his parents.

Through this personal story, Doctorow also conducts an analysis of the failure of American radicalism, of one generation to speak to another. By and large, the novel shows that 1960's radicals do not know much about the history of the left, and that the traditional left has done little to pass on its past, so that young men such as Daniel feel isolated, bereft, and angry about their lack of connection to a heritage of social protest.

Like *The Book of Daniel*, *Ragtime* is anchored in the story of a family—this time of a little boy who grows up at the turn of the century during events such as the development of motion pictures, polar exploration, and political upheavals led by radicals such as Emma Goldman. From his naïve viewpoint, the little boy observes the explosive changes and the stresses of a society that does not know how to handle its own dissenting elements—Coalhouse Walker, for example, a proud black man who is insulted by a group of white firemen and who (more in the style of the 1960's) resorts to violence and hostage taking, demanding that society recognize his human rights.

Ragtime is similar to *Welcome to Hard Times* in that it has a fairy-tale quality. The prose is quite simple, descriptive and declarative, so that Doctorow could almost begin with the phrase "once upon a time." It is clear, however, that his point is to link the past and the present, to show that the craving for mass entertainment at the beginning of the twentieth century naturally had its outlet in the invention of motion pictures, just as the urge of Arctic explorer Robert Peary and other explorers to roam the world had its industrial and societal counterpart in the mass production of the automobile. Repeatedly, Doctorow links the innovations in domestic life with great public adventures and events, fusing public and private affairs in an almost magical, uncanny manner.

The class distinctions that play an important role in *Ragtime* become the focal element of *Loon Lake* (1980), which, like *The Book of Daniel*, contains a double narrative perspective, shifting between the experience of a poet on a rich man's isolated estate and a poor man's picaresque adventures across 1930's America. The power of the materialist, the millionaire capitalist, is meant to be balanced by the imagination of the poet, but the novel fails to measure up to *Ragtime*'s astonishing feat of fusing the realms of fiction and history. The poetic interludes in *Loon Lake* are reminiscent of the introverted, stream-of-consciousness "Camera Eye" sections of novelist John Dos Passos' *U.S.A.* (1938), but they seem excessively obscure and introverted and disruptive of the novel's narrative pace.

Nevertheless, *Loon Lake* has a haunting, ineffable quality, evoking a metaphorical but almost tangible sense of history which is akin to the novel's image of the lake: a dazzling surface of ever-shifting and widening perspectives above glinting depths that are only suggested. History as mirror—refracting, distorting, highlighting, and obscuring human actions—is a palpable presence in *Loon Lake*. A great social novelist, Doctorow manages to describe every level and grouping of society in the soup kitchens, monasteries, mansions, and assembly lines of the United States between the two world wars.

In most of Doctorow's work there is a tension between a naïve, childlike point of view, with fresh perceptions, and an older, ironic, detached perspective. Sometimes this split is expressed in terms of dual first-person and third-person narration, as in *The Book of Daniel*. In *Ragtime*, the narrator seems simultaneously to be the little boy and his older self, both witnessing and remembering the past. *World Fair* and *Billy Bathgate* seem more conventional than these earlier novels, for they are told from the standpoint of two narrators, both mature men reviewing their youth. Yet both novels unfold with such immediacy that they appear to be taking place as their narrators reminisce.

THE BOOK OF DANIEL

First published: 1971
Type of work: Novel

In the turbulent 1960's, in the midst of social protest and calls for revolution, Daniel searches for the significance of his parents' execution for espionage.

The Book of Daniel is in many ways a political mystery story. As young children, Daniel and his sister lose their parents. Condemned as spies and betrayed by members of their own family, Daniel's parents are martyrs in the view of the left, which is sure they are innocent. As far as Daniel is concerned, however, his parents abandoned him, and he is doubtful that they understood the implications of their actions or how much their behavior actually played into the hands of the government which executed them.

Daniel finds it both fascinating and frustrating to try to piece together the past. When he finally tracks down the relative who informed on his parents, for example, Daniel finds that he is senile. So many years have passed that it is difficult either to re-create the feelings of another age or to determine the truth of the charges against his parents. Without a heritage he can share with others, Daniel feels isolated and without an identity. He wonders on what basis he can live his own life when he has such fundamental and apparently unanswerable questions about his own parents.

As a study of history, however, Daniel is capable of seeing things in terms larger than his own personal obsessions. The chapters of the novel alternate between first-person and third-person narration as Daniel himself swings from subjectivity to objectivity. His plight, he gradually realizes, is not so different from that of his country, which tends either to obliterate the past or to sentimentalize it. Daniel's images of his parents lack a certain substance, since they have become figures in Cold War ideological battles, and the truth often eludes Americans who are fed a steady diet of entertaining, pacific, and nostalgic pictures of the past.

Near the end of *The Book of Daniel*, there is a brilliant set-piece description of Disneyland, which comes to stand for the forces in American life that threaten a complex sense of history. At Disneyland, which resembles a film set, are arranged the figures and artifacts of American history, the symbols and the tokens of the national heritage, wrenched from their social and historical context, abstracted into a series of entertainments for customers who do not have to analyze what is presented to them. This spectacle of history substitutes for the real thing, demeaning the past and replacing it with a comfortable and convenient product that need only be enjoyed and consumed.

What fuels Daniel's anger is the way his parents allowed themselves to become symbols in the ideologies of the left and the right. Their willingness to sacrifice themselves, no matter what the cost to their family, appalls him. The human element, the complexity of loyalties to family and friends and country, is what distinguishes Doctorow's novel, taking it out of the realm of the merely political while at the same time asking the most fundamental questions about the relationship between ideology and individualism. Until Daniel comes to terms with the humanity of his parents, he finds it impossible to get on with his own life and to care for his wife and child. Only by reclaiming his mother and father in terms that are far more complex than those of their public immolation can Daniel function as a husband and father.

RAGTIME

First published: 1975
Type of work: Novel

At the beginning of the twentieth century, on the eve of world war and tremendous cultural changes, a proud black man defends his dignity by force.

Ragtime begins with a description of a comfortable American household in New Rochelle, New York, at the turn of the century. At the dinner table, Father, Mother, the little boy, and Mother's Younger Brother are interrupted by the visit of a young black man, Coalhouse Walker. Eventually, it is discovered that Walker is the father of the child who had been abandoned by a young black woman who, along with the child, has been given refuge in the household. The appearance of Walker changes everything in the family's life and eventually links the New Rochelle household directly to the fate of the nation. By not giving the family names, Doctorow emphasizes their role as representatives of white, middle-class life, gradually and inexorably drawn into the changing times of radicals, immigrants, and blacks.

Doctorow uses Walker as the agent of change. This proud black man is offended when his motor car is stopped by a group of unruly volunteer firemen who then block his way and (when he goes for assistance) deface his prized possession. Unable to obtain satisfaction from the law (he finds it impossible to file charges or to be taken seriously by the authorities), Walker takes justice into his own hands, recruiting a group of black comrades who devise an ingenious plan to occupy the J. P. Morgan Library in New York City and demand the return of Walker's car in pristine condition—or the precious building will be detonated with explosives.

While no such incident occurred in the years *Ragtime* covers, and it is unlikely that such an incident could have taken place, Doctorow is less concerned with realism than with the implications of historical change. His novel is a compression of history, a fable making the point that the Establishment in the twentieth century will eventually find it more and more difficult to ignore the new immigrants and blacks and to give them the runaround that Walker experiences. Thus the participation of Younger Brother—the only white man in Walker's gang—is again symbolic of what is about to happen in history: the joining together of white dissenters, radicals, and (in some cases) Communists with disaffected minorities who will demand their rights. Younger Brother, after all, chafes under the paternalistic, authoritarian household of his brother-in-law and sees in Walker the chance to overturn—or at least challenge—the status quo.

Indeed, *Ragtime* is studded with historical characters who, through their politics, their inventions, or their imaginations, disrupt the status quo. Emma Goldman, a Communist, Jacob Riis, a photographer of the slums, and Harry Houdini, the great escape artist, all figure in the novel, because each of them speaks to the public's dream of overcoming or breaking out of the status quo. Younger Brother, for example, is not only attracted to political activity but also to Evelyn Nesbit, the nubile model who excited public attention when her husband shot and murdered famous architect Stanford White because of White's alleged defilement of her. In turn, Doctorow has Nesbit form an infatuation with both Emma Goldman and with Tateh, the immigrant silhouette maker and (later) filmmaker, because each of them in different ways embodies romantic visions of America—of America as an equal and just society, as a land of dreams fulfilled.

The novel's intricate layering of historical and invented figures tends to dissolve the barriers between public and private life and between the wealthy and the poor. Doctorow is not concerned with whether such characters could in fact meet; rather, he is intent on demonstrating that in terms of the way people have experienced the United States there is a kind of imagination of the country that pervades every level of life. Evelyn Nesbit's dream of success, in other words, is much the same as the immigrant's, and so she eventually stars in one of Tateh's films. In the deepest sense of the word, Doctorow is a democratic novelist who shows that class divisions dissolve in the light of the commonality of American behavior, that the very things that split Americans apart are also the things that unite them. Walker's concern for his car is itself a very American concern—attaching his sense of dignity to a piece of machinery and making it an extension of himself. There is much humor and irony in Doctorow's treatment of America, but it is also the sly criticism of an insider, of a writer who revels in the country's contradictions and who shows that the myth of America, seen in its broadest terms, can encompass all groups, classes, and races of people.

WORLD'S FAIR

First published: 1985
Type of work: Novel

A remembrance of New York City in the 1930's, from the perspective of a boy writing about "The Typical American Boy" for an essay contest.

In comparison to Doctorow's earlier novels, *World's Fair* seems remarkably straightforward. It resembles a work of conventional nonfiction, and like a memoir, it is largely bound by a chronological structure. Much of the action is seen through the consciousness of a young boy, Edgar, growing up in the Bronx during the 1939-1940 World's Fair. Given the character's name and background, it is difficult not to conclude that Doctorow has himself and his family in mind. He had used his New Rochelle house as a model for the house in *Ragtime* and the mind of a young boy as the intuitive medium through which many of the domestic, private events of the novel would be filtered. Doctorow's interest in the way the fictional and factual impinge upon each other would naturally lead to this exercise in quasi-autobiography, in which the materials from his own background underpin the plot. The World's Fair becomes a metaphor for the boy's growing up and for the country's maturation. Unlike many American novelists, Doctorow does not merely criticize American materialism, seeing in the emphasis on things a soul-deadening culture which is antithetical to the artist's imagination. On the contrary, he enjoys playing with and observing the materiality of the United States—decrying, to be sure, the way in which the culture turns its important figures and events into toys and commercials for capitalism, but also capturing the American delight in inventiveness and machinery and honoring it. In *World's Fair*, he triumphantly combines the personal and the familiar aspects of life with the way a society celebrates itself. In doing so, he recovers the synthesis of history and literature that made *Ragtime* such a resounding success.

Compared with the characters in his other fiction, Edgar is unusual. He is a good, well-behaved boy with none of the rebelliousness that characterizes Younger Brother or Billy Bathgate. Yet society impinges just as significantly in *World's Fair* as it does in the other novels, with Edgar getting roughed up in his neighborhood for being a "Jewboy" and shaken up by the portentous crash of the German dirigible *Hindenburg*, which shows him how the apparent calm of his life and other American lives can be abruptly shattered by disaster.

As are Doctorow's other novels, *World's Fair* is full of fascinating period detail and places—the arrival of a water wagon, the Good Humor man, and a New York Giants game at the Polo Grounds. There is less plot, however, to hold the novel together. Essentially, the narrative turns on Edgar's anticipation of the fair, on his preparations for it, on his anxieties about whether his rather undependable father will take him, and on his chances of winning the essay contest. *World's Fair* is structured like a series of vignettes, the logic of which depends upon Edgar's sensibility rather than on the events themselves. In this respect, Doctorow reverses the pattern of *Ragtime*, in which human character is so definitely at one with the pattern of history. Called nostalgic and charming by many reviewers, *World's Fair* is somewhat surprising in that Doctorow does not analyze the ideological basis of the World's Fair, dissecting what it means for a modern technological society. The author in this work is much more concerned with the actual "feel" of experience, with a man remembering his youth, than with using it as a pretext for a political lesson.

BILLY BATHGATE

First published: 1989
Type of work: Novel

A Bronx boy grows up infatuated with Dutch Schultz and his gang, learning to survive and prosper even as the gangsters of his youth die out.

The first long sentence of *Billy Bathgate* launches right into the excitement of a scene in which Dutch Schultz is disposing of a disloyal associate, Bo Weinberg. The setting is described by fifteen-year-old Billy Bathgate, the novel's narrator, who is impressed with the smooth running of the Dutchman's criminal enterprise. A car drives up to a dark dock; without using any light or making a sound, Schultz's crew gets on the boat with Bo and his girl, Drew Preston. Schultz's control over the situation is awesome and inspiring for the young boy, who has been given the honor of running errands and performing other chores for the famous gang. He becomes their mascot and good luck charm.

Schultz has a way of utterly changing the face of things, and for a long time, working for him has a fairy-tale quality to it. Billy is enchanted by the sheer magic of the way Schultz gets things done. No sooner is Bo Weinberg overboard with his cement overshoes than Schultz is making love to Drew Preston—a socialite who is fascinated, for a while, by his presence and energy. She even accompanies him to Onondaga in upstate New York, where Schultz takes over a town, plying the locals with gifts and setting up a cozy atmosphere in preparation for what he rightly expects will be a favorable jury verdict in the case the government has brought against him for tax evasion.

Schultz's great strength, however, is also his great weakness. By making all of his business revolve around him, he fails to see how crime is becoming organized and corporate. His way of doing business is almost feudal—depending almost entirely on violence and on the loyalty of subordinates—and he has no grasp of how to put together an organization that can compete with the combinations of power being amassed by the government and by his rival, Lucky Luciano. Schultz wants to personalize everything so that it all evolves out of his own ego. That ego is unstable, however; on an impulse, he kills an uncooperative colleague in an Onondaga hotel. This is only one of many instances when he goes berserk and literally pounds his opponents into the floor.

Members of Schultz's gang—particularly his accountant Abbadabba Berman— sense that the old ways of doing things are nearly finished. Weinberg's defection is only the beginning of events which put Schultz on the defensive and which culminate in his gangland murder near the end of the novel. Berman tries to convince Schultz to do business in the new way, to recognize that he is part of a larger crime network, but Schultz can think only in terms of his own ambitions and calls off plans to amalgamate with Lucky Luciano and other gangsters. In compensation, perhaps, for Schultz's inability to adapt to new times, Berman turns to Billy, making him an apprentice and lavishing attention on the boy. Berman plies Billy with advice, gives him assignments that build his confidence and extend his knowledge of the business.

Through Berman and Preston, Billy gains perspective on Schultz. Preston, Billy finds, has her own sort of power and sense of ease. When she tires of Schultz, she simply leaves him, conveying to Billy the impression that Schultz's charisma has its limits. Billy never dares to think of actually leaving the gang, but he keeps his own counsel and is prepared to take care of himself when Schultz is murdered. At the death scene, in which Schultz, Berman, Lulu, and Irving have been shot, Billy learns from Berman the combination of the safe where Schultz has stashed much of his loot. Evasive about his subsequent career, Billy intimates at the end of the novel that he has indeed amassed the Dutchman's fortune, but he does not vouchsafe what he will do with it.

In this fast-paced adventure novel, which takes quick tours of the Bronx, upstate New York, Saratoga, and the docks of Manhattan, Doctorow supplies the color and the texture of the 1930's. As Billy prospers in the service of gangster Dutch Schultz and gets to know these different worlds, he finds it impossible to return as he was to his old neighborhood. He is immediately perceived as a different person. He dresses differently, carries himself differently, and has a consciousness of a world that extends far beyond the Bathgate Avenue from which he derives his assumed name. Billy becomes, in other words, a self-invented figure, transcending his origins not only in the actions he narrates but also in his very language, which is at once colloquial and formal, a blend of popular and sophisticated vocabulary that precisely captures the boy and the man who has become the narrator of this novel. In this quintessential American story, Doctorow has managed yet another stunning version of the hero's quest for identity and success.

Summary

E. L. Doctorow has shown himself to be a master stylist, a shrewd commentator on popular genres and political themes who maintains a strong sense of narrative and story telling. Indeed, his work is a major evocation and critique of the American mythos and a brilliant creation of new American fables. His experiments with point of view and with the relationship between history and fiction have marked him as a major innovator in contemporary fiction.

Bibliography

Kakutani, Michiko. "Do Facts and Fiction Mix?" *The New York Times Book Review*, January 27, 1980, pp. 2-3, 28-29.

Levine, Paul. *E. L. Doctorow*. London: Methuen, 1985.

Strout, Cushing. "Historizing Fiction and Fictionalizing History: The Case of E. L. Doctorow." *Prospects* (1980): 423-437.

Trenner, Richard. *E. L. Doctorow: Essays and Conversations*. Princeton, N.J.: Ontario Review Press, 1983.

Weber, Richard. "E. L. Doctorow: Myth Maker." *The New York Times Magazine*, October 20, 1985, pp. 25-26, 42-43, 74-77.

Carl Rollyson

JOHN DOS PASSOS

Born: Chicago, Illinois
January 14, 1896
Died: Baltimore, Maryland
September 28, 1970

Principal Literary Achievement

A pioneer in experimenting with forms of fiction, Dos Passos was one of the most important novelists of the modernist period in the 1920's and 1930's.

Biography

Born in Chicago, the illegitimate son of a wealthy lawyer of Portuguese descent and a mother whose family lived in Maryland and Virginia, John Roderigo Dos Passos grew up in the Washington, D.C., area. He attended private schools in England, Choate School, and later Harvard University. He was graduated from Harvard in 1916 and planned to study to be an architect, but when the United States entered World War I he joined a medical corps in France and later enlisted in the United States Army. After World War I he spent a number of years as a free-lance newspaper reporter.

Soon after the war, Dos Passos wrote his first novel, *One Man's Initiation—1917* (1920), based on his experiences as an ambulance driver; his second, *Three Soldiers* (1921), appeared soon after. Both these early works are bitter condemnations of the war and what it did to young Americans who happened to be caught in the violence. The central character in the first novel and all three of the soldiers depicted in the second are destroyed, physically or spiritually, by their experiences. In these novels, Dos Passos was already presenting a radical critique of the official view of the United States as the selfless defender of freedom for everyone.

Dos Passos would extend his criticism in his major work, beginning with his first genuinely experimental novel, *Manhattan Transfer* (1925), and continuing with new and unusual techniques in the three novels which formed his first trilogy: *The 42nd Parallel* (1930), *1919* (1932), and *The Big Money* (1936); they were collected as *U.S.A.* in 1937. During the 1920's, Dos Passos became more and more deeply involved in radical protests against what he saw as the degradation of American ideals. He served on the board of the Communist magazine *The New Masses* and contributed time and effort to a number of Communist causes, although he never joined the Communist Party. He was most disturbed by the Sacco-Vanzetti affair, a celebrated

case in the 1920's in which two immigrant anarchists were accused of murder during a robbery and sentenced to death. Many people at the time believed that their trial had been unfair, that evidence against them had been faked, and that they had been condemned because of their politics. Dos Passos was among the protesters, and he was jailed for picketing in 1927 prior to their execution.

Dos Passos eventually became disillusioned with left-wing politics, giving up his Communist activities in 1934; toward the end of the 1930's, he became increasingly alienated from his former causes. He traveled as a correspondent to Spain, where the Spanish Civil War had broken out in 1936. His sympathies were on the side of the Loyalist government, which was trying to suppress a rebellion by a group of insurgents led by army officers with the support of the Catholic church. The insurgents received military aid from Adolf Hitler's Germany and Benito Mussolini's Italy; the Loyalists were aided by the Soviet Union. Dos Passos found that the Loyalist government was dominated by Soviet agents and that the Communists were ruthlessly suppressing their opponents on the Loyalist side. He also was convinced that he had been lied to by the American novelist Ernest Hemingway about the fate of a mutual Spanish friend who, Dos Passos discovered, had been executed for opposing Communist domination.

Dos Passos was also dismayed by what he perceived as the betrayal of the labor movement in the United States. In *U.S.A.*, he had presented sympathetic portraits of union organizers and leaders who selflessly worked for the betterment of workers as well as scathing depictions of men who betrayed the workers, but he became convinced that as unions gained power they became corrupt organizations that deprived their members and others of freedoms. He expressed his disillusionment in a second trilogy, *District of Columbia* (1952), which consisted of *Adventures of a Young Man* (1939), *Number One* (1943), and *The Grand Design* (1949). They dealt with Spain, with the notorious corruption in governor Huey Long's Louisiana, and with the worse corruption in Washington, D.C. His most bitter portrayal of unions and their evils came in his last long novel, *Midcentury* (1961).

After World War II, he lived in the area around Washington and Baltimore and devoted much of his attention to historical writings. He expressed his profound admiration for one of the United States' founding fathers in *The Head and Heart of Thomas Jefferson* (1954) and wrote a more general history of revolutionary times in *The Men Who Made the Nation* (1957). He also wrote a number of autobiographical works, including *The Theme Is Freedom* (1956) and *Occasions and Protests* (1964). In the 1950's and 1960's he wrote regularly for *The National Review*, the conservative journal edited by William F. Buckley, Jr. When liberal friends such as Edmund Wilson, a longtime summer neighbor on Cape Cod, teased him about his new friends and commitments, Dos Passos replied that his overriding interest had always been, and remained, the freedom of the individual. He would support whatever movement or party seemed to him to share that dedication.

Dos Passos first married Katharine (Kay) Smith in 1929; she was killed in an automobile accident in 1947, while they were driving from Cape Cod to Virginia. He married Elizabeth Hamlin Holdridge in 1949. A daughter was born of that marriage in 1950.

Analysis

John Dos Passos was the most experimental of the major novelists of what critics now refer to as the period of "high modernism," which lasted roughly from 1910 until 1940. His great contemporaries in the American novel, Ernest Hemingway, F. Scott Fitzgerald, and William Faulkner, all concentrated on writing about specific areas or groups. Hemingway, during the 1920's, wrote mostly about expatriate Americans living in Europe and about such upper-class sports as big-game hunting and bullfighting. Fitzgerald, too, wrote about expatriates, but also about bored flappers and socialites, upper-class young people with too much money and too little to do. Faulkner, while using such experimental techniques as stream of consciousness, focused all of his attention on the Deep South, especially his own corner of northern Mississippi.

Dos Passos was looking for techniques which would enable him to portray the wide range of characters and economic situations to be found in American society. He was also looking for a style that would reflect the fast pace of modern life and the actual speech of its people. Even as early as *Three Soldiers* he was engaged in this pursuit, choosing as his principal characters a farm boy from Indiana, an esthete from the East Coast, and an Italian working-class man from San Francisco and making no attempt to combine their stories, except to make clear that all were destroyed by the machinelike nature of the modern army.

Dos Passos' experimentation took a major step forward in *Manhattan Transfer*, which also brought him wide public attention. He attempted to create a cross-section of urban life in the United States by introducing a wide range of characters. While much of the book's attention is devoted to a young newspaper reporter and a young woman who becomes an actress, depictions are also given of a young man from a farm who cannot find work, who becomes a bum and eventually dies, either accidentally or by suicide; a French immigrant who makes himself something of a success by marrying a widow who owns a delicatessen; a man who had once been a rich Wall Street investor but whose luck went bad and who sinks to the lowest levels of society; a war veteran who turns to crime; a milkman who is injured in an accident and uses the settlement as a springboard to a successful political career.

Each chapter in *Manhattan Transfer* is introduced by a brief section of impressionistic prose about some aspect of the city and its life which will appear in that chapter. For example, where a couple of the characters are to find their way to the waterfront and others are to arrive by ship in New York harbor, the opening segment depicts the shoreline and the dirty waters of the bay. In each chapter, as it proceeds, episodes in the lives of several of the characters are described, with occasional brief references to individuals who are mentioned only a single time. The intention is to produce a kaleidoscopic effect, a novel which will give the reader a vivid impression of what it is to live in a city as bustling and energetic and squalid as New York.

His most radical experiments are the techniques used in *U.S.A.* The prose style makes frequent use of a device he used sparingly in *Manhattan Transfer*, that of run-together words. The narrative segments move rapidly, with little attention to extended depictions of characters; the "Camera Eye" segments are more relaxed, and the "Newsreel" collages are jagged and sometimes almost incoherent as they skip from subject to subject.

In the novels which compose this trilogy, Dos Passos interweaves the stories of eleven major figures from various parts of the United States and various economic and social levels. Along with these narratives, three very different devices are employed. One is the "Newsreel," a collage of headlines from newspapers, brief stories of violence or betrayal, snatches of popular songs of the time, and quotations from public officials and from government reports. The second is the "Camera Eye," impressionistic pictures in vivid prose from the perspective of a single individual responding to the events of the times. The third consists of portraits of important historical figures of the time, from the industrialist Henry Ford and the financier J. Pierpont Morgan to the Socialist leader Eugene V. Debs and the economist Thorstein Veblen. Dos Passos' own views about politics and economics are most clearly suggested in these portraits.

MANHATTAN TRANSFER

First published: 1925
Type of work: Novel

Characters from all walks of life struggle with the tensions and pressures of life in New York City.

John Dos Passos, in *Manhattan Transfer*, tried to show what life was like between the last years of the nineteenth century and the early 1920's for a wide variety of people living in the largest of American cities, New York. At the center of the action are two characters, Ellen Thatcher, whose birth occurs in the novel's opening pages, and Jimmy Herf, who is first seen as a young boy. Her background is lower middle class; her father is an unsuccessful accountant, her mother an invalid who dies while Ellen is still a child. Jimmy's background is more wealthy, but his father is dead and his mother dies after a series of strokes. Instead of Yale or Harvard, he goes to Columbia University.

In the course of the novel, Ellen becomes a minor star in the theater and marries an actor who, it is revealed, is homosexual. She divorces him, and after a frustrating affair with a rich young alcoholic, she goes abroad with the Red Cross during World War I and meets Jimmy, whom she had known in New York. He has been a newspaper reporter. The two marry and have a son, but eventually they become bored with each other. Ellen has abandoned the theater and becomes a successful magazine editor. When they divorce, she reluctantly agrees to marry a longtime suitor,

George Baldwin, while Jimmy becomes increasingly restive as a reporter, and at the end he quits his job sets out to see the rest of America.

This thin plot is only a means for holding the novel together while Dos Passos provides glimpses of a number of very different lives. A few of these are from upper levels of society. Jimmy's aunt and her husband live well, and their son, James Merivale, becomes an officer in the war and then a stuffed-shirt banker. Phineas T. Blackhead and his partner, Densch, run an export-import business which seems very successful until the end of the novel, when it goes bankrupt. A few characters represent the lower depths of society. Bud Korpenning is a young farm boy who comes to the city after stealing his father's savings. He never finds a permanent job, drifting from handout to handout and eventually becoming a Bowery bum before falling, perhaps deliberately, from the Brooklyn Bridge. Anna Cohen, a poor Jewish girl, makes a meager living as a seamstress until she joins a strike against intolerable conditions and loses her job. She takes a job in a dress store and, dreaming of something better, is horribly burned in a fire. Dutch Robertson, a war veteran, and his girl, Francie, are barely surviving until he begins robbing stores. She joins him and is romanticized by the press as a "flapper bandit." They are caught when she gives birth to their baby.

Most of the characters, however, belong at some level of the middle class; a few of them rise. Gus McNiel is a milkman who negligently allows his cart to be hit by a train and is injured. An ambulance-chasing lawyer named George Baldwin sues, seduces McNiel's wife Nellie, and wins a large settlement for McNiel. The money is the springboard which launches McNiel on a successful political career. It also helps Baldwin to become a successful lawyer and eventually to be named district attorney. Another success, at least financially, is Congo Jake, a French sailor who becomes a bootlegger after retiring from the sea. Prohibition gives Congo Jake the opportunity for wealth; he marries a showgirl and offers to help Jimmy Herf financially after Jimmy has quit his job.

Others drop down or out in society. Jimmy's cousin, Joe Harland, was once one of the most successful gamblers on Wall Street, but his luck changed and he sinks lower and lower, unable finally even to hold onto a job as a night watchman. Ruth Prynne, one of Jimmy Herf's girlfriends, who at one time lived in the same boarding-house as Ellen, has a brief success as a singer but then loses her voice, resorting to dangerous treatments in doomed attempts to restore her career.

The picture given of New York life is sordid, whether it is depicted in the poetic tones of the introductions to each of the chapters in *Manhattan Transfer* or in the flat style of the narrative sections. Dos Passos' city is noisy, dirty, and dangerous. Characters such as Ellen find their lives unrewarding; others find them crushing. Somewhat confusingly, characters appear and disappear, sometimes without being given names, to emphasize the anonymity of city life for most people. The city is also pulsing with life, however; even as the author undercuts the glamour of show business and scoffs at the stodgy businessmen, the picture presented is gaudy, exciting, and challenging. Jimmy Herf feels a sense of relief when he cuts his ties to the city and heads west across the river, but what he leaves behind is, on balance, far more interesting than the unknown he is entering.

Manhattan Transfer contains less harsh social criticism than Dos Passos' other early novels, and far less than *U.S.A.* There is political corruption; Anna Cohen's boyfriend talks to her about the revolution and the need for solidarity among workers; society has no place for the Bud Korpennings and the Dutch Robertsons. Yet these are minor matters in this novel. What stands out is the vibrancy, the clatter, the feverish activity of the city.

U.S.A.

First published: *The 42nd Parallel*, 1930; *1919*, 1932; *The Big Money*, 1936
(as *U.S.A.*, 1937)

Type of work: Novel

Life in the United States from the 1890's to the Great Depression of the 1930's is depicted in an encyclopedic novel.

The three volumes which make up *U.S.A.* were originally published separately; the trilogy was published as a single novel in 1937. The themes introduced in the first volume run throughout the others: the corrupting influence of wealth and the desire for money; the humiliation and penury inflicted by American society on those who occupy the lower levels of that society; the pretentious fakery of most of those who profess to have artistic talent or inclinations; and the heroism of a few dedicated souls whose lives are ground down in the effort to serve others.

The techniques employed by Dos Passos in *U.S.A.* develop and expand upon those he used in *Manhattan Transfer.* A dozen different characters from various parts of the country and different levels of society are given one or more episodes during the course of the novel, and numerous other characters appear and disappear at various stages of the action. Frequently the paths of different characters intersect and run together. The narrative segments occupy less space than they do in *Manhattan Transfer*, as three other methods are given great significance.

In *The 42nd Parallel* there are nineteen sections of the "Newsreel," in which Dos Passos skillfully blends together newspaper headlines, snippets of popular songs, brief quotations from political speeches, and other material from the years between 1900 and 1917, when the novel ends. The "Newsreel" sections provide the authenticity of historical background. There are also, in this first volume, twenty-seven segments of "The Camera Eye," in which individuals' experiences are presented in a stream-of-consciousness technique, representing one perspective on the events of the passing years.

Finally, there are in this first volume nine brief portraits of prominent individuals from the same period of time: Eugene V. Debs, Socialist leader and frequent presidential candidate who was later imprisoned for opposing American participation in

World War I: Luther Burbank, "The Plant Wizard," who hybridized numerous vege-
tables and trees to the benefit of American agriculture; "Big Bill" Haywood, a radical labor organizer who moved from the Western Federation of Miners to the International Workers of the World (the IWW, or "Wobblies"), William Jennings Bryan,
"the boy orator of the Platte," famous for what was called his "cross of gold"
speech, leader of the Populist movement in the late nineteenth and early twentieth
centuries; and several others prominent in one field or another. Dos Passos' sympathies in these portraits are clearly with the rebels and the innovators. He is much
more ironic and dismissive in calling the section on steel magnate Andrew Carnegie
"Prince of Peace." He is also somewhat scornful of the idealistic inventor Charles
Steinmetz, who allowed himself and his inventions to be exploited by General Electric.

The same devices are used throughout *U.S.A.*, but there is a subtle shift in tone
between *1919* and *The Big Money*, noticeable in all four of the devices used by Dos
Passos. The subject of the narrative sections changes from "Mac," a journeyman
printer and part-time rebel, who disappears at the end of *The 42nd Parallel*, to
Charley Anderson, a midwesterner with skills as a mechanic who flies in World
War I, rises with the system in *The Big Money*, and is eventually crushed by it. The
sleazy public relations expert, J. Ward Moorehouse, becomes more important, as do
the women who are involved with him, the neurotic decorators Eleanor Stoddard
and Eveline Hutchins.

There is a parallel shift in the subjects chosen for the brief biographical sketches.
In *The 42nd Parallel* and *1919* these are, for the most part, devoted to individuals
who are presented as worthy of the reader's admiration: Debs, Haywood, and Burbank. In *1919* there are favorable depictions of John Reed, the left-wing American
journalist who went to Russia to report on the Russian Revolution and stayed on,
dying in Moscow and being buried in the Kremlin wall; other journalists such as
Randolph Bourne and Paxton Hibben, also radicals in their ways; and the IWW
organizer and writer of labor songs Joe Hill, who was framed for murder and executed in Utah after trying to organize miners. There are scathing portraits of Woodrow Wilson and the financier J. P. Morgan, but Dos Passos saves for last two figures
who share his admiration and his sympathy: The first is Wesley Everest, a logger and
organizer of a strike for the IWW in the Pacific Northwest, who was brutally lynched
after a violent episode in Centralia, Washington. The other is John Doe, the "Unknown Soldier," an ordinary American who was killed in World War I and made
into a hero in a patriotic burial ceremony which Dos Passos portrays as a kind of
ultimate exercise in hypocrisy.

In *The Big Money*, however, the emphasis has changed. There are fewer portraits,
and those that there are emphasize the corruption of the American Dream rather
than the heroics of those who, in the author's view, try to keep the dream alive. The
only sympathetic figures in the final volume are the pioneers in aviation, the Wright
Brothers; bitter social critic Thorstein Veblen; and the innovative architect Frank
Lloyd Wright. The dancer Isadora Duncan and the film actor Rudolph Valentino are

not so much admired as pitied. The subjects of the other depictions are scathingly portrayed as dehumanizers and exploiters and as defenders of a cruel and unfair economic system: Henry Ford, the efficiency expert Frederick W. Taylor, the newspaper tycoon William Randolph Hearst, and the stock market manipulator Samuel Insull.

The tone of the narrative sections becomes darker, as well. The central figure in the first half of *The 42nd Parallel* is Fenian McCreary, known as "Mac" once he leaves Chicago and begins his travels. Mac becomes a symbol of the entire novel. At one time or another he lives in every section of the country except the Deep South; he is balanced between his commitment to the kind of men who shared his life on the road and become involved in the IWW, and his middle-class aspirations: He wants a home and a "good life" for his wife and children. Eventually he moves to Mexico, where he sees a real revolution but does not take part in it. In the earlier years of the twentieth century, someone such as Mac can survive without making a definite commitment.

In later years, however, especially those which include the "roaring twenties," this kind of survival becomes less and less possible. Charley Anderson abandons his roots, has some success as a manufacturer, is drawn into the circle which includes Eveline Hutchins and Eleanor Stoddard, and eventually winds up with Margo Dowling, another major character who has been in the entertainment business and has become a gold-digger. Charley's business goes downhill as he drinks more and more, and eventualy he dies as the result of an automobile accident. Eveline Hutchins commits suicide. Richard Ellsworth Savage, who grew from a pleasant young boy to a career-minded toady in *1919*, becomes part of Moorehouse's enterprise and eventually gives in to what had been his suppressed homosexual inclinations. The young woman from Texas known as "Daughter" is tangentially involved in radical activities without being a radical herself; she goes abroad to do relief work after World War I, becomes involved with Savage, becomes pregnant by him, and is killed in an airplane crash.

The bitterness of the final volume is presented most directly in a "Camera Eye" segment toward the close of *The Big Money* dealing with the end of the Sacco-Vanzetti affair: "They have clubbed us off the street they are stronger they are rich they hire and fire the politicians the newspapereditors the old judges the small men with reputations the collegepresidents the wardheelers." Later in the same section the narrative voice says, "all right we are two nations," and at the end, "we stand defeated America." By this time, Dos Passos sees no hope in radical political movements. They have, in his view, self-destructed, and the society as a whole is headed for a disaster of which the 1929 stock market crash is only the first stage.

The final section of *The Big Money*, "Vag," presents a contrast between the two Americas, as Dos Passos saw them at the time. On the ground is an anonymous young man, out of work, half-starved, beaten by police, walking and hitchhiking across the country. In the air is an airplane carrying the rich, including a man who thinks only of wealth and power, who vomits up his dinner but does not mind—he is wealthy, so a single meal does not matter to him. The "Vag" is aware of the airplane, but the man in the plane is totally ignorant of the man on the ground. The two men and their circumstances represent the vast gulf that separates the two parts of the country.

Summary

John Dos Passos' reputation rests solidly on the novels he published between 1925 and 1939. In *Manhattan Transfer* and the three long novels that make up *U.S.A.*, he showed himself to be a daring and imaginative experimenter with prose style and a vivid depicter of the American scene. He does not present deep or penetrating analyses of his characters, but in part this results from the fact that he wishes to show that American society has a leveling influence that diminishes the differences between people's characters even as it exaggerates the economic and social differences between them. The picture Dos Passos provided of life in the United States in the first thirty years of the twentieth century remains lively and immediate. That picture, and the new directions he provided for prose style, secure for him a place among American novelists of modern times.

Bibliography

Carr, Virginia Spencer. *Dos Passos: A Life.* Garden City, N.Y.: Doubleday, 1984.

Clark, Michael. "The Structure of John Dos Passos' *U.S.A.*" *Arizona Quarterly* 38 (Autumn, 1982): 229-234.

Ludington, Townsend. *John Dos Passos: A Twentieth Century Odyssey.* New York: E. P. Dutton, 1980.

Rosen, Robert C. *John Dos Passos: Politics and the Writer.* Lincoln: University of Nebraska Press, 1982.

Sanders, David. *John Dos Passos: A Comprehensive Bibliography.* New York: Garland, 1985.

Spindler, Michael. "John Dos Passos and the Visual Arts." *Journal of American Studies* 15 (December, 1981): 391-406.

Wagner, Linda. *Dos Passos: Artist as American.* Austin: University of Texas Press, 1979.

John M. Muste

THEODORE DREISER

Born: Terre Haute, Indiana
August 27, 1871
Died: Los Angeles, California
December 28, 1945

Principal Literary Achievement
Although known as a naturalistic writer, Dreiser adapted the deterministic philosophy of naturalism by creating characters capable of weighing moral issues and making conscious decisions.

Biography
Theodore Herman Albert Dreiser was the twelfth of thirteen children belonging to John Paul Dreiser and Sarah Schnepp Dreiser. John Paul Dreiser, a weaver, had come from Mayhen, Germany, in the mid 1840's, settling in New England. After several years, he moved to a German community in Indiana, where he met Sarah, the daughter of a Mennonite farmer. Since Dreiser was unable to find work in this community, he and Sarah eloped to Dayton, Ohio, but returned to Fort Wayne, Indiana, before their first child was born.

At first, the elder Dreiser tried to build a secure life for his growing family, establishing his own woolen mill at Sullivan, Indiana, in 1867. Unfortunately, the mill burned to the ground just when it was starting to prosper. While Dreiser was supervising the building of a new mill, a ceiling beam slipped from the hands of a workman, striking him on the head. Following this accident, which resulted in what is now known as minimal brain dysfunction, Dreiser lost interest in his mill, as well as his ambition and his ability to hold a steady job. He became fanatical in the practice of his Catholic faith and extremely strict in the discipline of his children.

Sarah Dreiser has often been called the family's financial and emotional mainstay, keeping things together by taking in boarders and laundry. Biographers who knew the family well, however, report that she was inept in handling money, overly lenient with the children (perhaps in compensation for her husband's strictness), and given to fancy and superstition. Although Sarah could be a strong and supportive mother (as she demonstrated when her daughter Mame became pregnant), she could also be "lovingly cruel." When the children were naughty, for example, she threatened to abandon them, once even packing her bag and hiding in a cornfield while the younger ones cried hysterically.

Since Theodore was rather puny as a toddler, Sarah singled him out for special attention, often inviting him to sit at her feet while she sewed. This tender tableau also had a sinister side, however, for she would call the child's attention to her broken shoes, asking him if he did not pity his mother in her poverty. Perhaps because of this repeated experience, Theodore became very aware of women's clothing, especially the condition of their shoes—a detail frequently mentioned in his writing.

Thus, Theodore grew up in an atmosphere of financial instability and emotional conflict. The family moved frequently, which meant that the children's education suffered. Nevertheless, Theodore was an avid reader and educated himself. Although he had completed only one year of high school, he was admitted to Indiana University in 1889 as a special student. Not being academically inclined, however, he dropped out after one year.

During the 1890's, Dreiser worked as a feature reporter for a number of newspapers, among them the Chicago *Globe*, the St. Louis *Globe-Democrat* and *Republic*, the Pittsburgh *Dispatch*, and the New York *World*. In addition, he edited *Ev'ry Month*, a musical magazine, and contributed essays, poems, and stories to magazines such as *Harpers*, *Cosmopolitan*, *Munsey's*, and *Metropolitan*. While he strove for realism in his magazine stories, Dreiser always tinged them with a subtle sense of optimism.

Dreiser's friend Arthur Henry had been urging him to write a novel, but had no idea for a topic. Finally, while Dreiser was visiting at Henry's home, he took a piece of yellow paper and scribbled the title "Sister Carrie," evidently thinking of his sister Emma, whose real life experiences were similar to those of Carrie. From the title to the point when Carrie meets Hurstwood, the novel "wrote itself"; after the Hurstwood incident, however, it moved in a series of spurts and halts. Henry urged Dreiser on, occasionally writing bits of *Sister Carrie* himself to keep the novel going.

Sister Carrie was published by Doubleday in 1900, but its sales were suppressed for seven years on the grounds that it showed a despairing, animalistic view of humanity. The suppression of *Sister Carrie* discouraged Dreiser from trying another novel for nearly a decade, when he began work on *Jennie Gerhardt*, published in 1911. In the meantime, he continued to write short stories and became editor of *Smith's Magazine* and the *Butterick* trio, consisting of *Delineator*, *Designer*, and *New Ideas for Women*. Through the efforts of a literary agent named Flora Holly, *Sister Carrie* was republished in 1912; this time it was hailed as a "work of genius."

Although Dreiser is best known for his novels *Sister Carrie, Jennie Gerhardt, An American Tragedy* (1925), and the Cowperwood trilogy—*The Financier* (1912), *The Titan* (1914), and *The Stoic* (1947)—he also published collections of poems, stories, and essays, as well as several plays, a biography, and book-length treatises. Two of his novels, *The Bulwark* (1946) and *The Stoic*, were published posthumously.

In 1927, Dreiser visited the Soviet Union at the Russians' expense. Not entirely enchanted with this nation (he was appalled by the crowded and unsanitary housing), he nevertheless admired the Soviets' efforts to educate the workers and make their places of employment safe and clean. Dreiser's exposure to Soviet Communism "hit home" during the Great Depression. Throughout these bleak years, he traveled around the United States, writing and lecturing for reform in such areas as prison codes, birth control, and employment laws. Moreover, in 1931, the Department of International Labor Defense asked him to investigate labor conditions in the mines of Bell and Harlan Counties, Kentucky. These activities on behalf of the people may have induced Dreiser to join the Communist Party in 1945.

Dreiser married twice. His first wife was Sarah Osborne White, nicknamed "Jug." Unfortunately, Dreiser so idealized his wife that marital relations were difficult. They separated in 1910, and Dreiser took as his mistress Helen Patges, a young divorcée, whom he married after Jug's death in 1941. Dreiser himself died of a heart attack on December 28, 1945.

Analysis

Dreiser is best known as a leading American naturalist writer. Naturalism, a literary trend which began in France and reached the United States in the 1880's, depicted life realistically, often concentrating on the lower classes of society. Naturalism held that the lives of human beings were determined by circumstances and inborn traits, or drives. Thus, people acted purely on instinct, had no free will, and were unable to change. This philosophy of human life consequently gave naturalistic writing a depressing and pessimistic tone.

The name most frequently associated with French naturalism is Émile Zola, but when Dreiser wrote *Sister Carrie*, he had not read any of Zola's work. Neither had he read *McTeague* (1899), the recently published novel of American naturalist Frank Norris, who acclaimed *Sister Carrie* as "wonderful." Although Dreiser had read such writers as Honoré de Balzac, Charles Darwin, the philosopher Herbert Spencer, and the British novelist Thomas Hardy, it is doubtful that his view of human nature derived as much from the theories of others as from his own observations of his family and the persons he interviewed as a feature reporter. Events of fate, such as the mill fire and the brain injury that had wiped out his father's early ambition, had probably made it clear to Dreiser that people's lives are not entirely under their own control. Since three of his sisters had become mistresses and/or given birth to illegitimate children, he may have also reached the conclusion that human libido was a stronger force than any moral precepts established by church or society.

Nevertheless, Dreiser's works do not follow the theory of naturalism to the letter. Although his characters' lives and actions are strongly influenced by their youthful environments and their own innate personalities, he does not present them simply as animals or robots at the mercy of nature or outside forces; Dreiser's characters are real. They make thoughtful and conscious decisions—proving the existence of free will—even though these decisions are often guided by outside events, and some characters show the potential for positive change. Moreover, while Dreiser's works are somber, they are not totally pessimistic. Although the conclusions to *Sister Carrie*, *Jennie Gerhardt*, and *An American Tragedy* are far from the "happily ever after" variety, each contains a subtle hint of hope for the characters, provided the reader chooses to interpret them in that way.

Yet despite his deviations from theoretical naturalism, Dreiser still believed that most people are in the firm clutches of money and sex, which he considered the strongest and most basic of human drives. The drive toward money is obvious in all of Dreiser's major novels. Sex is equally powerful, but Dreiser presents it as more than a simple physical instinct. To the male characters, sexual conquests imply possession and confidence. After Jennie Gerhardt has yielded to her first lover, for example, he tells her that she "belongs" to him. Clyde, in *An American Tragedy*, assures himself that since one girl has given herself to him freely, there must be others willing to do the same.

Among Dreiser's female characters (with the possible exception of Roberta Alden, in *An American Tragedy*, who appears to regard it as a genuine physical pleasure as well as an expression of deep love), sex is viewed either as the means to an end or as an instrument of control. Sex as the gateway to a higher standard of living is a major theme in both *Sister Carrie* and *Jennie Gerhardt*, but its controlling aspect comes forth more obviously in *An American Tragedy*.

In Book 1, Clyde becomes attracted to a shop girl whose meager salary cannot afford an expensive fur coat she ardently desires. Not really caring for Clyde, but sensing his pliability regarding her wishes, she bribes him into buying the coat on the installation plan by promising sex once the coveted garment is in her possession.

Sondra Finchley uses sexual control in a more subtle form. She keeps Clyde at bay by insinuating that in the mores of her society—to which Clyde aspires to belong—sex does not occur before the wedding. While Dreiser had abandoned the practice of Catholicism quite early and no longer had faith in a personal God, his belief in the driving power of money and sex alienated him from all forms of organized religion. He believed that their moral teachings tried to change people from what nature intended them to be: sexual and material beings, enjoying the good, sensual things of life. Dreiser usually portrayed churches in a negative manner.

Many critics have objected that Dreiser's writing is cumbersome and overly descriptive. His descriptions, however, can often be enlightening. His detailed portrayals of street scenes in *Sister Carrie*, for example, give realistic pictures of Chicago and New York in the 1890's; his digression into the steps involved in shirt manufacturing in *An American Tragedy* provides information about that industry in the early twentieth century. Moreover, Dreiser's minute descriptions of certain characters, from their broken shoes to their frayed cuffs, help the reader to feel compassion for these people in the unfortunate circumstances which are probably beyond their control.

At times, Dreiser does tend to tell about his characters instead of "showing" them through their own words and actions. Furthermore, he frequently interrupts his narrative to philosophize on human nature in general. While it may be annoying to some readers, this habit serves a purpose. Not only does it arouse empathy for fictional characters, it also reminds the reader that the problems of these characters are those of the entire human race. Dreiser compensates for any heaviness in his style by producing tightly knit plots that move chronologically. Furthermore, while his novels contain a few symbols, he does not overload his writing with them. In some ways, therefore, his works are easier to read than modern novels. They continue to have value, for they treat human dramas that have always existed and will always exist.

SISTER CARRIE

First published: 1900
Type of work: Novel

A young woman uses her relationships with men as stepping stones in her quest for material beauty.

Although Carrie Meeber, the protagonist of *Sister Carrie*, may seem somewhat shallow in her preoccupation with clothing and popular entertainment, she has been called a seeker of beauty. Carrie has grown up in an impoverished rural district, probably knowing only the essentials of life. To her, luxuries such as fashionable clothes, theaters, and elegant restaurants are beautiful things.

At first, Carrie plans to acquire material beauty through her own efforts, working in Chicago. She soon learns, however, that her lack of training and experience qualifies her only for factory work, which does not pay well. Following a bout of flu, Carrie loses her job in a shoe factory (sick leave did not exist in 1889) and cannot find another position. During one of her futile job searches, she chances to encounter Charles Drouet, a traveling salesman whom she had met on the train to Chicago. Since Carrie is rather passive and pliable by nature, Charles easily persuades her to postpone her job search, have dinner with him, and let him buy her some nice clothes. Before long, Carrie has moved into this man's cozy apartment, enjoying material comforts she has never known, without having to scrabble for work.

When Carrie meets George Hurstwood, the manager of a prosperous saloon, however, she realizes that this man is superior to her present lover. Not only is Hurstwood more intelligent, but also his clothes are finer in quality—a clear indication that he can provide her with a higher form of material beauty. Attracted to Carrie, Hurstwood plans an elopement to New York. In order to execute this plan, he needs a supply of ready cash—something he lacks, since most of his money is in investments. This situation leads to a scene that exhibits Dreiser's belief in one's ability to weigh moral issues rather than only acting on impulse.

Closing the saloon one night, Hurstwood notices that the lock on the safe is not fastened. Tempted, he reaches in, takes out ten thousand dollars in bills, puts them back, then takes them out again. Aware that theft is intrinsically wrong as well as tremendously damaging to his reputation, he knows that he should replace the cash. Yet he hesitates, fondling the green paper that represents accessible spending power. Then an act of fate occurs that ends his conflict: The safe suddenly snaps shut, and he does not know the combination. Hurstwood decides to take the money but to send back most of it, retaining only enough to settle himself and Carrie in their new environment.

Once in New York, however, Hurstwood's luck changes, as he cannot find steady employment. Carrie becomes a chorus girl, eventually acquiring speaking parts in comedy shows. While her salary is modest, it is sufficient to cover essentials, such as rent, coal, and groceries. Resenting what she interprets as Hurstwood's laziness, however, and still on her search for material beauty, she spends all of her earnings on her wardrobe, so that the couple rapidly fall into debt. Eventually, Carrie and Hurstwood separate, and the latter, now homeless, commits suicide by gas inhalation.

In *Sister Carrie*, Dreiser shows his faith in the ability to change, as opposed to remaining in the "trap" of one's origin or inborn personality. Although Hurstwood's life ends tragically, he had exhibited progress in his youth. Starting as a bartender with little money, he worked his way into increasingly better positions, finally becoming the well-paid manager of a fashionable saloon. Carrie also changes—she loses her emotional dependence on men. When she happens to meet Charles Drouet in New York, he asks her to dinner. In former days, Carrie would have followed along, flattered by his enduring interest in her. This time, however, she declines, using a theater engagement as an excuse. Subsequent invitations from Drouet are also refused.

Robert Ames, a friend of Carrie, sees in her even greater potential for change. Robert points out that there is more to life than the acquisition of material luxuries. Having seen Carrie in comedy shows, he believes that she is capable of acting in more serious drama—a form of beauty that can transform people's lives and might bring true happiness to the actress. This gives Carrie something to think about, but whether she will act on Robert's advice is questionable, for Carrie is more a dreamer than a doer. Her tendency to dream is symbolized by the rocking chair—a frequent image throughout the novel. It is Carrie's wont to rock for hours, singing and dreaming of a rosy future. Hurstwood also uses the rocker, but to dream of his past.

While the rocking chair is the novel's primary symbol, Dreiser uses another, which reflects his awareness of the gulf between economic classes. Each evening, a homeless man called the Captain stands on a corner in the wealthy theater district. Surrounded by other homeless men, he begs for money so that each man might rent a bed for the night. The Captain's station emphasizes the great divergence between classes within the same vicinity.

Sister Carrie ends with an image of Carrie in her rocker, dreaming of "such happiness as [she] may never feel." The word "may" suggests ambiguity as to Carrie's future. She may remain a perpetual dreamer, or she may take Robert's advice and seek a form of beauty which could bring her lasting satisfaction.

JENNIE GERHARDT

First published: 1911
Type of work: Novel

Jennie, an unwed mother, becomes the mistress of an affluent man, who eventually leaves her to marry a wealthy widow.

Dreiser's second novel *Jennie Gerhardt*, is often considered his most popular, having sold more than five thousand copies in its first six months. Not only does the author "show" his characters through their own dialogue (rather than relying on description and narration), he also injects a bit of realistic humor in the "baby talk" conversations between a toddler and her grandfather. Moreover, he presents a heroine whose sexual liaisons stem not from a longing for possessions but from a sense of family responsibility.

Since Jennie's father is an unemployed glassblower with six children, she helps out by doing the laundry of George Brander, a senator who resides at a fashionable hotel. Having taken a fancy to Jennie, Brander tells her that if ever she or her family are in need, he will help. Thus, when Jennie's brother gets into trouble with the law, Brander gives Jennie the ten dollars bail that her parents cannot afford. In her relief and gratitude, Jennie yields herself to him completely.

Shortly afterward, Brander dies of heart failure and Jennie learns that she is pregnant. Although she is mortified by her condition, Jennie's maternal instinct comes through. Her strength during the pregnancy comes largely from the supportiveness of Mrs. Gerhardt, whose behavior Dreiser probably modeled on that of his own mother throughout the pregnancy of his sister Mame.

When her daughter, Vesta, is six months old, Jennie meets Lester Kane, heir to his father's flourishing carriage business. Lester is quickly attracted to Jennie and asks her to become his mistress, promising financial support to her family. This proposal throws Jennie into a conflict. Although the attraction is mutual, she has determined not to "fall" again. Yet her family is always short of money. Finally, fate intervenes, helping her to make a decision. Gerhardt, who has since found work, seriously burns his hands in a factory accident, to the extent that he will no longer be able to use them in the glassblowing trade. Thus, the major portion of the family's meager income is gone; knowing their need, Jennie accepts Lester's offer, lying to her parents that they have been secretly married.

In *Jennie Gerhardt*, Dreiser broaches two topics which he did not discuss in *Sister Carrie*. One is the issue of birth control: Dreading the idea of bearing another illegitimate child, Jennie tells Lester at the outset that she does not want a baby. Lester, who does not particularly want children himself, promises to protect her from this unwanted event. Dreiser also explores the compatibility of mates and the ability of partners to satisfy each other's needs. Unquestionably, Jennie provides

Lester with a comfortable home: For his part, Lester comes to care for Vesta, taking a genuine interest in this child of another man.

In time, however, fate disrupts their simple yet contented life. While traveling abroad with Jennie, Lester happens to encounter Letty Pace, a former girlfriend, now a rich widow. In his reunion with Letty, who comes from his own privileged background, Lester realizes how much he has missed high society, with its cultural interests and intellectual repartee. Since his father has already threatened to cut him from his will if he continues living with Jennie (promising only a pittance if he marries her), Lester begins thinking. Letty can obviously provide more social and intellectual stimulation than Jennie. Therefore, it might be financially and socially advantageous to leave his mistress and marry a woman of his own kind.

Lester's supposedly ideal marriage, however, does not bring him complete happiness, for despite her intelligence and social grace, Letty cannot offer Jennie's warm companionship—a situation suggesting that no one can entirely fulfill the needs of another. Ironically, it is Jennie who comes to Lester at the time of his sudden death, Letty being on a cruise and arriving home only in time for the funeral.

As in *Sister Carrie*, Dreiser's closing passage is somewhat ambiguous. After Vesta's death from typhoid, Jennie has adopted two orphans who "would marry and leave after a while, and then what? Days and days in endless reiteration, and then—?" Depending on the view of the reader, this conclusion can imply endless futility for Jennie, or, in time, the advent of a whole new life—something, perhaps, of which she has not yet dreamed.

AN AMERICAN TRAGEDY

First published: 1925
Type of work: Novel

Infatuated with a wealthy girl, Clyde Griffiths drowns his working-class lover, the mother of his unborn child—a crime which results in his execution.

An American Tragedy, Dreiser's longest novel, has often been hailed as his masterpiece. It is divided into three books, the first of which foreshadows the events of the second, while the third describes Clyde's trial. The protagonist is Clyde Griffiths, the son of street preachers who live in dire poverty. Thus, Clyde grows up longing for material things he can never attain except through his own efforts.

After a series of dead-end jobs, Clyde ventures to Lycurgus, New York, hoping for a place in his uncle's prosperous shirt factory. Before long, he becomes supervisor of the stamping room, where he meets Roberta Alden, a hardworking, pretty, vivacious young woman whose attraction to him matches his interest in her. After a few months of casual dating, the two become lovers and Roberta gets pregnant. In the meantime, however, Clyde has met Sondra Finchley, a girl of wealth and social prestige, whose way of life represents everything he has ever dreamed of. Infatuated with Sondra, but being pressured toward marriage by Roberta (who cannot obtain an abortion), Clyde feels himself in a trap. As in Dreiser's previous novels, however, two incidents of fate influence his actions.

The first is a news report of a drowning, in which the woman's body was found, but not the man's. Shortly after reading this, Clyde discovers a chain of isolated lakes north of the resort where the Finchleys have their summer home. It occurs to him that since Roberta cannot swim, an "accidental" drowning might be the way out of his predicament. Telling Roberta he will marry her, he plans a pre-wedding jaunt on one of these lonely lakes, choosing a boat that will easily overturn. When Roberta tries to draw closer to Clyde in the boat, he pushes her back, causing her to lose her balance and fall into the water. At this moment, Clyde experiences a fleeting change of heart. Reaching over to rescue Roberta, however, he upsets the boat, which hits her on the head, knocking her unconscious. Although Clyde might still have pulled Roberta from the water, a "voice" inside him says that fate has acted in his favor. Therefore, he lets her sink and heads back to Sondra.

When compared with *Sister Carrie* and *Jennie Gerhardt*, *An American Tragedy* seems closest to the spirit of naturalism, for Clyde appears to have no conscience. Dreiser foreshadows Clyde's indifference to murder in book 1. Clyde and some other youths are involved in an automobile accident which kills a child. No one, including Clyde, seems to care about the child. Their only concern is to get the car out of sight and then hide from the police, like hunted animals. Dreiser also refers several times to Clyde's "thin, sensitive hands," a symbolic reminder of his innate weakness that makes him run from a crisis. Finally, the author foreshadows Clyde's tendency to place his own needs over those of others. When his unwed sister Esta becomes pregnant, Mrs. Griffiths asks him for some money toward the "confinement." Although Clyde has fifty dollars in his pocket, he contributes a mere five, keeping the rest to buy his girlfriend a coat in return for her sexual favors.

In *An American Tragedy*, Dreiser strongly implies his own attitude toward religion. Before she can sleep with Clyde, Roberta must overcome the scruples of her church, which say that she will be a "bad girl" if she yields. Through Roberta's moral struggle, Dreiser suggests that the ethical teachings of organized religion are not in accord with the drives of human nature. Furthermore, he implies that religion is ineffective in bringing about desired results. In prison, some of the men condemned to die chant the prayers of their faiths, hoping for a favor from God; they still end up in the electric chair. Clyde's mother, who prays for her son's acquittal and tries to raise money for a second trial, fails in her efforts, and Clyde dies, doubtful of God's existence and peace in the hereafter.

Nevertheless, Dreiser suggests that for some, religion is a source of strength. Clyde's mother is an example, as is the Reverend Mr. McMillan, who visits Clyde in prison. Although Clyde cannot fully believe what McMillan tells him about making peace with God, he is drawn to the man's personal magnetism. McMillan's magnetism may derive, in part, from his deep religious faith.

The title of the novel is significant. Besides the youthful deaths of Roberta and

Clyde, it is a tragedy that no one can really understand the yearnings of another's heart. Clyde confesses to McMillan the true motive behind his crime: the material deprivation that drove him to an obsession with Sondra and her glittering world. McMillan, who has never experienced such strong longing for wealth, cannot understand, and he is unable to offer the court this evidence in Clyde's favor. Clyde's obsession with wealth also leads him to forfeit his chance for a warm and companionable marriage with Roberta. His matrimonial tragedy is particularly "American," for during the 1920's, the country was still recovering economically from World War I, and many saw wealth as their highest goal, sacrificing other joys.

The conclusion to this novel, like those of the others, is open to interpretation. *An American Tragedy* ends the way it begins, with the Griffiths preaching on a street corner. Now, however, they are accompanied by Esta's son, Russell, and two converts. In one sense, it looks as if everything is hopelessly the same. On the other hand, there is a glimmer of hope in Mrs. Griffiths' reflections concerning Russell. Before returning to the mission, Russell asks for money to buy an ice-cream cone. As he runs to the vendor, Mrs. Griffiths tells herself, "she must be kind to him, more liberal with him, not restrain him too much, as maybe, maybe, she had. . . . 'For *his* sake.' " It is possible, then, that she has learned something from her son's ordeal and that Russell's fate will not be a repetition of his Uncle Clyde's.

Summary

In all of his works, Dreiser portrayed society realistically. His observations of life taught him that human destiny is often affected by accidents of fate and by deep human yearnings or drives—particularly the drives toward money and sex. Yet Dreiser never felt that people are totally at the mercy of these forces, with no will of their own, even though individuals who are emotionally strong by nature seem more successful in coping with fate and drives than those who are passive or weak. Dreiser treated all of his characters with sympathy, however, proving himself to be a man of compassion.

Bibliography

Dreiser, Vera. *My Uncle Theodore*. New York: Nash, 1976.

Hakutani, Yoshinobu. *Young Dreiser: A Critical Study*. London: Associated University Presses, 1980.

Kazin, Alfred, and Charles Shapiro, eds. *The Stature of Theodore Dreiser: A Critical Survey of the Man and His Work*. Bloomington: Indiana University Press, 1955.

Kennell, Ruth E. *Theodore Dreiser and the Soviet Union, 1927-1945: A First-Hand Chronicle*. New York: International, 1969.

Pizer, Donald. *The Novels of Theodore Dreiser: A Critical Study*. Minneapolis: University of Minnesota Press, 1976.

Rebecca Stingley Hinton

PAUL LAURENCE DUNBAR

Born: Dayton, Ohio
June 27, 1872
Died: Dayton, Ohio
February 9, 1906

Principal Literary Achievement

At one time one of America's best-loved poets, Dunbar was the first African-American poet to gain a national and international reputation.

Biography

Paul Laurence Dunbar was born in Dayton, Ohio, on June 27, 1872, the son of Joshua and Matilda Glass Burton Murphy Dunbar, former slaves from Kentucky. Matilda Dunbar had two sons, William and Robert Murphy, by a previous marriage to R. Weeks Murphy prior to the emancipation; Paul Laurence Dunbar, born shortly after Matilda Murphy's marriage to Joshua Dunbar, was the only child of that union.

Dunbar's parents were divorced when he was still a small boy, and his father died when Dunbar was twelve. After her two older sons left home, Matilda Dunbar focused all of her attention on young Paul. Not only did she teach him to read, but she also exposed him to a number of literary works. More important, both mother and father passed on a number of stories from slavery days. These stories triggered a strong interest and imagination in Dunbar and became the basis for his most popular and enduring works.

Dunbar's interest in writing dated back to his high school days at Dayton's Central High School. Although he was the only black in his class, he was immensely popular. Dunbar's first published poem appeared when he was about sixteen years old, and as he continued publishing, he also became editor of the high school newspaper, class poet, class president, and president of the literary society. In addition, Dunbar founded the short-lived *Dayton Tattler*, a newspaper which reported news of Dayton's black community.

Because of a lack of funds, Dunbar was not able to attend college upon his graduation from high school in 1891; instead, he accepted a job as an elevator operator in the Callahan Building in downtown Dayton. This was one of very few reasonably respectable jobs open to blacks at the time. For his services, Dunbar earned only

four dollars per week, but the job gave him plenty of time to read and write poetry and to write articles that he published in various newspapers. In addition, Dunbar wrote several short stories during this early period.

Shortly before Dunbar's twentieth birthday, he got the break that brought him to the attention of the literary establishment and launched his career as the United States' foremost black poet. At the invitation of Helen Truesdale, Dunbar's former English teacher, he gave the welcoming address for the Western Association of Writers, then meeting in Dayton. The members were so impressed by Dunbar's eloquence and talent that he was asked to become a member of the association and was much praised by writers James Newton Matthews and James Whitcomb Riley. Later in 1892, Dunbar's friend and high school classmate, Orville Wright, encouraged him to publish a collection of his poems. *Oak and Ivy*, a collection of more than fifty poems, appeared early in 1893, published by Dayton's United Brethren Publishing House. The volume contained Dunbar's early dialect poems and sold reasonably well. To further his career and widen his audience, Dunbar began giving poetry readings throughout Ohio and later moved to Chicago, where he met a number of other important blacks, including Frederick Douglass, who had gathered for the occasion of the 1893 World's Columbian Exposition.

Upon returning to Dayton, Dunbar resumed his job as elevator operator and continued writing poems, a number of which appeared in his second volume, *Majors and Minors*, in 1895, along with several previously published poems. *Majors and Minors* received a glowing review from the novelist and influential critic William Dean Howells, which guaranteed his acceptance among the literary establishment of the United States. Later that year, Dunbar signed a contract with Dodd, Mead to publish *Lyrics of a Lowly Life* (1896), a collection of more than a hundred poems, most of which had appeared in *Oak and Ivy* and *Majors and Minors*, with an introduction by William Dean Howells. This became Dunbar's most successful book.

In 1897, Dunbar toured England, where he gave a number of successful readings. Upon his return to the United States, he began a clerkship at the Library of Congress in Washington, D.C., which lasted for a year and a half. During this time, he did a considerable amount of writing, publishing, among other things, two short story collections and a partly autobiographical novel, *The Uncalled* (1898).

In 1898, Dunbar married Alice Ruth Moore, a New Orleans poet and short story writer, with whom he had corresponded since 1895. The marriage was ill-fated because Moore's family was opposed to Dunbar's dark skin; after a frequently stormy marriage, the couple separated in 1902.

Beginning in 1898, Dunbar's health began to deteriorate rapidly. By 1899, he was suffering from tuberculosis and pneumonia and was near death. On the advice of doctors, he moved to Colorado, where he regained some of his strength and resumed his writing career. In 1900, Dunbar returned to Washington and continued to write short stories and novels in rapid succession: The Love of Landry (1900); *The Fanatics* (1901); and the best of his novels, *The Sport of the Gods* (1902).

Becoming increasingly ill and suffering from bouts of drinking and depression,

Dunbar left Washington for New York in 1902. From New York he traveled to Chicago, where, failing to achieve a reunion with his wife, he suffered a nervous breakdown. This was Dunbar's final period of decline, yet he continued to write and publish. In 1903, he return to Dayton, where he saw the publication of two more volumes of short fiction and one book of poetry. His health continued to worsen, and he died at his home on February 9, 1906.

Analysis

Paul Laurence Dunbar's poetry can be divided into two distinct classes: those poems written in Negro dialect and those written in standard English. The former, Dunbar wrote to gain an audience because of their popular appeal; in the latter, he expressed himself more as he believed a poet should. It is clear that Dunbar himself preferred the poems in standard English to the dialect poems, as seen in "The Poet" (1903): "But ah, the world, it turned to praise/ A jingle in a broken tongue." The praise for the dialect poems, often at the expense of those written in standard English, caused him considerable concern throughout his career.

In the dialect poems, Dunbar presents scenes from plantation life, mostly in the light, humorous, and lively manner of the plantation tradition popularized by white writers Joel Chandler Harris and Thomas Nelson Page. His characters are simple, good-natured, big-hearted folk who always speak in a dialect that Dunbar created. There is little overt protest in these poems, but often protest is subtly masked with the dialect.

Dunbar transforms the technique of masking into the theme of the mask in certain of his standard English poems, of which "We Wear the Mask" is the most obvious example. In addition, Dunbar eloquently addresses a variety of subjects, from love and death to nature and religion. The poems written in standard English are often lyrical and reflect a keen sensitivity on the part of the poet. Furthermore, these poems represent experiments with a number of different poetic forms as well as a mastery of rhyme and meter.

Similarly, Dunbar's short stories can be divided into two distinct types. First, there are the simple, lighthearted tales told in the plantation tradition—stories of a simple folk and their pleasures, pains, and sorrows. Then there are those stories written in a weak vein of protest but designed, nevertheless, to uphold the humanity of the black man. Regardless of type, however, the stories are structurally weak, and the characterization rarely transcends stereotype.

Dunbar's novels were largely unsuccessful. Three of them concern white characters: *The Uncalled*, *The Love of Landry*, and *The Fanatics*. The last novel, *The Sport of the Gods*, has black characters who are central to the story, but the plot is overly contrived and, while the characters are somewhat more complex, they are still largely stereotypes and thus fall short of creditable portrayals.

Regardless of genre, the one characteristic that stands out in all of Dunbar's writing is his sincerity, his deep regard for subject and craft. This, coupled with often delightful poems and stories, helped Dunbar achieve a high degree of popular success.

WHEN MALINDY SINGS

First published: 1895
Type of work: Poem

In old plantation days, one slave praises the singing talents of another slave, Malindy.

"When Malindy Sings" appeared in Dunbar's second collection of poems, *Majors and Minors*. Because it is a dialect piece, Dunbar placed it in the latter half of the collection, subtitled "Minors." Ironically, "When Malindy Sings" quickly became one of Dunbar's most popular poems and has since become perhaps his most anthologized dialect poem.

"When Malindy Sings" celebrates the black man's gift of song and was inspired by Dunbar's mother's constant singing of hymns and Negro spirituals. In particular, Dunbar cites the powerful melody and unmatchable phrasings as particular natural gifts of black singers.

The narrator, himself apparently a house servant, admonishes all to keep quiet as Malindy, probably a field slave, sings various songs of religious import. Miss Lucy, perhaps the plantation mistress, is told that her trained singing from a written score is no competition for Malindy's natural talent; indeed, the birds, though they sing sweetly, hush of their own accord when Malindy sings her superior melodies. Whenever Malindy sings, the narrator observes, it is a singular spiritual experience, one that should be taken advantage of every time.

In this early poem, Dunbar's gifts as a poet are evident: the meter and rhyme are regular, as are the quatrains that make up the poem. Furthermore, Dunbar is quite adept at creating images and imparting feeling through his use of sensory detail, talents he would continue to employ and capitalize upon in succeeding works.

WE WEAR THE MASK

First published: 1896
Type of work: Poem

Dunbar emphasizes the necessity for a black person to mask pain and suffering with a happy face.

"We Wear the Mask" is an often-anthologized poem that shows Dunbar at his best in his standard English poems. In this fifteen-line poem, he points specifically to the immense suffering of the black man and the necessity of painting on a happy face as a survival tactic. In so doing, Dunbar challenges the plantation tradition, of which he had become a well-known participant. In short, he emphasizes that slaves, while they may have appeared happy and docile, were in reality paradigms of suffering and strength. This could have applied as well to the suffering that Dunbar no doubt observed during his own lifetime, certainly one of the harshest periods in history for blacks in the United States.

Technically, the poem shows Dunbar as a mature and expert craftsman. It is written for the most part in strict iambic tetrameter lines with a repetitive rhyme pattern, but Dunbar interrupts this regular rhythm in the last lines of the second and third stanzas to deliver the jolting sobering statement, "We wear the mask." "We Wear the Mask" is perhaps the finest example of Dunbar's employment of masking as a theme. He would continue to use masking as both theme and technique throughout his writing career.

THE LYNCHING OF JUBE BENSON

First published: 1904
Type of work: Short story

Dr. Melville, a white doctor, expresses remorse over participating in the lynching of his black friend, Jube Benson, wrongly accused of raping Melville's fiancée.

"The Lynching of Jube Benson" appeared in one of Dunbar's last collections of short stories, *The Heart of Happy Hollow* (1904). The story, like many of his others, is set in the post-emancipation South and is written to uphold the humanity of the black man. As such, "The Lynching of Jube Benson" is perhaps his strongest piece of protest fiction.

In the library of a southern gentleman named Gordon Fairfax, Dr. Mclville, a relatively young medical doctor, and Handon Gay, a young newspaper reporter, are discussing various issues of the day, one of which is lynching. Gay expresses the desire to see one; Fairfax does not necessarily want to see one but would not avoid one if such an opportunity arose; Dr. Melville adamantly insists that he would avoid one, because, he relates to his companions, he had seen and taken part in one some seven years earlier, the lynching of Jube Benson.

At the time of the lynching, Dr. Melville was recently out of medical college and had moved to Brandon to open a medical practice among the white and black residents. Soon after his arrival, he began to fix his attentions on the young, pretty Annie Daly, daughter of a prosperous townsman from whom he rented office space. During this time, Dr. Melville also met Jube Benson, the black man who worked for the Dalys and who was fiercely devoted to young Annie.

Jube Benson became Dr. Melville's ally in his quest for the attentions of Annie Daly, to the point that he discouraged all other suitors. Also, during an outbreak of typhoid fever, which Dr. Melville contracts after treating most of the townspeople, Jube Benson serves as devoted nursemaid to the doctor.

One afternoon of the following summer, Dr. Melville returned to his house from a visit in a neighboring village to find Annie Daly beaten, raped, and near death. Dr. Melville fought to save her, but she died, but not before identifying her attacker as "That black——." Since Jube Benson was nowhere to be found, it was immediately assumed that he was the perpetrator of this vicious crime. A lynch mob formed immediately to find and punish Jube Benson.

Jube, who in reality had been to visit his own girlfriend, Lucy, was soon found, confronted with Annie's corpse, and immediately hanged despite his excuses and earnest pleas. Dr. Melville was the first to pull the rope.

No sooner had Jube's body swung from the tree limb than his brother, Ben Benson, arrived, dragging with him the real culprit, Tom Skinner, "The worst white ruffian in town," who had blackened his face with soot. Dr. Melville's efforts to revive Jube Benson were unsuccessful, and he felt all the more guilty when he reexamined Annie Daly and found the skin of a white man beneath her fingernails. He thus feels the burden of guilt because he helped murder an innocent man and a faithful friend. Seven years later, he still suffers from the guilt as he tells his companions, "Gentlemen, that was my last lynching."

The story is fast paced and is written with sharp, crisp prose that emphasizes the action. While Dunbar's characters fail to rise beyond stereotypes, in this story they are successful in communicating Dunbar's purpose, that of articulating his abhorrence of lynching.

Summary

Paul Laurence Dunbar strived to address real concerns about the lives of black people throughout his relatively short career. In his poetry, short stories, novels, and song lyrics, he was often caught between becoming an artistic or a popular success, yet Dunbar rarely compromised his sincerity in treating his subject matter or his craft. This fact has earned for him an enduring place in American literature.

Bibliography

Fox, Allan B. "Behind the Mask: Paul Laurence Dunbar's Poetry in Literary English." *Texas Quarterly* 14 (Summer, 1971): 7-19.

Laryea, Doris. "Paul Laurence Dunbar." In *Dictionary of Literary Biography.* Vol. 50, edited by Trudier Harris. Detroit: Gale Research, 1986.

Martin, Jay, ed. *A Singer in the Dawn: Reinterpretations of Paul Laurence Dunbar.* New York: Dodd, Mead, 1975.

Revell, Peter. *Paul Laurence Dunbar.* Boston: Twayne, 1979.

Turner, Darwin T. "Paul Laurence Dunbar: The Rejected Symbol." *Journal of Negro History* 52 (January, 1967): 1-13.

Warren J. Carson

ROBERT DUNCAN

Born: Oakland, California
January 7, 1919
Died: San Francisco, California
February 3, 1988

Principal Literary Achievement

Duncan is widely recognized as one of the most original voices of the twentieth century, and no modern American poet took his poetic office as seriously or made greater claims for the imagination's ability to create reality through language.

Biography

Robert Duncan was born in Oakland, California, on January 7, 1919, to Marguerite Wesley and Edward Howard Duncan. His mother died immediately following his birth as a result of an influenza epidemic. His father, a day laborer, was unable both to support and care for the child. Therefore, as an infant, Robert was put up for adoption and subsequently adopted by a family named Symmes. Mr. Symmes was a prominent architect who had offices in both Alameda and Bakersfield, California, where Robert spent his early childhood and adolescence.

The Symmes family was deeply involved in various forms of theosophy (a religious movement influenced by Buddhism). His adoptive mother's sister would frequently interpret children's stories, fairy tales, and myths with Gnostic and esoteric explanations to show young Robert the secret, deeper meanings of these seemingly harmless narratives. Duncan's grandmother had been an elder in a Hermetic religious order similar to Irish poet William Butler Yeats's Order of the Golden Dawn. These early childhood experiences remained with Duncan throughout his life and caused him to interpret practically all seemingly normal daily events as allegories corresponding to larger cosmic orders. Gnostic, hermetic, and alchemical lore continuously informed his imagination and became the groundwork for all of his major poetry. As Yeats's imagination found its sustenance in Celtic folklore and mythology, Duncan's spiritual core also found its center in his early apprehensions of his life as a spiritual enactment of mysterious powers he could only dimly perceive.

A sympathetic high school English teacher, Miss Edna Keough, spotted his obvious sensitivity to the beauty and seriousness of poetry; she helped him to envision it, as Duncan explained, "not as a cultural commodity or an exercise to improve

589

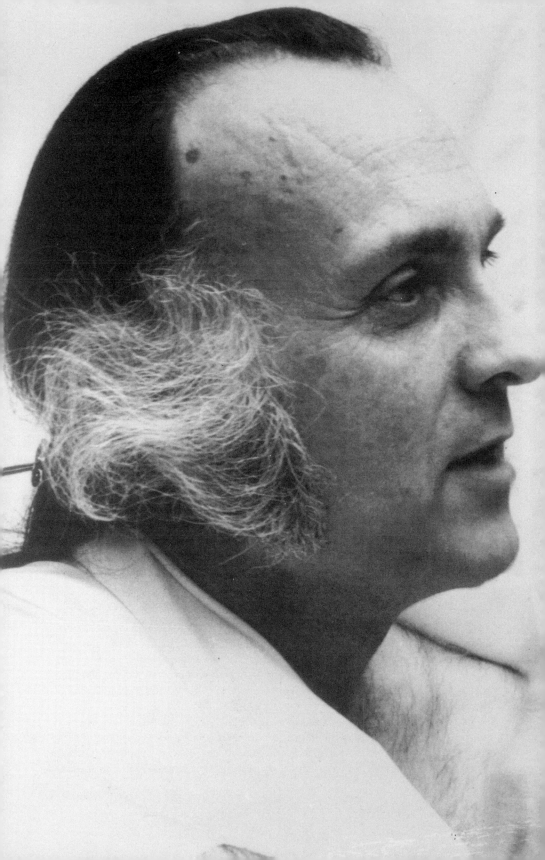

sensibility, but as a vital process of the spirit." She also introduced him to the dramatic monologues of Robert Browning, such as "My Last Duchess" and "The Bishop Orders His Tomb at St. Praxed's." Many of Duncan's early poems resemble in both form and tone those sophisticated works of Browning, poems that historians of English literature have called the first modern poems in the language. Ezra Pound, another spiritual mentor of Duncan during his college years, had also been heavily influenced by Robert Browning's ability to entertain multiple voices in his dramatic monologues, poetic devices that both he and Duncan practiced throughout their careers. Miss Keough also introduced the young Duncan to the work of a woman whose poetry became as vital to his own as that of Pound—Hilda Doolittle, or "H. D."

By the time he was graduated from Bakersfield High School, he had accepted his vocation as a poet and conducted himself accordingly as he began his college career at the University of California at Berkeley. He spent the years 1936 to 1938 there, where he published his first poems in a literary journal called *Occident*. He also lived an openly homosexual life-style and left California to follow his first lover to New York. In Manhattan he became involved with a group of young writers that included Anaïs Nin, Henry Miller, Kenneth Patchen, and George Barker, all of whom were considered avant-garde outsiders of modern literature at the time. He also helped edit and publish the famous *Experimental Review* with Sanders Russell in Woodstock, New York. His marriage to Marjorie McKee lasted only a short time. He and his fellow writers were influenced by the quirky genius of both the French artist, poet, and filmmaker Jean Cocteau and the English poet Edith Sitwell. In 1944, Duncan published an essay in Dwight Macdonald's journal, *Politics*, entitled "The Homosexual in Society," an essay which was simultaneously an admission of his own homosexual orientation and an argument for more humane treatment of homosexuals in general. After a storm of protests over such sexual honesty, Duncan returned to Berkeley in 1945 to resume his studies.

At Berkeley, he met and became part of a group of writers associated with the poet Kenneth Rexroth, who was highly critical of the literary establishment of the universities. At about the same time, Duncan also came under the intellectual tutelage of the great medieval and Renaissance historian Ernst Kantorowicz, an association so profound that much of Duncan's work from the Berkeley years onward reverberated with medieval and Renaissance themes and allusions. One of his first publications was called *Medieval Scenes* (1950), which attempted to evoke spiritually, via the creative process, "the eternal ones of the poem" in re-creating a specifically medieval mode or scene. Kantorowicz's brilliant lectures turned Duncan's attentions to medieval and Renaissance alchemy, which added considerable historical and philosophical depth to his earlier interests in Gnosticism and Hermeticism. It was also at this time that Duncan met and fell in love with a young art student named Jess Collins, with whom he spent the remainder of his life. Much of Duncan's later poetry frequently alludes to the joyfully fulfilling domestic scenes of the household that he and Jess created for themselves over a thirty-seven-year period.

Having gained a small but important poetic reputation, he was invited to teach at

Black Mountain College in North Carolina in 1956 by its rector, Charles Olson, himself a burgeoning poet and literary theorist. He subsequently returned to San Francisco and participated in the literary ferment which Allen Ginsberg and Jack Kerouac were creating as spokesmen for the Beat movement. Duncan became, over the years, the only writer whose concerns were broad enough for him to be considered a part of the Beat poets, the Black Mountain poets, and the poets of the San Francisco Renaissance.

Duncan published more than twenty-six volumes of poetry and numerous limited publications from small presses during his lifetime. His literary reputation with the larger reading public began with *The Opening of the Field* (1960), an especially auspicious first work since it contained a number of poems that are included in virtually all important anthologies of American literature. Duncan began a series of open-ended prose-poem commentaries on poetics called "The Structure of Rime" that he weaves throughout the other poetic texts in *The Opening of the Field*. This series continued without closure until his death in 1988. His next critically acclaimed volume of poetry was *Roots and Branches* (1964), which added not only eight more installments of "The Structure of Rime" but also several notable long poems, including "Apprehensions" and "The Continent," and a closet drama on theosophical themes called "Adam's Way." Both these earlier volumes show Duncan's poetic technique and range to be spectacularly accomplished and absolutely individual. *Bending the Bow* (1968) demonstrated Duncan's ability to articulate his rage against the Vietnam War while at the same time deepening and delineating the multiple themes of "The Structure of Rime." He also initiated a new open-ended series of poems called "Passages." After a self-imposed rule to publish no major volume for fifteen years, he produced the great works of his later years, *Ground Work I: Before the War* (1984) and *Ground Work II: In the Dark* (1987).

There is little doubt that Robert Duncan has taken his place as one of the major poets of modern American literature and that his complex but spiritually sustaining poetry will continue to inspire and nourish readers who view poetry as a serious spiritual enterprise rather than as the highly polished artifacts that fill up most poetry journals.

Analysis

The key to understanding the complex poetry and poetics of Robert Duncan can be found in his attitude toward his role as a poet, which for him was identical with his humanity. The primary task of both the poet and the man can be seen most clearly in Duncan's definition of the word "responsibility." Instead of giving the reader the standard dictionary definition of the word, he breaks it down etymologically—that is, into its most original and, therefore, obvious parts: "response-ability; or, keeping the ability to respond." His role or function is to respond to any and all movement or activity of the spirit: emotions, feelings (however small they may appear), hunches, impulses, daydreams, memories, echoes, verbal puns, and linguistic reverberations and resonances. Duncan's consciousness includes experiences of any kind because everything is eventual grist for his comprehensively Romantic imagination. He is, in short, open to all influences, and it is no accident that his first major volume of poetry was entitled *The Opening of the Field*.

No other American poet of this century takes his vocation as a poet as seriously as did Duncan. He viewed it as a literal "calling" to serve the imagination much in the mode of the medieval knight pledging his love and obedience to his Lady. For Duncan, "the Lady," the feminine creative element in a Jungian sense, the White Goddess as creator and destroyer that poet Robert Graves studied for years, is one of many embodiments of the imagination that Duncan locates himself within and speaks from each time he writes. The principal vehicle through which he activates his participation in this archetypal source is language itself. Language is the key in two ways. He speaks it and it speaks through him as poet; it is the order within which he experiences consciousness, both individual and universal, and also the agency through which he makes contact with his own and the collective unconscious. All of his major books of poetry can be understood as attempts to deepen and refine his commitment to his poetic office as embodied in language.

Because Duncan was reared in a family that believed in the basic fundamentals of theosophy—that spiritual worlds do exist and influence everyone's lives—he sees his poetic office as thaumaturgic or magic. A thaumaturge is a wonder worker, a caster of spells, a word that Duncan frequently puns with, reminding his reader that the present limited use of "spell"—a correct or incorrect spelling of a word—is a far cry from its older and much more important meaning as creating a condition of magic. As a verbal magician, he wishes to transport readers to spiritual orders or realms of which they are not conscious even though they are available if one possesses the right vision. Duncan's whole poetic project is to exhort his audience to attend to the source of reality as it is embodied in language, to pay attention to the dynamics of the linguistic structures in which everyone is involved on a daily basis. His spiritual orientations would suggest, for example, that Christianity drastically limited the scope of spiritual enquiry when it proposed Jesus Christ as the one and only designation for "the Word." Duncan would urge one, rather, to see that "the Word" is obviously about "words" and the unique structures they generate known as language.

One of Robert Duncan's spiritual sources over many years was his persistent study of certain Hebrew mystical texts such as the *Kabbalah* and the *Zohar*. One of his important early works, *Letters: Poems MCMLIII-MCMLVI* (1958) came out of a deep examination of the *Zohar*, a work in which ancient scholars searched the letters of the alphabet for their secret revelations. So Duncan's poems in *Letters* refer not to correspondence but rather to meditations and exercises on the letters of the alphabet, the most basic elements of language itself possessing their own creative powers that, with time and devoted concentration, can reveal mysteries of the cosmos. Since he trusted in the ability of language to reveal mystery, he went back to language's source, its individual letters, and examined how they are arranged and rearranged to "spell" out meaning. He found that the method used in the *Zohar* gave him "a new picture of language in which the letters of the Logos dance"; he quite consciously used the same method in *Letters*.

In 1966, Robert Duncan published a group of poems actually written between 1939 to 1946, calling it *The Years as Catches: First Poems (1939-1946)* (1966), and wrote an introduction in which he explained their influences and origins. He openly confessed that his etymological studies of words contribute heavily to the content of his poetry. The word "catch" contains various levels of interpretation, such as viewing his art as a "net of catches," fishing around hoping to "catch" something, and what "catches" him at work or "catches" his ear. His influences in the early poems are fairly obvious: John Milton, Ezra Pound, E.E. Cummings, Wallace Stevens, Gerard Manley Hopkins, and Laura Riding. More notable, however, is evidence that his imagination was and remained throughout his life very process oriented. The process of poem-making becomes a part of the subject matter of most of his major poems from these early works onward. The interplay generated between and among the various voices in the poem creates the tension that energizes the poem's movement; but instead of moving towards an orderly resolution or poetic product, the poems expand into multiple perspectives much in the manner of the *Cantos* of Ezra Pound (1917-1970).

The first volume of Duncan's poetry that drew national attention and critical acclaim was his *The Opening of the Field*, a book which many critics believe to be Duncan's finest single collection. It contains three poems that have been frequently anthologized and are viewed as typical Duncan poems: "Often I Am Permitted to Return to a Meadow," "The Dance," and "A Poem Beginning with a Line by Pindar." He also initiated, in the volume, a series of open-ended prose poems that constitute an ongoing discussion of the procedures of the poetic imagination and their relationship with the evolution of Duncan's interconnecting theories of rhyme and measure. The first thirteen of an eventual twenty-nine sections appear in this volume. The major themes that will be developed in all of his subsequent work are present in this volume.

The title of the work, *The Opening of the Field*, encapsulates the direction and scope of the collection. The individual poems are all interconnected by the possibilities of the activity of language when it is permitted to operate in an open field. The title and the organization of the work are direct responses to the kind of collection of individual poems that most poets had been producing during the era following World War II. These poems were highly crafted, closed systems, which the poet-critics involved in the so-called New Criticism were producing. Just as Allen Ginsberg's *Howl* (1956) opened up the possibility of an American poetry recalling and rekindling the open-form tradition of Walt Whitman, so Duncan's first major work exhorted American writers not to limit themselves to imitating conservative British models, but to permit expansion into American and continental European literary, artistic, and musical expressions. He also revealed his sources as coming out of a wisdom tradition of Gnosticism, Hermetic and alchemical texts, and theosophical lore. Indeed, the first poem in the collection, "Often I Am Permitted to Return to a

Meadow," presents virtually all the motifs that Duncan would develop during the remainder of his poetic career: origins, permission, fields and meadows, The Lady, dreams (the genesis of this poem was in a dream), boundaries, architecture, the Beloved, the Dance, and—most important—the poetic process itself.

Another project that *The Opening of the Field* initiates in its open organization is the possibility of an intertextual reading of many of its poems. One can read "A Poem Slow Beginning" as a gloss or comment on the first poem in the book, but "A Poem Slow Beginning" can also be read as a single poem with its own inner structure and thematic development. Both readings are valid; however, since this poem rests between the first two crucial "The Structure of Rime" sections and the next five, one can also view it as an example of what Duncan has been theorizing about in the first two and as a logical preparation of what he is about to discuss in the next five.

The next major volume that refines Duncan's highly complex poetic project of embodying the theme of process by enacting the dynamics of process itself is the highly romantic *Roots and Branches*, an obvious outgrowth of the poetic field of his previous book. Duncan concentrates on his poetic origins and inspirations, envisioning them as the "roots and branches" of the tree of language. Many of these branches go back to "branches" of study that helped formulate his mythopoeic imagination as a child, such as songs, fairy tales, myths, and the "old lore" that his spiritualist parents avidly studied. The language of this book is highly charged, almost baroque in its testings of the boundaries of expression. The long poem "Apprehensions" is not only one of his greatest poems but is also another example of how the poem's title simultaneously comments on and enacts the process of "apprehending" the cosmic event in the individual event.

Roots and Branches also includes, in keeping with Duncan's continuous return to origins, a number of blatant poetic imitations of his acknowledged literary masters. He writes sonnets based on Dante, poems imitating Percy Bysshe Shelley and the Latin poet Ovid, ballads that were obviously influenced by one of his contemporaries, Helen Adam, and a theosophical drama called "Adam's Way." In short, he wants to show his literary "roots" and their multiple "branchings" throughout his poetic career.

Duncan's next major collection is called *Bending the Bow*. The title continues the organic metaphor from the "field" in the first book to the "roots and branches" of his second to the "bow" carved from the wood of the tree of language into an instrument of war or into a bow across which stretch the strings of the lyre or harp which the ancient bards strummed as they declaimed their poetry. Duncan's attention moves from his preoccupation with origins to his rage over the American involvement in the Vietnam War. Much of the poetry of this volume consists of five additions to the series "The Structure of Rime" and of the beginning of what would eventually become his major poetic sequence, the "Passages" poems. The first thirty appear in *Bending the Bow* and interweave with both "The Structure of Rime" sequence and the other poems in the book.

Included in *Bending the Bow* is an introduction in which Duncan defines his idiosyncratic uses of some key terms such as "rime" and "measure" and explains his peculiar blending of political ideas and their relationship with his highly individual poetics. He defines what poetry is for him:

> The poem is not a stream of consciousness, but an area of composition in which I work with whatever comes into it. . . . So there is not only a melody of sounds but of images. Rimes, the reiterations of formations in the design, even puns, lead into complexities of the field. But now the poet works with a sense of parts fitting in relation to a design that is larger than the poems.

He then uses a scientific term "polysemous" (marked by a multiplicity of meaning) to further explain his unique understanding of form, while suggesting that Dante was the first consciously structuralist poet: "The artist, after Dante's poetics, works with all parts of the poem as *polysemous,* taking each thing of the composition as generative of meaning, a response to and a contribution to the building of form."

Duncan's two late works, *Ground Work I: Before the War* and *Ground Work II: In the Dark*, constitute a full flowering of all Duncan's poetic projects from his earliest work. In keeping with his relentless search for origins, he returns to the literal, organic source of the body and spirit, the ground of his being—earth itself. The work has come full circle from the "field" through the "roots and branches" to the leaves of his expression in the "bow" of his poetic lyre back to the earth. Walt Whitman's *Leaves of Grass* (1955) can always be read as a subtext in Duncan's work as both a metaphor for poetry and a reaffirmation of their mutual Romantic inheritance. Certain long poems, such as "The Santa Cruz Propositions," "The Dante Etudes," and the great hymn to homoerotic passion, "Circulations of the Song" from *Ground Work I: Before the War*, will undoubtedly become examples of how the late work of this great poet, though as dense as anything he ever produced, will reveal itself to those who view poetry as a vital activity of the spirit. The poetic sequence "The Regulators," in *Ground Work II: In the Dark*, is as sublime an attempt to synthesize the powers of nature and the imagination as its nineteenth century counterpart, Shelley's *Alastor: Or, The Spirit of Solitude* (1815).

THE STRUCTURE OF RIME

First published: 1960-1987
Type of work: Poetry

"The Structure of Rime" is interwoven throughout all the major poetic collections of Duncan's poems as a continuous discussion of his ever-changing poetic theory.

"The Structure of Rime" sections of his books were never gathered together in one specific volume, and Robert Duncan never wished them to be. Indeed, he wrote them as a series of ongoing prose-poem discussions of his poetics. The initial thirteen were interspersed throughout his first major collection, *The Opening of the Field*, the next seven were included in *Roots and Branches*, while five appeared in *Bending the Bow*. Three appeared in *Ground Work I*, with one final section in *Ground Work II*.

These highly complex open-form prose poems demonstrate Duncan's adherence to the poetry of open forms—that is, the more open the field of possibilities, the more inclusive it becomes. He also firmly believed in poet Robert Creeley's brilliantly comprehensive definition of both "form and content" when Creeley expanded upon poet Charles Olson's statement that "form is never more than an extension of content," a proposition that arguably closed the endlessly pedantic discussions over such obvious matters. These multiphasic works, along with many essays and the new formalistic ground broken with his "Passages" poems, both define and demonstrate Duncan's original ideas on what constitutes a long poem. Most major American poets from Whitman to the present had come to terms with the demands of the long poem: Ezra Pound in the *Cantos*, Robinson Jeffers in *The Women at Point Sur* (1927), Charles Olson in *The Maximus Poems* (1960), Harte Crane in *The Bridge* (1930), and many others. Duncan, however, produced not one but two major poetic sequences, which he interweaves throughout all of his work in a kind of DNA configuration. On several occasions, they actually become part of each other's process.

To further complicate the situation, Duncan himself has stated that neither "The Structure of Rime" nor "Passages" can be called "long poems": They are "large" poems. He questions the whole definition of what "long" means in regard to poetic form, explaining quite lucidly that his two works are "serial" works involved in the process of poem making. They are not a chronology or journey; their activity participates in neither a linear, circular, nor cyclic progression. They constitute exactly what Duncan proposed in his first book: a field, a large canvas or configuration that gathers meaning as it accumulates items. With the addition of each section, the area begins to radiate a kind of energy field, a field of memory which resonates correspondences which grow exponentially as it is added to. The field expands and enlarges as new combinations of patterns or motifs appear and these, in turn, begin to interconnect multiphasically.

In the first "The Structure of Rime," Duncan locates his primary task as a poet, "which is first a search in obedience" to language, a pledge that will, if he is steadfast, enable him to create himself out of words: "In the feet that measure the dance of my pages I hear cosmic intoxications of the man I will be." He further creates, in the next several sections, a mythological figure he calls the "Master of Rime," who engages him in a discussion of the nature of poetry and of time as destroyer, finally defining for Duncan the "Structure of Rime": "An absolute scale of resemblance and disresemblance establishes measures that are music in the actual world . . . the actual stars are music in the real world. This is the meaning of the music of the spheres." Duncan employs the first principle of alchemy throughout much of his poetry: "As above, so below," an orientation that enables him to view physical reality as an allegory of invisible worlds which only those possessing a spiritual vision can apprehend.

Throughout "The Structure of Rime" series in *The Opening of the Field*, he mythopoeically creates a world of his own and peoples it with figures from world mythology and theosophic lore: Adam and Eve; the garden with the cosmic ash tree, Yggdrasil, bleeding language from its branches; and the dance of the Heraclitean Fire whose "tongues" also speak. He then catalogs other figures, transforming their traditional roles into linguistic tasks; he transforms Chiron, the guide to Hades, into a syntactical grammarian. The natural cyclic movement of water from river to clouds to rain becomes a metaphor for the process of the activity of language. The poetic impulse becomes a fish in the sea of language, then a gopher and a snail struggling to create for themselves a home in the chaos of nature as archetypal memories erupt from beneath the earth and break the rocky surface. All these events remind the world of its origin, the sun, which subsequently became the source of man's first religions and his attempt to use language to express that ineffable relationship.

Since everything is perceived, named, and measured in language, it is evident that Duncan's use of the term "rime" refers to much more than similar sounds at the end of lines of poetry. Rather, "rime" designates any and all reiterations or repetitions that appear in these works and form a structure or pattern of some kind which, in short, humanizes the vast, unnameable void with language. Duncan can only experience his world if he can imagine it in terms of linguistic or musical orders, scales, or measures. His poetry contains its own measures, which are divided into rime and rhythm—both measurable and, therefore, knowable.

The remaining sections of "The Structure of Rime" further delineate their basic motifs throughout the rest of Duncan's work. "The Structure of Rime XIV" in *Roots and Branches*, however, appears as section 5 in a long poem called "Apprehensions," functioning as an active unit of both the single poem and a section of the series "The Structure of Rime." The combination works well, since "Apprehensions" concerns itself with memories of Duncan's childhood, especially the spiritualist influences of his parents. He also delves into the history of his grandfather's family and their migrations from the east to the northwest to the west, and how those patterns become a cave of remembrances and, therefore, a "cave of rimes!" Mythological figures from German folklore appear by way of composer Richard Wagner's *Parsifal* (1882) and its Grail quest as it moves through the poetry of French poet Paul Verlaine, resurfacing eventually in T. S. Eliot's *The Waste Land* (1922). True to Duncan's obsession with origins, he finds himself in the company of the originators of "sexual wound literature," Isis and Osiris. All the wounded figures in these legends could be cured if a questing hero, usually an innocent fool, speaks the loving and, therefore, "healing" words. The words must take the form of a question, and Duncan again locates the hidden and healing word "quest" within "question." The answer is in the "question" itself, since reality is always a matter of language continuously probing its sources for meaning.

PASSAGES

First published: 1968
Type of work: Poetry

The "Passages" poems are interwoven throughout Duncan's poetry after 1968 as interconnecting responses, but they can also be read within their own unique structure.

As in the case of "The Structure of Rime" series, Robert Duncan would not permit these poems to be collected into one volume. Indeed, he was so vehement about their nonsequential structure that he stopped numbering them after "Passages 37" so that readers would not be tempted to see any kind of evolving progressive structure. They share certain common functions with "The Structure of Rime" sections but are almost purely poetry, and they can be viewed as a poetic counterpart enacting the poetic process that "The Structure of Rime" sections probe and discuss. Looking at their mutual relationship also reveals a counterpoint, in a musical sense, that intermittently creates common measures and scales that Duncan would also consider a kind of "rime." One of the reasons for the expanding canvas of "Passages" is that Duncan no longer speaks through fictive voices and masks. It is his own highly musical, bardic voice speaking throughout; he has broken away from the kind of mythological personae that Ezra Pound and Charles Olson used throughout their long poems.

The first thirty "Passages" poems appeared in *Bending the Bow* in 1968 and immediately established Duncan as a master of long formal structures. The next ten were published in *Ground Work I: Before the War*, while the concluding thirteen are in *Ground Work II: In the Dark*. In all, fifty-three "Passages" poems appeared over a twenty-year period.

Part of the function of the first crucial "Passages" was a demonstration of Duncan's consistent habit within these works of talking about a topic while simultaneously activating that subject's archetypal reverberations and illustrating how a poem comes into being. "Passages 1" is entitled "Tribal Memories" and becomes, in effect, an invocation to the muse of memory, Mnemosyne, and a depiction of how she enters Duncan's afternoon nap with dreams of his individual poems, participating in the eternally recurring act of creation. In "Passages 2: At The Loom," Duncan further defines the poetic process in its relationship to his mind: "my mind a shuttle among/ set strings of the music/ lets a weft of dream grow in the day time,/ an increment of associations,/ luminous soft threads,/ the thrown glamor crossing and recrossing,/ the twisted sinews underlying the work." Not only has he continued the proposal of the preceding "Passages," he has also instructed the reader how to read his poems by comparing his imagination to the activity of a loom.

"Passages 3" interweaves Christ with his prototype, Osiris, archetypal twins that

Duncan uses throughout the collection. In the first thirty "Passages," old topics are reintroduced such as the Grail, alchemy, magic and puns on "spell," language, and homosexual dedication and passion, while new French masters, such as Victor Hugo and Jean Genet, appear. Throughout "Passages" 13-30, Duncan rails against the American involvement in Vietnam. In "Passages 21: The Multiversity," he bitterly condemns the military-industrial-university complex, identifying the Chancellor of the University of California, Clark Kerr, with William Blake's destructive "old Nobodaddy." Many of these poems are vehemently concerned with the political abuse of power by the rich and privileged, and Duncan explores in a deeply Freudian mode the connections between the etymological origins of "phallic" aggressiveness and the impulse toward "fascism" that the United States, to him, seemed to be demonstrating during those years in the 1960's. He boldly compares President Lyndon Johnson with both Adolf Hitler and repressive Soviet leader Josef Stalin.

In the later "Passages" that appeared in both *Ground Work* volumes, he moves away from the concerns of war and back to his search for origins. He moves comfortably from music and its source in utterance, vision, and dance, as subjects for the great "Tribunals Passages" to the more mundane concerns of "Passages 34: The Feast," which is obviously a recipe for cooking lamb. By changing the spelling of the word "EWE," he finds beneath it the name "EVE," transforming a seemingly casual dinner into a re-enactment of the Fall into consciousness and knowledge. The late "Passages" become extended meditations delving even more deeply into the "language beyond speech" and its ability to enter the pantheon of the spirits and the archetypal sea of words. Grief and ecstasy enter the work more intensely as his language brings him closer to the terror of the cosmological void in "Passages: Empedoklean Reveries": "There is a field of random energies from which we come." In the concluding "Passages" in *Ground Work II*, he finds himself a participant in the drama of wound literature in "In Blood's Domaine"; in his case, the wound is invisible. Indeed, because of complications from high blood pressure, Duncan died after several years of serious illness, ironically a "victim" of his own blood.

One of Duncan's last and most appropriate metaphors for his life was that of "a theme and variations," an early musical form from which all subsequent musical forms, such as the sonata and the symphony, emerged. In the final dark "Passages," he realizes that language does not come into the mind to be used by the poet. Rather, "Mind comes into this language as if into an Abyss." His two valedictory "Passages" are homages to vital sources of his imaginal and physical life: "The Muses" and his own circulatory system, with his heart at the center. His last "Passages" poem envisions the fluctuating dynamics of his entire creative mechanism, which he had earlier called the scales "of resemblance and disresemblance," and sees them still operating, but now with the "inflatus/deflatus" or the "blood/air pump" of his own weakening heart as it nourishes the "ex-change artist." He had found in the title of one of psychologist's James Hillman's books a perfect amalgamation of all his late themes as he embodied them and they embodied him: *The Thought of the Heart*.

Summary

There is little doubt that Robert Duncan's contributions to contemporary American poetry are unique; no other writer approaches the poetic office as an activity of the spirit with the intensity of Duncan's devotion. For him, poetry was as valid a way of exploring and knowing reality as chemistry or physics. His one consistent rule was that, though calling himself a traditionalist, he permitted the voices of his spiritual influences and ancestors to register their presences as long as he kept his poetic procedures open and trusted the changing structures of his primary source, language itself. He is unquestionably one of the major American Romantic poets since Walt Whitman.

Bibliography

Bertholf, Robert J. *Robert Duncan: A Descriptive Bibliography.* Santa Rosa, Calif.: Black Sparrow Press, 1986.

_____. "Robert Duncan: Blake's Contemporary Voice." In *William Blake and the Moderns,* edited by Robert J. Bertholf and Annette Levitt. Albany: State University of New York Press, 1982.

_____, ed. *Robert Duncan: Scales of the Marvelous.* New York: New Directions, 1979.

Cooley, Dennis. "Robert Duncan's Green Worlds." *Credences* 3 (March, 1980): 151-160.

Faas, Ekbert. *Young Robert Duncan: Portrait of the Poet as Homosexual in Society.* Santa Barbara, Calif.: Black Sparrow Press, 1983.

Johnson, Mark Andrew. *Robert Duncan.* Boston: Twayne, 1988. *Maps* 6 (1974). Special Duncan issue.

Nelson, Cary. "Between Openness and Loss: Form and Dissolution on Robert Duncan's Aesthetic." In *Our Last First Poets: Vision and History in Contemporary American Poetry.* Urbana: University of Illinois Press, 1981.

Paul, Sherman. "Robert Duncan." In *The Lost America of Love: Rereading Robert Creeley, Edward Dorn, and Robert Duncan.* Baton Rouge: Louisiana State University Press, 1981.

Weatherhead, A. Kingsley. "Robert Duncan and the Lyric." *Contemporary Literature* 16 (Spring, 1975): 163-174.

Patrick Meanor

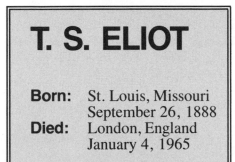

T. S. ELIOT

Born: St. Louis, Missouri
September 26, 1888
Died: London, England
January 4, 1965

Principal Literary Achievement

Critic, dramatist, and Nobel Laureate, Eliot was one of the foremost poets of the twentieth century; his startling originality heralded modernism and his poetic complexity continues to challenge readers.

Biography

Thomas Stearns Eliot was born in St. Louis, Missouri, on September 26, 1888, the son of Henry and Charlotte (Stearns) Eliot, whose ancestors were among the early settlers of seventeenth century Massachusetts. Eliot's grandfather, the Reverend William Greenleaf Eliot, left New England in 1834 to evangelize an outpost of civilization at St. Louis. There he founded the (first) Unitarian Church of the Messiah and Eliot Seminary which, under his leadership as chancellor (1870-1887), became Washington University. Eliot's early schooling at Smith Academy and his summers at coastal Rockport and Gloucester, Massachusetts, would inform the imagined landscapes of his subsequent poetry, as would his ancestral home in East Coker, Somerset, England. Eliot studied for a year at Milton Academy (Massachusetts) and then entered Harvard College, where he received the B.A. degree in 1909 and pursued a doctoral degree program from 1909 to 1914, in which he completed but did not defend a dissertation on F. H. Bradley's philosophy.

In 1910-1911, Eliot visited Germany and France and studied at the Sorbonne in Paris. In addition to his philosophical studies at Harvard, he explored several subjects, the Pali and Sanskrit languages among them. World War I halted his plans to study at Marburg, Germany, where he had received a fellowship stipend in 1914; instead, he transferred to the University of Oxford's Merton College. Two highly significant events followed: On September 22, 1914, he met the expatriate American poet Ezra Pound; on June 26, 1915, Eliot married Vivien Haigh-Wood. Pound, who observed that Eliot had already "trained himself *and* modernized himself *on his own*," was to become Eliot's lifelong friend and sometime editor, "the better craftsman" to whom Eliot dedicated *The Waste Land* (1922). Eliot's unhappy marriage was to last until Vivien's death in 1947, although Eliot wrote to her from America in

1933 announcing their official separation.

With his added fiscal responsibilities, Eliot left Oxford and embarked on a short-lived teaching career at High Wycombe Grammar School and Highgate School and as an extension lecturer for Oxford between 1915 and 1917. In March, 1917, he joined Lloyd's Bank, London, as a clerk in their Colonial and Foreign Department and, except for three months of sick leave in fall, 1921, remained there until 1925, when he became an editor with the publishing house of Faber and Gwynn (later, Faber and Faber). It has been suggested that his early career as a poet of somber things was directly influenced by his marriage, financial circumstances, and unchallenging work.

The period from 1916 to 1922 was marked by an extraordinary literary productivity. He regularly contributed essays and reviews to the *Athenaeum*, *The Dial*, *The Egoist*, *The Times Literary Supplement*, and other journals. Thanks to Pound's influence, his early poems, published in *Prufrock and Other Observations* (1917), *Poems* (1919), *Ara Vos Prec* (1920), and *The Waste Land* (1922), were published in British and American journals. This last poem reshaped the post-World War I literary world, made Eliot the obvious choice to be editor of the new journal *The Criterion* (1922-1939), and gained for him a lasting place among twentieth century poets.

A year after joining Faber and Gwynn, Eliot was Clark Lecturer at Trinity College, University of Cambridge, and a year later he underwent profound changes: In June, 1927, he joined the Church of England and within five months became a British subject. In his book *For Lancelot Andrews* (1928), he explained himself: "The general point of view may be described as classicist in literature, royalist in politics, and Anglo-Catholic in religion." Like most authorial statements, this may reflect more desire than achievement and may be less than accurate. It does, nevertheless, help account for an evolution in Eliot's poetic thought and concerns from "The Hollow Men" (1925) through *Four Quartets* (1943).

Eliot returned to the United States in 1932 and to his alma mater as Charles Eliot Norton Professor of Poetry at Harvard (1932-1933). While in America, he also obtained a legal separation from his wife. Before returning to England, he lectured at the University of Virginia on Christian apologetics, a topic that had already begun to suffuse his poetry and that was to inform much more of it, as well as his dramas. His work in the 1930's was largely given to spiritual topics such as those in the verse pageant plays, *The Rock: A Pageant Play* (1934) and *Murder in the Cathedral* (1935), and in the poems "Ash Wednesday" (1930) and the first of his *Four Quartets*, "Burnt Norton" (1939).

With "Burnt Norton" as a beginning, Eliot continued work on his *Four Quartets*, producing "East Coker" (1940), "The Dry Salvages" (1941), and "Little Gidding" (1942), and publishing them together in one volume in 1943. This was to be the last of his major poetic efforts; thereafter, he turned principally to prose and to writing verse dramas. The restoration of poetic drama to the stage was a project to which he had committed himself, as had Irish poet William Butler Yeats, in a conscious reaction to the vogue and influence of the realistic plays of Henrik Ibsen. In 1948, he was awarded both the British Order of Merit and the Nobel Prize in Literature.

More honors and distinctions were to follow in the 1950's and 1960's. He won the Hanseatic Goethe Prize (1954), the Dante Gold Medal (Florence, 1959), the Emerson-Thoreau Medal (American Academy of Arts and Sciences, 1959) and the U.S. Medal of Freedom (1964). He received honorary degrees from American, British, and other European colleges and universities. Another important change came to Eliot when he married Valerie Fletcher on January 10, 1957, a change decidedly for the better—it was a happy marriage. While he continued to write plays and essays, he wrote little poetry in the 1950's, *The Cultivation of Christmas Trees* (1954) standing as the sole volume of new poetry in this period.

Eliot died on January 4, 1965, survived by his wife, Valerie. A memorial to Eliot is in Poets' Corner, Westminster Abbey; his ashes are interred in the parish church of East Coker, Somerset, the church of his ancestors.

Analysis

Dante, Eliot once observed of the great Italian poet, his favorite writer, is "a poet to whom one grows up over a lifetime." So, too, is Eliot himself. Indeed, although he was a formidable, forceful, and original critic, a tireless advocate of Elizabethan and Jacobean drama, and a dramatist whose work endures, the one title he preferred was "poet." This is not to slight the other work but to emphasize the principal orientation and habit of mind from which his prose and drama sprang. He assessed his own critical work in "To Criticize the Critic," a lecture he presented at Leeds University in 1961, by distinguishing several categories of critics and placing himself among those whose criticism is a by-product of their creative activity.

Eliot's far-ranging critical work, like his poetry, dealt with artists and styles, writers and literature, that appealed to him and contained elements he would mine for his own poetic work. From the English religious and devotional work of the seventeenth century to the work of his contemporary, the classical scholar Gilbert Murray, from the French *Symboliste* poets of the nineteenth century to William Shakespeare, he interpreted literary production in ways that seemed original and fresh. His most notable critical concepts were the necessities of tradition, of impersonality in art, and of the poet's mind as a catalyst, as expressed in "Tradition and the Individual Talent" (1919), and of an objective correlative between ideas or emotions and the precise words to express them, which he discussed in "Hamlet" (1919).

Schooled in classical drama, a critic of Shakespeare (and of such dramatists as John Dryden as well as the Elizabethans and Jacobeans), and a poet who incorporated dramatic speech and situations into his poetry, Eliot came to write poetic drama only in the 1930's. His work includes the religious pageant plays *The Rock* and *Murder in the Cathedral*. The former is more static than dramatic, a choric piece that owes much to classical Greek drama. The latter is somewhat more dramatic, but it relies heavily on choric elements, a sermon, and a trial scene following the murder of the Archbishop of Canterbury. The sparsity of Eliot's stage directions allow for considerable latitude in handling elements of costume, set design, lighting, and stage "business" to heighten the drama of the play. While his later efforts, *The Family Reunion* (1939), *The Cocktail Party* (1949), *The Confidential Clerk* (1953), and *The Elder Statesman* (1958) enjoyed a brief vogue and are occasionally revived, *Murder in the Cathedral* remains his most popular play.

Eliot's poetry may be generally divided into three periods, the first beginning with his earliest efforts, the most famous of which is "The Love Song of J. Alfred Prufrock" (1915). "Gerontion" (1919) marks the inception of the second period, with *The Waste Land* as its apex and "The Hollow Men" as its terminus; it is also the terminus of what has been called his poetry of secular humanism. "Ash Wednesday" opens the final phase of his poetic practice, which may be characterized as one of Christian humanism. As with any attempt at poetic classification, this is a descriptive one that must be applied flexibly.

Eliot's early poetry, although steeped in tradition, was startlingly new and individual; his later poetry, similarly heavily informed by tradition, continued his own tradition of innovation. In a literary career that spanned more than half a century, he became the premier poet of his age, remembered especially for his three masterworks, "The Love Song of J. Alfred Prufrock," *The Waste Land*, and *Four Quartets*. From his earliest until his last poetry, he dealt with the essentially modernist themes of anxiety, depersonalization, the quest for identity and meaning, and the search for meaning through language, as well as with the timeless theme of love, both erotic and divine, and the physical and spiritual dualities of human existence.

Among the many influences on Eliot's poetry were the organizing structures used by the French *Symbolistes*, particularly Jules Laforgue, and the synaesthetic practice of musical poetry; influences on his finely honed expression included Ezra Pound, the French novelist Gustave Flaubert, and the English critic Walter Pater (whose influence Eliot was eager to disavow). The works he criticized and, in part, helped to revive were grist for his poetic mill; his poetry is filled with echoes of Shakespeare and seventeenth century dramatists, of the Metaphysical poets, of Dante, and of the poets of antiquity. Biblical and liturgical echoes also chime through in his poetry. Eliot's use of "the dead poets," as he called them, arose not so much from erudite pedantry as from a desire to belong to and alter the tradition in which he wrote. If his references and allusions at first appear obscure and arcane, a careful study of their place in his poems usually reveals that the one text complements or adjusts the meaning of the other.

Eliot also has a lighter side that surfaces in his appreciative essay of Marie Lloyd, the British music hall star, in his "five-finger exercises" of the 1930's, and, most popularly, in his *Old Possum's Book of Practical Cats* (1939), the foundation for Andrew Lloyd Webber's popular 1980's musical play, *Cats*. In a later, amused reassessment of his own critical work he could point to lapses that he said surfaced as "the occasional note of arrogance, of vehemence, of cocksureness or rudeness, the braggadocio of a mild-mannered man safely entrenched behind his typewriter." The humorous side of Eliot's work helps inform the ironic and sardonic elements of his more serious endeavors.

A consummate wordsmith and creator of memorable phrases, Eliot imbued his poetry with locutions that range from the gemlike to highly wrought goldsmith's work as he sought the phrase and sentence that is right, "where every word is at home." He consistently strove, as he wrote in "Little Gidding," to find "The common word, exact without vulgarity/ The formal word, precise but not pedantic/ The complete consort dancing together." His many poetic achievements have led him to be hailed as a poet's poet.

THE LOVE SONG OF J. ALFRED PRUFROCK

First published: 1915
Type of work: Poem

Prufrock invites the reader on an inward journey through the dreamscape of his mind.

The masterpiece of his poetic apprenticeship, "The Love Song of J. Alfred Prufrock" remains one of Eliot's most intriguing and challenging poems; it may be usefully examined by listening to the voices it embodies. Like much of the poetry of Robert Browning, it is a dramatic monologue; like the poetry of Jules Laforgue, it is a Symbolist poem that explores the narrator's stream of consciousness as he relates, in fragmented fashion, his seemingly random thoughts that are unified by the structure of the poem.

One key to this song of misprized, reluctant, hesitant love is in the epigraph from Dante's *Inferno* (XXVII) in which the speaker, Guido, reluctantly reveals the reason he is in Hell. While Prufrock finds it difficult to say what he means, he relates his thought as Guido had to Dante, without fear that his secret will be revealed to the living. The Dantean clue places the reader among the dead: This is one of the several suggestive possibilities for reading the poem and viewing its world as one of the circles that hold dead souls. The reader immediately enters what the critic Hugh Kenner has called a "zone of consciousness," not a realistic setting, and listens to a story that is not sequential: One is invited to share a dream with disturbing overtones.

The often perplexed reader needs to make numerous decisions about the teller and the tale. Is Prufrock actually addressing the reader, as Guido did Dante, or is he talking to himself? Is he any or all of the self-caricatures he contemplates—ragged claws, John the Baptist, Lazarus, Polonius? Is he bound on an erotic mission, a visit of social obligation, or merely an imaginary prowl through half-deserted streets; does he move at all from the spot where he begins his narrative, or is all animation suspended and all action only contemplated or remembered? The reader must negotiate these and similar questions, open to a variety of answers, to determine the speaker's identity and judge the situation in which he finds himself with Prufrock.

Similarly important are the sensory images that the voice projects, from the etherized patient to the ragged claws to the mermaids and one's own death by drowning, which involves all the senses until consciousness is extinguished. As the voices—Prufrock's, the women's, the woman's, the mermaids', Lazarus', John's—must be heard, so the images must be seen, the yellow fog and the seawater smelled and tasted, the motion of walking and the pressure of reclining felt along the nerves. Like many of Eliot's dramatic poems, this drama calls for total sensory involvement as the reader observes with the mind's eye the many scenes to which Prufrock refers.

Apart from its intrinsic significance, this poem foreshadows many of the concerns and techniques Eliot would explore and use in the remainder of his poetry. It stands, then, as a prelude to other work and, as Eliot would have it, is modified by that work.

GERONTION

First published: 1919
Type of work: Poem

Gerontion speaks the thoughts of a "dry brain in a dry season."

Like his earlier "Portraits of a Lady" (1917) and "The Love Song of J. Alfred Prufrock," the poem "Gerontion" is a dramatic but interior monologue in which the voice of the narrator is distinctly realized and his words reveal his character and the dramatic situation or scene in which he acts. A difficult poem, it may be approached as a collage, entered as one would a stream, in this case the stream of consciousness of the narrator, who is, literally, a "little old man." The narrator weaves personal history with more universal themes to form a meditative reverie of remembrance interspersed with remembered fragments from the Bible and from the Elizabethan and Jacobean dramatic poets William Shakespeare, Ben Jonson, George Chapman, Cyril Tourner, and Thomas Middleton. Other *dramatis personae* are the Jew, Christ, Mr. Silvero, Hakagawa, Mme. de Tornquist, Fraulein von Kulp, De Bailhache, Fresca, and Mrs. Cammel, as well as the anonymous boy who reads to the narrator.

Like the Fisher King of *The Waste Land* whom he prefigures, Gerontion is an old man waiting for rain, for rebirth in a period of aridity. Yet since the juvenescence of the year brings Christ the tiger who is eaten and who devours, there is some ambiguity and possibly some ambivalence about a rebirth that leads to death in a recurring cycle. There is also the equally large concern about action, phrased by one who denies that he has acted: He was not at the battle of Thermopylae (the hot gates), nor did he fight knee-deep in the salt marsh (possibly before the gates of windy Troy). He has, instead, been acted upon, driven by the trade winds to a sleepy corner.

The space/time continuum figures prominently in the poem. Eliot's use of space varies from the inner space of a dry brain, to the house, to the location of the house, to the Jew who has wandered from Antwerp to Brussels to London, to the ethnic origins of Hakagawa and company, to the celestial Ursa Major. Some of the characters, in a trope reminiscent of the poems of seventeenth century poet George Herbert, are gone into a world of light, whirled beyond the Bear's circuit in fractured atoms. Similarly, time is confused and variable as past, past remembered in the past and present, the present, and the future coalesce in the mind of the narrator. Similarly, the meditation on history and its gifts shuttles across time and raises ethical issues such as concerns over how and whether to act.

Above all, the poem represents an authorial attempt to present a speaker's attempt to order his experience, to make sense of the present in the light of the past, to think, and, in the act of thinking, to create meaning. What Gerontion does is essentially what the principal narrator of *The Waste Land* will do; he is shoring up fragments of language and of meaning against the ruins of a life.

THE WASTE LAND

First published: 1922
Type of work: Poem

The Waste Land explores human history and experience in a quest for regenerative wholeness.

The most celebrated poem of the twentieth century, *The Waste Land* epitomizes modernism—its anxious usurpation of previous texts in the literary tradition, its self-conscious desire to be new, its bleak analysis of the present as a post-lapsarian moment between a crumbling past and an uncertain future. Composed of five separate poems, the overarching poem is, in poetic range and effect, greater than the sum of these parts. Eliot combines many of the themes and techniques he had examined in his earlier work, themes such as aridity, sexuality, and living death, and techniques such as stream-of-consciousness, narration, historical, literary, and mythic allusions, and the dramatic monologue. As in his earlier works, he is intent upon voice and vision, but not to the exclusion of the other senses.

When he republished the poem in book form, also in 1922, he added more than fifty notes to it, some of which direct the reader to such sources as Jessie L. Weston's *From Ritual To Romance* (1920) and Sir James Frazer's *The Golden Bough* (1890-1915), the former for its handling of the Grail Quest and the waste land motifs, the latter for its expositions of vegetation myths and rituals. His note to line 218 helps explain the overall unity of the work and offers a useful starting place for a serious and necessary rereading of the poem by newcomers to the poem and to Eliot. "Tiresias," he wrote, "although a mere spectator and not indeed a 'character,' is yet the most important personage in the poem, uniting all the rest." All the male characters become one, all the women, one woman, "and the two sexes meet in Tiresias. What Tiresias *sees*, in fact, is the substance of the poem."

The poem's title, derived from the medieval Grail Quest, holds a clue: The questing reader must ask the right question of the Fisher King (who merges into Tiresias, the blind prophet of Thebes and, indeed, into the poet). The Greek and Latin epigraph concerns the Cumaean Sibyl who, asked by a boy what she wishes, states that she wishes to die—an impossibility, since she had asked of Apollo and been granted as many years as he had grains of sand in his hand. Unfortunately, she had not made the right first request: for eternal youth. One must, then, ask carefully. The Dantean dedication, to Ezra Pound, "the better craftsman," fuses ancient, medieval, and modern at the outset of the poem while acknowledging Pound's role in shaping the poem.

"The Burial of the Dead," part 1, contains a number of speakers, ranging from Marie to Madame Sosostris to Stetson, whose fragments of conversation in English, French, and German wind around ritual reenactments of burial and rebirth. From the Dantean vision of the dead walking over London bridge, to the dangerous business of doing a simple errand, to the buttonholing last line from the French poet Charles Baudelaire, in which the reader is addressed directly as hypocrite and brother, the atmosphere is menacing. Structurally, the poem contains varieties of motion to organize it: motion in time across days, months, seasons, years, and centuries, motion in change from youth to age, action to stillness, and death to rebirth, as Bernard Bergonzi has observed.

Part 2, "A Game of Chess," elaborates the themes of aridity and rebirth in the story of Lil's barren sexuality and Philomel's mythic reincarnation after sexual abuse, thus blending the mythic and the prosaic to reveal a relatively mindless luxury devoid of satisfying significance. Whether in the ornate boudoir that opens the sequence or the working-class pub that closes it, the pleasures of the world seem unsatisfying. In a memorable phrase that has rung through every English pub since their Victorian regulation, the barman's call for closing becomes, in the poet's hands, an advent call for change or a hastening of some final, eschatological closure: "*HURRY UP PLEASE ITS TIME.*"

In part 3, "The Fire Sermon," the poet deals with the refining fire of purgation, unites Western and Eastern mystical theology in Saint Augustine and the Buddha, and combines ancient and medieval literary tradition in Tiresias and the Fisher King. These higher quests are played off against the more sordid ones of Sweeney and Mrs. Porter, the typist and the carbuncular young man, and Mr. Eugenides ("wellborn" but decadent), as Tiresias begins to tie elements of the poem together.

The brief, ten-line "Death by Water," part 4, presents water as destroyer, cleanser, and paradoxical life-giver in the case of Phlebas, the Phoenician sailor who passes, two weeks dead, backwards through the stages of his age and youth and enters the whirlpool. This, too, Tiresias sees and possibly relates.

"What the Thunder Said," part 5, brings rain and its promise of rebirth. The thunder reverberates with the words of the Upanishads (Hindu philosophic writings) for "give, sympathize, control," keys to unlocking the prisons in which each individual is kept a solitary prisoner. The resolution offered to those journeying to Emmaus, to the Chapel Perilous, through "the present decay of eastern Europe," depends upon the trinity of commands or counsels from the thunder and becomes "the peace which passeth understanding" ("shantih," quoted from the Upanishads) repeated at the close of the poem.

Eliot's achievement in this highly sophisticated poem is the blending of the disparate elements of varied traditions into a unity that may itself be both an object lesson in and a plea for the necessity of artistic wholeness. This is one possible reading of the piece as a metapoetical work that points as much to itself as it does to the traditions in which it exists and which it, in turn, alters.

THE HOLLOW MEN

First published: 1925
Type of work: Poem

Eliot explores spiritual emptiness in a masquelike poem.

This poem of emptiness, "The Hollow Men," opens with a double epigraph, one from the novelist Joseph Conrad's *Heart of Darkness* (1902) and one from the traditional children's request for a penny on Guy Fawkes Day, November 5. The former seems intended to draw the reader to Conrad's short masterpiece and to the announcement of the death of Mr. Kurtz—perhaps the ultimate hollow man—to Charlie Marlow, the first narrator of that work. (Marlow had observed of London that it, too, was once one of the dark places of the world.) The latter epigraph also involves light and darkness, since it recalls the 1605 Gunpowder Plot, an alleged Roman Catholic attempt to blow up the English monarch and the houses of Parliament. The "guy" is a stuffed effigy of Guy Fawkes; the pennies collected by children are to purchase materials and fireworks to celebrate the ritual evening burning of the effigy. Both epigraphs allude to an emptiness, one spiritual and one physical.

Characteristically divided into five parts, the poem begins in a choric proclamation of emptiness, as if a chorus of stuffed men were appearing before the reader in a frozen *tableau vivant* that will quicken to a dance round in part 5, followed by an antiphonal and concluding with another dance round.

The playfulness of some of the motion implied in the poem is in sharp contrast to the words of the hollow men. The poem's first part also introduces the notion of a double kingdom of death, one in this world and one in the next.

The second part explores death's dream kingdom, sleep, and the hope that the speaker, one of the hollow men in soliloquy, would not meet eyes he would wish to avoid, eyes that he would prefer remain distant. Part 3 sets the reader in a dead land, a desert place of isolation that thwarts, like death's other kingdom, the ability to kiss, to express emotion. Part 4, filled with negation, describes a hollow valley, a broken jaw of lost kingdoms, where the hollow men gather silently on the beach of a tumid river and await the only hope of empty men, death.

The fifth part, the most complex and challenging, opens and closes with variants of children's game-songs. The first substitutes the prickly pear for the traditional mulberry bush; the last is a version of "London Bridge Is Falling Down." Both, if sung and danced by the effigies, produce even more incongruity between the song and the words, the action and the statement. Framed by these songs are the shadow verses of one chorus played off against another chorus repeating phrases and variants from the Anglican conclusion to the Lord's Prayer.

In his highly suggestive language and the character's elliptical speech, Eliot exposes an incompleteness that for these hollow men will be consummated not with the blaze and explosions customary on November 5 but with the inarticulate whimper that concludes the masque.

ASH WEDNESDAY

First published: 1930
Type of work: Poem

In a poem of intercession, the speaker reluctantly seeks conversion.

"Ash Wednesday" contains many traces of Eliot's newly found Anglo-Catholic orientation; he had officially joined the church in 1927. The poem's title comes from the Christian movable feast day celebrating the onset of Lent, forty days before Easter: It is a day of mortification of the flesh and of turning toward the spiritual. The poem exemplifies the tensions between the flesh and the spirit, borrowing much from Dante's medieval mysticism, as the story of conversion is told in a Symbolist dream, a favorite technique of Eliot. As in *The Waste Land*, characters merge; the Lady merges with other ladies, such as Ecclesia (church), Theologia (theology), and Beatrice (the blessed one, from Dante), possibly to represent the anima, or feminine principle.

The first portion of this six-part poem opens with a despairing lack of hope for conversion, followed by a prayer for mercy, a famous request for a holy indifference: "Teach us to care and not to care/ Teach us to sit still." It concludes with a refrain from the last sentence of the *Ave Maria*, "Holy Mary, Mother of God, pray for us sinners now and at the hour of our death." Eliot thus endows the poem with fragments of prayer (along with Shakespearean allusions), varied renunciations, and some recognition of the need for rejoicing. The negative assertion of hope's lack at the outset is modified by prayers which indicate a realization of the need for spiritual help.

Biblical references crowd part 2, forming a litany; the response to many of its phrases is the unvoiced but expected "Pray for us." In part 3, the speaker ascends a spiral staircase, past a devil and past a vision of an earthly paradise; this portion ends with the liturgical prayer before communion from the Mass of the Faithful, echoing phrases from one of the miracle stories about Jesus. Part 4 blends the biblical Mary with other female figures, asks for a redemption of time, and concludes with a phrase from the prayer *Salve, Regina*, which asks that Mary show us the fruit of her womb, Jesus, "after this our exile."

Part 5 is a meditation on the Word of God, the *Logos* from the Gospel according to John, that Eliot would amplify in *Four Quartets*. This is accompanied by the refrain from the *Improperia* of the Good Friday service, "O my people. . . ." The poem's final segment returns to the original state of mind of the narrator as the poet recapitulates the themes and images of the entire poem and ends with a phrase addressed to the Lord in the *Indulgentiam* of the Mass of the Catechumens, the early dialogue between priest and laity which asks God to forgive sins, show mercy, hear prayers, "and let my cry come unto Thee."

In many respects, Eliot's "Ash Wednesday" is a poetic public demonstration of a change of heart, an assertion of Christian desire balanced by a recognition of frailty, that ends with a striving, itself a conversion from the poem's opening posture.

FOUR QUARTETS

First published: 1943
Type of work: Poem

This sequence represents Eliot's most mature poetic statement on spiritual and artistic health.

Simpler, more direct in style than much of his early work, *Four Quartets* stands as the masterpiece of Eliot's poetic maturity and as an index of the extent to which his poetic concerns had changed and his spiritual concerns had deepened. Each poem of the group, as C. K. Stead has ably documented, is in five movements in quartet or sonata form. The first part of each concerns the movement of time in which fleeting moments of eternity flicker. Dissatisfaction with worldly experience is the keynote of each of the second parts. Part 3 is a spiritual quest for purgation and divestiture of worldly things. The lyric fourth part comments upon the need for spiritual intercession, while the concluding part probes the issue of artistic wholeness, an issue allied to the achievement of spiritual health.

Formed from lines originally written for *Murder in the Cathedral*, "Burnt Norton" (1939), the first of the sequence, is thematically linked to the play but goes beyond it as Eliot probes more deeply the motivation for action and the role of the poet as a participant in the *Logos* (Word). His epigraphs from the Greek philosopher Heraclitus concern the neglect of the law of reason (Logos) and cite the paradoxical phrase, "The way upward and downward are one and the same." A problematic proposition, "If all time is eternally present/ All time is unredeemable," is part of the poem's meditative opening, which also reiterates Thomas à Becket's line from the play, "human kind/ Cannot bear very much reality." The ascendent spirit and descendent body are the Heraclitean oppositions of part 2, in a continuing meditation on the limits of time and its eternity and the desire to purge the human condition of its limitations. In "a place of disaffection," the narrator seeks to approach the condition of fire with a "dry soul" (part 3); part 4 celebrates the dark night of the soul, "at the still point of the turning world." The final segment treats of words and music moving in time, artistic wholeness and spiritual health involving words as part of the Divine Logos, and love as a timeless present.

"East Coker" (1940) recalls Eliot's ancestral home in Somerset (it is also his burial place). Pursuing the poet's beginning in his end (1) and his role as craftsman of words (5), the poem contains a rueful look backward at "years largely wasted, years of *l'entre deux guerres*" essaying to learn to use words. In this poem, the focus is on the earth from which the poet springs; it has relevance to God the Son in some readings (as in the first of the poems, air is the dominant element), and some see direct relevance to God the Father. In this interpretation, the next poem, "The Dry Salvages" (1941), has as its motifs Mary, the Mother of God, and the element of water, and "Little Gidding" (1942), the element of fire and the Holy Ghost. These remain suggestive possibilities for interpretation, but they are supported by the texts.

"The Dry Salvages," a group of rocks off the Cape Ann coast, reflects the poet's early life in the United States, as does "the strong brown god," the Mississippi River at St. Louis. Much more explicitly religious in statement than the first two quartets, the poem has direct references to God and the Annunciation made to Mary (part 1), the tenets of Krishna (part 3), and the Queen of Heaven, *figlia del tuo figlio*, the "daughter of your son" (part 4). The occupation for the saint in part 5, "The point of intersection of the timeless/ With time," is also the poet's occupation, as Eliot continues to play out variations upon his themes.

His most famous poem in the sequence, "Little Gidding," is also his last major poetic statement. This place name is meant to evoke its seventeenth century associations as a center of spiritual life and its contemporary symbolism for the poet as the place of "the intersection of the timeless moment" (part 1). Encountering "the shade of some dead master," the speaker finds in the spirit's disillusionment yet another cause to reassess the poet's task: "To purify the language of the tribe" (part 2). The burden of the third part, that prayers and intercession are needful in the face of sin's inevitability, reinforces each of the prior third parts of the sequence. In the final segment, all birds coalesce to become one bird, as the Heraclitean fire of the epigraph is subsumed into the descent of the Holy Spirit at Pentecost. The final and often-quoted and anthologized hymn to poetic practice as a means of achieving unity and spiritual health concludes the poem and the sequence in a complete affirmation unprecedented in Eliot's poetry.

Taken together in the light of their ending, the poems of *Four Quartets* rank among the most highly accomplished works of devotional poetry and treatments of a poet's vision of poetry itself. With this sequence, Eliot capped his career as a poet.

MURDER IN THE CATHEDRAL

First produced: 1935 (first published, 1935)
Type of work: Play

Eliot dramatizes the killing of Thomas à Becket, archbishop of Canterbury.

Eliot's best-known and most-performed play, *Murder in the Cathedral* dramatizes the assassination of Thomas à Becket, archbishop of Canterbury, in A.D. 1170 at the hands of four knights and at the bidding of King Henry II. In this play, written for production at the Canterbury Festival, June, 1935, Eliot put into practice his long-held desire to reestablish verse drama as a viable form of theater, a wish shared by the Irish poet and playwright William Butler Yeats, whose work preceded Eliot's. Both sought to return poetry to the stage for historical and aesthetic reasons, since they viewed the popular realistic plays of the nineteenth and twentieth centuries as less desirable than poetic drama. Both writers have secured a lasting place in the history of modern drama.

Modeled upon the chorus of ancient Greek tragedy, the chorus that opens the play introduces the place and the time—the return from a seven-year exile of the archbishop, at odds with the king for whom he had served as chancellor. Three priests, a messenger, Thomas, and four tempters of some demoniac reasonableness fill out the players of the first act. These last, for echoic effect, should be read/played by the same actors who play the four knights in the third act: This was Eliot's original design, and it is one reason he altered the lines of the knights in the play's second edition (1937), the text now current.

The chorus of the women of Canterbury comments on the action and presents its own sense of foreboding, fear, and, at the play's end, desolation. The priests, who may be seen as chorus leaders, voice their own concerns and trepidations. They seek to act according to conventional wisdom, counsel Thomas to flee back to France, seek to protect him from martyrdom, and finally look to the martyr for spiritual help in a time of personal need for comfort.

Of greater dramatic interest is the interplay between Thomas and the tempters, who offer him fleshly delights and good times, earthly political power by regaining the chancellorship he had resigned upon becoming archbishop, temporal sovereignty by joining a coup against the king, and glorious triumph over the king by seeking martyrdom. Once the murder is committed—onstage (a break with classical and neoclassical traditions but quite Jacobean)—the knights offer the audience-turned-jury their defense of disinterestedness in carrying out the king's will; finally, they claim that Thomas has sought martyrdom and seek a verdict of "suicide while of Unsound Mind."

Throughout the play, Eliot's language echoes scriptural injunctions, parables, and situations. In his stage directions and dialogue, Eliot uses liturgical hymns and portions of the Anglo-Catholic Mass. The interlude between the two acts is a Christmas sermon stylistically reminiscent of those of the seventeenth century ministers John Donne and Lancelot Andrews.

TRADITION AND THE INDIVIDUAL TALENT

First published: 1919
Type of work: Essay

Eliot places the poet in a literary tradition and argues for the impersonality of art.

"Tradition and the Individual Talent," one of Eliot's early essays, typifies his critical stance and concerns; it quickly became what has been called his most influential single essay. Divided into three parts, appearing in *The Egoist* in September and December, 1919, the essay insists upon taking tradition into account when formulating criticism—"aesthetic, not merely historical criticism."

Eliot opens the essay by revivifying the word "tradition" and arguing that criticism, for which the French were then noted more than the English, in his view "is as inevitable as breathing." The first principle of criticism that he asserts is to focus not solely upon what is unique in a poet but upon what he shares with "the dead poets, his ancestors." This sharing, when it is not the mere and unquestioning following of established poetic practice, involves the historical sense, a sense that the whole of literary Europe and of one's own country "has a simultaneous existence and composes a simultaneous order."

A correlative principle is that no poet or artist has his complete meaning in isolation, but must be judged, for contrast and comparison, among the dead. As Eliot sees it, the order of art is complete before a new work of art is created, but with that new creation all the prior works forming an ideal order are modified and the order itself is altered.

One of the essay's memorable and enduring phrases concerns the objection that the living know so much more that the dead writers could have: Eliot counters by asserting, "Precisely, and they are that which we know." In gaining that knowledge, the artist engages in a "continual surrender" to tradition, and his progress "is a continual self-sacrifice, a continual extinction of personality." The definition of depersonalization that Eliot offers forms another of the essay's enduring phrases: As the novelist Gustave Flaubert and the English critic Walter Pater had written before him, Eliot seeks a scientific base for his works and likens the poet's mind to "a bit of finely filiated platinum . . . introduced into a chamber containing oxygen and sulphur dioxide."

The poet's mind, then, is a catalyst, as Eliot explains it in the essay's second part.

His point is that the poet's transforming mind stores up feelings, phrases, and images until all the particles that can form a new work of art come together to do so. The poet has not so much a personality to express as a medium for the expression of complex emotion that is separable from the poet's own emotions. Poetry, Eliot emphasizes, is not a turning loose of personal emotion but a consciously deliberate escape from it. The emotion of art, he reminds his readers in the essay's final section, is impersonal.

Summary

Eliot's multiyear quest "to purify the language of the tribe" found its reward in his reception of the Nobel Prize in Literature in 1948—"for the entire corpus," he supposed. A poet in the forefront of modernism whose later work sought to give life to a vigorous union of the poetic and the spiritual, Eliot's poetry, drama, and criticism remain cultural forces to which successive generations have had recourse in probing the same issues—sometimes disquieting issues—that Eliot had examined before them.

Bibliography

Bergonzi, Bernard. *T. S. Eliot*. New York: Macmillan, 1962.

Conlon, John J. "Eliot and Pater: Criticism in Transition." *English Literature in Transition* 25, no. 3 (1982): 169-177.

Matthews, T. S. *Great Tom*. New York: Harper & Row, 1973.

Matthiessen, F. O. *The Achievement of T. S. Eliot*. New York: Oxford University Press, 1969.

Meisel, Perry. *The Myth of the Modern*. New Haven, Conn.: Yale University Press, 1987.

Stead, C. K. *The New Poetic: Yeats to Eliot*. Philadelphia: University of Pennsylvania Press, 1975.

_____. *Pound, Yeats, and Eliot and the Modernist Movement*. New Brunswick, N.J.: Rutgers University Press, 1985.

John J. Conlon

RALPH ELLISON

Born: Oklahoma City, Oklahoma
March 1, 1914

Principal Literary Achievement
Ellison's novel *Invisible Man* is recognized as one of the finest achievements in modern American fiction as well as one of the most complete statements of the African-American experience.

Biography
Ralph Waldo Ellison was born in Oklahoma City, Oklahoma, on March 1, 1914. His father, Lewis, was an adventurous and accomplished man who had served in the military overseas and had lived in Abbeville, South Carolina, and Chattanooga, Tennessee, before moving to Oklahoma a short time after the former Indian territory achieved statehood. In Oklahoma City, Lewis Ellison worked in construction and started his own ice and coal business. Ellison's mother, Ida, who was known as "Brownie," was a political activist who campaigned for the Socialist party and against the segregationist policies of Oklahoma's governor, "Alfalfa Bill" Murray. After her husband's death, Ida Ellison supported Ralph and his younger brother Herbert by working at a variety of jobs. Although the family was sometimes short of money, Ellison and his younger brother did not have deprived childhoods.

Ellison benefited from the advantages of the Oklahoma public schools but took odd jobs to pay for supplemental education. His particular interest was music; in return for yard work, Ellison received lessons from Ludwig Hebestreit, the conductor of the Oklahoma City Orchestra. At nineteen, with the dream of becoming a composer, he accepted a state scholarship and used it to attend Tuskegee Institute in Alabama.

Unlike the protagonist of *Invisible Man* (1952), Ellison was not expelled from Tuskegee, but like the character he later created, Ellison was not graduated. Instead, he traveled to New York City in 1936 to find work during the summer between his junior and senior years, intending to return to Tuskegee in the fall. Soon after his arrival in New York, however, Ellison met Alain Locke and Langston Hughes, major literary figures of the Harlem Renaissance. Through his acquaintance with Hughes, Ellison was introduced to Richard Wright, who encouraged Ellison to write and published Ellison's first review in *New Challenge*, a journal that Wright edited.

Ellison supported himself with a variety of jobs during his first years in Harlem.

In 1938, he joined the Federal Writer's Project, where he and others employed by the Living Lore Unit gathered urban folklore materials. This experience introduced Ellison to the richness of black urban culture and provided him with a wealth of folklore materials that he used effectively in *Invisible Man*. In the early 1940's, Ellison published several short stories. During World War II, he served as a cook on a merchant marine ship. At the war's end, he traveled to New Hampshire to rest, and there he began work on *Invisible Man*. With the financial assistance of a Rosenwald Foundation grant, Ellison worked on the novel for several years, publishing it in 1952.

Invisible Man was controversial, attacked by militants as reactionary and banned from schools because of its explicit descriptions of black life. Critics, however, generally agreed on the book's significance. In 1965, a poll of literary critics named it the outstanding book written by an American in the previous twenty years, placing it ahead of works by William Faulkner, Ernest Hemingway, and Saul Bellow. Ellison received many awards for his work, including the National Book Award (1953), the Russwurm Award (1953), an Academy of Arts and Letters fellowship to Rome (1955-1957), and the Medal of Freedom (1969); he was also named a Chevalier de l'Ordre des Artes et Lettres (1970).

In 1958, Ellison accepted a teaching position at Bard College. In subsequent years he taught at Rutgers University, the University of Chicago, and New York University, from which he retired in 1979. He has accepted numerous honorary doctorates and published two collections of essays. The essays in *Shadow and Act* (1964) focus on three topics: African-American literature and folklore, African-American music, and the interrelation of African-American culture and the broader culture of the United States. *Going to the Territory* (1986) collected sixteen reviews, essays, and speeches that Ellison had published previously.

Since the 1960's, Ellison has worked on a second novel that he reputedly plans to publish as a trilogy. His work on the novel was disrupted when about 350 pages of its thousand-page manuscript were destroyed in a house fire in 1967. Several selections from the book have been published in journals.

Analysis

The central theme of Ralph Ellison's writing is the search for identity, a search that he sees as central to American literature and the American experience. He has said that "the nature of our society is such that we are prevented from knowing who we are," and in *Invisible Man* this struggle toward self-definition is applied to individuals, groups, and the society as a whole. The particular genius of *Invisible Man* is Ellison's ability to interweave these individual, communal, and national quests into a single, complex vision.

On the level of the individual, *Invisible Man* is, in Ellison's words, a clash of "innocence and human error, a struggle through illusion to reality." In this sense, the book is part of the literary tradition of initiation tales, stories of young men or women who confront the larger world beyond the security of home and attempt to

define themselves in these new terms. Through the misadventures of his naïve protagonist, Ellison stresses the individual's need to free himself from the powerful
influence of societal stereotypes and demonstrates the multiple levels of deception
that must be overcome before an individual can achieve self-awareness. Ellison describes the major flaw of his protagonist as an "unquestioning willingness to do
what is required of him by others as a way to success." Although Ellison's hero is
repeatedly manipulated, betrayed, and deceived, Ellison shows that an individual is
not trapped by geography, time, or place. He optimistically asserts that human beings can overcome these obstacles to independence if they are willing to accept the
responsibility to judge existence independently.

Invisible Man is also concerned with the communal effort of African Americans
to define their cultural identity. The novel surveys the history of African-American
experience and alludes directly or indirectly to historical figures who serve as contradictory models for Ellison's protagonist. Some of the novel's effect is surely lost
on readers who do not recognize the parallels drawn between Booker T. Washington
and the Founder, between Marcus Garvey and Ras the Destroyer, or between Frederick Douglass and the narrator's grandfather. W. E. B. DuBois's description of the
doubleness of the African-American experience fits the *Invisible Man*'s narrator, and
DuBois's assertion that the central fact of an African American's experience is the
"longing to attain self-conscious manhood, to merge his double self into a better
and truer self" stands as a summary of the novel's overriding action.

Ellison does not restrict himself to the concerns of African Americans, however,
because he believes that African-American culture is an inextricable part of American culture. Thus, *Invisible Man* shows how the struggles of the narrator as an individual and as a representative of an ethnic minority are paralleled by the struggle of
the nation to define and redefine itself. Ellison's frequently expressed opinion that
African-American culture's assimilation by the dominant culture of the United States
is inevitable and salutary has led some African-American critics to attack him as
reactionary. The suspicion that he has "sold out" has also been fed by his broad
popularity among white readers and his acceptance of teaching positions at predominantly white universities.

The breadth and diversity of *Invisible Man* make it possible to fit Ellison's novel
into several American literary traditions. As part of the vernacular tradition, exemplified by Mark Twain and Ernest Hemingway, Ellison skillfully reproduces the
various speech patterns and rich folklore of rural and urban African Americans. As
part of the Symbolist tradition, exemplified by Herman Melville and T. S. Eliot, Ellison builds his novel around a full set of provocative and multifaceted symbols. As
part of the tradition of African-American literature, Ellison echoes the theme of
DuBois's *The Souls of Black Folk* (1903), reproduces the northward flight to freedom in Frederick Douglass' *Narrative of the Life of Frederick Douglass* (1845),
explores the ambiguity of identity as James Weldon Johnson did in *The Autobiography of an Ex-Colored Man* (1912), and appropriates the striking underground metaphor of Richard Wright's "The Man Who Lived Underground" (1944).

In *Invisible Man*, Ellison employs a "jazz" style in which an improvisation of rhetorical forms is played against his central theme. Letters, speeches, sermons, songs, nursery rhymes, and dreams are used throughout the novel, and the novel's style adjusts to match the changing consciousness and circumstances of the protagonist. In the early chapters, Ellison employs a direct, didactic style similar to that of the social-realist protest novels of the 1930's and 1940's. In the middle portions of the novel, after the narrator moves to New York City, Ellison's prose becomes more expressionistic, reflecting the narrator's introspection. In the last section of the novel, as the story moves toward the climactic race riot in Harlem, the prose becomes surreal, emphasizing the darkly comic absurdities of American existence. In all sections, the book is enriched by Ellison's versatile use of symbols that focus attention on his major themes while underscoring the ambiguous nature of the human condition.

Structurally, *Invisible Man* is episodic and cyclic, presenting the reader with versions of a basic pattern of disillusionment enacted in increasingly complex social environments. In each cycle, the narrator eagerly accepts an identity provided by a deceitful mentor and eventually experiences a revelation that shatters the illusory identity he has adopted. This repeated pattern demonstrates the pervasiveness of racism and self-interest and convinces the narrator that he must find his individual answers and stop looking to others.

Although *Invisible Man* addresses some of the most serious concerns of American society, it is also a comic novel in which Ellison relies on both the traditional picaresque humor of initiation and the rough-edged and often disguised humor of urban African Americans. Its dark comedy, sophisticated play of rhetorical forms, complex use of symbolism, and original examination of difficult social issues distinguish the book as a masterpiece of modern fiction.

INVISIBLE MAN

First published: 1952
Type of work: Novel

An ambitious but naïve black youth journeys through American society in search of his identity.

Ralph Ellison's *Invisible Man* is framed by a prologue and an epilogue that are set at a time after the completion of the novel's central action. The novel's picaresque story of a young black man's misadventures is presented as a memoir written by an older, more experienced embodiment of the protagonist. The narrator of the prologue and epilogue has withdrawn into a state he calls "hibernation" after surviving the multiple deceptions and betrayals that he recounts in his memoir. As he says, "the end is the beginning and lies far ahead."

The prologue foreshadows the novel's action. It prepares the reader for the narrator's final condition; focuses the reader's attention on the major themes of truth, responsibility, and freedom; and introduces the reader to the double consciousness that operates in the book. Throughout the novel, the naïve assumptions of the youthful protagonist are counterbalanced by the cynical judgments of his more mature self, creating an ironic double perspective.

The broken narrator to whom the reader is introduced in the prologue is hiding in an underground room, stealing power from the Monopolated Power Company to light the thousands of bulbs he has strung up. An angry and damaged man, he explains his frustration at his "invisibility," a quality that prevents others from seeing anything but "surroundings, themselves, or figments of their imagination." The narrator experiences a desperate need to convince himself that he does "exist in the real world." As he listens to Louis Armstrong's recording of "What Did I Do to Be so Black and Blue?" he dreams and then recounts his experiences.

The first episode, which goes back to his graduation from a black high school in the South, is a representative anecdote, a story that sets the pattern and themes of subsequent misadventures. Throughout *Invisible Man*, the young hero builds illusory expectations based on the deceitful promises of people who set themselves up as his mentors. In each cycle, he is eventually disillusioned by a dramatic revelation of deceit and sent spiraling toward his final confrontation with himself.

In the initial episode, he is invited to repeat his valedictory speech before the white leaders of the town. These men, however, humiliate him and some other black youths by forcing them to engage in a "battle royal," a blindfolded fist fight in which the last standing participant is victorious. They also tempt the black youths to fight for counterfeit coins tossed on an electrified rug and they rudely disregard the protagonist's remarks when he is finally allowed to speak. The episode demonstrates how racist leaders control African Americans by encouraging them to direct their anger at one another and by rewarding acceptably submissive behavior such as the protagonist's speech about "social responsibility." Although the corrupt and even bestial nature of these men is clear to the reader, the protagonist is blinded by his eagerness to succeed, and he gratefully accepts the briefcase he is given after his speech.

The episode develops the ocular symbols of blindness/sight, darkness/light that are used in the novel to describe the protagonist's invisibility and his stumbling quest for truth. It also introduces the briefcase, a symbol of his naïve effort to accept prescribed identities. The briefcase stays with him until the end of the novel, accumulating objects and documents to represent the false identities he assumes. These two symbols are united at the end of the novel when he burns the contents of his briefcase in order to see in his underground hideout.

At the black college that the protagonist attends, he is introduced to the misuse of black power. Dr. Bledsoe, the ruthless college president (whose name implies his deracinated disregard for other African Americans), is blindly idolized by the protagonist, for whom the college is a paradise of reason and culture. The protagonist says that "within the quiet greenness I possessed the only identity I had ever known."

When he mishandles a visiting white trustee named Norton, however, by allowing him to hear Jim Trueblood's shocking tale of incest and taking him to a brothel where they are beset by a group of World War I veterans, Dr. Bledsoe banishes the protagonist from the collegiate Eden. It is only later, after fruitless efforts to find employment in New York City, that the protagonist discovers that Bledsoe's supposed letters of recommendation have betrayed him.

The revelation of Dr. Bledsoe's perfidy destroys the narrator's dream of returning to the college, so he accepts a job with Liberty Paints, determined to make his own way. The factory, which is a microcosm of capitalist America, produces Optic White, "the purest white that can be found." Optic White will "cover just about anything" and is purchased in large amounts by the government, but the secret ingredient is a small amount of black base that is produced in a boiler room by an aging African American named Lucius Brockaway. The protagonist is assigned to Brockaway, but the veteran employee's paranoid suspicion that his new helper is a company spy and the protagonist's resentment at being assigned to an African-American supervisor result in a fight. As the two fight, pressure builds until the boilers explode.

The protagonist awakes in the factory's infirmary, where masked doctors discuss ways to make him pliable. Half-conscious, the narrator is dimly aware of the doctors' efforts at behavior modification, but their bizarre treatment only succeeds at stripping away layers of superficial personality and revealing a changed man who looks at the world with "wild infant's eyes." In this reborn state, the dazed hero is adopted by Mary Rambo, the maternal owner of a boarding house in Harlem. Mary's nurturing restores the protagonist and awakens his sensitivity to injustice. When he comes across an elderly couple being evicted from their apartment, he speaks up in their behalf, stirring a gathering crowd to resist the eviction.

The protagonist's effective oratory is overheard by Jack, a leader of the Brotherhood, an organization that closely resembles the Communist party. Jack recruits the protagonist and makes him the party's new spokesperson in Harlem. Armed with a new name supplied by the Brotherhood, the protagonist eagerly takes on his organizational duties, dreaming that he will become a modern Frederick Douglass (a nineteenth century black leader). He successfully builds Brotherhood membership in Harlem and effectively competes with rival organizations such as that led by Ras the Destroyer, an African-American nationalist who is reminiscent of the historical Marcus Garvey, but instead of being rewarded, the protagonist is suddenly reassigned to a downtown position. The protagonist's protests result in a climactic showdown, at which Jack plucks out his glass eye, demonstrating at once the organization's demand of personal sacrifice and his own blindness.

Eventually, the protagonist realizes that he is being used by Jack, that the Brotherhood is willing to sacrifice the progress made in Harlem for the larger ends of the party, and that his dream of becoming another Frederick Douglass is a sham. With another prescribed identity deflated, he suddenly finds that he is being mistaken for the protean character Rinehart, a mysterious con man who is at once a minister and a pimp, a man whose name suggests the ambiguous relation of inner and outer realities. The protagonist considers adopting the cynicism of Rinehart, a decision that would end the search for a true identity, but he concludes that he cannot abandon his own conscience. As the book nears its conclusion, the protagonist runs through a race riot that the Brotherhood has encouraged. Pursued by armed men, he finds sanctuary underground, where he is forced to burn the symbolic contents of his briefcase in order to see. He thus destroys the prescribed identities that others have supplied for him in order to prepare for the "hibernation" during which he hopes to discover himself.

Invisible Man's epilogue completes the frame begun in the novel's prologue, returning the reader to the subterranean narrator of the memoir, who says that although the world outside is as deceitful and dangerous as ever, the process of telling his story has made him "better understand my relation to it and it to me." He has come to accept the responsibility of determining his own identity and rejects formulaic responses to injustice. He advises his reader that "too much of your life will be lost, its meaning lost unless you approach it as much through love as through hate," and he now sees his own life as "one of infinite possibilities." Thus, at the novel's conclusion, the narrator is preparing to reenter the world. As Ellison has said, his narrator "comes up from underground because the act of writing and thinking necessitated it."

Summary

Although Ellison has modestly claimed that *Invisible Man* is "not an important novel," the book has demonstrated its ability to speak to a variety of readers for four decades. Ellison is the rare example of an author who continues to be ranked among America's greatest fiction writers because of the quality of a single novel.

Invisible Man earned for Ellison a special place in African-American literature because the novel goes beyond the thematic and rhetorical limitations of the protest novel, extending the story of the African-American experience to all Americans. The novel's concluding question, "Who knows but that, on the lower frequencies, I speak for you?" underscores this universality.

Bibliography

Covo, Jacqueline. *The Blinking Eye: Ralph Waldo Ellison and His American, French, German, and Italian Critics, 1952-1971.* Metuchen, N.J.: Scarecrow Press, 1974.

Gottesman, Ronald. *The Merrill Studies in "Invisible Man".* Columbus: Charles E. Merrill, 1971.

Gray, Valerie Bonita. *"Invisible Man's" Literary Heritage: "Benito Cereno" and "Moby Dick."* Amsterdam, the Netherlands: Rodopi, 1978.

Hersey, John. *Ralph Ellison: A Collection of Critical Essays.* Englewood Cliffs, N.J.: Prentice-Hall, 1974.

List, Robert N. *Dedalus in Harlem: The Joyce-Ellison Connection.* Washington, D.C.:

University Press of America, 1982.

McSweeney, Kerry. *"Invisible Man": Race and Identity.* Boston: G. K. Hall, 1988.

Nadel, Alan. *Invisible Criticism: Ralph Ellison and the American Canon.* Iowa City: University of Iowa Press, 1988.

O'Meally, Robert G. *The Craft of Ralph Ellison.* Cambridge, Mass.: Harvard University Press, 1980.

Reilly, John M., ed. *Twentieth Century Interpretations of "Invisible Man."* Englewood Cliffs, N.J.: Prentice-Hall, 1970.

Trimmer, Joseph, ed. *A Casebook on Ralph Ellison's "Invisible Man."* New York: Crowell, 1972.

Carl Brucker

RALPH WALDO EMERSON

Born: Boston, Massachusetts
May 25, 1803
Died: Concord, Massachusetts
April 27, 1882

Principal Literary Achievement

One of the most influential figures in American literary history, Emerson used essentially everyday language to articulate his thought, thereby consummating the art of prosaic discourse.

Biography

Ralph Waldo Emerson was born in Boston, Massachusetts, on May 25, 1803, the third son of the Reverend William Emerson and Ruth Haskins Emerson. Stern and disciplined, his parents normally refrained from displaying intense affection in the family, as so many Bostonians did at the beginning of the nineteenth century. Partly because of this upbringing, coldness, as Emerson himself noted throughout his life, became a distinct feature of his character, later, perhaps unconsciously, making him search in his writing for a spiritual life rich in sentiment. Characteristic of his time, Emerson was enrolled in a Dame school at two and in the Boston Public Latin school at nine. While in the Latin school, he displayed unusual talent in declamation, a gift which eventually paved his way to becoming a great speaker. His aunt Mary Moody Emerson, who lived intermittently with his family for a considerable length of time during his childhood, greatly influenced Emerson in encouraging him to set high goals and do things which he might otherwise be afraid to do. The early death of his father in 1811 left the family in poverty to the extent that he had to share an overcoat with his younger brother. This impoverishment, however, disciplined him all the more.

In 1817 Emerson, then fourteen, entered Harvard College. In his third year at Harvard, he began keeping a journal, an endeavor which would last for more than fifty years, often serving as the source of ideas for his literary writing. In his last year, he distinguished himself by being chosen as class poet and winning second prize in the Boylston competition for delivering a dissertation on ethical philosophy. After being graduated in 1821, Emerson taught at his elder brother's school for

young ladies for three years, earning enough money for him to return to Harvard in 1825 to pursue studies in theology. His reading of Michel de Montaigne, a French Renaissance writer, at the beginning of 1825 made him believe that good essays can be written in plain language. In 1826, Emerson preached with approbation his first sermon from his uncle's pulpit, an episode which marked the beginning of his long career as a speaker. Shortly after this sermon, bad health forced him to travel to the South for better climate and a quick recovery. Not until 1829, when Emerson became somewhat sure of his health, was he ordained as a junior pastor to the Unitarian ministry and began to preach regularly.

In 1827, he had met Ellen Tucker and, after a short courtship, married her in 1829 regardless of her rapidly deteriorating health caused by tuberculosis (a disease which plagued their era). As expected, this marriage soon ended with Ellen's death in 1831. The bereaved Emerson was thus able, as the beneficiary of his wife's will, to receive a sufficient amount of money for him to live without having to hold a regular job—an event which enabled him to concentrate on his literary creativity. The following year witnessed a turning point in Emerson's thought. Unsatisfied with the conventional Christian form of worship and now somewhat assured of his future livelihood, he resigned his pastorate at the Second Church in Boston, stating that he could no longer administer communion as a ritual. Apart from the emotional turmoil Emerson experienced from the loss of his beloved wife and the resignation of his pastorate, his own health was failing him in 1832; he eventually embarked upon a journey of recovery to Europe at the end of this year. While in Europe, he visited some of the important literary figures of his time, such as the renowned English poets William Wordsworth and Samuel Taylor Coleridge and the Scottish essayist Thomas Carlyle, with whom Emerson was to correspond for the rest of his life. Shortly after returning from Europe, Emerson began his career as a lecturer and settled at Concord, Massachusetts, where he lived until his death. In 1835, after specifying his conditions—to remain a poet and to live in the countryside—he married Lydia Jackson of Plymouth, who had to compete with the memory of his first wife for Emerson's respect and affection.

The following years, between 1836 and 1842, witnessed one of the most creative periods in Emerson's life. The publication of his first book, *Nature*, in 1836, though it was short, established him as a prose writer. The series of lectures he gave in the following two years, such as "The Philosophy of History," "The American Scholar," "Divinity School Address," and "Literary Ethics," helped him to gain recognition. Because of his unorthodox stance toward Christianity, expressed in the "Divinity School Address" delivered at Harvard in 1838, Emerson received ruthless criticisms from some conservative believers and was barred from giving any lectures at his alma mater until almost thirty years later. The publication of his *Essays: First Series* in 1841 further established him as a major figure in American literature. As a result of his growing fame, Emerson gradually became the literary leader of his time, though he preferred to lead people to themselves rather than to himself. Compared with his prose, his poetry gained recognition much more slowly. Not until the end of

1846, when his first collection of poems was published, did his poetry receive some serious attention. Although Emerson regarded himself mainly as a poet, his poetry never gained as much prestige as did his essays.

From October, 1847, to July, 1848, Emerson, already internationally known, made his second trip to Europe, visiting friends and giving lectures while in England. Many of his impressions on this trip eventually found expression in his *English Traits* (1856). Later works, often of inferior quality, continued to appear during his remaining years. A few years after the end of the Civil War, a war characterized by unprecedented casualties in American history that certainly disturbed him, the aging Emerson began to lose his memory. The burning of his house in Concord in 1872 accentuated the decline of his health. His last decade brought about the continuous growth of Emerson's reputation along with the failure of his faculties. He died in 1882 at the age of seventy-nine.

Analysis

Throughout his literary career, Emerson consistently advocated the idea of self-reliance, of making self the ultimate judge of things in this world. The self he celebrates, however, is not the same as the individual self, which threatens to become selfishness, but an autonomous spirit which wills to act according to universal moral laws. This spirit, which is located in all objects, may grow as a result of communion with nature. Like many Romantics, who give nature an essential role in their intrinsic lives by treating it either as an equal partner with, or as a substitute for, God, Emerson often expresses a passion for nature, as can be seen in his famous work *Nature* (1836). His love for nature appears to be the expression of his heart based on nature's utilitarian value; however, his reason tells him otherwise. In his analytical reasoning, he follows the argument of traditional idealism in conceiving nature as an ephemeral phenomenon without independent existence. As a result of the conflict between his intellect and his emotion, Emerson remains essentially indecisive as to the ontological being of nature. From his early work *Nature* to the publication of *Letters and Social Aims* (1876), he consistently uses the image of shadows to illustrate the essence of nature. What is emphasized in an equally consistent manner throughout Emerson's life is the utilitarian value, both spiritual and physical, of nature to man. Because of the extremely important role that it enjoys in a person's daily life, Emerson cannot afford to part with nature, which is emotionally close to him, nor can he follow the traditional doctrine of idealism without misgivings. His love for nature often makes him doubt the statement of idealism, and these emotions force him to endow nature with life—hence, the persistent tension between emotion and intellect in Emerson. When his reason gains ascendancy, he will deny that nature has a soul. Once his emotion becomes dominant, however, he will not hesitate to attribute a spirit or apply the metaphorical expression of transcendence to nature.

In "The Over-Soul" (1842), Emerson works out the framework for his idea of oneness, a metaphysical basis for the celebration of ego. The Over-Soul is the embodiment of wisdom, virtue, power, and beauty, among which virtue is supreme. To be the partner of the Creator—or to be a creator—one's duty lies only in assuring the unceasing circular flow between one's own soul and the Over-Soul. It follows that when Emerson says in his "Divinity School Address" that the man who renounces himself comes to himself, he means only the renunciation of the willful interference with the free flowing of the universal spirit, not biblical self-denial. To obey the soul, according to Emerson, one's acts would naturally arrange themselves by irresistible magnetism in a straight line. Because of the constant communication with and participation of the divine essence of the universe, each individual becomes part of the essence and is, thus, self-sufficient in every moment of his existence. Since the divinity of the Over-Soul is inherent in the soul of each individual, one fulfills this divinity by being true to the transcendental spirit in oneself and by keeping it free from the harmful interpositions of one's own artificial will. Virtue is not, as is made clear in "Spiritual Laws" (1841), the product of conscious calculation and should not be interfered with by our will.

Applied to history, the idea of the Over-Soul leads to a subjective view of the past. History, according to Emerson, is only a record of the universal mind, and its task is to find the expression of one's soul. Under this notion, what is called history is actually biography. A similarly moralistic view characterizes his theory of art. Although Emerson's theory of the Over-Soul lays the groundwork for Walt Whitman's "Song of Myself" (1855), his view of art focuses more on a poet's character than on the work of art. What characterizes a poet, according to Emerson, is the power to perceive the unity of nature and the ability to impart his impression of it through imagination. As every person is susceptible to the work of the Over-Soul and possesses imagination, every person is thus potentially a poet. In cultivating his power and exercising his imagination, the poet should communicate with nature. Because of his ability to see the essence of this world and his power to employ signs to express it, the poet animates and illuminates other people and thus becomes a spiritual emancipator. The prestige which the poet enjoys, however, is not exclusive: It is equally shared by the hero and the sage. These three sovereigns—the namer, the doer, and the knower—are simply different names for the highest progeny of the Over-Soul.

A change has been noted in Emerson's thought in his later period, when fate and limitation are emphasized. Emerson speaks of fate with awe; nevertheless, his tone remains defiant. Apart from or in spite of the emphasis on fate, assertions of thought and will are frequently made in his later works, as is demonstrated by the posthumous book *Natural History of Intellect and Other Papers* (1893), which primarily concerns the soul rather than the exterior world. Even in the essays "Fate" and "Illusions" (1860), where limitation is a major concern, the fundamental views expressed are still those which characterize his early period. As a counterbalance to the idea of illusion, sincerity is invoked by Emerson in his later works. With the recognition of this limitation as well as the corresponding stress on will and thought, Emerson's doctrines thus become more profound.

It has been noted that every work of Emerson appears to contain all of his major ideas. His works are, indeed, often a highly crystallized form of writing resulting from the long process of modifications based on his audiences' different responses. Because of the complexity of ideas, his essays often convey the impression of great diversity without clear logical connections. The central statements—usually simple, short, and concise—tend to be the most powerful expressions, calling for no lengthy modifier yet yielding great insight. Emerson's masterly command of everyday language continues to be a wonder in American literature.

NATURE

First published: 1836
Type of work: Essay

Through communion with nature, one is able to transcend oneself and this world and achieve union with the divine essence of the universe.

Composed of an introduction and eight chapters, *Nature*, Emerson's first book, contains all the fundamental ideas which were to be developed at length later in his life. The dominant theme of this work—the harmony between man and nature— also became the theoretical basis of many literary works composed after it in the nineteenth century United States.

The treatise begins with a criticism of reliance on the past and a suggestion to depend on oneself to explore this world. In explaining the reason for self-trust, Emerson espouses a dualistic view of this universe, which, according to him, is divided into two parts: one, the self, which represents the soul, the other, the exterior world, which he terms nature, the latter being subordinated to the former. Perfect correspondence, in his view, exists between these two parts, a link which makes one's communication with the outside world possible. To him, nature is all benevolence; community, by contrast, often signifies waywardness. In communicating with nature, he believes, one is able to purge oneself of all cares and eventually achieve a mystical union with the universe. Apart from spiritual nourishment, nature provides an individual's material needs. At higher levels, it further fulfills one's aesthetic sentiment, serves as the vehicle of thought, and disciplines one's mind. Under the heading "Beauty," which constitutes the third chapter, a theory of aesthetics is advanced. Emerson distinguishes three kinds of beauty in nature: the beauty of exterior forms, which is the lowest kind; spiritual beauty, with virtue as its essence; and the intellectual beauty characterized by a search for the absolute order of things. Characteristic of Emerson, unity can be found among these three kinds of beauty, which, at the ultimate level, are but different expressions of the same essence: "God is the all-fair. Truth, and goodness, and beauty, are but different faces of the same All." The equation of beauty, truth, and virtue is typical of Romantic aesthetics.

In discussing the use of nature as the vehicle of thought, Emerson further illustrates the correspondence between nature and soul, and matter and mind, using this link as the basis for his theory of language. According to him, language originally came from and should remain in close contact with natural images or facts. A language characterized by, or a discourse drawing heavily upon, vivid images is thus most desirable. Because of the identification of beauty, truth, and virtue as different expressions of the Creator, the corruption of a man's character is necessarily followed by his corrupted use of language. Viewed in this light, people with strong minds who lead a simple life in the countryside cannot but have an advantage in the use of powerful language over people residing in the city, who are prone to be distracted by the material world.

After language, discipline—another use of nature at a still higher level—occurs. Following Coleridge and some of the nineteenth century German idealists, Emerson distinguishes two kinds of cognitive faculties: one, reason, which perceives the analogy that unites matter and mind, the other, understanding, which discerns the characteristics of things. Apart from the reiteration of the tremendous healing power of nature, which is esteemed as a religious preacher, the idea of unity is presented. It is Emerson's belief that what unites nature and soul, matter and mind, is a moral sentiment, sometimes called the Creator, the Universal Spirit, or the Supreme Being, which both pervades and transcends the two different parts of the universe. The ultimate discipline that one receives from nature, he maintains, should be the recognition and acceptance of this Universal Spirit underlying both the world and the self. The tremendous importance which nature commands in his thought prompts Emerson to discuss its metaphysical status in the sixth chapter, entitled "Idealism." Before exploring this issue, he makes it clear that whether nature substantially exists or is simply a reflection of one's mind is not exactly settled and makes little difference to him in terms of his love for nature. He then proceeds, however, to maintain that senses or understanding based on senses tends to make one believe in the absolute existence of nature, whereas reason, the better cognitive faculty, modifies this belief. The further distinction between a sensual man, who is confined by the material world, and a poet, who frees himself with imagination from the domination of the material world, shows that Emerson favors the view that nature does not have absolute existence. The discussion of the issue eventually ends with the reiteration of the superiority of the soul and trust in God, whose creation of nature is to be regarded for man's emancipation. Having emphatically asserted the superiority of the soul, Emerson gives the following chapter the title "Spirit" to indicate that the essential function of nature is to lead one back to the Universal Spirit. In order to do so, one needs to employ a creative imagination rather than a mechanical analysis to achieve communion with nature: "a guess is often more fruitful than an indisputable affirmation, and . . . a dream may let us deeper into the secret of nature than a hundred concerted experiments." The problem with this world, according to him, can only be a problem with self. In concluding *Nature* Emerson therefore exhorts one to achieve unity with nature, to trust in oneself, and eventually to create one's own world.

THE AMERICAN SCHOLAR

First published: 1837
Type of work: Lecture

The American scholar should avoid being enslaved to the past or foreign influences, instructing people to rely upon the self as the ever-dependable source of inspiration.

In 1837, Emerson was invited to deliver the address "The American Scholar," one of the most influential American addresses made at his time, to the Harvard chapter of Phi Beta Kappa; the same topic of the address had been prescribed year after year since his boyhood. When Emerson urged American scholars at the beginning of his address to create an original literature free from European influence, he was to some extent reiterating a conventional theme. The creation of an original literature, Emerson maintained, however, would have to be based on an inner spirit of self-reliance—the opening and concluding theme of *Nature*. The primary concern of this address is thus with an intellectual's spiritual cultivation—the eventual goal being "Man Thinking"—rather than the actual composition of literary works. In the discussion of the scholar's education, three kinds of influence are mentioned: nature, books, and action. Of primary importance, permanent nature corresponds to one's mind, hence it should be studied for the enhancement of the understanding of the self. The close relationship between the soul and nature is explained here in terms of a seal and print. The second source of influence is the mind of the past, which can best be seen in books. Emerson criticizes those scholars who allow themselves to be dominated by the past great minds to the extent that they think for the historical figures rather than for themselves, thereby becoming bookworms instead of "Man Thinking." As a result, creative reading is advocated for one's own inspiration. Because of his belief in the union of the self with the Universal Spirit, he further urges scholars to communicate with it first, drawing upon its creative force to compose their own original books. Only when one encounters difficulty in communicating with this spirit or God directly, he insists, should one depend on books. Action is considered the third source of influence upon the scholar. In encouraging a scholar to act, Emerson not only emphasizes the importance of the actual experience for one's mental growth but also, and especially, attempts to identify a man of action with a contemplative mind, a hero with a poet. After illustrating the three kinds of influence upon the scholar, Emerson describes the scholar's duty, which is to guide people to find the universal mind within themselves and to achieve unity with it. To be qualified for such a work, the scholar would naturally need to be confident and self-trusting: "In self-trust all the virtues are comprehended." When one looks within and becomes a master of oneself, Emerson states, one actually examines all minds and becomes a master of all men. Because of the unceasing manifestation of the

Universal Spirit in every object, the here and now is thus greatly emphasized. Instead of looking to great minds in the past and from afar, he prefers to embrace the lowly and common in the present—a common Romantic theme. To conclude, Emerson repeats the theme of self-reliance on the most grandiloquent level, assuring his audience that "if the single man plant himself indomitably on his instincts, and there abide, the huge world will come round to him."

SELF-RELIANCE

First published: 1841
Type of work: Essay

Because of the inherent moral sentiment, which partakes of the divine spirit, the best principle for behavior is to trust one's own intuition.

In his book entitled *Essays*, "Self-Reliance" follows "History" so that a balanced and self-contained unit can be created out of these two. Abounding with short aphorisms, the essay begins with an admonition to believe in the true self, which is considered in essence identical with the Universal Spirit: "Trust thyself: every heart vibrates to that iron string." Emerson then holds infancy, which is favorably contrasted with adulthood, as a model for one to follow in the cultivation of a spirit of independence or nonconformity. His metaphorical use of a babe as a model of nonconformity is a radical twist of Christ's elevation of it as an emblem of total dependence on God. As does Wordsworth, Emerson regards a person's growth normally as a process of losing one's moral sentiment or spirit of nonconformity. Society is considered to have an adverse effect on the growth of each individual's independent spirit, whereas solitude may contribute to it. Senseless philanthropy, which encourages dependence on outside help, is thus also thought to be detrimental. When Emerson states that one should live by one's instinct, whether or not it be from the devil, he is attempting to use exaggeration to shock his audience; his idea is that the inherent moral sentiment, which makes one self-sufficient, cannot come from the devil. Total trust in one's emotions may well result in contradiction when one's emotions change, however; noting this, Emerson simply retorts that life itself is an organic process, inevitably involving contradiction. Acting in accordance with true feeling, he believes, will automatically bring about a sound life. Viewed in light of self, history is thus the biography of a few unusually powerful figures. Having emphasized the importance of nonconformity, he begins to explore the philosophical basis for self-reliance. According to Emerson, there is an instinct or intuition in each individual drawing upon the Universal Spirit as the ever-dependable guiding principle. Because of the identification of intuition with the Universal Spirit, one is simply following its command when one acts in accordance with one's intuition. The presence of the self-sufficing and self-contained Universal Spirit in each individual thus justifies one's living in and for the present without having to refer either to the past or to the future.

Whereas Christ alone has traditionally been regarded as the Word made flesh, Emer--
son regards every man potentially as a reincarnation of the Word. Consequently,
regret of the past and prayer for the future as a means to effect private ends are both
diseases of human will and should be avoided. Traveling with the hope to see something greater than the self, in Emerson's view, would simply be senseless. As a result
of this moralistic view, society, like nature, may change but never advance. Typical
of his conclusions, the end of this essay, which repeats the theme of self-reliance and
predicts the subjugation of Chance under human will based on self-reliance, sounds
greatly optimistic.

THE OVER-SOUL

First published: 1841
Type of work: Essay

The Over-Soul underlies the universe, giving birth to and justifying the existence of all the objects.

Greatly influenced by a third century neo-Platonist philosopher, Plotinus, "The
Over-Soul" explicates one of Emerson's essential ideas, one on which his entire
thought is based. Beginning with an approval of a life based on hope, Emerson posits
the idea of unity or "Over-Soul" as the metaphysical basis for the existence of everything. According to him, the Over-Soul is a perfect self-sufficing universal force, the
origin of which is unknown and the essence of which is characterized through wisdom, virtue, power, and beauty, giving sustenance to all objects. Maintained by this
force, all objects are thus self-sufficient in every moment of their existence, having
no need to concern themselves with the future. With no hearkening back to the past
and no anticipation of the future, the meaning of one's ever-progressive life simply
exists in the "here and now."

Because of the unifying power of the Over-Soul, differences between objects can
be eradicated: "The act of seeing and the thing seen, the seer and the spectacle, the
subject and the object, are one." In explaining the nature of this universal spirit,
Emerson makes a distinction between the natural self—the body and its faculties—
and the transcendental spirit residing in each individual and animating the natural
self. This transcendental spirit, he emphasizes, cannot be defined by the intellect; it
can be detected only with the intuition. A child, who acts according to instinct, is
thus celebrated as the model for the reception of this spirit. As the ultimate force in
this universe, the Over-Soul ought to be obeyed as the absolute commander of the
self, since it can guide one to lead a most sound life. The movement of the universe
in this sense can be interpreted as the ceaseless communication between each individual soul and the Over-Soul. The more one communicates with the universal soul,
the more powerful one may become. Jesus, who, according to Emerson, heeded the
voice from the spirit within oneself, is held as a perfect example of such a communi-

cation between the individual soul and the Over-Soul. A genius is simply the person who lets the spirit flow into the intellect and then speaks from within. In order to communicate with this universal spirit, one needs only to be plain and true, since it normally descends upon the lowly and simple, the type of people who consistently received Emerson's attention since the composition of *Nature.*

Echoing a statement from the Hindu sacred text, the *Upanishads*, Emerson maintains that one may also partake of divinity from communicating with the divine force: "The simplest person who in his integrity worships God, becomes God." The presence of this universal spirit in each individual thus makes it imperative for one to look not without but within for the source of inspiration. Viewed in this light, the greatness of renowned poets lies thus in their ability to remind people of the immense resource under their control and to instruct them to disregard all their achievements. All exterior authority, be what it may, Emerson states, should be disregarded; only the self guided by the Over-Soul is to be trusted. The orthodox faith based on exterior authority is interpreted at the end of the essay as a result of the withdrawal of the soul and the decline of religion. To be a master of the world around him, Emerson concludes, a person has to achieve unity with the divine soul and follow the dictate of his own heart.

FATE

First published: 1860
Type of work: Essay

Although fate is a horrendous force in this world, mind and will are equally powerful and can subjugate fate to a good use.

A great change occurred in Emerson's thought in his later life, as can be demonstrated in the essay "Fate." Whereas freedom and optimism were emphasized in his early life, fate and limitation eventually became his great concern. Having, in his later life, read much Oriental literature, which greatly emphasizes the power of fate, Emerson felt it necessary to reckon with this subject and include it in his thought. Unlike his earlier essays, which nearly always begin with an optimistic trust in the potentiality of the self, "Fate" begins with an emphasis on obstacles, which are described as immovable and which individuals would inevitably experience in their attempt to achieve goals. To avoid the misunderstanding that he has radically changed his view regarding the grand nature of mankind, which had been effectively advocated during most of his life, Emerson affirms the importance of liberty immediately after his opening statement on the significance of fate.

The ideal principle, according to him, is to strike a balance between liberty and fate, rather than over-emphasize either of them. After setting forth this principle, Emerson turns his attention back to fate, citing Hinduism, Calvinism, and Greek tragedy as examples for their emphatic treatment of this grim aspect of life. Contrary to his earlier idea, Nature—equated with fate in this essay—is now perceived as potentially rough and dangerous. He describes various kinds of limitations—environment, race, physique, character, and sometimes thought. In order to illustrate the importance of fate, Emerson even makes an overstatement that one is predetermined the moment one is born. A criticism is further made on the narrow focus of his own previous thought (the optimism emphasizing the power of the self) with the recognition that circumstance, the negative side which one cannot fully control, ought to be considered. According to Emerson, fate manifests itself in both matter and mind, the latter being affected in a much more subtle way.

Having elaborated the significance of fate, he begins to assert liberty again: "Intellect annuls Fate." To counteract fate, one is advised first to transform it intrinsically by regarding it as a positive force working for one's ultimate good rather than a negative force. Furthermore, one should draw upon the ever-resourceful universal force, the moral sentiment within oneself, to take oneself out of bondage into freedom. Only by so doing, Emerson maintains, can one expect to reconcile fate and freedom: "Person makes event, and event person." After analyzing the way to reconcile the opposite forces of fate and freedom, he moves a step further in holding that one can subjugate fate to one's will because event is only the exteriorization of the soul—an idea which is in agreement with his early thought. In doing so, he applies the law of cause and effect to human life, regarding the soul as the cause and event as its effect. Nature, in his view, best serves those who concentrate on refining their moral sentiment. The essay concludes with an assertion of the balanced interplay of fate and freedom, giving the enduring impression that by trusting oneself, one is eventually able to become what one wants to be: "Let us build altars to the Blessed Unity which holds nature and souls in perfect solution."

THE RHODORA

First published: 1839
Type of work: Poem

Beauty needs no rational justification for its self-sufficient existence.

Consisting of sixteen lines, "The Rhodora" is one of Emerson's most admired poems. The major theme in this poem, a work written two years before *Nature*, can be found in many of his later works as well as in the Romantic literature of his time. As indicated by the subtitle, "On Being Asked, Whence Is the Flower?" the poem has a philosophical import concerning the existence of the flower. A spiritual communication between humankind and nature appears at the very beginning (represented by sea winds, a favorite theme in Emerson's works), when the speaker states that the sea winds in May "pierced our solitudes." A common image in Romantic poetry, the wind often connotes inspiration. In this regard, the opening statement may also imply that the poet was inspired by the muse through his communication with nature, thereby beginning his creative process—an act which corresponds with the growing season of May in the outside world, as is mentioned in the poem. Freed from solitude by the sea winds, the speaker notices the Rhodora—a rather obscure flower—blooming in the woods in a somewhat private location ordinarily unlikely to catch one's attention. The presence of this flower, the spelling of which is capitalized throughout the poem to emphasize its significance as the symbol of beauty, is described as pleasing to both land and water. The service which the Rhodora offers to the world almost involves self-sacrifice, as is reflected in the description of the pleasure that its fallen petals were able to give to the pool: "The purple petals, fallen in the pool/ Made the black water with their beauty gay." After examining the objects on land and water, Emerson proceeds to note the creature in the sky, the "red-bird," courting the flower, thereby making his poem symbolically comprehensive of all the objects in this world. A radical transition occurs at the center of this poem; whereas the first half essentially describes various objects with the focus on the beauty of the Rhodora, the second half primarily concerns the metaphysical meaning of the flower. Further division exists in the second half, which contains two sets of questions and answers, each set occurring every four lines. Corresponding to this structural pattern, the tenses also shift from the past in the first half to the present mixed with the past in the second. Furthermore, the rhyme scheme of *aabbcdcd*, which occurs twice in the poem, reinforces the theme of the dichotomy between nature and self (the description of the Rhodora and the inquiry about the metaphysical meaning of its existence) and the correspondence between them.

Emerson begins the second half with an apostrophe to the Rhodora, asking in the name of the "sages" why its beauty is wasted on earth and sky. The reason, central to this poem as well as to Emerson's thought, is that the flower is self-sufficient, existing for its own sake; "Tell them, dear, that if eyes were made for seeing,/ Then Beauty is its own excuse for being." By refusing to justify the being of the flower with analytical rationalization, activity which characterizes the sages, the poet implies that intuition or instinct rather than rationalization is necessary for leading a satisfactory life. A similar question is posed in the last four lines, where the Rhodora is regarded as the rival of the rose, a favorite flower in Western tradition. The rivalry between the Rhodora and the rose possibly signifies a contrast between the lowly and plain and the high and flamboyant in stylistics, the former being the poet's choice. The concluding answer may be given by the Rhodora as well as the speaker, or by the latter speaking for both: "But, in my simple ignorance, suppose/ The self-same Power that brought me there brought you." The poet's affirmation of the quality of simple ignorance represented by the flower indicates his predilection to use the lowly and humble as the basis of his aesthetics, a theme presaged by the seclusive setting. The eventual naming of the Power, which unifies various objects in the universe, not only serves as a link between the poet and the flower—a spiritual rapport between man and nature already seen at the beginning—but also hearkens back to the subtitle of the poem, thereby giving the poem a highly structured unity.

BRAHMA

First published: 1857
Type of work: Poem

The universal spirit Brahma is effable and transcends the dichotomy of a person's thinking.

Greatly influenced by a sacred text of Hinduism, *Katha-Upanishad*, "Brahma" is a philosophical explication of the universal spirit by that name. The poetic form of elegiac quatrain is used to represent the solemn nature of the subject. Throughout the poem, Brahma appears as the only speaker, sustaining the continuity of the work. That the spirit is the only speaker signifies not only its absolute nature but also its sustaining power, upon which the existence of the entire universe—metaphorically, the poem—is based. The poem begins by examining the common-sensical view that the spirit ends with one's death. Even though the body may be destroyed, Brahma, which resides in each individual as the fountain of life, never ceases to exist: "If the red slayer think he slays,/ Or if the slain think he is slain,/ They know not well the subtle ways/ I keep." When the body is destroyed, the poet maintains, the spirit will appear again, likely in a different form. By employing the examples of both the slayer and the slain, the speaker is suggesting not only the prevalence of their view (that the spirit may not be eternal) but also the dichotomy that normally characterizes a person's perception.

The dichotomy recurs in the second stanza, in which opposite notions such as far and near, shadow and sunlight, vanishing and appearing, and shame and fame are juxtaposed. To the speaker, who unifies the universe, the seemingly unbridgeable differences between opposite concepts can be perfectly resolved; hence, the paradoxical statements. Brahma's great power is further described in the third stanza, where the spirit states that it comprehends yet transcends everything—both "the doubter and the doubt," the subject and object, and matter and mind. In addition, the rhyme scheme befittingly reinforces the spirit's interweaving power, yielding a sense of wonder based on unusual metrical symmetry.

Different from the otherworldly spirit in Hinduism, however, the transcendental spirit represented by Brahma in this poem leads the follower not to heaven but to this world. By using the conjunction "but" in the last stanza, Emerson prepares his reader for his own interpretation of the universal spirit. The concluding statement that justifies self-sufficient existence in this world, "But thou, meek lover of the good!/ Find me, and turn thy back on heaven," makes this poem characteristically Emersonian.

Summary

Emerson's thought is characterized by optimism and tremendous hope for mankind. Although some critics, represented by George Santayana, believe that he failed to reckon with the force of evil, his advocacy of looking within and acting sincerely as the ultimate mode of behavior still appeals to the modern age. Especially in a society dominated by technology, Emerson's poetic vision of the transcendent mind offers an intriguing alternate way of life emphasizing the spirit. Furthermore, the dynamic style primarily based on powerful short sentences, insightful aphorisms, and natural transitions makes Emerson unequivocally one of the greatest essayists of all time.

Bibliography

Barish, Evelyn. *Emerson: The Roots of Prophecy.* Princeton, N.J.: Princeton University Press, 1989.

Bishop, Jonathan. *Emerson on the Soul.* Cambridge, Mass.: Harvard University Press, 1964.

Konvitz, Milton R., and Stephen E. Whicher, eds. *Emerson: A Collection of Critical Essays.* Englewood Cliffs, N.J.: Prentice-Hall, 1962.

McAleer, John J. *Ralph Waldo Emerson: Days of Encounter.* Boston: Little, Brown, 1984.

Paul, Sherman. *Emerson's Angle of Vision: Man and Nature in American Experience.* Cambridge, Mass.: Harvard University Press, 1952.

Porter, David. *Emerson and Literary Change.* Cambridge, Mass.: Harvard University Press, 1978.

Rusk, Ralph L. *The Life of Ralph Waldo Emerson.* New York: Columbia University Press, 1949.

Waggoner, Hyatt H. *Emerson as Poet.* Princeton, N.J.: Princeton University Press, 1974.

Whicher, Stephen. *Freedom and Fate: An Inner Life of Ralph Waldo Emerson.* Philadelphia: University of Pennsylvania Press, 1953.

Yoder, R. A. *Emerson and the Orphic Poet in America.* Berkeley: University of California Press, 1978.

Vincent Yang

LOUISE ERDRICH

Born: Little Falls, Minnesota
July 6, 1954

Principal Literary Achievement

Drawing on her Chippewa and German-immigrant heritage, Erdrich, in her novels and poetry, has created a wide-ranging chronicle of Native-American and white experience in twentieth century North Dakota.

Biography

Although born in Minnesota, Louise Erdrich grew up in Wahpeton, a small town in southeastern North Dakota, just across the Red River from her native state. Her father, Ralph Erdrich, was a German immigrant who taught in the Wahpeton Bureau of Indian Affairs boarding school. Her mother, Rita Journeau Erdrich, a three-quarters Chippewa Indian, also worked at the school. Erdrich was the oldest of seven children, and in her youth her parents encouraged her interest in writing by paying her a nickel for her stories and binding them in homemade book form.

Erdrich's mixed religious and cultural background provided a rich foundation for her poetry and fiction. Along with the Indian boarding school, there were two convents in Wahpeton, and Erdrich commented in 1985 and 1986 interviews that she had a "gothic-Catholic childhood," including a close relationship with her paternal grandmother, who embraced "a dark, very Catholic kind of mysticism." Erdrich also paid frequent visits to her Chippewa relatives on the Turtle Mountain Reservation in north-central North Dakota. There her maternal grandfather served as tribal chairman, and he participated in both traditional Chippewa religion and Roman Catholicism.

In 1972, Erdrich enrolled at Dartmouth College in New Hampshire, arriving on the same day that Michael Dorris, her future husband, came to campus to teach anthropology. Nine years her senior, Dorris later became a tenured professor and head of the Native American Studies Program at Dartmouth. Erdrich majored in creative writing, and though she took a course from Dorris in her junior year, she has stated that she did not form a close relationship with him or take a strong interest in her Indian heritage, until years later.

Encouraged at Dartmouth by prizes for her poetry and fiction, Erdrich decided to pursue writing as her career. During and immediately after her college years, she worked at a variety of jobs in the Northeast and in North Dakota to support herself

and broaden her experience of the world. These jobs included waiting tables, working in a mental hospital, teaching poetry in prisons and schools, and editing an Indian newspaper. In 1978, Erdrich entered a creative writing program at Johns Hopkins University, and after earning her M.A. in 1979, she returned to Dartmouth to give a poetry reading. This visit sparked a closer friendship with Dorris, and in 1981 they were married.

Louise Erdrich and Michael Dorris devoted their lives to ambitious family, literary, and humanitarian goals. Like Erdrich, Dorris is three-eighths Indian, and years before his marriage to Erdrich he adopted three Indian infants from Midwestern reservations. Dorris and Erdrich produced three more children.

Erdrich and her husband collaborate on virtually all the works that either one publishes—whether fiction, poetry, or nonfiction. They conceive of subjects, plots, and characters together; one does the writing, and the other helps in the editing stage, which may involve as many as seven drafts. Their first major literary success came in 1982, when Erdrich's story "The World's Greatest Fishermen" won the five-thousand-dollar first prize in the Nelson Algren fiction competition. Set in 1981, this story involves members of two Chippewa families (the Kashpaws and the Morrisseys), and Erdrich and Dorris built on the success of the story by conceiving others that intertwined its characters with members of three other Chippewa and mixed-blood families in the years from 1934 to 1984. The stories appeared in prestigious magazines such as *The Atlantic Monthly* and the *Kenyon Review*, and two were selected for honorary anthologies: "Scales," for *Best American Short Stories, 1983* (1983), and "Saint Marie," for *Prize Stories 1985: The O. Henry Awards* (1985).

In 1984, the year she turned thirty, Louise Erdrich gave birth to her first child, became pregnant with her second, and published two books. *Jacklight*, a collection of forty poems and four folktales, met with high critical praise. When Erdrich collected fourteen of the Chippewa family stories and presented them as a novel, *Love Medicine* became a national best-seller and won several prizes, including the 1984 National Book Critics Circle Award for Fiction.

The success of *Love Medicine* encouraged Erdrich and Dorris to plan three more novels chronicling the interwoven lives of Chippewas and whites in twentieth century North Dakota. The second novel, *The Beet Queen* (1986), ranges over a slightly earlier period (1932-1972) than *Love Medicine* and focuses less on native Americans than on whites and their small-town lives. The third novel in the tetralogy, *Tracks* (1988), goes further back in time to 1912-1924, when members of the Chippewa and mixed-blood families of *Love Medicine* are engaged in a bitter struggle for survival. Although neither *The Beet Queen* nor *Tracks* was as monumental a success as *Love Medicine*, both were highly praised by critics and became best-sellers. In addition, two stories from *Tracks* were reprinted in honorary anthologies: "Fleur," in *Prize Stories 1987: The O. Henry Awards* (1987), and "Snares," in *Best American Short Stories, 1988* (1988).

Along with the North Dakota novels that have been the main source of Erdrich's fame, she and her husband have also been involved with other literary and humanitarian projects. In 1987, Dorris published his first novel, *A Yellow Raft in Blue Water*, a story of three Indian women. The couple spent a year in Montana while Dorris conducted research on fetal alcohol syndrome (FAS), a group of physical and psychological symptoms that afflict many Indian children, including one of Dorris' adopted sons. In 1989, Dorris published a study of FAS, *The Broken Cord*, and he and Erdrich have donated money and campaigned for legislation to combat this debilitating disease. Also in 1989, Erdrich published her second volume of poetry, *Baptism of Desire*. The book did not receive as much critical attention as her earlier works, though the poems and folktales in it deal vividly with many of Erdrich's recurring themes: sexual and spiritual desire, and birth and parenting.

Analysis

In a 1985 essay entitled "Where I Ought to Be: A Writer's Sense of Place," Louise Erdrich wrote that the essence of her writing emerges from her attachment to a specific locale: North Dakota, the site of a Chippewa reservation and of the neighboring white communities founded by European immigrants. In this essay, Erdrich also defines her mission as a writer by comparing it with the function of a traditional storyteller in tribal cultures such as that of the native American:

> In a tribal view of the world, where one place has been inhabited for generations, the landscape becomes enlivened by a sense of group and family history. Unlike most contemporary writers, a traditional storyteller fixes listeners in an unchanging landscape combined of myth and reality. People and place are inseparable.

Although three-eighths Chippewa, Erdrich has not aspired to become precisely this kind of traditional storyteller. She realizes only too keenly that the tribal view in its pure form is no longer tenable for American Indians, because the "unchanging" relationship of Indian people and landscape, of myth and reality, has been destroyed by the massive dislocations and changes brought by European settlement and nineteenth and twentieth century "progress." On the other hand, Erdrich's writing does create a contemporary neo-tribal view by dramatizing the intricate relatedness of people and place in her North Dakota locale. The central paradox of her work is that, though her characters often feel disconnected and isolated, the works themselves reveal how deeply interrelated these people are—both with their North Dakota homeland (the landscape and the spirits that inhabit it) and with other people (their contemporaries and their ancestors).

One way in which Erdrich reveals this relatedness is in her precise use of setting. Virtually every poem and story gains in effectiveness from the way in which details of location, season, time of day, and weather reflect the emotional state or social situation of her characters. The often extreme elements of the North Dakota environment—its flat plains and dense forests; its marshes and lakes; its scalding, dry summers and frigid, snowy winters; its rivers that vacillate between raging spring torrents and late summer trickles—all function dramatically in Erdrich's work.

Animals are another feature of her North Dakota locale that Erdrich uses to dramatize relationships among humans and of humans with their environment. In traditional Indian myths and folktales, animals and humans are often closely related—even interchangeable. Erdrich's poetry often draws on this aspect of her Indian literary heritage both for individual figures of speech and as the narrative basis for entire poems. For example, Erdrich sets the poem "A Love Medicine" on a night when the Red River reaches flood stage; she describes her sister Theresa, a young woman seeking sexual experience who is oblivious to possible disaster, in this way:

> Theresa goes out in green halter and chains
> that glitter at her throat.
> This dragonfly, my sister,
> she belongs more than I
> to this night of rising water.

Erdrich's presentation of animals and of the supernatural in her fiction is more complex than in her poetry and is related to the unusual mixture of realism and exaggeration in her fiction. Rather than boldly asserting the metaphoric or mystical connections of animals and people as she does in her poetry, her stories and novels generally begin by establishing a realistic base of recognizably ordinary people, settings, and actions. As her tales develop, however, these people become involved in events and perceptions that appear to the reader quite extraordinary—exaggerated in ways that may seem deluded or mystical, grotesque or magical, comic or tragic, or some strange mixture of these.

The chapter (or story) entitled "Love Medicine" in Erdrich's first novel is a rich illustration of this mixture of realism and exaggeration, as well as of other characteristic features of her fiction. In this story, the young man Lipsha Morrissey begins by reflecting on how mundane his life has been: "I never really done much with my life, I suppose. I never had a television." Under pressure from his grandmother, Marie Lazarre Kashpaw, who wants to rein in her husband Nector's straying affections, Lipsha tries to concoct a love potion based on the hearts of Canadian geese— birds that mate for life. The story develops comically as Lipsha fails to shoot down the wild geese he thinks he needs and instead substitutes turkey hearts that he buys in a supermarket. The story then takes a grotesque, tragicomic turn, however, when a suspicious and reluctant Nector chokes to death on a turkey heart that Marie nags him into eating.

The story leaves the reader wondering how to interpret Nector's death. Is it evidence of the power of traditional Indian spiritualism, an ironic punishment of Marie for trying to trick her husband into loving her, or mere monstrous bad luck? As so often in her fiction, Erdrich refrains from any authorial comment that would provide a direct or conclusive answer to the mysteries (often involving the supernatural) that she presents. Instead, she relies on a first-person (or, occasionally, third-person limited) point of view, and she concentrates on dramatizing what the characters think and feel about the mysteries in their lives. In "Love Medicine," Lipsha and Marie share a sense of guilt over Nector's death until, in another surprising twist, his ghost returns to visit them. Lipsha's interpretation of this event is so moving and profound that it seems a more meaningful act of "love medicine" than the supernatural magic he had earlier failed to perform:

> Love medicine ain't what brings him back to you, Grandma. No, it's something else. He loved you over time and distance, but he went off so quick he never got the chance to tell you how he loves you, how he doesn't blame you, how he understands. It's true feeling, not no magic. No supermarket heart could have brung him back.

One other element of Erdrich's fiction is often praised by critics: her poetic, often lyrical style. Erdrich intensifies many moments in her tales through an aptly chosen image or figure of speech, yet she is also a master at drawing such poetically heightened language from her characters' experience. For example, in "Love Medicine," after Lipsha has encountered the spirit of his dead grandfather, he compares life to a kind of clothing that he knows well:

> Your life feels different on you, once you greet death and understand your heart's position. You wear your life like a garment from the mission bundle sale ever after—lightly because you realize you never paid nothing for it, cherishing because you know you won't ever come by such a bargain again.

Erdrich often ends her stories with a lyrical flourish, a series of images that extends feelings and themes in vivid, though sometimes oblique and unexpected ways. One example is the end of "Love Medicine," where Lipsha decides to pull some dandelions as a way of reconnecting his life with the forces of nature. Rather than ending the story with clear narrative sentences that neatly tie up a conclusion, Erdrich ends with a curious series of sentence fragments, images of what Lipsha sees that invite interpretation like lines in a poem: "The spiked leaves full of bitter mother's milk. A buried root. A nuisance people dig up and throw in the sun to wither. A globe of frail seeds that's indestructible."

JACKLIGHT

First published: 1984
Type of work: Poem

In the harsh glare of "jacklight," animals emerge from the woods and beckon hunters to follow them back into a realm of mystery.

"Jacklight," the opening and title poem in Louise Erdrich's first book of verse, is a haunting dramatization of male-female and of white-Indian relations. The poem begins with a note that "the same Chippewa word is used both for flirting and for hunting game," so that the encounter between hunters and animals enacted in the poem is also an allegory for sexual gamesmanship between men and women. The title refers to an artificial light, such as a flashlight, used in hunting or fishing at night; this detail, along with a number of others, suggests that the poem is also an allegory of an encounter between white and Indian cultures. Erdrich does not indicate whether the male hunters in the poem are white or Indian, but in either case their equipment and character traits clearly suggest aggressive and exploitative aspects of white culture.

The poem begins not with the hunters going into the woods, but with the animals coming out—perhaps because of their curiosity, flirtatiousness, or trusting openness:

> We have come to the edge of the woods,
> out of brown grass where we slept, unseen,
> out of knotted twigs, out of leaves creaked shut,
> out of hiding.

In these lines and throughout the poem, Erdrich's use of assonance and consonance (such as "Out . . . brown," "knotted twigs," "leaves creaked") and of parallel syntax (such as the repetition of "out of") creates a charged atmosphere that suggests repeated, ritualistic behavior.

The harsh assaultiveness of males and of white culture is portrayed in the beams of the jacklights, which "clenched to a fist of light that pointed,/ searched out, divided us." The perverse power of this jacklight, in contrast with the powers of nature, is such that the animals (or females, or Indians) are compelled into separation from their group. Although the animals in the poem smell many repulsive aspects of the hunters ("the raw steel of their gun barrels," "their tongues of sour barley," "the itch underneath the caked guts on their clothes"), they do not retreat. Erdrich seems to be suggesting that women (if they want to have husbands) and Indians (if they want to avoid total destruction by the advancing white culture) have no choice but to deal with such brutishness.

In the last two stanzas, however, the animals declare that it is time for some concessions:

> We have come here too long.
>
> It is their turn now,
> their turn to follow us. Listen,
> they put down their equipment.
> It is useless in the tall brush.
> And now they take the first steps, not knowing
> how deep the woods are and lightless.

For the male who is in search of a female, or the white in confrontation with an Indian, or the reader who may be white or male and about to enter the world of a female Indian poet, there must be a willingness to deal with complexities and mysteries for which their "equipment" or preconceptions are inadequate. Yet Erdrich's readers may also be assured that though "the woods" of her poetry may seem "deep" and at times "lightless," they always contain authentic rewards of feeling and experience.

LOVE MEDICINE

First published: 1984
Type of work: Novel

In the years from 1934 to 1984, members of five Chippewa and mixed-blood families struggle to attain a sense of belonging through love, religion, home, and family.

Love Medicine is both the title and the main thematic thread that ties fourteen diverse short stories into a novel. Although it refers specifically to traditional Indian magic in one story, in a broader sense "love medicine" refers to the different kinds of spiritual power that enable Erdrich's Chippewa and mixed-blood characters to transcend—however momentarily—the grim circumstances of their lives. Trapped on their shrinking reservation by racism and poverty, plagued by alcoholism, disintegrating families, and violence, some of Erdrich's characters nevertheless discover forms of "love medicine" that can help to sustain them.

The opening story, "The World's Greatest Fishermen," begins with an episode of "love medicine" corrupted and thwarted. Although June Kashpaw was once a woman of striking beauty and feisty spirit, in 1981 she has sunk to the level of picking up men in an oil boomtown. Hoping at first that a man she meets will be "different" from others who have used and discarded her, then trying to walk to the reservation through a snowstorm, June fails in her last attempts to attain two goals that other characters will also seek throughout the novel: love and home. Although she appears only briefly in this and one other story, June Kashpaw is nevertheless a central character in the novel, for she embodies the potential power of spirit and love in ways that impress and haunt the other characters.

Part 2 of "The World's Greatest Fishermen" introduces many of the other major characters of *Love Medicine*, as June's relatives gather together several months after her death. On the one hand, several characters seem sympathetic because of their closeness to June and their kind treatment of each other. Albertine Johnson, who narrates the story and remembers her Aunt June lovingly, has gone through a wild phase of her own and is now a nursing student. Eli Kashpaw, Albertine's great-uncle who was largely responsible for rearing June, is a tough and sharp-minded old man who has maintained a traditional Chippewa existence as a hunter and fisherman. Lipsha Morrissey, who, though he seems not to know it, is June's illegitimate son, is a sensitive, self-educated young man who acts warmly toward Albertine. In contrast to these characters are others who are flawed or unsympathetic when seen through the eyes of Albertine, who would like to feel that her family is pulling together after June's death. Zelda and Aurelia, Albertine's gossipy mother and aunt, host the family gathering but do little to make Albertine feel at home. Albertine admires "Grandpa," Zelda's father Nector Kashpaw, for having once been an effective tribal chairman, but in contrast to his brother Eli, Nector has become so senile that Albertine cannot communicate with him. Gordie Kashpaw, the husband whom June left, is a pleasant fellow, but also a hapless drunk. Finally, in marked contrast to Lipsha, June's legitimate son King is a volatile bully. Although King gains some sympathy when he voices his grief over his mother's death, his horrifying acts of violence—abusing his wife Lynette, battering his new car, smashing the pies prepared for the family dinner—leave Albertine (and the reader) with a dismayed sense of a family in shambles.

Love Medicine then moves back in time from 1981, and its stories proceed in chronological order from 1934 to 1984, presenting ten earlier episodes in the lives of the Kashpaws and related families and three later episodes that follow the events in "The World's Greatest Fishermen." "Saint Marie" concerns a poor white girl, Marie Lazarre, who in 1934 enters Sacred Heart Convent and a violent love-hate relationship with Sister Leopolda. In "Wild Geese," also set in 1934, Nector Kashpaw is infatuated with Lulu Nanapush, but his affections swerve unexpectedly when he encounters Marie Lazarre on the road outside her convent. By 1948, the time of "The Beads," Marie has married Nector, had three children (Aurelia, Zelda, and Gordie), and agreed to rear her niece June. Marie, however, encounters difficulties: Nector is drinking and philandering, and June, after almost committing suicide in a children's hanging game, leaves to be brought up by Eli in the woods. "Lulu's Boys," set in 1957, reveals that the amorous Lulu Lamartine (née Nanapush) had married Henry Lamartine but bore eight sons by different fathers; years later, she still has a mysterious sexual hold over Henry's brother Beverly. Meanwhile, in "The Plunge of the Brave," also set in 1957, Nector recalls the development of his five-year affair with Lulu and tries to leave his wife Marie for her, but the result is that he accidentally burns Lulu's house to the ground.

The offspring of these Kashpaws and Lamartines also have their problems. In "The Bridge," set in 1973, Albertine Johnson runs away from home and becomes lovers with Henry Lamartine, Jr., one of Lulu's sons, who is a troubled Vietnam veteran. "The Red Convertible," set in 1974, also involves Henry Jr., as Lyman Lamartine tries unsuccessfully to bring his brother out of the dark personality changes that Vietnam has wrought in him. On a lighter note, "Scales," set in 1980, is a hilarious account of the romance between Dot Adare, an obese white clerk at a truck weighing station, and Gerry Nanapush, one of Lulu's sons who is a most unusual convict; enormously fat, amazingly expert at escaping from jail, but totally inept at avoiding capture. "A Crown of Thorns," which overlaps the time of "The World's Greatest Fishermen" in 1981, traces the harrowing and bizarre decline of Gordie Kashpaw into alcoholism after June's death.

Although in these earlier *Love Medicine* stories the positive powers of love and spirit are more often frustrated than fulfilled, in the last three stories several characters achieve breakthroughs that bring members of the different families together in moving and hopeful ways. In "Love Medicine," set in 1982, Lipsha Morrissey reaches out lovingly to his grandmother Marie and to the ghosts of Nector and June. In "The Good Tears," set in 1983, Lulu undergoes a serious eye operation and is cared for by Marie, who forgives her for being Nector's longtime extramarital lover. Finally, in "Crossing the Water," set in 1984, Lipsha Morrissey mentions that Lulu and Marie have joined forces in campaigning for Indian rights, and he helps his father Gerry Nanapush escape to Canada. As Lipsha heads home to the reservation, he comes to appreciate the rich heritage of love, spirit, and wiliness that he has inherited from his diverse patchwork of Chippewa relatives—especially from his grandmother Lulu, his aunt Marie, and his parents June Kashpaw and Gerry Nanapush.

THE BEET QUEEN

First published: 1986
Type of work: Novel

In a North Dakota small town in the years 1932-1972, two orphaned children, along with their relatives and friends, struggle in attempts to sustain love and family.

In *The Beet Queen*, Erdrich shifts her main focus from the native American to the European immigrant side of her background and creates in impressive detail the fictional town of Argus (modeled on Wahpeton, where she grew up, but located closer to the Chippewa reservation). The novel captures both the flat surfaces of life in small-town North Dakota and the wild incidents and strange passions that seem all the more startling, comic, and heartrending for their appearance in such a mundane environment.

As in *Love Medicine*, in *The Beet Queen* Erdrich uses first- and third-person-limited narration to present the diverse points of view of numerous characters. In this novel, however, she focuses more closely on a few main characters (four, later expanded to six) and devotes more time to their childhoods. In this way, the novel conveys a richly detailed perspective on how the dynamics of family and friendship affect her characters over time.

Like *Love Medicine*, *The Beet Queen* begins with a vividly symbolic episode, shifts back in time, and then proceeds chronologically through a series of decades. The opening scene, "The Branch," dramatizes two contrasting approaches to life that many characters will enact throughout the novel. On a cold spring day in 1932, two orphans, Mary and Karl Adare, arrive by freight train in Argus. As they seek the way to the butcher shop owned by their aunt and uncle, Mary "trudge[s] solidly forward," while Karl stops to embrace a tree that already has its spring blossoms. When they are attacked by a dog, Mary runs ahead, continuing her search for the butcher shop, while Karl runs back to hop the train once again. As the archetypal plodder of the novel, Mary continues to "trudge solidly forward" throughout; she is careful, determined, and self-reliant in pursuit of her goals. On the other hand, Karl is the principal dreamer—impressionable, prone to escapist impulses, and dependent on others to catch him when he falls.

The Adare family history shows that Karl is following a pattern set by his mother Adelaide, while Mary grows in reaction against this pattern. Like Karl, Adelaide is physically beautiful but self-indulgent and impulsive. Driven to desperation by her hard luck in the early years of the Depression, Adelaide startles a fairground crowd by abandoning her three children (Mary, Karl, and an unnamed newborn son) to fly away with the Great Omar, an airplane stunt pilot.

In Argus, Mary tangles with yet another beautiful, self-centered dreamer: her cousin Sita Kozka, who resents the attention that her parents Pete and Fritzie and her best friend Celestine James pay to Mary. Yet Mary prevails and carves a solid niche for herself among Pete, Fritzie, and Celestine, who like Mary believe in a strong work ethic and lack Sita's pretentious airs.

A number of episodes gratify the reader with triumphs for Mary and comeuppances for the less sympathetic characters Karl, Adelaide, and Sita. Mary becomes famous for a miracle at her school (she falls and cracks the ice in the image of Jesus), gains Celestine as a close friend, and in time becomes manager of the Kozka butcher shop. By contrast, Karl becomes a drifter who finds only sordid momentary pleasure in brief homosexual affairs, and he twice recklessly injures himself. Meanwhile, Adelaide marries Omar and settles in Florida, but she becomes moody and subject to violent rages. Similarly, Sita fails in her vainglorious attempts to become a model and to establish a fashionable French restaurant; she escapes her first marriage through divorce and becomes insane and suicidal during her second.

Yet even as Erdrich charts the strange and sometimes grotesque downfalls of her flighty characters, she also develops her more sympathetic ones in ways that suggest that the opposite approach to life does not guarantee happiness either. Mary fails in her attempt to attract Russell Kashpaw (the Chippewa half-brother of Celestine), and she develops into an exotically dressed eccentric who is obsessed with predicting the future and controlling others. Like Mary, Celestine James and Wallace Pfef are hard-working and successful in business, but their loneliness drives them to ill-advised affairs with Karl, and he causes each of them considerable grief. In addition, the affair of Celestine and Karl results in the birth of Dot Adare (who grows up to be the obese lover of Gerry Nanapush in the story "Scales" in *Love Medicine*; since Celestine, Mary, and Wallace all spoil the child, Dot turns out, in Wallace's words, to have "all of her family's worst qualities . . . Mary's stubborn, abrupt ways, Sita's vanity, Celestine's occasional cruelties, Karl's lack of responsibility." As a teenager, Dot herself comes to grief when she is mortified to learn that Wallace has rigged the election for Queen of the Argus Beet Festival so that she, an unpopular and ludicrously unlikely candidate, will win.

In addition to the defeats and disappointments that all the characters bear, Erdrich dramatizes the joy that these characters derive from life. The compensations of family and friendship—ephemeral and vulnerable as these may be—turn out to be significant for all the characters at various times in the story, particularly at the end. The irrepressible vitality of these people, troublesome as they often are to one another, keeps the reader involved and entertained throughout the novel.

TRACKS

First published: 1988
Type of work: Novel

In the years between 1912 and 1924, Chippewa Indians struggle to maintain control of their lives and their lands despite the ravages of plagues, starvation, internecine feuding, and white encroachment.

Tracks is Louise Erdrich's most concentrated, intense, and mystical novel. It is the shortest, it covers the shortest period of time (1912-1924), and it alternates between only two first-person narrators (compared with seven and six in the preceding novels). This compression serves the story well, for the human stakes are high. At first, and periodically throughout the novel, the Chippewa characters fear for their very survival, as smallpox, tuberculosis, severe winters, starvation, and feuds with mixed-blood families bring them close to extinction. Later in the novel, government taxes and political chicanery threaten the Chippewas' ownership of their family homesteads. In response, Erdrich's Chippewa characters use all the powers at their command—including the traditional mystical powers of the old ways—to try to survive and maintain their control over the land.

Nanapush, one of the novel's two narrators, is an old Chippewa whom Erdrich names after the trickster rabbit in tribal mythology that repeatedly delivers the Chippewas from threatening monsters. In *Tracks*, Erdrich's Nanapush often does credit to his mythological model by wielding the trickster rabbit's powers of deliverance, wiliness, and humor. First, he saves Fleur Pillager, a starving seventeen-year-old girl and the sole survivor of a Chippewa clan that others fear because the clan is legendary for practicing dark magic. Then he twice delivers young Eli Kashpaw from the sufferings of love by advising him how to win Fleur's heart. Nanapush is also instrumental in saving the extended family that forms around Fleur, Eli, and himself. This family grows to five when Fleur gives birth to a daughter, Lulu, and Eli's mother Margaret Kashpaw becomes Nanapush's bedmate. As these five come close to starvation in the winter of 1918, Nanapush sends Eli out to hunt an elk, and in one of the most extraordinary passages of the novel, Nanapush summons a power vision of Eli hunting that the old man imagines is guiding Eli to the kill. Nanapush also demonstrates the humor associated with his mythological model in his wry tone as a narrator, his sharp wit in conversation, and the tricks that he plays on his mixed-blood antagonists.

Foremost among these antagonists is the novel's other narrator, Pauline Pukwan. A "skinny big-nosed girl with staring eyes," Pauline circulates in Argus from the Kozkas' butcher shop to the Sacred Heart Convent, and on the reservation from the Nanapush-Pillager-Kashpaw group to the Morrissey and Lazarre clans. At first attracted to Fleur by the beauty and sexual power that she herself lacks, Pauline later takes an envious revenge by concocting a love potion that seems to drive Fleur's husband Eli and Sophie Morrissey to become lovers. The word "seems" must be used because Pauline's account of her perceptions, actions, and powers is sometimes so distorted that she becomes an unreliable narrator. She is so torn between desires for inclusion and revenge, between the earthy sexual and spiritual powers of the Chippewas on the one hand and the self-mortifying, otherworldly religion of the Catholic nuns on the other, that her character and narration at times go over the edge into Gothic dementia. Ironically, Pauline gives birth out of wedlock to a girl named Marie, and at the end of her narrative Pauline enters the convent to become Sister Leopolda—the cruel nun who in *Love Medicine* influences her own daughter, Marie Lazarre, to grow into a similarly warped personality, torn between fanatical Catholic piety and earthy sexuality.

Although Erdrich clearly feels passionately about the sufferings visited on her Chippewa characters in *Tracks*, she treats this politically charged material with her usual disciplined restraint. Her dispassionate, deadpan use of first-person narrators (never intruding with her own authorial commentary) matches the understated, stoic attitude that Nanapush adopts toward the numerous waves of hardship and betrayal that the Chippewas must endure. It is also a measure of Erdrich's impressive lack of sentimentality that in the struggle over Chippewa family lands that occupies the last quarter of the novel, it is not merely the whites and their mixed-blood accomplices who rob the Indians. In a startling act of betrayal, Margaret and Nector Kashpaw misappropriate the money that the Nanapush-Pillager-Kashpaw group had raised together, using it to secure the Kashpaw lands but letting the hereditary Pillager lands fall prey to lumber interests.

If in some ways *Tracks* seems to conclude with a feeling of fragmentation and defeat, in other ways it strikes positive notes of solidarity and survival, especially when considered in relation to *Love Medicine* and *The Beet Queen*. Fleur disappears, leaving her husband and daughter, but Nanapush uses his wiliness to become tribal chairman and then to retrieve Lulu from a distant boarding school. At the end, the reader is reminded that Nanapush has addressed his entire narrative to Lulu: The old man hopes that his story will convince Lulu to embrace the memory of Fleur, "the one you will not call mother."

Summary

If Louise Erdrich had been born two hundred years earlier, she might have become a traditional Chippewa storyteller, whose tales would have reminded her listeners of their unchanging relationship to the land and to the mythic and legendary characters that inhabited it. Now, several generations removed from such a stable and undamaged culture, Erdrich nevertheless creates a richly neo-tribal view of people and place. In her poetry and fiction, Erdrich shows the profound interrelatedness of her characters—Indian and white, contemporaries and ancestors, both with one another and with their North Dakota homeland.

Bibliography

Bly, Robert. "Another World Breaks Through." *The New York Times Book Review* 92 (August 21, 1986): 2.

Erdrich, Louise. "Where I Ought to Be: A Writer's Sense of Place." *The New York Times Book Review* 91 (July 28, 1985): 1, 23-24.

Jahner, Elaine. Review of *Love Medicine. Parabola* 10 (May, 1985): 96, 98, 100.

Portales, Marco. "People with Holes in Their Lives." *The New York Times Book Review* 90 (December 23, 1984): 6.

Rubins, Josh. "Foundling Fiction." *The New York Review of Books* 33 (January 15, 1987): 14-15.

Strouse, Jean. "In the Heart of the Heartland." *The New York Times Book Review* 94 (October 2, 1988): 1, 41-42.

Towers, Robert. "Roughing It." *The New York Review of Books* 35 (November 19, 1988): 40-41.

_____. "Uprooted." *The New York Review of Books* 32 (April 11, 1985): 36-37.

Wickenden, Dorothy. "Off the Reservation." *The New Republic* 195 (October 6, 1986): 46-48.

Wright, Carolyne. "Women Poets: Seven New Voices from Small Presses." *Northwest Review* 23, no. 1 (1985): 118-133.

Terry L. Andrews

JAMES T. FARRELL

Born: Chicago, Illinois
February 27, 1904
Died: New York, New York
August 22, 1979

Principal Literary Achievement
The literary heir of Theodore Dreiser, Farrell wrote naturalistic fiction about the lower classes in Chicago and the effect of the environment on his protagonists.

Biography
James T. Farrell was born in Chicago, Illinois, on February 27, 1904, the son of James and Mary Daly Farrell. Although Farrell's father was a hard-working Chicago teamster and served as a symbol of the toil and troubles of the working classes in Farrell's fiction, he did not make enough money to support his large family—six of fifteen children lived to maturity. As a result of the financial pressure, Farrell was moved to his maternal grandparents' house at the age of three. That move, from dire poverty to some affluence, did provide him with material advantages, but at the cost of a normal family life. Later in life, Farrell observed that he was both in the events he wrote about and outside them, a situation that produced the identity problems he treats in his young protagonists.

He was educated in Catholic parochial schools. In grammar school, he was active and proficient in sports, particularly baseball and boxing, and thereby succeeded in partially overcoming his early loneliness. Farrell's other great early interest was religion, though his enthusiasm was primarily the product of his relationship with Sister Magdalen, the Sister Bertha of *Young Lonigan: A Boyhood in Chicago Streets* (1932), who encouraged him and prompted his academic interests. He attended the nearby St. Cyril High School, where he took the four-year scholastic course, which focused on the "classics" and religion. While he early criticized the authoritarian rigidity of his "miseducation," he later noted that it had instilled moral values in him. At St. Cyril he was outstanding in athletics and writing (he wrote his first Danny O'Neill story there), but despite his achievements, he still did not receive the acceptance he sought—he was still, in part, the "misfit."

After graduation in 1923, he worked at an express company, but in 1924 he also enrolled in night classes at De Paul University, where he first read the work of

Theodore Dreiser, the single greatest influence on his work. In the following year, with funds saved from his job as a gasoline attendant, he entered the University of Chicago, which radically changed his life. He became an avid reader, particularly in the social sciences: Sigmund Freud, Friedrich Nietzsche, Thorstein Veblen, and John Dewey transformed his devout Catholicism into a pragmatic naturalism, and novelists Dreiser, Ernest Hemingway, Sherwood Anderson, and James Joyce provided examples of literary naturalism and inspired his own literary ambitions. Farrell wrote book reviews and, in 1929, placed one of his stories in *Blues*, a little magazine, and commenced his work on *Studs Lonigan*.

After his story "Studs" appeared in *This Quarter*, a Paris journal, Farrell and his wife Dorothy, whom he married in 1931, left for Paris, where, despite initial financial problems and personal calamities (his son Sean died only five days after birth), his writing career finally prospered. After moving to the suburb of Sceaux-Robinson, he revised *Young Lonigan*, wrote most of *Gas-House McGinty* (1933), and finished many short stories, which soon appeared in *The New Review, The American Mercury*, and *Story*, among other publications. During this fruitful period, Farrell also received the welcome encouragement of Ezra Pound.

After he returned to New York in 1932, Farrell experienced a meteoric rise in reputation; the 1930's became, despite a lifetime of literary productivity, his literary decade. His novels appeared with astonishing regularity: *Young Lonigan, Gas-House McGinty, The Young Manhood of Studs Lonigan* (1934), *Judgment Day* (1935), and the culminating *Studs Lonigan: A Trilogy* (1935). He was awarded a Guggenheim fellowship in 1936, and in 1937 he received a Book of the Month Club fellowship for *Studs Lonigan*. His second major series, the books concerned with Danny O'Neill, began with the publication of *A World I Never Made* (1936). The O'Neill novel was the target of censorship; although Farrell and Vanguard Press, Farrell's regular publisher, were cleared of the charges against them, the censorship issue continued to plague Farrell throughout his career.

As a writer with strong sociopolitical views, it was inevitable that Farrell would be embroiled in the political controversies of the times. He joined the League of American Writers, a Communist-controlled organization, in 1935, and in 1936 supported the Socialist ticket; yet in spite of early left-wing praise for his "proletarian" writing, he was no doctrinaire Communist. He opposed the Communist literary critics, such as Granville Hicks, who equated left-wing propaganda with literary merit. His *A Note on Literary Criticism* (1936) espoused the dual function of literature: It should have both aesthetic and functional purposes. He retained his liberal views and spent the rest of his life working for various liberal causes and organizations; for example, he served as chairman of the Civil Rights Defense Committee (1941) and the Committee Against Jim Crow in Military Training (1950).

Although he peaked in popularity during the 1930's, Farrell continued his writing until his death of a heart attack in New York City on August 22, 1979. More than twenty-five novels, almost twenty collections of short stories, two volumes of poetry, and some ten volumes of prose, including literary criticism, personal essays, satirical prose under his Fogarty pseudonym, and a book about the Chicago White Sox flowed from a man who wrote almost every day of his life. Because he was before the public eye as a practicing writer and a political activist, he continued to receive both critical recognition and honorary degrees from such institutions as the University of Oxford, Columbia University, and the University of Chicago—the last particularly appropriate in the light of his early years there.

Analysis

The literary heir of Theodore Dreiser, Farrell is the epitome of the naturalistic writer whose protagonists' behavior is shaped by their social, psychological, political, and financial environment. In his essay "Some Observations on Naturalism, So Called, in Fiction" (1950), Farrell defines his concept of naturalism: "By naturalism I mean that whatever happens in this world must ultimately be explainable in terms of events in this world." The definition effectively distinguishes his fiction from those naturalistic novelists such as Frank Norris who frequently resort to the supernatural or mystical in shaping their plots. Moreover, Farrell documents his novels, piling up realistic details that circumscribe his characters' choices, making them victims of their environment.

Farrell's world is, for the most part, Chicago's South Side, where he grew up; his Irish Catholic protagonists closely resemble their creator, particularly when the Danny O'Neills and Bernard Carrs are intellectuals and writers confronting the role of the artist in an alien society. Even the Studs Lonigan figures, who are less articulate and more passive, are alienated (though they ironically belong to a gang) and isolated from their peers by their insecurity and their insistence on being stereotypical tough guys rather than individuals. The Farrell protagonist is often alone and typically alienated from self; consequently, he is a person divided into outer toughness and an inner tenderness, which must be consciously repressed. Despite his somewhat simplistic notion of personality, Farrell does succeed in creating unforgettable characters.

Although Farrell was praised by left-wing critics, some of them avowed Communists, he viewed literature as distinct from propaganda. His novels do have a sociopolitical message and do indict society, but Farrell was not naïve about what literature could accomplish. His aim was to inform his readers, to lead them to discover truths about themselves and their society, rather than to change that society. His readers discover characters who are ill-equipped to control the rapidly changing world of the 1930's and 1940's and who cling stubbornly to ineffective but traditional beliefs in family, patriotism, capitalism, religion, and the American Dream.

His characters' inability to cope is tied directly to their stunted lives and minds, which have been destroyed not only by their physical environment but also by their spiritual and domestic environment. While Chicago is not a "character" in Farrell's novels, the city permeates the books and restricts the characters' world. The priests mouth platitudes about morality and Catholic education, and these clichés, repeated often enough, provide solace to their parishioners. There is material, spiritual, and mental poverty on the South Side, where the characters react to their problems with formulas, homilies, and conventional wisdom. Innovation and creativity are absent, and when the rote answers do not work, silence or physical force is the result. Unless the Farrell protagonist is a writer, there can be no inner life, no stream of consciousness because the characters literally do not think.

Relationships between men and women consequently are shallow and superficial, with each sex responding to the other in terms of stereotypes. Farrell's males are sentimental but insensitive, violent but insecure; they tend to regard women as either spiritual creatures or tramps rather than as individuals. Women, on the other hand, mourn the loss of love and redirect their energies and ambitions to their children, whom they view with naïve idealism.

Characterization is Farrell's strength; plot and style are his weaknesses. At best, the plots are episodic, and often the subplots are only tangential to the story because they develop a political message or some social criticism. The main plot concerns the maturation and attendant alienation and debilitation of the "hero." The movement toward tragedy or pathos is inexorable; though the protagonist has free will, it is so circumscribed by his environment that it is theoretical rather than actual. The style is only a bit less predictable; there is a decided lack of subtlety, much repetition, and dated slang, most of which is taken from the 1930's and 1940's. One of the most frequent criticisms of Farrell is that his novels never escaped from those decades.

For the most part, Farrell's novels focus on character, which he believes is "all important" in the novel, and most of his characters are provided with lengthy biographies. The plots proceed chronologically, but they are often juxtaposed with newspaper headlines and stories, as well as with anecdotes about characters who do not appear elsewhere in the novel. These techniques indicate the Dreiser influence on both Farrell's content (urban determinism) and style. An added Dreiser technique is the fragmentation of chapters, which become in some novels a series of snippets that work cumulatively to produce both an emotional effect and a commentary on the plot and the characters, themselves fragmented beings.

The newspaper stories, newsreels, and films that appear, often with elaborate plots that serve as counterpoint to his narrative, reflect Farrell's preoccupation with the impact of the media on American life. Characters are guided by newspaper stories, and they are shaped by Hollywood's version of the truth and provided with emotional escapes. Readers are also, through the ironic clash between a character's vision and the real world, made aware of a character's illusions and inevitable failure. For Farrell, to learn about others is to learn about oneself. In "The Function of the Novel," he writes, "One of the major functions of the novel is to help us in gaining this expanded image of ourselves."

YOUNG LONIGAN

First published: 1932
Type of work: Novel

In the 1910's in Chicago, a young man is torn between his tough-guy image and his "softer side" and struggles to find his true identity.

Young Lonigan: A Boyhood in Chicago Streets, the first volume of the *Studs Lonigan* trilogy, concerns Studs's development from his graduation from St. Patrick's Grammar School to the end of the year he was supposed to attend Loyola High school. Farrell is unsparing in his criticism of the platitudes mouthed by the Catholic priests (the influence of Irish novelist James Joyce is particularly evident in Father Gilhooley's graduation address) and repeated by parents who bask in "burgher comfort" as they naïvely contemplate their children's glowing futures. (In reality, Frank "Weary" Reilley becomes a sadistic rapist rather than a lawyer, and William "Studs" Lonigan hardly fulfills his mother's ambition to have him become a priest.)

Farrell is primarily concerned with Studs's struggle to create and maintain an identity, even if that tough-guy image is at odds with the "real" Studs. Sections 1 and 2 begin with Studs appropriately before a mirror contemplating his "image." Studs is relieved when he looks "like Studs Lonigan was supposed to look," the way he must appear to win peer acceptance; here, as elsewhere, the ties between Studs and Farrell are quite evident. Although he later assures himself, "He was STUDS LONIGAN," he does have lingering doubts about his true self: "He wished he was somebody else." For his peers, Studs is, despite being rather small, a tough guy whose reputation depends on his successful fights with Weary Reilley and Red Kelley.

Studs fears that he is a misfit, someone with a split personality, someone who has a "mushy," "queer," "soft" side that he must repress. This romantic, poetic (if poetry were not beyond the relatively inarticulate Studs) side is associated with "angelic" Lucy Scanlon, the epitome of the "purer" Catholic girls, the "higher creatures." Farrell writes, "But the tough outside part of Studs told the tender inside part of him that nobody really knew, that he had better forget all that bull." When he and Lucy go to the park, which Farrell describes in terms of escape, of flight from self, Studs allows his "tender" side the ascendancy, but this idyllic interlude is followed by Studs, again the victim of peer pressure, coarsely rejecting Lucy. At the end of the novel, Studs unconsciously mourns the lost Lucy, while his father, whom Studs is beginning to resemble, procrastinates again about taking his wife for a night out—thus, Farrell prepares his readers for the further adventures of Studs Lonigan.

THE YOUNG MANHOOD OF STUDS LONIGAN

First published: 1934
Type of work: Novel

As a young man passes from adolescence to adulthood, his self-doubt and fears increase, leading him to self-destructive behavior.

In *The Young Manhood of Studs Lonigan*, the second novel of the trilogy, Farrell continues the saga. Though the title mentions Studs's "young manhood," Farrell depicts his protagonist as a boy in search of manhood. When he and some friends try to enlist in the Army, the recruiter advises them to "get your diapers pinned on," and when he attempts, as Lonewolf Lonigan, a hold-up, the "victim" states, "Son, you better put that toy away." Even when he is in his twenties, Lucy tells him that he is "just like a little boy," an image at odds with his created persona.

The self-doubt, fear, and identity problems first mentioned in *Young Lonigan* are developed in greater detail in the second novel: "He was a hero in his own mind. He was miserable." As he ages, Studs seems more uncertain of his identity; he sees himself as Lonewolf Lonigan, Yukon Lonigan (an image inspired by a film), and K. O. Lonigan (a boxer), but then as Pig Lonigan and Slob Lonigan as his self-pity increases. Studs seems to fear being "found out," and his tough-guy façade crumbles when he is outfought by young Morgan. Although Studs occasionally feels "mushy" when he dates Lucy, his coarse "outer" nature again destroys their relationship, and his contempt for his social-climbing sisters really marks his own sense of inferiority.

While he still focuses on Studs, Farrell gives his second novel more sociopolitical context than he had included in *Young Lonigan*. Farrell depicts changing neighborhoods and the heightening of racial tensions, the blacklisting of unionists such as Mr. Le Gare, and the political persecution of "unAmerican" ideas such as Communism. The Irish-American community in Chicago, paranoid about race and Communism, retreats, as Studs does, to patriotism, white supremacy, and the Church. Farrell suggests, however, through Father Shannon's morally edifying sermons, that the Church is ineffective—when the religious revival is over, the community's finest young Catholic men get drunk and look for women. There is little to believe in, as the plight of Danny O'Neill, the young University of Chicago intellectual, suggests; he rejects society's political and religious values but has nothing with which to replace them.

The novel concludes with a New Year's party at which Weary Reilley rapes Irene and a drunken Studs lies in the gutter, causing his pneumonia. This party is followed by an italicized chapter (this novel is more experimental in style, with its snippets of chapters and choruslike italicized chapters) in which Stephen Lewis, a young black, reenacts Studs's behavior in *Young Lonigan*. Times and characters change, but the behavior, values, and themes remain constant.

JUDGMENT DAY

First published: 1935
Type of work: Novel

A young man's self-inflicted physical problems and his incapacity for action lead to his early death in a hostile environment.

Judgment Day, which begins with a "devotion to be said at the beginning of the mass for the dead," is the third volume of the *Studs Lonigan* trilogy. It begins, appropriately, with Shrimp Haggerty's funeral and ends with Studs's death, but the novel also chronicles the death of the American Dream and the fall of the middle-class Irish Catholic community in Chicago. Farrell elaborates on the racism and political intolerance of the first two novels and adds anti-Semitism to the ills that afflict not only his characters but also American society in general.

In the course of *Judgment Day*, Studs declines physically, suffers a heart attack, cannot find work during the Depression, and finally dies, but not before impregnating his intended bride, Catherine. Although he still looks to his past exploits as the key to his identity, the self-doubt and fear increase until even his Walter Mitty dreams of being a champion golfer and a secret service agent falter: Even his imagination fails him. He cannot ignore the baseball game in which he fails miserably, thereby signaling the end of the athletic prowess that helped shape his identity. As in the second novel, he attends a film in which he empathizes with the hero; but this time the title of the film, *Doomed Victory*, and the hero's death ironically foreshadow Studs's life and death.

In *Judgment Day*, Studs seems to have lost his unrealized poetic nature and becomes almost inarticulate. Unable to communicate with Catherine, he enjoys "a vision of himself as a strong man whose words always meant something," yet his squabbles with her usually result from his silences. He also is unable to act and watches his stock plummet in value until he realizes that he is trapped financially, sexually, and vocationally. Standing before the mirror, a self-pitying Studs ironically tells his image, "You're the real stuff." Whatever Studs is, he is the product of his environment and is his father's son—a procrastinating, sentimental person who believes in the fraternity of the St. Christopher Society, the platitudes of the church, and the American Dream (itself symbolized by a dance marathon). All fail him, as they have failed his father, and as they will fail his brother, who emulates Studs.

Summary

In "On the Function of the Novel," Farrell writes, "Novels can enable us to gain a fuller sense of participation in the culture of our own time, and in the history of human thought and feeling." Like Dreiser, Farrell realistically documents a time, the 1930's, and a place, Chicago's South Side, in order to indict a society by chronicling events that produce alienated, fragmented human beings. He depicts the chronological maturation and the arrested emotional and spiritual development of his young protagonists, who cannot articulate their feelings, who cling precariously to stereotypical images of themselves, and who are ridden by self-doubt and fear.

Bibliography

Beach, Joseph Warren. *American Fiction, 1920-1940*. New York: Macmillan, 1941.

Bogardus, Ralph F., and Fred Hobson, eds. *Literature at the Barricades: The American Writer in the 1930's*. Tuscaloosa: University of Alabama Press, 1982.

Branch, Edgar M. *James T. Farrell*. Minneapolis: University of Minnesota Press, 1963.

_____. *James T. Farrell*. New York: Twayne, 1971.

Gelfast, Blanche H. *The American City Novel*. Norman: University of Oklahoma Press, 1954.

Kazin, Alfred. *On Native Grounds: An Interpretation of Modern American Prose Literature*. New York: Reynal and Hitchcock, 1942.

Pizer, Donald. *Twentieth Century American Literary Naturalism: An Interpretation*. Carbondale: Southern Illinois University Press, 1982.

Walcutt, Charles C. *American Literary Naturalism: A Divided Stream*. Minneapolis: University of Minnesota Press, 1956.

Wald, Alan M. *James T. Farrell: The Revolutionary Socialist Years*. New York: New York University Press, 1978.

Thomas L. Erskine

WILLIAM FAULKNER

Born: New Albany, Mississippi
September 25, 1897
Died: Byhalia, Mississippi
July 6, 1962

Principal Literary Achievement

Faulkner, internationally acclaimed as one of America's foremost novelists, is also noted for his short stories and novellas.

Biography

William Faulkner was born William Cuthbert Falkner in New Albany, Mississippi, September 25, 1897, to Murry C. and Maud Butler Falkner; he was the oldest of four children, all boys. The family moved in 1898 to nearby Ripley and in 1902 to Oxford, Mississippi, the author's primary home throughout his life. His father's employment included being treasurer of a railroad, owner of businesses, and administrator of the local University of Mississippi. Faulkner's early loves included trains, horses, hunting, and reading. In adolescence, after years of truancy and low performance, he quit high school in his senior year. Friendship with the future lawyer Phil Stone and frequenting the university campus were positive influences.

In 1918, Faulkner left Oxford to work in Connecticut at an arms factory; rejected by the army as too short and too small, he joined the Royal Canadian Air Force, training as a cadet in Toronto, Canada, until the end of World War I.

He traveled in the United States and abroad, worked as the university postmaster, attended the university as a special student, and began publishing poems in university and other periodicals. In New Orleans, he was befriended by Sherwood Anderson. Important works published early in his career were a collection of poems, *The Marble Faun* (1924), and two novels, *Soldiers' Pay* (1926) and *Mosquitoes* (1927). Three works in progress during 1927 treated the places and people of Faulkner's future work: Yoknapatawpha County, the Compsons, the Sartorises, and the Snopeses; Faulkner had taken Anderson's advice to return home and write about what he knew.

The years 1929 through 1937 mark the first major phase of Faulkner's career. *Flags in the Dust* (not published until 1973), his first "Yoknapatawpha" novel, had been rejected; it was shortened, revised, and published as *Sartoris* (1929). A few months later his greatest novel, *The Sound and the Fury* (1929), also appeared. In

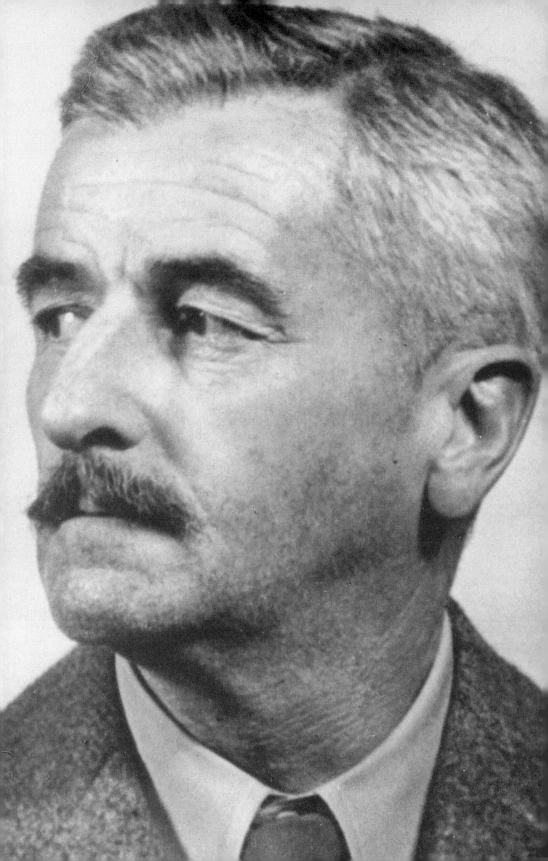

anger over its poor reception, Faulkner wrote *Sanctuary*, a violent, salacious novel. It was rejected as unfit for publication. That same year he married the recently divorced Estelle Franklin; following a honeymoon, they and her two children lived on the University of Mississippi campus; working and writing in the boiler room, Faulkner published *As I Lay Dying* (1930). Starting with "A Rose for Emily" (1930), he began publishing short stories in national magazines (no less than forty-eight appeared in six years, including some of his best stories). Republishing of his works in England and translations elsewhere (the French versions of Maurice Coindreau, for example) added to his international reputation; it would be some time before his own country recognized him. A severely revised *Sanctuary* was published in 1931, as was the first of many collections of stories, *These 13*.

In 1932, Faulkner launched a second career, one which would compete for his time and presence for the next thirteen years: He became a Hollywood scriptwriter. Also in 1932, *Light in August* was published and Faulkner's father died, making Faulkner the head of the Falkner family. The next year, his daughter Jill was born. He took flying lessons; soon he would be a pilot, own a plane, help establish the local airport, and give flying lessons. Another volume of poems, *A Green Bough* (1933), and a second collection, *Dr. Martino and Other Stories* (1934), were published. His works often served as the bases for films: In 1933, the story "Turn About" (1932) became *Today We Live*; *Sanctuary* became *The Story of Temple Drake*. In 1935, Faulkner's brother Dean died in a crash of Faulkner's plane. *Pylon* (1935) is a novel set in New Orleans (under another name) about flyers. Publication of *Absalom, Absalom!* (1936) marked the end of production of the earlier major novels. During this time Faulkner supported a wife, three children, Dean's widow and daughter, and two black servants (Uncle Ned and Caroline Barr, known as Mammie Callie) primarily by selling short stories and writing film scripts. In 1929 he had purchased a large antebellum house, the Sheegog place, renaming it Rowan Oak (or Rowanoak); he restored the house and did the landscaping himself. In 1937, he purchased Bailey Woods and renamed it the Greenfield Farm.

The second major period seems to have begun with the publishing of *The Unvanquished* (1938), a novel of the Civil War that utilizes six previously published stories and one written for this work. Faulkner became less private in his life and in his ideas. His works became more philosophical and at times even moralistic. *The Wild Palms* (1939) is actually two novellas with alternating chapters. The first of the Snopes trilogy, *The Hamlet*, appeared in 1940. It was followed by a novel incorporating stories about black people, *Go Down, Moses* (1942). In 1939, the first of many honors came with Faulkner's election to the National Institute of Letters.

During the next twenty years, Faulkner's final period, he became increasingly a public person, speaking out on racial segregation and representing the United States as an ambassador of goodwill in places as diverse as Japan, Venezuela, and Europe. In 1945 he was finally released from a contract to write scripts; in the meantime his contributions to magazines had become fewer. In 1947 he conducted classroom interviews at the University of Mississippi. Later he would become writer-in-residence, doing the same at the University of Virginia and buying a home in Charlottesville. He received the Nobel Prize in Literature in 1950 and the Pulitzer Prize in 1955; the French bestowed membership in the Legion of Honor upon him. His daughter married Paul D. Summers, Jr., in 1954; there were three grandsons born between 1956 and 1961. Faulkner died in Byhalia, Mississippi, July 6, 1962, while undergoing medical treatment following a fall from a horse.

Works published after 1942 include the novels *Intruder in the Dust* (1947), *Requiem for a Nun* (1951), *A Fable* (1954), *The Town* (1957), *The Mansion* (1959), and *The Reivers* (1962). Collections include *The Portable Faulkner* (1946), *Collected Short Stories of William Faulkner* (1950), and *Big Woods* (1955); also appearing after 1942 were occasional stories, letters to editors, and essays in periodicals. Numerous works, such as collections of interviews, letters, previously unpublished works, biographies, and new editions, have appeared since Faulkner's death.

Analysis

Faulkner's works, like their creator, are highly complex. His style has caused much difficulty for readers, especially if *The Sound and the Fury, Light in August, As I Lay Dying,* or *Absalom, Absalom!* is the reader's introduction to Faulkner. These best of his earlier Yoknapatawpha novels vary in structure but are alike in one point—an obscurity that results from unusual, complicated organization and presentation. *The Sound and the Fury* has multiple narrators, extended streams of consciousness, and subtle time shifts; it is divided into four at times seemingly disconnected parts. *Light in August* has three narratives interwoven, with past and present intermixed. *As I Lay Dying* is a series of numerous brief chapters, each a stream of consciousness, usually but not always by a member of the Bundren family. *Absalom, Absalom!* is told using various levels of time and narrator viewpoint.

Faulkner himself and some of his major critics have recommended *The Unvanquished* as the best starting place. In spite of multiple narratives, real and metaphorical, there is one narrator: Bayard Sartoris, an old man recalling experiences of his early life during the American Civil War. Several viewpoints are presented, but all by him. Time is interrupted by an occasional flashback or digression, but generally the thrust is chronological, once the digressive nature of the entire narrative is recognized. Violence and hardship are moderated by generous doses of good-natured humor. Focus is on two races, blacks and various classes of Mississippi whites. Since Bayard Sartoris is a rather normal adolescent through much of the plot, his viewpoint is not tedious. Another good entree into Faulkner is *Intruder in the Dust*, in which traditional form of single narrator and chronological time are, with some lapses, followed.

Place is extremely important to Faulkner; in most of his better works his setting is his fictional Yoknapatawpha County (based in part on his own home county of Lafayette) with its town of Jefferson, largely Oxford renamed and without the state university (he moves Oxford and the university to another site). Faulkner utilizes local people, including members of his own family: His grandfather, J. W. T. Falkner, becomes old Bayard Sartoris; his great-grandfather, a mythic figure with a shady past, a record of violence, Civil War experience and public leadership, becomes Colonel John Sartoris. V.K. Surratt, Faulkner's genial peddler/story teller, is lifted from real life and temporarily given his real name. Various other characters are based on one or more real people. Similarly, the narratives are based on tales, often traditions handed down by his family or others.

In turn, he might borrow freely from history or classical mythology, from existentialism, psychology, the Bible, or any of the numerous books that he read. Next to the Bible, he most often mentioned Miguel de Cervantes (author of *Don Quixote*), the sixteenth century Spanish writer; other influences included Charles Dickens, Mark Twain, and Polish-British novelist Joseph Conrad. Following the philosophy of Henri Bergson, the French thinker, Faulkner did not view time as chronological. Having watched a man write the Lord's Prayer on the head of a pin, Faulkner sought to write the history of the human soul in one sentence. Faulkner's style is often verbose, especially if a talkative narrator is speaking or a troubled individual is pouring out thoughts in a stream of consciousness. There may even be an occasional sentence that goes on for pages. The later novels, with obvious exceptions (the commissary section of "The Bear" in *Go Down, Moses*, for example), and the short stories are written in a style much more readable than some of the earlier novels.

Although Faulkner's writing is recognized as excellent by critics in both the United States and abroad, it should be noted that his work is uneven; this fact is especially obvious since almost everything he wrote is now available, including apprenticeship poems and stories. Even his mature work, however, is somewhat uneven; critics regard his earlier Yoknapatawpha novels and a few later ones such as *The Hamlet* and *Go Down, Moses*, for example, to be of better literary quality than the apprenticeship novels (*Soldiers' Pay* and *Mosquitoes*) or *Pylon*.

Faulkner's philosophy has been difficult for many critics. He believed in God but did not pretend to be a Christian. He borrowed freely from the Bible, yet used as parallels to Christ uncouth characters such as Joe Christmas in *Light in August*. His attitude toward race, especially toward black and white relations, angered whites and blacks, integrationists and segregationists. He was in favor of moderate, gradual integration. In his works, he often treats the themes of incest and miscegenation; sometimes they are combined, as in *Absalom, Absalom!* His attitude toward the South combines regional pride with shame at offenses past and present. His complex treatment avoids the two extremes that one often finds in works about the South—squalid poverty on the one hand, magnolias and hooped skirts on the other. His setting is more a particular region—northern Mississippi—than the entire South. A most successful regional writer, he nevertheless achieves universality by combining the local perspective with a broad treatment of the human condition. Both a Greek stoic and a Christian humanist, he believed in the worth of the individual, most especially his ability to endure and prevail; thus, in spite of much darkness in Faulkner's works, they possess an overriding optimism in an age of pessimistic trends in literature.

SARTORIS

First published: 1929
Type of work: Novel

A troubled World War I ace returns home to seek and eventually find a violent death.

Sartoris, Faulkner's first published mature novel, and the first to treat the people and places of his fictional county of Yoknapatawpha, is a fitting introduction to his settings and characters. The title is the name of one of his leading families. In one sense, young Bayard Sartoris is the protagonist; in another, it is the entire Sartoris family (at least the first, second, and fourth generations). Also introduced are two members of the Snopes clan—Flem and Byron, employees of old Bayard Sartoris' bank. Protagonists of an interwoven subplot are the Benbows—brother and sister Horace and Narcissa; other characters include the MacCallums (spelled McCallum in later works). The setting begins in Jefferson, the county seat of Yoknapatawpha, and moves to other parts of the region (and occasionally other parts of the United States) in the main narrative, but shifts to the Civil War and World War I in digressions.

Colonel John Sartoris, the legendary ancestor of the two Bayards, was modeled after Faulkner's great-grandfather, Colonel William C. Falkner, a colorful adventurer of the periods before, during, and after the Civil War. Colonel Sartoris' twin brother, Bayard, was killed while engaged in a prank during the Civil War; Colonel John's presence still permeates the atmosphere three generations later. Old Bayard is passive and nonviolent. Young Bayard experiences guilt because he has seen his twin brother John's plane shot down; he is also driven by the Sartoris penchant for violent endings—partly fatalism, partly recklessness. He drives his car too fast, endangering himself and his passengers. Once he drives off a bridge and breaks his ribs; another time he drives over a cliff and back onto the road, only to learn he has caused his grandfather, old Bayard, to die of a heart attack.

The Benbow house is in Jefferson, as are the cemetery, the courthouse, the church, and other places of interest. Horace is a young lawyer recently returned from war experience as a YMCA worker in Italy; he is interested in poetry and art, bringing a glassblowing apparatus home with him. He becomes involved with another family, Harry and Belle Mitchell and their daughter, little Belle. Eventually Belle divorces Harry and marries Horace. Narcissa and Horace are very close, with strong emotional ties to each other. She is friends with old Bayard's aunt, Miss Jenny DuPre, whose common sense offers a contrast to the Sartoris attitudes and actions. Byron Snopes writes anonymous letters to Narcissa, eventually breaking into her house and stealing an undergarment. He, like his people, is low-bred, amoral, and grasping.

The Sartoris family is also treated at length in *The Unvanquished*; the Benbows are among the important characters of *Sanctuary.* The MacCallums (McCallums) are the protagonists of the short story "The Tall Men" (1941). In *Sartoris*, their hill farm home more than fourteen miles north of Jefferson becomes young Bayard's refuge after old Bayard's death. Here drinking and hunting (two of Faulkner's favorite avocations) take place. Another family, a nameless and poverty-stricken black family, share their hospitality on Christmas Day. They stand in contrast to others in the novel who are stereotypes of black characters in literature and drama of the time. Following the death of young Bayard, who has foolheartedly flight-tested an unsafe plane in Dayton, Ohio, the focus is on Benbow Sartoris, who represents a new generation of the family. Bayard's wife Narcissa has named the son Benbow in hopes that he will avoid the curse of the Sartoris men.

THE SOUND AND THE FURY

First published: 1929
Type of work: Novel

A once-distinguished family degenerates and eventually disintegrates.

The Sound and the Fury is about another family, the Compsons; like the Sartorises, they are of the aristocratic social level, the planter class. Unlike the Sartorises, who live four miles north of Jefferson, they live in town. They consist of Mr. and Mrs. Compson and four children: Quentin, the oldest son, commits suicide while a student at Harvard University; he is attracted to his sister Caddy. Benjy, born Maury, is an idiot son. Jason, the youngest son, is grasping and amoral, without feeling for other people. The other important members of the household are Miss Quentin, Caddy's illegitimate daughter (named for her uncle), and the black female servant Dilsey, modeled to a great extent after the Falkner family's Mammy Callie.

Faulkner's most esoteric novel, especially through the first two of the four parts, *The Sound and the Fury* is his most difficult to read, causing problems for both scholar and beginner. Obviously modeled after James Joyce's novel *Ulysses* (1922), it consists of three streams of consciousness, each by a male character, followed by a fourth section in omniscient viewpoint with strong partial focus on a female. Part 1 unfolds the thoughts and emotions of Benjy, who on his birthday (he is thirty-three), Saturday, April 7, 1928, confuses the present with the past of 1910. His pasture, sold to pay for Caddy's wedding and Quentin's education at Harvard, is now a golf course; players' shouts to their caddies remind him of his sister and of his former dependence on her.

Quentin's section is set at the earlier time of Thursday, June 2, 1910. During the events before his death, he tears the hands off his watch, wanders through the town, becomes friends with a young girl, has a violent confrontation as he tries to find her people, and eventually dresses and brushes his teeth before killing himself. His death results from his inability to accept his sister's infidelity, an act foreshadowed by an experience on the day of their grandmother's wake: Climbing up to look in the window after having sat in the mud, she has revealed her soiled drawers.

Jason's section is less esoteric, more direct, because it pours out the thoughts of a crass, greedy, cruel man who is unimaginative. Remaining at home after the deaths of Quentin and his father, he works in a business. He extorts money from Caddy by insisting that she avoid contact with her daughter and by threatening to expose Miss Quentin's background. The money that Caddy sends her, Jason takes for his own. His section is set in the present: Friday, April 6, 1928, the day before Benjy's birthday and two days before Easter. Miss Quentin, now seventeen, runs off with a man from a carnival, stealing money from Jason, who ironically had previously stolen it from her. Much of the section serves to characterize Jason, especially his contempt toward Quentin, Benjy, Caddy, Miss Quentin, Dilsey, women in general, and nearly everyone else. Throughout the sections, the parents and a relative, Uncle Maury, are also characterized: The father fails to assume authority, the mother is a whining, dependent hypochondriac, the uncle is an immoral ne'er-do-well.

Jason's conflict with Dilsey, who tries vainly to keep the family from disintegrating, and his pursuit of Miss Quentin are depicted in both the third and fourth sections. The latter, sometimes called the Dilsey section in spite of its third person narrator, reaches its grand climax in Dilsey's worship experience on Easter Sunday morning, April 8, 1928, the day after Benjy's birthday. She takes Benjy with her and walks to the Second Baptist Church, the black church, where a small, unattractive substitute minister preaches. In the course of Reverend Sheegog's sermon, she reaches a state of ecstasy—one of the rare genuine religious experiences in all of Faulkner's work. The setting of the days of Easter week, though not in chronological order, parallel those in Dante's *The Divine Comedy* (c. 1320). The year 1928 reflects a Faulkner custom often employed: to make the time of writing the present in a work in progress.

SANCTUARY

First published: 1931
Type of work: Novel

Characters are the victims of murder, rape, lynching, and miscarriages of justice.

In 1929, while angered at the poor reception of his *The Sound and the Fury* (and possibly the previous rejection of *Flags in the Dust*), Faulkner wrote a first version of *Sanctuary* as the most violent, most salacious novel possible, in order to make money. Later, Phil Stone, his lawyer friend and mentor, persuaded him that the work was unworthy of the author of *The Sound and the Fury* or of the short stories "Rose for Emily" and "That Evening Sun Go Down" (1931). Faulkner did extensive revision, toning down the violence and sex (although much remains) and rewriting *Sanc-*

tuary as a work of excellent literary quality. Whereas the earlier version had been rejected, the later was published.

Main characters include Horace Benbow and, to a lesser extent, his sister Narcissa, already seen in *Sartoris*. She is living in the family home with Aunt Sally (no blood kin); he is out in the country, a troubled soul separated from his wife Belle and her daughter Little Belle. He comes to some property closely guarded by a criminal element of people: Popeye is an amoral, almost inhuman, unfeeling psychotic killer, a petty gangster; Lee Goodwin is a bootlegger in business with Popeye; Ruby Lamar is his wife. Horace is sexually attracted to Ruby. Eventually, he is allowed to leave the premises.

Later, Gowan Stevens, a self-centered young Virginia man, gets drunk and causes Temple Drake, an eighteen-year-old college girl who is the daughter of a judge, to forfeit a trip to a football game. Eventually, they too find themselves in Goodwin's place, Gowan too drunk to cope and Temple, warned by Ruby of her danger and shocked by the men she observes, hysterical, running all around the place.

One of the men is murdered by Popeye, who attacks Temple and later holds her captive in a Memphis brothel. Lee Goodwin is imprisoned in Jefferson for the murder, and Horace agrees to defend him, presumably to be paid in services by Goodwin's wife if he is acquitted. Horace is not the proper attorney, since not only is he not a criminal lawyer but also he is personally involved. Narcissa betrays Horace's confidence to her, as does state senator Snopes, with the result that a politically ambitious prosecuting attorney gets Temple freed (from Popeye), and he, rather than Horace, uses her as a witness: Her false testimony that Goodwin is the murderer, in the emotional climate created by her revelation that she has been raped with a corncob, causes mass hysteria in the courtroom. Horace does not even cross-examine her. Goodwin is later taken from jail and, in Horace's presence, burned to death in the courthouse square. Popeye, who has escaped prosecution for this and other murders, is later arrested and convicted for one that he did not commit. His early life, in the manner of that of Joe Christmas in *Light in August*, is revealed as he awaits execution in Florida. His death is poetic justice.

Certainly, the plot is effective enough, especially for those who like mystery, crime, violence, and sex, but the question remains whether *Sanctuary* as published is more than a violent, salacious fiction. A literary novel is a proper balance of three elements, all fully effected: a structured plot, clearly realized (delineated) characters, and manners (the characterization of a society in a particular time and place). *Sanctuary* is highly effective in all three respects. The plot is structured effectively. The manners of both the criminal class and the respectable people are delineated. Ruby is the wife of a criminal and is herself a former prostitute, but she is a faithful wife to an unworthy husband who was untrue to her while in the armed forces; her prostitution was to earn money to free him from prison. She shows concern and a gruff type of kindness to intruders into her sordid world; she shows courage by telling Horace about Popeye and Temple. She is also willing to pay in the only way she can to free her husband.

The genteel class are also of mixed virtue. Both Horace and Gowan are immoral and given to drink. They are both weak men who bring violence to others by their weakness yet bear no responsibility for their actions. Temple, who could prevent her rape and a man's murder simply by walking away from Goodwin's place, succumbs to panic and fails to act. Once she is in court, her father is concerned that she testify no longer; he should know that testimony without privilege of cross-examination is a travesty. The presiding judge should certainly know that it is inadmissible as evidence. Horace puts his lust ahead of his client's life. Narcissa is willing to let an innocent man die so that her brother can return to her—or to his wife—rather than becoming involved with a fallen woman. The characters function within the plot as individuals and as members of a society.

LIGHT IN AUGUST

First published: 1932
Type of work: Novel

A man of uncertain race and origins turns to violence and is himself a victim of violence.

Light in August, Faulkner's fifth Yoknapatawpha novel, brings together in and near Jefferson characters with varying backgrounds and personalities, but with one common bond—they all have deep-seated problems. Lena Grove arrives in town from Alabama pregnant but unmarried in search of Lucas Burch, the father of her child. She finds instead Byron Bunch, a good man who is timid and withdrawn. Burch, using the name Brown, has just burned Miss Joanna Burden's house to cover her murder by Joe Christmas, who has killed Joanna after being her lover for three years. Joe had lived at her place while being partners with Brown in the bootleg whiskey business. Gail Hightower, a defrocked minister who has withdrawn from society after its rejection and mistreatment of him, now has a different religion— ancestor worship of his Civil War grandfather's memory. He is friends with Bunch, who involves him with Lena (he delivers her baby) and with Joe (he lies when Joe takes refuge in his house attempting to prevent the fugitive's murder at the hands of his pursuers). The leader of the three-man posse pursuing Joe is Percy Grimm, a deputized young man who has a stormtrooper mentality years before Adolf Hitler's rise to power. He shoots the armed Joe Christmas and mutilates his body.

Much of the novel is devoted to the events and people that have influenced Joe's character. The son of a Mexican (or black) carnival worker and Doc Hines's granddaughter, he is left at a Memphis orphanage on Christmas Day (thus his assumed name). His questionable parentage and his age (thirty-three when arriving in Jefferson), together with his name, suggest parallels to Jesus. The parallels were even more obvious in earlier versions, but Faulkner later toned them down. The use of biblical matter paralleling Jesus or some other biblical character or incident with an opposite type of person is a Faulknerian technique known as an inversion. Doc Hines takes a job at the orphanage so that he can watch the boy. Hines is an extreme religious fanatic and a racist; he tells people that Joe is a Negro. Joe's foster parents, the MacEacherns, are strict Calvinists, Mr. MacEachern harshly so.

The belief in Joe's black blood, though it is never actually established in the novel, is focus for much of the action. Doc Hines's attitude is primarily racist. Joe himself has ambivalent feelings: At times he calls himself a Negro, but he always functions as a white man in a white-dominated society. After killing Joanna, Joe disturbs worship at a Negro church, thinking to establish himself in their society but only terrifying them and doing violence to one of the worshipers.

The novel closes as it opened, quietly, with the focus on Lena Grove. The final chapter is told by a furniture maker and dealer who has given Lena, Byron Bunch, and the baby a ride from Mississippi to Jackson, Tennessee. Byron cannot get her to marry him, and he is unsuccessful in his attempt to rape her, but he continues to be her traveling companion.

ABSALOM, ABSALOM!

First published: 1936
Type of work: Novel

A man with dreams of affluence and family dynasty sees everything crumble around him.

Absalom, Absalom!, another Yoknapatawpha novel and another work with multiple structure, has different levels of narrator viewpoint; Quentin Compson and his Canadian roommate at Harvard University are the primary level. Shreve McCannon has asked Quentin to tell him about Mississippi; the result is a story told in true Quentin fashion. It is far from chronological; sometimes he speaks from his own observation, but most often he repeats a secondhand narrative as given him by Miss Rosa Coldfield, Jason Compson III, and others. Some gaps are filled in by the boys' speculative dialogue.

The story is about Thomas Sutpen, who as a young man left his western Virginia home and was severely rebuked by a black servant at a tidewater Virginia mansion. Emotionally scarred, he traveled to the West Indies, where he married the daughter of a wealthy planter and became a man of wealth himself. Discovering that his wife was part black, he left her and traveled to Mississippi. The novel opens with Miss Rosa's earliest childhood memory of Sutpen, who has married her sister. His violent manner of driving his horses up to the front of the church outrages the townspeople; his cockfights and brutal boxing matches have left her with a sense of terror. He has fathered a daughter, Judith, and a son, Henry, by this marriage, and he dreams of family, dynasty, and great wealth. A few miles out from Jefferson, he has built a mansion and established a large plantation; he has brought many slaves with him.

Problems arise when Charles Bon is brought into the family: He is the son of Sutpen by Sutpen's previous marriage. His friendship with Henry and his budding relationship with Judith present the problems of incest and miscegenation.

Sutpen is generally regarded more highly throughout the novel than he is in the eyes of Miss Rosa, who despises him because he has offered to marry her on the condition that she will give him a son. He is characterized as a worthy soldier, being elected commander of the battalion organized and led by Colonel John Sartoris. When, after the Civil War, he is threatened by a vigilante committee, he faces down the group. He cannot cope, however, with the disintegration of his family and his fortune. The end of the novel is uncertain; Quentin describes having found the aged Henry, who has been hiding at the old Sutpen place after killing Charles Bon. A sequel to *Absalom, Absalom!* is the short story "Wash," which tells of the death of Sutpen at the hands of a "poor white" employee and drinking companion, Wash Jones, whose daughter Millie's child Sutpen has fathered and spurned. In typical Faulkner fashion, the story was published in 1934, two years before the novel.

THE BEAR

First published: 1942
Type of work: Novella

A boy is initiated into manhood and participates in the killing of a great bear that symbolizes the wilderness.

"The Bear" is Faulkner's best-known and most highly regarded story; it takes its place among his wilderness narratives, such as *Old Man* (one of the two novellas that make up *The Wild Palms*), "Red Leaves" (1930), the best of Faulkner's Indian stories, and the escape of the black architect in *Absalom, Absalom!* Its genesis is typical of Faulkner's writing and publishing career: He utilized his material to the greatest degree. A short story entitled "Lion" appeared in 1934; it was enlarged in 1941 and 1942 as "The Bear," to be a section of the novel *Go Down, Moses.* A shortened form was published in a magazine in 1942; then, two days later, the novel appeared, with what is sometimes called "The Bear II" included. Since this contained section 4, which adds to the novel but detracts from the hunting story, the novel version without section 4 was anthologized in *Big Woods* in 1955; with section 4, it appeared in *Three Famous Short Novels* in 1961.

The work symbolizes the destruction of the wilderness. It is also concerned with the mythic initiation of a boy, young Isaac (Ike) McCaslin, into manhood. In the later versions, Quentin Compson as narrator is dropped in favor of omniscient narration, and "the boy" becomes Ike. The magazine and novel versions differ in that the bear is killed only in the latter. Old Ben is a mythic two-toed bear that has eluded hunters for years; Lion is the huge dog the appearance of which foreshadows the end. Sam Fathers, Major De Spain, General Compson, McCaslin Edmunds, and

Boon Hogganbeck are among those chasing but not killing Old Ben; the major's hunting camp is on what was once Thomas Sutpen's estate. McCaslin (Cass) is Ike's older cousin; Sam, an Indian of noble blood, is Ike's friend and wilderness mentor; Boon is a big man (partly of plebeian Indian blood) with the mind of a child.

The time of the opening and of the climactic killing of Ben is 1883, when Ike is sixteen. Through digressions, previous events are related: At ten, Ike had gone on his first hunt with the men; at eleven, he had seen Ben for the first time. At thirteen, he killed his first deer and underwent initiation when Sam marked his face with the blood; when he was fourteen, the special dog, Lion, was brought into camp; when he was fifteen, Lion attacked Ben and Ben was wounded by a gun. Comic interludes have to do with Boon—his attitude toward Lion and his ineptitude with a gun. Section 4, sometimes called "The Land," consists of one sixteen-hundred-word sentence unfolding a dialogue between Ike (now twenty-one) and Cass regarding ownership of the land: Ike will waive his right to his inheritance. The brief final section is two years after the last hunt on this land; Ike at nineteen revisits the site (two years before section 4) to find Boon under a lone tree full of squirrels: Having broken his gun, Boon is clubbing at the squirrels and shouting at would-be intruders. The high serious tone of the novella gives way to the comic, seeming to contrast the awe and majesty of the now-departed wilderness with the civilization that has taken its place.

SPOTTED HORSES

First published: 1931
Type of work: Short story

People experience injury and loss when they are sold wild horses.

As did "*The Bear*," Faulkner's "Spotted Horses" evolved over a period of years. As early as 1927 and 1928, he was writing about the Snopeses in a work entitled "Father Abraham" (it was never published as such). In *Flags in the Dust* and *Sartoris*, Flem and Byron Snopes appear as minor characters. The first-published fuller treatment of Flem was in the short story version of "Spotted Horses" in 1931. Originally entitled "Aria Con Amore," it had been revised into this version for *Scribners*. It was also enlarged into a novella and was included as a key episode in the first Snopes novel, *The Hamlet*, in 1940. Five years later, parts were included in Malcolm Cowley's collection *The Portable Faulkner*.

"Spotted Horses," then, marks the beginning of the Snopes stories (others include "Barn Burning," 1939, and "Mule in the Yard," 1934) and (as part of *The Hamlet*) the Snopes novels. Flem's rise from obscurity to prominence and affluence is the subject of the Snopes trilogy (*The Hamlet*, *The Town*, and *The Mansion*); his first important stride is his gaining ascendancy over the Varners; by marrying the pregnant Eula, he gains not only a most desirable woman but also opportunities for advancement. "Spotted Horses" opens with Flem, Eula, and her baby returning from a honeymoon in Texas. They bring with them a stranger, the Texan Buck Hipps, and a string of wild pinto horses straight from the range.

In this work Faulkner utilizes some of the people and places of *As I Lay Dying*, including the farmers of Frenchman's Bend. In addition to the Snopeses and Varners are the Armstids, the Littlejohns, and others. V. K. Suratt is an outsider but no stranger; he has already appeared briefly in *Sartoris* (by *The Hamlet*, his name will be V. K. Ratliff). Here, he is driving a wagon pulled by a mixed team. Buck Hipps is a congenial but tough man; he carries a pistol in his pocket and continually eats ginger snaps. The setting, Frenchman's Bend, is based on the region in and around Taylor, southeast of Oxford. One might consider the community the protagonist. and Flem the antagonist. As elsewhere, Faulkner effectively blends violence with robust humor. The horse auction and the farmers' attempts to claim their purchases cause inconvenience, injury, and property damage. Faulkner based the story on a real-life incident that had happened in Ripley. As a boy, after outgrowing his pony, Faulkner himself had purchased and tamed one of these very horses; it became his first horse.

Summary

William Faulkner wrote more than nineteen novels and dozens of stories. His best have established him as one of the great novelists and storytellers. Each work is complete in itself, yet his works also inform and relate to one another. His variety is vast: Settings range from the Civil War to the twentieth century, from Mississippi to war-torn France. He utilized the people and places of his own region to write on universal themes, creating not only characters but also entire families and communities. His reputation has grown steadily, first in Europe and Japan, later in the United States and the rest of the world.

Bibliography

Blotner, Joseph. *Faulkner: A Biography*. 2 vols. New York: Random House, 1974.

Brooks, Cleanth. *William Faulkner: The Yoknapatawpha Country*. New Haven, Conn.: Yale University Press, 1963.

Gresset, Michel. *A Faulkner Chronology*. Translated by Arthur B. Sharff. Jackson: University Press of Mississippi, 1985.

McHaney, Thomas L. *William Faulkner: A Reference Guide*. Boston: G. K. Hall, 1976.

Milgate, Michael. *The Achievement of William Faulkner*. New York: Random House, 1963.

Pilkington, John. *The Heart of Yoknapatawpha*. Jackson: University Press of Mississippi, 1981.

Tuck, Dorothy. *Crowell's Handbook of Faulkner*. New York: Thomas Y. Crowell, 1964.

George W. Van Devender

F. SCOTT FITZGERALD

Born: St. Paul, Minnesota
September 24, 1886
Died: Hollywood, California
December 21, 1940

Principal Literary Achievement
An outstanding stylist and acute social observer, Fitzgerald captured the essence of American life between World War I and World War II.

Biography

Francis Scott Key Fitzgerald, one of the most talented and tragic of American writers, was born on September 24, 1886, in St. Paul, Minnesota. His father, Edward, was unsuccessful in a variety of enterprises, and the family moved numerous times until Fitzgerald's mother inherited sufficient money for them to settle in one of the more exclusive neighborhoods of St. Paul; even as a young boy, Fitzgerald was acutely aware that his mother, rather than his father, provided the financial foundation of the family. It was a situation—a wife's inherited money—which was to recur frequently in his writing.

In 1911, Fitzgerald entered Newman School, a Catholic institution in Hackensack, New Jersey. It was there that he decided upon Princeton University as the ideal college, thus beginning one strand that would run throughout his writing, especially in his earlier works and his popular first novel, *This Side of Paradise*, with its collegiate setting. It was also at Newman that Fitzgerald met and was encouraged in his literary ambitions by Father Sigourney Fay, a priest who became one of the most important influences upon Fitzgerald's development. Father Fay strengthened the young Fitzgerald's sense of a noble character as an essential element in achieving high goals—and of the accompanying dangers of anything that would weaken that character, disrupt its resolve, or corrupt its nature: the lure of unearned wealth, sins of the flesh, moral weakness. These beliefs were also woven deep into Fitzgerald's psyche and found repeated, perhaps obsessive, expression in his fiction.

After he entered Princeton in the fall of 1913, Fitzgerald was active in the literary and social activities of the college; he was a talented and frequent contributor to the shows of the Triangle Club and the literary magazines. Perhaps as a result, his

grades were marginal at best, causing him to drop out for a semester during his junior year, returning to Princeton a year behind his classmates.

By then another goal had presented itself: With the entry of the United States into World War I, Fitzgerald had determined to join the army. He was commissioned as a second lieutenant in October, 1917. He started the first draft of a novel provisionally entitled "The Romantic Egotist," which, greatly reworked, would become *This Side of Paradise*. In June, 1918, Fitzgerald was transferred to Camp Sheridan near Montgomery, Alabama, where he met and fell in love with Zelda Sayre, the young and beautiful daughter of a distinguished Southern family. Fitzgerald received orders for Europe, but the war ended before he sailed for France.

The engagement with Zelda flickered on and off while Fitzgerald was discharged from the army, worked briefly in advertising in New York, sold his first commercial short stories, and continued with his novel. In September, 1919, *This Side of Paradise* (1920) was accepted by Scribner's; the editor who made the decision, Maxwell Perkins, was one of the most discerning and influential figures in publishing during the period, and he was to have a close professional association with Fitzgerald for many years. Fitzgerald also began publishing short stories in *The Saturday Evening Post*, one of the most popular and highly paying magazines of the time. Now a success, Fitzgerald married Zelda in New York City on April 3, 1920.

Scribner's had published *This Side of Paradise* the month before, and the novel was an immediate success, making its twenty-three-year-old author a critical and commercial success. Later in 1920, Fitzgerald's first collection of short stories, *Flappers and Philosophers*, was also published. Young, wealthy, and in love, the Fitzgeralds lived well on their income during a period when the United States was shaking free of the past and entering a self-consciously new period, the "jazz age." F. Scott Fitzgerald was its chronicler: His second collection of stories, published in 1922, was entitled *Tales of the Jazz Age*. Residing in a succession of rented houses, traveling to Europe, living the good life, and beginning to drink perhaps more than he should, Fitzgerald still found time to write. His second novel, *The Beautiful and Damned*, came out in 1922, and he tried a play, *The Vegetable: Or, From President to Postman*, which was unsuccessful; it closed at its tryout in Atlantic City in November, 1923. Undeterred, he began work on his third, and probably most important, novel, *The Great Gatsby*, which was published in 1925, bringing its author the best critical reception he received during his lifetime.

The Fitzgeralds continued to travel, often living for months at a time in Europe, where they associated with literary figures such as Ernest Hemingway and James Joyce. Perhaps because of his drinking, perhaps because of Zelda's steadily deteriorating mental and emotional condition, Fitzgerald practically abandoned the novel to concentrate on short stories; while among these were some masterpieces, there are many which were written quickly (although well) for money. In a sense, Fitzgerald was succumbing to the temptations against which Father Fay had warned him earlier in his life.

In April, 1930, Zelda Fitzgerald had her first serious mental breakdown; she was placed in a Swiss clinic, and it was not until September, 1931, that the couple returned to the United States. Zelda's condition did not improve; in early 1932, she went into a clinic of the Johns Hopkins Hospital in Baltimore. In the meantime, Fitzgerald had turned this stuff of personal tragedy into the material for art, and his fourth novel, *Tender Is the Night*, which concerned a mental patient and her doctor/ husband, was published in April, 1934. It met with a mixed reception, and Fitzgerald continued his slide into alcoholism, while Zelda was moved from clinic to clinic.

Although Fitzgerald had been successful as a novelist and was one of the most highly paid short story writers of the time, the couple's expensive life-style and the costs of Zelda's care had plunged him deeply into debt. In the summer of 1937, he took a course that was often, if reluctantly, followed by serious authors of his time: He went to Hollywood as a scriptwriter. He was not a success, but he did begin work on another novel, *The Last Tycoon* (1941), which used the motion picture world, modern America's greatest example of the power of illusion, as its theme. He was working on the novel when he died on December 21, 1940, of a heart attack. Eight years later, after dying in a fire that destroyed the North Carolina clinic where she was staying, Zelda Sayre Fitzgerald was buried beside her husband.

Analysis

In one of the most haunting passages of *The Great Gatsby*, the narrator, Nick Carraway, sees his mysterious neighbor perform a strange ritual:

> [H]e stretched out his arms toward the dark water in a curious way, and, far as I was from him, I could have sworn he was trembling. Involuntarily I glanced seaward—and distinguished nothing except a single green light, minute and far away, that might have been the end of a dock. When I looked once more for Gatsby he had vanished, and I was alone again in the unquiet darkness.

What Gatsby is trying to do in the novel, literally as well as symbolically, is reach out to recapture the past. For Gatsby, that past is embodied in Daisy Buchanan, the woman he loved as a young lieutenant while stationed in her hometown in the South. He loves her still and, as a rich man, hopes to regain her and in doing so recapture his youthful dreams and promise.

It is a scene and a dream that runs throughout Fitzgerald's fiction. All of his heroes carry that sense of the lost past, of misspent promise. They are outsiders in some form or other—usually because they come from the lower or middle class— and they are further set apart because of the high goals and exacting standards they have set for themselves. From Amory Blaine, in Fitzgerald's first novel, through Monroe Stahr, in his last, left unfinished at the time of his death, Fitzgerald created protagonists who aspired to be larger than life, but who were destroyed by the commonplace existence they sought to rise above. In a sense, these fictional characters have many of the attributes of their author; in particular, they share with him a keen sense of morality and destiny that applies particularly to them. When they fail, betrayed by human lapses into drink or by the dark promise of sex, they find themselves on a downward spiral, often overindulging in the failings that distracted them initially. Their tragedies are largely self-made, as they become victims of their own romantic moralism.

This romantic moralism is especially painful in the relationship between men and women. A love which begins as strengthening, almost magical in its nature, turns out badly; the woman is frequently the agent of the hero's downfall. Anthony Patch, in *The Beautiful and Damned*, sinks into dissipation after his marriage to Gloria Gilbert. Dick Diver, the brilliant and promising young psychiatrist in *Tender Is the Night*, is undermined personally and professionally when he marries his patient, the rich heiress Nicole Warren. Most notably of all, Jay Gatsby is literally destroyed because of his love for Daisy: shot dead in his own swimming pool at the end of a series of sordid and entangling events that never would have occurred except for Gatsby's obsessed pursuit of her.

The style in which these tragedies are told is one of the most famous in American literature: a brilliant, sensuous, lyrical prose that re-creates for the reader the sense of emotional ecstasy and despair felt by the Fitzgerald character. As he developed as a writer, Fitzgerald's style gained in strength and clarity, dropping much of its earlier, self-conscious rhetoric but retaining its beauty, until it became a powerful and supple instrument that captured both particular insights and wide-ranging social observations.

Perhaps because Fitzgerald felt so keenly his own role as an outsider, he had a sharp and most perceptive view of American social mores. A large part of the power—and a cause for the immediate success—of *This Side of Paradise* was its fresh, vivid portrayal of college life, presenting it in a more realistic fashion than ever before. Whether etching the characters of heedless expatriates on the French Riviera, giving sharp, thumbnail portraits of New York gangsters, or presenting the excesses of the irresponsibly rich during the jazz age, Fitzgerald was a master of creating accurate, indelible images of American life—what they wore, drove, drank, and sang—during his time. His writings are a social history of the first rank.

These were the qualities which won for Fitzgerald success early in his career and which, for a while, made him the most popular and highly paid writer of his day. He was especially gifted in the short story form, finding it particularly suited to his skills in crafting characters who have come to a point of crisis in their lives, a crisis that requires them to make a choice that will, almost inevitably, destroy their youthful dreams. The best of these stories, such as "The Rich Boy," "The Diamond as Big as the Ritz," or "Babylon Revisited," are recognized as authentic masterpieces.

All Fitzgerald's writings come, sooner or later, to the themes which he explored throughout his career: early promise betrayed, the romantic hero broken by the indifferent world, love lost, and the impossibility of recapturing the past. These are themes woven deep into the American mind as well, and in pursuing them Fitzgerald is perhaps the most "American" author in the literature of the United States.

In the end, that dual sense of promise and loss, innocence and fall, is Fitzgerald's characteristic tone. It sounds strongest in *The Great Gatsby*:

I thought of Gatsby's wonder when he first picked out the green light at the end of Daisy's dock. He had come a long way to this blue lawn, and his dream must have seemed so close that he could hardly fail to grasp it. He did not know that it was already behind him, somewhere back in that vast obscurity beyond the city, where the dark fields of the republic rolled on under the night.

Gatsby, like Fitzgerald's other heroes, is ignorant of his loss until the realization of it destroys him. In a very American sense, the message of F. Scott Fitzgerald is that knowledge is tragedy but that such tragedy summons forth true greatness.

THIS SIDE OF PARADISE

First published: 1920
Type of work: Novel

The intellectual and moral development of Amory Blaine, from his pampered childhood to his early manhood.

This Side of Paradise, Fitzgerald's first novel, made him an enormously successful popular author when he was only twenty-three years old. The combination of romanticism and realism, mingled with a fresh—and for the time—sometimes startling depiction of college life, caught the attention of the reading public and made the novel representative of an entire generation.

This Side of Paradise is loose and episodic, a collection of vivid scenes which do not fuse into a well-structured novel. It is divided into two sections: "The Romantic Egotist" (the title of the novel's first draft) and "The Education of a Personage." The first takes Amory Blaine from his childhood through his years at Princeton University and concerns his intellectual and moral development.

Convinced that he has a great, if obscure, destiny, Amory is greatly influenced by a Catholic priest, Father Darcy, who awakens him to the reality and power of evil. Darcy is based upon Father Sigourney Fay, who exerted a comparable influence on Fitzgerald himself. In the novel, this moral and spiritual education is dramatized by incidents which appear supernatural, as when Amory is pursued by a diabolic figure through the streets of New York. Perhaps a remnant of Father Fay's moralism, the sense of sin and the power of sex are mixed in Amory's mind in an inextricable, if often confusing fashion.

The second section is restricted to one year, 1919, and concentrates on Amory's character development, which it traces by following his adventures after service in World War I. Since Fitzgerald had no experience of combat, he wisely omitted any actual description of Amory in the conflict. In book 2, Amory's courtship of Rosalind Connage is ended after the sudden loss of his family fortune. Having weathered this traumatic event, Amory undergoes another supernatural experience, involving the death of Father Darcy and again related to his confused feelings about sex, sin, morality, and destiny. Yet the death of Father Darcy frees Amory, in a sense, and at the end of the novel he gazes on the lights of Princeton and vows to begin his real search for his unknown but surely glorious destiny.

Readers responded to several different aspects of *This Side of Paradise*. It was one of the first novels to use the college setting in a realistic way—as opposed to the simplistic "Dink Stover at Yale" genre—and, although later generations were to see it as sentimental, even naïve, Fitzgerald's contemporaries were treated to a fresh and innovative point of view concerning the young. His scenes of college life, enticing to younger readers, were even thought shocking by some—including the president of Princeton, John Grier Hibben, who wrote Fitzgerald an aggrieved letter.

Hibben was troubled that *This Side of Paradise* seemed to emphasize the facile and superficial aspects of Princeton life. On the other hand, it should be noted that Fitzgerald's novel is highly concerned with the development of Amory Blaine's intellect. A recurrent theme in *This Side of Paradise* is the importance of reading in forming character: One critic has counted sixty-four book titles and the names of ninety-eight authors in the novel. In this concern with its hero's intellectual growth, *This Side of Paradise* is very similar to another influential novel of the period, James Joyce's *A Portrait of the Artist as a Young Man* (1916). Both books startled many by their blend of the mental and physical desires of their protagonists, including what was for the times a frank approach to sexual awakening.

Also startling to many readers, long accustomed to conventional portraits of women, were the manners and actions of Fitzgerald's female characters. Such young women as Eleanor Savage, a heedless and self-indulgent romantic, for example, were far removed from conventional morality. Actually, this realistic aspect of the novel fit quite well with the highly moral, even religious, sentiments of Amory Blaine concerning sex by underscoring the dangerous power of physical desires.

The style of the novel, remarked upon by many critics, remains its most distinguishing feature. Although *This Side of Paradise* is in many passages highly rhetorical, even excessively so, it contains the essential qualities of Fitzgerald's writing: the precise social observation aptly rendered, the flowing, rhythmic passages, and the presentation of abstract ideals embodied in specific individuals. In his later books and stories, Fitzgerald refined and developed these attributes, but they are clearly present from the start of his career.

THE BEAUTIFUL AND DAMNED

First published: 1922
Type of work: Novel

The moral characters of a young couple disintegrate as they wait to inherit a vast fortune.

The Beautiful and Damned, Fitzgerald's second novel, follows the decline—fiscal, physical, and moral—of Anthony and Gloria Patch. Like so many of Fitzgerald's figures, the Patches are destroyed by great wealth; the irony in this novel is that they are undone not by the possession of money but merely by expecting it.

Anthony, the only heir of his wealthy grandfather, Adam Patch, is a young Harvard University graduate who lives on money left by his father and disdains work because he believes nothing is equal to his supposed abilities. He marries the beautiful Gloria Gilbert, and they sink into a pointless and destructive life, squandering their income in an endless round of parties and extravagant expenses. When the grandfather, an inflexible and intolerant reformer, walks in unexpectedly on one of their gin-soaked parties, he writes Anthony out of his will; following his death, the Patches must sue to claim the inheritance which lured them into destruction. At the novel's end, they triumph, but the cost has been high: Gloria's beauty has been coarsened and Anthony's mind snapped by worry and drink.

Anthony and Gloria are selfish, self-indulgent characters who begin the novel with some perverse appeal but quickly deteriorate under the influence of greed, excess, and alcohol. As they move through their pointless round of pleasures, they demand wilder and stronger stimulation, but this in turn only confirms them in their downward spiral. Rejected as officer material when the United States enters World War I, Anthony is later drafted and, while on training in the South, has an affair with a local woman. In the meantime, Gloria fails to win the film role she covets, which had been offered to her by a former admirer. All in all, the aptly named Patches made shreds of their lives.

A strong sense of moralism runs though all Fitzgerald's works, and in *The Beautiful and Damned* it is married to the sophisticated, modern style of *This Side of Paradise*. The two elements are not cleanly fused, and this causes difficulties with the novel, chiefly with the view Fitzgerald takes of the main characters. The third-person narrator veers between bemused appreciation of Anthony and Gloria as unapologetic hedonists, and hardly veiled disapproval of their waste of talent and lives. In the earlier portions of the book, Fitzgerald seems to have some sort of respect for the code the Patches have adopted for themselves, but as their lives and code cheapen, the tone of the book becomes harsher. It seems that even dissipation has its standards.

As with most of Fitzgerald's writings, *The Beautiful and Damned* has many autobiographical elements. Quite a few of the pleasure-seeking, carefree antics of Anthony and Gloria—at least in the earlier sections of the novel—are based on the escapades of Fitzgerald and his wife, Zelda. In the second portion of the novel, Anthony is stationed in the South and has a love affair with a local girl; this also echoes Fitzgerald's own history, but with significant exceptions. Fitzgerald was an officer, while Anthony Patch is an enlisted man; Dot, Anthony's lover, is a common sort of woman, quite unlike the aristocratic Zelda. Most notably, Anthony and Dot have a simple but sordid relationship, unlike the romantic passion of which Fitzgerald and Zelda believed themselves to be the central characters.

Although *The Beautiful and Damned* is a more structured and planned book than *This Side of Paradise*, it still shows Fitzgerald as a writer learning the difficult skills of crafting a novel. Too often uncertain and wavering in its tone and point of view, overwritten in many of its descriptive passages, the book is redeemed by the power of its depiction of the deterioration of the Patches, who emerge for the reader as flawed but vividly memorable characters.

THE GREAT GATSBY

First published: 1925
Type of work: Novel

Seeking to recapture his lost early love and all that she symbolizes, a man is destroyed.

The Great Gatsby is Fitzgerald's finest novel, an almost perfect artistic creation which is perhaps the single most American novel of its time. It should be seen as the ultimate vehicle for the themes which form the central concerns of Fitzgerald's career, and indeed of so much of the United States' national life: lost hope, the corruption of innocence by money, and the impossibility of recapturing the past. These elements are fused together by Fitzgerald's eloquent yet careful prose in a novel which transcends its period and has become a touchstone of American literature.

Nick Carraway, the first-person narrator of the novel, lives on Long Island, New York, next door to the enormous mansion of a mysterious man named Gatsby, who throws gaudy, glittering parties. Wild, improbable rumors circulate about Gatsby, but when Nick meets him, he finds himself charmed and intrigued. Nick learns that Gatsby is in love with Nick's cousin, Daisy Buchanan, whom Gatsby met while stationed in her hometown in the South during World War I. Gatsby seeks to rekindle that earlier love in Daisy, now married to a coarse, brutal husband, Tom. The effort fails, and Gatsby becomes entangled in the lives of the Buchanans and is killed, shot by the confused and grieving husband of Tom's mistress. Gatsby's glowing dream ends in sordid confusion.

In this novel Fitzgerald relies on a narrative technique which he clearly learned from the works of the English writer Joseph Conrad: He gradually unveils Gatsby's story as Nick pieces it together a bit at a time. Each chapter allows Nick, and the reader, more insight into Gatsby's past and his true character. The facts are sifted from rumors and speculation until Jay Gatsby, born Gatz, is revealed as a flawed, but still great, hero.

Like so many of Fitzgerald's heroes, Gatsby is a romantic, a man who began with a high, even exalted, vision of himself and his destiny. He aspires to greatness, which he associates with Daisy. If he can win her, then he will have somehow achieved his goal. Gatsby's wealth, his mansion, his parties, his possessions, even his heroism in battle are but means to achieve his ultimate end. Gatsby is mistaken, however, in his belief that money can buy happiness or that he can recapture his past. His story is clearly a version of the traditional American myth, poor boy makes good, but is it a distorted version or an accurate one? Fitzgerald leaves this ambiguity unresolved, which adds to the power of his novel.

As a romantic, Jay Gatsby does not understand how money actually works in American life. He believes that if he is rich, then Daisy can be his. This is displayed most powerfully and poignantly in the scene where Gatsby shows Daisy and Nick the shirts he has tailored for him in London: He hauls them out in a rainbow of color and fabric, almost filling the room with the tangible yet useless symbols of his wealth. The shirts cause Daisy to cry, but they do not win her; they cannot let Gatsby realize his dream.

Gatsby has amassed his money by dealings with gangsters, yet he remains an innocent figure—he is a romantic, in other words. Ironically, Daisy Buchanan, his great love, is a much more realistic, hard-headed character. She understands money and what it means in American society, because it is her nature; she was born into it. Gatsby intuitively recognizes this, although he cannot fully accept it, when he remarks to Nick that Daisy's voice "is full of money." Gatsby will not admit this essential fact because it would destroy his conception of Daisy. In the end, this willful blindness helps lead to his destruction.

Actually, both Gatsby and Daisy are incapable of seeing the whole of reality, since he is a romantic and she, a cynic. This conflict is found in the other characters of the novel as well and is a key to *The Great Gatsby*. Fitzgerald uses a variety of symbolic scenes and images to express the blindness that the characters impose upon themselves. Gatsby's ostentatious material possessions are aspects of illusion. So is the green light at the end of Daisy's dock, the light which Gatsby gazes upon but cannot reach.

Other symbolic touches illuminate the book: the ash heaps which litter the landscape between Long Island and New York, for example, or the eyes of Doctor Ecleberg, found on a billboard dominating the valley of the ash heaps. The ash heaps are a reference to the vanity of life (and a nod at T. S. Eliot's poem *The Waste Land*, published in 1922), and the eyes a comment on the blindness of the book's characters, who do not fully understand what they behold.

While such devices add to the depth of *The Great Gatsby*, its true power derives from it being a quintessentially American novel, full of American characters and American themes. Nick Carraway, the midwestern narrator, encounters the sophistication of the East: New York, gangsters, the promise and hollowness of wealth. Tom and Daisy Buchanan, insulated by their money, do what they want without consequence, showing no remorse for their actions and no concern for those they have harmed. Jay Gatsby, like the hero in a story by Horatio Alger, rises from being a penniless youth through ambition and good fortune, only to discover that his wealth cannot buy what he most desires—and is, in fact, the very agent of his destruction. They are all American characters in an American setting.

Fitzgerald's skill as a novelist was at its peak with *The Great Gatsby*, and this is shown best in his command of the book's structure. By using Nick Carraway as the first-person narrator, Fitzgerald establishes a central focus for the novel, a character who is partly involved with the plot but partly a commentator upon it. Nick is presented as an honest, reliable person, and his perceptions and judgments are accepted by the reader. Nick ties the novel together, and through him it makes sense. Most important, Nick's solid, midwestern common sense validates Gatsby as a character despite Gatsby's outrageous background and fabulous adventures. In the end, if Nick Carraway accepts Gatsby and approves of him—and he does—so does the reader.

Nick's approval is what allows Gatsby to be called "great," but his greatness has a curious, puzzling quality to it, since it cannot be easily or completely defined. Gatsby certainly lacks many of the qualities and fails many of the tests normally associated with greatness, but he redeems this by his exalted conception of himself. It is to this romantic image of Gatsby that both Nick and the reader respond.

TENDER IS THE NIGHT

First published: 1934
Type of work: Novel

The career and character of a brilliant young psychiatrist are undermined by wealth and an irresponsible life-style.

Nine years elapsed between the publication of *The Great Gatsby* and *Tender Is the Night*, and during that time Fitzgerald worked on his fourth novel in several stages, completing the final version in about a year. It is an ambitious novel, a multilayered work which charts the moral and psychological decline of Dick Diver, a young and promising American psychiatrist, set against the background of American expatriates in Europe during the 1920's. In a sense, Fitzgerald is tracing two parallel cases of decay—an individual's and a generation's.

Tender Is the Night is divided into three books and covers the years 1925 through 1929. Dick and Nicole Diver are the center of an amusing circle of friends, including the alcoholic composer Abe North, who has never fulfilled his early promise, and the sinister mercenary, Tommy Barban, who is in love with Nicole. Through a flashback, Fitzgerald reveals that Nicole was originally Dick's patient, placed in his care after being traumatized by being raped by her father.

It is an essential part of Dick Diver's personality to feel loved and needed, and this causes him to marry Nicole. The dual pressures of being Nicole's husband and her doctor, combined with the lure of Nicole's inherited fortune, undermine Dick's dedication to his work. Using Nicole's money, Dick becomes partner in a psychiatric clinic in the Swiss Alps but is unable to concentrate on his duties. In the meantime, the master treatise which he has long planned goes unwritten, and he sinks deeper into pointless and frenzied activity, fueled by alcohol. As his career sinks further into decline, Dick reaches bottom, symbolized by a drunken brawl and arrest in Rome. The Divers return to the Riviera, the scene of their earlier triumphs, but to no avail: Nicole leaves Dick for Tommy Barban, and Dick returns to the United States, losing himself in obscurity as an unsuccessful doctor, wandering from town to small town.

In *Tender Is the Night*, Fitzgerald returns to the technique he employed so successfully in *The Great Gatsby*, that of gradually revealing the full nature of his characters—in this case, by the use of flashbacks. This allows the reader to become almost a participant in creating the novel, building the characters while reading. The method does have one drawback, as some critics have noted, in that it makes the deterioration of Dick Diver difficult to understand and accept. It requires careful reading to discern that the flaw in Dick's character is his desire—almost a compulsion—to be loved and needed. It is this which draws him into his fatal relationship with Nicole Warren.

Dick's decline occurs on two levels, personal and professional, and both are directly connected with his wife. Nicole had originally been his patient, a deeply disturbed young woman whose personality was fragile and whose grasp of reality was uncertain. As the novel progresses, Nicole grows stronger psychologically and more distant from Dick emotionally. As his wife comes to depend upon him less, Dick loses his purpose. He begins to drink more—and more irresponsibly. He has an affair with a young American actress, less out of physical desire than from the need to find someone who depends upon him and will admire him, as Nicole had done. His once promising professional career also fades, and the important book that he had planned to write is never finished. The clinic, bought with Nicole's money, slips out of his control, and he must let it go. He ends up a failure, no longer respected (or even known) by his peers.

This trajectory follows a pattern familiar in Fitzgerald's works. A hero with a high conception of his potential is diverted from his original purpose and wastes his gifts. The growing realization that he is squandering his talents only hastens the process and causes the downward slide to accelerate. Alcohol and unearned money are essential elements in the collapse, and although they do not cause the hero's fall, they certainly speed it along.

This pattern shows Fitzgerald's romantic moralism, which flows through all of his novels. Women, in particular women with inherited money, are often agents of moral destruction, diverting the hero from his goals. Without Nicole's wealth, Dick Diver is an acute and resourceful psychiatrist, skillful and capable in exploring the human mind and its discontents. When the Warren fortune takes hold, Dick loses his vision, literally becoming incapable of understanding the psychology of people, including himself. Once a diver into the mind, as his symbolic name indicates, he has gotten out of his depth.

An ambitious and sensitive novel, *Tender Is the Night* has a keen sense of character, especially for the two main figures. The structure of the book, which moves back and forth in time, and the way in which Fitzgerald gradually reveals important information, however, have been confusing to some readers. Some critics have believed that these are damaging flaws and that a more straightforward, chronological approach would have been better. Fitzgerald himself considered this possibility after the novel was published, even reworking it for reissue in a revised form. Still, given the complex theme and psychological aspects of the work, the original presentation is undoubtedly the more appropriate. *Tender Is the Night* is a complex novel because the human mind and heart are themselves complex, complicated, and mysterious.

THE DIAMOND AS BIG AS THE RITZ

First published: 1922
Type of work: Short story

A young man falls in love with the daughter of the world's richest man and is nearly destroyed.

"The Diamond as Big as the Ritz" is Fitzgerald's most successful fantasy story, a genre in which he worked mainly during the early phase of his career. While it contains what might be read as a happy ending, the story carries many of the tragic elements inherent in Fitzgerald's most enduring theme: how a young man is destroyed by the wealth of the woman he loves.

The plot of "The Diamond as Big as the Ritz" is relatively simple. John T. Unger, a young man from the small midwestern town of Hades, is sent by his ambitious parents to the exclusive eastern school of St. Midas. There he makes friends with Percy Washington and is invited to spend the summer at the Washington estate in the far West. Unger learns that the Washingtons are literally the richest family in the world, because they own a flawless diamond that is as large as the Ritz-Carlton Hotel. There is also a darker side to this fortune: To protect it, the Washingtons have made their estate a fortress, completely isolated from the outside world, and intruders are held captive in a giant cage.

While in this strange combination of luxury and prison, Unger meets and falls in love with Kismine, Percy's sixteen-year-old sister. From Kismine, Unger learns that all invited visitors to the Washington estate are murdered before they can leave. As Unger and Kismine flee, the place is attacked by airplanes, led there by one of the prisoners who managed to escape. The fabulous estate is destroyed as Unger and Kismine discover they have fled with worthless rhinestones instead of diamonds; they are free but penniless.

"The Diamond as Big as the Ritz" is a story full of symbolic and allegorical touches, many of them dealing with the soul-destroying potential of wealth. The hero, named Unger, is avid for more than his hometown can offer, and he seems to find it in Kismine Washington: young, beautiful, and heiress to a great fortune. The Washington fortune has become a prison for the family, however: They are isolated from the world, guarded by blacks who have been tricked into believing that slavery still exists. There is an obvious parallel between the two kinds of bondage, a parallel ironically emphasized by the family name of Washington, so closely associated with American freedom.

Wealth is also destructive in a religious sense. The train that carries Unger and Washington stops at the town of Fish, which has a population of only twelve men, who await the arrival of the train as a mystical event directed by the "Great Brakeman." (The fish was an early Christian symbol for Jesus, who urged his followers to renounce wealth, often in extremely pointed terms.) Yet these twelve have no real belief: By mere proximity to the Washingtons, these counterparts to the twelve apostles have been drained of all faith.

Even more emphatic are the baneful effects of incalculable wealth on the family. Their land is literally nowhere, since they have taken extraordinary measures to keep it off even official government maps. To protect their secret, the Washingtons are ready to perpetuate slavery, imprison the innocent, and even commit murder, including fratricide. When the estate is about to be overrun, Percy's father offers a bribe to God—an enormous gem, backed by promises of human sacrifice—and then destroys his estate himself, rather than submit.

These various elements, which do not quite fit together in a consistently coherent fashion, are united by Fitzgerald's use of both fantasy and realistic descriptions, which allow the reader to accept the fairy-tale premises of the story. In a sense, "The Diamond as Big as the Ritz" is a magical counterpart to the more realistic *The Great Gatsby*, and the two explore many of the same themes and concerns.

THE LAST OF THE BELLES

First published: 1929
Type of work: Short story

A romantic young army lieutenant and a Southern belle learn that dreams are destroyed by time.

"The Last of the Belles" combines autobiographical elements of Fitzgerald's courtship of Zelda Sayre and his theme of the lost dreams of youthful promise. Beautiful, blond, and vivacious, Ailie Calhoun captivates all the young officers who meet her in the small Georgia town of Tarleton, where they are in training for World War I. Many pursue her, including the narrator, Andy, and one young man may even have killed himself in a plane crash because of her. Ailie is perversely attracted to and at the same time repelled by Earl Schoen, an uncouth Yankee who is alien to everything she has known. In the end, she rejects them all but is herself rejected by time and the modern world, which leaves her as the last of the traditional southern belles, a memory of what was once youthful and applauded.

The tone of the story is wistful and elegiac. All the events are in the past, which heightens the sense of lost opportunity and gives added emphasis to the connections between Fitzgerald's own life and the fictional work. At the end of the story Andy returns to Tarleton and, with Ailie, revisits the now desolate site of the abandoned army camp. Andy wanders there, "in the knee-deep underbrush, looking for my youth in a clapboard or a strip of roofing or a rusty tomato can," another of Fitzgerald's heroes wondering what became of his youthful dreams and promise.

BABYLON REVISITED

First published: 1931
Type of work: Short story

A reformed alcoholic tries to regain his daughter and start life anew, but his efforts are undermined by his past.

Charlie Wales, the central character of "Babylon Revisited," is a man who lived high and wildly in Paris during the late 1920's and then lost everything with the Great Depression, including his wife and daughter. After the death of his wife, perhaps hastened when, in a drunken rage, he locked her out of their apartment during a snowstorm, Charlie had given guardianship of his daughter, Honoria, to his sister-in-law. When the story opens, Charlie has returned to Paris to regain Honoria. Just when it seems he has convinced his suspicious relatives that he is indeed reformed, Charlie has his hopes dashed by the unexpected and disastrous arrival of two drinking companions from the bad old days. At the story's end Charlie maintains his sobriety, determined to continue in his attempts to regain his daughter.

Once again, Fitzgerald's theme is the waste of promise, fueled by the harmful effects of alcoholic indulgence. In this story, the theme is made explicit as Charlie Wales comes to realize the meaning of the word dissipate: "to dissipate into thin air; to make nothing out of something." Paris, the place where this wasting has taken place, is for Charlie Wales a Babylon, a city of wasting—not only materially, but morally and spiritually as well. Wales has repaired some of the effects of that dissipation—he has partially restored his finances and is once again sober—but the story ends with both Charlie and the reader uncertain if the most tragic loss can be restored and father and daughter reunited.

The character of Charlie Wales is an important part of "Babylon Revisited," because he is believable and sympathetic, a full-rounded individual who is presented through suggestion and inference, dialogue and reference. As the story moves in and out of Charlie's present and past, the reader comes to understand more than is openly told, largely through Fitzgerald's selection of relevant details.

Fitzgerald's style in "Babylon Revisited" is remarkable: In place of the lush, romantic prose of earlier stories such as "The Diamond as Big as the Ritz," he uses a spare, careful technique that conveys intense and often painful emotions through understatement and implication. The language is supple and powerful, so graceful that the reader is almost unaware of it, but a close and attentive study shows that Fitzgerald has achieved a masterpiece of the modern short story.

Summary

Fitzgerald was an acute social observer and an incomparable stylist. His central concern was with the individual whose promise is destroyed by an uncaring or hostile world, a destruction made possible by some inherent flaw in an otherwise noble nature. Fitzgerald's writings all have this viewpoint, which can best be described as romantic moralism.

Immensely popular with his first novel, highly successful with his short stories, and critically acclaimed for his masterpiece, *The Great Gatsby*, F. Scott Fitzgerald has come to be recognized as one of American literature's premier authors and the creator of some of its most memorable and individual characters. Although his work is clearly a product of and a reflection of its time, Fitzgerald's best efforts transcend that specific period to become universal.

Bibliography

Bruccoli, Matthew. *Some Sort of Epic Grandeur.* New York: Harcourt Brace Jovanovich, 1981.

Kazan, Alfred, ed. *F. Scott Fitzgerald: The Man and the Work.* Cleveland, Ohio: World, 1951.

Mizenor, Arthur, ed. *F. Scott Fitzgerald: A Collection of Critical Essays.* Englewood Cliffs, N.J.: Prentice-Hall, 1963.

_____. *The Far Side of Paradise.* Boston: Houghton Mifflin, 1951.

Turnbull, Andrew. *Scott Fitzgerald.* New York: Charles Scribner's Sons, 1962.

Michael Witkoski

BENJAMIN FRANKLIN

Born: Boston, Massachusetts
January 17, 1706
Died: Philadelphia, Pennsylvania
April 17, 1790

Principal Literary Achievement

Franklin's writings attest his intellect: He is the epitome of the Age of Reason in his ability to take philosophical ideas and formulate them, through his prose, into a practical, efficient, yet beneficent life-style.

Biography

Benjamin Franklin was born in Boston, Massachusetts, on January 17, 1706, to Josiah and Abiah Folger Franklin. His father, a candle and soap maker, was a devout Puritan who left England for the colonies during the religious upheavals of the 1600's. Benjamin was the tenth son of a family of sixteen (Josiah had seven children by a first wife, who died about 1700). The elder Franklin encouraged Benjamin to pursue the ministry; unfortunately, economic circumstances forced Josiah to abandon not only that idea but also the idea of Benjamin's even attending grammar school. Young Benjamin detested his father's avocation, however, and asked permission to go to sea. Josiah compromised by allowing Benjamin to become an apprentice to his older brother James, a successful printer, who operated a thriving business as publisher of a newspaper, the *New England Courant*. Under James's tutelage, Benjamin acquired great skill in the trade and furthered his love of books and learning through a number of James's customers. Eventually, Franklin took up the pen himself, and in 1722, James published his sixteen-year-old brother's fourteen satirical "Do Good" essays, modeled, in part, on Joseph Addison and Richard Steele's London periodical *The Spectator*. Franklin adopted a pseudonym, as was the custom of the day, of "Silence Do Good," a young widow, who offered "her" opinion on a variety of topics, including fashion, religion, temperance, and education. Most scholars point to these essays as the genesis of Franklin's literary career; in fact, many see the essays as the finest literature to be found in early eighteenth-century New England.

In spite of this success, Franklin had a serious disagreement with his brother over the terms of his indenture in 1723 and left Boston for Philadelphia late that year. After an unproductive stint as a journeyman printer, Franklin sailed for London and

worked as a typesetter for one of London's finest printing houses. It was there that he developed his intellectual acumen and published numerous pamphlet essays, in his own name, on religious and philosophical controversies of the day.

Returning to Philadelphia in 1726, Franklin was immediately hired as a print shop manager. He also formed a literary-social club, called the Junto, in which members wrote essays to share with all members of the group; Franklin's organizational efforts became the impetus for America's first circulating library, which began operation as the Library Company of Philadelphia in 1731.

Franklin's business acumen, bolstered by a strong penchant for honesty, enabled him to buy out the newspaper of his first Philadelphia employer in 1729 and purchase his own business. His new paper, *The Pennsylvania Gazette*, frequently graced by Franklin's intuitive essays, such as "A Scolding Wife," became immensely popular. In 1732, after years of planning, Franklin launched his own almanac, *Poor Richard's Almanack*, loosely based on a version his brother James had begun in Boston a few years earlier. Not only did *Poor Richard's Almanack* offer calendars, weather forecasts, and astronomical figures, as all almanacs do, but it also included the wise and pithy sayings for which Franklin is known. This "extra" made *Poor Richard's Almanack* a success in Pennsylvania and throughout the Colonies, assuring Franklin's financial success.

Poor Richard's Almanack became the forum for many of Franklin's greatest literary successes and afforded him the opportunity to explore other areas that interested him, specifically science and public service. He was appointed clerk of the Pennsylvania Assembly and Philadelphia postmaster. Incurring the wrath of pacifist Quakers in the colony, Franklin proposed a "Military Defense Association" to protect Philadelphia from French and Spanish privateers roaming near the mouth of the Delaware river. By the late 1740's, Franklin was particularly interested in electricity and its uses, and his famous kite experiment was described in detail in *Experiments and Observations on Electricity* (1751).

In 1757, Franklin was appointed envoy to England by the Assembly, with the express purpose of settling a tax dispute between Pennsylvania and England. It was during this mission that Franklin first began to consider the debilitating system under which England's colonies found themselves. For the next fifteen years, Franklin published numerous pamphlets on English-colonial policies, many of which drew praise from Edmund Burke, a British statesman sympathetic toward the American colonies.

In 1771, on one of Franklin's diplomatic missions to London, he began his autobiography, which he entitled "*Memoirs*." It begins as an extended letter to his son William, later colonial governor of New Jersey. Franklin had two children, Francis Folger and Sarah, from his common-law marriage of forty-four years to Deborah Reed. William was Franklin's illegitimate son and not only later a governor, but also an outspoken Tory, hotly opposed to the revolutionary fervor of his father.

The remainder of Franklin's life involved serving the rebellious colonies and, later, the new republic. He served as delegate to the Second Continental Congress and on the committee that drafted the Declaration of Independence. In 1776, Franklin was appointed minister to France and secured crucial support for the revolution from Louis XVI. When the war ended in 1781, Franklin negotiated and signed the Treaty of Paris, ensuring America's independence. Franklin's last public activity was as a delegate to the Constitutional Convention in 1785. When he died in 1790, twenty thousand people attended his funeral, indicating his status as perhaps the greatest American of the eighteenth century.

Analysis

Franklin's intellectual and literary prowess was achieved in an era known for its philosophical advances. The eighteenth century is frequently called the beginning of the "modern era" in philosophy, an ideal also found in the literature of the era, whether Colonial, British, or Continental. The century is thus known as the "Enlightenment," or "The Age of Reason." Two factors—or, more specifically, two intellectuals—epitomize this era. Sir Isaac Newton (1642-1727), English mathematician and astronomer, made revolutionary scientific discoveries concerning light and gravitation and formulated the basis of modern calculus. His unsurpassed genius changed humankind's view of itself and its capabilities: Individuals can practically, rationally, and reasonably order their world for the benefit of all human beings. The English philosopher John Locke (1632-1704) formulated these attitudes into his *Essay Concerning Human Understanding* (1689). Locke's basic thesis asserts that man is born devoid of any preformed ideas or perceptions; in essence, he is a *tabula rasa*, or "blank slate." Through experience, as perceived through the senses, man develops knowledge.

This theory, revised and amended by numerous philosophers of the century, calls into serious question the previously believed role of God in man's life. With the traditional idea of Christian predestiny called into question, a new attitude toward the Creator was developed to coincide with these new philosophical advances. This "religion," termed Deism, espoused a belief in a "clockwork universe," in which the Creator provided the spark to create the heavens but then took an inactive role in its operation. Thus, man, through reason (not through a reliance on revelation), has the sole responsibility to arrange his affairs, both personally and socially. Many American colonists adhered to this philosophy, most notably Thomas Jefferson, the radical revolutionary Thomas Paine, and Benjamin Franklin. Early in his autobiography, Franklin concludes after much study that he had become "a thorough Deist."

Franklin, however, took his Enlightenment ideas a step further than most of his scholarly contemporaries. While the philosophers of the era were content to argue among themselves about the nature of man, Franklin believed in bringing these new philosophical and scientific ideas to the common people. Franklin's wit, coupled with his intellect, had an immediate appeal to his readership. His maxims and aphorisms in *Poor Richard's Almanack* made the colonists laugh, but also revealed some of their foibles. Franklin's *Autobiography* is essentially a story of the application of rationality, practicality, and wise frugality to everyday life. Also inherent in Franklin's writings is the belief in the innate liberty of the common man and the right of that man to pursue his own destiny.

Many twentieth-century intellectuals have taken exception to what they see as Franklin's "materialism." German sociologist Max Weber's Marxist interpretation takes issue with the aims of Franklin's philosophy:

> It (the earning of money) is thought of purely as an end in itself. . . . [I]t appears entirely transcendental and absolutely irrational. Man is dominated by the making of money, by acquisition as the ultimate purpose of his life.

It is unfortunate that such criticism has evolved not as much from Franklin and his writings, as from readers who believe Franklin's philosophy somehow justifies abject materialism. In fact, the true character of Benjamin Franklin reveals a man concerned about society and its treatment of humankind. His concern for public education, public safety, and public health made Philadelphia the most modern city not only in the Colonies, but also in the entire Western world. Franklin also refused to apply for patents for many of his inventions, thus making them more accessible to the general public. Thus, Franklin's philosophy not only defined the American ideal but also defined the entire concept of human progress.

AUTOBIOGRAPHY

First published: Part 1, 1790; complete, 1818
Type of work: Autobiography

Franklin's *Autobiography*, begun in 1771, presents his thoughts on practicality, frugality, and Enlightenment ideals.

Franklin's *Autobiography* is divided into three parts, with a short addendum added a few months before Franklin's death in 1790. Each has a distinct thematic purpose and thus serves, in part, to make the work an important philosophical and historical tract. Part 1 is, in essence, an extended letter to Franklin's son William, written in England in 1771. It recounts Franklin's ancestry, his early days in Boston and Philadelphia, and his first journey to London in 1724. In fact, *Autobiography* is by far the best source for information on Franklin's early life. Part 1 ends with Franklin's marriage to Deborah and the beginning of his subscription library in late 1730, when he was twenty-four years old. Franklin ends part 1 with this explanatory note:

> Thus far was written with the Intention express'd in the Beginning and therefore contains several little family Anecdotes of no Importance to others. . . . The Affairs of the Revolution occasion'd the Interruption.

In spite of this rejoinder, there are important ideas developed in part 1. Franklin concludes that, after a youthful prank brought parental admonishment, that, "tho' I pleaded the Usefulness of the Work, mine convinc'd me that nothing was useful which was not honest." Part 1 also discussed Franklin's Deistic inclinations and his predilection for the art of disputation, which is similar to modern-day debate. Franklin thus believed in the mind's ability to use logic and reason over and above strong emotions. He comments:

> . . . therefore I took a Delight in it [disputing], practic'd it continually and grew very artful and expert in drawing People of even superior Knowledge into Concessions the Consequences of which they did not foresee . . . and so obtaining Victories that neither myself nor my Cause always deserved.

One should not conclude that Franklin had a thoroughly optimistic view of human nature; too many of Franklin's "friends" took advantage of his good nature and left him with their debts or with other embarrassing situations. Franklin, however, frequently blamed himself for allowing such situations—and others, such as his failure to pursue his courtship of Deborah actively after first meeting her, and he terms such faults *errata*, a term that appears frequently in part 1.

Part 2 is less autobiographical and more philosophical than part 1, but no less revealing of Franklin's character. Franklin's Philadelphia friend Abel James encouraged Benjamin in 1782 to follow through on his idea of continuing the *Autobiography*, with the idea of depicting, in Franklin's words, "My Manner of acting to engage People in this and future Undertakings." The essence of part 2 can be found in Franklin's discussion of his attempts to achieve "moral perfection," "a bold and arduous project." He devised a list of thirteen virtues, such as temperance, industry, moderation, and humility, and included a precise definition for each. He then ordered them in a vertical list, according to the theory that "the previous Acquisition of some might facilitate the Acquisition of certain others." A list of the days of the week then composed the horizontal axis of the chart. Each of the virtues has its own separate chart, thus allowing Franklin to concentrate on a particular virtue for those seven days. Theoretically, at the end of thirteen weeks and after a religious maintenance of the charts, noting all transgressions at the appropriate points, moral perfection, an attribute attainable by "people in all religions," would be achieved.

This "Book of Virtues" was joined by Franklin's "Scheme of Order," an organizational plan to meet each workday, to complete his precise scheme of living. Was Franklin himself able to realize the edicts of moral perfection? He comments:

> In Truth I found myself incorrigible with respect to Order; and now I am grown old, and my Memory bad, I feel very sensibly the want of it. But on the whole, tho' I never arrived at the Perfection I had been so ambitious of obtaining, but fell far short of it, yet I was by the Endeavour made a better and happier Man than I otherwise should have been, if I had not attempted it. . . .

Part 3 does not have the literary value of the first two parts, but it is an intriguing recollection of Franklin's career as a public administrator. It particularly focuses on Franklin's efforts as Pennsylvania representative to British General William Braddock in a plan to lease civilian "waggons and baggage horses" to the British Army in 1755. The plan nearly failed as a result of Braddock's arrogant contempt for the colonists. This incident had a profound effect on Franklin's future attitudes toward Great Britain.

POOR RICHARD'S ALMANACK

First published: 1733; in annual editions until 1758
Type of work: Almanac and maxim book

An American institution of proverbs, maxims, poems, and anecdotes on how to achieve "moral perfection."

Essentially *Poor Richard's Almanack* embodies all the themes of the *Autobiography* in a witty and accessible format. Franklin's literary influence on *Poor Richard's Almanack* comes in a variety of forms: Proverbs, epigrams, rhymes, and aphorisms abound in each edition, usually interspersed among the calendars, weather forecasts, and astronomical charts. Each edition opens with a letter from the almanac's alleged author, one "Richard Saunders" (another Franklin pseudonym). He was "excessive poor" but fascinated with the heavens. Influenced by his wife, who could not bear "to sit spinning in her Shift of Tow," he was compelled to publish his observations. Thus, Franklin presents to his readership—"middling people" who had to work long and hard to save and prosper—one of their own, a man of humble means in search of moral perfection and its resultant prosperity.

Few of Franklin's sayings in *Poor Richard's Almanack* were original. He borrowed many of them from larger poetic works written within the preceding five or ten years; the poetic satirists Alexander Pope, John Dryden, and Jonathan Swift are heavily borrowed from but revised by Franklin to fit the needs and tastes of his readership. Many of these sayings have become oft-repeated foundations of American cultural heritage: "A true friend is the best possession"; "Don't misinform your Doctor nor your Lawyer"; "Don't throw stones at your neighbors, if your own windows are glass"; "Fish and visitors stink in 3 days"; "Haste makes waste"; "Eat to live, and not live to eat." Scholars point to the role that experience plays in the sayings found in *Poor Richard's Almanack*: It is not scholarly pursuits, but wise, practical living that paves the road to virtue. Although there were allusions to Deism ("Serving God is doing Good to Man, but praying is Thought an easier Service, and therefore more generally chosen") and the theories of Locke, Newton, and the essayist Francis Bacon, they were versed in language that indicated that such ideas could be acquired through experience—which includes, in the Lockean sense, observation. Thus, those colonists (and there were a great many) who did not have access to books could gain much contemporary philosophical and literary thought through "Mr. Saunders'" *Almanack*.

Franklin's sayings, while not original in themselves, were revised to adapt to the emerging working class of the American colonies. Such an infusion of philosophical ideas dealing with equality helped give the American colonies the intellectual impetus for the Revolution that occurred less than twenty years after the last edition of *Poor Richard's Almanack* was published.

One final note as to the popularity of *Poor Richard's Almanack* concerns the Revolutionary War naval hero John Paul Jones, who waited for months in France for a refitted man-of-war promised to him by the French monarchy to aid the independence effort. Finally, Jones recalled a maxim from *Poor Richard's Almanack*, "If you'd have it done, go; if not, send," and he marched to Versailles and demanded the vessel. The resulting warship was christened *Bonhomme Richard* in appreciation of the influence of *Poor Richard's Almanack* on the indomitable Jones.

Summary

George Washington and Benjamin Franklin are two of the many American colonial figures who have ascended to near-mythological figures in the cultural heritage of the United States. Washington earns such status by dint of his dominating, yet humble, leadership skills. Franklin, on the other hand, ascends primarily because of his intellectual accomplishments, which focused and adapted the philosophy of the century to the needs of a raw, colonial power. The American colonies were the epitome of the Enlightenment. Reasonable, rational, practical, and, above all, determined to assure liberty for all inhabitants, the Pennsylvania readership of *Poor Richard's Almanack* represented the realization of Franklin's belief in an ordered, modern society.

Bibliography

Aldridge, Alfred Own. *Benjamin Franklin: Philosopher and Man*. Philadelphia: J. B. Lippincott, 1965.

Granger, Bruce Ingham. *Benjamin Franklin: An American Man of Letters*. Ithaca, N.Y.: Cornell University Press, 1964.

Seavey, Ormond. *Becoming Benjamin Franklin: The Autobiography and the Life*. University Park: Pennsylvania State University Press, 1988.

Van Doren, Carl. *Benjamin Franklin*. Reprint. New York: Viking Press, 1973.

Zall, Paul M. *Franklin's Autobiography: A Model Life*. Boston: Twayne, 1989.

Richard S. Keating

PHILIP FRENEAU

Born: New York, New York
January 2, 1752
Died: Freehold, New Jersey
December 18, 1832

Principal Literary Achievement

Although he was an indefatigable journalist and political propagandist, Freneau earned the title "poet of the American Revolution" because of his sincere patriotism and his satiric treatment of royalist attitudes.

Biography

Freneau's family heritage was French Huguenot (Protestant); his father's family migrated to New York in 1705, became members of the city's respected and influential Huguenot community, and established a profitable agency for wines imported from Bordeaux, France, and the Madeira Islands. Pierre Fresneau (Philip changed the spelling of the family surname) carried on this business with his brother, but upon his marriage to Agnes Watson he commenced his interest in the dry goods business. Philip Morin Fresneau was born on Frankfort Street, New York, on January 2, 1752; he was the first of his parents' five children. Later in the same year, the family moved to the hamlet of Mount Pleasant, near present-day Matawan, New Jersey, which was centrally located for the crucial New Jersey campaigns of the War of Independence—at Trenton, Princeton, and Monmouth.

When Philip was fifteen, his father died, and the future poet inscribed at the end of Pierre's letter-book, "Here ends a book of vexation, disappointments, loss, and plagues that sunk the author to his grave short of 50 years." Philip's father left the family in unenviable financial straits. Philip's education, however, had not been jeopardized as his father's financial situation deteriorated: He had been sent to a Latin school in Penolopen, New Jersey, headed by the Reverend Alexander Mitchell, a friend of John Witherspoon, the newly appointed president of the College of New Jersey (now Princeton University), subsequently one of the signers of the Declaration of Independence. Although it was intended that Philip should prepare for a career in the church, his associations at Princeton (where he was admitted as a sophomore) militated against such a serene career: He was a roommate of James Madison; he became a close friend of Hugh Brackenridge, a future novelist; and he heard numerous sermons by Witherspoon, a leading theologian, philosopher, and

703

rhetorician, who was to write much in favor of the Revolution. Freneau and Brack-enridge were joint authors of "The Rising Glory of America," a long poem read at their commencement in 1771.

After graduation, Freneau taught school briefly, studied for the ministry desulto-rily, toyed with Deism, and penned several satires of British manners and adminis-tration before (early in 1776) sailing for the West Indies, where he was briefly a privateer. His "A Political Litany," written in 1775, is hardly above doggerel level, but the sentiments are genuine. In eight stanzas, the poet asks the Lord to deliver his countrymen from sixteen pestilences that range from Lord North and Admiral Mon-tagu to bishops and slaves; however, his poems that resulted from his West Indian experiences are generally more socially significant, less petulant, and better com-posed: "The Beauties of Santa Cruz" is one.

Perhaps feeling embarrassed by his absence from North America during the tem-pestuous days of the infant revolution, Freneau returned to New Jersey in July, 1778, just after the Battle of Monmouth. He enlisted as a private in the militia but saw lit-tle action, though he was in the coastal patrol infantry. He was promoted to the rank of sergeant, was wounded in the knee, and ended his military service on May 1, 1780.

Shortly thereafter, aboard the privateer *Aurora*, bound for the West Indies, he was captured by a British frigate and incarcerated in a prison ship, H.M.S. *Scorpion*, and later in a hospital ship in New York Harbor for six weeks. Immediately upon his release, he returned to his family home in Mount Pleasant and wrote in prose *Some Account of the Capture of the Ship "Aurora"* (not published until 1899) and in verse "The British Prison Ship" (1781), which detailed his detention in six hundred lines of heroic couplets. Canto 3 ("The Hospital Prison Ship") describes the conditions on board with poignant phrase and vivid image:

> On the hard floors these wasted objects laid,
> There tossed and tumbled in the dismal shade,
> There no soft voice their bitter fate bemoaned,
> And Death strode stately, while the victims groaned.

This tribulation cast Freneau as an implacable enemy of the British and as an earnest and prolific propagandist for the revolutionary cause; henceforth, it was universally acknowledged that he wrote only with unquestioned sincerity.

After a brief recuperation, Freneau went to Philadelphia, where he worked for about a year as a printer and assistant editor of *The Freeman's Journal*, becoming a prolific contributor to the periodical. In 1786, Francis Bailey, editor of *The Free-man's Journal*, published *The Poems of Philip Freneau*, and two years later the *Mis-cellaneous Works of Mr. Philip Freneau*.

Meanwhile, however, Freneau had worked as a clerk in the Philadelphia post office, translated Abbé Claude Robin's *New Travels Through North-America* (1784) from the original French, shipped to Jamaica as a deckhand aboard the *Dromelly* (and almost drowned in a hurricane), and became master of the *Monmouth, Indus-*

try, and *Columbia*, which sailed between New York and Philadelphia and southern and Caribbean ports. He retired from the sea in 1789.

In March, 1790, Freneau took a position on the staff of the *Daily Advertiser* in New York, and a month later he married Eleanor Forman, daughter of a well-established Monmouth County family of Scots background, at Middletown Point, New Jersey. Within the following years, the first of the couple's four daughters was born and Freneau (on the urging of James Madison) accepted an appointment as clerk for foreign languages to Thomas Jefferson—at a minuscule salary. While working in Philadelphia, Freneau inaugurated the *National Gazette*, a twice-weekly publication that endorsed Thomas Paine's philosophy and the French revolutionists. Soon Alexander Hamilton attacked the *Gazette* and proposed that Freneau was merely a front for Jefferson; both men publicly denied the charge. Jefferson declared Freneau to be the person who "saved our constitution, which was fast galloping into monarchy," while George Washington and the federalists referred to him as "that rascal Freneau." Toward the end of 1793, Philadelphia saw an outbreak of yellow fever; Freneau resigned his clerkship, closed his *Gazette*, and returned to New Jersey, where he edited the *Jersey Chronicle* for a short time, issued a unique *Monmouth Almanac*, and published his *Poems Written Between the years 1786 and 1774* (1795).

Freneau missed the "polite taste" and political environment of Philadelphia in Monmouth County, to which he once referred as a "crude and barbarous part of the country." Freneau soon headed once more for the seas briefly—none of his vocations seeming to be capable of significant endurance. After a decade of acting as a sea captain, Freneau retired in 1807, largely because of the effects of the Embargo Act. Thereafter he returned to his New Jersey home and worked as an occasional laborer and tinker, contributed essays to the *Aurora* (under the pseudonym Old Soldier), published poems and essays in the *True American* in Trenton, and issued two collections of new poems (in 1809 and 1815). His home burned down in October, 1818, so he moved to a farm near Freehold. Freneau died in a blizzard on December 18, 1832.

Analysis

As an undergraduate poet, Freneau imitated the standard British poets; in his *Poems* (1786), he conveniently dated many of his compositions, so one can see his progression of interest from John Dryden and Alexander Pope to John Milton as models in both subject matter and technique. One of his best early lyrics, "The Power of Fancy" (dated 1770), suggests a conscious imitation of Milton's "L'Allegro" and "Il Penseroso" in its use of tetrametrical couplets, variously iambic and trochaic, although Joseph Warton's poem of the same title, written in 1746, may well have been an inspiration.

"The Power of Fancy" is a long poem for a beginning poet, though its 154 lines hardly exceed the limitation imposed by Edgar Allan Poe's theory of verse composition, for it can, with ease, be read at a single sitting. The poem is noteworthy for its fusion of the elements of the classical (in form and allusions) with those of the

Romantic writers, whose philosophy and technique were not yet enunciated: there is praise for fancy as a transforming force; there is the introduction of dreaming as a device; there is the use of the distant and hence exotic, and there is a pervasive mood of melancholy. Furthermore, Freneau offers in this poem an early glimpse of his slowly developing Deist (or Unitarian) tendencies, which are perhaps most clearly stated in his poem "On the Uniformity and Perfection of Nature," one of his last. None of his other undergraduate poems has similar interest or quality.

In "The American Village," Freneau imitates the British poet Oliver Goldsmith's "The Deserted Village" (which had been published two years earlier), but whereas Goldsmith's poem is melancholy, Freneau's is optimistic and confident of the future of America and speaks of "this land with rising pomp divine" and "its own splendor." Thus, by 1772 Freneau was expressing his regional chauvinism; he was already displaying his special attachment to his American homeland.

Before long, poems expressing simple pride and faith in the American colonies gave way to somewhat bellicose political verse, to statements of the theme that the North Americans valued the "godlike glory to be free" (a phrase in his "American Liberty"). By 1778, Freneau was writing the verse that earned for him the title "poet of the American Revolution": "American Independence" likened King George III to Cain, Nero, and Herod; in couplets that must have reminded some readers of the work of Thomas Gray, Freneau wrote: "Full many a corpse lies rotting on the plain,/ That ne'er shall see its little brood again." Here the juxtaposition of images of the battlefront campaigns and the violated domestic tranquility show Freneau at his most brilliant achievement as a patriotic and propagandistic poet. The poet was somewhat ambivalent about engaging in the military conflict himself, and, in his "The Beauties of Santa Cruz," written during his privateering period, he both urged his fellow colonials to leave "the bloody plains and iron glooms" for "the climes which youthful Eden saw" and praised those who remained to "repel the tyrant who thy peace invades." Similarly, within the poem he vacillates between viewing the island of Santa Cruz as an edenic refuge and seeing it as a source of evil—slavery, avarice, indolence, and the annihilation of the native inhabitants.

From 1780 to 1790 Freneau produced some of his most commendable and lasting verse, both political and lyric. "The British Prison Ship," occasioned by the poet's capture and imprisonment in New York Harbor aboard the British ships *Scorpion* and *Hunter*, has the immediacy of a personal *cri de coeur* yet also offers detailed and reliable eyewitness evidence of the maltreatment of his fellow prisoners. It closes with a rousing appeal for revenge. No less rousing are the poems that memorialize the victory of John Paul Jones over the British warship *Seraphis* (September 23, 1779) and to the memory of those who fell in the action of September 8, 1781, under General Greene in South Carolina. In the first poem are the lines,

> Go on, great man, to daunt the foe,
> And bid the haughty Britons know
> They to our thirteen stars shall bend.

The second poem praises the "conquering genius," General Greene, and commends to "A brighter sunshine of their own" the "patriot band" who fought with him.

"The House of Night," written while Freneau was in the West Indies, was initially published in 1779 in seventy-three six-line iambic pentameter stanzas; it was subsequently expanded to 136 stanzas (816 lines). In an "Advertisement" (an authorial statement), Freneau indicates that the poem was founded upon scripture ("the last enemy that shall be conquered is death"); he sets the poem at midnight in a solitary place that was once "beautiful and joyous"—perfectly suited for "the death of Death." The poem concludes, he notes, "with a few reflexions on the impropriety of a too great attachment to the present life." Throughout his life, Freneau toyed with the poem, adding lines and removing stanzas until in its 1786 version the death of Death was totally expunged. Yet this remarkable composition was the first significant American poem to be written on the abstraction Death. It anticipates Poe in its pervasive Romanticism, its tone and atmosphere, though it is also in a direct line of descent from the "graveyard poets" of Britain of the immediately preceding years.

Several "reform" poems were written in the same decade; of them, "To Sir Toby," which describes and condemns the practices of slave-owners in Jamaica, is a good example. "If there exists a hell," Freneau opens, "Sir Toby's slaves enjoy that portion here." Branding, whipping, chaining, imprisonment, and starvation—all the indignities and punishments inflicted upon the "black herd" are listed and condemned. "On the Anniversary of the Storming of the Bastille" is another of the poems that resulted from Freneau's intense interest in reform causes, but it is somewhat more philosophical and indicates a developing serenity in the poet's disposition.

That serenity became more apparent when Freneau took as subject matter the themes of nature, transience, and personal identity; it gave rise to some of his most pleasing lyrics, poems truly personal in essence, informed by a genuine rather than a spurious religious concern, and demonstrating his highest gifts in imagination and statement. Among those must be included "The Wild Honey Suckle"—generally agreed to be his most accomplished lyric—"The Indian Burying Ground," and "On the Uniformity and Perfection of Nature." Hardly inferior are "To a Caty-did" and "On a Honey Bee Drinking from a Glass of Wine and Drowned Therein," in which there is an unaccustomed levity to be found within the generally austere and mordant lines.

From the trenchant critic of the status quo before the American Revolution, Freneau became the true voice of the stalwarts of the rebellion; toward the end of his life he again became evangelical—but for the status quo ruled over by Nature rather than by Britain. "No imperfection can be found/ In all that is, above, around," he wrote, and concluded that in the dominion of Nature, "*all is right*." In this conclusion he predated Robert Browning.

ON MR. PAINE'S RIGHTS OF MAN

First published: 1791
Type of work: Poem

The rights of the common man are inconsistent with monarchy, and the new republic in North America will be the guardian of man's rights.

This poem, which is sometimes published under the title "To a Republican, with Mr. Paine's *Rights of Man*," was written immediately after the publication of Thomas Paine's great and influential book in defense of the French Revolution. It was later included in Freneau's *Poems* (1809). In many ways, the poem is uncharacteristic of Freneau: While trenchant in its criticism of monarchy and enthusiastic in its endorsement of Paine's thinking, it is neither overtly satiric nor especially lyrical, though it does make reference to the laws of Nature and to personified Virtue. As might be expected, it makes no allusion to God: It is, therefore, essentially a rationalist-deist poem on the morality of the national polity.

Further, the structure of the poem is a departure from the usual forms that Freneau used: The fifty lines are divided into four stanzas of ten, fourteen, ten, and sixteen lines of iambic pentameter that are end-rhymed—that is, in closed couplets. The first three stanzas bemoan the ugly fate of the "sacred Rights of Man" as they have been travestied by monarchs; the final two celebrate the great plan for the enunciation and protection of the natural rights of the common man that was contained in Paine's treatise and was being worked out in the new Constitution of the United States, which is addressed as "Columbia."

Just as "A Political Litany" and "To Sir Toby" are characterized by catalogs of deficiencies and shortcomings, so too is "On Mr. Paine's Rights of Man." Kings are presented as the source of discord, murder, slavery, knavery, plunder, and—worst of all—the restraint of freedom and "Nature's law reversed." The indictment is detailed and extensive. For example, after complaining that ships are ordered to sail the distant seas on royal orders, Freneau states that the benefits of these voyages, the proceeds of the "plundered prize," are used not to benefit mankind but "the strumpet," or they serve "to glut the king." These abuses of royal prerogatives are neither unusual nor passing: The reader is invited to scan the record of history for confirmation, for the poet is sure that he will be inflamed "with kindling rage" to see the rights of man aspersed and freedom restrained. The "manly page" of Paine and the reasoned argument of his treatise will not fail to convince any reader of the soundness of his thesis.

Then comes the bifurcation in the poem: In rather traditional Enlightenment manner, Freneau, having presented the present condition, offers a glimpse of the corrections to be obtained by pursuing the course proposed by Paine. Though the final stanza has sixteen lines, it is in the form of a rather loosely constructed sonnet. It opens with an apostrophe to Columbia and then lists some of the future's great boons: Without a king, the colonists—now American citizens—will peacefully and profitably till the fields to their own advantage. They have already "traced the unbounded sea," and they have instituted the rule of law, which is honored by one and all. Freneau does not conclude with a listing of the immediate advantages of the new social order, however; he offers a list of responsibilities for the newly independent Americans. These include the restraint of the politically ambitious, and the propagation of a few basic truths: that kings are vain, that warfare inevitably brings ruin to a republic, and that monarchies subsist by waging war.

Then, in the concluding four lines, Freneau offers a magnificent view of the goals and future of the United States in language of undoubted sincerity. There is no suggestion of cliché or slogan, no inflated or bombastic vocabulary, no circumlocution or literary idiom—only the simple language of the new man of the new republic enunciating the rights of every man to such things as life, liberty, property, and the pursuit of happiness:

> So shall our nation, form'd on Virtue's plan,
> Remain the guardian of the Rights of Man,
> A vast Republic, famed through every clime,
> Without a king, to see the end of time.

THE WILD HONEY SUCKLE

First published: 1786
Type of work: Poem

The wild honeysuckle growing in the country grieves the poet because its beauty is so short-lived.

Although "The Wild Honey Suckle" is now the most frequently reprinted and quoted of Freneau's poems, it was seldom reprinted in the poet's lifetime. The consensus both in the United States and abroad is that this is the poet's best lyric and is perhaps his most accomplished verse composition. Yet it is a comparatively short poem: It has only four six-line stanzas of iambic tetrameter arranged in the quite traditional rhyme scheme *ababcc*. The first two stanzas sing of the joys of growing in the country ("this silent, dull retreat"), where no careless bypasser will threaten the flower's gentle existence, its comeliness in the gentle shade of the woods. The poet stresses that this secluded location is "Nature's" design: The shade is to guard the plant, which is to "shun the vulgar eye"; that is, it is personified and admonished to assume an attitude of modesty despite its beauty.

The third stanza develops the image introduced in the penultimate line of the second stanza, that "quietly the summer goes." That is, an analogy is proposed between the life and death of the honeysuckle and the life and death of mankind; in both, one can see existence "declining to repose" (death). As if to place the death of the individual flower in perspective, Freneau suggests that even the flowers that bloomed in the Garden of Eden—which were no more beautiful than the native flower of the North American countryside—were killed off by the "[u]npitying frosts" of autumn. Of Eden's flowers there is no vestige; of the wild honeysuckle, also, there will be no trace.

The concluding stanza offers the traditional philosophical observation, or resolution of the situation presented in the preceding stanzas. It notes that the flower had its origins in morning suns and evening dews, developing from a pre-Edenic void; it will have its death knell from the same natural moisture and light—the ultimate paradox of life itself. Further, to place the lifespan of flower or man in perspective, the poet concludes with admirable logic that since the flower came from nothing, it can have lost nothing at death: It (and humankind) moves only from void to void, and "[t]he space between is but an hour"—the twinkling of an eye of "[t]he frail duration of a flower." Decay and death are immutable and universal, are irreversible, yet the disappearance of a thing of beauty, whether a wild honeysuckle or a beautiful young woman, is a melancholy phenomenon. In fact, the tone of the entire poem is one of melancholy; the use of personification (which is used in even the opening apostrophe, "Fair flower," and continues unabated throughout the poem) makes the analogy between flower and individual inescapable. The poet goes further, however, and makes the particular universal: The wild honeysuckle appropriately represents all the unseen, unacknowledged things of beauty that have ever existed and have died.

The poem has more than the traditional sense of the loss of beauty to recommend it, however: It has a serenity, a sense of awe and loss that is rare, and it combines native subject matter with the poet's personal philosophy of the transience of all human experiences without being circumscribed by the language of the English pre-Romantics such as William Collins and Thomas Gray and the great Scots poet Robert Burns.

Summary

Satiric verse that is inspired by temporary or parochial concerns is seldom able to outlive the special circumstances that occasioned it: This is the reason for the almost total exclusion from anthologies today of Philip Freneau's vitriolic verse of the Revolutionary years. Undoubtedly he was one of the most popular poets of his time and place and deserved his title, the "poet of the American Revolution." With the passage of time, however, his lyrical poems, in which he sang of the beauties of nature with the feeling and intensity of the British Romantic poets, are those that have remained of interest to readers. Some half-dozen beautiful lyrics represent a praiseworthy accomplishment and assure Freneau of a small but permanent place in American literature.

Bibliography

Adkins, Nelson F. *Philip Freneau and the Cosmic Enigma: The Religious and Philo-sophical Speculations of an American Poet*. New York: New York University Press, 1949.

Axelrad, Jacob. *Philip Freneau: Champion of Democracy*. Austin: University of Texas Press, 1967.

Bowden, Mary Weatherspoon. *Philip Freneau*. Boston: Twayne, 1976.

Forman, Samuel E. *The Political Activities of Philip Freneau*. New York: Arno, 1974.

Leary, Lewis. *That Rascal Freneau: A Study in Literary Failure*. New York: Octagon, 1964.

Marsh, Philip M. *Philip Freneau: Poet and Journalist*. Minneapolis: Dillon Press, 1967.

_____. *The Works of Philip Freneau: A Critical Study*. Metuchen, N.J.: Scarecrow Press, 1968.

Nickson, Richard. *Philip Freneau: Poet of the Revolution*. Trenton, N.J.: Historical Commission, 1981.

Marian B. McLeod

ROBERT FROST

Born: San Francisco, California
March 26, 1874
Died: Boston, Massachusetts
January 29, 1963

Principal Literary Achievement

Although he was nearly forty when his first book was published, Frost came to be acknowledged within his lifetime as one of America's greatest poets.

Biography

Famed as a New England poet, Robert Lee Frost was actually born in San Francisco on March 26, 1874, and named for a great Confederate general. His father, William Prescott Frost, Jr., was a footloose journalist who as a teenager had tried to run away from his Lawrence, Massachusetts, home and join the Confederate Army. When he died in 1885, Isabelle Moodie Frost brought young Rob and his sister Jeanie back to Lawrence, where her late husband's parents still lived. Frost's poem "Once by the Pacific" demonstrates that the West Coast did help shape the poet's imagination, but he grew to maturity in Lawrence, where he was graduated second in his high school class behind Elinor Miriam White in 1892; shortly thereafter the two became engaged.

After attending Dartmouth College briefly, Frost took a series of odd jobs, which included newspaper reporting and teaching in a school conducted by his mother. In 1894, he published his first poem, "My Butterfly," in a periodical called *The Independent*. He gathered this poem with four others he had composed into a little book called *Twilight*, which he presented to Elinor White as a preview of what he hoped would be substantial success as a poet. He married Elinor in 1895 and was already a father when he entered Harvard College as a special student in 1897. Although he again failed to graduate and in fact later boasted of walking away from two colleges, Frost was a good student in his two years at Harvard, and what he learned of classical poetry certainly furthered his poetic development.

The Frosts' early married years were difficult ones. Their first son died in 1900, but four other children were born between 1899 and 1905. While continuing to write poetry, Frost supported his family by farming in West Derry, New Hampshire, teaching at nearby Pinkerton Academy, and accepting financial assistance from his paternal grandfather, who left him a generous annuity when he died in 1901.

713

After more than a decade of this modest and obscure life, Frost made a momentous decision in 1912. He decided to move his family to England, where, benefiting from the promotional efforts of his fellow American expatriate Ezra Pound, he published *A Boy's Will* (1913) and *North of Boston* (1914). He also developed friendships with other writers, particularly the English poet Edward Thomas. When the Frosts returned to the United States in 1915, he was finally gaining recognition as a poet.

Frost still hoped to combine farming and poetry and lived for several years after his return in Franconia, New Hampshire, and in South Shaftesbury, Vermont, but increasingly he played the role of a gentleman farmer. His 1923 volume, *New Hampshire: A Poem with Notes and Grace Notes*, which won the Pulitzer Prize the following year, made much of "the need of being versed in country things." Having gained access to the literary and academic worlds, however, he undertook at this point three years as a poet-in-residence at Amherst College and two more at the University of Michigan. He later taught at both Amherst and Harvard, one of the colleges from which he had failed to graduate. His favorite activity became the performing of his own poems before chiefly academic audiences. Developing a chatty, informal style of discussing his poems that proved highly popular, he gained the reputation as he grew older, of a cheerful, homespun philosopher—a pose that is belied, however, both by his poetry and by the conflicts of his personal life.

A number of poems in his 1928 book *West-Running Brook*, among them "Bereft," "Acquainted with the Night," and "Tree at My Window," reflect a troubled spirit. Frost sensed in himself a precarious mental balance and feared a breakdown such as the one that led to the institutionalization of his sister Jeanie. Later his son Carol committed suicide, and his daughter Irma had to be confined for mental disorder. There were other tragedies—the deaths of his daughter Marjorie of puerperal fever in 1934 and of his wife in 1938, which devastated him.

His career, however, continued in high gear. His *Collected Poems* (1930) earned for him another Pulitzer Prize, as did *A Further Range* (1936), though critics disputed whether Frost's title could justly be regarded as an allusion to the extension of his poetic range or simply to another range of New England mountains. In the 1930's, when arguments raged over whether a poet ought to articulate a social commitment, Frost continued to write about solitary and rural figures, but "Departmental" wryly examines the subject of bureaucracy, and "Provide, Provide" twits those who would depend on the social legislation of Franklin D. Roosevelt's administration for their security.

In the 1940's Frost published two new books of poems, *A Witness Tree* (1942) and *Steeple Bush* (1947), as well as two masques—short dramatic works—on "reason" and "mercy," respectively. By the time of *Steeple Bush*, Frost was seventy-three; his output slowed to a trickle, but honors flowed in. Both the Universities of Oxford and Cambridge made him a Doctor of Letters in 1957; he was named the Consultant in Poetry to the Library of Congress in 1958, and he read a poem at the inauguration of President John F. Kennedy in 1961.

The last year of his long life proved to be a capstone. He brought out a final book of poems, *In the Clearing* (1962), and in late summer of that year he visited the Soviet Union as a good-will ambassador. The trip proved a difficult ordeal for the eighty-eight-year-old poet, however, and soon afterward his health declined rapidly. In December, he entered Peter Bent Brigham Hospital in Boston; he died on January 29, 1963.

Analysis

Robert Frost is that rare twentieth century poet who achieved both enormous popularity and critical acclaim. In an introductory essay to his collected poems, Frost insists that a poem "will forever keep its freshness as a metal keeps its fragrance. It can never lose its sense of a meaning that once unfolded by surprise as it went," an observation that applies to most of his three hundred-odd poems. Once his work came into circulation, its freshness and deceptive simplicity captivated audiences that shied away from more difficult poets such as T. S. Eliot and Wallace Stevens, while astute critics came to recognize the subtlety of thought and feeling that so often pervade these "simple" poems.

North of Boston ranks among the most original books of American poetry. Its title suggests its locale; one of the titles Frost originally proposed for it, *Farm Servants*, indicates its typical subject matter. Most of its best-known poems— "Mending Wall," "The Death of the Hired Man," "Home Burial," "The Wood-Pile"—are in blank verse (unrhymed iambic pentameter). The language consists of everyday words, Frost having discarded the "poetic" vocabulary that he had occasionally used in *A Boy's Will*. None of these features was new in poetry, but in combination they result in strikingly innovative poetry.

The works in this volume represent the conscious application of a theory which Frost set forth most directly in several letters to a friend named John Bartlett. He aimed to accommodate what he called "the sound of sense" to blank verse. He noted that many casual utterances of the people among whom he lived fell into a basically iambic rhythm: "She thinks I have no eye for these," "My father used to say," "Never you say a thing like that to a man," and so on. Writing poetry involved listening for and adapting to meter—what Frost called "sentence sounds." In this way Frost created poems that did not only talk about rural New Englanders but also enacted them. Ten of the sixteen poems in *North of Boston* consist almost entirely of dialogue, one is a monologue, and several others incorporate colloquial lines. Many readers do not even notice that the poems all "scan" according to the rules of iambic meter, but it is there, a firm substratum to Frost's "sound of sense."

To Frost's credit, he refused merely to repeat the effects of this book in subsequent work. While he continued from time to time to base poems on dialogue— especially between husband and wife—dialogue does not dominate any of his later books. *Mountain Interval* (1916), his first book to appear originally in the United States, offers much greater variety in form: sonnets, poems in four- and five-line rhymed stanzas, poems written in short lines, and others in patterns made up of lines of different lengths. Several, including "The Road Not Taken" and "The Sound of Trees," are reflective poems that raise deep questions and provide teasing or ambiguous answers in a fashion that delighted Frost. They also remind the reader that many of life's important questions do not have answers both simple and unfailingly satisfying.

A number of Frost's poems celebrate encounters with nature. The first poem in his first book, "Into My Own," and the last poem in his final book, an untitled one beginning "In winter in the woods alone," depict a solitary person entering the woods, while in the long stretch between those poems the one that may be his best known of all, "Stopping by Woods on a Snowy Evening," portrays the desire to do so. On one level, Frost can be seen as simply continuing the love affair with the wilderness so common in American mythology, whose literary manifestations include such classics as James Fenimore Cooper's Leatherstocking Tales (1823-1841) and Mark Twain's *The Adventures of Huckleberry Finn* (1884). On another level, the woodsman—independent, defiant of urban artificiality, at one with nature—is one of Frost's conceptions of himself. These poems convey a number of themes and even more attitudes. The woods can be a place for restoration of the spirit through vigorous activity and communion with nature, the locus of deep and sometimes sinister psychic forces, or a happy hunting ground for analogies of the human condition generally. Frost portrays both the perils and joys of isolation.

A considerable portion of Frost's poems are set either in winter or at night or both. These are the times that tend to isolate people, to throw them on their own resources, to encourage reflection. Those readers who think that these reflections are always mild and cheerful have not read his poems carefully enough. In *West-Running Brook*, a group of poems gathered under the epigraph *"Fiat Nox"* ("let there be night") suggests something of Frost's nocturnal range. These poems include "Acceptance," "Once by the Pacific," "Bereft," "Tree at My Window," and "Acquainted with the Night."

Frost is also a daylight observer of ordinary people and their ways. The relationships of husbands and wives interested him particularly, and his range is wide, from the telepathic harmony of a couple in "The Telephone" to the marital disintegration of "Home Burial." Perhaps no other poet has portrayed the give and take of marriage so variously and so vividly. His world is also one of neighbors, passing tramps, and even garrulous witches. Neither children nor sophisticated adults appear very often in his poetry. Rooted in the countryside, his writing focuses on simple things and people. He used language with the same economy and precision his characters display in their use of the scythe, the axe, and the pitchfork. Demonstrating how much can be done by the skillful application of simple tools, Robert Frost has left to an increasingly industrialized and impersonal society a valuable legacy of poems celebrating basic emotions and relationships.

HOME BURIAL

First published: 1914
Type of work: Poem

Under the strain of their child's recent death, a young couple try vainly to communicate.

"Home Burial" is an intensely dramatic poem about a bereaved and increasingly estranged married couple. The husband has just returned from burying their young son in a family plot of the sort that served northern New Englanders as cemeteries for generations. He mounts the stairs toward his wife "until she cowered under him." What follows is a bitter exchange. The wife, unable to understand his failure to express grief vocally, accuses him of indifference to their loss; he, rankled by what he considers a groundless charge, tries blunderingly to assure her, but they fail to comprehend each other. At the end of the poem she is threatening to leave and find someone else who can console her, while he threatens, "I'll follow and bring you back by force. I will!—."

The poem is nearly all dialogue except for a few sections of description which work like stage directions in a play, serving to relate the couple spatially and to underline by movement and gestures the tension between them. Although the poem does not require staging, it is easily stageable, so dramatically is it presented. The reader surmises that the two really do love—or at least have loved—each other and that the difficulties between them have resulted not from willful malice but from clashes of temperament and different training. The man is expected to be stoical, tight-lipped in adversity. Having learned to hide his feelings, he is unable to express them in a way recognizable to his wife, with her different emotional orientation. She has watched with a kind of horror his energetic digging at the gravesite; he has made the gravel "leap up . . . and land so lightly." She cannot understand that he has converted his frustration into a relevant and necessary physical activity, as men have traditionally learned to do. Nor does she realize that a seemingly callous remark of his about the rotting of birch fences may well constitute an oblique way of referring to the demise of the child that he has helped make. Instead she draws the conclusion that, because he does not grieve overtly as she does, he has no feelings. Because he is inexpert at oral communication, he cannot say the kind of thing that might alleviate her grief. The poem becomes a painful study in misinterpretation that is in the process of leading to the disintegration of a marriage.

The poem is also a brilliant example of Frost's success at unobtrusively adapting a vignette from life to the formal requirements of blank verse. In the early twentieth century, avant-garde poets were strongly resisting traditional verse poems, but Frost had his own way of escaping the tyrannizing effects of meter. Although "Home Burial" and the other blank verse poems in *North of Boston* look conventional on the page, and although the poet's firm iambic support for the dialogue is readily apparent to well-versed readers, it is easy to forget that something such as the wife's "There you go sneering now!" followed by his "I'm not, I'm not!" is a more or less "regular" pentameter line as well as an easily imaginable bit of argument between two disaffected people. Frost showed that ordinary people could inhabit a poem, could talk and argue and move convincingly within a medium that William Shakespeare and John Milton in the sixteenth and seventeenth centuries had tended to reserve for aristocrats and angels.

Unlike a play, Frost's dramatic poem has no resolution. Will the wife leave, as she threatens? If so, will he restrain her by force as he threatens, or will he resign himself to the status quo as he has before? It is not Frost's intention to solve this marital problem. He had known conflict in his own marriage and observed it in other marriages; he certainly knew the ways in which spouses might resolve or fail to resolve their conflicts. What he chose to do was provide an opportunity to eavesdrop on a bereaved couple at an agonizing moment and feel their passion and frustration.

THE ROAD NOT TAKEN

First published: 1915
Type of work: Poem

A traveler through life reflects on a past choice of route "that has made all the difference."

The first poem in Frost's book *Mountain Interval*, "The Road Not Taken," has long been a favorite. Like many of his poems it seems simple, but it is not exactly straightforward, and even perceptive readers have disagreed considerably over its best interpretation. It looks like a personal poem about a decision of vast importance, but there is evidence to the contrary both inside and outside the poem. Frost has created a richly mysterious reading experience out of a marvelous economy of means.

The first significant thing about "The Road Not Taken" is its title, which presumably refers to an unexercised option—something about which the speaker can only speculate. The traveler comes to a fork in a road through a "yellow wood" and wishes he could somehow manage to "travel both" routes; he rejects that aspiration as impractical, however, at least for the day at hand. The road he selects is "the one less traveled by," suggesting the decision of an individualist, someone little inclined to follow the crowd. Almost immediately, however, he seems to contradict his own judgment: "Though as for that the passing there/ Had worn them really about the same." The poet appears to imply that the decision is based on evidence that is, or comes close to being, an illusion.

The contradictions continue. He decides to save the first, (perhaps) more traveled route for another day, but then confesses that he does not think it probable that he will return, implying that this seemingly casual and inconsequential choice is really likely to be crucial—one of the choices of life that involve commitment or lead to the necessity of other choices that will divert the traveler forever from the original stopping place. In the final stanza, the traveler says that he will be "telling this with a sigh," which may connote regret. His choice, in any event, "has made all the difference." The tone of this stanza, coupled with the title, strongly suggests that the traveler, if not regretting his choice, at least laments the possibilities that the necessity of making a choice leaves unfulfilled.

Has Frost in mind a particular and irrevocable choice of his own life, and if so, what feeling in this poem of mixed feelings, should be regarded as dominant? There is no way of identifying such a specific decision from the evidence of the poem itself. Although a prejudice exists in favor of identifying the "I" of the poem with the author in the absence of evidence to the contrary, the speaker may not be Frost at all. On more than one occasion the poet claimed that this poem was about his friend Edward Thomas, a man inclined to indecisiveness out of a strong—and, as Frost thought, amusing—habit of dwelling on the irrevocability of decisions. If so, the reference in the poem's final stanza to "telling" of the experience "with a sigh/ Somewhere ages and ages hence" might be read not only as the boast of Robert Frost, who "tells" it as long as people read the poem, but also as a perpetual revelation of Thomas, also a fine poet.

What is clear is that the speaker is at least a person like Thomas in some respects (though there may well be some of Frost in him also). Critics of this poem are likely always to argue whether it is an affirmation of the crucial nature of the choices people must make on the road of life or a gentle satire on the sort of temperament that always insists on struggling with such choices. The extent of the poet's sympathy with the traveler also remains an open question.

Frost composed this poem in four five-line stanzas with only two end rhymes in each stanza (abaab). The flexible iambic meter has four strong beats to the line. Of the technical achievements in "The Road Not Taken," one in particular shows Frost's skill at enforcing meaning through form. The poem ends,

> Two roads diverged in a wood, and I—
> I took the one less traveled by,
> And that has made all the difference.

The indecision of the speaker—his divided state of mind—is heightened by the repetition of "I," split by the line division and emphasized by the rhyme and pause. It is an effect possible only in a rhymed and metrical poem—and thus a good argument for the continuing viability of traditional forms.

THE OVEN BIRD

First published: 1916
Type of work: Poem

In the call of a forest bird, the listener discerns the theme of diminishment.

"The Oven Bird" is an irregular sonnet that explores in various ways the problem of "what to make of a diminished thing." The poet does not refer to the bird directly by its other common name of "teacher bird" (based on the resemblance of its reiterated call to the word "teacher") but attributes to the bird an instructive discourse about diminishment, the downward thrust of things. In the middle of summer, this bird reminds one of the fall (specifically the petal fall) that is already past and of the fall to come.

Like many of Frost's poems, this one is built on paradox. This bird can be said to sing, but it is not particularly tuneful. Its repeated call in a trochaic, or falling, rhythm does not have the upward lilt that humans generally consider cheerful or merry. The bird is a twentieth century teacher—not the old-fashioned lecturer, but the modern one who contrives to induce the pupils to teach themselves. Like the teacher, the bird "knows," and in knowing frames the kind of question that is intended to provoke thought, although without any guarantee of easy resolution. Paradoxically, the process of learning becomes one of discovering that some questions must be struggled with unendingly. Like the teacher bird, the poem supplies no answers.

Literally, the "diminished thing" of the poem is the weather and the natural year. The sonnet is full of words and phrases such as "old," "early petal-fall," "down in showers," "dust is over all," and "the bird would cease," that suggest decline in the natural order. Knowing that people persist in interpreting nature in human terms, the poet can safely assume that the poem will be read as referring to the diminishment of human hopes, of life itself. Frost reinforces his theme by using a proportion of diminishment: "for flowers/ Mid-summer is to spring as one to ten." As expectations turn into past events and remaining possibilities steadily diminish, any thoughtful person must ponder "what to make" of that which is left.

Frost also enforces his theme rhythmically. He crosses the usual iambic rising rhythm with trochaic words—words with first-syllable accents. "Singer," "flowers," "summer," "petal"—in fact, all the two-syllable words of the poem carry this accent. These words, nevertheless, are all placed in positions that contribute to an iambic movement which might be taken as suggesting that, despite the declines and falls, both the cycle of seasons and human hopes endure.

The typical English sonnet ends in a rhymed couplet which often sums up or tops off the poem and gives a feeling of finality. This poem does have two couplets, but neither is at the end. It seems to be part of Frost's strategy to avoid any sense of completeness or finality. Whatever continues, continues to diminish, but while the process continues, something always remains. The only regular quatrain (the sort of rhyming unit one expects to find in a sonnet three times before the couplet) is the four lines that fall at the end. What to make of this feature is one of the persisting questions about this haunting poem.

BIRCHES

First published: 1916
Type of work: Poem

The tension between earthly satisfactions and higher aspirations emerges from the recollection of a childhood game.

In "Birches," the speaker's attention is first caught by a cluster of bent birch trees that he knows were bowed by ice storms. The sight reminds him of his boyhood sport of swinging on birch trees, although such an activity does not permanently bow them. Swinging on birches is a form of play that can be done alone, the competition strictly between child and tree. It is a sport requiring poise and good judgment; for a safe and satisfactory ride, one must climb to the very top of the tree and "launch out" at just the right moment. A country boy might expect to master all the birches on his father's land.

The speaker dreams of swinging on birches again. From the perspective of adulthood, he envies his childhood capacity for launching out anew, making a new beginning on a new tree. In his mind, the game has become a way of escaping from earth, where life sometimes seems to be a "pathless wood"—but he knows that such a game is not a permanent escape from earth and that part of the fun is "coming back," for life is not always a pathless wood, and the earth from which he contemplates escaping is "the right place for love." The mature man thus recognizes a symbolic value that he could not have consciously realized when he was young enough to be a swinger of birches.

The poem consists of fifty-nine easily flowing blank verse lines. Though "Birches" has no formal divisions, it can be separated into three almost equal parts: the observation and description of trees bent by winter storms, the recollection of the techniques of birch-swinging, and the grown man's dream, energized by his awareness of the claims of both "earth" and "heaven." Each part leads casually to the next: "But I was going to say" to the second part, "It's when I'm weary of considerations" to the third.

The poem is marvelously vivid and concrete in its descriptions of both ice storms and child's play. The stir of the trees after acquiring their load of ice "cracks and crazes their enamel"; casting their load off, they leave "heaps of broken glass." The reader is made to see the boy "kicking his way down through the air" and the man "weeping/ From a twig's having lashed it [his eye] open." Black and white are used suggestively and, as often in Frost, somewhat ambiguously. The white birches are first seen against the background of "straighter darker trees." The sun shining on the ice coating of the tree trunks turns them prismatic. The boy climbs "black branches up a snow-white trunk/ *Toward* heaven" ("toward" being significantly italicized, for heaven is not attainable), the white intimating the pure and heavenly aspiration, the black, the necessary physical, earthly steps, the "going and coming back."

Far from being the simple reminiscence of a sentimental adult, the poem not only acknowledges that returning to the birch-swinging of childhood is a "dream" but also assesses the significance of the game from a mature viewpoint. Part of maturity is coming to understand and articulate the profundity of early experience.

DUST OF SNOW

First published: 1921
Type of work: Poem

A small event on a winter walk unexpectedly changes a person's day for the better.

Frost was proud of his small, compact poems that say much more than they seem to say; his 1923 volume *New Hampshire* gathers several of these, including "Fire and Ice," "Nothing Gold Can Stay," and one of the shortest of all, "Dust of Snow." Once sentence long, it occupies eight short lines and contains only thirty-four words, all but two of them monosyllabic, and all of them part of even a young child's vocabulary.

> The way a crow
> Shook down on me
> The dust of snow
> From a hemlock tree
>
> Has given my heart
> A change of mood
> And saved some part
> Of a day I had rued.

Much of the effect of this poem derives from its paradoxes or seeming contradictions, the first of which is in the title. Although the phrase "a dusting of snow" is common in weather reports, dust usually calls forth notions of something dirty and unpleasant, quite unlike the dust of snow.

It is also paradoxical that the speaker's mood is initially so negative on a presumably fine winter day after a fresh snowfall, but he has so far "rued" this day. Even more paradoxically, the agent responsible for provoking a change for the better is a bird normally contemned: the large, black, raucous crow. Even its important function as a devourer of carrion does not summon forth a favorable image. In medieval times the crow often symbolized the devil, and its larger cousin, the raven, was employed by Edgar Allan Poe and other writers to create a sinister or melancholy mood. This crow, however, rescues the speaker from his previously rueful mood.

One paradox that Frost did not intend occurred to a woman who heard him read "Dust of Snow" and responded, "Very sinister poem!" When the puzzled author asked her why, she replied, "Hemlock—Socrates, you know," alluding to the poison which the ancient Greek philosopher was required to drink after his trial. Not only had Frost intended no such suggestion, it contradicts the effect of the poem as a whole. Socrates' hemlock was quite a different thing from the tree inhabited by Frost's crow, and the woman's misinterpretation exemplifies an important point: not all the possible suggestions of a word or image are necessarily applicable in a given context. Frost depends on his reader to use imagination responsibly and to exclude meaning that will not make sense in a poem.

The rhyme and meter of this short poem contribute much to its effect. The firm iambic beat is established in the first three lines, but Frost knew exactly when to vary the rhythm to avoid a sing-song effect; thus there is an extra syllable (in a different place) in each of the next two lines, and after two more regular lines, the last line consists of two anapests. Furthermore, the rhyming words are important ones, and the most surprising one, "rued," is reserved until the end. The reader is left with a memorable impression of an unexpected boon from an unlikely source. To be "saved" by a crow, because of its unexpectedness, is more delightful than being saved by a song sparrow.

TREE AT MY WINDOW

First published: 1928
Type of work: Poem

A person who has known trouble recognizes a kindred spirit in the tree outside his window.

"Tree at My Window" differs from most of Frost's nature poems in its locale. Instead of being out in the fields or woods, the speaker is looking out his bedroom window at a nearby tree. He closes his window at night, but out of love for the tree he does not draw the curtain. This is an unmistakably modern nature poem. Whereas the transcendentalists of the nineteenth century had regarded nature as profound, the speaker here specifically denies the possibility of the tree speaking wisdom. Instead, he compares the conditions of man and tree. He has seen the tree "taken and tossed" by storm, and if the tree can be imagined as having looked in at him asleep, it has seen him "taken and swept/ and all but lost." That which brought them together is styled "fate"—but an imaginative fate, because of their respective concerns with "outer" and "inner weather."

He sees the tree not as an instructor but as a comrade, a fellow sufferer. Between Frost and the transcendentalist faith in nature as a teacher lies a scientific revolution that denies the possibility of "sermons in stones," and it is clear that the tree is physically, the man only metaphorically, storm-tossed. This metaphor, an old contrivance of poets, remains a potent one when used freshly as it is here. The speaker's storm is only a dream, but dreams can be deeply disturbing; psychology insists that they may be very significant. "Inner weather" reflects a recurring theme in Frost, who in his personal life had to grapple with the maintenance of psychic balance. Inner doubt and conflict dominate a number of poems from Frost's middle years, including, in his 1928 book *West-Running Brook*, "Bereft" and "Acquainted with the Night"; "Desert Places," in his next book, *A Further Range*, describes personal fear. In "Tree at My Window," the kinship with nature is even more therapeutic and steadying than it was in the earlier "Birches." Both tree and man have been "tossed" but survive. Frost would reassert nature's steadying influence in later poems such as "One Step Backward Taken" and "Take Something Like a Star," both in the 1947 *Steeple Bush*.

"Tree at My Window" has a distinctive form. First glance reveals it to be a neat, compact poem which uses the abba rhyme scheme made famous by Alfred, Lord Tennyson in his long poem *In Memoriam* (1850). The first three lines of each quatrain are tetrameter lines, while the last line has either two or three strong beats. The rhythmical variations, however, are quite unusual. Frost once observed that there are only two meters in English, strict iambic and loose iambic. This poem is definitely the latter. Out of the sixteen lines only two—both short ones—are indisputably regular; Frost worked extra unstressed syllables into most of the lines. Again, Frost found a way to be rhythmically innovative without losing the sense of a traditional poetic structure.

DEPARTMENTAL

First published: 1936
Type of work: Poem

Observing the "funeral" of an ant leads to a recognition of the strengths and weaknesses of human institutions.

"Departmental," a Frost poem of the 1930's, typifies its author in several ways. It is playful, full of clever rhymes, and closely observant of a natural scene that mirrors aspects of human life. In this Depression-era poem, Frost focuses on the popular theme of social organization. It is almost a fable, though it implies rather than states its moral.

To follow an ant on a tablecloth, the poem says, is immediately to see dutiful and specialized behavior. "Departmental" focuses on the ants' way of dealing with death. If a particular ant finds a dead moth, his only obligation is to report it to "the hive's enquiry squad." Even when he encounters the body of another ant, he merely informs the proper authorities, who arrange for a "solemn mortician" to bring the body back home and give it a dignified burial while the rest of the colony continue about their business: "It couldn't be called ungentle./ But how thoroughly departmental."

As observed, the ant colony excludes a host of what one considers human reactions. There is no "surprise" at death, no pausing to mourn or reflect on its meaning. The ant does not slow down, is not at all "impressed." Other than a formal report, there is no talk, no standing around and staring, as one expects at the scene of a fatal accident. Everything is routine, designated behavior and prescribed ritual. Ants are efficient; they eschew all the impractical reactions of human beings. Frost's ants are not cruel, but they are unfeeling and robotic in their reactions to death, as though it has been decreed that death is, after all, a commonplace event that should not be allowed to interrupt duty or waste the time of the populace.

Thus Frost calls attention to a basic difference between ants (at least as humans perceive them) and humans. The fact that death is common does not, for humans, negate its profundity. Human reactions are often not profound and seldom "useful," but they betoken the human way of experiencing life. The ceremony of a funeral service, moreover, brings together in common cause people who otherwise may have few opportunities to socialize; such differences hover in the background of Frost's poem.

The differences between ant and human conduct, however, also call attention to the bureaucratic or "departmental" likenesses. The ant world of Frost's poem has been constructed with frequent analogies to specialized human institutions: janizaries, commissaries, courts, and the "state" funeral of a deceased dignitary. Ant behavior cannot be described successfully, it seems, without reference to concepts totally beyond the range of ants. Unlike ants, who do it instinctively, human beings have to learn to be efficient and impersonal, but because humans are capable of modifying their social norms, they run the risk of damaging specifically human ideas and feelings when they adopt the modes of social insects. Ants must be "departmental"; people do not have to be. Like an ancient fable, the poem amuses, then challenges its reader by comparing human conduct to that of other branches of the animal kingdom.

The lines are iambic trimeter, with a liberal sprinkling of anapestic feet. Rhymes are prominent, chiefly in couplets, occasionally triplets, with one quadruplet. A number of them— "any" and "antennae," "atwiddle" and "middle," for example— are the sort of feminine rhymes that often serve to reinforce humor. It was axiomatic with Frost to convey inner seriousness with outer humor. "Departmental" shows him avoiding the sugar-coated pill by blending the "sugar"—the delight—and the "pill"—the enlightenment—in a poem that appears light and droll but that slyly satirizes a prevalent human weakness: a tendency to design human institutions inhumanely.

DESIGN

First published: 1936
Type of work: Poem

The question of whether there exists a comprehensible plan or design in nature is a baffling one.

"Design" was completed for the 1936 volume *A Further Range*, but Frost had completed an earlier version of the poem as far back as 1912 without attempting to publish it. In the tradition of New England Puritanism, it details closely a small event in nature and attempts to interpret its meaning for man. Since the revolution in scientific thought stimulated by Charles Darwin's *On the Origin of Species* (1859), however, poetry of this sort has been less likely to underline a received article of Christian or other transcendent faith. Frost's poem is a questioning one in the form of an Italian sonnet whose octave, or first eight-line unit, is balanced against the closing six-line sestet.

The speaker comes upon "a dimpled spider, fat and white" that has captured and killed a moth against the background of a white flower called a heal-all. The octave describes the scene, which is all "in white" (to quote a phrase not in the poem that stood as Frost's original title for it). The description is ironic: The disarmingly attractive spider and the moth are "characters of death and blight/ Mixed ready to begin the morning right." The spider is also compared to a snowflake, and the very name of the flower suggests the opposite of "death and blight."

The sestet asks three questions, the third of which seems to answer the first two but is then qualified in the last line: Why did the killing take place on a white flower, what brought the spider and moth together, and was the event part of a sinister design? The final line of the sonnet then implies another question: Can such a small event of nature properly be considered as part of any design, either good or evil.

The answers to these questions hinge on the meaning of "design." Before Darwin, the idea that the processes of nature both generally and in particular reveal a great design of the Creator prevailed in the Western world; overwhelmingly, this design was viewed as benevolent. A sparrow "shall not fall on the ground without your Father," Jesus told his disciples. A few dissidents might have argued that God was malign or that the devil had gained control, but even they would take for granted a designing intelligence. Nineteenth century scientific thought changed all this by dispensing with design and the necessity of a designer in favor of concepts such as Darwin's "natural selection." Frost's poem shows the influence of the late nineteenth century American philosopher William James, who, while rejecting the simple Christian affirmation of a designer involved in every detail of creation, sought to retain the concept of design as a "seeing force" rather than a "blind force." Frost appears to be mocking the idea of design in "small" events such as the confrontation of an individual spider and moth, but he characteristically leaves his most important questions unanswered.

The pattern of the poem is that of a traditional sonnet: descriptive octave followed by reflective sestet. Because of what he has been taught, the observer of the spider's triumph both sees and reflects differently from a person of any earlier time. The poem dramatizes the impossibility of maintaining a view of God and nature similar to the one that satisifed people of past generations. At the same time, it embodies the difficulty of reinterpreting nature in a satisfactory way.

Summary

The poetry of Robert Frost has accomplished a feat rare in the twentieth century: It has received both critical acclaim and widespread popular acceptance. His poetry expresses common emotional and sentient experiences so simply and directly that its authenticity affects readers without expertise in reading poetry; the subtlety of his thought and the sublimity of his art are appreciated by those who ponder his work. The rural character or meditative speaker in a Frost poem represents not merely a person the poet has met or a mood he has felt but humanity in the process of being itself or discovering itself.

Bibliography

Barry, Elaine, ed. *Robert Frost on Writing*. New Brunswick, N.J.: Rutgers University Press, 1973.

Brower, Reuben. *The Poetry of Robert Frost: Constellations of Intention*. New York: Oxford University Press, 1963.

Gould, Jean. *Robert Frost: The Aim Was Song*. New York: Dodd, Mead, 1964.

Pritchard, William H. *Frost: A Literary Life Reconsidered*. New York: Oxford University Press, 1984.

Sergeant, Elizabeth Shepley. *Robert Frost: The Trial by Existence*. New York: Holt, Rinehart and Winston, 1960.

Squires, Radcliffe. *The Major Themes of Robert Frost*. Ann Arbor: University of Michigan Press, 1963.

Thompson, Lawrance R. *Robert Frost: The Early Years, 1874-1915*. New York: Holt, Rinehart and Winston, 1966.

_____. *Robert Frost: The Years of Triumph, 1915-1938*. New York: Holt, Rinehart and Winston, 1971.

Thompson, Lawrance, and R. H. Winnick. *Robert Frost: The Later Years, 1938-1963*. New York: Holt, Rinehart and Winston, 1976.

Van Egmond, Peter. *The Critical Reception of Robert Frost*. Boston: G. K. Hall, 1974.

Robert P. Ellis

WILLIAM GADDIS

Born: New York, New York
December 29, 1922

Principal Literary Achievement

Gaddis' innovative uses of dialogue in fiction and his sharply barbed satires of American society have confirmed his standing as a major American novelist.

Biography

William Thomas Gaddis was born in New York City on December 29, 1922, the only child of parents who were divorced when he was three years old. His mother soon moved to Massapequa, Long Island, where Gaddis was reared in a house that would eventually serve as a model for the Bast house in his second novel, *JR* (1975). On his mother's side, Gaddis' family were Quakers, but he himself was brought up in a strict Calvinist tradition upon which he would draw for his first novel, *The Recognitions* (1955).

An intensely private man, Gaddis has granted few interviews, and little is known about his life. He has always preferred that his novels speak for themselves. It is known, however, that between the ages of five and thirteen, Gaddis was educated at a boarding school in Berlin, Connecticut, and that he later attended Farmingdale High School in Long Island. These experiences appear to have provided material for the vividly anguished recollections of his fictional character Jack Gibbs in *JR*, who cynically laments a lonely and emotionally unsatisfying childhood. Indeed, in all three of Gaddis' novels much of the alienation, disorder, and strife that sets the narratives in motion and besets the characters has its beginning in the absence or death of the protagonists' fathers.

While in high school, Gaddis contracted a rare disease, erythema grave, upon whose symptoms of high fever and delusions he draws for Wyatt Gwyon, the protagonist of his first novel. Though easily cured with modern drugs, a kidney disorder that was a side effect of his treatment left Gaddis unfit for military service in World War II. Throughout the war he was a student at Harvard University. Enrolling in September, 1941, Gaddis majored in English literature, joined the staff of the *Lampoon* (a satirical campus magazine) in 1943, and then, beginning in September 1944, took over the prestigious post of *Lampoon* president. This work provided Gaddis his first outlet for publication. His early pieces covered a wide range of forms: reviews, verse parodies, essays, short fictions, and satires of such forms as the scientific report.

Gaddis' Harvard career was cut short in his senior year. He and a drinking companion tangled with the Cambridge police, word of it came to the college dean, and both students were asked to resign. Gaddis then took up residence in New York, in Greenwich Village, and for two years worked as a "fact checker" at *The New Yorker* magazine. Years later, he noted how this otherwise boring job taught him the virtue of paying close attention to details of reference and allusion. Late in 1947, Gaddis left New York and began a five-year sojourn through Mexico, Central America, and Europe, working his way as a machinist, briefly carrying a rifle during a civil war in Costa Rica, and beginning work on his first novel—through it all, he occasionally returned to the family residence on Long Island. Again these events were transmuted into fiction: They provide the experiences of Otto and Wyatt in *The Recognitions*.

The year 1950 found Gaddis in Paris writing radio scripts for United Nations Educational, Scientific, and Cultural Organization (UNESCO) broadcasts. There he had briefly put *The Recognitions* aside to publish his first magazine work, a humorous article about player pianos for *The Atlantic Monthly*, but on returning to the United States in 1951, he resumed work on the novel, secured a publisher's advance that allowed him to write full time on what was becoming a very long manuscript, and fell in with the Beat Generation writers—Jack Kerouac, Gregory Corso, Chandler Brossard, and others then residing in Greenwich Village. Gaddis finished *The Recognitions* in 1954; it was published in March, 1955, only after some in-house disputes about whether the book should be cut or should be published at all.

Reactions to *The Recognitions* were greatly disappointing to Gaddis, as reviewers seemed rarely to have gotten beyond its length and difficulties of plot and reference. Still more disappointing were the sales figures. In hardcover and paper, the novel would sell fewer than seven thousand copies in its initial run, would top those figures only slightly with a 1962 re-release, and for years thereafter would be known among a limited group of writers and critics as a darkly satirical novel that brilliantly forecast the black humor fictions of the 1960's.

During this time (when he was once classed among "ten neglected writers"), Gaddis nevertheless remained very active. He occasionally supported himself by writing for business and industry. When awarded a National Institute of Arts and Letters grant in 1963, he had a play and several novels either written or in progress, including another long novel, a satire of American finance that evidently became *JR*. Scholarly essays analyzing his first novel also began to appear, and when *JR* was published in 1975, it was to universal acclaim. This novel, another long and trying fiction that one critic called "a masterpiece of acoustical collage," won Gaddis a National Book Award in 1976. Further compensation for the years of relative neglect came in 1982, with the award of a prestigious MacArthur Foundation "Genius Grant" as well as with the first widespread scholarly attention to his writing.

During the 1970's and 1980's, Gaddis taught literature and creative writing at Bard College, published several more magazine pieces, and completed his third novel, *Carpenter's Gothic* (1985), which uses as its setting the Victorian house Gaddis owns in Piermont, New York. Easily the most accessible of his novels, because of its brevity, *Carpenter's Gothic* is nevertheless as difficult in its collage methods and as dark in its satire as either of Gaddis' earlier fictions. It underscores his reputation as a satirist of American idealism in the tradition of Mark Twain and Herman Melville.

Analysis

In "The Rush for Second Place," an April, 1981, essay for *Harper's* magazine, Gaddis spells out the central concern of his fictions. "The real marvel of our complex technological world," he writes, is "that anything goes right at all." Events seem to follow a law of entropy: The more complex the system or message, the greater the chance for disorganization or error. Thus, in a contemporary United States grown hugely complex, there is "failure so massive," Gaddis argues, that no one is accountable and few things seem "worth doing well" any more.

From these convictions spring some of the main difficulties in reading Gaddis' fictions. The initial difficulties are of style, and they chiefly involve the complex allusions woven into the fabric of his dialogues and brief descriptive passages, but they involve as well Gaddis' experiments with dialogue.

The allusiveness of Gaddis' writing was a notable trait from the beginning. *The Recognitions* quotes and makes other forms of indirect reference to a wide range of texts: Snippets of T. S. Eliot's poetry appear alongside other literary allusions, but the principal field of reference is that of religious myth and mysticism. Gaddis draws from secondary works of scholarship such as Robert Grave's *The White Goddess* (1948) and James Frazer's massive *The Golden Bough* (1890-1915), as well as from an impressive range of primary texts by the Catholic church fathers (saints Clement and Ignatius), and other sources such as the Koran, *The Egyptian Book of the Dead*, and books on occult beliefs and practices. For his second novel, *JR*, Gaddis once more cast a wide net, bringing into play allusions to pre-Socratic philosophy, the poetry of Tennyson, and Germanic mythology—especially as it was popularly embodied in nineteenth century German composer Richard Wagner's operatic cycle *Der Ring des Nibelungen* (The Ring of the Nibelung). Initial reviews of *The Recognitions* were perhaps harshest in judging these seemingly overdone scholarly tendencies in Gaddis' writing. Nevertheless, a first-time reader of his novels does well to keep in mind that this allusive quality serves Gaddis' aim of satirizing the uses of Western knowledge; a number of the allusions mouthed by characters are drawn from dictionaries of quotations and clearly participate in Gaddis' broad satire of those who pretend to learnedness. Taken at a distance, the allusions to world mythologies are also crucial to Gaddis' great theme. They evoke a technologized, modern world in which meaning has shattered into "sound bites" or fragments of political and social dogma or even into mere errors; it is a world in which individuals long, often nostalgically, for totalizing messages, for the very stuff that myth provides.

The second stylistic difficulty of Gaddis' writing springs from his experiments with dialogue. Along with James Joyce, and especially along with contemporary American authors such as Donald Barthelme and William Burroughs, Gaddis has stripped his characters' direct speech of any conventional markers: He has eliminated not only the quotation marks (which is the first thing the reader notices), but also markers such as speakers' names, details about voice inflections, gestural counterparts, or contextual details identifying the localities of speech. (The "he said, laughingly, from his chair" types of phrases common to the realistic novel have simply been erased from Gaddis' work.) All these narrative particulars may still be embedded in the characters' direct discourse (or, as well, they may not be). A Gaddis novel thus demands a much more active reader to reconstruct these ordinary signs of narrative art; eventually, in fact, one begins to know the voices by means of identifying tics, such as Jack Bast's expletives or J. R. Vansant's repeated exclamations ("Well holy!") in *JR*. The result is an auditory performance of human speech, in all its fragmentariness, as if recorded by some omnipresent instrument. From these minimal but very potent semblances of speech, one is able to imagine a world, including the knotted woof of the characters' pasts as they are criss-crossed by the accelerated and very noisy warp of present events.

Gaddis began to develop these rapid-fire dialogues in *The Recognitions*, with chapters set in the crowded and artistically pretentious nightclubs of Greenwich Village. These scenes of his first novel, composing a minor percentage of the text, are among its most memorably ludicrous for their disconnectedness and qualities of humorous counterpoint. In *JR* and *Carpenter's Gothic*, the technique has virtually taken over. Gaddis' second novel even dispenses with conventional markers of scene and time change, traditionally handled in fiction by chapter endings and beginnings or by the descriptive interventions of an omniscient narrator. Instead, across its several months of story time and 726 pages of text, *JR* is one seamless, nonstop ride on the babbling tongues of Americans in the year 1971. To block out chronologically separate scenes, chapter divisions are restored in *Carpenter's Gothic*; otherwise the technique is unchanged.

In large measure, the boldness of Gaddis' techniques may be gauged by remembering that he is, foremost, a satirist. In traditional narrative satire, it is the function of omniscient intervention both to point out clearly and to judge plainly the exemplars of folly and vice. Gaddis refuses to do this. He will, however, weave into each fiction a voice that points the finger and unceremoniously judges; such are the characters named Willy in *The Recognitions*, Jack Gibbs in *JR*, and McCandless in *Carpenter's Gothic*, who variously serve as Gaddis' outraged mouthpieces. Yet theirs are merely other voices among the din, so the lack of an omniscient standpoint still leaves the task of moral judgment to the reader.

Doubtless, this is exactly the point. As immensely complex "messages" in narrative, and charged as they are on the hyperspeeds and incompletions of contemporary technological culture, Gaddis' novels ask the reader to confront forms of "failure so massive" that they would initially seem to defy order or meaning. Having confronted them, though, the reader's next task is to begin tracing lines of organization, and eventually to see that someone can indeed be held "accountable." In *The Recognitions*, Gaddis holds up before readers a massive indictment of fakery in all reaches of American culture; in *JR*, his target is the failure of democratic capitalism as an

American ideal; and in *Carpenter's Gothic*, his subject is the degrading of American millennial ideals by popular media, religions, and politics. Defined by thematic intentions such as these, the three novels Gaddis published in thirty years make literary claims of major importance.

THE RECOGNITIONS

First published: 1955
Type of work: Novel

An artist searches for authenticity and order in a contemporary culture defined by its myriad counterfeits and its decline into disorder.

The Recognitions takes its title from a third century theological romance inscribed by St. Clement, whose story concerned a neophyte's search for true religious experience in the midst of a corrupted empire. Set in the contemporary United States, and mainly in New York City, Gaddis' novel nevertheless finds parallels (as one character notes) with "Caligula's Rome, with a new circus of vulgar bestialized suffering in the newspapers." Across 958 densely written pages, the text narrates the story of Wyatt Gwyon's maturation, both aesthetic and spiritual.

Like all of Gaddis' novels, this one begins with contested lines of descent. From the side of his mother, Camilla (who wanted to name him Stephen), Wyatt has inherited an artistic temperament. From his father, a Calvinist minister, he inherits a severe sense of the damnation of man and of his own guilt in particular. During a sojourn in Spain, his mother dies mysteriously when Wyatt is three, and later the raging fevers of a mysterious childhood illness (drawn from memories of Gaddis' own bout with erythema grave) seem to confirm his Calvinist side; it is Wyatt's gift for drawing, however, that seems to pull his spirit back to health. Wyatt opts for divinity school, like his father, but paints in secret and eventually leaves the United States for Europe to study painting. There Wyatt is oblivious to styles of modernist art, and his best works are "recognitions" of the Flemish masters of the late middle ages. Disparaged by fashionable critics for this work, Wyatt gives it up, returns to the United States, and settles for mere draftsman's work and a mindless marriage.

Lapsing into cynical despair over his failures, Wyatt is discovered by an art dealer, Recktall Brown, who proposes to employ the young man's talents in creating almost faultless forgeries of the Flemish masters, which forgeries he moreover proposes to have "authenticated" by his associate, a corrupted art critic named Basil Valentine. The circle of this plan closes when Wyatt's canvasses bring spectacular prices and, indeed, even a perverse recognition of his talents. Plunged into the relentless work demanded of him by this counterfeiting ring, Wyatt also falls into the pretentious bohemian demimonde of Greenwich Village, and these chapters provide Gaddis opportunities for some of his most corrosive satires of an art world driven by egotism and profit motives. In this middle portion of the novel, Wyatt is virtually surrounded by frauds: Frank Sinisterra, a counterfeiter; Otto Pivner, a failed playwright who fakes a war injury, and whose only artistic motive is pecuniary gain; Agnes Deigh, an overweight matron of the art world who encourages artists by feeding their conflicting physical and spiritual needs.

Increasingly depressed because of his corruption by money and the semblances of fame in this society, Wyatt considers resuming his divinity studies. The break finally comes after he witnesses Brown's ludicrous death, in a fake suit of medieval armor, as well as after he causes—or so he mistakenly thinks—the death of Basil Valentine. Wyatt flees America once again, on the same boat which had evidently brought his father home from Spain after Camilla's untimely death; Wyatt eventually winds up at the same Spanish monastery, at Estremadura, where his mother is buried. Here Wyatt closes a different kind of circle. Not only does he change his name to Stephen, as his mother intended; he also leaves behind the seemingly ceaseless guilt about the conflict of matter and spirit which is his inheritance from his father. Wyatt resumes a relationship with a Spanish mistress from his first European trip and commits himself to rearing a child of that union; yet he also resumes his theological studies. He accepts the need for earned income, yet he continues with the painting which had been so corrupted by greed. The novel thus ends with tenuous assertions of balance, though on a very small scale. Wyatt/Stephen, his tiny family, their meager belongings, and few paintings suggest a balance achievable only in minimalist forms—a recurring theme in Gaddis' later work.

Wyatt/Stephen's solution stands opposite the enormously detailed world that Gaddis realizes in this very large tapestry. Gaddis' satirical target is a society in which, as Frank Sinisterra notes, "Everything's middlemen. Everything's cheap work and middlemen wherever you look. They're the ones who take the profit." Elsewhere, Recktall Brown (whose name fixes his identity, as do the monikers given to other characters) plans "a novel factory, a sort of assembly line" for fictions that will be patchworked from other texts, for (as he asks), "What hasn't been written before?" The dialogue of Otto Pivner's play is plagiarized from Wyatt's abstruse bar-room speeches, themselves bursting with quotations and allusions. Wyatt's quest is to get outside these vicious circles. In his last scene, he stands within his monastery room and releases a bird from his cupped hands. The confused creature momentarily flutters before Wyatt's most recent painting—an artwork that has given up the apparently ceaseless mirroring of other artworks to become, instead, like a window. This is the most that Gaddis' dark novel will provide by way of positive values.

JR

First published: 1975
Type of work: Novel

A sixth grader fed on promises of success absurdly builds a mega-corporation that spins toward catastrophe and nearly pulls an artist down with it.

In *JR*, the society of "middlemen" has spread, virus-like, and the resulting depreciation of all values is Gaddis' main theme. The characters' desires for commercial and aesthetic success highlight a crisis in values: Artistic significations (words and musical sounds, for example) are conflated with money, and a monetized culture further governed by the principal of usury (the extracting of "interest") diminishes things all around. In this novel, therefore, money almost literally talks, and does so in relentless, rapid-fire sentences that threaten to drown out meaning. Edward Bast, the artist figure of this novel, must struggle relentlessly to free himself from these conditions. Mostly he struggles with a vastly institutionalized usury that drives him, at novel's end, into a feverish delirium (brought on by exhaustion and pneumonia) that recalls Wyatt's at the beginning of *The Recognitions.*

JR opens in the Long Island home of Bast's two aging aunts, who are engaged with a lawyer in discussing the settlement of the estate of Thomas Bast—their brother, Edward's father, and the owner of a business that manufactures piano rolls. Thomas has died intestate, and thus, as in Gaddis' first novel, the constituting theme is inheritance. Edward's appears to be a purely financial legacy, but the characters' dialogues unfold complications: Edward Bast's first wife bore him a daughter, Stella, with claims on the estate; it also becomes evident that Thomas' second wife, Nellie, may have conceived Edward during an adulterous affair with Thomas' brother, James. Edward might therefore lay claim to the Bast wealth through either, or both, of these potential fathers. The overriding question, however, is whether he will choose to inherit the gifts of art or money.

Enter J. R. Vansant, a sixth grader at the Long Island school where Bast has been hired to teach music—absurdly, he is teaching Wagner's *The Ring of the Nibelung* for an upcoming performance. JR's part of the opera is, significantly, that of Alberich, the grotesque gnome who renounces love for money and sets out to enslave men by possessing the golden ring of the Nibelung. Having just returned from a field trip to a Wall Street brokerage house, JR is filled with dreams of unlimited financial success. A bit of epithetic advice proffered by one of the cynical brokers—"buy for credit, sell for cash"—inspires JR. Scanning the newspaper want ads, working from a phone booth, and aided by an unwitting Edward Bast, JR purchases (on credit) four-and-a-half million surplus picnic forks from the U.S. Air Force, and as quickly sells them (for cash) to the Army. His ventures burgeon from that point, as JR acquires bankrupt companies, empty mining claims, an entire bankrupted New England mill town full of pensioned employees, a chain of nursing homes that services the pensioned millworkers (and is tied to another chain of funeral homes), as well as the Bast family company. In sum, "The JR Family of Companies" (as it is eventually known) balloons around the empty, the incomplete, the aged, and the dead. Yet it is wildly successful. By novel's end, when JR's enterprise comes crashing down, it triggers a national financial crisis.

JR functions as the consummate middleman in a society of cynical dealers. Along the way, Gaddis' satire takes aim at Wall Street, at government, and especially at school administrators driven by chances to profit at the same kinds of "business tie-ins" that JR finagles. The novel's most consistent voice for this corrosive satire is Jack Gibbs, a science teacher at JR's school. He first appears in the text while trying to teach students the concept of entropy, which predicts the ultimate thermodynamic degradation of any closed system. This theory sets forward a crucial analogy in Gaddis' novel: In the closed (adulterous and nearly incestuous) system of the Bast family, entropy has seemed to lay their entire estate to waste, and that result is duplicated in the equally closed "family" of JR's companies, or indeed throughout the economy of which JR's ventures are simply a part. Gibbs rages against these abuses and he tries (and in the course of the novel fails) both to love and to write. Thus, he exits the novel an impotent, sickly figure who cannot arrest the general decay, a failure he shares with a swarm of would-be artists around him.

Bast's story is more suggestive, however. Though plunged into the chaos of JR's school and business dealings, Bast struggles to compose a vastly orchestrated opera. Frustrated and broke, he barters his services on Wall Street by agreeing to write the musical accompaniment to a documentary film. Failing at both of these—in short, failing at both art and money—Bast begins limiting his artistic work. In succession he starts, and leaves aside, a cantata, and then a suite. His frantic involvements as JR's "financial manager" drag him down until, exhausted and feverish in the hospital, he composes a brief solo work for cello. Initially he tosses this work in a hospital trash can, but leaving the hospital he rescues the composition for the simple reason that a deceased roommate had liked the "idea" of Bast's music.

As in *The Recognitions*, then, Gaddis ends his second novel with suggestions that his artistic-hero has at last managed to get "outside" the social contradictions hemming him in, and has done so chiefly by working in a minimalist form. Even so, Gaddis gives his Alberich, JR, the last word. He is a public celebrity now, working the college lecture circuit, appearing in parades and on talk shows, and even contemplating writing a book. His business emerges from the chaos just as recuperated as Bast's aesthetic spirit. Gaddis' satire has thus turned darker: His artist exits the novel a shambling and harried figure, as money triumphs over all.

CARPENTER'S GOTHIC

First published: 1985
Type of work: Novel

A nexus of political, journalistic, and religious affiliations spin the United States uncontrollably toward a nuclear holocaust in Africa, aided by a Vietnam veteran.

Gaddis' third novel in as many decades, *Carpenter's Gothic* is also his bleakest satire. Its style, as well as its theme of cultural entropy in a civilization where meaning and value are utterly degraded in a complex "media-scape," are consistent developments for him. While no plot summary can succeed in conveying the rich tapestry of characters, events, and cultural detailing in his work, this novel is not only briefer (at 262 pages) but also more focused—and therefore more readable—than either of Gaddis' prior fictions. For many readers, it therefore constitutes the best door into the writer's work.

The story centers on the last four weeks in the life of Elizabeth Vorakers Booth, a former debutante and the daughter of a mineral tycoon. Her father's suicide, nine years earlier, had been a desperate attempt to block the U.S. Senate's investigation of various briberies, manipulations of the media, and monopolistic dealings in Africa that assured his company's success. Liz's husband Paul, a Vietnam veteran, transacted F. R. Vorakers' bribes, and he met (and seduced) Liz while testifying before the Congress after her father's death.

The novel thus opens, as do Gaddis' prior fictions, with complications resulting from a father having died more or less intestate. Desperately frustrated that fortunes are either tied up in lawsuits or manipulated by a network of self-serving associates, Paul Booth rages against his fate, meanwhile goading Liz into pursuing any available tidbits the estate lawyers might give up and prodding her further into a lawsuit he has brought against an airline responsible (he claims) for his loss of Liz's "marital services" when she was injured (four years previously) in a plane crash. Meanwhile, he has attached himself as a "media consultant" to one Reverend Ude, a fundamentalist preacher whose South Carolina television ministry is rapidly burgeoning into an influential social and political force. Yet Paul and Liz are verging on bankruptcy. She approaches their ruin with a pathetic resignation, but Paul drunkenly schemes and rages either at Liz, at the morning newspaper, or at the incessantly ringing telephone, in dialogues that unfold entirely within the Booths' Hudson Valley rental house, the curiously pieced-together "Carpenter's Gothic" which they have rented from a Mr. McCandless.

With McCandless' entry into the novel, events begin to close in on the characters, as always happens in a Gaddis novel. McCandless, a sometime geologist, teacher, and writer, had surveyed the very southeast African mineral fields in which the Vorakers Reserve Company had consolidated its fortunes years ago, and in which the Reverend Ude is now building missions for a great "harvest of souls" expected during "the Rapture," or anticipated Second Coming of Christ. McCandless is being pursued by both the Internal Revenue Service for back taxes and the Central Intelligence Agency for information about those African territories. He arrives one autumn morning to gather some papers from a locked room. A shambling, weary man, an incessant smoker and an alcoholic, McCandless is nevertheless a romantic mystery man to Liz, who straightaway takes him to bed.

Occasionally bursting into the claustrophobic and chaotic spaces of the novel is Liz's younger brother, Billy, a curious mix of cynicism and idealism. He is so taken by McCandless' drunken tirades against the nexus of American media, government institutions, and popular religions that he goes off to Africa himself—where he is killed when his plane is gunned down by terrorists. Events spin toward catastrophe. Reverend Ude is under investigation for bribing a senator to grant a new television license, and the media skewer Ude for drowning a boy who had presented himself for baptism. In southeast Africa, civil war erupts. Liz learns that all of her stored personal belongings, her final links to family and tradition, were auctioned off.

The end comes on several fronts at once. McCandless, having accepted a CIA offer (or bribe) for his papers, simply exits the narrative after failing to persuade Liz to leave with him. She dies of a heart attack, the warning symptoms of which Gaddis has planted from the novel's beginning. While doubtless symbolizing an absolute loss of empathy and love in this fictional world, even Liz's heart attack is ironized when it is erroneously identified as having taken place during a burglary. Paul wastes no time in moving to claim any inheritance due Billy and Liz, and he exits the novel using the same seductive approach on Liz's best friend that he used on Liz nine years earlier. In Africa, political events explode: U.S. forces are poised to strike in protection of "national interests"; indeed, apocalypse looms as senators and media commentators laud the use of nuclear weapons—a "10 K 'DEMO' BOMB OFF AFRICA COAST," as one headline puts the news.

With this novel, Gaddis brings his satire toward a kind of limit. There is nothing darker or more bitter in his work than McCandless' ragings against the failures of American democracy. Other than the cynical exits of Paul and McCandless, there seems no way out of this novel's dilemmas, and there is no generative artwork either, however minimal. Yet this most recent novel clarifies how Gaddis' great subject has always been the United States: the crushing weight of its mass society on the individual, the corruption of its civic institutions, the monetization and hence the counterfeiting of all values, and therefore the loss of its cultural inheritance. These remain the great themes of his satire.

Summary

It has often been noted that a satirist functions as the infuriated conscience of his or her national culture. The novels of William Gaddis attest the accuracy of that statement.

Gaddis' principal subject concerns the terms of failure in America. Like F. Scott Fitzgerald, Mark Twain, or Herman Melville, Gaddis takes issue with the democratic ideal that success in great things shall come to all Americans who simply work hard for it. Throughout his writing runs the counter-conviction that even small successes come only through hard-fought moral, aesthetic, and spiritual struggles.

Bibliography

Auchincloss, Louis. "Recognizing Gaddis." *The New York Times Magazine*, November 15, 1987, pp. 36, 38, 41, 54, 58.

Karl, Frederick R. *American Fictions, 1940-1980*. New York: Harper & Row, 1983.

Kuehl, John, and Steven Moore, eds. *In Recognition of William Gaddis*. Syracuse, N.Y.: Syracuse University Press, 1984.

Moore, Steven. *A Reader's Guide to William Gaddis's "The Recognitions."* Lincoln: University of Nebraska Press, 1982.
_____. *William Gaddis.* Boston: Twayne, 1989.
Review of Contemporary Fiction 2 (Summer, 1982). Special Gaddis and Nicholas Mosley issue.
Tanner, Tony. *City of Words: American Fiction, 1950-1979.* New York: Harper & Row, 1971.

Steven Weisenburger

JOHN GARDNER

Born: Batavia, New York
July 21, 1933
Died: Susquehanna, Pennsylvania
September 14, 1982

Principal Literary Achievement

Believing that literature should make a serious contribution to human life, Gardner combined philosophical and moral concerns in fiction that emphasized the complexities of everyday existence.

Biography

John Gardner's father was a dairy farmer and part-time preacher; his mother was a high school literature teacher. From these two, Gardner inherited and combined down-to-earth realism, life-affirming moral vision, and the belief in the power of art not only to reflect the human condition but to affect it as well. Gardner learned early the redemptive power of art. When he was twelve years old, he accidentally killed his younger brother by running over the boy with a tractor used on the family farm. In response to this tragedy Gardner turned to art—first music and then writing; he would later explain his serious, almost religious devotion to literature in terms of this early experience, when writing was literally his salvation.

Gardner received his bachelor's degree from Washington University in St. Louis. Recognized for his intellectual brilliance and promise, he was named a Woodrow Wilson fellow at the University of Iowa, and he earned his MA from there in 1956, his doctorate in 1958. Although Iowa was widely known for its creative writing program—and Gardner did participate in it—his degree was in classical and medieval literature, and his earliest publications were primarily scholarly, rather than creative.

Yet while Gardner was teaching at various schools across the country and publishing academic articles on Old English texts and early classics such as the works of the Gawain Poet and the Wakefield cycle of mystery plays, he was also diligently writing his own fiction. More than diligently, in fact, since Gardner was compulsive in his need to write, completing more than twenty volumes during his relatively short life. His novels were rejected by numerous publishers, however, and Gardner, who was a firm believer in the serious nature of art, became dismayed at the state of current literature, which he believed populated by superficial, nihilistic writers who shirked

art's essentially moral responsibilities. Largely out of response to this, and to avoid dejection—the redemptive power of art again—he began work on a manifesto of his artistic creed; when it was eventually published, after Gardner's acclaim, it would cause considerable turmoil and even damage his reputation.

In the meantime Gardner persevered with his efforts, and was at last successful in 1966 with *The Resurrection*, his first published novel, which, however, drew little attention. *The Wreckage of Agathon*, his second novel (1970), was only slightly better received. It was his third effort, *Grendel* (1971), which retold the Beowulf saga (c. A.D. 1000) from the monster's point of view, that first won for Gardner critical and popular recognition; significantly enough, it was also the first of his novels to be illustrated, a device which he retained throughout his career.

In 1972, Gardner published *The Sunlight Dialogues*, a massive, philosophical novel which used ancient Mesopotamian myth and modern American complexity to comment upon universal human themes of law and justice, the rights of the individual, and the needs of society. Although recognized as a work of daring originality and philosophical speculation, *The Sunlight Dialogues* was nominated for no major literary awards, something which caused some furor and discussion in the literary world. Partially in response to this, but more in recognition of its own considerable merits, Gardner's 1976 novel, *October Light*, won the National Book Critics Circle Award, perhaps the most respected of all American literary honors.

The prolific Gardner wrote in every genre: criticism, novels, short stories, biography, children's books, libretti for operas (*Frankenstein*, 1979, is his most notable attempt, but there were several others), poetry, translations and academic studies.

His two-volume biography and critical study of Chaucer caused some arguments, mainly in academic circles, over the question of possible plagiarism: Had Gardner cited his sources fully enough, or had he merely adapted earlier scholarship without proper credit? Gardner himself freely admitted that he had drawn on earlier scholars, pointing out that he was essentially a popularizer—shown by his technique in the Chaucer biography, which included novelistic touches.

Even more of a controversy was stirred with the publication of *On Moral Fiction* in 1978. As noted, the book was largely written while Gardner was unpublished and frustrated, and, as he said, "I was furious, just enraged, at those guys with big reputations, and I wrote a vituperative, angry book. Most of it I got wrong." What he did not get wrong, according to many perceptive readers, was the insistence that art has a moral function—moral in the sense that it must affirm life by addressing serious issues in a serious (but not necessarily solemn) fashion. The books' message was much in keeping with traditional Western views of literature, but Gardner's willingness to question the accepted authors of modern American writing stirred great bitterness in the literary establishment. A number of the negative reviews which his subsequent books received were generated by this controversy, which lasted until the end of his life.

Gardner's personal life, which often seemed secondary to his artistic one, was turbulent and unsettled. Often at odds with authority, he scorned academic tweed to roar about campus on his motorcycle, wearing a black leather jacket and blue jeans. He had problems with drinking, a bout with cancer, and a running feud with the Internal Revenue Service over unpaid back taxes. He was twice married and twice divorced. With Joan Patterson, whom he married in 1953, he had two children, Joel and Lucy; Joel took the photographs which illustrated Gardner's last book, *Mickelsson's Ghosts* (1982). His second marriage was to Elizabeth Rosenberg, an English professor and cofounder with Gardner of the publication *MSS*, which specialized in discovering new literary talent.

On September 14, 1982, only four days before he planned to marry again, Gardner rounded a curve near his home and lost control of the Harley-Davidson motorcycle he was riding. He was killed in the accident.

Analysis

For John Gardner, art, and in particular literature, was more than a career: It was in almost the religious sense a vocation, a calling of a chosen individual. He also believed that art has a profound and lasting impact on those who receive it, whether they are watchers of plays, listeners to music, viewers of paintings, or readers of novels. For these reasons, reinforced by his personal experience, Gardner felt that art was essentially serious—although it could be playful—and that true art, art that is valid and lasts, must therefore be moral art.

Moral art meant art that affirms and reinforces all that is best in human nature. Literature in particular has a special place, because among all the arts it has the possibility of being the most vivid and closely felt, and so has the greatest impact. In his own novels and short stories, Gardner sought to embody this artistic philosophy, and his book of criticism, *On Moral Fiction*, is an outspoken and uncompromising defense of the kind of writing he considered worthwhile and an unsparing assault on that which he considered merely facile, trivial, or downright harmful.

Gardner's touchstone of good writing was a standard easy to articulate but difficult to execute: It must create a "vivid and continuous dream" for the reader. Mere verbal dexterity, adherence to fashionable but pointless literary trends, or any technique or device that obscured the artist's ability to perceive and re-create the truth of human existence destroyed such a dream. In his brief book *On Becoming a Novelist* (1983), Gardner gives a summary of the characteristics of true writing:

> It is "generous" in the sense that it is complete and self-contained: it answers, either explicitly or by implication, every reasonable question the reader can ask. It does not leave us hanging, unless the narrative itself justifies its inconclusiveness. It does not play pointlessly subtle games in which storytelling is confused with puzzle-making. It does not "test" the reader by demanding that he bring with him some special knowledge without which the events make no sense. In short, it seeks, without pandering, to satisfy and please. It is intellectually and emotionally significant.

In his own novels, Gardner attempted to achieve these goals by concentrating upon his characters and by entering into the mind and heart of each of them so that he could present their points of view to the reader. These presentations were made without overt judgment, even with characters whose moral nature might be questionable, or whose motives and ends were warped or distorted. Such intrusive judgments would, Gardner felt, have prejudiced the reader's vision and interrupted the dream. His view was summed up in the quotation from the *I Ching* found at the beginning of *The Sunlight Dialogues*: "The earth in its devotions carries all things, good and evil, without exception."

So, in *Grendel*, Gardner tells the story from the point of view of what most would call a monster, an inhuman beast who yet, when seen clearly, has something of a soul and the aspirations of a poet. In his two "pastoral novels," *Nickel Mountain: A Pastoral Novel* (1973) and *October Light*, Gardner moves among the various characters, filtering the story through each of their perceptions in turn, and so allowing a comprehensive and generous vision not only of individuals but also of a community to emerge. No single person has a monopoly on the truth, so the only valid vision — other than God's — must be a communal vision.

This sense of community is a powerful and recurrent theme in Gardner's fiction, and characters who find themselves in despair, without purpose, or acting in ways which even they sense are evil, are those who have cut themselves off from their community. Thus James Page, in *October Light*, descends into bitterness, drunken rage, and nearly murder when he rejects his community. In a similar but not quite as dramatic fashion (although she does attempt to kill her brother), Sally Page Abbott, James's sister, suffers significant moral decline when she locks herself in her room, literally isolated. Significantly, Sally's moral deterioration is hastened by reading a cheap, trashy novel, the kind whose bleak and cynical vision Gardner despised as being truly immoral art.

The positive power of community, on the other hand, is pervasive in Gardner's novels, where it is frequently linked with the concept of the natural world as a kind of moral center; the two, community and nature, are joined by the power of art. For Gardner, art does not necessarily mean the creation of beautiful objects, but includes the honest observation and appreciation of the world. Henry Soames, the central character of *Nickel Mountain*, becomes such an artist during the course of the novel, discovering the enduring values of the Catskill Mountains and the people around him. In doing so, Henry actually saves his own life, drawing away from a self-imposed early death from compulsive overeating and resulting heart problems.

In Gardner's novels, a condition such as Henry's weakened heart is both actual and symbolic. Gardner's fiction is crammed with images and situations which carry far more than their literal meaning and create a multilayered and complex structure that suggests more than it states. Gardner is also a master of metaphor (for Aristotle, the supreme test of an artist) and uses it in very effective fashion, making the natural world a vast array of symbols without detracting from its concrete presence or tangible existence — without disturbing what the philosopher William James called, in words Gardner often cited, "the buzzing, blooming confusion."

High moral seriousness, a deep interest in philosophy and its relationship to everyday life, and everyday life itself as lived by fully realized, completely human characters: These are the hallmarks of John Gardner's fiction. In his novels, he has re-created a world where the individual and the community exist in the special order of nature, mediated by the saving power of true art.

GRENDEL

First published: 1971
Type of work: Novel

The Beowulf legend is retold by the monster, who muses on the meaning of human life and art.

In *Grendel*, Gardner takes one of the mainstays of Western literature, the Old English epic *Beowulf*, and gives it a dramatic new vision by telling it from the point of view (and through the words) of the monster. In this way he is able to present the story anew but also to make telling comments on his enduring theme, the place and power of art in human life.

Beginning the novel as a brute, barely articulate figure, Grendel is exposed to art and its powers by two competing forces. On the one hand, there is the human he calls the Shaper, the blind poet of the mead hall; allied with the Shaper is Wealtheow, the beautiful queen. These two are embodiments of the positive power of art to raise human beings—or even creatures such as Grendel—beyond the pointless round of mere existence. Yet Grendel is profoundly troubled by them and by the power they wield and comes to prefer their opposite number. The Old Dragon represents another aspect of art, its negative side, since he holds the universe to be meaningless, a random collection of events without purpose, its creatures without dignity.

There is thus a truly philosophical dimension to the novel—as is always the case with Gardner's fiction—and in Grendel, Gardner has composed a satirical portrait of the noted modern philosopher, Jean-Paul Sartre, whose theory known as existentialism posited a meaningless world, a vision close to the Dragon's bleak theories. In accepting this view, Grendel closes himself to the effects of what Gardner termed "moral fiction"—that is, literature which transcends limitations, makes sense of life, and is redemptive in an almost religious sense. Lacking this view, Grendel attempts to force meaning upon the world by violence: He ravages the lands of King Hrothgar, kills his men, wastes his crops, and defiles his queen Wealtheow. In the end, however, Grendel is overcome by an unnamed hero—Beowulf—who is not only physically powerful but also morally superior, precisely because he has accepted and can use the art which Grendel fears and rejects.

The novel operates on several different levels. On the surface it is an exciting adventure, a literary tour de force. Below that it is a serious meditation on the power and place of art in human life. To signal these layers, Gardner employs numerous symbols and recurring thematic devices through the short book, and these give

Grendel power and resonance greater than its length suggests.

Christian imagery and Norse mythology are mingled throughout the novel, most frequently in scenes where Grendel encounters trees: hiding in them, being caught in their branches, hanging from them. The chief god of Scandinavian myth, Odin, is closely associated with trees and with sacrifice by hanging from a tree; closely parallel to this are Christian beliefs in the sacrificial death of Christ on the cross, often referred to as a tree. Repeated use of such symbolism gives the novel a complexity and density more like poetry than fiction, since each word is capable of handling several different meanings.

The structure of the novel is ingenious as well. Each of the twelve chapters is dominated by a symbol of the Zodiac, starting with the ram (Aries) and progressing through the year to the sign of the fish (Pisces). Once again there are the references to Christianity—the lamb and the fish are both signs of Christ—and a natural movement through the year, from spring to fall. The number twelve crops up repeatedly in the novel, a unifying technique which Gardner adopted from early English literature.

In the end, however, despite the intricate cleverness with which the novel is written, its main power lies in two points: its brilliantly evocative use of language, especially in the creation of Grendel as a character, and the battle between two powerful views of art and human life—one negative, the other, positive.

THE SUNLIGHT DIALOGUES

First published: 1972
Type of work: Novel

During the course of a police investigation, two men with greatly differing philosophies debate the meaning of human life and morality.

The Sunlight Dialogues was Gardner's first major success in his writing career—a best-seller for a number of weeks and a critically acclaimed serious novel of ideas. A long novel, it has a considerable amount of action, but it also contains extensive passages of discussion and debate on moral and philosophical issues, which is characteristic of Gardner's fiction, always deeply concerned with how abstract matters translate into the everyday human situation.

The novel centers on the confrontation between representatives of two differing points of view; one is a chief of police, the other a "magician," and their dispute concerns law and order, the universe, and humanity's place in that universe. The police chief, Fred Clumly, and the magician, known for most of the novel only as the Sunlight Man, thus become not only individuals, but also representatives of much more.

The Sunlight Man is actually Taggert Hodge, member of a prominent local family now in decline. Taggert, who had fled the town of Batavia sixteen years previously, has returned for his own version of revenge and redemption; Clumly is drawn into this against his will, but once entered into the pursuit of the Sunlight Man, he becomes caught up in an even larger chase, that of the elusive truth. In a sense captive to his strange relationship with the Sunlight Man, Clumly allows his life and work to collapse, worrying his blind wife, Esther, and angering the mayor and council, who eventually fire him. He joins the Sunlight Man for a final meeting at Stony Hill, the family home of the Hodges, now in decline, and the two men come to a half-spoken agreement. Later the Sunlight Man tries to surrender to the police; by mistake he is killed, shot, (significantly enough) through the heart.

To express the search for meaning and order in which the Sunlight Man and Clumly engage, Gardner fashions his work around four dialogues between Clumly and the Sunlight Man in which far-ranging moral and philosophical issues are discussed. Using the contrast between ancient Babylonian and Jewish cultures, Gardner outlines the differences between justice and law, freedom and order, the individual and society. While Clumly and the Sunlight Man seem opposites, they actually have much in common. Both are disfigured physically (hairlessness for Clumly, fire burns for the Sunlight Man), each has a handicapped wife (the sheriff's is blind, his opponent's, insane) and both are isolated from their fellow human beings, cut off from the larger community. The dialogues between the two are partially their fumbling, only partially conscious attempts to break through this isolation.

A vast novel with a multitude of characters, *The Sunlight Dialogues* is carefully constructed, filled with parallels of character and plot. The main supporter of order, Chief Clumly, pursues a criminal and has discussions with him; Will Hodge, another proponent of law, has a series of his own "dialogues" with a counterculture character named Freeman. Walter Boyle, a small-time thief who has an alternate identity (and thus is in one person a contract between law and outlaw, order and disorder) has another set of confrontations with the boarder who seduces his wife. In this fashion, Gardner re-emphasizes the impact that ideas and ideals can have on actual human life.

Two themes are emphasized in *The Sunlight Dialogues*. The first is one Gardner uses in several of his novels, the need to establish meaning for life in the face of death. This theme flows from his first published novel, *The Resurrection*, through his last, *Mickelsson's Ghosts* (1982), and is a central component of *The Sunlight Dialogues*; here, as in the other works mentioned, Gardner resolved the conflict by the union, or at least acceptance, of seeming opposites through the power of love.

A second theme is the conflict between order and anarchy, society and the individual, law and justice. Clumly champions the first, a heritage Gardner identifies with ancient Jewish culture. The Sunlight Man speaks for the second, which is linked with the Babylonian world. While Gardner's novel suggests that these two widely divergent viewpoints may be combined in some fashion, it is also realistic in admitting that they might simply be ignored or forgotten by an indifferent world: At the end of the novel the Sunlight Man is dead, Chief Clumly is fired, and the events are soon relegated to the past. Still, Gardner insists, the effort is worthwhile, and true art is that effort to reconcile what seems irreconcilable.

The Sunlight Dialogues is the centerpiece of Gardner's works; it is his most ambitious and successful novel, filled with well-created, memorable characters in a believable setting. Its publication brought him his first popular recognition and firmly established his standing as a novelist who could handle ideas, realistic description of action, and the creation of distinct individuals.

NICKEL MOUNTAIN

First published: 1973
Type of work: Novel

By showing love and compassion to an unmarried mother and her son, a man regains his sense of community and accepts the natural world.

Although *Nickel Mountain* was published in 1973, it was begun when Gardner was nineteen years old; despite numerous revisions, therefore, the novel is among the author's earliest work, and it shows clearly that the basic themes of his fiction were present from the start: the need for love and compassion, the ability of the true artist to adopt the point of view of others, and the need to affirm all that life contains.

The story in *Nickel Mountain* is that of Henry Soames, the three-hundred-pound owner of the Stop-Off Cafe, a little eatery deep in the Catskill Mountains of New York State. Henry, gnawed by vague despair, given to heart problems—both literally and metaphorically—receives a new chance at life when he marries Callie Wells, a sixteen-year-old waitress left pregnant by her boyfriend. The novel follows Henry, Callie, and their son, Jimmy, through a year of life and the lives of their neighbors in a small, agricultural community. Although a number of highly dramatic incidents occur, including accidental deaths, personal tragedies, and a devastating drought, the core of the plot is how Henry comes to accept life and love again; he becomes, in a sense, what Gardner would term a true artist.

In counterpoint to Henry's growing acceptance of the world are the characters Simon Bale and George Loomis. Both men are soured and embittered by the world: Bale's wife died when their house burned, while Loomis was wounded in Korea, jilted by a Japanese prostitute, and has lost an arm in a farm accident. The symbolically named Simon Bale has become a religious fanatic, but his faith brings no joy, only frustration and gloom. He wishes to be a disciple of the Lord (hence the "Simon," reflecting the original name of the apostle Peter), but his influence is harmful (baleful). Henry Soames, who is frequently compared to Jesus, takes Bale into his house but is unable to bring love into the man's soul. In the end, Bale dies—perhaps an accident, perhaps a disguised suicide—by falling down the stairs at Henry's house. Twisted faith has killed the man, and he ends up literally twisted and crushed at the bottom of the steps.

George Loomis also withdraws from the world, retreating into his sense of the past. He lives in the house which has been in his family for more than two hundred years, and he derives his greatest pleasure from fondling the family heirlooms. Things, rather than people, have become his life. Early in the novel George has the opportunity to marry Callie—in fact, Henry himself makes the suggestion—but he rejects it, a symbolic rejection of the world outside his dark and shuttered prison. Like Simon Bale, George Loomis represents an alternative which Henry Soames wisely rejects.

Nickel Mountain is subtitled "A Pastoral," and through the subtitle Gardner is indulging in a characteristic multilayered use of language. On the one hand, the novel is literally a pastoral in the sense that it fits into the requirements of a particular literary genre that stretches back to classical Greece: The action takes place in the country, the characters are farmers and their families, cities are seen as embodiments of evil, while nature is the only source of goodness and true morality. All of these elements are present in *Nickel Mountain*.

On the other hand, the novel is "pastoral" in a religious sense. Henry Soames is the pastor, or good shepherd of his small family, and by extension, of the entire community around Nickel Mountain. Numerous comparisons between Henry and Jesus are made in the book, most notably to Christ's willingness to be crucified for the sake of humanity. In the novel's climactic scene, the members of the farming community gather at the Stop-Off to wait for the rain they desperately need, and they sing "Happy Birthday" to Henry. The reader will sense the parallel between Christ's birth—which ensured salvation—and Henry's, which in a sense redeems his neighbors. Simply by singing the song they feel better, and later it does indeed rain. Still, *Nickel Mountain* does not advocate any particular religious doctrine or specific beliefs. Rather, it emphasizes that belief itself is important and that the varieties and particularities which individuals may select should all be tolerated, respected, and encouraged as long as they aspire to moral goodness and love.

OCTOBER LIGHT

First published: 1976
Type of work: Novel

The feud between an old man and his sister re-enacts the American Revolution and depicts the conflict between changing values.

Published in 1976, *October Light* was in one sense Gardner's bicentennial novel, a symbolic retelling of the American Revolution through the lives of two elderly Vermont residents, James Page and his sister, Sally Page Abbott. The struggle between the two recapitulates, in miniature, the conflict between the colonists and Great Britain, while the small New England community where they live comes to represent the United States—its past and its promise.

On another, deeper, level the novel focuses on a theme which Gardner found compelling, and which is the basis for his pastoral novels: the power of nature to act as a moral force and become the positive center for human life, strengthening that which is best, and serving as a guide. Nature cannot accomplish this alone, but needs to be mediated by art, and that art, as *October Light* makes explicit, must be moral art—moral fiction.

Fiction must be moral because fiction is powerful, capable of affecting lives and societies. In *October Light* this power is displayed in two fashions. First is the hostile, visceral reaction James Page has to modern media, especially television. The feud between Page and his sister starts when he blows apart her television with a blast from his shotgun. Later, enraged by the shows he sees in a bar, Page gets drunk, violent, and destroys his truck in an accident on the winding mountain road.

The second fashion through which Gardner shows the power of literature is by his device of a novel within the novel, a cheap crime/science fiction thriller called *The Smugglers of Lost Souls' Rock*. This trashy paperback is found by Sally after she has taken refuge in her room, and as she reads its tawdry tale of sex, violence, and crime, her view of life and her perceptions are coarsened and debased. Eventually she plans, with cold-blooded but fortunately inept determination, to kill her brother. This attempted murder, Gardner implies, is caused as much by the book she was reading as the situation in which Sally finds herself.

The conflict between James Page and his sister operates on several levels simultaneously. On one, as noted, there are the parallels between them and the American Revolution. Some of these are specific, as when James Page destroys his sister's television, thereby depriving her of freedom of speech. Numerous other connections, more or less explicit, are scattered throughout the book. There is also the struggle between the old America and the new, in which the older sibling (Sally, who is eighty) ironically represents the future: She watches television, approves of nuclear power plants, and supports the Equal Rights Amendment to the Constitution; naturally James finds all of these abhorrent, perversions of traditional American values. Through careful modulation of his plot and a gradual softening in the positions of these two characters, Gardner suggests that there is room—and need—for compromise.

The "immoral fiction" of the antinovel embedded within the book rejects this, for it represents a United States where compromise has been rejected and all values, past and present, have been rejected as well. Quoting an imaginary review, *The Smugglers of Lost Souls' Rock* is "a sick book, as sick and evil as life in America." Gardner believes that such indeed would be the state of an America that could neither maintain its worthy traditions from the past nor recognize new strengths of the future.

Finally, there is the resolution of the conflict between James and Sally, past and present, America and Britain, through the power of nature as interpreted by art. *October Light* contains some of Gardner's most lyrical and evocative descriptions of the landscape and the patterned order of rural life, and this sets the characters within a world where healing is possible through nature's power and within the confines of a shared community of human beings. This community is symbolized in the novel by a party held to reconcile Sally and James; although neither attends in person, the bond which it calls forth works on them, and reconciliation is achieved. As is always the case in Gardner's fiction, isolation within one's self leads to despair; rejoining the larger community brings strength and joy. In *October Light*, the community envisioned becomes as close as a family and as widespread as America.

MICKELSSON'S GHOSTS

First published: 1982
Type of work: Novel

Disillusioned and despairing, a philosopher sets about restoring an old house and, at the same time, his life.

Recognized throughout his career as a philosophical novelist, fascinated with abstract ideas and how they are embodied in specific characters, Gardner returned explicitly to this kind of fiction in the final novel he published during his lifetime, *Mickelsson's Ghosts*. It is literally the story of a philosopher, Peter Mickelsson, and his attempts to restore meaning and purpose to his life—intellectually, morally and emotionally.

Mickelsson is a professor of philosophy at the State University of New York at Binghamton, the school where Gardner himself was teaching at the time of his death. Significantly, Mickelsson's specialty is ethics, but neither ethics nor intellect stirs him any more, and his personal life is a shambles: separated from his family, hounded by the Internal Revenue Service, drinking too much and too often, and wandering the streets alone at night, unable to sleep. While on one of these aimless nocturnal rambles, Mickelsson savagely kills a dog that startles him, and, startled by his descent into violence, he decides to move to the country, hoping to regain some order and purpose to his life.

Mickelsson buys a run-down farmhouse in the Endless Mountains, just across the border in Pennsylvania, and begins to restore it, but he finds this harder than he anticipated, just as he finds it difficult to bring clarity back to his own life. The nearby town of Susquehanna (again there is the echo of Gardner's own life) may be the site of an illegal toxic waste dump; the countryside is infested with sinister, mysterious Mormons; Mickelsson further complicates his own life by his dual affairs with Jessica Stark, a fellow Binghamton professor, and Donnie Matthews, a young prostitute in town. Inevitably, the farmhouse turns out to be haunted, and Mickelsson begins having windy debates with spirits, including the shades of famous philosophers.

Mickelsson reaches a crisis when he accidentally kills a man—an old, fat bank robber whose money Mickelsson needs to pay for Donnie's abortion. With this death and Donnie's subsequent flight from town, Mickelsson has reached bottom, and he can at last begin to put his life truly in order. At the novel's end, he returns to Jessica Stark, and they make love in a scene of ambiguous but hopeful resolution.

In many ways *Mickelsson's Ghosts* returns Gardner to his first published novel, *The Resurrection*, which was also about a philosopher trying to get his life in order; in a sense, the book rounds out Gardner's career with the concerns which occupied him in all his writings: the need for community, the search for truly human values, and the place of art as a guide. The book is autobiographical in many aspects, set in the same locale where Gardner lived, and with Peter Mickelsson facing many of the same troubles which dogged John Gardner. The combination of these two forces, aristic and personal, and the fact that *Mickelsson's Ghosts* was Gardner's final novel give the book a particular poignancy.

This poignancy is reinforced by the symbolic device of ghosts which figures so prominently in the book. In a sense, Mickelsson himself is a ghost, a man who has died, not yet literally but intellectually and emotionally. As is the nature of ghosts, he wanders through the world able to see and be seen, but unable to touch or make full human contact. In all of Gardner's fiction, process is a vital element, and in *Mickelsson's Ghosts* the basic process is the one whereby its hero regains his humanity.

The key element in that process is the power of love, mediated by art. Art in this novel takes two forms: Mickelsson's study of philosophy and his restoration of the old farmhouse. Both are initially useless, because Mickelsson attempts them in isolation; it is only when he admits others into his life—Donnie, Jessica Stark, the townspeople—that art and love can perform their true function and make Peter Mickelsson more than a ghost.

ON MORAL FICTION

First published: 1978
Type of work: Literary criticism

A summary and spirited defense of the intellectual and philosophical principles of Gardner's own writing.

On Moral Fiction is actually two books: One is a philosophical and aesthetic study of literature—in fact, of all forms of art—which attempts to define its purpose, explain its effects, and establish its values. In maintaining that fiction is at its basis serious and important, Gardner's work is squarely in the tradition of texts as old as Aristotle's *Poetics* (fourth century B.C.), Longinus' *On the Sublime* (first century A.D.), and Sir Philip Sidney's masterpiece of English Renaissance prose and thought, *The Defense of Poetry* (1595).

The second book, which is much shorter and is actually a series of illustrative examples, consists of Gardner's evaluation of contemporary American writers, nearly all of whom he brusquely dismisses as having failed to adhere to the moral and artistic standards that he champions. In examining the work of such highly regarded authors as John Barth, John Updike, Norman Mailer, and E. L. Doctorow, Gardner is unsparing in his criticism and perhaps intemperate in his tone. It was this aspect of *On Moral Fiction*—especially its polemical style—which caused such controversy about the book and which clearly damaged Gardner's reputation with many in the literary establishment.

The philosophical and artistic arguments of *On Moral Fiction* are certainly not new, and, while they might strike some readers as old-fashioned, they are clearly within a Western literary tradition that is thousands of years old, dating back to the ancient Greeks. True art, according to Gardner, is moral art, moral in the sense that it affirms and reinforces the dignity and purpose of human life, without falling into the trap of easy sentimentality. In the face of inevitable death—of individuals, civilization, perhaps of the world itself—true art finds and celebrates that which is worthwhile. Gardner maintains that in doing this art is didactic—that is, it teaches its beholders to become better human beings. Once again, his line of reasoning follows traditional thought, and in this case the line reaches back to Aristotle and his theories of the effects of art on the spectator.

In Gardner's words, "Art rediscovers, generation by generation, what is necessary for humanness." In the process of rediscovery, art conveys the necessary information as elegantly as possible to those who hear it, see it, or read it. Art teaches while it entertains. In one sense art, especially literature, can be seen as exhausted, because there are no new stories, no truly original characters left; however, Gardner spurns the despair some of his contemporaries have over this fact, because it is basically unimportant. The real value of art is in its restatement of essential and timeless truths which should never be forgotten but which, ironically, would be if not for art:

> Insofar as literature is a telling of new stories, literature has been "exhausted" for centuries; but insofar as literature tells archetypal stories in an attempt to understand once more their truth—translate their wisdom for another generation—literature will be exhausted only when we all, in our foolish arrogance, abandon it.

Gardner's most trenchant and even vitriolic criticism of his fellow writers was based upon this very premise: They had abandoned traditional writing—traditional not necessarily in the stylistic sense, but traditional in its central concerns. The two aspects, however, content and technique, are linked, because Gardner believed that writers as different as John Barth and Donald Barthelme, or J. P. Donleavy and William Gass, had become enamored of language for its own sake, neglecting its fundamental role as a vehicle for the presentation of character and archetypal truths. Gardner dismissed the vast majority of modern American writing as "toy fiction," and in doing so, he incurred the wrath of the cultural establishment which had accepted and validated the writers and works he attacked.

Gardner's conception of what constituted moral art in practice, however, almost required such an unsparing critique as he made in *On Moral Fiction*. In his view, the essential method of literary art had been abandoned. That method was the process of art: As the writer comes to understand his or her characters, their values, their points of view, then truth is revealed. In this way, the real artist breaks through the illusion of isolation and subjectivity which has weakened so much of modern writing.

"Nothing in the world is universal anymore; there is neither wisdom nor stability, and faithfulness is dead." So laments a despairing character in Gardner's novel *The Sunlight Dialogues*. This is the point that Gardner claims far too many modern writers have accepted. Their response has been to trivialize literature, to make it only a game of words and word play, irony for its own sake. Gardner rejected this view, and in *On Moral Fiction* he set forth a philosophical and artistic program for the redemption of literature, a program that would affirm not only art, but what art itself affirms, human life.

Summary

The key to all of Gardner's work was summed up in the title of his book *On Moral Fiction*. Gardner believed, with passionate intensity, that art was absolutely vital to human life and that it had a powerful and profound influence upon both those who created it and those who received it. In Gardner's view, moral art affirms and reinforces that which is best in human nature: understanding of others, compassion, and love. It does not pretend to resolve the terrible complexities and tragedies of the human condition into simplistic answers or a single point of view. Rather, it embraces the "buzzing, blooming confusion" of the world and helps make sense of it.

Bibliography

Butts, Leonard. *The Novels of John Gardner*. Baton Rouge: Louisiana State University Press, 1988.

Cowart, David. *Arches and Light*. Carbondale: Southern Illinois University Press, 1983.

Henderson, Jeff, ed. *Thor's Hammer: Essays on John Gardner*. Conway: University of Central Arkansas Press, 1985.

Morace, Robert A., and Kathryn VanSpanckeren, eds. *John Gardner*. Carbondale: Southern Illinois University Press, 1982.

Morris, Gregory L. *A World of Order and Light*. Athens: University of Georgia Press, 1984.

Michael Witkoski

WILLIAM GIBSON

Born: New York, New York
November 13, 1914

Principal Literary Achievement
Gibson has dramatized much of the life of Helen Keller and is the author of two very successful Broadway plays.

Biography
William Gibson was born in the Bronx, New York City, on November 13, 1914. His father, a mailroom clerk and a talented amateur pianist, died during Gibson's childhood, and his Irish Catholic mother had to work as a scrubwoman to support the family. *A Mass for the Dead* (1968) is a heartfelt chronicle of Gibson's childhood and adolescence. Emulating his father, Gibson learned to play the piano as a child and in his early writing days worked as a piano teacher and as a performer to supplement his income. His lifelong interest in music is reflected in his work on the libretto for the operetta *The Ruby* (1955) and the text for the 1964 musical *Golden Boy*. By the time he was sixteen, Gibson had graduated from Townsend Harris Hall, a Manhattan public high school for gifted boys, and had begun work at what later became known as City College of the City University of New York. Gibson did not like college, however, and dropped out after two years.

In 1940, at twenty-six, Gibson married Margaret Brenman, a psychoanalyst, whose work with the Menninger Clinic had led them to Topeka, Kansas. At the Topeka Civic Theatre, Gibson had his first plays performed, a one-act verse drama about the Apostle Peter, *I Lay in Zion* (1943), *Dinny and the Witches* (1945), and *A Cry of Players* (1948). *Dinny and the Witches* was revised and produced off-Broadway in 1959 but was panned by critics and closed after only twenty-nine performances. *A Cry of Players* was also produced in New York City at Lincoln Center in 1968 but enjoyed only moderate success.

In the 1940's, however, Gibson had not settled on being a playwright. He was also writing short stories and poems—he won the Harriet Monroe Memorial Prize for a group of poems published in *Poetry* in 1945 and published, through Oxford University Press, a collection of poems entitled *Winter Crook* in 1948. Eventually, he also wrote a novel, *The Cobweb* (1954), which he sold to Metro Goldwyn-Mayer, earning enough to buy a home in Stockbridge, Massachusetts, where his wife Margaret had taken a new job.

In Massachusetts, Gibson turned again to drama and in 1956 completed the play that would launch his meteoric Broadway career. *Two for the Seesaw* (1958) is the story of a brief love affair between a Nebraska lawyer separated from his wife and a New York dancer down on her luck. The play was completed with the encouragement of Arthur Penn and appeared on Broadway with established star Henry Fonda playing Jerry Ryan and Anne Bancroft, then a newcomer, portraying Gittel Mosca. The play was a huge success, running for 750 performances and grossing more than $2 million in its two-year run. Though the play drew critical praise, Gibson considered the four-year process "the most odious experience of my life" because commercial pressures had forced him to alter the script drastically. He records the story of the writing, casting, rehearsal, and production of the play in *The Seesaw Log: A Chronicle of the Stage Production* (1959); his unflattering portrait of Henry Fonda remains striking and controversial. Touring companies took the play around the world, a film version of the play appeared in 1962, and a musical version of the play was mounted on Broadway in 1973, rewarding Gibson with a considerable amount of money for his aggravation.

Before 1959 was over, Gibson already had another Broadway hit. *The Miracle Worker* (1959) is the amazing story of how Annie Sullivan helps the deaf and blind Helen Keller to acquire language at the age of six, despite Helen's inability to experience anything outside her own mind except what she can touch. The script had originally been a teleplay, appearing on CBS's *Playhouse 90* anthology series and winning the Sylvania Award in 1957 as the year's best television drama. Gibson rewrote the play for the stage, and it appeared on Broadway in 1959 with Anne Bancroft as Annie Sullivan and Patty Duke as Helen Keller. *The Miracle Worker* was Gibson's second great success, running for close to two years and then, like *Two for the Seesaw*, enjoying a transformation to the screen in 1962. In a few short years in the late 1950's, William Gibson had become a significant new playwright.

Thereafter, Gibson's career slowed significantly. The off-Broadway version of *Dinny and the Witches* (1959) was not a success. In 1964, after the death of his friend Clifford Odets, Gibson was hired to complete the book for the musical version of Odets' *Golden Boy*, which was only moderately successful on Broadway despite the bravura performance of Sammy Davis, Jr. In 1966, Gibson cofounded the Berkshire Theatre Festival in Stockbridge, Massachusetts, which in 1969 produced his *John and Abigail*, a play based on the letters of John and Abigail Adams, but Gibson eventually considered the play a disaster. It was remounted in 1971 in Washington, D.C., under the title *American Primitive.* In the 1970's and 1980's a number of plays followed—*The Body and the Wheel* (1974), *The Butterfingers Angel* (1974), *Golda* (1977), *Goodly Creatures* (1980), *Monday After the Miracle* (1982), *Handy Andy* (1984), and *Raggedy Ann and Andy* (1984)—but none achieved the success of his earlier plays. *Monday After the Miracle*, a sequel to *The Miracle Worker*, premiered in South Africa and was featured at the Spoleto Festival in Charleston, South Carolina, before being mounted in New York City, but on Broadway it was not received well either by the critics or the public.

Analysis

William Gibson's literary career is noteworthy partly because he has worked successfully in a very wide variety of literary forms and has added to American popular literature a most unusual investigation into the nature of human love.

The diversity of Gibson's literary efforts includes poetry (*Winter Crook*), a novel, (*The Cobweb*), screenplay adaptations of his own works (*The Cobweb*, *The Miracle Worker*), the teleplay version of *The Miracle Worker*, an operetta (*The Ruby*), a Broadway musical (*Golden Boy*), and numerous nonfiction pieces: *The Seesaw Log*, *A Mass for the Dead*, *Shakespeare's Game* (1978), and *A Season in Heaven: Being a Log of an Expedition after That Legendary Beast, Cosmic Consciousness* (1974). The diversity within his nonfiction corpus is also striking. The last title, for example, is an account of a visit to the Maharishi International University in La Antilla, Spain, where Gibson studied transcendental meditation with the Maharishi Mahesh Yogi and regained the Catholicism of his youth, while *Shakespeare's Game* is an exercise in practical criticism, with Gibson demonstrating how Shakespeare's plays fit his personal theory of drama. Gibson's theatrical work is no less diverse, ranging from the fantastical quality of *Dinny and the Witches* (in which a trumpet player and Central Park witches stop the passage of time) to the domestic realism of *The Miracle Worker* and the ritualism of the liturgical passion play *The Body and the Wheel*. The most consistent format in which Gibson has worked has been biographical drama, but the range of materials and treatment even in that area has been wide as well, ranging from *A Cry of Players*, where Gibson focuses on the youthful Shakespeare and works with very sparse historical materials, to *Golda*, where Gibson writes during Golda Meir's lifetime about the famous Prime Minister of Israel and the Arab-Israeli Yom Kippur War.

On the other hand, there is a remarkable consistency in Gibson's subject matter, as many of his works are investigations into the complex nature of human love. *The Cobweb*, set in a mental institution, explores the emotional bonds between members of the psychiatric staff and their patients, with the imagery of the novel's title suggesting ways in which these complex relationships can be as treacherous as they are supportive. *A Mass for the Dead* is an attempt to come to terms with the complex love Gibson felt for his parents, and *A Cry of Players* hypothesizes about how a rocky marital love between the young Shakespeare and his older bride, Anne Hathaway, might have led to Shakespeare's theatrical career in London.

Perhaps Gibson's most provocative treatment of love comes in *Monday After the Miracle*, the sequel to *The Miracle Worker*, where he investigates a complex emotional triangle. In this play, Helen Keller is twenty-three years old and Annie Sullivan is thirty-seven. Twenty-five-year-old John May enters the household to help edit Helen's publications, and both women fall in love with John. John marries Annie, but his presence alters forever the love between the two women, and the play ends with the marriage's failure, with John turning to drink and leaving, and with Annie and Helen launching a new and highly profitable venture—an exhausting series of lecture tours for Helen—that brings Helen and Annie back together in the kind of relationship they had before John arrived.

Yet the resolution of the action is not satisfactory even for Helen and Annie. In the last scene, Helen recites for Annie, her "Teacher," a poem that sums up her life: "Teacher. And once again, Teacher. . . . [I]t will be my answer, in the dark. When death, calls." Helen has her new work, but she may never know love with a man. Annie has Helen again, but not her life as wife and mother, and it is fairly clear that both Annie and Helen have taken the energy they have for human love and sublimated it into their work, substituting work for the special intimacy that comes with marriage. John's stark summary captures the bleakness of the play's resolution:

> Love. John loves Teacher. Teacher loves Helen. Helen and Teacher love John, and John loves Helen and Teacher. John and Helen and Teacher are one huge love-turd. . . . Yes. It's next to murder, isn't it. Love.

Given the bleakness of this resolution, it is not surprising that *Monday After the Miracle* was not a commercial success. Most audiences demand a clear uplift at the end of a play, not the kind of stark examination that Gibson offers, provocative as it might be.

THE MIRACLE WORKER

First produced: 1957 (first published, 1959)
Type of work: Play

Helen Keller, blind, deaf, and unaware of the connection between words and things, learns to talk with the help of Annie Sullivan.

In *The Miracle Worker*, Gibson dramatizes the first month of Helen Keller's life with Annie Sullivan. By the age of six, the blind, deaf, and silent Helen is a savage child, gobbling food with her hands off any plate that she wants to invade around the family dinner table, even wrestling a young playmate to the ground and attacking her with scissors. Helen's family, the Kellers of Tuscumbia, Alabama, indulge nearly all of Helen's demands until they hire Annie Sullivan from the Perkins Institute for the Blind to be Helen's teacher and companion.

Herself only twenty years old and formerly blind, Annie insists upon civilizing Helen's behavior, much to the consternation of the family, who see Annie's treatment of Helen as brutally strict. Annie insists that the family's tenderness is misguided pity rather than love, that a superior love for Helen will respect her potential and demand that she live up to it. After a protracted struggle over Helen's table manners, for example, Annie is able to teach Helen to fold her napkin and use a spoon rather than her hands to eat from her own plate; however, the willful Helen returns to her more savage ways whenever she senses the family's indulgence, so Annie insists that she be permitted to teach Helen in isolation for two weeks.

In a garden house behind the family dwelling, Annie succeeds in calming Helen somewhat and teaches her a "finger-game," spelling words into Helen's palm, even though Helen does not understand that the words correspond to things in the world outside her. The family is satisfied with the progress, but Annie insists that Helen is capable of more, that she cannot be fully human until she understands the connection between words and things and begins using language. In an emotional last scene, Helen regresses at the dinner table and empties a pitcher of water on her teacher. When Annie forces Helen to fill the pitcher from a pump in the back yard, the miracle occurs: Helen feels the water cascading over her hand, feels Annie spelling the word into her palm, and says, "Wah. Wah." Within minutes, Helen is clambering around the back yard, demanding to know the names of things. Finally, she spells "teacher" and identifies the word with Annie. As the play ends, Annie embraces Helen and whispers a sentence that she will eventually be able to spell into Helen's palm, "I, love, Helen. Forever, and—ever."

A play of power and eloquence, *The Miracle Worker* is still often revived by regional and amateur theater groups. In the story of Helen Keller and Annie Sullivan, Gibson creates an image of the indomitable human spirit and the power of language while suggesting that love includes discipline and is based more on respect for a person's potential than on indulgence of a person's weakness or handicaps.

TWO FOR THE SEESAW

First produced: 1958 (first published, 1959)
Type of work: Play

A brief romance between a Nebraska lawyer and a New York dancer ends with the lawyer returning to his estranged wife.

Two for the Seesaw is about an eight-month romance between a thirty-three-year-old Nebraska lawyer who has left his wife and an aspiring New York dancer of twenty-nine. Jerry Ryan has come to New York to escape a stifling marriage poisoned by a father-in-law whose money and influence makes Jerry feel dependent and trapped. While Jerry's wife awaits the divorce, Jerry wanders the New York streets and museums, going to films and living on the five hundred dollars he brought from Nebraska. Then he meets Gittel Mosca. Young, vivacious, but unsettled as she pursues her illusory hope of becoming a famous dancer, Gittel's romantic entanglements have always been brief and superficial until she meets Jerry. Their romance, though tempestuous, is intense and appears potentially redeeming for both. After becoming Gittel's lover, Jerry takes a job in a law office and plans to reassume his legal career in New York, while Gittel rents a loft and gives dance lessons, with Jerry eventually moving in and sharing Gittel's apartment. After Jerry's divorce becomes final, however, his wife decides that she wants to attempt again to make the marriage work, and Jerry decides to leave Gittel and return to Nebraska. He will try to resurrect his marriage under terms that do not involve dependence on his father-in-law. Jerry and Gittel part as friends, thankful for what they have gained from one another.

The original title of *Two for the Seesaw* was *After the Verb to Love*, which Gibson used as a curtain line for the end of the play: "After the verb to love, to help is the sweetest in the tongue." With Gibson, love is not the clichéd, windswept passion of Hollywood or the soap operas. The prosaic concern for another's well-being and the desire to aid is, for Gibson, a more concrete and realistic way to define love. Gibson is also precise about what he means by "help." Jerry received one kind of help from his father-in-law, but it was not love because the help created a feeling of dependence and inferiority. The help to which Jerry refers is what Jerry and Gittel helped each other learn through their relationship. Gittel helped Jerry regain his sense of independence and self-esteem, while Jerry helped Gittel gain the self-respect she needed to insist on real romance rather than shallow, exploitive relationships.

Gibson's conclusion, however, does not strike the audience or the reader as particularly uplifting, despite what the dialogue asserts. The play remains unsettling because after Jerry returns to his wife, Gittel is left behind with no prospects—a realistic but not particularly comforting or uplifting conclusion. Although Gibson attempts to soften Jerry's departure with Gittel's proclamation that the relationship has done her "a world of good," the sense of Gittel's abandonment is perhaps a vestige of Gibson's original script. In the original script, Gibson intended Jerry to be a much more ruthless character, a "taker" rather than a "giver," and in *The Seesaw Log*, Gibson relates how Henry Fonda, who played Jerry, and Arthur Penn, the director of the Broadway production, demanded that Jerry be made more sensitive and sympathetic. Whether the final script is superior or inferior to the script with which Gibson began remains unsettled, but it is clear that Gibson retained even in the final script the disturbing portrait of the failure of love rather than of its success.

Summary

William Gibson is a writer of great diversity and intensity. Two of his plays, *The Miracle Worker* and *Two for the Seesaw* are particularly stageworthy, and *Monday After the Miracle* is a play with significant dramatic potential. Gibson's prose pieces, especially *A Mass for the Dead*, and *The Seesaw Log: A Chronicle of the Stage Production*, display considerable emotion of very different kinds, and as a specialist in biographical drama, Gibson is both an innovator and a master practitioner. As a writer focusing on the theme of love, Gibson is usually provocative and unconventional.

Bibliography

Clark, Tim. "After the Miracle Worker: Portrait of a Playwright." *Yankee* 46 (May, 1982): 66.

James, T. F. "Millionaire Class of Young Writers." *Cosmopolitan* 145 (August, 1958): 40-43.

Moe, Christian H. "William Gibson." In *Contemporary Dramatists*, edited by James Vinson. 4th ed. New York: St. James, 1988.

"On the Seesaw." *The New Yorker* 33 (February 15, 1958): 23-24.

Plummer, William, and Maria Wilhelm. "An Activist and Her Playwright Husband Address the Nuclear Peril with His Words and Her Deeds." *People* 24 (October 14, 1985): 65-66.

Terry Nienhuis

ALLEN GINSBERG

Born: Newark, New Jersey
June 3, 1926

Principal Literary Achievement

Ginsberg is a visionary poet of American English whose singular use of language, rhythm, and subject has made him a major figure in the cultural, political, and literary life of the United States.

Biography

Irwin Allen Ginsberg was born in Newark, New Jersey, the second son of Louis Ginsberg, a lyric poet and teacher, and Naomi Levy Ginsberg, a teacher and political activist. His family moved to Paterson, New Jersey, in 1929, the year his mother was hospitalized for mental stress for the first time, and Ginsberg attended primary school in Paterson. He published two pieces in the Easter issue of the Central High School magazine, *The Spectator*, his first public work, in 1941. When he transferred to Eastside High School, he became president of both the Debating Society and the Dramatic Society before he was graduated in 1943. He entered Columbia University as a pre-law student, hoping to pursue a career in labor law, and he studied with Lionel Trilling and Mark Van Doren, who were partially responsible for shifting his focus toward literature. His schoolmates at Columbia included Jack Kerouac, and he met William Burroughs in New York City during his first year there. With Kerouac and Burroughs, among others, Ginsberg formulated a philosophical discourse which they called "The New Vision," a precursor of the Beat generation precepts he exemplified in his later work.

In 1945, he was suspended from Columbia for permitting Kerouac to stay in his room overnight, and he worked temporarily as a welder, dishwasher, assistant at the Gotham Book Mart, and apprentice seaman in the merchant marine. He was readmitted in 1946 and became assistant editor of the *Columbia Review*, in which he published poems, stories, and book reviews. Ginsberg spent the summer of 1947 traveling to Colorado to visit Neal Cassady, the model for Kerouac's Dean Moriarty character in *On the Road* (1957), and he was graduated with a B.A. from Columbia in 1948. Later in that year, he had a vision of the English Romantic poet William Blake speaking to him directly—partially a product of Ginsberg's fairly extensive experimentation with hallucinogenic substances, partially an expression of his intense literary and philosophical considerations of the nature of the cosmos. Gins-

berg became involved in several quasi-criminal activities as a part of an underground (or as Kerouac called it, "subterranean") existence, and he committed himself to an eight-month stay in Columbia Presbyterian Psychiatric Institute as a means of avoiding prosecution. During his stay he met Carl Solomon, the man to whom "Howl" (1956) is addressed.

After moving in with his father and stepmother in 1950, he sent a letter and some poems to William Carlos Williams, who was living nearby in Rutherford, New Jersey. Williams provided guidance and encouragement, and while Ginsberg traveled to Mexico and Europe during the early 1950's, he continued to work on his poetry. In 1953, he moved to the Lower East Side of Manhattan, which was to become his home ground for the next five decades, and worked as a copyboy at the *New York World-Telegram*. He spent much of 1954 living in Mexico and then San Francisco, where he worked briefly as a market researcher and met Lawrence Ferlinghetti, the poet and publisher of City Lights Books, which would issue Ginsberg's poetry for the next quarter century. He also met Peter Orlovsky, who became his closest friend and lover in an enduring relationship. In 1955, Ginsberg moved to Berkeley, California, where he wrote his tribute to Walt Whitman, "A Supermarket in California," and organized the now-legendary landmark reading of October 13 at the Six Gallery, where he joined Gary Snyder, Philip Lamantia, Michael McClure, and Philip Whalen to read "Howl" in public for the first time. His mother Naomi died in 1956, the year that *Howl and Other Poems* was published, and Ginsberg spent the next two years traveling extensively, promoting the work of friends, defending the *Howl* volume against charges of obscenity, and working on "Kaddish," his celebration of his mother, published in 1961.

The media had discovered the artists whom they grouped under the title "Beatniks" in the late 1950's, and Ginsberg began to appear in magazines and films as an exemplar and proponent of this literary movement. Ginsberg continued to travel widely, reading and discussing the books that he and his friends—Gregory Corso, Leroi Jones (later Amiri Baraka), Herbert Huncke, Diana di Prima—were trying to publish. He visited South America and India in the early 1960's, then Great Britain, where he met and performed with the Beatles. He revived his friendship with Neal Cassady when a bus driven by Cassady carried Ken Kesey—author of *One Flew over the Cuckoo's Nest* (1962)—and the Merry Pranksters across the country to New York in 1964. In 1963, he published his third collection of poems, *Reality Sandwiches*, as well as an exchange of letters with William Burroughs (*The Yage Letters*) on their experiences with the liquid mind-altering substance yage. His interest in the use of materials such as this led him to form LeMar (Organization to Legalize Marijuana) in 1964 with the poet Ed Sanders.

Because of his often critical comments about politics in the United States, the Communist governments of Cuba and Czechoslovakia invited Ginsberg to visit under the mistaken assumption that he would approve of their repressive regimes. In 1965, Ginsberg visited Cuba and was expelled when he challenged the totalitarian aspects of Cuban society, and then visited Prague, where he was chosen "King of

May" by a hundred thousand Czechs before being expelled for his "unusual sex politics dream opinions," as he put it in the poem "Kral Majales."

At the same time that he was becoming increasingly specific about his differences with the government about its policies in Vietnam, Ginsberg was also becoming a patron of sorts in forming the Committee on Poetry, a nonprofit foundation to assist other writers. In 1967, he was arrested at an anti-draft demonstration; he also interviewed Ezra Pound, the most influential modernist poet in American literature, in Spoleto, Italy. He published *Planet News* in 1968, a volume including all the poetry he had written in the 1960's, and he was directly involved in the massive political protests at the Democratic National Convention in Chicago in the summer of 1968.

As the 1960's drew to a close, Ginsberg was becoming recognized more widely as an important figure in American literature. In 1969, he was awarded a National Institute of Arts and Letters grant for poetry, and in 1971, he served as a judge on the National Book Awards panel for poetry. In the early 1970's, he spent some time on a farm in upstate New York and published *The Fall of America: Poems of These States, 1965-1971* (1972) poems written during the previous six years. His interest in Buddhism, going back to his visit to India which was presented in *Indian Journals: March 1962-May 1963* in 1970, culminated in an acceptance of the teaching of Buddha under the instruction of Chögyam Trungpa, a religious figure from Tibet who initiated him with the name "Lion of Dharma." In 1974, *The Fall of America* won the National Book Award, and Ginsberg began to teach at the Naropa Institute in Boulder, Colorado, in a school he named "The Jack Kerouac Disembodied School of Poetics."

Continuing to work in areas not traditionally associated with conventional literary expression, Ginsberg joined Bob Dylan's Rolling Thunder Review as a percussionist-poet in 1975 and recorded much of his own work, as well as some poetry by Blake, with various types of musical accompaniment. In 1978, he published *Mind Breaths* and joined a protest at the Rocky Flat nuclear trigger factory, an activity that led to the composition of his "Plutonian Ode." As the decade closed, Ginsberg's increasing celebrity and accomplishment were honored by a gold medal from the National Arts Club Academy and induction into the American Academy of Arts and Letters.

Ginsberg continued to travel, teach, and perform during the early 1980's, publishing poems written during the preceding three years in *Plutonian Ode: Poems, 1977-1980* (1982) and then achieving stature as a major figure in American letters with the publication of his *Collected Poems, 1947-1980* in 1984, a volume received with wide attention and respect by both academic critics and the national media. In 1986, he was appointed distinguished professor at Brooklyn College, and he published *White Shroud*, an epilogue to "Kaddish" plus other poems from the early 1980's. In 1987, he appeared in several segments of the Public Broadcasting Service (PBS) *Voices and Visions* series on American poets; as the decade drew to a close, he began a collaboration with the composer Philip Glass that led to a release in 1990 of a chamber opera called *Hydrogen Jukebox* (a phrase from "Howl"), which placed many of his well-known poems in inventive musical settings. As the twentieth century moved into its last decade, Ginsberg, no longer considered a wild madman of language, was recognized as an active force in American culture and an elder sage of American letters.

Analysis

When "Howl" was published, Allen Ginsberg sent a copy to his former teacher at Columbia University, Lionel Trilling, a man widely regarded as one of the foremost professors of American literature. Trilling, who was fond of Ginsberg and wanted to encourage him, wrote in May, 1956, "I'm afraid I have to tell you that I don't like the poems at all. I hesitate before saying that they seem to me quite dull . . . [but] I am being sincere when I say they are dull." The significance of Trilling's reply is not simply that he was unable to appreciate an exceptional poem but that he was unprepared to recognize the qualities of an entire tradition in American literature. Trilling's training and experience had prepared him to respond with intelligence and insight to poems which the academic critical establishment regarded as important, but the influence of the New Critics—the writers who followed the teaching of such men as Cleanth Brooks, Robert Penn Warren, and John Crowe Ransom—left a line of poetic expression from Walt Whitman through Ezra Pound and on to Charles Olson, Marianne Moore, William Carlos Williams, and now Ginsberg essentially invisible. When Ginsberg finished "Howl," many poets outside the academic and publishing network of power were extraordinarily enthusiastic (Kenneth Rexroth said that the poem would make Ginsberg famous "bridge to bridge," meaning across the entire continent), but many critics and professors attacked it as formless and haphazard, the work of an uneducated buffoon. This particularly angered Ginsberg, who expected some misunderstanding but was especially disappointed that his own careful analysis of poetry in the English language and his efforts to find an appropriate structure for his thoughts had been so completely missed.

In addition to Trilling, Ginsberg sent a copy to his old mentor William Carlos Williams with a letter pointing out "what I have done with the long line," his basic rhythmic measure, a unit of breath which replaced the more familiar meter as a means of organizing the images of the poem. He believed that this "line" had what he called an "elastic" quality that permitted "spontaneity" and that its "rhythmical buildup" would lead to a "release of emotion," a human quality which he believed had been removed from the formal and often ironic stance taken by twentieth century poetry. Although Whitman obviously was one of his models in his attempt to reclaim the life of an ordinary citizen as a subject as well as for his characteristically long-breath lines, Ginsberg also mentioned American poet Hart Crane and English Romantic poets Percy Bysshe Shelley (citing his *Epipsychidion*, 1821, in particular) and William Wordsworth ("Tintern Abbey") as influences. While he was describing his modernist method of composition as "observing the flashings on the mind" and casually dismissing most editing by issuing the dictum "First thought, best thought," he also insisted on pointing out his lifelong familiarity with the traditional "bearded poets of the nineteenth century" that he had read in his father's home.

This solid background with conventional poetry was missed at first by critics who were overwhelmed by the originality of Ginsberg's writing and by his insistence on including all of his primary concerns—his amalgam of religions (Jewish/Buddhist/Hindu), his homosexuality, his radical politics, and his particular current literary enthusiasms—in his writing. When Ginsberg spoke of "compositional self exploration," he was challenging the idea that the poet worked everything out beforehand and selected an approved form to contain his thoughts. Ginsberg was, instead, one of the first proponents of Charles Olson's well-known definition that "form is never more than an extension of content," seeking to "graph the movement of his own mind" without the limitations of grammatical, syntactical, or quasi-literary conceptions about what was and was not poetic.

Ginsberg's intentions were ultimately to remake or restore American poetry, "to open the field" to its fullest dimensions. The mass media's misguided view of Ginsberg as a somewhat pathetic jester was obliterated by Ginsberg's *Collected Poems, 1947-1980*, which made it clear just how much a part of the main current of American poetry Ginsberg had become. It was not a matter of Ginsberg's ideas replacing previous orthodoxy as a dominant mode, but rather of a recognition that the approaches and ideas upon which Ginsberg insisted must be given the serious attention they require. From the sequence of what Ginsberg called "strong-breath'd poems," one might also derive a kind of counter-strain of lyrics which would not be "peaks of inspiration" in the most profound sense, but which exhibit Ginsberg's zany, Keatonesque comic spirit and his heartfelt commingling of sadness and sweetness. They also demonstrate his extremely sharp eye for detail amid the intricate landscape of American culture and his consistently inventive use of contemporary American speech on all levels, mixed with a classic English-American diction. The poems included in this mode begin with "A Strange New Cottage in Berkeley" and "A Supermarket in California" (1956), which Ginsberg describes as one poem in two parts that he wrote to satisfy his curiosity about whether "short quiet lyrical poems could be written using the long line." The poignance of Ginsberg's lament in "A Supermarket in California" for the promise of an earlier America still alive among symbols of contemporary American decay, and his homage to Whitman in the poem's conclusion, in which he addresses Whitman as "lonely old courage-teacher," evoke a mood of lyric innocence that is sustained by poems throughout his career.

The comic nature of Ginsberg's work, often using his poetic persona as the source and object of the joke, is evident in poems such as "Yes and It's Hopeless" (1973), "Junk Mail" (1976), and "Personals Ad" (1990), and especially in "I Am a Victim of Telephone" (1964), where his reveries are constantly interrupted by the telephone, which demands he respond immediately because "my husband's gone my boyfriend's busted forever my poetry was/ rejected." Since Ginsberg is essentially serious, however, his use of comic situations tends to underscore and to temper his earnestness so that when he vows in "America" (1956) that "I'm putting my queer shoulder to the wheel," his humor works as both a defense against a hostile world and as an expression of his modesty beneath his almost epic claims. In addition, the comic moods of his poems are often a product of his sheer delight in the weirdness of existence, another aspect of his ultimately optimistic and even exuberantly enthusiastic response to the world.

A major part of Ginsberg's world has always been his friends and literary companions, and they too figure prominently in his poetry. Cassady, Orlovsky, Kesey, and Burroughs are mentioned in various poems and dedications to collections, but the poem which unites generations of artists with a similar sensibility is "Death News" (1963). Ginsberg, upon learning of William Carlos Williams' death, recalls an earlier occasion when he, Kerouac, Gregory Corso, and Orlovsky sat "on sofa in living room" and asked for "wise words." Williams' wisdom— "There's a lot of bastards out there"—moves Ginsberg toward a celebration of the older poet in which he recognizes Williams' ability to retain humaneness in his life and art even though he is aware of the "bastards." From this lesson, Ginsberg proceeds to a series of reconciliations, including the theological (conflicting religious backgrounds), the local with the eternal, and most important in this context, the generational, as there is a mutuality of feeling and respect between the poets of two ages.

A similar Whitmanic generosity of spirit is displayed in "Who Be Kind To" (1965), a poem in which Ginsberg goes beyond the sympathy he extends to his friends to offer love to an often hostile environment. The community of underground artists with whom Ginsberg began his writing has broadened to include many members of the more traditional cultural enclaves, but there is still a very destructive force at large in the United States that Ginsberg has always opposed; in poems such as "Bayonne Entering NYC" (1966) or "Death on All Fronts" (1969), the ugliness and lethal pollution of the world is presented as a sickness to be challenged with the mind-awakening strength of the soul. This is what Ginsberg has always tried to do in his poetry, beginning with "Howl," which identified and described the psychic disaster, on through all the other poems that have uncovered and examined fears and desires denied and repressed and have then demanded that these impulses be accepted as a part of the totality of human experience.

HOWL

First published: 1956
Type of work: Poem

The poet laments the loss of sensitive young people destroyed by society, castigates the forces behind the destruction, and concludes in a spirit of affirmation.

When Lawrence Ferlinghetti heard "Howl" for the first time, he wrote Ginsberg a note asking for the manuscript so that he could publish it and repeated Ralph Waldo Emerson's words to Walt Whitman upon the publication of *Leaves of Grass* in 1855: "I greet you at the beginning of a great career"; many others shared his enthusiasm.

The tremendous energy that Ginsberg had generated with his images and gathered with his rhythmic structure was impossible to avoid, but while those who were open to all the possibilities of "language charged with meaning" (in Ezra Pound's famous phrase) were excited and inspired by the poem, a very strong counterreaction among academic critics and others frightened or appalled by Ginsberg's subject matter and approach produced some very harsh criticism.

Norman Podhoretz attacked "Howl" for "its glorification of madness, drugs and homosexuality, and . . . its contempt and hatred for anything and everything generally deemed healthy, normal or decent." Ginsberg felt that the poem spoke for itself in terms of his ideas and attitudes, but what bothered him was how the poetic qualities behind its composition seemed to have been overlooked in the furor. Even if he saw himself as a poet who, in the ancient sense, was a prophet who offered insight which could guide his race, he was, initially, a poet. Therefore, it was his "craft or sullen art" (as Dylan Thomas put it) which he offered as his proclamation of intention, and when it was misunderstood, Ginsberg explained or taught the poem himself.

His work prior to 1955 had consisted primarily of imitations of earlier poets or variations on early modernist styles. Then, in a crucial moment of self-awareness, he decided "to follow my romantic inspiration—Hebraic-Melvillian bardic breath." His plan was to write down (or "scribble") images flashing across his perceptual circuits in an overview of his entire life experience. From the famous first line, "I saw the best minds of my generation . . . ," Ginsberg compressed or condensed the life stories of his acquaintances—students, artists, drop-outs, madmen, junkies, and other mutants deviating from the conventional expectations of the muted 1950's—into what he called "a huge sad comedy of wild phrasing." He used the word "who" to maintain a rhythmic pulse and to establish a base from which he could leap into rhapsodic spasms of language:

> angelheaded hipsters burning for the ancient heavenly connection
> to the starry dynamo in the machinery of night,
> who poverty and tatters and hollow-eyed and high sat up smoking
> in the supernatural darkness of cold-water flats floating
> across the tops of cities contemplating jazz.

When he realized that it would be difficult to sustain such a long line, he juxtaposed disparate items and elements in a kind of verbal associative collage. He likened his technique to a haiku that involved a clash of images which maintained an element of mystery while putting "iron poetry back into the line." The first part of the poem was designed to be a lament for what Ginsberg felt were "lamblike youths" who had been psychically slaughtered by American society, and it was conceived in a "speech-rhythm prosody to build up large organic structures."

In the second section, Ginsberg identified "an image of the robot skullface of Moloch," which he used as a symbol for the devouring power of every destructive, inhuman, and death-driven feature of American life. His plan was to use a version of a stanza form, which he divided further by inserting and repeating the word "Moloch" as a form of punctuation; within each stanzaic unit, he defined the attributes of Moloch in order to form a picture of what he called "the monster of mental consciousness." Ginsberg builds this section to a climax of exclamation before temporarily releasing some of the accumulated tension in a vision of a breakdown or breakthrough where the social contract can no longer bind the diverse impulses of energy into any coherent arrangement. The lingering effect of the section is that of a ritual of exorcism, an incantation that develops a spell of sorts through the effect of a chant that alters consciousness.

Part 3 takes as its subject Carl Solomon, an old friend of Ginsberg from the time he spent in the Columbia Psychiatric Institute, who is the conspectus of all the "best minds" of part 1, a victim/hero of modern American life to whom Ginsberg pledges a unity of spiritual allegiance in his incarceration in Rockland Mental Hospital. Ginsberg took the form of this section from Christopher Smart, whose poem "Jubilate Agno" ("rejoice in the lamb") of the eighteenth century used a statement-counterstatement stanza which Ginsberg appropriated so that "I'm with you in Rockland" is followed by "where . . ." in a "litany of affirmation." Ginsberg described the third part as "pyramidal, with a graduated longer response to the fixed base," and the last image of the poem depicts Solomon at the door of Ginsberg's "cottage/ in the Western night." The poem does not end with a period, however, suggesting the almost utopian hopes for a better future which Ginsberg maintained. Even if the poem now seems almost overwrought in spots, it contains the central concerns of Ginsberg's work: the intense interest in sound appropriate to a poet firmly in the oral tradition, a fierce condemnation of the worst of American politics, a commitment to an explicit statement of erotic intention, and a rapturous reaction to the wonder of the universe akin to religious ecstasy.

KADDISH

First published: 1961
Type of work: Poem

The poet offers the traditional Jewish prayer for the dead as a celebration of his mother's life and his feeling for her suffering.

One of the central formative experiences of Allen Ginsberg's life was the decline into madness of his mother, Naomi, a wrenching psychic ordeal that he internalized for the first four decades of his life before confronting his feelings in the poem "Kaddish," which he composed in bursts of confessional exhilaration from 1958 through 1961. The trigger for the central narrative section of the poem, a biographical recollection of his mother's life, was a night spent listening to jazz, ingesting marijuana and methamphetamine, and reading passages from an old bar mitzvah book.

Ginsberg then walked out into New York City, and with his mind racing with the rhythms of the Hebrew prayers, he found himself covering the same ground his mother had known in her early youth. As his thoughts turned to her life, and to his inability to talk to her directly as an adult, he remembered that she had been buried three years before without the traditional Kaddish, the prayer for the dead. Determined to honor her memory before God, to face his own doubts about death and about his relationship with his mother, and to come to terms with his life to that point, Ginsberg began with a direct exposition of his feelings, "Strange now to think of you, gone," and withheld nothing as he re-created the full emotional depth of their life together.

"Kaddish" is both an extended elegy and a dual biography. For the poet himself, it is a "release of particulars," the "recollections that rose in my heart," which he views with a mixture of lingering nostalgia for childhood and a dread of how details apprehended in innocence take on a darker cast when seen in terms of the course of a person's life. His own journey from early youth to his present middle age is a parallel to the path that Naomi took from a youthful beauty, "her long hair wound with flowers—smiling—playing lullabies on mandolin," to Naomi "At forty, varicosed, nude, fat, doomed." Her madness and paranoia, which baffled and frightened him in his youth, are now a lurking threat to his own mental stability, especially since he has experienced visions and hallucinations of awesome power. The direction of their lives, of everyone's life, is toward "the names of Death in many mind-worlds," and it is this awesome certainty that has driven Ginsberg to open the paths to his subconscious. Rebuked by his mother's madness in life, and by her silence now, the poet thinks with gratitude of his mother no longer suffering, but he realizes that he will not find any kind of peace because he still has not "written your history."

The central incident in the second section concerns the trip that the twelve-year-old Ginsberg took with his mother on a public bus to a rest home. The awful implications of unpredictability and confusion in the presence of one who is supposed to provide stability turn the child into a quasi-adult, but one without guidance or education. While not blaming himself for his inability to handle the situation, he knows (even at the age of fifteen, the actual time of the trip) that an inescapable incursion of the chaotic has been planted permanently in his mind. In this lengthy narrative, carried along image by image through the power of Ginsberg's imaginative use of language, the world in which the poet developed his mind and began to shape his art comes into focus. It is a picture of American life in the late 1930's and early 1940's, and as Naomi retreats into madness, Ginsberg recalls how his political ideals, nascent poetic instincts, and sense of himself grew toward the poet who is writing this psychic history.

As the section concludes, Ginsberg turns his complete attention to his mother, indicating her madness by the seemingly logical but disjointed fragments of her conversation that he reproduces and using the power of very graphic physical details of the body's collapse as a metaphor for the decay of the mind. The extreme frankness with which Ginsberg describes his mother in a state of increasing deterioration is jolting in its candor, but it also functions as a seal of authenticity, implying an overall veracity, since the most painful of memories have been reconstructed.

The long decline that his mother suffered is so stunning that the poet is moved to prayer in the face of his helplessness, introducing the literal Hebrew words of the Kaddish, providing the prayer that the world withheld at her death. His own contribution, though, is not only to create a context of appropriateness for the ancient words but also to supply in language his own appreciation of his mother's best qualities. As the long second section moves toward a conclusion, Ginsberg employs a familiar poetic motif, setting the power of language in celebration of the beautiful against the agony of circumstance. Returning to some of the more traditional features of the elegiac mode (modeled on Shelley's *Adonais*, 1821), which he has held in reserve, Ginsberg declares,

> holy mother, now you smile on your love, your world
> is born anew, children run naked in the field spotted with
> dandelions,

and sings,

> O glorious muse that bore me from the womb, gave
>   suck first mystic
> life & taught me talk and music, from whose pained head I first
> took Vision—

and concludes:

>   Now wear your naked-
> ness forever, white flowers in your hair, your marriage
>   sealed behind the sky
> —no revolution might destroy that maidenhood—
> O beautiful Garbo of my Karma.

The closing lines of this part quote a letter that Ginsberg received from his mother only days before her final stroke, in which she tells him "the key" is "in the sunlight in the window." The image of light immediately precedes her salutation, "Love,/ your mother," that Ginsberg ratifies, "which is Naomi—" as an acknowledgment of his own love.

The last section of the poem is called "Hymmnn," and it is divided into three parts. The first is a prayer for blessing that examines the "key" image, the second a recapitulation of some of his mother's attributes in a catalog of her characteristics, and the third what Ginsberg called "another variation of the litany form" in which the poem ends in waves of "pure emotive sound" varying the words "Lord lord lord" and "caw caw caw." The poem is not really complete for Ginsberg, as he added a reflection on it in "White Shroud" (1983) and has suggested that other parts may yet appear as well. It is not a really difficult poem, but it is not a comfortable one either, and in resisting all the temptations to use centuries of sentimental associations with motherhood, Ginsberg has placed an archetypal relationship in a vivid and original light, reaching depths of feeling rarely touched except in the most powerful art.

KRAL MAJALES

First published: 1965
Type of work: Poem

In accepting the Czechoslovakian honor of "King of May," Ginsberg attacks the evils of both Communism and capitalism and extols the life-giving powers of art.

Among the links in the "chain of strong-breath'd poems," "Kral Majales" contains some of Ginsberg's strongest affirmations of human love as a force sufficient to overcome the powers of evil. The poem was written in May, 1965, after Ginsberg had been "sent from Havana" when his hosts found that he was not sympathetic to their suppression of unconventional behavior, and then "sent from Prague" when the authorities became nervous that a hundred thousand Czech citizens were deliriously cheering a bearded, anarchic American poet who was advocating action directly opposed to the political workings of their drab dictatorship. Ginsberg had been chosen as King of May by students and intellectuals in an ancient custom that had endured centuries of upheaval and conquest by foreign empires.

The poem begins as a comic rant juxtaposing the foolishness of capitalists who "proffer Napalm and money in green suitcases to the Naked" with his disappointment in the actuality of a Communist government after hearing his mother "reading patiently out of Communist fairy book." Instead of a worker's paradise, the Communists "create heavy industry but the heart is also heavy." After a balance of images condemning the idiocy of both sides, Ginsberg shifts the tone of the poem completely; he sets against the darkness of modern industrial decay at its most deadly the life-giving properties of the office with which he has been honored and which he honors in the poem. In a great list, he describes the King of May—himself, in this current incarnation—as a mythic savior who offers the powers of art, love, invention, true religion, and the excitement of language in action. Using the phrase "I am" to keep the beat, his long line pulses with energy; the method of juxtaposition utilized in "Howl" is even more concentrated and direct:

> And I am the King of May, which is the power of sexual youth,
> and I am the King of May, which is industry in eloquence and
> action in amour,
> and I am the King of May, which is long hair of Adam and the

Beard of my own body
and I am the King of May, which is Kral Majales in the Czecho-
    slovakian tongue,
and I am the King of May, which is old Human poesy, and
    100,000 people chose my name.

Ginsberg goes on to cite his other qualifications, including an inclusive, ecumenical vision of religion, labeling himself a "Buddhist Jew/ who worships the Sacred Heart of Christ the blue body of Krishna the straight back of Ram/ the beads of Chango the Nigerian singing Shiva Shiva in a manner which I have invented." "Kral Majales" concludes with the almost breathless excitement of the poet arriving at "Albion's airfield" still vibrating with the excitement of the poem's composition.

Summary

Allen Ginsberg works in the tradition begun by Walt Whitman, in which the poet is not only a master of language and literature but also a singer whose voice carries the spirit of a nation's speech and thought. A self-proclaimed "poet as priest" whose congregation is his country's citizenry, Ginsberg has never lost sight of his initial vision of a cosmos where the full range of human possibility can be made manifest through the unrestricted explorations of the mind and body. In opposition to the evils of the modern age, Ginsberg has tried to create a kingdom of love leading toward a utopian universe that is alive in his poetry. Like Whitman, the "dear father graybeard" who guides him, he has never lost the courage to proclaim his heart's truth in his poetry.

Bibliography

Hyde, Lewis, ed. *On the Poetry of Allen Ginsberg*. Ann Arbor: University of Michigan Press, 1984.

Kramer, Jane. *Allen Ginsberg in America*. New York: Random House, 1969.

Merrill, Thomas F. *Allen Ginsberg*. New York: Twayne, 1969.

Miles, Barry. *Ginsberg: A Biography*. New York: Simon & Schuster, 1989.

Molesworth, Charles. *The Fierce Embrace*. Columbia: University of Missouri Press, 1979.

Morgan, Bill, and Bob Rosenthal, eds. *Best Minds: A Tribute to Allen Ginsberg*. New York: Lospecchio, 1986.

Mottram, Eric. *Allen Ginsberg in the Sixties*. Brighton, England: Unicorn Press, 1972.

Portuges, Paul. *The Visionary Poetics of Allen Ginsberg*. Santa Barbara, Calif.: Ross-Erikson, 1978.

Leon Lewis

NIKKI GIOVANNI

Born: Knoxville, Tennessee
June 7, 1943

Principal Literary Achievement

Nikki Giovanni is best known as the most enduring of the 1960's black revolutionary poets, but she has continued to grow in importance and esteem during subsequent years.

Biography

Nikki Giovanni was born Yolande Cornelia Giovanni, Jr., in Knoxville, Tennessee, on June 7, 1943, the younger of two daughters of Gus and Yolande Giovanni. As a child, Giovanni moved with her parents to the black middle-class suburbs of Cincinnati, Ohio, where her mother worked as a supervisor for the Welfare Department and her father worked as a social worker. Some of the most memorable days, however, were the summers she spent back in Knoxville with her maternal grandparents, John Brown and Louvenia Terrell Watson. Many of these experiences figure importantly in some of Giovanni's poems, most notably, "Knoxville, Tennessee" (1969).

As a young girl, Giovanni began to display certain traits that would characterize her and her poetry after she became an adult— brashness, assertiveness, and outspokenness among them. These traits can perhaps be seen most clearly in Giovanni's fierce determination to protect her older sister, Gary, whom she idolized. Furthermore, these traits may have been inherited from, or at least encouraged by, her grandmother, Louvenia Watson, herself assertive and outspoken, as one learns in Giovanni's autobiographical statement, *Gemini: An Extended Autobiographical Statement on My First Twenty-Five Years of Being a Black Poet* (1971). As Nikki Giovanni grew older, these traits merged into the one which brought her to the attention of both the literary world and the political establishment during the 1960's—militance.

Upon being graduated from high school in 1960, Giovanni entered Fisk University, a historically black college located in Nashville, Tennessee, but was dismissed from the school in February, 1961, because her poor attitude was not consistent with that expected of Fisk women. She returned to Fisk in 1964, where she excelled as a scholar, became active in student literary circles, and became involved in campus politics, soon establishing at Fisk a chapter of SNCC (Student Nonviolent Coordinating Committee), a prominent organization in the Civil Rights movement. This

was the first display of the revolutionary spirit for which she would become so well known in the next few years.

Also at Fisk, Nikki Giovanni became editor of *Élan*, the campus literary publication, and participated in the Fisk Writers Workshop. This workshop for younger writers was directed by John Oliver Killens, an important African-American novelist and critic. Through these activities, Giovanni began to develop her feelings and talents as a poet of intense sensitivity. Further, her interest in the various struggles of black people for social, political, cultural, and economic liberation became much more pronounced.

Giovanni was graduated from Fisk magna cum laude with a bachelor's degree in history during the winter commencement exercises held in early February, 1967. Following graduation she returned to Cincinnati, but within a few weeks received the news of her beloved grandmother's death in Knoxville. This event profoundly affected Giovanni, immediately making her ill, but also triggering a more far-reaching and longer-lasting anger that would characterize the majority of her early poetry. From her grandmother's death, Giovanni became more aware of the plight of powerless people in the United States. Her grandmother had been forced to move from her home at 400 Mulvaney Street when an urban renewal project relocated her neighborhood to make way for new commercial development. Although the new house had more amenities—a bigger backyard, the reader is told in *Gemini*—Louvenia Watson was never happy, because the house was not "home." She had simply had to leave behind too many memories, and she withered and died as a result of this displacement.

During the late spring and early summer of 1967, Giovanni became involved in organizing Cincinnati's black community and established the first Black Arts Festival in that city. Through this activity her black awareness became more keenly pronounced, and though she would have preferred to continue her activities in the black community, Giovanni's mother, supported by her father, delivered the ultimatum that she either go to work or go to graduate school. Neither alternative was attractive to Giovanni at the time, but she entered the School of Social Work at the University of Pennsylvania. Later she attended Columbia University in New York and began teaching at Queens College, also in New York. During this period, Giovanni received several grants, notably from the Ford Foundation and the National Foundation for the Arts.

In 1968, Giovanni published *Black Feeling, Black Talk*, her first book of poems. This was followed by *Black Judgement* (1968), which was combined with its predecessor into a single volume, *Black Feeling, Black Talk, Black Judgment* in 1970. These first poems are mostly characterized by Giovanni's black revolutionary ideas and spirit, and they quickly established her as one of the most able spokespersons of the Black Arts cultural movement. Another event that underscored Giovanni's new independence and her revolutionary stance was her decision to have a child, though yet unmarried, an unpopular choice even during the turbulent 1960's. Her son, Tommy, was born in Cincinnati on August 31, 1969, while Giovanni was visiting her parents during Labor Day vacation. Tommy soon became the center for most of the poet's artistic and spiritual concerns.

In 1970, Giovanni published her third book of poems, *Re: Creation*, which continued in the revolutionary vein, and followed in a rather rapid succession the combined volume of her first two works, her autobiographical statement, *Gemini*, and a book of poems for children, *Spin a Soft Black Song: Poems for Children*, both issued in 1971, and both dedicated to her son. Giovanni's national reputation and popularity were further established in 1971 when the record album *Truth Is on the Way* was released; it featured Giovanni reading her poems to the background of black gospel music, itself an up-and-coming art form, sung by the New York Community Choir under the direction of Benny Diggs. The album was a monumental success, and Nikki Giovanni began to be in great demand throughout the country, especially on college campuses. In addition, she was recognized in many national magazines, including *Ebony*, *Jet*, and *Mademoiselle*, and was awarded numerous distinctions, including the key to the city of Gary, Indiana. In April, 1972, she had an honorary doctorate degree conferred upon her by Wilberforce University in Ohio, the nation's oldest historically black college.

Also in 1972, the immensely popular book of poems, *My House: Poems*, appeared, and its enthusiastic reception further enhanced the poet's reputation. In 1973, Giovanni issued a new collection of poems for children, many previously published, under the title *Ego-Tripping and Other Poems for Young People*. This book increased Giovanni's popularity among younger readers and gained for her continued respect among other readers as well.

During 1973 and 1974, the transcriptions of two important exchanges between Nikki Giovanni and older established black writers were published. The first, a conversation with James Baldwin, the novelist and essayist, had actually taken place late in 1971. It was published in 1973 as *A Dialogue: James Baldwin and Nikki Giovanni* and was a spirited exchange of ideas between the two writers on a number of topics of interest to black people, including black male/female relationships, black literature and the black liberation movement, and religion and the black community. The second exchange was with the poet and novelist Margaret Walker, published in 1974 as *A Poetic Equation: Conversations Between Nikki Giovanni and Margaret Walker*, and it contained much more intense and heated discussions on the present and future states of black people in America and the role of black literature in the black liberation movement, among other topics. Giovanni emerged from these discussions as the clear spokesperson for new trends in black literature; she gained, in addition, much admiration and respect from an older generation of writers.

Giovanni continued her steady stream of publications of poetry collections with *The Women and the Men* (1975), followed by *Cotton Candy on a Rainy Day* (1978); more children's poems, *Vacation Time* (1980); *Those Who Ride the Night Winds* (1983); and a book of prose, *Sacred Cows and Other Edibles* (1988). With each successive book, Giovanni displays a new phase of writing that reflects an ever-developing poetic sensibility.

Giovanni is a perennial favorite on the college lecture circuit and delights in sharing her thoughts and insights with others, especially the young. In addition, she is in great demand as a teacher, having taught at a number of colleges and universities, including Rutgers University and Virginia Polytechnic Institute. She continues to write, speak, and publish regularly and is indeed one of the most popular poets of her generation.

Analysis

Nikki Giovanni's poetry is largely the chronicle of the development of a contemporary black poet, and each volume reflects her concerns and sensibilities at various phases of her development. The poems are always written in free verse and employ plain, simple, direct language with a strong rhythmic sense and an often playful, yet meaningful, manipulation of words. All of these are characteristics of the revolutionary black poetry of the 1960's and 1970's that sought to speak directly to the black community to motivate black people to become liberated.

Giovanni's first two books of poems, *Black Feeling, Black Talk*, and *Black Judgement*, both published in 1968 (and combined into a single volume in 1970), contain poems that speak primarily from a revolutionary stance. The poems, like their author, are young, angry, and assertive, and their very titles are often suggestive of their subject matter. "Black Separatism," "Black Power," "Of Liberation," "Revolutionary Music," and "Beautiful Black Man" are examples of some of the more revolutionary poems of Giovanni's early period. The two poems that show her at her most bitter point are "Poem (No Name No. 2)" and "The True Import of Present Dialogue, Black vs. Negro." These poems point to Giovanni's rejection of safe, comfortable middle-class values in favor of the revolutionary values associated with black liberation. These and other poems written in a similar vein brought Giovanni to the forefront of the Black Arts cultural revolution of the 1960's, and she became one of its most ardent and celebrated spokespersons.

While Nikki Giovanni's early poems tend to fall into the revolutionary category, from the beginning she has also been concerned with family, love, childhood, experiences, and friendship. Poems such as "Nikki-Rosa" and "Knoxville, Tennessee," speak of the importance of family but also insist on the importance of self-definition, another concern that is found often in Giovanni's work. This self-definition, or concern for the individual, having been announced in the early collections and developed more fully in *Gemini*, is at the center of the 1972 collection, *My House*, and figures importantly in each subsequent work—most notably in *Cotton Candy on a Rainy Day* and *Those Who Ride the Night Winds*.

In her prose works, particularly the autobiographical statement *Gemini* and a later volume of miscellaneous essays titled *Sacred Cows and Other Edibles*, Giovanni employs the characteristic crisp, direct, simple language and the often playful style and conversational tone that are found in her poems. In fact, her poems are often so prosaic and her prose so poetic that if one were to hear instead of read Giovanni, one would hardly be able to tell the difference in genre.

Whatever mode of expression Giovanni elects to use, the thing that is the most obvious is the artist's sincerity. Giovanni not only believes in her ideas, but she also is fiercely committed to her craft; moreover, she wants her readers to believe and be committed as well. Thus, reading Giovanni is often like reading a big sister or a best friend—you trust her judgment, you share her vision, and you appreciate her wisdom and concern.

THE TRUE IMPORT OF PRESENT DIALOGUE, BLACK VS. NEGRO

First published: 1968
Type of work: Poem

The speaker in the poem challenges black people to reject complacency for revolution.

"The True Import of Present Dialogue, Black vs. Negro" challenges black people to reject their middle-class complacency and adopt an angry revolutionary spirit in the quest for liberation of the black community. The title establishes the polarization of opposing attitudes among blacks during the Civil Rights movement of the 1960's— on the one hand, "Black," or those of a more revolutionary bent, and, on the other hand, "Negro," or those with a more bourgeois mentality. Here Giovanni insists that the revolutionary approach is the only one that will guarantee a meaningful future for black youth, who will be the beneficiaries of their efforts to liberate the black community from domination and possibly annihilation.

How does one adopt a revolutionary stance? By becoming angry enough to kill, according to Giovanni, but while the possibility exists for literally killing someone, what she really means is killing in the sense of rejecting values, habits, and actions that have kept blacks enslaved. These include certain religious practices, economic habits, and behavioral characteristics that black people must "kill" if they are to be free from continued oppression by the white majority.

The poem is effective in its badgering repetition of "Can You Kill"; similarly, the harsh, often revolting language underscores the urgency of the poet's message, which she states succinctly in the last two lines:

> Learn to kill niggers
> Learn to be Black men.

NIKKI-ROSA

First published: 1969
Type of Work: Poem

The poet reflects on what it means to grow up black.

"Nikki-Rosa," like many of Nikki Giovanni's poems, is full of the poet's own experiences. This poem talks about growing up black and the pleasures and pains inherent in the process. The poem was perhaps prompted by the tendency of white biographers of black people to point out only what seems to be wrong in black families and in black communities. The tone is reflective and critical but not bitter, although Giovanni very matter-of-factly observes that

> I really hope no white person ever has cause
> to write about me
> because they never understand.

Giovanni flatly rejects white interpretations of black life because they come from different frames of reference with different values and simply are incapable of truly assessing what it is to grow up as a black child in a black family in a black community. Giovanni concludes:

> Black love is Black wealth and they'll
> probably talk about my hard childhood
> and never understand that
> all the while I was quite happy.

Here Giovanni establishes her reverence for black folk culture. Furthermore, in addressing a number of realities for poor people, ranging from having no indoor toilets to bathing in galvanized tubs, alcoholism, and domestic violence, Giovanni asserts that "it isn't poverty that concerns you/ . . . but only that everybody is together." The theme of the communal nature of black communities as something to be celebrated and preserved resounds in much of Giovanni's work.

MY HOUSE

First published: 1972
Type of work: Poem

The poet stresses individuality and self expression.

"My House" is the title poem of Giovanni's 1972 book of poems and concludes the collection with a forthright statement of the poet's freedom to live by her own rules. Furthermore, she is willing and capable of accepting the responsibilities for her choices, as is clear when Giovanni asserts that "i run the kitchen/ and i can stand the heat."

On the surface, "My House" seems to be hodge-podge, a haphazard collection of comments on everything from love to individuality to the inadequacy of the English language to express emotions. A more careful reading, however, uncovers a more conscious blend of seeming incongruent parts, akin to the quilting motif used in the poem, into a bold statement of independence. This concern for individual worth and self-expression that characterize the poems in *My House* becomes even more pronounced in subsequent works. For example, in "My House," Giovanni adopts a stance shared by many later feminists, that of challenging the idea of the male as name-giver. This challenge is evident when the speaker asserts:

> i mean it's my house
> and i want to fry pork chops
> and bake sweet potatoes
> and call them yams.

Precisely put, since this is her house, she will accept no compromise; thus, she asserts the validity of a female name-giver, and, by extension, the validity of an Afrocentric perspective in American culture (varieties of what are commonly called "sweet potatoes" in American culture are known as "yams" in African cultures). Here again, Giovanni offers a revolutionary interpretation of black life in America. She underscores this interpretation emphatically as she vows to

> smile at old men and call
> it revolution cause what's real
> is really real.

"My House" is one of Giovanni's most popular poems and shows her at once at her most playful and most serious self.

I WROTE A GOOD OMELET

First published: 1983
Type of work: Poem

The speaker is delightfully confused after a wonderful experience with love.

"I Wrote a Good Omelet" also shows Nikki Giovanni at her playful best. The speaker has had a spectacularly jolting encounter with love and has everything confused. She tells the reader, "I goed on red . . . and stopped on green . . . after loving you." In short, things were never the same, but filled with ecstasy, passion, and delight.

Stylistically, "I Wrote a Good Omelet" is representative of the entire collection *Those Who Ride the Night Winds*. In this book, the poems are longer, more prosaic, and frequently punctuated with ellipses. Furthermore, they mark a continued growth in the poet, at once becoming more introspective and showing an even more pronounced spirit of the individual than previous poems.

GEMINI

First published: 1971
Type of work: Autobiography

Giovanni presents memories and observations of the first twenty-five years of her life.

Gemini, so titled because of the sign of the zodiac under which Nikki Giovanni was born, is subtitled *An Extended Autobiographical Statement on My First Twenty-Five Years of Being a Black Poet*. As such *Gemini* is not a strictly chronological autobiography in the usual sense; rather, it is a collection of carefully selected and arranged recollections and observations that helped her develop into the black revolutionary poet that she was at the time of its writing. Published when Giovanni was twenty-eight, most of the pieces had indeed been written several years earlier, when she reflected on having turned twenty-five.

The book is divided into thirteen sections and covers everything from a history of her grandparents, John Brown and Louvenia Watson, to an appreciation of actress, singer, and black icon, Lena Horne, to an appraisal of the early black novelist and short story writer Charles Waddell Chesnutt, to a review of a book on black music by black writer Phyll Garland that Giovanni finds severely limited. Through these comments and especially in the last section, "Gemini—A Prolonged Autobiographical Statement on Why," Giovanni grapples with various aspects of her thoughts and feelings in an attempt to explain and justify her stance as a revolutionary. She is, however, never apologetic; rather, she speaks her mind very matter-of-factly in the characteristic Giovanni manner.

One important revelation in *Gemini* is her commitment to preserving family history. This is established in the first section of the book, "400 Mulvaney Street," a short account of her maternal grandparents with a special emphasis on the grandmother, Louvenia Terrell Watson, herself something of a revolutionary, who influenced Giovanni tremendously. Giovanni intimates later in *Gemini* that her grandparents migrated to Knoxville, Tennessee, from Georgia to escape the consequences of her grandmother's outspokenness, but as she reflects on how Mrs. Watson lived and died, Giovanni resolves that "Tommy, my son, must know about this. He must know we come from somewhere. That we belong."

Another section of *Gemini* that is especially important is "Don't Have a Baby till You Read This," about Giovanni's decision to have a child without being married and the accompanying responsibilities and adjustments. Family had always been important to Giovanni, and while she concluded that marriage was an unattractive prospect, she did want to experience motherhood—thus the decision to have a child, born Thomas Watson Giovanni in 1969. The numerous adjustments the entire family must make are often comic, but more important, Tommy becomes the absolute central focus of Giovanni's life and occupies an important station in the larger family as well. Giovanni's devotion to her son is indeed admirable.

Gemini alternates between superficial observation and whimsical comment on the one hand to deep philosophical analysis on the other. Like her poems, though, *Gemini* contains the same unquestionable sincerity, the same clarity of vision, and the same precision of statement. Most important, *Gemini* goes a long way toward explaining the revolutionary psyche and simplifying many of the artistic complexities of one of the finest poets of the contemporary world.

Summary

Nikki Giovanni has been aptly called a child of the 1960's and a woman of the 1970's; however, the most frequent title bestowed upon her is the Princess of Black Poetry. From articulating concerns of the black liberation movement to championing the individual, Giovanni has emerged as a keen interpreter of contemporary times.

Bibliography

Bell, Bernard W. "New Black Poetry: A Double-Edged Sword." *College Language Association Journal* 15 (September, 1971): 37-43.

Davis, Arthur P. "The New Poetry of Black Hate." In *Modern Black Poets: A Collection of Critical Essays*, edited by Donald B. Gibson. Englewood Cliffs, N.J.: Prentice-Hall, 1973.

Palmer, R. Roderick. "The Poetry of Three Revolutionists: Don L. Lee, Sonia Sanchez, and Nikki Giovanni." *College Language Association Journal* 15 (September, 1971): 25-36.

Rosenthal, Lois. "Writing as Breathing: Nikki Giovanni." *Writers Digest*, February, 1989, 30-34.

Stokes, Stephanie. " 'My House': Nikki Giovanni." *Essence* 12 (August, 1981): 84-88.

Thompson, Cordell. "Nikki Giovanni: Black Rebel with Power in Poetry." *Jet*, May 25, 1972, 18-24.

Warren J. Carson

ELLEN GLASGOW

Born: Richmond, Virginia
April 22, 1873
Died: Richmond, Virginia
November 21, 1945

Principal Literary Achievement

With her ironic juxtaposition of moral idealism and unflinching realism, Ellen Glasgow is considered the founder of the modern Southern literary tradition.

Biography

Ellen Glasgow was born in Richmond, Virginia, on April 22, 1873, to Anne Jane Glasgow and Francis Thomas Glasgow, manager of Tredegar Iron Works. Ellen was the eighth of ten children. During her childhood, she was particularly sensitive to the nervousness and depression from which her gentle, aristocratic mother suffered, undoubtedly the result of Anne Glasgow's almost incessant childbearing. This experience was to motivate Ellen's later work for women's rights and was clearly reflected in her fiction.

Ironically, in temperament, Glasgow was more like her father than her mother. Even though she rejected her Calvinistic faith, she retained a strong ethical sense, which is evident throughout her works. Furthermore, her own fierce independence of thought and rebelliousness of spirit were the very qualities which had motivated her Presbyterian ancestors in their defiance of monarchs.

In lieu of the usual formal instruction, Glasgow was educated by relatives and, perhaps even more important, was allowed to choose books at will from her father's extensive library. When she was still a child, she began to write. Although later she accused her family of lacking sympathy for her ambitions, Glasgow was probably exaggerating their unkindness. Always delicate, always aware of her mother's unhappiness, Glasgow seemed destined to develop a sense of alienation. Even while she was flirting and dancing at the innumerable balls to which a young lady of a good Richmond family would be invited, she was becoming more and more convinced that her real interests were creative and intellectual.

Guided by George Walter McCormack, the husband of her sister Cary Glasgow McCormack, she read the works of philosophers, economists, playwrights, and novelists. She also continued to write. When she was eighteen, she took a novel that she had written to a New York agent, but when he made advances to her, she was so

angry that she destroyed the manuscript. When Glasgow was twenty, she was so shattered by her mother's sudden death from typhoid fever that she destroyed the manuscript of another novel. Fortunately, after two years had passed, she reconsidered and reconstructed the work. This novel, her first full-length work to be published, *The Descendant*, appeared anonymously in 1897. With its illegitimate, politically radical hero and its independent, art-student heroine, both Southerners in New York, *The Descendant* was a marked departure from the sentimental, nostalgic novels which had come to be expected from Southern writers. The book was well received and sold well. It was followed in 1898 by *Phases of an Inferior Planet*, which took another Southern girl, in this case a singer, to New York and explored her doomed relationship with another intelligent, alienated hero. Partly because of inherent flaws, partly because of her publisher's failure to advertise it, *Phases of an Inferior Planet* was unsuccessful.

For the setting of her third book, Glasgow wisely turned back to her native Virginia. *The Voice of the People* (1900) is significant because it is the first of a series of novels that analyze Virginia society rather than simply voicing Glasgow's anger with the social and religious expectations that threatened her freedom. In later works, Glasgow viewed her society from various angles. In *The Battle-Ground* (1902), she turned back to the Civil War period for her story, and in *The Deliverance* (1904), she wrote about the Reconstruction era. In neither book was there any regret for what she saw as a social structure which had been based on repression and had condemned its women to frustration and despair.

Despite problems with her hearing, which was to culminate in total deafness by the time she was forty, Glasgow later called the period between 1899 and 1905 the happiest of her life. Her works were best-sellers, as well as winning praise from critics; she was being compared with such literary giants as American writers Hamlin Garland, Stephen Crane, and Theodore Dreiser. Furthermore, she was involved in the great love affair of her life. Although the man was married, Glasgow and he met for romantic intervals, such as the summertime rendezvous in the Swiss Alps which she described so rhapsodically in her autobiography. When the relationship ended in 1905, she was shattered. The books that followed, *The Wheel of Life* (1906), *The Ancient Law* (1908), and *The Romance of a Plain Man* (1909), lack the energy of Glasgow's later works. Even her three-year engagement to the Episcopal minister Frank Ilsley Paradise, which was broken in 1909, did not assuage her grief over the loss of her illicit lover.

There were other losses during this period. In 1909, Glasgow's brother Frank committed suicide. Within a year, her beloved sister Cary developed cancer; her death was slow and agonizing. After the end had come, Glasgow fled from Richmond to New York, where she lived for five years. The novels published during that period, *The Miller of Old Church* (1911) and *Virginia* (1913), indicate that Glasgow had regained her old creative energy.

After her father's death in 1916, Glasgow moved back to the family home in Richmond, where she spent the rest of her life. On the surface, her situation seemed ideal. With the money she had inherited, she could live well and travel whenever she liked; she was not dependent on the success of her literary works. She was entrenched in Richmond society, and, perhaps more important to her, she had made numerous friends in the literary world. In 1918, however, Glasgow attempted to commit suicide. She was evidently distraught by the involvement of her fiancé, the prominent Richmond lawyer Henry Watkins Anderson, with Queen Marie of Rumania. This episode, along with Glasgow's general depression about the war and its aftermath, resulted in a period of unimpressive literary output.

With *Barren Ground* (1925), it was evident that Glasgow had recovered. During the decade which followed, most of her best novels were published—*The Romantic Comedians* (1926), *They Stooped to Folly* (1929), *The Sheltered Life* (1932), and *Vein of Iron* (1935). During this period, she won many honors; however, perhaps her most significant achievement, other than her novels, was her leadership in the first Southern Writers Conference, held in 1931 at the University of Virginia, over which she presided.

At the end of the decade, Ellen Glasgow's health declined, and once again her works reflected the diminution of creative energy. Even though it won a Pulitzer Prize, *In This Our Life* (1941) is less impressive than Glasgow's earlier works. On November 21, 1945, Glasgow died. She left in manuscript an autobiography, later published as *The Woman Within* (1954), which, though it appears to have many factual errors, provides important insights into the psychological makeup of an important Southern realist.

Analysis

Throughout her life, Ellen Glasgow considered herself to be a searcher for truth, and it was this quest that motivated her writing. As she frequently pointed out, her novels began with ideas. Over a long gestation period, those ideas became embodied in character and scene and finally coalesced into a plot. Then the actual writing process would begin, and during that process, the world Glasgow was creating became more real to her than the actual world in which she lived. When the book was finished, she felt a sense of deprivation, almost a death; the only remedy was to begin another novel.

This summary of her creative process makes it clear that to Glasgow, fiction was indeed an imitation of reality; however, she was not interested in presenting a mere slice of life. Her works always had an intellectual basis. That fact accounts for the artistic failure of early works such as *Phases of an Inferior Planet*, in which characters do not achieve a real existence but merely illustrate ideas. For example, the heroine of that novel, Mariana Musin, is the daughter of a Presbyterian father and a Catholic mother, whose religious differences eventually destroy their love for each other. After she goes to New York to become an opera singer, Mariana meets, marries, and parts from a teacher, Anthony Algarcife, who later goes into the priesthood and becomes the most famous preacher in New York. Algarcife is noted for his brilliant essays in rebuttal to a series of anti-religious articles, which he himself is actually writing. Despite the novel's portrayal of romantic love, grinding poverty, the death of a baby, and final reunion, the characters never become real enough to inspire sympathy; they are pasteboard symbols of alienation, illustrating the evils of institutional religion.

By the time she wrote her third novel, *The Voice of the People*, Glasgow had learned to let her characters come alive and to suggest her ideas through those characters. From her own life, Glasgow could draw on very real conflicts, but she no longer protested shrilly; she was able to examine the ironies which were so evident in her culture. One of Glasgow's major themes is her view of Southern history as a conflict between two traditions, that of the pleasure-loving cavalier and that of the rigidly righteous but strong Calvinist. In *The Voice of the People* and in *The Deliverance*, she shows how people of her mother's aristocratic stock live upon lies, embracing an illusory past. In *Vein of Iron*, on the other hand, the heroine discovers that neither the past, nor even love, can get one through life—only strength of character can. In the South, Glasgow stresses, that came not from the cavaliers, who are far more appealing, but from the rigid and dour Scots-Irish Calvinists.

Another theme which pervades Glasgow's work is the conflict between the Old South and the New South. In her Civil War novel, *The Battle-Ground*, Glasgow described the dying society, as well as the war which doomed it, realistically, not sentimentally. At the end of the book, the survivors seem to be relieved that they no longer are burdened by the past. The same conflict is treated comically in *The Romantic Comedians*, which follows the male protagonist, a gentleman of the old school, from shock to shock as he moves forward in time into a world that he does not understand.

A third major theme of Glasgow involves the conflict between the expectations for women, as the objects of male chivalry, and their need for independence. In her first two novels, women rebel by leaving the South for New York, where they pursue careers and live bohemian lives. In later books, however, women fight their battles on the South, on home territory. In *The Battle-Ground*, Betty Ambler has learned her own worth through hardship. When the man she loves returns from war, it is clear that he will never be able to imprison her again by referring to the code of chivalry.

Although Glasgow's themes change little from work to work, her tone varies greatly from novel to novel. It is amazing, for example, that a work as grim as *Barren Ground* should have been followed by two comedies of manners, *The Romantic Comedians* and *They Stooped to Folly*, and then by a work that is only somewhat more serious, *The Sheltered Life*, which was followed by the near-tragedy of *Vein of Iron*. Immediately before she wrote *Barren Ground*, the founder of Southern realism had even participated in the writing of a romance, but since her collaborator was Henry Anderson, her fiancé, that lapse may be understandable.

Throughout all of her work, whatever the tone, Glasgow is a careful plotter and scene builder, as well as an expert in revealing character through the spoken and the unspoken word. Her skill is illustrated in the initial scene of *The Romantic Comedians*, which takes place at a grave on Easter Sunday. At the beginning of the scene, the widower, Judge Gamaliel Bland Honeywell, is moaning a sentimental formula for his grief, while vainly attempting to remember his wife's face. At the end of the scene, he leaves the cemetery, almost simultaneously musing about his dislike of old women and contemplating the virtues of the old social system, which women of his generation support. It is spring. At the end of the book, after the judge has very nearly died as a result of his disastrous marriage to a young girl, Glasgow repeats the elements of that first scene—the judge's conservatism, his antipathy to old women of his own age, his consciousness of spring, and finally, his response to a young woman. Even though Glasgow stressed the intellectual content of her works, this level of writing illustrates the fact that she had worked hard to become a superb craftsman. From her third novel on, her readers expected artistry from Glasgow as well as challenging ideas.

BARREN GROUND

First published: 1925
Type of work: Novel

For thirty years, Dorinda Oakley vainly seeks happiness through human love but finally discovers contentment in her relationship with the land.

Barren Ground, Ellen Glasgow's favorite among her novels and the most auto-biographical of them, is the story of Dorinda Oakley, a woman who spends her life in the pursuit of happiness, only to discover that happiness comes through the rejection of human relationships. The book was written after Glasgow's suicide attempt; it is significant that she sent her unfaithful fiancé a copy of the book, which concludes with Dorinda's statement that she is happy to be finished with love.

Barren Ground is set in the Shenandoah Valley of Virginia, where there are few aristocrats, and the chief distinction among men is their stewardship of their farms. James Ellgood, for example, is a fine stock farmer, and his family prospers accordingly. On the other hand, a doctor in the neighborhood has let his large farm go to ruin because he spends his time drinking instead of taking care of it. The case of Dorinda's father is somewhat different: Although he is a hard worker, he is a poor white, reared in poverty and ignorance, fearful of change, and therefore unable and unwilling to improve his land. His children seem doomed to live as he lived—in misery and frustration. Seeing him as he is, Dorinda's mother hates the man she married for love (marrying below herself), and she hopes that she can persuade Dorinda not to make the same mistake.

Unfortunately, Dorinda is aware that she will never again be so young and pretty as she is at twenty, and despite her mother's warnings, she believes that she must use her power to win a husband. The young man she chooses to charm is the doctor's son, who, beneath his sophisticated exterior, is actually as weak as his father. After proposing to Dorinda, he leaves town; when he returns, he has been persuaded to marry someone else. The betrayal devastates Dorinda. She turns against the God who was her mother's consolation, and she turns against men. From that time on, she is barren ground, incapable of response. Although in her preface, Glasgow praises Dorinda as a character who has learned to live without hope or joy—merely to endure life—the reader is likely to find Dorinda's denial of love and even of sex a tragic denial of life.

Ironically, after she has lost the capacity to love, Dorinda is courted by several men who, unlike her first love, are strong, unselfish, and responsible. The first of them is a young doctor, whom she meets in New York, where she has been living and working after her flight from home. He senses her frigidity, but he hopes eventually to win her love. It is clear that Dorinda must fight to deny her emotional self; when she attends a concert, she is intensely moved. If there is a chance for love, however, it is thwarted by fate. Dorinda is called home because her father has had a stroke and her mother needs her help.

Actually, Dorinda is not unwilling to return home. During her stay in New York, she has been reading books on agriculture, and she has an idea that the farm could be made profitable. More than that, Dorinda muses, she can dare to give her heart to the farm; because it is not human, it will not betray her.

After both of her parents have died, worn out from poverty and hard work, she agrees to marry the storekeeper Nathan Pedlar, an intelligent, resourceful man who has always been devoted to her. Dorinda has only one condition: that it will be a marriage in name only. Nathan and Dorinda are happy together; in a sense, Nathan does eventually win Dorinda, but he must die to do it. In a train wreck, he saves the lives of many passengers, but sacrifices his own. Now a hero, now no physical threat, he is given what love Dorinda has to give. Her first love was an illusion; her last love is a mythical figure.

In an attempt at a happy ending, Glasgow gives Dorinda a peculiar revenge. When her former lover, the doctor's son, now ruined and destitute, is about to be sent to the poor house, Dorinda chooses to take him in and to see that he is cared for until his death. The fact that, although she is kind, her former lover must realize that she is completely indifferent to him gives her great pleasure.

In her conclusion, Glasgow has Dorinda realize that a woman can be happy without love as long as she has a spirit of adventure. Presumably that is the spirit that enabled Dorinda to try new ideas on the farm. It is clear to the reader, however, that in reality Dorinda's contentment derives simply from the knowledge of her own strength. This revelation, which comes to Dorinda at the age of fifty, is exactly the bleak conclusion that Glasgow herself had reached in her forties, when she began to write the novel.

THE ROMANTIC COMEDIANS

First published: 1926
Type of work: Novel

A widower in his sixties spurns the woman who has spent her life waiting for him in order to marry a twenty-three-year-old girl, with disastrous results.

The Romantic Comedians was the first of Ellen Glasgow's comic novels—written, she said later, to amuse herself. The pleasure she had in writing it was shared by her readers; *The Romantic Comedians* was one of her best-selling novels.

Like *Barren Ground*, *The Romantic Comedians* deals with the conflict between men and women in a society that defines their roles and their relationships. While *Barren Ground* was tragic in tone, however, *The Romantic Comedians* is comic. The protagonist of *Barren Ground* was a woman who could find contentment in life only by denying her natural feelings; the central character in *The Romantic Comedians* is a man who, despite the disastrous results of his marriage to a young woman, at the end of the book is still pursuing happiness and the opposite sex. Interestingly, although the tone of the earlier novel is tragic, Glasgow obviously considers the ending a happy one, while in the second novel, although the tone is comic, it is suggested at the end of the book that the next young woman with whom the protagonist becomes involved will probably be the death of him.

In *The Romantic Comedians*, as in all Glasgow's other fiction, the conflict between the sexes is an integral part of the conflict between an old world, which is dying, and a new world, which is coming into being. Despite his pride in what he considers enlightened views, the protagonist of the novel, sixty-five-year-old Judge Gamaliel Bland Honeywell, lives by the standards of the Old South and is appalled at the moral decay that he sees all around him. In his world, women of good family adhered to rigid rules and were rewarded for good conduct with the respect and protection of the men in their class. As an example of proper conduct, the judge need look no further than the memory of his late wife, Cordelia Honeywell. After her death, Queenborough society expects the judge to marry another exemplary lady, Amanda Lightfoot, who had been his fiancée until a foolish quarrel severed the engagement; she has remained unmarried, cherishing her love for him and spending her time in good works during the thirty-six years of his marriage to Cordelia.

If Cordelia and Amanda represent the ideal of the Old South, the impoverished widow Bella Upchurch represents the reality. Unlike Amanda, who never had to worry about money, Bella does not intend to suffer for love; instead, she will use the weakness of men to get the money she desperately desires. She decides to play her highest card and expose the judge to the charms of her twenty-three-year-old daughter, Annabel Upchurch, who is inexperienced enough to think that there is no more to marriage than pretty clothes and compliments, and who is devoted enough to be generous to her mother, who will then not have to be burdened with another husband.

There is yet another major woman character in Glasgow's comedy—Edmonia Bredalbane, the judge's twin sister. While Bella and Annabel play the part of the helpless Southern lady, Edmonia flaunts her freedom. As she comments to her brother, while he spent his life doing his duty and living up to the ideal of the Old South, she devoted hers to pleasure. Edmonia has caused scandal on two continents, used up four husbands, and acquired considerable wealth. Back in Queenborough (Glasgow's fictional name for Richmond), Edmonia is completely open about her past; it is clear that it is age, not morality, which has prevented her from continuing her hedonistic life.

The judge will not listen to the advice of Edmonia, who is fond of him and concerned about his vulnerability. As a realist, she understands that her brother is too old to change his way of thinking, to abandon the chivalric code by which he has lived. Therefore, Edmonia urges her brother to marry someone who will share his standards and make him comfortable in his declining years. The still-attractive Amanda is the obvious choice. When Edmonia sees the judge's infatuation with Annabel, she foresees disaster, and she begs him to break off the relationship; however, the judge insists on marrying youth, in the person of Annabel.

The central portion of the book proves that Edmonia was right. At first, all is harmonious. Then Annabel becomes bored with mere possessions. There are quarrels about their life-style. The judge has limited energy, while Annabel's is limitless. When she gives in to him, she is bored and petulant; when he gives in to her, he is crotchety and becomes ill. Eventually, Annabel becomes involved with a man of her own age and leaves the judge. At the end of the book, he considers taking the sensible course of action and returning to Amanda. In the final pages, however, the sap is rising again, and the judge is eyeing his young nurse. The female protagonist in *Barren Ground* became wiser as she became older, but the male protagonist of *The Romantic Comedians* never does achieve self-knowledge or an understanding of the real world in which he lives.

VEIN OF IRON

First published: 1935
Type of work: Novel

Surmounting disappointments and hardships, a strong woman perseveres to find happiness.

Vein of Iron stresses one of Glasgow's dominant themes: that only the strong can make it through the hardships of life. As in many other Glasgow novels, including *Barren Ground*, the most obvious of these hardships is the lack of money. Ada Fincastle, the protagonist of *Vein of Iron*, has been aware of her family's financial situation from her earliest years. Her father, however, unlike Dorinda's father, is an educated man; indeed, his intellectual gifts have been his downfall. A Presbyterian minister, he had published a brilliant but unconventional book; as a result, he lost his church and his profession, and he had to move back to his Appalachian home, where he lives with his mother, attempting to support the household on what he can make as a schoolmaster. Ada's childhood is summed up by her disappointment when her father brings her a cheap doll for Christmas instead of the one with real hair on which she had set her heart. Her character is summed up by the comment made at that time—that the child has a single heart. Although that singleness of affection means that Ada will never be happy with the wrong doll, in later life it enables her to cling to her love for Ralph McBride until together they find happiness.

The love story of Ada Fincastle and Ralph McBride begins in their childhood, when they are schoolfellows. By the time Ada is twenty, she knows that she is in love with Ralph, who is then a young law student. After a quarrel, however, Ralph gets involved with another girl; when he is found in a compromising situation, he is forced by her parents to marry her. Years pass; Ralph goes into military service during World War I; when he returns home on leave, separated from his wife but not yet divorced, he and Ada spend some idyllic days together in a mountain cabin before Ralph returns to his unit.

When Ada becomes pregnant, the good Christians of her community treat her like an outcast. Eventually, Ada, her father, her aunt, and her little son move to Queenborough, where Ada can find a job in a store while her father again turns to teaching. Although this is a very difficult period for Ada, she endures. When Ralph at last finds her and the son he did not know he had, it seems that her trials are over.

Yet the pattern repeats itself. Once again, Ralph gets involved with a woman; this time, he is injured in an accident. Ten years of savings go for his medical care. Then, just as the family is getting back on its feet, the Depression bursts upon them. The plight of the McBrides, who have always worked hard and saved what they could, only to lose their jobs and their savings, is repeated over and over. Ironically, Ralph and Ada show a strength in adversity that is lacking in her once-wealthy kinfolk, who once snubbed her and now must accept her generosity.

At the end of the novel, Ralph and Ada move back to their old Appalachian home. Even though they will probably always be poor and even though the first glow of love is gone, they realize that they have found happiness in their love for each other. The comparison with *Barren Ground* is obvious. In *Vein of Iron*, the protagonist's first love is basically a man of character (although he has his weaknesses) who never ceases loving her. In turn, she retains her capacity to love and, though it brings her heartaches, in the end that openness gives her contentment. Although much in the two plots is similar—the disappointment in love, the illicit sexual relationships resulting in pregnancy, the unstable and unhappy family situations, and the haunting poverty—the heroines, though both strong, react in very different ways to life's hardships. Where Dorinda denies her emotional being, Ada draws strength from it. Not only her ancestry, but also her own willingness to love gives her the iron to endure.

Summary

Whether she is writing serious works or comic, satirical novels, Ellen Glasgow's primary goal is to show life as it is. Like the Southern realists who followed her, Glasgow invents plots full of missed chances and chance decisions that lead to alienation and tragedy. Her characters often destroy themselves by deluding themselves; by the time they attain self-knowledge, it is often too late to salvage their lives. Furthermore, Glasgow presents the societies in which her characters live as repressive and hypocritical, particularly in their treatment of women, whom they pretend to revere but actually enslave.

Bibliography

Glasgow, Ellen. *The Woman Within*. New York: Harcourt Brace, 1954.

Godbold, E. Stanly, Jr. *Ellen Glasgow and the Woman Within*. Baton Rouge: Louisiana State University Press, 1972.

Holman, C. Hugh. "Ellen Glasgow and the Southern Literary Tradition." In *Southern Writers: Appraisals in Our Time*, edited by R. C. Simonini, Jr. Charlottesville: University Press of Virginia, 1964.

_____. *The Roots of Southern Writing: Essays on the Literature of the American South*. Athens: University of Georgia Press, 1972.

McDonald, Edgar E. "The Ambivalent Heart: Literary Revival in Richmond." In *The History of Southern Literature*, edited by Louis D. Rubin, Jr., et al. Baton Rouge: Louisiana State University Press, 1985.

McDowell, Frederick P. W. *Ellen Glasgow and the Ironic Art of Fiction*. Madison: University of Wisconsin Press, 1963.

Rosemary M. Canfield Reisman

MARY GORDON

Born: Far Rockaway, New York
December 8, 1949

Principal Literary Achievement
Gordon is a brilliant stylist whose fiction explores human love and its limitations and the familial, religious, and cultural legacies impinging upon modern American individuals and communities.

Biography

Mary Catherine Gordon was born in Far Rockaway, New York on December 8, 1949. Her mother, Anna Gagliano Gordon, was a devout Catholic and the daughter of Italian and Irish immigrants. David Gordon, her father, was born in Ohio and converted from Judaism to the Catholic Church in the 1930's.

As a young child, Mary Gordon was cared for by her father, who stayed at home with her while her mother, an admirable and courageous woman, worked, despite the crippling effects of childhood polio, to support the family as a legal secretary. David Gordon, a lively and literate man, educated at Harvard University, enthusiastically fostered his daughter's intellectual development. He died when she was seven, but he had already begun to teach her French, Greek, and philosophy. She was also influenced by his intense devotion to Catholicism.

After her father's death, Mary Gordon attended Holy Name of Mary School in her predominantly Catholic working-class neighborhood in Valley Stream, Long Island. She had literary aspirations quite early and dreamt while in grade school of becoming both a poet and a nun. As a teenager, she rebelled against the church but continued her literary efforts while she attended Mary Louis Academy, a Catholic girls' school in Queens. In 1967, Gordon won a scholarship to Barnard College of Columbia University, which she was eager to attend in order to escape her sheltered Catholic community. She has stated that her experiences at Barnard, especially in the novelist Elizabeth Hardwick's creative writing course, changed her life. Hardwick advised Gordon, who at the time was writing nothing but poetry, to switch to prose. She did so after being graduated from Barnard in 1971 and enrolling in the writing program at Syracuse University, where she received her M.A. in 1973. While continuing at Syracuse in the English Ph.D program, she met James Brain, a British anthropologist whom she married in 1974.

Between 1975 and 1988, Gordon published some sixty-five short stories, reviews,

and other articles. Twenty of her short stories were reprinted in the volume *Temporary Shelter* (1987). Many of those stories address themes that recur in her novels— human love and loss, parent-child relationships, and the Irish immigrant experience in the United States.

Gordon began writing her first novel, *Final Payments*, in 1975 while she was an instructor of freshman composition at Dutchess Community College in Poughkeepsie, New York, from 1974 to 1978. She rewrote the novel a number of times, and it was rejected by several publishers. Finally Elizabeth Hardwick suggested that she change the narration from third person to first person. After she did so, Random House published the novel in the spring of 1978. Like her subsequent novels, *Final Payments* was a critical and popular success.

Gordon's first marriage ended in divorce; in 1979, she married Arthur Cash, an English professor, and moved to New Paltz, New York. She began teaching at Amherst College in Massachusetts. At the same time, she was writing her second novel, *The Company of Women*, published in 1980. *Men and Angels*, her third novel, appeared in 1985, and *The Other Side*, her fourth, in 1989. She began teaching courses at Barnard College in 1988. Mary Gordon has two children, Anna Gordon and David Dess Gordon. Her other interests include musical theater.

Mary Gordon has acknowledged a number of influences on her work. Among the earliest were the language of religious devotions, the language and structure of the Roman Catholic Mass, which she attended daily, the small world of Roman Catholicism in which she grew up, and stories of saints' lives—which afforded vivid images of heroic women not dependent upon men for their identities. She has cited James Joyce's *Dubliners* (1914), the novels of Virginia Woolf, Margaret Drabble, and J. F. Powers, and Simone Weil's *Waiting for God* (1951) as influential upon her fiction. Among Catholic writers she especially admires Georges Bernanos, the author of *Journal d'un cure de campagne* (1936; Diary of a Country Priest, 1937), which she considers the greatest of religious novels. Her favorite twentieth century novelist is Virginia Woolf, and among writers of the past she admires Jane Austen above all.

Analysis

To categorize Mary Gordon as simply an American Irish-Catholic novelist is too narrow. She is, as well, a feminist, a lyrical realist, an astute diagnostician of human relationships, and a brilliant prose stylist. Yet her ethnic and religious heritage figures prominently in her fiction as both source and subject.

Just as Gordon addresses her own background in much of her fiction, so all of her major characters try to come to terms with their pasts. Concern with one's past, especially one's childhood, has been a salient feature of Western literature and society at least since the late eighteenth century. In the twentieth century, this concern has been closely connected with the predominant schools of modern psychology, particularly the Freudian. Mary Gordon is rare among late twentieth century novelists in that she does not embed her explorations of human life in psychological theory at the expense of its spiritual and theological dimensions. Indeed, scripture, rather than psychological theory, is frequently Gordon's reference point.

Gordon does not equate art, including the art of fiction, with religion or even with morality. She has written:

> An experience to be properly religious must include three things: an ethical component, the possibility of full participation by the entire human community and acknowledgment of the existence of a life beyond the human. Art need do none of these things, although it may.

These three dimensions of religious experience emerge as implicit or explicit concerns in all of Gordon's novels.

The strongest ethical component in Gordon's novels is their close examination of human love. She has commented that "love is the source of any moral vision that's worth anything." She effectively dramatizes the dynamics of love between friends and between parents and children as well as the challenges posed by those people who are apparently unlovable. She has been criticized for delineating romantic and marital relationships sketchily in the first three novels, but the marriage of Ellen and Vincent MacNamara in *The Other Side* is presented vividly and in depth.

Gordon's depiction of communities is a natural extension of her treatments of individual relationships. *The Company of Women* and *The Other Side* are especially remarkable as detailed and realistic examinations of the ways in which communities succeed or fail and of their influence upon children. Gordon pays particular attention to figures who attempt to dominate their communities—Father Cyprian and Robert Cavendish in *The Company of Women*, for example, and Ellen MacNamara in *The Other Side*. The religious ideal of "full participation by the entire human community" remains largely unrealized in Gordon's novels, since their characters typically endeavor to protect their identities by excluding others. This ideal of full participation is always implicit, however, and is frequently dreamed of by Gordon's characters.

Most of Gordon's major characters acknowledge the existence or at least ponder seriously the possibility of a life beyond the human. Those characters reared as traditional Catholics struggle with questions that are closely related to faith in a supreme being. How best can one know God? Who or what is authoritative, in a world where the authority of the Church is weakened or absent? Part of Gordon's project as a novelist is, it seems, to dramatize individuals in the context of their subjectivity. Consequently, one narrative convention that she consistently avoids is that of the omniscient narrator who speaks in a morally normative voice. Instead, she has the reader listen to her characters' first-person voices or to their interior monologues as they strive to see life steadily and wholly, while limited in their vision by ideological, psychological, or circumstantial blinders.

Gordon's prose style, in its solidity of physical detail, its abundance of metaphors and similes, militates constantly against what she has called the "twin dangers of the religious life," dualism and abstractionism. One thinks, for example, of the wealth of detail about Catholic schooling in the first two novels and about Vincent MacNamara's work on the New York subways in *The Other Side*. Gordon's most engaging characters tend to be witty—revealing a lively appreciation of life in the physical human world. In *Final Payments*, for example, Liz assesses Isabel Moore's disastrous hairstyle thus: "Who did your hair? Annette Funicello?" Isabel reflects, "It was a miracle to me, the solidity of that joke. Even the cutting edge of it was a miracle. And our laughter was solid. It stirred the air and hung above us like rings of bone that shivered in the cold, gradual morning." In her fiction, Gordon strives to find images to render "the highest possible justice to the visible world." She is eager, she says,

> to get the right rhythm for the inner life, and the combination of image and rhythm to pin down an internal state is terribly important to me. At least as important as any sort of moral report of the world.

FINAL PAYMENTS

First published: 1978
Type of work: Novel

A young woman comes to terms with her past after the death of her father, an invalid whom she nursed for eleven years.

Final Payments begins and ends with its central character and narrator, Isabel Moore, contemplating the death of her father. For eleven years before his death, she cared for him in his illness. Now, at age thirty, she is determined to invent a life for herself. Before she can embrace life fully, however, Isabel must learn to acknowledge and accept the risks it poses and must come to terms with the legacy she has inherited.

This legacy is cultural, philosophical, emotional, and material. Isabel was reared in a conservative Irish-Catholic neighborhood in Queens, New York. Motherless from age two, she spent her childhood intensely influenced by her father, Joe Moore, a brilliant and opinionated professor vehement in his traditional Catholicism, and by Margaret Casey, their unattractive, life-denying housekeeper, whose jealous devotion to Isabel's father was as strong as her dislike and disapproval of Isabel, who came to return these feelings. Isabel's intelligence, wit, elegance, and even her disdain for housework were cultivated in calculated opposition to Margaret's ways.

Behind Joe Moore's authority stood the authority of the Church and its educational system, from which Isabel inherited her intellectual legacy. Entailed in this legacy are a respect for authority and a valuing of love as synonymous with life. Isabel learned to love her father in part because he was so certain he was right, but such authority breeds rebellion and courts betrayal. At nineteen, Isabel betrayed her father by having an affair with David Lowe, his favorite student. Three weeks after finding the couple in bed together, Joe Moore suffered a stroke, and for the next eleven years Isabel lived a life of expiation, nursing him and keeping house.

Isabel knew that she had violated the moral standards of both her father and the Church. She comes to confront the conflicts that arise between otherworldly spiritual imperatives and earthly needs. Isabel is perplexed by her desire for pleasure. Is pleasure a good? If not, why does it exist? Is it something for which one must always pay in the end? Isabel has been taught that love is self-sacrifice and that it is the key to identity. How, then, can one live, if the only way to have an identity is to sacrifice one's very being? Throughout the novel, Isabel contemplates Jesus' paradoxical dictum that one must lose one's life in order to save it.

Her father's death leaves Isabel free, but stunned and confused; she is as yet unable to acknowledge the full import of losing him, and at his funeral she does not weep. The middle chapters of *Final Payments* chronicle her first attempts to move forward. She is aided by two women friends, Eleanor and Liz, whose love and support contrast significantly with Joe Moore's unbearable emotional demands. She buys new clothes, sells the house she inherited, sets up her own apartment, and secures a job investigating home health care for the elderly; she reflects constantly about the needs of the people with whom she works.

In most of her relationships, Isabel has felt cheated in the act of giving and guilty in the act of getting. Her years of nursing her father left her feeling that she had given up her life for him. Her guilt-inducing relationship with David Lowe is repeated in kind after her father's death. First she humiliates herself by having sex with Liz's husband. After Liz forgives her, Isabel proceeds to fall in love with a married man, Hugh Slade. When Hugh's wife finds out about the affair and confronts her, the guilt-ridden Isabel embarks upon yet another course of expiation.

Isabel chooses the life of a martyr, believing that it will be her salvation. She goes to live with Margaret Cascy, devoting herself to the one person she is least capable of loving. She suffers Margaret's insults and ingratitude; she sacrifices her own beauty by overeating and gaining an enormous amount of weight and by acquiescing to Margaret's malicious suggestion that she get her beautiful long hair cut and styled unattractively. Depressed, she spends most of her time sleeping. At this low point, Isabel is aided by what is best in her past: her friends and her Catholic habits of mind. Her old friend Father Mulcahy warns her that she is sinning by killing herself slowly. Clearly, losing one's life in order to find it is not to be equated with destroying oneself, body and spirit.

The import of her own self-destructiveness comes to Isabel in a way that is full of saving ironies. Jealous about Isabel's visit from Father Mulcahy, Margaret insinuates that Isabel has been behaving improperly with the priest. In the raging quarrel that ensues, Isabel is reminded of a gospel passage: "The poor you have always with you: but me you have not always." She interprets Jesus' words as meaning that the pleasures of life must be taken, because death will deprive a person of them soon enough. She realizes that she has been trying to second-guess death, to give up all she loves so that she will never lose it. On Good Friday, she comes to acknowledge in Christ's death the mortality of everyone she has loved. Only now is she able to weep for her father. She realizes that "the greatest love meant only, finally, the greatest danger." In accepting the danger of loss, Isabel affirms life and love.

Isabel then makes her final payment to her past, losing her old life to find renewal in relinquishing her material legacy. She gives Margaret a check for twenty-thousand dollars, the money she received from the sale of her father's house. She rejects strict orthodoxy and returns to her friends. In doing so she preserves the spiritual core of her past; from her Catholic legacy there emerges a Christian redemption.

THE COMPANY OF WOMEN

First published: 1981
Type of work: Novel

A girl reared by a company of Catholic women and their spiritual adviser searches for "ordinary human happiness."

The New York Catholic upbringing of Felicitas Taylor, *The Company of Women*'s central character, is in one respect a near photographic negative of that of Isabel Moore in *Final Payments*. Whereas Isabel was motherless and reared by her widowed father, Felicitas' father is dead, and she has not only a mother but three godmothers as well. Each of these women has been independent of a husband for many years. The practical and wise Charlotte Taylor has worked as a secretary to support Felicitas since her father died six months after she was born. Good-humored Mary Rose is a motion-picture theater usher whose husband has been confined for thirty years to an asylum after suffering a mental breakdown. Clare, an elegant, independent-minded woman, manages a Manhattan leather-goods store. Elizabeth, fragile and impractical, is a schoolteacher full of imagination and a love for poetry. Hovering in the shadows, never really one of this company of women, is Muriel, reminiscent of both the bitter uninvited godmother in "Sleeping Beauty" and the jealous housekeeper, Margaret Casey, in *Final Payments*. These women came to know one another through Father Cyprian, a conservative Catholic priest whose retreats for working women they attended during the late 1930's. Father Cyprian is like Joe Moore in *Final Payments* in his respect for the Church, his anger at modern society, and his role as an authority figure over the women in his life.

Part 1 of the novel is set in 1963. Its narrative weaves in and out of the minds of these various characters. Love, community, and continuity between generations are crucial themes. Felicitas is the central focus of concern; at fourteen, she is seen by Father Cyprian and the company of women as their hope for the future. Father Cyprian makes her his protégée, teaching her theology and skills such as carpentry that are unconventional for a woman. Cyprian's weaknesses—he is bullheaded, dictatorial, and self-centered—distress Felicitas; even so, she becomes enveloped in his love and determined never to leave him.

Leave him she does, however, when, in 1969-1970 (part 2 of the novel) Felicitas enrolls at Barnard College to study classics. Meanwhile she has rebelled against her upbringing; she has discarded her faith and has been secretly attending peace marches. At Barnard, Felicitas discovers the counterculture. She becomes infatuated with Robert Cavendish, her handsome and charismatic political science professor, who takes her first to bed and then to live at his apartment, which he shares with two young women and a small child named—a sign of the times—Mao. Mary Gordon sets up Felicitas' life with Robert and his friends in a deliberate contrast to her childhood. Robert himself is a parodic, shallow version of Father Cyprian; both men dominate the women with whom they surround themselves.

What Felicitas seeks consistently is what she calls "ordinary human happiness." She senses that love, especially in the context of human community, is the key to such happiness, but Robert's commune proves itself as false and inadequate a community as Robert is a lover. Spurning an exclusive relationship, he goads Felicitas to sleep with someone else. Finding herself pregnant and unsure of who fathered the fetus, she seeks an abortion, illegal in 1970. Horrified at seeing a woman being hustled out of the backstreet clinic, ill and bleeding from a botched procedure, Felicitas rushes home to her mother.

The novel shifts abruptly at this point to part 3, set seven years later, in 1977. Felicitas and her mother are living in western New York near Father Cyprian's retirement home. Elizabeth, Clare, and Muriel live nearby. The group's hopes are now focused on Felicitas' daughter Linda. Felicitas' project is to prepare Linda for "ordinary" human life, in contrast to the ways in which Father Cyprian trained her to be extraordinary. She plans to marry Leo, a local hardware store owner, to give Linda a father and a "normal" home. True to her name, Felicitas tries to pass her hope for happiness on to Linda.

Part 3 is a series of interior monologues by the major characters, through whose points of view (told in the third person) the earlier events of the novel were presented. The change to first-person narration is striking: Gordon gives each character his or her own last word completely unmediated. The closing monologue is, appropriately, that of Linda, who represents the future. She muses about love and wonders what happens to it after death. Her final words are "We are not dying." Like those words, *The Company of Women* offers a qualified affirmation of life on earth, celebrating its possibilities and recognizing its limitations.

MEN AND ANGELS
First published: 1985
Type of work: Novel

The need to give and receive love is dramatized through the tragic relationship of a professional woman and the mentally disturbed babysitter of her children.

In *Men and Angels,* Mary Gordon continues her examination of human love and its limitations and of female identity. She explores these issues in the contexts of work, friendship, motherhood, and male-female relationships. Set in the 1980's in the fictitious small college town of Selby, Massachusetts, this novel dramatizes, in alternating chapters, the sharply contrasting perspectives of two women, Laura Post and Anne Foster. Although in this novel Gordon moves beyond the world of New York Irish Catholicism, she gives this complex and compelling novel a well-defined religious perspective. Its title and epigraph are the words of Saint Paul: "Though I speak with the tongues of men and of angels, and have not charity, I am become as sounding brass, or a tinkling cymbal."

At the outset, neither Laura Post nor Anne Foster fully understands Saint Paul's words; neither has come to terms effectively with her own needs to love and to be loved. The spiritual conditions of both women fail to empower them: Laura's spirituality is diseased, while Anne's is undeveloped. Their relationship proves to be a fatal combination.

Rejected cruelly in childhood by her mother and neglected by her father, twenty-year-old Laura Post has drifted into the byways of fundamentalist and charismatic religious cults. She has come to address the absence of human love in her life by convincing herself that the Holy Spirit has summoned her to teach children that such love—especially family love—is unimportant. Armed with her Bible, from which she has gleaned texts that seem to reinforce this conviction, Laura comes to Selby, where she meets Anne Foster, who, despite some misgivings, hires her as a live-in babysitter for her children, Peter, age nine, and Sarah, age six. Laura soon becomes enamored of Anne and imagines that the Holy Spirit is calling her to save Anne's soul by freeing her from her family so that Anne can live alone with Laura, who will lead her to the Lord. On the surface, Laura is reliable and diligent in her babysitting and household chores, but Anne distrusts her and finds her unlikable and intrusive. One day Anne's suspicions prove to be well-founded when Laura endangers the children's lives by leading them onto thin ice. Enraged, Anne fires Laura immediately. In despair, Laura takes revenge by carving Anne's name on her wrists and bleeding to death in the bathtub. She leaves the water running, and Anne and her children return home to find a pool of bloodied water in the living room. Peter discovers Laura's dead body.

The chapters that are narrated from Laura's point of view powerfully dramatize the workings of an unbalanced mind obsessed with terrible memories and longings. Laura's thoughts are rendered in sentences whose syntactical simplicity conveys her inability to reason effectually. She is haunted by biblical passages and stories whose sense she passionately contorts. Anne's chapters are, perforce, more deeply reflective than Laura's. One dimension of Anne's experience that broadens and deepens her perspective is her work. Anne is an art historian who is studying the work of Caroline Watson, a neglected but brilliant twentieth century artist. She discovers that Caroline neglected and discouraged her son Stephen, a frustrated artist who killed himself. Caroline's efforts to forge a career for herself lead Anne to reflect upon her own professional life. Although she is determined not to sacrifice her love and care for her children in favor of her career, her life becomes ironically parallel to Caroline's by virtue of Laura's suicide.

Although Anne believed at first that her anger in firing Laura was justified, and although Laura was indeed more dangerous than she could have suspected, she is left understanding that, Laura's madness notwithstanding, in her failure to love Laura she is at least partly responsible for her death. Anne has indeed proved capable of loving others—friends, her husband, her children—and that love has been returned, even if, as in the case of her marriage, imperfectly at times. Laura, however, was seemingly unlovable; even after her death, Anne can mourn for her, but does not find that she loves her, and she is perplexed by this limitation. She is perplexed as well by her new understanding of the ways in which mother love—the strongest of human bonds—is limited. She realizes that no matter how fervently she may love her children, there are myriad ways in which she cannot protect them from the world's ravages or from their own mistakes.

THE OTHER SIDE

First published: 1989
Type of work: Novel

Four generations of an Irish-American immigrant family struggle with their emotional legacies of love and anger.

Mary Gordon's fourth novel is one of the most vivid presentations in American fiction of the experiences of Irish immigrants in the twentieth century. Centering on the life histories of Vincent and Ellen MacNamara and depicting the lives of their children, grandchildren, and great-grandchildren as well, *The Other Side* is also an intricate and perceptive examination of the dynamics of familial relationships.

Unlike the conventional generational sagas of popular fiction, *The Other Side* is not linear in structure. The novel focuses on a single day in August, 1985, at the home in Queens Village, New York, in which Ellen and Vincent MacNamara have lived since 1922. The extended family has gathered to welcome the eighty-eight-year-old Vincent home from his long stay in a nursing home, where he has been recovering from a broken hip he suffered when Ellen, a stroke victim suffering from mental disorientation, knocked him to the floor. Although Vincent prefers the friendly community of the nursing home, he is returning home to fulfill a promise he made to Ellen sixty years ago, that he would let her die in her own bed, with him there, rather than among strangers. Moving back and forth in time through the inner reflections of diverse family members, Gordon pieces together a patterned whole whose configurations resemble those of an elaborate patchwork quilt. The novel is divided into five long sections. Sections 1, 3, and 5 shift in focus from one character to another; their variety of viewpoints balances section 2, told from Ellen's perspective, and section 4, told from Vincent's.

Vincent is motivated primarily by love—for his wife, for his children and grand-children, for his friends, and for life itself. He seeks genuine enjoyment for himself and for those he loves, and although he is a very old man, he is hungry for life. Vincent's problem is that he can no longer afford Ellen any enjoyment beyond her satisfaction, which she probably will be unable to communicate to him and indeed may never be able fully to feel, of knowing that he has kept his promise not to abandon her. In the final sentence of the novel, as Vincent enters Ellen's room, the reader finds that "he believes that she can see him, but he's not quite sure." Vincent's power of loving is a power of protectiveness, a crucial issue in Gordon's fiction.

Paradoxically, the emotion that has ruled Ellen's life was, in its inception, also protective in kind, even though most of the results have been destructive. Ellen has lived most of her life in passionate anger. As a child in Ireland, she was enraged by her father's abandonment of her mother, who was driven half mad by a series of failed pregnancies. Eventually her rage empowered her to leave Ireland for America, on "the other side" of the Atlantic, and to find a new life, but she never put this rage behind her. Despite her husband's protective love and his integrity, she diffused her rage toward other targets—priests, employers, politicians, her daughters, even Vincent himself. Ellen's anger comes down hard upon the succeeding generations of MacNamaras, for Vincent's love proves insufficient as a shield. Her rage is almost palpable in its active force, while Vincent's love is, in comparison, passive. The power to wound, Gordon implies, is stronger than the power to heal.

The other sections of the novel show how the rest of the family has fared. Ironically, John, the only child of hers whom Ellen could love, died in World War II. Her daughter Magdalene suffers from agoraphobia and alcoholism. Theresa, her other daughter, tries to hide her malice and anger at her mother's failure to love her behind a façade of charismatic religiosity. All the descendants of Ellen and Vincent Mac-Namara are scarred in some critical way. Two of them, in particular, however, emerge as potential survivors—Dan and Cam, grandchildren whom Ellen took into her home and fostered. Cam has inherited her grandmother's energy, but it has emerged not as rage but as resourcefulness in the face of difficulty. Despite child-lessness, a sexless marriage, and a selfishly domineering mother, Cam has succeeded in defining a satisfying life for herself; she has a lover who cherishes her, professional fulfillment, and the personal strengths of self-respect, keen intelligence, and lively wit. Dan, her cousin and partner in law practice, reveals tenderness and reflectiveness that are like his grandfather's: "He sees the wholeness of all life, the intricate connecting tissue. It is this, this terrible endeavor, this impossible endeavor. Simply to live a life." Dan's response to his family and even his clients is that he "would like to embrace them all. He would like to say: You must believe this. I understand you all." This same faith, vision, understanding, and compassion are implicit throughout *The Other Side*; they are the essence of Mary Gordon's outlook.

Summary

From *Final Payments* to *The Other Side*, Mary Gordon's literary techniques become increasingly complex and experimental, especially in her approach to structure and point of view. Her outlook on life broadens, deepens, and darkens. The fact that life is chancy and perplexing becomes successively more apparent in her fiction. While her characters' futures appear less and less promising, those individuals nevertheless remain affirmative of human life on earth, as does their author. As the world of organized religion recedes in terms of setting and theme in the course of her novels, Gordon's religious perspective becomes more subtly implicit.

Bibliography

Cooper-Clark, Diana. "An Interview with Mary Gordon." *Commonweal* 107 (May 9, 1980): 270-273.

Gordon, Mary. "Getting from Here to There: A Writer's Reflections on a Religious Past." In *Spiritual Quests: The Art and Craft of Religious Writing*, edited by William Zinsser. Boston: Houghton Mifflin, 1988.

Keyishian, M. Deiter. "Radical Damage: An Interview with Mary Gordon." *The Literary Review* 32 (Fall, 1988): 69-82.

Mahon, Eleanor B. "The Displaced Balance: Mary Gordon's *Men and Angels*. In *Mother Puzzles: Daughters and Mothers in Contemporary American Literature*, edited by Mickey Pearlman. Westport, Conn.: Greenwood Press, 1989.

Mahon, John W. "A Bibliography of Writings about Mary Gordon." In *American Women Writing Fiction: Memory, Identity, Family, Space*, edited by Mickey Pearlman. Lexington: University Press of Kentucky, 1989.

_____. "Mary Gordon: The Struggle with Love." In *American Women Writing Fiction: Memory, Identity, Family, Space*, edited by Mickey Pearlman. Lexington: University Press of Kentucky, 1989.

Suleiman, Susan Rubin. "On Maternal Splitting: A Propos of Mary Gordon's *Men and Angels.*" *Signs: Journal of Women in Culture and Society* 14 (Autumn, 1988): 25-41.

Ward, Susan. "In Search of 'Ordinary Human Happiness': Rebellion and Affirmation in Mary Gordon's Novels." In *Faith of a (Woman) Writer*, edited by Alice Kessler-Harris and William McBrien. Westport, Conn.: Greenwood Press, 1988.

Wymward, Eleanor B. "Mary Gordon: Her Religious Sensibility." *Cross Currents: A Yearbook of Central European Culture* 37 (Summer/Fall 1987): 147-158.

Eileen Tess Tyler

DASHIELL HAMMETT

Born: St. Mary's County, Maryland
May 27, 1894
Died: New York, New York
January 10, 1961

Principal Literary Achievement

Hammett's creation of the hard-boiled detective and the corrupt world in which he works laid the foundations for a new subgenre of detective fiction and introduced the tough, cynical private eye in American popular mythology.

Biography

Dashiell Hammett was born Samuel Dashiell Hammett on May 27, 1894, in St. Mary's County, Maryland, to Richard Thomas and Annie Bond Dashiell Hammett. The family moved first to Philadelphia and then to Baltimore, where Hammett attended public school and, in 1908, one semester of high school at Baltimore Polytechnic Institute. His family never did well financially, and Hammett was forced to leave school to find work at the age of fourteen; this marked the end of his formal education. He held several different jobs for short periods of time until 1915, when he became an operative for the Pinkerton National Detective Agency, the turning point of his life and the event that provided him with the background for the writing of his realistic detective fiction. Hammett left Pinkerton's to join the Army in 1918, reaching the rank of sergeant by the time of his discharge in 1919. He then returned to detective work, but hospitalization for pulmonary tuberculosis in 1920 interrupted his work and eventually ended it in 1921, shortly after his marriage to Josephine Annis Dolan, a nurse he had met while at the hospital. They had two daughters, Mary Jane, born in 1921, and Josephine Rebecca, born in 1926.

While trying to support himself and his family with a small government disability pension and a series of part-time jobs, Hammett began publishing short stories in *The Smart Set* in 1922 and published the first Continental Op story, "Arson Plus," in 1923 in *Black Mask*, the pulp magazine specializing in mystery and crime fiction that would publish his first four novels in serial form. The appearance of the first two novels in book form in 1929 made him a successful writer, and the next two, following quickly on that success, made him internationally famous. During this time, Hammett moved away from his family, at least initially on the advice of a doctor to keep his younger daughter from being exposed to his tuberculosis, and in 1930 he

went to Hollywood as a screenwriter.

It was then, at the height of his fame, that he met Lillian Hellman, with whom he had a close relationship until his death. Hellman was near the beginning of her distinguished career as a playwright, screenwriter, and essayist and was to be aided considerably in her work by Hammett's expertise as an editor and critic. He, however, was almost finished as a creative writer, publishing only one more novel, *The Thin Man*, in 1934, and writing no fiction in the last twenty-seven years of his life other than a fifty-page fragment of a novel called *Tulip*. Although he stopped writing novels and stories, royalties from his previous books and from a series of sixteen popular films and three weekly radio shows based on his characters and stories, as well as occasional screenwriting and a daily comic strip, *Secret Agent X-9*, provided him with income and public exposure. In 1954, his income from these various sources was more than eighty thousand dollars, an enormous sum for that time and an indicator of how popular his work had become. Hammett also taught courses in mystery writing at the Jefferson School of Social Science from 1946 to 1956.

The reasons that Hammett suddenly stopped writing after a series of five best-selling novels will probably never be known, but his involvement in left-wing politics, dating from the 1930's, has often been cited as a factor. He was under investigation by the Federal Bureau of Investigation as a suspected Communist from the 1930's until his death, despite his volunteering for the Army again after the outbreak of World War II and serving from 1942 until 1945. In 1946, he was elected president of the New York Civil Rights Congress, a position he held until the middle 1950's. Given the national temper at that time, any left-wing political involvement was dangerous, and in 1951 Hammett received a six-month sentence in federal prison for refusing to answer questions about the Civil Rights Congress bail fund— questions to which, according to Hellman, he did not know the answers. Hammett was also called to testify before Joseph McCarthy's Senate subcommittee in 1953 and before a New York State legislative committee in 1955, both times in connection with his presumed role as a Communist sympathizer. During these years, as direct or indirect results of his being branded as a Communist, his books went out of print, his radio shows were taken off the air, and his income was attached by the Internal Revenue Service for alleged income tax infractions. In a word, he was blacklisted. He spent his remaining years in poor health and poverty, living with Hellman and other friends until his death on January 10, 1961. The year before his death, his reported income was thirty dollars. It is perhaps ironic after all of the government persecution to which he was subjected that Hammett, as a veteran of two wars, was buried as a hero in Arlington National Cemetery on January 13.

Analysis

Before Dashiell Hammett laid the foundation of the modern realistic detective novel, virtually all detective fiction had been designed on the pattern established by the American writer Edgar Allan Poe in three short stories written between 1841 and 1844: "The Murders in the Rue Morgue," "The Mystery of Marie Rogêt," and "The

Purloined Letter." The basic ingredients of the formula were simple: a brilliant but eccentric amateur detective, his trusty but somewhat pedestrian companion and chronicler, an even more pedestrian police force, and an intricate and bizarre crime. The solution of the puzzle, generally set up as something of a game or contest to be played out between the author and the reader, called for a complex series of logical deductions drawn by the scientific detective on the basis of an equally complex series of subtle clues. According to what came to constitute the rules of this game, these clues were to be available to the detective's companion, who was also the narrator, and through him to the reader, who would derive interest and pleasure from the attempt to beat the detective to the solution. The canonical popular version of this classical tradition of the mystery as a puzzle to be solved is the English writer Arthur Conan Doyle's Sherlock Holmes series, although purists have objected that essential information available to Holmes is often withheld from the reader, which constitutes "cheating" on the part of the author. The success of the series paved the way for similar work by other English writers such as Agatha Christie. Although this classical model was invented by the American Poe and practiced by several American mystery writers, its predominance among English writers has led to its being thought of as the English school, in opposition to a more realistic type of mystery being written around the 1920's by a small group of American writers.

Dashiell Hammett proved to be the master of the new kind of detective story, written in reaction against the English model. As Raymond Chandler, one of Hammett's most notable literary descendants, remarked in his seminal essay on the two schools, "The Simple Art of Murder," "Hammett gave murder back to the kind of people that commit it for reasons, not just to provide a corpse; and with the means at hand, not hand-wrought dueling pistols, curare and tropical fish." Rather than serving as the vehicle for an intentionally bewildering set of clues and an often implausible solution, the realistic story of detection shifted the emphases to characterization, action, and, especially, rapid-fire and colloquial dialogue, as opposed to the flat characters, slow pace, and stilted set speeches of the classical school. Just as the entire classical formula was complete in Poe's earliest stories, the essentials of the realistic model are found complete in Hammett's earliest work, almost from the first of his thirty-five stories that feature an operative for the Continental Detective Agency, known to the reader only as the Continental Op. Although Hammett's contribution extends well beyond the codification of this model—indeed, much of his significance lies in his questioning and modifying of these conventions in his own novels—a sketch of these ingredients highlights the nature of his innovations.

Hammett's familiarity with the classical paradigm is established in the seventy-three reviews of detective novels he wrote for the *Saturday Review of Literature* and the *New York Evening Post* between 1927 and 1930; his rejection of it is thorough. In fact, he specifically contrasted his theory of the detective with that of Conan Doyle in describing Sam Spade, the protagonist of Hammett's *The Maltese Falcon* (1930), a description applicable to the Continental Op as well:

For your private detective does not . . . want to be an erudite solver of riddles in the Sherlock Holmes manner; he wants to be a hard and shifty fellow, able to take care of himself in any situation, able to get the best of anybody he comes in contact with, whether criminal, innocent by-stander, or client.

Hammett's Continental Op is distinctly unglamorous and unintellectual. The Op is pushing forty, is about five feet, six or seven inches tall, weighs one hundred and ninety pounds, and works as a modestly paid operative of the Continental Detective Agency, a fictional firm loosely modeled on the Pinkerton organization. Although certainly not stupid, the Op relies on routine police procedures and direct, often violent action rather than elaborate chains of logic to track down criminals. The colorful amateur detective is replaced by the professional, anonymous, and colorless Op, who has no history, no family, no hobbies or interests outside his work, and no social life beyond an occasional poker game with police officers or other detectives. In a 1925 short story, "The Gutting of Couffignal," the Op gives his most extensive discussion of his ideas about his work:

Now I'm a detective because I happen to like the work. . . . I don't know anything else, don't enjoy anything else, don't want to know or enjoy anything else. . . . You think I'm a man and you're a woman. That's wrong. I'm a manhunter and you're something that has been running in front of me. There's nothing human about it. You might as well expect a hound to play tiddly-winks with the fox he's caught.

Hammett humorously underscored the difference in methods in a 1924 short story, "The Tenth Clew," which parodies the classical detective plot with a set of nine bewildering clues, including a victim missing his left shoe and collar buttons, a mysterious list of names, a bizarre murder weapon (the victim was beaten to death with a typewriter), and so on. The solution, the "tenth clue," is to ignore all nine of these confusing and, as it turns out, phony clues and to use standard methods such as the surveillance of suspects to find the killer. The Op relies on methodical routine, long hours, and action to get results, not on reasoning alone. Rather than presenting a brilliant alternative to unimaginative police methods, the Op often follows their standard procedures.

Just as the detective is different in Hammett, so are the crimes and criminals. The world of the traditional mystery is one of security and regularity, disrupted temporarily by the aberrant event of the crime. Once the detective solves the crime through the application of reason, normalcy is restored. The worldview implicit in this plot was obviously comforting for a largely middle-class English readership at the turn of the century but was remote from the experience of the generation of American readers who had just survived World War I. The world of the hard-boiled detective, as conceived by an author who had been through the horrors of that war, is one in which criminal behavior is the norm rather than the exception. There are usually several crimes and several criminals, and the society is not an orderly one temporarily disrupted but a deeply corrupt one that will not be redeemed or even much changed after the particular set of crimes being investigated is solved.

RED HARVEST

First published: 1927-1928 (serial), 1929
Type of work: Novel

The Continental Op resorts to desperate methods to clean up organized crime and political corruption in a small mining town.

Red Harvest, Hammett's first novel, is now generally regarded as one of his best. The case begins when the Continental Op is sent to the small Montana mining town of Personville (called "Poisonville" by those who know it) at the request of Donald Willsson, the publisher of the town's newspapers. Willsson, who had been using the newspapers as a platform from which to fight civic corruption, is murdered before the Op can meet him and find out what he was hired to do. The Op manages to persuade Elihu Willsson, Donald's father and the owner of most of the property in the town, including the newspapers and the mines, to hire him to investigate crime and political corruption in Personville. As it turns out, Donald Willsson's murder was at the hands of a jealous bank teller who mistakenly believed that Willsson was having an affair with the teller's former girlfriend, Dinah Brand. When Elihu Willsson learns that his son's death was entirely unrelated to the organized crime in the town, he tries to call the Op off the case; in fact, Willsson himself is deeply involved in the corruption and could be caught up in the investigation. By this time, however, there is no turning back; the Op has become too deeply enmeshed in the web of power and corruption that includes not only his own client, but also the local bootleggers, gamblers, hired gunmen, and even the chief of police.

As the title suggests, this is the most violent of the novels; the twenty-first of its twenty-seven chapters is entitled "The Seventeenth Murder" (in its original serial publication in the pulp magazine *Black Mask*, it had been the nineteenth), and the series of killings has by no means ended at that point. The difference between the neat puzzles to be solved by deduction in the classical model and the confusing multiplicity of crimes and criminals in the hard-boiled novel of detection is underscored when Dinah Brand, who becomes the Op's ally and, the text implies, romantic interest, comments directly on the Op's methods:

> "So that's the way you scientific detectives work. My God! for a fat, middle-aged, hard-boiled pig-headed guy you've got the vaguest way of doing things I ever heard of."
> "Plans are all right sometimes," I said. "And sometimes just stirring things up is all right—if you're tough enough to survive, and keep your eyes open so you'll see what you want when it comes up to the top."

The moral corruption that permeates the town seems to be contagious, eventually affecting even the Op, who arranges several murders himself by playing off the rival factions against each other, largely by misinforming them about each other's intentions. Indeed, it is only at the end of the novel that the reader, along with the Op, learns that he did not commit the seventeenth murder (of Dinah Brand) while under the influence of a mixture of laudanum and gin. This type of suspense is possible because of Hammett's decision to use a severely restricted first-person narration by the Op to tell the story; the reader sees and hears only as much as the Op does and knows far less. The story is told almost entirely through terse, objective descriptions and dialogue. The Op seldom reveals his thoughts directly and only occasionally discusses them with other characters. The reader's task of interpretation is complicated by the fact that most of the dialogue in the novel is between characters who are intentionally trying to mislead and confuse each other. The reader's limitation to and identification with the Op's point of view creates much of the book's interest, especially when the Op appears to be falling under the contagion of corruption himself, becoming poisoned morally by "Poisonville" and turning into a bloodthirsty killer not much different from the criminals he is supposed to be combating.

At the book's close, most of the major characters have been murdered. Rather than emphasizing a tidy solution to the case—recall that the murder he was originally hired to investigate is solved quite early in the book and has little to do with the main plot—the ending clearly suggests that the pattern of pervasive corruption will continue relatively unchanged; Elihu Willsson is still in control of the local government and the town is "all nice and clean and ready to go to the dogs again." Political corruption, fueled by the rich industrialist, is the norm, not the aberration. Many critics have seen evidence of Hammett's Marxist views even in this early work because of this implicit critique of capitalist society. This morally evil, or at best neutral, world within which the hard-boiled detective lives and works and the patent corruption of the public legal system places added importance on his private code of ethics, the only standard of behavior to which he holds himself.

THE MALTESE FALCON

First published: 1929-1930 (serial), 1930
Type of work: Novel

Sam Spade, investigating the murder of his partner, becomes involved in the search for the priceless jeweled statue of a falcon.

Although he appeared only in *The Maltese Falcon* and three short stories, Sam Spade has become Hammett's best-known creation, largely as a result of Humphrey Bogart's portrayal of him in John Huston's scrupulously faithful film version (the third made of the book). After writing a second and somewhat weaker Continental Op novel, *The Dain Curse* (1929), Hammett turned to an entirely objective third-person narration for his next two novels, *The Maltese Falcon* and *The Glass Key* (1931), describing details of gesture and expression from the outside, as with a camera-eye point of view, but never revealing characters' thoughts or motives. This

shift removes even the few traces of interpretation and analysis that had been provided by the taciturn Op and makes the analysis of the character of the detective
himself the central concern of critics. The question that readers of *The Maltese
Falcon* must work to answer is not "who committed the crime?" but "what sort of
man is Sam Spade?"

The story begins when a beautiful woman calling herself Miss Wonderly hires
private detective Sam Spade and his partner, Miles Archer, to follow a man named
Floyd Thursby, ostensibly to help her find her missing sister, who has run away with
Thursby. Archer is murdered that night, and shortly afterward Thursby is murdered
as well. Miss Wonderly, whose real name is Brigid O'Shaughnessy, turns out to be
involved in a complicated plot to steal a priceless jeweled statue of a falcon, and
Thursby was her accomplice. Other parties pursuing the falcon appear as the narrative progresses, chief among them the colorful figures of Joel Cairo, one of the first
homosexual characters portrayed in an American novel, and Caspar Gutman, the
unforgettable Fat Man, who is the mastermind behind the search for the falcon.
Unlike Hammett's first two novels, *The Maltese Falcon* contains comparatively little
violence (the sixteenth of the twenty chapters is entitled "The Third Murder," in
distinct contrast to the excesses of *Red Harvest*), and most of that occurs "offstage,"
reported rather than directly depicted. The emphasis is on Spade's gradual uncover-
ing of the complex relations among the various criminals rather than on simply
determining who killed Thursby (the police and the rest of the interested parties
draw the obvious conclusion early in the book that Thursby killed Archer), and also
on the criminals' and police department's (as well as the reader's) attempts to determine Spade's own motives and intentions. Hammett's objective narration limits the
reader's knowledge to the same set of lies and half-truths that the characters must
sift through themselves to learn the facts of the story.

In fact, Archer's death, the initial crime to be solved, is probably dismissed as of
little concern by most readers once the story gets under way, until it is revealed at
the end that he was really murdered by Brigid O'Shaughnessy, with whom Spade has
since apparently fallen in love. In the novel's dramatic conclusion, Spade turns his
lover over to the police as Archer's murderer. The reasoning that leads Spade to
solve the crime is based upon clues available from the start, suggesting that he may
have known of her guilt all along, since before they became lovers. The question
remains open as to whether he has really fallen in love but is forced by his rigid
personal code of ethics to turn her in or whether he has been coldbloodedly manip-
ulating her throughout in order to solve the case; the evidence of the text suggests
paradoxically that both hypotheses may be partially true.

Spade's long delay in solving the case raises other questions: Is he crooked himself, hoping to get rich by helping the gang of thieves recover the falcon, or is he
merely playing along with them to further his investigation? After all, it is only after
the falcon proves worthless and the offers of vast sums of money that have been
made to him for its recovery have been withdrawn that Spade turns in the criminals.
Add to these disquieting concerns the points that he was having an affair with his

partner's wife, Ida (and that he liked neither of them), and that he purposely obstructs the police investigation at every stage until he is ready to reveal his solution, and the result is that the mystery of the novel resides far more in understanding the character of the protagonist than in resolving the plot. This interest in exploring character rather than in finding the killer is extended in Hammett's fourth novel, *The Glass Key*, which does not even have a detective, featuring instead a gambler, Ned Beaumont, as its protagonist; it is as much a psychological novel as a mystery.

THE THIN MAN

First published: 1933 (serial), 1934
Type of work: Novel

Nick Charles, a retired private detective, and his wife, Nora, become caught up in the investigation of the disappearance of a wealthy scientist.

Hammett's fifth and final novel, *The Thin Man*, is a return to first-person narration, as Nick Charles narrates the story of a case he unwillingly takes on while vacationing. Charles retired from the Trans-American Detective Agency six years before the action of the book begins in order to manage the businesses that his young wife, Nora, inherited from her father shortly after they were married. They are spending the Christmas holidays in New York City, primarily to avoid spending them with Nora's family on the West Coast. While Charles is in many respects another example of the hard-boiled detective, the novel is unique in its light comic tone, which fitted it for popular adaptations in a series of "Thin Man" films. In the book, however, the thin man of the title is actually the missing inventor, Clyde Wynant, not the detective. The description that Charles gives of Wynant ("Tall—over six feet—and one of the thinnest men I've ever seen. He must be about fifty now, and his hair was almost white when I knew him.") fits Hammett himself, except for his age, and he posed for the picture on the jacket of the first edition of the book, perhaps furthering the popular misconception that the title refers to the detective.

In other respects, the author and his protagonist are quite similar, sharing the same age and the same background as detectives. Their personal lives are also similar: The centerpiece of the book is the relationship between the worldly and jaded Charles and his young and enthusiastic wife Nora, one of the few happy marriages depicted in modern fiction. Their relationship is clearly based on that between Hammett and Lillian Hellman, to whom the book is dedicated. Gertrude Stein once remarked that Hammett was the only American novelist who wrote well about women, and Nora is one more example of the series of interesting and complex women characters featured in Hammett's fiction, extending from Dinah Brand in *Red Harvest* through Brigid O'Shaughnessy in *The Maltese Falcon*.

Wynant's disappearance is ascribed at first to his well-known eccentricity but becomes ominous when his secretary and former lover, Julia Wolf, is found murdered. Charles had previously done some detective work for Wynant and his lawyer, Herbert Macaulay, and his past association with the other members of the Wynant family (Wynant's ex-wife, Mimi, and his children, Dorothy and Gilbert) leads them to consult him about the case. One of the book's comic motifs is Charles' continuing and unsuccessful attempt to convince people that he really has retired and has no interest in working on the murder or disappearance. Eventually, he is drawn into the investigation against his will and solves the case. As in Hammett's earlier novels, suspense is created by the use of a deadpan first-person narrator, who reports all the relevant facts but seldom reveals to the reader what he thinks about them except in conversation with other characters (from whom he is as often as not withholding his conclusions as well).

Summary

Raymond Chandler observed that Dashiell Hammett "took murder out of the Venetian vase and dropped it into the alley." The two main ingredients of his breakthrough are the creation of the hard-boiled detective, a ruthless and often violent man who is bound, not by the law, but only by his own rigid and private code of ethics, and the perfection of an almost entirely objective narrative style, restricted primarily to terse descriptions and crisp, idiomatic dialogue, revealing the characters' thoughts and emotions only between the lines. Hammett's creation of the hard-boiled detective and the corrupt world in which he works provided the inspiration for Hammett's most noteworthy successors, Raymond Chandler and Ross Macdonald, and introduced the tough, cynical private eye into American popular mythology.

Bibliography

Chandler, Raymond. "The Simple Art of Murder." *The Atlantic Monthly* 174 (December, 1944): 53-59.

Dooley, Dennis. *Dashiell Hammett*. New York: Frederick Ungar, 1984.

Gregory, Sinda. *Private Investigations: The Novels of Dashiell Hammett*. Carbondale: Southern Illinois University Press, 1985.

Johnson, Diane. *Dashiell Hammett: A Life*. New York: Random House, 1983.

Layman, Richard. *Shadow Man: The Life of Dashiell Hammett*. New York: Harcourt Brace Jovanovich, 1981.

Marling, William. *Dashiell Hammett*. Boston: Twayne, 1983.

Nolan, William F. *Dashiell Hammett: A Casebook*. Santa Barbara, Calif.: McNally & Loftin, 1969.

_____. *Hammett: A Life at the Edge*. New York: Congdon & Weed, 1983.

Symons, Julian. *Dashiell Hammett*. New York: Harcourt Brace Jovanovich, 1985.

Wolfe, Peter. *Beams Falling: The Art of Dashiell Hammett*. Bowling Green, Ohio: Bowling Green University Popular Press, 1980.

William Nelles

LORRAINE HANSBERRY

Born: Chicago, Illinois
May 19, 1930
Died: New York, New York
January 12, 1965

Principal Literary Achievement

The writer of only two plays performed during her lifetime, Hansberry established a black authorial presence in the previously white commercial theater on Broadway.

Biography

Lorraine Vivian Hansberry was born on May 19, 1930, into an upper-middle-class black family living on Chicago's racially segregated south side. Her father, Carl, was a United States deputy marshall who ran unsuccessfully for Congress; her mother, Nannie, was a Republican ward committee member who gave her daughter a white fur coat for her fifth Christmas, which provoked taunts by her classmates. In the late 1930's the family purchased a home in a white neighborhood, inciting open hostility that resulted in a brick flung through a window, barely missing Lorraine. Although the state courts ordered their eviction, Carl successfully appealed the decision to the Supreme Court, which struck down restrictive covenants based on race.

During Lorraine's years at Englewood High School, frequent visitors to the family home included the black sociologist, W. E. B. Du Bois, author of the classic *The Souls of Black Folk* (1903), under whom she would later study African history; the prominent Shakespearean actor and activist Paul Robeson; and Langston Hughes, poet and playwright of the Harlem Renaissance. After the sudden death of her father in Mexico in 1946, Lorraine became intrigued by the work of her uncle, William Leo Hansberry, a professor of African studies. Following high school, Lorraine enrolled at the University of Wisconsin, where she saw the Irish dramatist Sean O'Casey's *Juno and the Paycock* (1924)—which would greatly influence both her philosophy and theatrical style—and where she chaired the Young Progressives of America, who supported third-party candidate Henry Wallace for President in 1948.

Without graduating from college, Lorraine left the Midwest to settle in New York City, where she took courses at the New School for Social Research and became a writer and later associate editor of *Freedom* magazine, contributing articles on women, Africa, and various social issues, many of which later provided background

for her plays. She was even substitute speaker at a peace conference in Uruguay for Robeson, the publisher of *Freedom*, whose passport had been revoked (he was viewed by the government as a Communist sympathizer during the McCarthy era), resulting in the revocation of her own. After her interracial marriage to Robert Nemiroff in 1953, who became her staunchest supporter, they settled in Greenwich Village, where Lorraine worked at various jobs, including teaching black literature; Nemiroff's success as coauthor of a popular tune, "Cindy, Oh, Cindy," freed her to become a full-time writer.

When *A Raisin in the Sun* opened to critical praise on May 11, 1959, it became the first play by a black author to achieve commercial success on Broadway. As James Baldwin, himself an African-American novelist and playwright, remarked: "I had never in my life seen so many black people in the theater. And the reason was that never before, in the entire history of the American theater, had so much of the truth of black people's lives been seen on the stage." The play ran for 530 performances and won the New York Drama Critics Circle Award, making Hansberry the first black, only the fifth woman, and the youngest playwright so honored. (The film version, for which Hansberry wrote the screenplay, received the Cannes Film Festival Award in 1961; a 1973 musical version by Nemiroff, entitled *Raisin*, won the Tony Award for best musical that season.)

After the phenomenal success of her first effort, Hansberry pursued various writing projects: *The Drinking Gourd* (1972), a teleplay commissioned by NBC but never produced, in which a slave's determination to read and write is punished by blinding; *What Use Are Flowers?* (1972), a never-produced fable about relearning the civilizing arts following a nuclear holocaust; *The Movement: Documentary of a Struggle for Equality* (1964), a product of her involvement with student activists in the freedom crusades during the Civil Rights era; *Les Blancs* (1970) an unfinished drama about the moral dilemma of armed revolution for African independence, which Nemiroff revised for a brief Broadway run in 1970; "Toussaint," a dramatic fragment about the Haitian revolutionary; and *The Sign in Sidney Brustein's Window* (1964), her only other play produced during her lifetime. Kept alive largely through the legendary efforts of her theatrical colleagues following a mixed critical reception, *The Sign in Sidney Brustein's Window* closed after 101 performances on the night Hansberry died, January 12, 1965.

During the early 1970's, selections from the entire range of Hansberry's writings became widely known via *To Be Young, Gifted, and Black: Lorraine Hansberry in Her Own Words*, compiled by Nemiroff, then adapted for the off-Broadway stage—where it enjoyed a long run in 1969 before a two-year national tour—and for publication as a book in 1970. Its title captures the qualities that ensure Hansberry's continued prominence among post-World War II American playwrights.

Analysis

In "The Negro Writer and His Roots: Toward a New Romanticism" (1959), a speech delivered shortly before *A Raisin in the Sun* premiered in New York, Lorraine

Hansberry outlined her artistic credo as well as analyzed the roots of her political radicalism. She asserted the responsibility of black writers to disprove certain myths widespread on the American scene. They must challenge the faulty assumptions that art should not be social in its impetus; that individuals exist independent of their socio-cultural environment; that the values of middle class, industrialized society necessarily represent those of the lower class; and that the United States has un-limited time to eradicate inequality among its citizens. As her mentor, W. E. B. Du Bois foretold, "the problem of the Twentieth Century is the problem of the color line."

As is true in her plays as well, Hansberry's perspective in the essay is a balanced one; blacks themselves can be slaves to a perverted materialism rather than cham-pions of freedom, prone to color prejudice of their own, to romanticizing the sen-suality and sleaziness of urban black life, and to apologizing for having been vic-timized in the past. Yet, having accepted all that, it remains true that "in this most hostile nation," her black sisters and brothers are not really free citizens who enjoy equal job opportunities and who can vote without harassment or partake of other basic rights of American life. Therefore, along with her protagonist in *The Sign in Sidney Brustein's Window*, she proclaims: "The 'why' of why we are here is an intrigue for adolescents; the 'how' is what must command the living. Which is why I have lately become an insurgent again."

Hansberry opened her talk by quoting from Sean O'Casey, whose ghetto melo-dramas about the powerlessness of oppressed Dublin families living in the midst of enormous political upheaval are forerunners of plays such as *A Raisin in the Sun*. Hansberry treasured O'Casey for his compassionate humanity, ironic humor, and implied belief in human potentiality despite failures and foibles. Also influential was the Norwegian playwright Henrik Ibsen, whose realistic, well-made problem dramas exemplify Hansberry's dictum "that there are *no* plays which are not social and no plays that do not have a thesis."

Rather than embrace naturalism, which aspires to a photographic representation of "the world as it is," Hansberry espouses a realism which incorporates "what is *possible* . . . because that is part of reality too." Further, a realistic framework allows for the inclusion of highly symbolic scenes—for example, those in which her protagonists attempt to reach back to some primeval energy: in *A Raisin in the Sun*, Walter's primitive dance on the table; in *The Sign in Sidney Brustein's Window*, Sid-ney's dreamlike retreat into Appalachia; in *Les Blancs*, Tshembe's ritualistic union with the African warrior god. Just as Hansberry mistrusts a naturalism that subordi-nates free choice to a biological or environmental determinism, so, too, does she reject the absurdism popularized by the post-War French intellectuals; she intended her television fable, *What Use Are Flowers?*, in fact, as a response to Samuel Beck-ett's *En attendant Godot* (1952; *Waiting for Godot*, 1954), the chief dramatic em-bodiment of the philosophy that life is meaningless, senseless, without purpose. In her plays, Hansberry champions meaningful advance over hopeless repetition, faith over despair, engagement over acquiescence.

In *A Raisin in the Sun*, Beneatha, the college-age daughter in the Younger family, debates with Asagai, her Nigerian friend, the question of historical change; whereas she argues that "there isn't any real progress . . . there is only one large circle that we march in, around and around," he corrects her, claiming, "It isn't a circle—it is simply a long line . . . one that reaches into infinity." In *The Sign in Sidney Brustein's Window*, Hansberry satirizes absurdism when David writes a successful play that is set inside a refrigerator; in the face of its philosophy of isolation, alienation, and desolation, Sidney must discover a reason to go on. In *Les Blancs*, withdrawal into a safe Eurocentrism is challenged when Tshembe must return to his African roots and take up the cause of independence from Western colonialism, through violent means if necessary.

The philosophical position that Hansberry develops might best be termed a rational humanism. Although she understands the widespread need for religious belief and even "rather admire[s] this human quality to make our own crutches as long as we need them," she (like Beneatha) puts her belief firmly in "man . . . who makes miracles!" In short, "Man exalts himself by his achievements . . . and his power to . . . *reason!*" Hansberry treasures as the highest virtues individual dignity and integrity, a mantle hard won through suffering and not always easy to bear once achieved.

To show her protagonists' dynamism as they pursue this end, Hansberry structures her plays using a series of plot reversals that continually challenge the characters to question and move away from the status quo. Insofar as her characters create their essence—what they are—through the moral choices that they make, Hansberry's dramas might be termed existential. The triumph over the seeming absurdity of life is not only possible but necessary if humankind is to prevail. Above all else, as Sidney Brustein's sister-in-law Mavis remarks, "ordinary people" look ultimately to the creative artist to provide "understanding . . . in this quite dreadful world." It is a challenge that Hansberry consistently meets.

A RAISIN IN THE SUN

First produced: 1959 (first published, 1959)
Type of work: Play

The dilemmas posed by a black family's move into a white neighborhood provide opportunities and occasion for growth into adulthood.

A Raisin in the Sun is a moving drama about securing one's dignity within a system that discriminates against, even enslaves, its racial minorities. Crowded into a tenement apartment, Lena ("Mama") Younger and her adult children—a son, Walter Lee, Jr. (husband of Ruth and father of Travis) and a daughter, Beneatha—await the arrival of a ten-thousand-dollar insurance payment on Walter, Sr., in the expectation that dreams long deferred might be realized. As the children lay claims to the money—he for buying into a liquor store, she for her medical school tuition—Mama acts on the family's need for a place to hold them together, purchasing a home in a white neighborhood.

Another leading black dramatist, Amiri Baraka (LeRoi Jones), wrote of his play *Dutchman* (1964) that it concerns "the difficulty of becoming a man in America." The same is true of *A Raisin in the Sun*, since Walter Lee attempts to define a rightful position for himself. A chauffeur for a well-to-do white, he feels himself restricted not only by class and racial boundaries but also by a mother who will not condone his business venture and a wife who seems not to support his pursuit of the dream. To his mother's dismay, he equates money with life, having things with being somebody; he tries to live by white values, as exemplified in George Murchison, Beneatha's assimilationist suitor. Like Willy Loman in Arthur Miller's *Death of a Salesman* (1949), Walter looks to material success to satisfy essentially spiritual longings, not understanding that his own dream is flawed by the same class and sexual biases as that of his oppressors.

When Mama realizes what her son's perceived lack of power is doing to him as a man, she entrusts the remaining insurance money to Walter, who is promptly bilked of it by his partner in the liquor store scheme. In his desperation, he tells the representative of the white community association that they will take money not to move into the neighborhood. When Mama insists, however, that he sign away his self-respect in front of his son, he chooses instead the dignity due him as the son of a hardworking father and reiterates their choice to move.

Hansberry's three female characters vary. Beneatha, a mild self-parody of the artist herself when she was ten years younger, seeks identity as an adult by rebelling against the traditional religion of her mother; as a woman by her determination to become a doctor and her refusal to be any man's sexual plaything; and as a black proud of her race by adopting an Afro hairstyle and being committed to the notion of African independence. Of all Hansberry's characters, she best displays the author's womanist, early feminist stance.

Ruth, on the other hand, though overjoyed at the thought of having a home of her own, will continue in a role subordinate to her husband. Pregnant with the baby whom she considered aborting when it appeared that Walter's love for her had dried up, she is determined to strap the child to her back if necessary to work as a domestic and help meet the mortgage payments. Mama, with her dignified hat and the lone geranium she nurtures as her piece of the garden promised as a sign of the dream's attainment, is the continuing source of strength and active endurance who categorically rejects Booker T. Washington's policy of submission. As Hansberry said of her so eloquently:

[Lena] is the black matriarch incarnate; the bulwark of the Negro family since slavery. . . . It is she who . . . scrubs the floors of the nation in order to create black diplomats and university professors. . . . [I]t is she who drives the young into the fire hoses. And one day she simply refuses to move to the back of the bus in Montgomery.

Mama's literary descendant in Hansberry's works is the slave Rissa in *Drinking Gourd*, who allows her owner to die while arming her son for the escape north.

Although the Younger family's spiritual condition has changed, their material condition has not altered much—as symbolized by the worn furniture they move to the new home. They remain mired in subservient jobs and are likely to face, as Hansberry's family did, bricks through windows from their racist neighbors; an earlier version of the play, in fact, ended just that way. So *A Raisin in the Sun*, rather than naïvely support integration or allow its audiences to applaud, and thus escape, protest directed against themselves, in reality is more subversive. "The dream denied," as the last line of the Hughes poem that gives the play its title reminds, might not "dry up like a raisin in the sun," but rather "*explode*"—as the United States would in the 1960's.

THE SIGN IN SIDNEY BRUSTEIN'S WINDOW

First produced: 1964 (first published, 1965)
Type of work: Play

A political activist who loses faith in a corrupt system rejects disillusionment and recommits himself when he sees that moral choices can still be made.

The Sign in Sidney Brustein's Window initially appears to be a departure from the playwright's first success, *A Raisin in the Sun*. Rather than focus on a working-class family in a black ghetto, it examines an ethnically and racially mixed cross section of the liberal intelligentsia in the bohemian world of New York's Greenwich Village. Yet its chief concern remains the existential choices that propel characters toward a mature morality in what Iris, Sidney's wife, terms "a dirty world." Specifically, it inquires to what extent one is willing to turn oneself into a saleable commodity, as Walter Lee in *A Raisin in the Sun* thinks of doing.

As the play opens, Sidney enters with the remnants of a failed restaurant venture, now determined to "presume no commitment, disavow all engagement." Before long, he has bought a newspaper, promising to "steer clear of politics"; he desires most of all to retreat, banjo in hand, to the mountains of Appalachia, there to have Iris dance for him. Yet soon he is supporting Wally O'Hara for political office, complete with a sign in the window and a campaign song at rallies. When Wally unexpectedly wins, Iris reveals that he is under the control of the corrupt political bosses, causing Sidney to despair. Where before he had mocked the philosophical position of the absurdists embodied in the plays of his neighbor, David, now he falls into cynical derision himself.

His naïveté about public matters is complicated by his deteriorating relationship with Iris, whom he belittles and fails to encourage in her acting career. Desperate to make it within the Establishment, she will do commercials rather than serious work, even—in the first of several moral lapses these characters display—spouting erroneous claims about home-permanent products. Recognizing her anguish, Sidney attempts to bribe David into including a role for her in his new play, promising in return a rave newspaper review. Though he rebukes Sidney's offer, later David is willing, in an effort to satisfy the desires of his homosexual lover, to proposition Iris' sister Gloria into being a voyeur to their lovemaking. Finally, Gloria herself is rejected by Alton, the black whom she hopes will marry her, when he discovers that she has been a highly paid call girl, a commodity like his enslaved grandmother; he will not take as wife "a white man's leavings."

Sidney learns to care again in a most unexpected way. Gloria, whose father called her a "tramp" on his deathbed and who insisted that Alton know the truth about her, refuses to demean herself as David wishes; she knows that she is "better than this," and, hoping that her father will forgive her, commits suicide. Her decision to die rather than suffer further indignity teaches Sidney that he must not continue to go through life without taking a firm stand and that out of sorrow can come strength.

The father of Iris, Gloria, and the feisty if bigoted Mavis—the oldest of the three sisters, who chooses to stay in a loveless marriage—had changed their last name to Parodus. Referring literally to the chorus in Greek tragedy, the name here symbolizes all those who would watch from the sidelines, distanced and uninvolved. Despite evidence to the contrary, Hansberry insists, through Gloria's impact upon Sidney, that "people want to be better than they are," that humankind must not fear commitment because of the pain it exacts, but must rebel against passivity and inaction. A commitment tempered by knowledge will be firmer than one built on naïve and untested idealism. *The Sign in Sidney Brustein's Window* may be less neatly plotted and more philosophical than *A Raisin in the Sun*, and so less immediately engaging of the emotions; nevertheless, it makes a powerful impact.

Summary

To some readers, Lorraine Hansberry has appeared more interested in gaining acceptance from the largely white literary establishment than in speaking out unabashedly for the oppressed black minority. Her plays, however, reveal the falsity of this impression: She not only refuses to soothe her audience's guilt over their responsibility for past inequities but also increasingly challenges them to adopt a radical, even an openly revolutionary stance to ending those injustices.

A biographer once wrote of Lillian Hellman, another important American dramatist: "She was, is, a lasting voice, and when all the storms . . . are done, it will still be heard. She has a final place. She is a writer." These words could serve equally appropriately as Lorraine Hansberry's epitaph.

Bibliography

Abramson, Doris E. *Negro Playwrights in the American Theatre, 1925-1959.* New York: Columbia University Press, 1967.

Bigsby, C. W. E. *Confrontation and Commitment: A Study of Contemporary American Drama, 1959-1966.* Columbia: University of Missouri Press, 1968.

Cheney, Anne. *Lorraine Hansberry.* Boston: Twayne, 1974.

Wilkerson, Margaret B. "The Dark Vision of Lorraine Hansberry: Excerpts from a Literary Biography." *The Massachusetts Review* 28 (Winter, 1987): 642-650.

_____. "*A Raisin in the Sun*: Anniversary of an American Classic." *Theatre Journal* 38 (December, 1986): 441-452.

Thomas P. Adler

BRET HARTE

Born: Albany, New York
August 25, 1836
Died: Camberley, Surrey, England
May 5, 1902

Principal Literary Achievement

Known as a romantic short fiction writer and a realistic literary critic, Bret Harte developed plots and character types that formed the base for hundreds of Western books and films.

Biography

Francis Bret Harte was born in Albany, New York, on August 25, 1836, to Henry Philip (a schoolteacher) and Elizabeth Rebecca Ostrander Hart; the last name was changed to Harte in 1844. Bret, the third born of the Hartes' four children, was in ill health from ages six to ten, during which time he read avidly. He was particularly influenced by the writing of British author Charles Dickens. His first poem to be published, "Autumnal Musings," was printed in the *New York Sunday Atlas* when he was eleven. Bret attended eight different schools before he ended his formal schooling at the age of thirteen for financial reasons.

In 1845, after the death of Bret's father, the family moved to Brooklyn. After becoming engaged to Andrew Williams, Elizabeth Harte moved to Oakland, California, in 1853, where they were married. A year later, Bret and his younger sister Margaret joined their mother in California. Bret stayed there until 1870.

Bret Harte began working at odd jobs when he was thirteen and was self-supporting by the time he was fifteen or sixteen. In 1857, when he moved to Union (now Arcata), California, Harte seriously began his career in journalism. He worked for the newspaper in Union from 1858 to 1860. He was forced out of town after the February 26, 1860, issue of the newspaper, *The Northern Californian*, in which Harte, in the editor's absence, published an account of the Mad River Indian massacre of 1860, the slaughter by local whites of all the Indians attending a three-day religious festival. Harte, outraged at the "cowardice" and "cruelty" of the attack, intimated that another local editor and Eureka's sheriff were behind the attack. Some sources say Harte had to leave town instantly, barely escaping with his life; others say he was forced to leave within the month.

On August 11, 1862, Harte married Anna Griswold, an older woman who was

well established in her musical career. Neither family approved of the marriage. Bret and Anna had four children: Griswold (1863), Francis (1865), Jessamy (1873), and Ethel (1875). In 1871, the Hartes left San Francisco for Chicago. Harte never returned to California, and he even avoided friends from the West. In 1875, Harte began keeping an apartment separate from his family. After that time, the Hartes had a sort of genteel Victorian divorce, although neither took legal action.

During the eleven years that Harte lived in San Francisco, he was a prolific writer. In 1868, he became the first editor of the *Overland Monthly*, California's first quality literary journal. Before the publication of the second issue, he had a battle with a proofreader about "The Luck of Roaring Camp," one of the stories for which Harte is most remembered. She wanted the story omitted because it contained a prostitute and profanity. Harte threatened to resign as editor if the story were not published. The publisher backed Harte, thus furthering realism in American literature.

Harte met numerous literary figures in the United States. Among them were William Dean Howells, Ralph Waldo Emerson, Henry Wadsworth Longfellow, Oliver Wendell Holmes, James Russell Lowell, Louis Agassiz, and Julia Ward Howe. Perhaps his closest friend among well-known writers, however, was Samuel Clemens (Mark Twain). In 1876, however, after Clemens and Harte jointly wrote and produced the unsuccessful play *Ah Sin*, a dramatization of Harte's "Heathen Chinee," they had a falling out.

Bret Harte lived extravagantly, as a celebrity, and his work dried up. He was surrounded by scandal concerning his indebtedness, drinking, and partying. During this time, in Chicago, he tried unsuccessfully to write plays and novels. Curiously, *Gabriel Conroy* (1876), a novel, failed in the United States but went through several editions in Germany. In desperation over debts, Harte began a lecture tour of the United States, but he was contemptuous of his audiences and soon had a reputation as a not very entertaining lecturer.

In July of 1878, President Rutherford B. Hayes appointed Harte to a consulship in Crefeld, Germany. Harte moved to Germany without his family and neglected his position, making frequent trips to London on the pretext of ill health. There he met George Eliot, Thomas Hardy, Henry James, and Arthur and Marguerite Van de Velde. In 1880, he was transferred to Glasgow, but he did not like the murky weather there and again neglected his duties. In 1885, President Grover Cleveland relieved Harte of his consulship for "inattention to duty."

At the invitation of Marguerite Van de Velde, Harte moved in with the Van de Veldes; he remained living there, even after Arthur's death in 1892, despite the scandal that the arrangement caused in Victorian England. Having taken up his writing again in 1882, Harte continued to write at the Van de Veldes', and he published a small volume of fiction every year until his death. Although Harte moved to a house a few doors away from Marguerite Van de Velde shortly before his wife Anna arrived in London in 1898, Bret and Anna did not live together. Some sources say that Anna declined to live with him; others hold that he did not invite her to live with him. Harte saw his wife and his daughter Ethel, who was studying music in

Paris, a few times at his son Frank's home in London, but the gatherings led to quarrels. After Bret Harte hemorrhaged and died of throat cancer on May 5, 1902, it was Marguerite Van de Velde who disposed of his ashes.

Analysis

Bret Harte, a writer who featured local color and depictions of the California Gold Rush in his short stories, created stock characters who were villains externally and saints internally. Many of his protagonists are estranged from their own culture, such as the outcasts in "The Outcasts of Poker Flat." Harte's writing has been praised for its fresh humor, good prose (rarely was it inflated and self-conscious), and command of dialect. Wallace Stegner, in his introduction to *The Outcasts of Poker Flat and Other Tales*, summarizes why Harte, despite his critics, has lasted:

> Humor, economy, mastery of a prose instrument and a compact fictional form, a trick
> of paradox and color, a chosen (later compulsive) subject matter full of romantic glamor,
> a faculty for creating types that have become the stock in trade of a whole entertain-
> ment industry—these are surely enough to account for Harte's lasting. But there is
> something more. He made a world. . . . It was at once recognizable as plausible, co-
> hesive, self-contained.

Much has been said of Harte's narrative strategy. He constantly uses a third-person narrator, creating a distance between himself and his characters. Also contributing to the distance between the author and the characters is that Harte used almost no autobiographical incidents in his stories, though he claimed in an interview that all the characters existed in real life even if he may not have been able to label each specifically. This distancing is, in part, what allowed him to leave profanity and a prostitute in "The Luck of Roaring Camp"; however, such distance makes his characters types more than individuals.

Harte also paints vivid California settings in his stories. Oddly enough, as many readers have observed, the settings are not identifiable with real locations in California. Somewhat ironically, Harte, primarily a city dweller, was not intimate with the area now called Bret Harte country; he created a mythic landscape that was nevertheless appealing to the audiences of American realism.

One of Bret Harte's recurrent themes is anti-racism. Throughout his life, Harte was contemptuous of racial hypocrisy. In 1860, he was forced out of Union, California, as a result of his journalistic attack on the white men who massacred the Indians at Mad River. During the Civil War, he helped the Reverend Thomas Starr King work for the abolitionists. Anti-racist themes run through many of Harte's short stories, plays, and poems. Another theme Harte explored is the influence of civilization on the West. Harte's characters, those who "civilized" the West, show that there is good in the worst people. In his private life, however, Harte had a low opinion of his audiences. Perhaps because Harte so carefully distanced himself from the protagonists and other characters of his stories, his paradoxical views seem not to create a deep ambivalence in the stories.

Bret Harte, by all accounts, was fundamentally an Easterner who wrote about the California of Gold Rush days. Criticism of his work lacks variety, with most critics concurring that his best work was that done before 1872, primarily the short stories and a series of seventeen parodies. Some attention is given to his poetry, especially a dialect poem, "Plain Language from Truthful James," better known as "The Heathen Chinee." Harte rose to sudden popularity after his publication of "The Outcasts of Poker Flat," but only after the story received praise from the East. His fall from popularity was also fairly sudden.

Some critics argue that the stories that Harte wrote during the last twenty years of his life were of comparable quality to the early work but that those stories, written in England, were less popular because the audience changed during Harte's literary career while his formula did not. In 1885, Harte wrote in a letter that his popularity, though strong in England, had fallen off in America. During the last years of his life, he lost touch with main currents in American and world literature. Nevertheless, Harte developed the stock Western characters that are found in hundreds of Western stories and motion pictures. Harte created a mythic West that has endured far beyond the Gold Rush.

THE LUCK OF ROARING CAMP

First published: 1868
Type of work: Short story

The story follows the transformation of a male mining community that ends up caring for an orphaned infant until the baby's death in a spring flood.

"The Luck of Roaring Camp," written in Bret Harte's characteristic narrative style, begins with a depiction of approximately a hundred men standing outside a shack in which "Cherokee Sal" is giving birth unattended. Because there are no other women in the mining community, Kentuck, "a prominent citizen," sends Stumpy, a bigamist seeking refuge in the lawless Roaring Camp, in to help Sal. Stumpy has "had experience in them things."

While Stumpy tries to help Sal, the other men of Roaring Camp wait outside, smoking pipes and wagering on the survival of Sal and the infant and on the gender of the child. Characteristic of Bret Harte's Gold Rush tales, the sketch of the opening scene is vivid, showing the men on the hill facing the cabin illuminated by the moon and their campfire. This scene draws readers into the suspense of the action.

The cry of the infant breaks the suspense, causing celebration among the men, but their enthusiasm is dampened by Cherokee Sal's death within the hour. Stumpy takes up a collection for the infant as the men file through the cabin, pay their last respects to Sal, and look at the infant. Kentuck is delighted, and cusses to show it, when the baby clutches his finger. Kentuck turns to Sandy Tipton, another of the men, and says, "He rastled with my finger, . . . the d—d little cuss!" It was this opening scene with the prostitute Sal and the cussing Kentuck that caused the conflict between Bret Harte and the proofreader of the *Overland Monthly.*

Fittingly, the men of Roaring Camp become, as one, father to the orphan, though Stumpy becomes the main caregiver. The men of Roaring Camp soon hold a rowdy christening for the child and name him Thomas Luck, the luck of Roaring Camp. The final pages of the story sketch the men of Roaring Camp becoming attached to the infant Tommy Luck. As their attachment grows, the men become more proper and keep the camp and themselves cleaner. The expressman tells stories in other camps of the transformation of Roaring Camp. He concludes, "They've got vines and flowers round their houses, and they wash themselves twice a day. But they're mighty rough on strangers, and they worship an Ingin baby."

The washing becomes a sort of gruesome irony when the spring thaws flood the riverbanks and wash away Stumpy's cabin, drowning Stumpy and setting Kentuck and the child adrift in the river. When Kentuck and the child are found, Kentuck, clutching Tommy Luck, is told that the child is dead and that he, too, is dying. Kentuck, still clutching the "frail babe," takes "The Luck" with him and drifts away into the "shadowy river" of death.

Such is the story that created the turmoil in the second issue of the *Overland Monthly.* In an interview in 1894, Harte said of the conflict that the publisher feared that the story might imperil the magazine's future. Harte, however, concluded that if the story were not suitable, then he was not the suitable editor for the magazine; Harte prevailed. When the story appeared, Harte said, public reaction was strong:

> The religious papers were unanimous in declaring it immoral, and they published columns in its disfavor. The local press, reflecting the pride of a young and new community, could not see why stories should be printed by their representative magazine which put the community into such unfavorable contrast with the effete civilization of the East. They would have none of it!

Harte concludes, however, that a month later, when Fields & Osgood, Boston publishers, sent him a letter offering to publish future works of the author of "The Luck of Roaring Camp," the tide of criticism turned. Once Boston endorsed the story, Harte said, "San Francisco was properly proud of it."

THE OUTCASTS OF POKER FLAT

First published: 1869
Type of work: Short story

The story follows the fate of four outcasts and a young couple eloping when the group is caught in a snowstorm.

"The Outcasts of Poker Flat" opens as John Oakhurst, a gambler (and a minor character from Harte's earlier "The Luck of Roaring Camp"), steps onto the main street of Poker Flat on November 23, 1850. He realizes that the citizens of Poker Flat are continuing their purge of undesirable elements and that he may be among the next lynched or driven out of town. He observes, ironically, their vigilante tactics and concludes that the town is "experiencing a spasm of virtuous reaction, quite as lawless and ungovernable as any of the acts that had provoked it."

Oakhurst, a stock character in later Westerns, is correct in his observations and faces the judgment calmly. He is the prototype of the philosophical gambler who occurs in Westerns and in country and western music. Oakhurst, along with a young woman known as "The Duchess," another older woman called Mother Shipton, and a robber and drunkard called "Uncle Billy," is escorted to the edge of Poker Flat and forbidden to return. With no provisions except liquor and with winter approaching, they leave Poker Flat and travel toward another mining camp, Sandy Bar, that is "distant a day's severe travel." Though Oakhurst, always the gentleman, exchanges his riding horse with the Duchess' mule, she grows tired by midday and insists that she will go no further. Despite Oakhurst's better judgment, the group stops.

After the two women and Uncle Billy drink themselves into oblivion, Oakhurst, who does not drink, contemplates the group of outcasts. It is a moment of awareness: "As he gazed at his recumbent fellow exiles, the loneliness begotten of his pariah trade, his habits of life, his very vices, for the first time seriously oppressed him." Still, it does not occur to Oakhurst to desert "his weaker and more pitiable companions."

As Oakhurst contemplates, he is interrupted by the arrival of Tom Simson, "The Innocent," who recognizes Oakhurst as the gambler who returned Tom's forty dollars and steered him away from gambling. Tom is with Piney Woods, "a stout, comely damsel of fifteen." They plan to marry in Poker Flat.

Tom and Piney (the "virgin"), unaware of the nature of the group of outcasts, decide to stop for the night. They are carrying provisions that they unload into a nearby dilapidated shack in preparation for the night's stay. The couple provides a contrast to the outcasts and, later, they are the vehicle for revealing better sides of Oakhurst, Mother Shipton, and The Duchess.

During the night, a snowstorm moves in, and Uncle Billy slips out of the camp with the provisions mule. Early the next morning, Oakhurst discovers the theft, but to protect the innocents, he says that Uncle Billy has gone for provisions. The Duchess and Mother Shipton, fully aware of what has happened, go along with Oakhurst's story.

Harte sketches the following days, during which the group is snowed in, with compassion and humor. Tom calls the Duchess "Mrs. Oakhurst," Mother Shipton sneaks off to curse the smoke rising from the distant Poker Flat, Piney's chatter makes the Duchess blush through her heavy makeup, and, finally, Tom retells Homer's *Iliad* in vernacular to entertain the group.

The deaths of the outcasts are clearly foreshadowed, but the dignity of their last actions reflects Harte's recurrent theme that there is good in the worst of people, Uncle Billy appearing an exception. Mother Shipton starves herself to save her provisions for Piney. Oakhurst builds snowshoes so Tom can go for help and then accompanies Tom on the first part of the journey. After Tom has gone on, Oakhurst shoots himself, presumably so he will not take the provisions the others need to survive. The Duchess, who remains behind with Piney, finally realizes that death is approaching. The way they are found tells the story of their deaths: "And so reclining, the younger and purer pillowing the head of her soiled sister upon her virgin breast, they fell asleep." Hart includes a final theme of redemption by adding that an "equal peace . . . dwelt upon them."

Oakhurst, a gambler to the end, had "settled himself coolly to the losing game before him." The final image is of him. He has pinned the deuce of clubs with his epitaph written on it to a tree with his bowie knife. Harte's narrator concludes of John Oakhurst that he was "at once the strongest and yet the weakest of the outcasts of Poker Flat."

Summary

"The Luck of Roaring Camp" and "The Outcasts of Poker Flat" are among the best of the colorful Gold Rush tales for which Bret Harte is most remembered. The stories, sometimes regarded more as parables or myths than short stories, demonstrate the strong narrative and descriptive style and the stock characters that Harte contributed to modern Western stories and films.

The stories that capture the California Gold Rush years as they never were were written by a writer who never experienced them; in that sense, Harte created the Gold Rush. His work endures. Even today, he has an international audience that enjoys his mythic California Gold Rush.

Bibliography

Duckett, Margaret. *Mark Twain and Bret Harte.* Norman: University of Oklahoma Press, 1964.

Harte, Bret. *The Gold Rush Story Teller.* Oakland, Calif.: Star Rover House, 1986.

Golemba, Henry L. "Bret Harte." In *American Short Story Writers Before 1880,* edited by Bobby Ellen Kimbel. Vol. 74 in *Dictionary of Literary Biography.* Detroit: Gale Research, 1988.

Morrow, Patrick. *Bret Harte.* Boise, Idaho: Boise State College Press, 1972.

O'Connor, Richard. *Bret Harte: A Biography.* Boston: Little, Brown, 1966.

Stewart, George R., Jr. *Bret Harte: Argonaut and Exile.* Boston: Houghton Mifflin, 1931.

Carol Franks

MAGILL'S
SURVEY
OF
AMERICAN
LITERATURE

GLOSSARY

Absurdism: A philosophical attitude underlining the alienation that humans experience in what absurdists see as a universe devoid of meaning; literature of the absurd often purposely lacks logic, coherence, and intelligibility.

Act: One of the major divisions of a play or opera; the typical number of acts in a play ranges from one to four.

Agrarianism: A movement of the 1920's and 1930's in which John Crowe Ransom, Allen Tate, Robert Penn Warren, and other Southern writers championed the agrarian society of their region against the industrialized society of the North.

Allegory: A literary mode in which a second level of meaning (wherein characters, events, and settings represent abstractions) is encoded within the narrative.

Alliteration: The repetition of consonant sounds focused at the beginning of syllables, as in: "Large *m*annered *m*otions of his *m*ythy *m*ind."

Allusion: A reference to a historical event or to another literary text that adds dimension or meaning to a literary work.

Alter ego: A character's other self—sometimes a double, sometimes another side of the character's personality, sometimes a dear and constant companion.

Ambiguity: The capacity of language to sustain multiple meanings; ambiguity can add to both the richness and the concentration of literary language.

Angst: A pervasive feeling of anxiety and depression, often associated with the moral and spiritual uncertainties of the twentieth century.

Antagonist: The major character or force in opposition to the protagonist or hero.

Antihero: A fictional figure who tries to define himself and to establish his own codes, or a protagonist who simply lacks traditional heroic qualities.

Apostrophe: A poetic device in which the speaker addresses either someone not physically present or something not physically capable of hearing the words addressed.

Aside: A short passage generally spoken by one dramatic character in an undertone, or directed to the audience, so as not to be heard by the other characters onstage.

Assonance: A term for the association of words with identical vowel sounds but different consonants; "stars," "arms," and "park," for example, all contain identical "a" (and "ar") sounds.

Atmosphere: The general mood or tone of a work; it is often associated with setting, but can also be established by action or dialogue.

Autobiography: A form of nonfiction writing in which the author narrates events of his or her own life.

Avant-garde: A term describing works intended to expand the conventions of a genre through the experimental treatment of form and/or content.

Bardic voice: A passionate poetic voice modeled after that of a bard, or tribal poet/singer, who composed lyric or epic poetry to honor a chief or recite tribal history.

Bildungsroman: Sometimes called the "novel of education," the *Bildungsroman* focuses on the growth of a young protagonist who is learning about the world and finding his place in life; typical examples are James Joyce's *A Portrait of the Artist as a Young Man* (1916) and Thomas Wolfe's *Look Homeward, Angel* (1929).

Biography: Nonfiction that details the events of a particular individual's life.

Black humor: A general term of modern origin that refers to a form of "sick humor" that is intended to produce laughter out of the morbid and the taboo.

Blank verse: Lines of unrhymed iambic pentameter; it is a poetic form that allows much flexibility, and it has been used since the Elizabethan era.

Caesura: A pause or break in a poem; it is most commonly indicated by a punctuation mark such as a comma, dash, semicolon, or period.

Canon: A generally accepted list of literary works; it may refer to works by a single author or works in a genre. The literary canon often refers to the texts that are thought to belong on university reading lists.

Catharsis: A term from Aristotle's *Poetics* referring to the purgation of the spectators' emotions of pity and fear as aroused by the actions of the tragic hero.

Character: A personage appearing in any literary or dramatic work.

Chorus: An individual or group sometimes used in drama to comment on the action; the chorus was used extensively in classical Greek drama.

Classicism: A literary stance or value system consciously based on classical Greek and Roman literature; it generally denotes a cluster of values including formal discipline, restrained expression, reverence for tradition, and an objective rather than a subjective orientation.

Climax: The moment in a work of fiction or drama at which the action reaches its highest intensity and is resolved.

Comedy: A lighter form of drama that aims chiefly to amuse and that ends happily; comedic forms range from physical (slapstick) humor to subtle intellectual humor.

Comedy of manners: A type of drama which treats humorously, and often satirically, the behavior within an artificial, highly sophisticated society.

Comic relief: A humorous incident or scene in an otherwise serious or tragic work intended to release the reader's or audience's tensions through laughter without detracting from the serious material.

Conceit: One type of metaphor, the conceit is used for comparisons which are highly intellectualized. When T. S. Eliot, for example, says that winding streets are like a tedious argument of insidious intent, there is no clear connection between the two, so the reader must apply abstract logic to fill in the missing links.

Confessional poetry: Autobiographical poetry in which personal revelation provides a basis for the intellectual or theoretical study of moral, religious, or aesthetic concerns.

Conflation: The fusion of variant readings of a text into a composite whole.

Conflict: The struggle that develops as a result of the opposition between the protagonist and another person, the natural world, society, or some force within the self.

Connotation: A type of meaning that depends on the associative meanings of a word beyond its formal definition. (*See also* Denotation.)

Conventions: All those devices of stylization, compression, and selection that constitute the necessary differences between art and life.

Counterplot: A secondary action coincident with the major action of a fictional or dramatic work. The counterplot is generally a reflection on or variation of the main action and is strongly integrated into the whole of the work.

Couplet: Any two succeeding lines of poetry that rhyme.

Cubism: In literature, a style of poetry, such as that of E. E. Cummings and Archibald MacLeish, which first fragments an experience, then rearranges its elements into some new artistic entity.

Dactyl: A metrical foot in which a stressed syllable is followed by two unstressed syllables; an example of a dactyllic line is "After the pangs of a desperate lover."

Deconstruction: An extremely influential contemporary school of criticism based on the works of the French philosopher Jacques Derrida. Deconstruction treats literary works as unconscious reflections of the myths of Western culture; the primary myth is that there is a meaningful world which language signifies or represents. The Deconstructionist critic is often concerned with showing how a literary text tacitly subverts the very assumptions or myths on which it ostensibly rests.

Denotation: The explicit, formal definition of a word, exclusive of its implications and emotional associations. (*See also* Connotation.)

Denouement: Originally French, this word literally means "unknotting" or "untying" and is another term for the catastrophe or resolution of a dramatic action, the solution or clarification of a plot.

Detective story: In the so-called "classic" detective story, the focus is on a crime solved by a detective through interpretation of evidence and clever reasoning. Many modern practitioners of the genre, however, have deemphasized the puzzle-like qualities, stressing instead characterization, theme, and other elements of mainstream fiction.

Determinism: The belief that a person's actions are essentially determined by biological and environmental factors, with free will playing a negligible role. (*See also* Naturalism.)

Deus ex machina: Latin, meaning "god out of a machine." In the Greek theater, it referred to the use of a god lowered by means of a mechanism onto the stage to untangle the plot or save the hero. It has come to signify any artificial device for the easy resolution of dramatic difficulties.

Dialogue: Speech exchanged between characters or even, in a looser sense, the thoughts of a single character.

Dime novel: A type of inexpensive book very popular in the late nineteenth century that told a formulaic tale of war, adventure, or romance.

Domestic tragedy: A serious and usually realistic play with lower-class or middle-class characters and milieu, typically dealing with personal or domestic concerns.

Donnée: From the French verb meaning "to give," the term refers to the premise or the given set of circumstances from which the plot will proceed.

Drama: Any work designed to be represented on a stage by actors. More specifically, the term has come to signify a play of a serious nature and intent which may end either happily (comedy) or unhappily (tragedy).

Dramatic irony: A form of irony that most typically occurs when the spoken lines of a character are perceived by the audience to have a double meaning or when the audience knows more about a situation than the character knows.

Dramatic monologue: A poem in which the narrator addresses a silent persona whose presence greatly influences what the narrator tells the reader.

Dramatis personae: The characters in a play; often it refers to a printed list defining the characters and their relationships.

Dramaturgy: The composition of plays; the term is occasionally used to refer to the performance or acting of plays.

Dream vision: A poem presented as a dream in which the poet-dreamer envisions people and events that frequently have allegorical overtones.

Dualism: A theory that the universe is explicable in terms of two basic, conflicting entities, such as good and evil, mind and matter, or the physical and the spiritual.

Elegy: The elegy and pastoral elegy are distinguishable by their subject matter, not their form. The elegy is usually a long, rhymed, strophic poem whose subject is meditation upon death or a lamentable theme; the pastoral elegy uses a pastoral scene to sing of death or love.

Elizabethan: Of or referring to the reign of Queen Elizabeth I of England, lasting from 1558 to 1603, a period of important artistic achievements; William Shakespeare was an Elizabethan playwright.

End-stop: When a punctuated pause occurs at the end of a line of poetry, the line is said to be end-stopped.

Enjambment: When a line of poetry is not end-stopped and instead carries over to the next line, the line is said to be enjambed.

Epic: This term usually refers to a long narrative poem which presents the exploits of a central figure of high position; it is also used to designate a long novel that has the style or structure usually associated with an epic.

Epilogue: A closing section or speech at the end of a play or other literary work that makes some reflection on the preceding action.

Episodic narrative: A work that is held together primarily by a loose connection of self-sufficient episodes. Picaresque novels often have an episodic structure.

Epithalamion: A bridal song or poem, a genre deriving from the poets of antiquity.

Essay: A nonfiction work, usually short, that analyzes or interprets a particular subject or idea; it is often written from a personal point of view.

Existentialism: A philosophical and literary term for a group of attitudes surrounding the idea that existence precedes essence; according to Jean-Paul Sartre, "man is nothing else but what he makes himself." Existential literature exhibits an awareness of the absurdity of the universe and is preoccupied with the single ethical choice that determines the meaning of a person's existence.

Expressionism: A movement in the arts, especially in German painting, dominant in the decade following World War I; external reality is consciously distorted in order to portray the world as it is "viewed emotionally."

Fabulation: The act of lying to invent or tell a fable, sometimes used to designate the fable itself.

Fantastic: The fantastic has been defined as a genre that lies between the "uncanny" and the "marvelous." All three genres embody the familiar world but present an event that cannot be explained by the laws of the familiar world.

Farce: A play that evokes laughter through such low-comedy devices as physical humor, rough wit, and ridiculous and improbable situations and characters.

First person: A point of view in which the narrator of a story or poem addresses the reader directly, often using the pronoun "I," thereby allowing the reader direct access to the narrator's thoughts.

Flashback: A scene in a fictional or dramatic work depicting events that occurred at an earlier time.

Foot: A rhythmic unit of poetry consisting of two or three syllables grouped together; the most common foot in English is the iamb, composed of one unstressed syllable attached to one stressed syllable.

Foreshadowing: A device used to create suspense or dramatic irony by indicating through suggestion what will take place in the future.

Formalism: A school of literary criticism which particularly emphasizes the form of the work of art—that is, the type or genre to which it belongs.

Frame story: A story that provides a framework for another story (or stories) told within it.

Free verse: A poem that does not conform to such traditional conventions as meter or rhyme, and that does not establish any pattern within itself, is said to be a "free verse" poem.

Genre: A type or category of literature, such as tragedy, novel, memoir, poem, or essay; a genre has a particular set of conventions and expectations.

Genre fiction: Categories of popular fiction such as the mystery, the romance, and the Western; although the term can be used in a neutral sense, "genre fiction" is often used dismissively to refer to fiction in which the writer is bound by more or less rigid conventions.

Gothic novel: A form of fiction developed in the eighteenth century that focuses on horror and the supernatural.

Grotesque: Characterized by a breakup of the everyday world by mysterious forces, the form differs from fantasy in that the reader is not sure whether to react with humor or with horror.

Half rhyme. *See* Slant rhyme.

Hamartia. *See* Tragic flaw.

Harlem Renaissance: A flowering of black American writing, in all literary genres, in the 1930's and 1940's.

Hero/Heroine: The most important character in a drama or other literary work. Popularly, the term has come to refer to a character who possesses extraordinary prowess or virtue, but as a technical term it simply indicates the central participant in a dramatic action. (*See also* Protagonist.)

Heroic couplet: A pair of rhyming iambic pentameter lines traditionally used in epic poetry; a heroic couplet often serves as a self-contained witticism or pithy observation.

Historical novel: A novel that depicts past events, usually public in nature, and that features real as well as fictional people; the relationship between fiction and history in the form varies greatly depending on the author.

Hubris: Excessive pride, the characteristic in tragic heroes such as Oedipus, Doctor Faustus, and Macbeth that leads them to transgress moral codes or ignore warnings. (*See also* Tragic flaw.)

Humanism: A man-centered rather than god-centered view of the universe that usually stresses reason, restraint, and human values; in the Renaissance, humanism devoted itself to the revival of the life, thought, language, and literature of ancient Greece and Rome.

Hyperbole: The use of gross exaggeration for rhetorical effect, based upon the assumption that the reader will not respond to the exaggeration literally.

Iamb: The basic metric foot of the English language, the iamb associates one unstressed syllable with one stressed syllable. The line "So long as men can breathe or eyes can see" is composed of five iambs (a form called iambic pentameter).

Imagery: The simulation of sensory perception through figurative language; imagery can be controlled to create emotional or intellectual effects.

Imagism: A school of poetry prominent in Great Britain and North America between 1909 and 1918. The objectives of Imagism were accurate description, objective presentation, concentration and economy, new rhythms, freedom of choice in subject matter, and suggestion rather than explanation.

Interior monologue: The speech of a character designed to introduce the reader directly to the character's internal life; it differs from other monologues in that it attempts to reproduce thought before logical organization is imposed upon it.

Irony: An effect that occurs when a writer's or a character's real meaning is different from (and frequently opposite to) his or her apparent meaning. (*See also* Dramatic irony.)

Jazz Age: The 1920's, a period of prosperity, sweeping social change, frequent excess, and youthful rebellion, for which F. Scott Fitzgerald is the acknowledged spokesman.

Künstlerroman: An apprenticeship novel in which the protagonist, a young artist, faces the conflicts of growing up and coming to understand the purpose of his life and art.

Leitmotif: The repetition in a work of literature of a word, phrase, or image which serves to establish the tone or otherwise unify the piece.

Line: A rhythmical unit within a poem between the foot and the poem's larger structural units; the words or feet in a line are usually in a single row.

Lyric poetry: Poetry that is generally short, adaptable to metrical variation, and personal in theme; it may explore deeply personal feelings about life.

Magical realism: Imaginary or fantastic scenes and occurrences presented in a meticulously realistic style.

Melodrama: A play in which characters are clearly either virtuous or evil and are pitted against one another in suspenseful, often sensational situations.

Memoir: A piece of autobiographical writing which emphasizes important events in which the author has participated and prominent people whom the author has known.

Metafiction: Fiction that manifests a reflexive tendency and shows a consciousness of itself as an artificial creation; such terms as "postmodernist fiction," "antifiction," and "surfiction" also refer to this type of fiction.

Metaphor: A figure of speech in which two different things are identified with each other, as in the T. S. Eliot line, "The whole earth is our hospital"; the term is also widely used to identify many kinds of analogies.

Metaphysical poetry: A type of poetry that stresses the intellectual over the emotional; it is marked by irony, paradox, and striking comparisons of dissimilar things, the latter frequently being farfetched to the point of eccentricity.

Meter: The rhythmic pattern of language when it is formed into lines of poetry; when the rhythm of language is organized and regulated so as to affect the meaning and emotional response to the words, the rhythm has been refined into meter.

Mise-en-scène: The staging of a drama, including scenery, costumes, movable furniture (properties), and, by extension, the positions (blocking) and gestures of the actors.

Mock-heroic style: A form of burlesque in which a trivial subject is absurdly elevated through use of the meter, diction, and familiar devices of the epic poem.

Modernism: An international movement in the arts which began in the early years of the twentieth century; modernism in general was characterized by its international idiom, by its interest in cultures distant in space or time, by its emphasis on formal experimentation, and by its sense of dislocation and radical change.

Monologue: An extended speech by one character in a drama. If the character is alone onstage, unheard by other characters, the monologue is more specifically referred to as a soliloquy.

Musical comedy: A theatrical form mingling song, dance, and spoken dialogue which was developed in the United States in the twentieth century; it was derived from vaudeville and operetta.

Myth: Anonymous traditional stories dealing with basic human concepts and fundamentally opposing principles; a myth is often constructed as a story that tells of supposedly historical events.

Narrator: The character who recounts the story in a work of fiction.

Naturalism: The application of the principles of scientific determinism to fiction. Although it usually refers more to the choice of subject matter than to technical conventions, conventions associated with the movement center on the author's attempt to be precise and objective in description and detail, regardless of whether the events described are sordid or shocking. (*See also* Determinism.)

Neoclassicism: The type of classicism that dominated English literature from the Restoration to the late eighteenth century. Modeling itself on the literature of ancient Greece and Rome, neoclassicism exalts the virtues of proportion, unity, harmony, grace, decorum, taste, manners, and restraint; it values realism and reason.

New Criticism: A reaction against the "old criticism" that either saw art as self-expression, applied extrinsic criteria of morality and value, or gave credence to the professed intentions of the author. The New Criticism regards a work of art as an autonomous object, a self-contained universe. It holds that a close reading of literary texts will reveal their meanings and the complexities of their verbal texture as well as the oppositions and tensions balanced in the text.

New journalism: Writing that largely abandons the traditional objectivity of journalism in order to express the subjective response of the observer.

Nonfiction novel: A novel such as Truman Capote's *In Cold Blood*, which, though taking actual people and events as its subject matter, uses fictional techniques to develop the narrative.

Novel: A long fictional form that is generally concerned with individual characterization and with presenting a social world and a detailed environment.

Novel of ideas: A novel in which the characters, plot, and dialogue serve to develop some controlling idea or to present the clash of ideas.

Novel of manners: The classic example of the form might be the novels of Jane Austen, wherein the customs and conventions of a social group of a particular time and place are realistically, and often satirically, portrayed.

Novella, novelle, nouvelle, novelette: These terms usually refer to that form of fiction which is said to be longer than a short story and shorter than a novel; "novella" is the term usually used to refer to American works in this genre.

Ode: A lyric poem that treats a unified subject with elevated emotion and seriousness of purpose, usually ending with a satisfactory resolution.

Old Criticism: Criticism predating the New Criticism and bringing extrinsic criteria to bear on the analysis of literature as authorial self-expression (Romanticism), critical self-expression (Impressionism), or work that is dependent upon moral or ethical absolutes (new humanism).

Omniscient narration: A godlike point of view from which the narrator sees all and knows everything there is to know about the story and its characters.

One-act play: A short, unified dramatic work, the one-act play is usually quite limited in number of characters and scene changes; the action often revolves around a single incident or event.

Opera: A complex combination of various art forms, opera is a form of dramatic entertainment consisting of a play set to music.

Original Sin: A concept of the innate depravity of man's nature resulting from Adam's sin and fall from grace.

Paradox: A statement that initially seems to be illogical or self-contradictory yet eventually proves to embody a complex truth.

Parataxis: The placing of clauses or phrases in a series without the use of coordinating or subordinating terms.

Pathos: The quality in a character that evokes pity or sorrow from the observer.

Pentameter: A line of poetry consisting of five recognizable rhythmic units called feet.

Picaresque novel: A form of fiction that involves a central rogue figure, or picaro, who usually tells his own story. The plot structure is normally episodic, and the episodes usually focus on how the picaro lives by his wits.

Plot: The sequence of the occurrence of events in a dramatic action. A plot may be unified around a single action, but it may also consist of a series of disconnected incidents; it is then referred to as "episodic."

Poem: A unified composition that uses the rhythms and sounds of language, as well as devices such as metaphor, to communicate emotions and experiences to the reader or hearer.

Point of view: The perspective from which a story is presented to the reader. In simplest terms, it refers to whether narration is first-person (directly addressed to the reader as if told by one involved in the narrative) or third-person (usually a more objective, distanced perspective).

Postmodernism: The term is loosely applied to various artistic movements which have followed so-called high modernism, represented by such giants as James Joyce and Pablo Picasso. The term is frequently applied to the works of writers (such as Thomas Pynchon and John Barth) who exhibit a self-conscious awareness of their predecessors as well as a reflexive treatment of fictional form.

Prose poem: A type of poem, usually less than a page in length, that appears on the page like prose; there is great stylistic and thematic variety within the genre.

Protagonist: Originally, in the Greek drama, the "first actor," who played the leading role. The term has come to signify the most important character in a drama or story. It is not unusual for there to be more than one protagonist in a work. (*See also* Hero/Heroine.)

Psychoanalytic theory: A tremendously influential theory of the unconscious developed by Sigmund Freud, it divides the human psyche into three components—the id, the ego, and the superego. In this theory, the psyche represses instinctual and sexual desires, and channels (sublimates) those desires into socially acceptable behavior.

Psychological novel: A form of fiction in which character, especially the inner life of characters, is the primary focus. The form has characterized much of the work of James Joyce, Virginia Woolf, and William Faulkner.

Psychological realism: A type of realism that tries to reproduce the complex psychological motivations behind human behavior; writers in the late nineteenth and early twentieth centuries were particularly influenced by Sigmund Freud's theories. (*See also* Psychoanalytic theory.)

Pun: A pun occurs when words which have similar pronunciations have entirely different meanings; a pun can establish a connection between two meanings or contexts that the reader would not ordinarily make. The result may be a striking connection or simply a humorously accidental connection.

Quatrain: Any four-line stanza is a quatrain; other than the couplet, the quatrain is the most common type of stanza.

Rationalism: A system of thought which seeks truth through the exercise of reason rather than by means of emotional response or revelation.

Realism: A literary technique in which the primary convention is to render an illusion of fidelity to external reality. Realism is often identified as the primary method of the novel form; the realist movement in the late nineteenth century coincided with the full development of the novel form.

Regional novel: Any novel in which the character of a given geographical region plays a decisive role; the Southern United States, for example, has fostered a strong regional tradition.

Representationalism: An approach to drama that seeks to create the illusion of reality onstage through realistic characters, situations, and settings.

Revue: A theatrical production, typically consisting of sketches, song, and dance, which often comments satirically upon personalities and events of the day; generally there is no plot involved.

Rhyme: A full rhyme comprises two or more words that have the same vowel sound and that end with the same consonant sound: "Hat" and "cat" is a full rhyme, as is "laughter" and "after." Rhyme is also used more broadly as a term for any correspondence in sound between syllables in poetry. (*See also* Slant rhyme.)

Rhyme scheme: Poems which establish a pattern of rhyme have a "rhyme scheme," designated by lowercase letters; the rhyme scheme of ottava rima, for example, is abababcc. Traditional stanza forms are categorized by their rhyme scheme and base meter.

Roman à clef: A fiction wherein actual persons, often celebrities of some sort, are thinly disguised.

Romance: The romance usually differs from the novel form in that the focus is on symbolic events and representational characters rather than on "as-if-real" characters and events. Character is often highly stylized, serving as a function of the plot.

Romantic comedy: A play in which love is the central motive of the dramatic action. The term often refers to plays of the Elizabethan period, such as William Shakespeare's *As You Like It* and *A Midsummer Night's Dream*, but it has also been applied to any modern work that contains similar features.

Romanticism: A widespread cultural movement in the late-eighteenth and early-nineteenth centuries, Romanticism is frequently contrasted with classicism. The term generally suggests primitivism, an interest in folklore, a reverence for nature, a fascination with the demoniac and the macabre, and an assertion of the preeminence of the imagination.

Satire: Satire employs the comedic devices of wit, irony, and exaggeration to expose and condemn human folly, vice, and stupidity.

Scene: In drama, a division of action within an act (some plays are divided only into scenes instead of acts). Sometimes scene division indicates a change of setting or locale; sometimes it simply indicates the entrances and exits of characters.

Science fiction: Fiction in which real or imagined scientific developments or certain givens (such as physical laws, psychological principles, or social conditions) form the basis of an imaginative projection, frequently into the future.

Sentimental novel: A form of fiction popular in the eighteenth century in which emotionalism and optimism are the primary characteristics. The best-known examples are Samuel Richardson's *Pamela* (1740-1741) and Oliver Goldsmith's *The Vicar of Wakefield* (1766).

Sentimentalism: A term used to describe any emotional response that is excessive and disproportionate to its impetus or occasion. It also refers to the eighteenth century idea that human beings are essentially benevolent, devoid of Original Sin and basic depravity.

Setting: The time and place in which the action of a literary work happens. The term also applies to the physical elements of a theatrical production, such as scenery and properties.

Short story: A concise work of fiction, shorter than a novella, that is usually more concerned with mood, effect, or a single event than with plot or extensive characterization.

Simile: Loosely defined, a simile is a type of metaphor which signals a comparison by the use of the words "like" or "as." Shakespeare's line, "My mistress' eyes are nothing like the sun," establishes a comparison between the woman's eyes and the sun, and is a simile.

Slant rhyme: A slant rhyme, or half rhyme, occurs when words with identical consonants but different vowel sounds are associated; "fall" and "well," and "table" and "bauble" are slant rhymes.

Slapstick: Low comedy in which physical action (such as a kick in the rear, tripping, and knocking over people or objects) evokes laughter.

Social realism: A type of realism in which the social and economic conditions in which characters live figure prominently in their situations, actions, and outlooks.

Soliloquy: An extended speech delivered by a character alone onstage, unheard by other characters. Soliloquy is a form of monologue, and it typically reveals the intimate thoughts and emotions of the speaker.

Sonnet: A traditional poetic form that is almost always composed of fourteen lines of rhymed iambic pentameter; a turning point usually divides the poem into two parts, with the first part presenting a situation and the second part reflecting on it.

Southern Gothic: A term applied to the scenes of decay, incest, madness, and violence often found in the fiction of William Faulkner, Erskine Caldwell, and other Southern writers.

Speaker: The voice which speaks the words of a poem—sometimes a fictional character in an invented situation, sometimes the author speaking directly to the reader, sometimes the author speaking from behind the disguise of a persona.

Stanza: When lines of poetry are meant to be taken as a unit, and the unit recurs throughout the poem, that unit is called a stanza; a four-line unit is one common stanza.

Stream of consciousness: The depiction of the thought processes of a character, insofar as this is possible, without any mediating structures. The metaphor of consciousness as a "stream" suggests a rush of thoughts and images governed by free association rather than by strictly rational development; the term is often used loosely as a synonym for interior monologue.

Stress: When more emphasis is placed on one syllable in a line of poetry than on another syllable, that syllable is said to be stressed.

Subplot: A secondary action coincident with the main action of a fictional or dramatic work. A subplot may be a reflection upon the main action, but it may also be largely unrelated. (*See also* Counterplot.)

Surrealism: An approach to literature and art that startlingly combines seemingly incompatible elements; surrealist writing usually has a bizarre, dreamlike, or nightmarish quality.

Symbol: A literary symbol is an image that stands for something else; it may evoke a cluster of meanings rather than a single specific meaning.

Symbolism: A literary movement encompassing the work of a group of French writers in the latter half of the nineteenth century, a group that included Charles Baudelaire, Stéphane Mallarmé, and Paul Verlaine. According to Symbolism, there is a mystical correspondence between the natural and spiritual worlds.

Syntax: A linguistic term used to describe the study of the ways in which words are arranged sequentially to produce grammatical units such as phrases, clauses, and sentences.

Tableau: A silent, stationary grouping of performers in a theatrical performance.

Terza rima: A rhyming three-line stanza form in which the middle line of one stanza rhymes with the first line of the following stanza.

Tetrameter: A line of poetry consisting of four recognizable rhythmic units called feet.

Theater of the absurd: The general name given to plays that express a basic belief that life is illogical, irrational, formless, and contradictory and that man is without meaning or purpose. This perspective often leads to the abandonment of traditional theatrical forms and coherent dialogue.

Theme: Loosely defined as what a literary work means. The theme of W. B. Yeats's poem "Sailing to Byzantium," for example, might be interpreted as the failure of man's attempt to isolate himself within the world of art.

Thespian: Another term for an actor; also, of or relating to the theater. The word derives from Thespis, by tradition the first actor of the Greek theater.

Third person: Third-person narration is related from a point of view more distant from the story than first-person narration; the narrator is not an identifiable "I" persona. A third-person point of view may be limited or omniscient ("all-knowing").

Three unities. *See* Unities.

Tone: Tone usually refers to the dominant mood of a work. (*See also* Atmosphere.)

Tragedy: A form of drama that is serious in action and intent and that involves disastrous events and death; classical Greek drama observed specific guidelines for tragedy, but the term is now sometimes applied to a range of dramatic or fictional situations.

Tragic flaw: Also known as hamartia, it is the weakness or error in judgment in a tragic hero or protagonist that causes the character's downfall; it may proceed from ignorance or a moral fault. Excessive pride (hubris) is one traditional tragic flaw.

Travel literature: Writing which emphasizes the author's subjective response to places visited, especially faraway, exotic, and culturally different locales.

Trimeter: A line of poetry consisting of three recognizable rhythmic units called feet.

Trochee: One of the most common feet in English poetry, the trochee associates one stressed syllable with one unstressed syllable, as in the line, "Double, double, toil and trouble."

Unities: A set of rules for proper dramatic construction formulated by European Renaissance drama critics and derived from classical Greek concepts: A play should have no scenes or subplots irrelevant to the central action, should not cover a period of more than twenty-four hours, and should not occur in more than one place.

Verisimilitude: The attempt to have the readers of a literary work believe that it conforms to reality rather than to its own laws.

Verse: A generic term for poetry; verse also refers in a narrower sense to poetry that is humorous or merely superficial, as in "greeting-card verse."

Verse paragraph: A division within a poem that is created by logic or syntax rather than by form; verse paragraphs are important for determining the movement of a poem and the logical association between ideas.

Victorian novel: Although the Victorian period extended from 1837 to 1901, the term "Victorian novel" does not include works from the later decades of Queen Victoria's reign. The term loosely refers to the sprawling works of novelists such as Charles Dickens and William Makepeace Thackeray, which are characterized by a broad social canvas.

Villanelle: The villanelle is a French verse form assimilated by English prosody. It is usually composed of nineteen lines divided into five tercets and a quatrain, rhyming aba, bba, aba, aba, abaa.

Well-made play: A type of play constructed according to a nineteenth century French formula; the plot often revolves around a secret (revealed at the end) known only to some of the characters. Misunderstanding, suspense, and coincidence are among the devices used.

Western novel: The Western novel is defined by a relatively predictable combination of conventions and recurring themes. These predictable elements, familiar from television and film Westerns, differentiate the Western from historical novels and other works which may be set in the Old West.

Worldview: Frequently rendered as the German *weltanschauung*, it is a comprehensive set of beliefs or assumptions by means of which one interprets what goes on in the world.

LIST OF AUTHORS

LIST OF AUTHORS